# Research Design and Methods

## *A Process Approach*

### TENTH EDITION

Kenneth S. Bordens
Bruce B. Abbott
*Indiana University—Purdue University Fort Wayne*

RESEARCH DESIGN AND METHODS: A PROCESS APPROACH, TENTH EDITION

Published by McGraw-Hill Education, 2 Penn Plaza, New York, NY 10121. Copyright © 2018 by McGraw-Hill Education. All rights reserved. Printed in the United States of America. Previous editions © 2014, 2011, and 2008. No part of this publication may be reproduced or distributed in any form or by any means, or stored in a database or retrieval system, without the prior written consent of McGraw-Hill Education, including, but not limited to, in any network or other electronic storage or transmission, or broadcast for distance learning.

Some ancillaries, including electronic and print components, may not be available to customers outside the United States.

This book is printed on acid-free paper.

1 2 3 4 5 6 7 8 9 LCR 21 20 19 18 17

ISBN 978-1-259-84474-4
MHID 1-259-84474-9

Chief Product Officer, SVP Products & Markets: *G. Scott Virkler*
Vice President, General Manager, Products & Markets: *Michael Ryan*
Vice President, Content Design & Delivery: *Betsy Whalen*
Managing Director: *David Patterson*
Director: *William Glass*
Brand Manager: *Jamie Laferrera*
Director, Product Development: *Meghan Campbell*
Product Developer: *Alexander Preiss*
Marketing Manager: *Meredith Leo*
Director, Content Design & Delivery: *Terri Schiesl*
Program Manager: *Debra Hash*
Content Project Managers: *Jeni McAtee, George Theofanopoulos, Karen Jozefowicz*
Buyer: *Laura M. Fuller*
Content Licensing Specialist: *Lori Slattery*
Cover Image: © *Olesya Karakotsya/123RF*
Compositor: *Aptara®, Inc.*
Printer: *LSC Communications*

All credits appearing on page or at the end of the book are considered to be an extension of the copyright page.

**Library of Congress Cataloging-in-Publication Data**

Names: Bordens, Kenneth S., author. | Abbott, Bruce B., author.
Title: Research design and methods: a process approach / Kenneth Bordens.
Description: Tenth edition. | Dubuque, IA : McGraw-Hill Education, 2018. |
    Revised edition of the authors' Research design and methods, [2014]
Identifiers: LCCN 2016053273| ISBN 9781259844744 (alk. paper) | ISBN
    1259844749 (alk. paper)
Subjects: LCSH: Psychology—Research. | Psychology—Research—Methodology. |
    BISAC: PSYCHOLOGY / General.
Classification: LCC BF76.5 .B67 2017 | DDC 150.72—dc23 LC record available at https://lccn.loc.gov/2016053273

The Internet addresses listed in the text were accurate at the time of publication. The inclusion of a website does not indicate an endorsement by the authors or McGraw-Hill Education, and McGraw-Hill Education does not guarantee the accuracy of the information presented at these sites.

mheducation.com/highered

*We dedicate this book to our wives, Ricky Karen Bordens and Stephanie Abbott, and to our children and grandchildren.*

# CONTENTS

## Chapter 3:  Getting Ideas for Research    58

## Chapter 6:  Choosing and Using Research Subjects    162

## Chapter 7: Understanding Ethical Issues in the Research Process    199

## Chapter 10: Using Between-Subjects and Within-Subjects Experimental Designs   300

## Chapter 11: Using Specialized Research Designs   336

## Chapter 14:  Using Inferential Statistics    433

## Chapter 15:  Using Multivariate Design and Analysis    470

# *PREFACE*

This, the tenth edition of *Research Design and Methods: A Process Approach*, retains the general theme that characterized prior editions. As before, we take students through the research process, from getting and developing a research idea, to designing and conducting a study, through analyzing and reporting data. Our goals continue to be to present students with information on the research process in a lively and engaging way and to highlight the numerous decisions they must make when designing and conducting research. We also continue to stress how their early decisions in the process affect how data are collected, analyzed, and interpreted later in the research process. Additionally, we have continued the emphasis on the importance of ethical conduct, both in the treatment of research subjects and in the conduct of research and reporting research results.

In this edition we have rewritten material to improve clarity and organization, provided new examples, updated the material in numerous areas to reflect changes in current requirements and practice, and added more than 70 new references.

## CHANGES IN THE TENTH EDITION

The substantive changes in the Tenth Edition are listed below by chapter. Listed changes do not include minor improvements that were made in writing and organization.

## CHAPTER 1: EXPLAINING BEHAVIOR

The sections on protoscience and pseudoscience have been updated. A new section has been added on the emergence of new, conflicting information as a reason why a scientific explanation may fail. There is also an updated example of research on distracted walking (Byington & Schwebel, 2013).

## CHAPTER 2: DEVELOPING AND EVALUATING THEORIES OF BEHAVIOR

The section of theory versus hypothesis has been rewritten. We added a section on theory versus law to deal with laws less quantitative.

## CHAPTER 3: GETTING IDEAS FOR RESEARCH

The section on theory as a source of research ideas has been partially rewritten to use a different example based on the Rescorla-Wagner theory of conditioning. A new figure presents a graph showing the overexpectation effect predicted by the Rescorla-Wagner model of classical conditioning.

The section on primary versus secondary sources focusing on the danger of relying too heavily on secondary sources is now illustrated by a new example based on misrepresentations of the "Little Albert" study by Watson and Rayner.

The sections on identifying whether a scholarly journal is refereed or nonrefereed, and how to determine the quality of a journal, were updated to reflect information available on the Internet. The section on other sources of research information has been updated to include mention of Internet sources.

The entire main section on performing library research has been revised and updated in recognition of students' greater familiarity with digital resources. A new figure shows an image of the screen during a search using PsycINFO via EBSCOhost. An early portion of the section on reading a research report discussing obtaining a copy has been shortened to reflect the ease of obtaining pdf copies of reports via search engines and other Internet sources.

The section on statistical significance now mentions preregistration as a technique designed to reduce the file-drawer phenomenon.

The introductory portion of the section on peer review has been expanded and a new final portion added to address suggestions for improving the process. A new figure shows survey results showing percentage of authors reporting problems with peer review, broken down by type of problem.

The section on values reflected in research has been partially rewritten and a new section added on combatting values and ideological homogeneity in science. A new table addresses areas in which ideological bias can be addressed.

## CHAPTER 4: CHOOSING A RESEARCH DESIGN

There is a new example of correlational research: playing violent video games and bullying (Lam, Cheng, & Liu, 2013). There is also a new example of experimental research: playing violent video games and aggression (Hollingdale & Greitemeyer, 2014). A new example of a study involving simulation has been added (Bode & Codling, 2013).

## CHAPTER 5: MAKING SYSTEMATIC OBSERVATIONS

The description of "Clever Hans" has been rewritten and a photograph added showing Hans and his owner, Wilhelm Von Osten. A paragraph describing automation of experiments using computers was deleted as it is now felt to be unnecessary.

## CHAPTER 6: CHOOSING AND USING RESEARCH SUBJECTS

The section on nonrandom sampling has been updated. The section on debriefing now discusses situations in which it may be ethically permissible to forego debriefing.

Public opinion about the use of animals in research has been updated to reflect the results of more recent polling on the subject. The list of characteristics relating to attitudes toward animal research has been expanded. Use of "organ on a chip" technology added a technique that may reduce the use of animals in medical research.

## CHAPTER 7: UNDERSTANDING ETHICAL ISSUES IN THE RESEARCH PROCESS

A paragraph was added to the section reviewing government regulations relating to ethics, calling attention to the Ethical Research Involving Children (ERIC) project.

The section covering Internet research and ethical research practice was expanded to include mention of the guidelines put out by the Association of Internet Researchers (AoIR). The main points are provided in a new table.

The section discussing the Institutional Review Board (IRB) has been expanded to mention that some IRBs may require you to file annual reports of your progress on your research, and to note that some journals now require submission of your IRB proposal and approval before they will send your paper out for review. Final notes on the IRB have been expanded to note how IRB requirements and actions may act as a hindrance to research.

The table showing the APA Ethical Code for the Care and Use of Animal Subjects has been updated to reflect the 2012 revision and has been placed in a new table.

The section on research misconduct now has a paragraph discussing how fraudulent results can find their way into popular culture and as a result, become difficult to root out. The section on dealing with research fraud now opens by discussing how fraud can be detected. The same section now lists five ways that journals can help to guard against research fraud and expands the discussion of whistleblowers to include the Office of Research Integrity's *Whistleblower Bill of Rights.*

## CHAPTER 8: DOING NONEXPERIMENTAL RESEARCH

The section on conducting observational research has been largely rewritten, including a revised section on establishing the accuracy and reliability of observations. The initial portion of the section on designing a questionnaire now includes advice to "put yourself in a respondent's state of mind." The subsection discussing open-ended questions has been expanded to differentiate several categories of open-ended questions. The subsection on restricted items now includes four general guidelines to follow when writing restricted items.

## CHAPTER 9: DOING SURVEY RESEARCH

The section offering a final note on survey techniques now notes that hard-copy mail surveys remain popular as they continue to be effective in producing relatively high participation rates. In the section on simple random sampling, problems are noted arising from the popularity of electronic forms of communication, including cell phones and social media. The section on sample size has been rewritten.

## CHAPTER 10: USING BETWEEN-SUBJECTS AND WITHIN-SUBJECTS EXPERIMENTAL DESIGNS

In the section on randomizing error variance across groups, a paragraph was added about the fact that random assignment permits using inferential statistics to assess reliability. The following brief section on inferential statistics has been deleted. A new example of a single-factor randomized groups design has been provided (Guéguen, 2015). The factorial between-subjects design is illustrated with a new example (Rayner, Baxter, & Ilicic, 2015). Two new figures illustrate the design and present a graph of the results. An experiment by Gowin, Swann, Moeller, and Lane (2010) now illustrates the within-subjects factorial design.

## CHAPTER 11: USING SPECIALIZED RESEARCH DESIGNS

No substantive changes were made.

## CHAPTER 12: USING SINGLE-SUBJECT DESIGNS

No substantive changes were made.

## CHAPTER 13: DESCRIBING DATA

The bar and line graphs for results of a multifactor design now display error bars around treatment means, based on a figure from a new study (Waldum & McDaniel, 2016). The table showing hypothetical scores from an introductory psychology class has been replaced by a stemplot of the same data so that students do not have to refer back several pages to the histogram of the same data, and grades have been added as labels to the score ranges.

## CHAPTER 14: USING INFERENTIAL STATISTICS

The chapter has been reorganized to place the sections covering the power of a statistical test and statistical versus practical significance at the end of the section on the logic of inferential statistics. The introductory portion of the section on the logic of inferential statistics has been streamlined. The section on statistical significance has been rewritten.

The section on the meaning of statistical significance has been retitled as "Balancing Type I versus Type II Errors" to better capture its content. The example illustrating the use of $t$ tests (Hess, Marwitz, & Kreutzer, 2003) has been extended to include a measure of power. A new section addressing the Bayesian approach to statistical analysis has been added just above the section on alternatives to inferential statistics. The Chapter Summary has been rewritten to better reflect the content of the chapter.

## CHAPTER 15: USING MULTIVARIATE DESIGN AND ANALYSIS

The figure illustrating the logic of partial correlation has been revised. The section on structural equation modeling now introduces the term "measured variable" as used in SEM.

## CHAPTER 16: REPORTING YOUR RESEARCH RESULTS

The section on getting ready to write has been revised to address electronic submission of papers to journals. The Results Section information now specifies what to do if you are using less well-known statistics. An example of reference formatting mistakes that can arise by block-copying references from a database (PsycINFO) has been added to the Reference Section discussion. The section on avoiding biased language now encourages writers to investigate whether certain terms may now be considered preferable to those previously deemed acceptable. The section on telling the world about your results has been rewritten and updated.

**■ connect**

The tenth edition of *Research Design and Methods: A Process Approach* is now available online with Connect, McGraw-Hill Education's integrated assignment and assessment platform. Connect also offers SmartBook for the new edition, which is the first adaptive reading experience proven to improve grades and help students study more effectively. All of the title's website and ancillary content is also available through Connect, including:

- An Instructor's Manual for each chapter.
- A full Test Bank of multiple-choice questions that test students on central concepts and ideas in each chapter.
- Lecture Slides for instructor use in class.

# Required=Results

## McGraw-Hill Connect®
## Learn Without Limits

Connect is a teaching and learning platform that is proven to deliver better results for students and instructors.

Connect empowers students by continually adapting to deliver precisely what they need, when they need it, and how they need it, so your class time is more engaging and effective.

73% of instructors who use **Connect** require it; instructor satisfaction **increases** by 28% when **Connect** is required.

### Connect's Impact on Retention Rates, Pass Rates, and Average Exam Scores

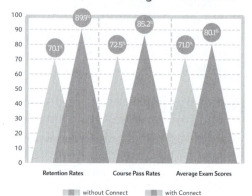

Using **Connect** improves retention rates by **19.8%**, passing rates by **12.7%**, and exam scores by **9.1%**.

# Analytics

## Connect Insight®

Connect Insight is Connect's new one-of-a-kind visual analytics dashboard—now available for both instructors and students—that provides at-a-glance information regarding student performance, which is immediately actionable. By presenting assignment, assessment, and topical performance results together with a time metric that is easily visible for aggregate or individual results, Connect Insight gives the user the ability to take a just-in-time approach to teaching and learning, which was never before available. Connect Insight presents data that empowers students and helps instructors improve class performance in a way that is efficient and effective.

### Impact on Final Course Grade Distribution

| without Connect | | with Connect |
|---|---|---|
| 22.9% | A | 31.0% |
| 27.4% | B | 34.3% |
| 22.9% | C | 18.7% |
| 11.5% | D | 6.1% |
| 15.4% | F | 9.9% |

Students can view their results for any **Connect** course.

# Mobile

Connect's new, intuitive mobile interface gives students and instructors flexible and convenient, anytime–anywhere access to all components of the Connect platform.

# Adaptive

## THE **ADAPTIVE** **READING EXPERIENCE** DESIGNED TO TRANSFORM THE WAY STUDENTS READ

More students earn **A's** and **B's** when they use McGraw-Hill Education **Adaptive** products.

## SmartBook®

Proven to help students improve grades and study more efficiently, SmartBook contains the same content within the print book, but actively tailors that content to the needs of the individual. SmartBook's adaptive technology provides precise, personalized instruction on what the student should do next, guiding the student to master and remember key concepts, targeting gaps in knowledge and offering customized feedback, and driving the student toward comprehension and retention of the subject matter. Available on tablets, SmartBook puts learning at the student's fingertips—anywhere, anytime.

Over **8 billion questions** have been answered, making McGraw-Hill Education products more intelligent, reliable, and precise.

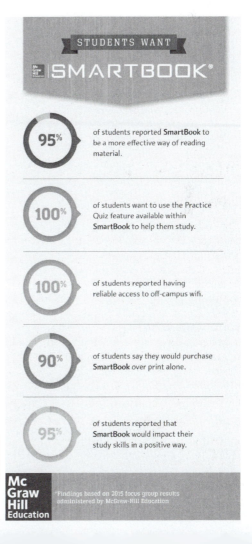

STUDENTS WANT

**SMARTBOOK®**

**95%** of students reported **SmartBook** to be a more effective way of reading material.

**100%** of students want to use the Practice Quiz feature available within **SmartBook** to help them study.

**100%** of students reported having reliable access to off-campus wifi.

**90%** of students say they would purchase **SmartBook** over print alone.

**95%** of students reported that **SmartBook** would impact their study skills in a positive way.

Mc Graw Hill Education

*Findings based on 2015 focus group results administered by McGraw-Hill Education

**www.mheducation.com**

## ACKNOWLEDGMENTS

After ten editions, the list is long of those to whom we owe our thanks—past reviewers, editors, colleagues, and students who have contributed their time and talents to improve the text and make it successful. For the tenth edition we especially wish to single Jamie Laferrera, Brand Manager at McGraw, to Freelance Editors Erin Guendelsberger and Poornima Harikumar of ANSR Source; to our copy editor, Susan Nodine; to our Project Manager Sarita Yadav; to our indexer, Vikas Makkar; and to those other members of the McGraw-Hill staff who worked on the ancillaries and organized the text website where these resources are made available to students and instructors.

Finally, we offer a special thanks to our wives, Stephanie Abbott and Ricky Karen Bordens, for their support and encouragement, and to our families.

**Kenneth S. Bordens**
**Bruce B. Abbott**

# Explaining Behavior

On September 21, 2008, after a day of playing basketball with his friends, 14-year-old Christopher Cepeda and four of his buddies began their journey home on foot. Along the way they came to a busy stretch of Highway 27, where a grassy median separated four lanes of traffic that sped by at 65 mph. The boys made it safely across the two northbound lanes and, upon seeing a tan, 1998 Buick sedan approaching in the southbound lane, they paused in the median. Christopher, distracted as he typed out a text message on his cell phone, never saw the car and stepped out into its path. The car struck the young teenager, throwing him into the windshield and then onto the pavement. In spite of the quick response from local emergency crews, Christopher succumbed to his injuries.

A number of states have enacted laws banning the practice of texting while driving. Studies have demonstrated that texting while driving results in a degradation of driving skills (e.g., Drews, Pasupathi, & Strayer, 2008). Attention has now shifted to the problem of "distracted walking." This occurs when a person is so engrossed in doing something on a cell phone that the distracted person fails to identify potentially dangerous conditions. Sometimes the consequences of walking while using a cell phone are harmless, even funny. For example, a video posted on YouTube shows a young woman walking in a mall who is so engrossed in her cell phone that she doesn't notice a fountain and falls right into it. We can all laugh at the poor woman's fate, knowing that she was not seriously hurt. However, as in the case of Christopher Cepeda, distracted walking can have tragic consequences.

It seems obvious why texting while walking may lead to accidents: Distracted by the task of reading or composing messages, the person fails to notice potential dangers such as obstacles in the pathway or oncoming vehicles. Yet, most of the time, we somehow manage to engage in a variety of activities while walking—including interacting with a cell phone—without suffering nasty consequences.

Why does cell phone use while walking sometimes lead to accidents but more often does not? Attempting to answer this question, we could engage in endless speculation. Is it simply a matter of chance? Do some individuals become more absorbed in their activities on the cell phone than others and thus become less likely to notice a potential danger? Does the specific activity on the phone matter (e.g., texting as opposed to talking)? Are drugs and alcohol a factor?

Questions such as these almost cry out for answers. This is where science and scientists come in. Whereas most of us content ourselves with answers that merely *seem* reasonable, scientists go well beyond mere speculation: They formulate ways to determine clearly the relationship between such factors and one's ability to walk safely while interacting on a cell phone and then design research studies to test those relationships.

This book is about how the initial curiosity sparked by an event such as the Cepeda accident gets transformed into a testable research question and eventually into a research study yielding data that are analyzed. Only through this process can we move beyond dinner table speculations and into the realm of scientific explanation.

## WHAT IS SCIENCE, AND WHAT DO SCIENTISTS DO?

The terms *science* and *scientist* probably conjure up a variety of images in your mind. A common image is that of a person in a white lab coat surrounded by bubbling flasks and test tubes, working diligently to discover a cure for some dreaded disease. Alternatively, our lab-coated scientist might be involved in some evil endeavor that will threaten humankind. Books, movies, and television have provided such images. Just think about the classic horror films of the 1940s and 1950s (e.g., *Frankenstein*), and it is not hard to see where some of these images come from.

Although these images may be entertaining, they do not accurately capture what science actually is and what real scientists do. Simply put, **science** is a set of methods used to collect information about phenomena in a particular area of interest and build a reliable base of knowledge about them. This knowledge is acquired via *research,* which involves a scientist identifying a phenomenon to study, developing hypotheses, conducting a study to collect data, analyzing the data, and disseminating the results. Science also involves developing theories to help better describe, explain, and organize scientific information that is collected. At the heart of any science (psychology included) is information that is obtained through observation and measurement of phenomena. So, for example, if I want to know if text messaging while walking is a serious threat to safety, I must go out and make relevant observations. Science also requires that any explanations for phenomena can be modified and corrected if new information becomes available. Nothing in science is taken as an absolute truth. And, regardless of what you may have seen in the media, there is no such thing as "settled science." All scientific observations, conclusions, and theories are *always* open to modification and perhaps even abandonment as new evidence arises.

Of course, a **scientist** is someone who does science. A scientist is a person who adopts the methods of science in his or her quest for knowledge. However, this simple definition does not capture what scientists do. Despite the stereotyped image of the scientist hunkered over bubbling flasks, scientists engage in a wide range of activities designed to acquire knowledge in their fields. These activities take place in a variety of settings and for a variety of reasons. For example, you have scientists who work for pharmaceutical companies trying to discover new medications for the diseases that afflict humans. You have scientists who brave the bitter cold of the Arctic to take ice samples that they can use to track the course of global climate change. You have scientists who sit in observatories with their telescopes pointed to the heavens, searching for and classifying celestial bodies. You have scientists who sit for hours in carefully constructed blinds observing and recording the natural behavior of animals in the wild. You have scientists who work at universities and conduct studies to acquire knowledge in their chosen fields (e.g., psychology, biology, or physics). In short, science is a diverse activity involving a diverse group of people doing a wide range of things. Despite these differences, all scientists have a common goal: to acquire knowledge through the application of scientific methods and techniques.

## Science as a Way of Thinking

It is important for you to understand that science is not just a means of acquiring knowledge; it is also a way of thinking and of viewing the world. A scientist approaches a problem by carefully defining its parameters, seeking out relevant information, and subjecting proposed solutions to rigorous testing. The scientific view of the world leads a person to be skeptical about what he or she reads or hears in the popular media. Having a scientific outlook leads a person to question the validity of provocative statements made in the media and to find out what scientific studies say about those statements. In short, an individual with a scientific outlook does not accept everything at face value.

Let's see how thinking like a scientist might be applied. Imagine that you are having difficulty relaxing while taking important exams, resulting in poor performance. One night while watching television you see an advertisement for something that might help you relax. According to the advertisement, a new extract of lavender has been discovered that, when inhaled, will help you relax. There are several testimonials from users of the product to back up the claims made in the ad. The question is whether to shell out the money for the lavender scent.

A person who is *not* thinking like a scientist will pull out a credit card and place the order. A person who *is* thinking like a scientist will question the validity of the claims made in the ad and make an effort to find out whether the lavender scent will in fact reduce stress and improve performance. This involves taking the time and making the effort to track down relevant research on the effectiveness of aromatherapy, specifically the effects of lavender scent on stress. Imagine you do a quick literature search and find an article by Howard and Hughes (2008) that tested the effect of a lavender scent against a placebo scent (a scent without any purported therapeutic value) and against no scent on stress responses. Howard and Hughes, you discover, found that scents had no effect on stress unless participants were specifically led to expect the scents to have an effect. In short, the effect of the lavender scent could be explained by expectation effects. So, you decide to save your money.

This is but one example of how thinking like a scientist leads one to question a claim and look for *empirical evidence*—evidence based on observation or experimentation—to verify that claim. There are many other situations where thinking like a scientist can better allow you to evaluate the validity of a claim or a conclusion. For example, during an election year we are bombarded with poll after poll about candidates and who is in the lead. Rather than accepting on face value that candidate X has a lead over candidate Y, you should obtain a copy of the actual survey results (often available online at the pollster's website), and then look at the sample employed and how the questions were worded. As we will see in later chapters, biased samples and question wording can affect the validity of survey findings.

## How Do Scientists Do Science?

In their quest for knowledge about a phenomenon, scientists can use a wide variety of techniques, each suited to a particular purpose. Take the question about using a cell phone while walking. You, as a scientist, could approach this issue in several ways. For example, you could examine health records on injuries incurred while talking on a cell phone during walking. You would then examine your data to see if there is a relationship between using a cell phone and being injured while walking. If you found that there was a greater frequency of accidents when using a cell phone, this would verify the role of cell phones in pedestrian accident injuries.

Another way you could approach this problem is to conduct a controlled experiment. You could have participants navigate through a controlled environment while either using or not using a cell phone. If you find that participants bump into more objects when using a cell phone, you would have verified the effects of distracted walking on accidents.

## QUESTIONS TO PONDER

1. What is science, and what do scientists do?
2. What is meant by the statement that science is a way of thinking? (Explain.)
3. How do scientists obtain knowledge on issues that interest them?

## Basic and Applied Research

Scientists work in a variety of areas to identify phenomena and develop valid explanations for them. The goals established by scientists working within a given field of research may vary according to the nature of the research problem being considered. For example, the goal of some scientists is to discover general laws that explain particular classes of behaviors. In the course of developing those laws, psychologists study behavior in specific situations and attempt to isolate the variables affecting behavior. Other scientists within the field are more interested in tackling practical problems than in finding general laws. For example, they might be interested in determining which of several therapy techniques is best for treating severe phobias.

An important distinction has been made between basic research and applied research along the lines just presented.

*Basic Research*   **Basic research** is conducted to investigate issues relevant to the confirmation or disconfirmation of theoretical or empirical positions. The major goal of basic research is to acquire general information about a phenomenon, with little emphasis placed on applications to real-world examples of the phenomenon (Yaremko, Harari, Harrison, & Lynn, 1982). For example, research on the memory process may be conducted to test the efficacy of interference as a viable theory of forgetting. The researcher would be interested in discovering something about the forgetting process while testing the validity of a theoretical position. Applying the results to forgetting in a real-world situation would be of less immediate interest.

*Applied Research*    The focus of **applied research** is somewhat different from that of basic research. Although you may still work from a theory when formulating your hypotheses, your primary goal is to generate information that can be applied directly to a real-world problem. A study by Jodi Quas and her colleagues (2007) provides a nice example of an applied study. In a number of criminal and civil trials, children may be called to testify about something (such as abuse) that may have happened to them. One concern is that children's memories may not be as accurate as adult memories or that it may be easier to implant memories into children than adults. Quas et al. investigated a number of factors that can affect the accuracy of children's memory. They found that children who were interviewed multiple times about an event that never occurred showed greater memory accuracy and less susceptibility to suggestion than children interviewed once. Results such as these can help law enforcement officers design interviews for children that will maximize memory accuracy. Further examples of applied research can be found in the areas of clinical, environmental, and industrial psychology (among others).

*Overlap Between Basic and Applied Research*    The distinction between applied and basic research is not always clear. Some research areas have both basic and applied aspects. The Quas et al. study provides a good example of research that has both applied and basic implications. Their results can inform law enforcement personnel and others who may have to interview young children how to best approach the interview process. In addition to these applied implications, this research has basic implications as well because the results tell us something about developmental changes in how memory works and the factors that affect memory accuracy.

Even applied research is not independent of theories and other research in psychology. The defining quality of applied research is that the researcher attempts to conduct a study the results of which can be applied directly to a real-world event. To accomplish this task, you must choose a research strategy that maximizes the applicability of findings.

## Framing a Problem in Scientific Terms

Kelly (1963) characterized each person as a scientist who develops a set of strategies for determining the causes of behavior observed. We humans are curious about our world and like to have explanations for the things that happen to us and others. After reading about Christopher Cepeda's accident, you may have thought about potential explanations for the accident. For example, you might have questioned whether using a cell phone while walking is uniquely distracting compared to other distractions (e.g., talking with friends).

Usually, the explanations we come up with are based on little information and mainly reflect personal opinions and biases. The everyday strategies we use to explain what we observe frequently lack the rigor to qualify as truly scientific approaches. In most cases, the explanations for everyday events are made on the spot, with little attention given to ensuring their accuracy. We simply develop an explanation and, satisfied with its plausibility, adopt it as true. We do not consider exploring whether our explanation is correct or whether there might be other, better explanations.

If we do give more thought to our explanations, we often base our thinking on hearsay, conjecture, anecdotal evidence, or unverified sources of information. These revised explanations, even though they reduce transient curiosity, remain untested and are thus of questionable validity. In the Christopher Cepeda case, you might come to the conclusion that texting while walking distracts a person from important environmental cues that signal danger. Although this explanation seems plausible (and may even be correct!), without careful testing it remains mere speculation. To make matters worse, we have a tendency to look for information that will confirm our prior beliefs and assumptions and to ignore or downplay information that does not conform to those beliefs and assumptions. So, if you believe that texting on cell phones causes pedestrian accidents, you might seek out newspaper articles that report on such accidents and fail to investigate the extent to which texting while walking does not lead to an accident. At the same time, you may ignore information that conflicts with your beliefs. The human tendency to seek out information that confirms what is already believed is known as **confirmation bias**.

Unfounded but commonly accepted explanations for behavior can have widespread consequences when the explanations become the basis for social policy. For example, segregation of Blacks in the South was based on stereotypes of assumed racial differences in intelligence and moral judgment. These beliefs sound ludicrous today and have failed to survive a scientific analysis. Such mistakes might have been avoided if lawmakers of the time had relied on objective information rather than on prejudice.

To avoid the trap of easy, untested explanations for behavior, we need to abandon the informal, unsystematic approach to explanation and adopt an approach that has proven its ability to find explanations of great power and generality. This approach, called the *scientific method,* and how you can apply it to answer questions about behavior are the central topics of this book.

## LEARNING ABOUT RESEARCH: WHY SHOULD YOU CARE?

Students sometimes express the sentiment that learning about research is a waste of time because they do not plan on a career in science. Although it is true that a strong background in science is essential if you plan to further your career in psychology after you graduate, it is also true that knowing about science is important even if you do *not* plan to become a researcher.

The layperson is bombarded by science every day. When you read about the controversy over stem-cell research or climate change, you are being exposed to science. When you read about a "scientific" poll on a political issue, you are being exposed to science. When you hear about a new cure for a disease, you are being exposed to science. When you are persuaded to buy one product over another, you are being exposed to science. Science, on one level or another, permeates our everyday lives. To deal rationally with your world, you must be able to analyze critically the information thrown at you and separate scientifically verified facts from unverified conjecture.

Often, popular media such as television news programs present segments that *appear* scientific but on further scrutiny turn out to be flawed. One example was a segment on the ABC television news show *20/20* on sexual functions in women after a hysterectomy. In the segment, three women discussed their post-hysterectomy sexual dysfunction. One woman reported, "It got to the point where I couldn't have sex. I mean, it was so painful . . . we couldn't do it." The testimonials of the three patients were backed up by a number of medical experts who discussed the link between hysterectomy and sexual dysfunction.

Had you watched this segment and looked no further, you would have come away with the impression that post-hysterectomy sexual dysfunction is common. After all, all the women interviewed experienced it, and the experts supported them. However, your impression would not be correct. When we examine the research on post-hysterectomy sexual functioning, the picture is not nearly as clear as the one portrayed in the *20/20* segment. In fact, there are studies showing that after hysterectomy, women may report an *improvement* in sexual function (Rhodes, Kjerulff, Langenberg, & Guzinski, 1999). Other studies show that the type of hysterectomy a woman has undergone makes a difference. If the surgery involves removing the cervix (a total hysterectomy), there is more sexual dysfunction after surgery than if the cervix is left intact (Saini, Kuczynski, Gretz, & Sills, 2002). Finally, the Boston University School of Medicine's Institute for Sexual Medicine reports that of 1,200 women seen at its Center for Sexual Medicine, very few of them complained of post-hysterectomy sexual dysfunction (Goldstein, 2003).

As this examples suggests, whether you plan a career in research or not, it is to your benefit to learn how research is done. This will put you in a position to evaluate information that you encounter that is supposedly based on "science."

## EXPLORING THE CAUSES OF BEHAVIOR

Psychology is the science of behavior and mental processes. The major goals of psychology are (1) to build an organized body of knowledge about its subject matter and (2) to describe mental and behavioral processes and develop reliable explanations for these processes. For example, psychologists interested in aggression and the media would build a storehouse of knowledge concerning how various types of media violence (e.g., movies, television shows, cartoons, or violent video games) affect aggressive behavior. If it were shown that exposure to violence in the media increases aggression, the psychologist would seek to explain how this occurs.

How do you, as a scientist, go about adding to this storehouse of knowledge? The principal method for acquiring knowledge and uncovering causes of behavior is *research*. You identify a problem and then systematically set out to collect information about the problem and develop explanations.

Robert Cialdini (1994) offers a simple yet effective analogy to describe the process of studying behavior: He likens science to a hunting trip. Before you go out to "bag" your prey, you must first scout out the area within which you are going to hunt. On a hunting trip, scouting involves determining the type and number of prey available in an area. Cialdini suggests that in science "scouting" involves making systematic observations of naturally occurring behavior.

Sometimes scouting may not be necessary. Sometimes the prey falls right into your lap without you having to go out and find it. Cialdini tells a story of a young woman who was soliciting for a charity. Initially, Cialdini declined to give a donation. However, after the young woman told him that "even a penny would help," he found himself digging into his wallet. As he reflected on this experience, he got to wondering why he gave a donation after the "even a penny would help" statement. This led him to a series of studies on the dynamics of compliance. In a similar manner, as you read about the Christopher Cepeda case, you might already have begun to wonder about the factors that contribute to distraction-related accidents. As we describe in Chapter 3, "scouting" can involve considering many sources.

The second step that Cialdini identifies is "trapping." After you have identified a problem that interests you, the next thing to do is identify the factors that might affect the behavior that you have scouted. Then, much like a hunter closing in on prey, you systematically study the phenomenon and identify the factors that are crucial to explaining that phenomenon. For example, after wondering whether talking on a cell phone while walking causes accidents, you could set up an experiment to test this. You could have participants walk through a building over a predesignated route. Participants in one condition would walk through the building while talking on a cell phone, and participants in another would do the task without talking on a cell phone. You could record the number of times a participant bumps into objects while walking through the building. If you find that participants talking on a cell phone bump into more objects than those not talking on a cell phone, you have evidence that talking on a cell phone while walking causes pedestrians to make more potentially dangerous errors while walking.

## QUESTIONS TO PONDER

1. How do basic and applied research differ, and how are they similar?

2. How are problems framed in research terms?

3. What is confirmation bias, and what are its implications for understanding behavior?

4. Why should you care about learning about research, even if you are not planning a career in research?

5. What are the two steps suggested by Cialdini (1994) for exploring the causes of behavior, and how do they relate to explaining behavior?

# EXPLAINING BEHAVIOR

Imagine that, after narrowly avoiding being hit by a car when you stepped into an intersection while texting on your phone, you find yourself depressed, unable to sleep, and lacking appetite. After a few weeks of feeling miserable, you find a therapist whom you have heard can help alleviate your symptoms. On the day of your appointment you meet with your new therapist. You begin by mapping out a therapy plan with your therapist. You and she identify stressful events you have experienced, current situations that are distressing to you, and events in your past that might relate to your current symptoms. Next you identify an incident that is causing you the most distress (in this case, your near-accident) and your therapist has you visualize things relating to your memory of the event. She also has you try to reexperience the sensations and emotions related to the accident.

So far you are pretty satisfied with your therapy session because your therapist is using techniques you have read about and that are successful in relieving symptoms like yours. What occurs next, however, puzzles you. Your therapist has you follow her finger with your eyes as she moves it rapidly back and forth across your field of vision. Suddenly, she stops and tells you to let your mind go blank and attend to any thoughts, feelings, or sensations that come to mind. You are starting to wonder just what is going on. Whatever you come up with, your therapist tells you to visualize and has you follow her finger once again with your eyes. On your way home after the session you wonder just what the finger exercise was all about.

When you get home, you do some research on the Internet and find that your therapist was using a technique called Eye Movement Desensitization and Reprocessing (EMDR) therapy. You read that the eye movements are supposed to reduce the patient's symptoms rapidly. Because you did not experience this, you decide to look into what is known about EMDR therapy. What you find surprises you. You find a number of websites touting the effectiveness of EMDR. You read testimonials from therapists and patients claiming major successes using the treatment. You also learn that many clinical psychologists doubt that the eye movements are a necessary component of the therapy. In response, advocates of EMDR have challenged critics to prove that EMDR does not work. They suggest that those testing EMDR are not properly trained in the technique, so it will not work for them. They also suggest that the eye movements are not necessary and that other forms of stimulation, such as the therapist tapping her fingers on the client's leg, will work. You are becoming skeptical. What you want to find is some real scientific evidence concerning EMDR.

## Science, Protoscience, Nonscience, and Pseudoscience

We have noted that one goal of science is to develop explanations for behavior. This goal is shared by other disciplines as well. For example, historians may attempt to explain why Robert E. Lee ordered Pickett's Charge on the final day of the Battle of Gettysburg. Any explanation would be based on reading and interpreting historical documents and records. However, unless such explanations can be submitted to empirical testing, they are not considered scientific.

What distinguishes a true established science from protoscience, nonscience, and pseudoscience? The difference lies in the methods used to collect information and draw conclusions from it. A true, established science relies on established scientific methods to acquire information and adheres to certain rules when determining the validity of information acquired.

**Protoscience** is a term given to science at the edges of current scientific understanding (Sohl, 2004). Sometimes this form of science is called "fringe science" because it deals with issues and phenomena at the fringes of established science (Sohl, 2004). Protosciences often use the scientific method to test ideas. According to Sohl, protoscience has the potential to develop into true science if the phenomena being studied receive legitimate scientific support; this happened in areas such as computer science and epigenetics. On the other hand, protoscience can descend into pseudoscience if claims made cannot be empirically verified. In yet other cases, not enough evidence is available to establish a field as scientific. For example, after actor Christopher Reeve suffered a spinal injury that left him paralyzed from the neck down, new treatments were being explored in which spinal cord patients exercised paralyzed limbs on special equipment. Many of these patients showed recovery of some sensory and/or motor functions. However, to be considered scientifically valid, the efficacy of this therapy, while potentially exciting for patients, must be verified via carefully conducted studies. A recent review of existing studies suggests that exercise can improve muscle tone and improve existing capabilities (Lu, Battistuzzo, Zoghi, & Galea, 2015). However, there is little evidence that exercise can help spinal patients recover lost functions (Hicks et al., 2011). Although there are instances where protoscience has advanced to the status of true science, there are others where seemingly scientific areas descended into the realm of pseudoscience (e.g., alchemy and astrology).

A *nonscience* can be a legitimate academic discipline (like philosophy) that applies systematic techniques to the acquisition of information. For example, philosophers may differ on what they consider to be ethical behavior and may support their positions through logical argument. However, they lack any empirical test through which one view or another might be supported, and so the question of what is ethical cannot be addressed through scientific means.

Pseudoscience is another animal altogether. The term **pseudoscience** literally means "false science." According to Robert Carroll (2006), "pseudoscience is [a] set of ideas based on theories put forth as scientific when they are not scientific" (http://skepdic.com/pseudosc.html). It is important to note that true science and pseudoscience differ more in degree than in kind, with blurred boundaries between them (Lilienfeld, Lynn, & Lohr, 2003). What this means is that science and pseudoscience share many characteristics. For example, both may attempt to provide support for an idea. However, the methods of pseudoscience do not have the same rigor or standards required of a true science. Some notorious examples of pseudoscience include phrenology (determining personality by reading the bumps on one's head), eye movement desensitization and reprocessing therapy (EMDR—moving one's eyes back and forth rapidly while thinking about a problem), and astrology (using the position of the stars and planets to explain behavior and predict the future).

Scott Lilienfeld (2005) lists several qualities that define a pseudoscience:

- Using situation-specific hypotheses to explain away falsification of a pseudoscientific idea or claim;

- Having no mechanisms for self-correction and consequent stagnation of ideas or claims;

- Relying on confirming one's beliefs rather than disconfirming them;

- Shifting the burden of proof to skeptics and critics away from the proponent of an idea or a claim;

- Relying on nonscientific anecdotal evidence and testimonials to support an idea or claim;

- Avoiding the peer review process that would scientifically evaluate ideas and claims;

- Failing to build on an existing base of scientific knowledge;

- Using impressive-sounding jargon that lends false credibility to ideas and claims;

- Failing to specify conditions under which ideas or claims would not hold true.

Lilienfeld points out that no one criterion from this list is sufficient to classify an idea or claim as pseudoscientific. However, the greater the number of the aforementioned qualities an idea or claim possesses, the more confident you can be that the idea or claim is based on pseudoscience and not legitimate science.

Rory Coker (2007) provides a nice contrast between a true science and a pseudoscience. He identifies several crucial differences between science and pseudoscience that can help you assess whether an idea or claim is truly scientific or based on pseudoscientific beliefs. This contrast is shown in Table 1-1. Coker also suggests several additional characteristics of pseudoscience. First, pseudoscience often is unconcerned with facts and "spouts" dubious facts when necessary. Second, what research is conducted on an idea or claim is usually sloppy and does not include independent investigations to check its sources. Third, pseudoscience inevitably defaults to absurd explanations when pressed for an explanation of an idea or claim. Fourth, by leaving out critical facts pseudoscience creates mysteries that are difficult to solve. You can find a full list of these and other characteristics of pseudoscience at www.quackwatch. org/01QuackeryRelatedTopics/pseudo.html.

One area in which pseudoscience has become a concern is in the treatment of mental and behavioral disorders (Lilienfeld, 2015). There is ample evidence that evidence-based treatments have a significant, positive effect on treating disorders. For example, there is considerable scientific support for the success of cognitive-behavioral therapy (Lee & Hunsley, 2015). However, throughout the history of psychiatry and clinical psychology, there have been numerous treatments based on little empirical evidence or on pseudoscience, such as gluten-free diets to treat autism spectrum disorders (Lilienfeld, 2015). Now, you might be thinking what harm is there in trying such treatments? If it helps one child with autism, isn't it worth it? Lilienfeld points out that there are two liabilities in adopting treatments based on pseudoscience. First, such treatments may actually cause more harm than good. Lilienfeld gives the example of

**TABLE 1-1   Distinguishing Science from Pseudoscience**

| SCIENCE | PSEUDOSCIENCE |
|---|---|
| Findings published in peer-reviewed publications using standards for honesty and accuracy aimed at scientists. | Findings disseminated to general public via sources that are not peer reviewed. No prepublication review for precision or accuracy. |
| Experiments must be precisely described and be reproducible. Reliable results are demanded. | Studies, if any, are vaguely defined and cannot be reproduced easily. Results cannot be reproduced |
| Scientific failures are carefully scrutinized and studied for reasons for failure. | Failures are ignored, minimized, explained away, rationalized, or hidden. |
| Over time and continued research, more and more is learned about scientific phenomena. | No underlying mechanisms are identified and no new research is done. No progress is made and nothing concrete is learned. |
| Idiosyncratic findings and blunders "average out" and do not affect the actual phenomenon under study. | Idiosyncratic findings and blunders provide the only identifiable phenomena. |
| Scientists convince others based on evidence and research findings, making the best case permitted by existing data. Old ideas discarded in the light of new evidence. | Attempts to convince based on belief and faith rather than facts. Belief encouraged in spite of facts, not because of them. Ideas never discarded, regardless of the evidence. |
| Scientist has no personal stake in a specific outcome of a study. | Serious conflicts of interest. Pseudoscientist makes his or her living off of pseudoscientific products or services. |

SOURCE: Coker, 2007, https://webspace.utexas.edu/cokerwr/www/index.html/distinguish.htm

"scared straight" programs, which exposed youthful offenders to harsh prison environments. According to Lilienfeld, research evidence suggests that such programs can actually lead to more crime. Second, the time and energy devoted to poorly supported treatments sap valuable resources that could be better directed toward treatments that are more effective. The bottom line is that relying on information and treatments that do not have a solid foundation in science can be dangerous.

## Scientific Explanations

Contrast pseudoscience with how a true science operates. A true science attempts to develop scientific explanations to explain phenomena within its domain. Simply put, a **scientific explanation** is an explanation based on the application of accepted scientific methods. Scientific explanations differ in several important ways from nonscientific and pseudoscientific explanations that rely more on common sense or faith. Let's take a look at how science approaches a question like the effectiveness of EMDR therapy.

EMDR therapy was developed by Francine Shapiro. Shapiro noticed that when she was experiencing a disturbing thought, her eyes were involuntarily moving rapidly. She noticed further that when she brought her eye movements under voluntary control while thinking a traumatic thought, anxiety was reduced (Shapiro, 1989). Based on her experience, Shapiro proposed EMDR as a new therapy for individuals suffering from posttraumatic stress disorder (PTSD). Shapiro speculated that traumatic events "upset the excitatory/inhibitory balance in the brain, causing a pathological change in the neural elements" (Shapiro, 1989, p. 216). Shapiro speculated that the eye movements used in EMDR coupled with traumatic thoughts restored the neural balance and reversed the brain pathology caused by the trauma. In short, eye movements were believed to be central to the power of EMDR to bring about rapid and dramatic reductions in PTSD symptoms.

Shapiro (1989) provided some evidence for the effectiveness of EMDR therapy in the form of a case study. Based on her research and her case studies, Shapiro concluded that EMDR was a unique, effective new therapy for PTSD. Other researchers did not agree. They pointed out that Shapiro's evidence (and evidence provided by others) was based on flawed research. Because EMDR was rapidly gaining popularity, it was necessary to test rigorously the claims made by advocates of EMDR that eye movements were essential to successful outcomes. Two researchers, George Renfrey and C. Richard Spates (1994), tested the claim that eye movements were a necessary component of EMDR therapy. Their study provides an excellent example of how scientists go about their business of uncovering true scientific explanations.

In their experiment Renfrey and Spates "deconstructed" the EMDR technique into its components. Patients with PTSD were randomly assigned to one of three conditions in the study. Some patients were assigned to a standard EMDR condition. Other patients were assigned to an automated EMDR condition in which eye movements were induced by having patients shift their eyes back and forth between two alternating lights. The remaining patients were assigned to a no eye movement group in which the patients fixated their eyes on a stationary light. In all three conditions all of the other essential elements of EMDR therapy (visualizing and thinking about a traumatic event) were maintained. Measures of heart rate and anxiety were obtained from patients. Renfrey and Spates found that there was no difference between the three treatment groups on any of the measures, leading them to conclude that "eye movements are not an essential component of the intervention" (Renfrey & Spates, 1994, p. 238). Subsequent research confirmed this conclusion (Davidson & Parker, 2001).

In contrast to nonscience and pseudoscience, a true science attempts to develop scientific explanations for behavior through the application of the scientific method and specific scientific research designs, just as Renfrey and Spates (1994) did when they tested the role of eye movements in EMDR therapy. Scientific explanations are the only ones accepted by scientists because they have a unique blend of characteristics that sets them apart from other explanations. Let's take a look at those characteristics next.

*Scientific Explanations Are Empirical*      An explanation is *empirical* if it is based on the evidence of the senses. To qualify as scientific, an explanation must be based on objective and systematic observation, often carried out under carefully controlled conditions. The observable events and conditions referred to in the explanation must be capable of verification by others.

*Scientific Explanations Are Rational*    An explanation is *rational* if it follows the rules of logic and is consistent with known facts. If the explanation makes assumptions that are known to be false, commits logical errors in drawing conclusions from its assumptions, or is inconsistent with established fact, then it does not qualify as scientific.

*Scientific Explanations Are Testable*    A scientific explanation should either be verifiable through direct observation or lead to specific predictions about what should occur under conditions not yet observed. An explanation is *testable* if confidence in the explanation could be undermined by a failure to observe the predicted outcome. One should be able to imagine outcomes that would disprove the explanation.

*Scientific Explanations Are Parsimonious*    Often more than one explanation is offered for an observed behavior. When this occurs, scientists prefer the **parsimonious explanation**, the one that explains behavior with the fewest number of assumptions.

*Scientific Explanations Are General*    Scientists prefer explanations of broad explanatory power over those that "work" only within a limited set of circumstances.

*Scientific Explanations Are Tentative*    Scientists may have confidence in their explanations, but they are nevertheless willing to entertain the possibility that an explanation is faulty. This attitude was strengthened in the past century by the realization that even Newton's conception of the universe, one of the most strongly supported views in scientific history, had to be replaced when new evidence showed that some of its predictions were wrong.

*Scientific Explanations Are Rigorously Evaluated*    This characteristic derives from the other characteristics listed, but it is important enough to deserve its own place in our list. Scientific explanations are constantly evaluated for consistency with the evidence and with known principles, for parsimony, and for generality. Attempts are made to extend the scope of the explanation to cover broader areas and to include more factors. As plausible alternatives appear, these are pitted against the old explanations in a continual battle for the "survival of the fittest." In this way, even accepted explanations may be overthrown in favor of views that are more general, more parsimonious, or more consistent with observation.

## QUESTIONS TO PONDER

1. How do science, protoscience, nonscience, and pseudoscience differ?
2. What are the defining characteristics of pseudoscience?
3. What are the main characteristics of scientific explanations? (Describe each.)

## Commonsense Explanations Versus Scientific Explanations

During the course of everyday experience, we develop explanations of the events we see going on around us. Largely, these explanations are based on the limited information available from the observed event and what our previous experience has told us is true. These rather loose explanations can be classified as **commonsense explanations** because they are based on our own sense of what is true about the world around us. Of course, scientific explanations and commonsense explanations have something in common: They both start with an observation of events in the real world. However, the two types of explanations differ in the level of proof required to support the explanation. Commonsense explanations tend to be accepted at face value, whereas scientific explanations are subjected to rigorous research scrutiny.

Take the case of Tamir Rice, which occurred in 2015. Rice was a Black 12-year-old boy who was shot by a White police officer who believed that Rice had a real gun, when the gun was actually a realistic toy gun. Many in the Black community believed that the officer's behavior was racially motivated. The implication was that if Rice had been White, he would not have been shot by the police officer. That a police officer's racial prejudice might make him or her quicker to pull the trigger on a minority suspect might seem to be a viable explanation for what happened in the Tamir Rice case. Although this explanation may have some intuitive appeal, several factors disqualify it as a scientific explanation.

First, the "racism" explanation was not based on careful, systematic observation. Instead, it was based on what some *believe* to be true of the relationship between race and a police officer's behavior. Consequently, the explanation may have been derived from biased, incomplete, or limited evidence (if from any evidence at all). Second, it was not examined to determine its consistency with other available observations. Third, no effort was made to evaluate it against plausible alternative explanations. Fourth, no predictions were derived from the explanation and tested. Fifth, no attempt was made to determine how well the explanation accounted for similar behavior in a variety of other circumstances. Those who accepted this explanation did so simply because it appeared to make sense of the police officer's behavior and was consistent with their preexisting beliefs about how the police treat Black suspects. Because commonsense explanations are not rigorously evaluated, they are likely to be incomplete, inconsistent with other evidence, lacking in generality, and probably wrong. This is certainly the case with the "racism" explanation.

Although commonsense explanations may "feel right" and give us a sense that we understand a behavior, they may lack the power to apply across a variety of apparently similar situations. To see how commonsense explanations may fail to provide a truly general account of behavior, consider the following event.

On October 31, 2012, Halloween partygoers in the crowded Madrid Arena in Spain were having a great time. Suddenly, someone threw firecrackers into the arena. Partygoers believed that the firecrackers were gunshots and started to flee toward the one available exit. As the crowd surged forward in their panicked state, three people were crushed to death in the stampede. One witness who survived reported, "There were people screaming, crushed, as security guards tried to pull out those who were trapped." As a student of psychology, you may already be formulating explanations for why normally rational human beings would behave mindlessly in this situation. Clearly, lives would have been saved had the patrons of the Madrid Arena filed out in an orderly fashion. How would you explain the tragedy?

A logical and "obvious" answer is that the partygoers believed their lives to be in danger and wanted to leave the arena as quickly as possible. In this view, the panic inside the arena was motivated by a desire to survive.

Notice that the explanation at this point is probably adequate to explain the crowd behavior under the specific conditions inside the arena and perhaps to explain the same behavior under other life-threatening conditions. However, the explanation is probably too situation specific to serve as a general scientific explanation of irrational crowd behavior. It cannot explain, for example, the following incident.

On January 24, 2010, in Duisburg, Germany fans were lined up waiting to get into the Love Parade Festival. The festival is a very popular event where fans revel to the latest Techno music. The only entrance to the festival was through a tunnel leading to the parade grounds where the festival was taking place. As the parade grounds filled up, police attempted to halt the flow of additional people into the festival. The crowd in the tunnel began to grow and surge forward. In the end, 17 people were crushed to death. The tunnel was so densely packed that it took police some time to get to the victims.

Clearly, the explanation for irrational crowd behavior at the Madrid Arena cannot be applied to the Duisburg tragedy. People were not going to die if they failed to get into the arena. What seemed a reasonable explanation for irrational crowd behavior in the Madrid Arena case must be discarded.

You must look for common elements to explain such similar yet diverse events. In both situations, the available rewards were perceived to be limited. A powerful reward (avoiding pain and death) in the Madrid Arena undoubtedly was perceived as attainable only for a brief time. Similarly, in Duisburg the perceived reward (getting into a festival), although not essential for survival, was also available for a limited time only. In both cases, apparently irrational behavior resulted as large numbers of people individually attempted to maximize the probability of obtaining the reward.

The new tentative explanation for the irrational behavior now centers on the perceived availability of rewards rather than situation-specific variables. This new tentative explanation has been tested in research and has received some support.

As these examples illustrate, simple commonsense explanations may not apply beyond the specific situations that spawned them. The scientist interested in irrational crowd behavior would look for a more general concept (such as perceived availability of rewards) to explain observed behavior. That is not to say that simple, obvious explanations are always incorrect. However, when you are looking for an explanation that transcends situation-specific variables, you often must look beyond simple, commonsense explanations.

## Belief-Based Explanations Versus Scientific Explanations

Explanations for behavior often arise not from common sense or scientific observation but from individuals or groups who (through indoctrination, upbringing, or personal need) have accepted on faith the truth of their beliefs. You may agree or disagree with those beliefs, but you should be aware that explanations offered by science and **belief-based explanations** are fundamentally different.

Explanations based on belief are accepted because they come from a trusted source or appear to be consistent with the larger framework of belief. No evidence is required. If evidence suggests that the explanation is incorrect, then the evidence is discarded or reinterpreted to make it appear consistent with the belief. For example, certain religions hold that Earth was created only a few thousand years ago. The discovery of fossilized remains of dinosaurs and other creatures (apparently millions of years old) challenged this belief. To explain the existence of these remains, people defending the belief suggest that fossils are actually natural rock formations that resemble bones or that the fossils are the remains of the victims of the Great Flood. Thus, rather than calling the belief into question, apparently contrary evidence is interpreted to appear consistent with the belief.

This willingness to apply a different *post hoc* (after-the-fact) explanation to reconcile each conflicting observation with a belief leads to an unparsimonious patchwork quilt of explanations that lacks generality, fails to produce testable predictions about future findings, and often requires that one assumes the common occurrence of highly unlikely events. Scientific explanations of the same phenomena, in contrast, logically organize the observed facts by means of a few parsimonious assumptions and lead to testable predictions.

Nowhere is the contrast between these two approaches more striking than in the debate between evolutionary biologists and the so-called creation scientists, whose explanation for fossils was previously mentioned. To take one example, consider the recent discoveries based on gene sequencing, which reveal the degree of genetic similarity among various species. These observations and some simple assumptions about the rate of mutation in the genetic material allowed biologists to develop "family trees" indicating how long ago the various species separated from one another. The trees drawn up from the gene-sequencing data agree amazingly well with and to a large degree were predicted by the trees assembled from the fossil record. In contrast, because creationists assume that all animals alive today have always had their current form and that fossils represent the remains of animals killed in the Great Flood, their view could not have predicted relationships found in the genetic material. Instead, they must invent yet another *post hoc* explanation to make these new findings appear consistent with their beliefs.

In addition to the differences described thus far, scientific and belief-based explanations also differ in tentativeness. Whereas explanations based on belief are simply *assumed* to be true, scientific explanations are accepted because they are consistent with existing objective evidence and have survived rigorous testing against plausible alternatives. Scientists accept the possibility that better explanations may turn up or that new tests may show that the current explanation is inadequate.

Scientific explanations also differ from belief-based explanations in the subject areas for which explanations are offered. Whereas explanations based on belief may seek to answer virtually any question, scientific explanations are limited to addressing those questions that can be answered by means of objective observations. For example, what happens to a person after death and why suffering exists in the world are explained by religion, but such questions remain outside the realm of scientific explanation. No objective tests or observations can be performed to answer these questions within the confines of the scientific method. Science offers no explanation for such questions, and you must rely on faith or belief for answers. However, for questions that can be settled on the basis of objective observation, scientific explanations generally have provided more satisfactory and useful accounts of behavior than those provided by a priori beliefs.

## QUESTIONS TO PONDER

1. How do scientific and commonsense explanations differ?
2. How do belief-based and scientific explanations differ?
3. What kinds of questions do scientists refrain from investigating? Why do scientists refrain from studying these issues?

## WHEN SCIENTIFIC EXPLANATIONS FAIL

Scientific explanation is preferable to other kinds of explanation when scientific methods can be applied. Using a scientific approach maximizes the chances of discovering the best explanation for an observed behavioral phenomenon. Despite the application of the most rigorous scientific methods, instances do occur in which the explanation offered by a scientist is not valid. Scientific explanations are sometimes flawed. Understanding some of the pitfalls inherent to developing scientific explanations will help you avoid arriving at flawed or incorrect explanations for behavior.

### Failures Due to Faulty Inference

Explanations may fail because developing them involves an inference process. We make observations and then infer the causes for the observed behavior. This inference process always involves the danger of incorrectly inferring the underlying mechanisms that control behavior.

The problem of faulty inference is illustrated in a satirical book by David Macaulay (1979) called *Motel of the Mysteries*. In this book, a scientist (Howard Carson) uncovers the remnants of our civilization 5,000 years from now. Carson unearths a motel and begins the task of explaining what our civilization was like, based on the artifacts found in the motel.

Among the items unearthed were various bathroom plumbing devices: a plunger, a showerhead, and a spout. These items were assumed by Carson to be musical instruments. The archaeologist describes the items as follows:

> The two trumpets [the showerhead and spout] . . . were found attached to the wall of the inner chamber at the end of the sarcophagus. They were both coated with a silver substance similar to that used on the ornamental pieces of the metal animals. Music was played by forcing water from the sacred spring through the

trumpets under great pressure. Pitch was controlled by a large silver handle marked HC. . . . The [other] instrument [the plunger] is probably of the percussion family, but as yet the method of playing it remains a mystery. It is, however, beautifully crafted of wood and rubber. (Macaulay, 1979, p. 68)

By hypothesizing that various plumbing devices served as ceremonial musical instruments, Macaulay's archaeologist has reached a number of inaccurate conclusions. Although the *Motel of the Mysteries* example is pure fiction, real-life examples of inference gone wrong abound in science, and psychology is no exception. R. E. Fancher (1985) described the following example in his book *The Intelligence Men: Makers of the IQ Controversy*. During World War I, the U.S. Army administered group intelligence tests under the direction of Robert Yerkes. More than 1.75 million men had taken either the Alpha or Beta version of the test by the end of the war and provided an excellent statistical sample from which conclusions could be drawn about the abilities of U.S. men of that era.

The results were shocking. Analysis of the data revealed that the average army recruit had a mental age of 13 years—3 years below the "average adult" mental age of 16 and only 1 year above the upper limit for moronity. Fancher described Yerkes's interpretation as follows:

Rather than interpreting his results to mean that there was something wrong with the standard, or that the army scores had been artificially depressed by . . . the failure to re-test most low Alpha scorers on Beta, as was supposed to have been the case, Yerkes asserted that the "native intelligence" of the average recruit was shockingly low. The tests, he said, were "originally intended, and now definitely known, to measure native intellectual ability. They are to some extent influenced by educational acquirement, but in the main the soldier's inborn intelligence and not the accidents of environment determined his mental rating or grade." Accordingly, a very substantial proportion of the soldiers in the U.S. Army were actually morons. (1985, p. 127)

In fact, Yerkes's assertions about the tests were not in any sense established, and indeed the data provided evidence against Yerkes's conclusion. For example, poorly educated recruits from rural areas scored lower than their better-educated city cousins. Yerkes's tests had failed to consider the differences in educational opportunities among recruits. As a result, Yerkes and his followers inappropriately concluded that the average intellectual ability of Americans was deteriorating.

In the Yerkes example, faulty conclusions were drawn because the conclusions were based on unfounded assumptions concerning the ability of the tests to unambiguously measure intelligence. The researchers failed to consider possible *alternative explanations* for observed effects. Although the intelligence of U.S. Army recruits may in fact have been distressingly low, an alternative explanation centering on environmental factors such as educational level would have been equally plausible. These two rival explanations (real decline in intelligence versus lack of educational experience) should have been subjected to the proper tests to determine which was more plausible. Later, this book discusses how developing, testing, and eliminating such rival hypotheses are crucial elements of the scientific method.

## Pseudoexplanations

Failing to consider alternative explanations is not the only danger waiting to befall the unwary scientist. In formulating valid scientific explanations for behavioral events, it is important to avoid the trap of **pseudoexplanation**. In seeking to provide explanations for behavior, psychologists sometimes offer positions, theories, and explanations that do nothing more than provide an alternative label for the behavioral event. One notorious example was the attempt to explain aggression with the concept of an instinct. According to this position, people (and animals) behave aggressively because of an aggressive instinct. Although this explanation may have intuitive appeal, it does not serve as a valid scientific explanation.

Figure 1-1 illustrates the problem with such an explanation. Notice that the observed behavior (aggression) is used to prove the existence of the aggressive instinct. The concept of instinct is then used to explain the aggressive behavior.

This form of reasoning is called a **circular explanation**, or **tautology**. It does not provide a true explanation but rather merely provides another label (instinct) for a class of observed behavior (aggression). Animals are aggressive because they have aggressive instincts. How do we know they have aggressive instincts? Because they are aggressive! Thus, all we are saying is that animals are aggressive because of a tendency to behave aggressively. Obviously, this is not an explanation.

You might expect only novice behavioral scientists to be prone to using pseudoexplanations. However, even professional behavioral scientists have proposed "explanations" for behavioral phenomena that are really pseudoexplanations. In a 1970 article, Martin Seligman proposed a continuum of preparedness to help explain why an animal can learn some associations easily (such as between taste and illness) and other associations only with great difficulty (such as between taste and electric shock).

According to Seligman's analysis, the animal may be biologically prepared to learn some associations (those learned quickly) and contraprepared to learn others (those learned slowly, if at all). Thus, some animals may have difficulty acquiring an association between taste and shock because they are contraprepared by evolution to associate the two.

As with the use of instinct to explain aggression, the continuum-of-preparedness notion seems intuitively correct. Indeed, it does serve as a potentially valid explanation

**FIGURE 1-1**   A circular explanation. The observed behavior is "explained" by a concept, but the behavior itself is used as proof of the existence of the explanatory concept.

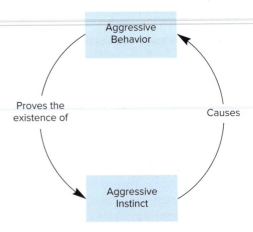

for the observed differences in learning rates. But it does not qualify as a true explanation as it is stated. Refer to Figure 1-1 and substitute "quickly or slowly acquired association" for "aggressive behavior" and "continuum of preparedness" for "aggressive instinct." As presently stated, the continuum-of-preparedness explanation is circular: Animals learn a particular association with difficulty because they are contraprepared to learn it. How do you know they are contraprepared? You know because they have difficulty learning.

How can you avoid falling into the trap of proposing and accepting pseudo-explanations? When evaluating a proposed explanation, ask yourself whether or not the researcher has provided *independent measures* of the behavior of interest (such as difficulty learning an association) *and* the proposed explanatory concept (such as the continuum of preparedness). For example, if you could find an independent measure of preparedness that does *not* involve the animal's ability to form an association, then the explanation in terms of preparedness would qualify as a true explanation. If you can determine the animal's preparedness only by observing its ability to form a particular association, the proposed explanation is circular. Rather than explaining the differing rates of learning, the statement actually serves only to define the types of preparedness.

Developing independent measures for the explanatory concept and the behavior to be explained may not be easy. For example, in the continuum-of-preparedness case, it may take some creative thought to develop a measure of preparedness that is independent of the observed behavior. The same is true for the concept of an instinct.

As these examples have illustrated, even scientific explanations may fail. However, you should not conclude that such explanations are no better than those derived from other sources. Living, behaving organisms are complex systems whose observable workings provide only clues to their inner processes. Given the available evidence, you make your best guess. It should not be surprising that these guesses are often wrong. As these conjectures are evaluated against new evidence, even the failures serve to rule out plausible alternatives and to prepare the way for better guesses. As a result, science has a strong tendency to converge on valid explanations as research progresses. Such progress in understanding is a hallmark of the scientific method.

## The Emergence of New, Conflicting Information

Previously, we made the points that humans have a strong need to explain what they experience and that scientific explanations are tentative. Sometimes science provides us with a scientific explanation, only to have it called into question when new scientific evidence emerges. The new information requires us to modify what we previously believed to be true. Unfortunately, humans can be remarkably resistant to modifying existing beliefs in the face of new evidence. Social psychologists call this phenomenon *belief perseverance.*

A good example of belief perseverance was the "science" of cereology, which was proposed to account for crop circles that appeared most notably in England. In an attempt to explain the crop circles, a whole science developed involving scientists taking various measurements to help explain where the mysterious circles came from. Scientists published their results in journals and presented their findings at conferences. Eventually, two men came forward and said that after visiting the local pub, they went out into fields and made the circles using a rope and a wooden board. Despite this new information, the cereologists were reluctant to give up their science.

The cereology example may seem silly to you, but the point is important. In many instances in science, we must abandon scientific explanations when new, contradictory evidence emerges. We made the point earlier that there is no such thing as "settled science." Scientists are and must always be willing to modify their explanations and beliefs in the face of new information.

Let's see how this might apply to another situation: the Tamir Rice case discussed earlier. The popular explanation for why the police officer shot Rice was that Rice was Black. If you had done a literature search, you would have found a study done by Correll, Park, Judd, and Wittenbrink (2002) using a technique called the shooter paradigm. In the shooter paradigm, participants play a computer game in which they must decide whether to shoot or not shoot (by pressing one or another key on the keyboard) an armed or unarmed suspect who appears on the screen. In some cases the suspect is Black and in others White. The main measure used by Correll et al. was reaction time: how quickly the participants chose to shoot or not shoot the suspect. Correll et al. found that White participants shot armed Black targets more quickly than armed White targets and decided not to shoot unarmed White targets more quickly than unarmed Black targets. Aha, you might claim: Here is scientific proof that racism was involved in Rice's death. Not so fast!

One study does not provide us with the final answer to any question. In fact, if you look further into the literature, you will find a study published in 2013 by Lois James, Bryan Vila, and Ken Daratha using the shooter paradigm. Unlike Correll et al., James and her colleagues used a realistic simulator and had participants use a laser pistol to shoot at suspects. They also included a sample of untrained civilians and trained police and military personnel. The main finding of interest here is that White participants took longer to shoot Black suspects than White suspects and were more likely *not* to shoot armed Black suspects than armed White suspects. Based on these findings, we must question our confidence in our original explanation for the Rice shooting. We must always be willing to consider new information and modify existing explanations based on it.

## QUESTIONS TO PONDER

1. How can faulty inference invalidate a scientific explanation?
2. What are pseudoexplanations, and how do you avoid them?

## METHODS OF INQUIRY

Before a scientist can offer valid and general explanations for behavior, he or she must gather information about the behavior of interest. Knowledge about behavior can be acquired by several methods, including the method of authority, the rational method, and the scientific method.

## The Method of Authority

After reading about the Madrid Arena tragedy, you might conduct an Internet search or call your former social psychology professor in search of information to help explain the irrational behavior inside the arena. When you use expert sources (whether books or people), you are using the **method of authority**. Using the method of authority involves consulting some source that you consider authoritative on the issue in question (e.g., consulting books, television, religious leaders, scientists, or the Internet).

Although useful in the early stages of acquiring knowledge, the method of authority does not always provide valid answers to questions about behavior for at least two reasons. First, the source that you consult may not be truly authoritative. Some persons are more than willing to give you their "expert" opinions on any topic, no matter how little they actually know about it (writers are no exception). Internet sources are particularly suspect. Anyone can post anything they want on the Internet. Consequently, you cannot be certain that information you obtain there is valid. (We cover this issue in more detail in Chapter 3.) Second, sources often are biased by a particular point of view. A sociologist may offer a different explanation for the Madrid Arena tragedy from the one offered by a behaviorally oriented psychologist. For these reasons, the method of authority by itself is not adequate for producing reliable explanations.

Although the method of authority is not the final word in the search for explanations of behavior, the method does play an important role in the acquisition of scientific knowledge. Information that you obtain from authorities on a topic can familiarize you with the problem, the available evidence, and the proposed explanations. With this information, you could generate new ideas about causes of behavior. However, these ideas must then be subjected to rigorous scientific scrutiny rather than being accepted at face value.

## The Rational Method

René Descartes proposed in the 17th century that valid conclusions about the universe could be drawn through the use of pure reason, a doctrine called *rationalism.* This proposal was quite revolutionary at the time because most scholars of the day relied heavily on the method of authority to answer questions. Descartes' method began with skepticism, a willingness to doubt the truth of every belief. Descartes noted, as an example, that it was even possible to doubt the existence of the universe. What you perceive, he reasoned, could be an illusion. Could you prove otherwise?

After establishing doubt, Descartes moved to the next stage of his method: the search for "self-evident truths," statements that *must* be true because to assume otherwise would contradict logic. Descartes reasoned that if the universe around him did not really exist, then perhaps he himself also did not exist. It was immediately obvious to Descartes that this idea contradicted logic—it was self-evidently true that if he did not exist, he certainly could not be thinking about the question of his own existence. And it was just as self-evidently true that he was indeed thinking.

These two self-evident truths can be used as assumptions from which deductive logic will yield a firm conclusion:

Assumption 1: Something that thinks must exist.

Assumption 2: I am thinking.

Conclusion: I exist.

Using only his powers of reasoning, Descartes had identified two statements whose truth logically cannot be doubted, and from them he was able to deduce a conclusion that is equally bulletproof. It is bulletproof because, if the assumptions are true and you make no logical errors, deduction guarantees the truth of the conclusion. By the way, this particular example of the use of his method was immortalized by Descartes in the declaration *"Cogito, ergo sum"* (Latin for "I think, therefore I am"). If you've heard that phrase before and wondered what it meant, now you know.

Descartes' method came to be called the **rational method** because it depends on logical reasoning rather than on authority or the evidence of one's senses. Although the method satisfied Descartes, we must approach "knowledge" acquired in this way with caution. The power of the rational method lies in logically deduced conclusions from self-evident truths. Unfortunately, precious few self-evident truths can serve as assumptions in a logical system. If one (or both) of the assumptions used in the deduction process is incorrect, the logically deduced conclusion will be invalid.

Because of its shortcomings, the rational method is not used to develop scientific explanations. However, it still plays an important role in science. The tentative ideas that we form about the relationship between variables are often deduced from earlier assumptions. For example, having learned that fleeing from a fire or trying to get into a crowded arena causes irrational behavior, we may deduce that "perceived availability of reinforcers" (escaping death or getting a front-row seat) is responsible for such behavior. Rather than accepting such a deduction as correct, however, the scientist puts the deduction to empirical test.

## The Scientific Method

Braithwaite (1953) proposed that the function of a science is to "establish general laws covering the behavior of the empirical events with which the science in question is concerned" (p. 1). According to Braithwaite, a science should allow us to fuse together information concerning separately occurring events and to make reliable predictions about future, unknown events. One goal of psychology is to establish general laws of behavior that help explain and predict behavioral events that occur in a variety of situations.

Although explanations for behavior and general laws cannot be adequately formulated by relying solely on authoritative sources and using deductive reasoning, these methods (when combined with other features) form the basis for the most powerful approach to knowledge yet developed: the **scientific method**. This method comprises a series of four cyclical steps that you can repeatedly execute as you pursue the solution to a scientific problem (Yaremko et al., 1982, p. 212). These steps are (1) observing a phenomenon, (2) formulating tentative explanations or statements of cause and effect, (3) further observing or experimenting (or both) to rule out alternative explanations, and (4) refining and retesting the explanations.

*Observing a Phenomenon*    The starting point for using the scientific method is to observe the behavior of interest. This first step is essentially what Cialdini (1994) called "scouting" in which some behavior or event catches your attention. These preliminary observations of behavior and of potential causes for that behavior can take a variety of forms. In the case of the effects of cell phone distraction while walking, your initial musings about Christopher Cepeda's accident may have led you to think more carefully about the role of distraction on the ability to perform a complex task. Your curiosity might have been further piqued when divided attention was discussed in your cognitive psychology class or when you read about another case where cell phone distraction was a suspected cause of an accident. Or you might even have known some-one who was nearly killed in an accident while talking on his cell phone and attempt-ing to cross a street at the same time. In any of these cases, your curiosity might be energized so that you begin to formulate hypotheses about what factors affect the behavior you have observed.

Through the process of observation, you identify variables that appear to have an important influence on behavior. A **variable** is any characteristic or quantity that can take on two or more values. For example, whether a participant is talking on a cell phone or not while walking is a variable. Remember that in order for something to be considered a variable it must be capable of taking on *at least* two values (e.g., talking on a cell phone or not talking on a cell phone). A characteristic or quantity that takes on only one value is known as a *constant*.

*Formulating Tentative Explanations*      After identifying an interesting phenomenon to study, your next step is to develop one or more tentative explanations that seem consistent with your observations. In science these tentative explanations often include a statement of the relationship between two or more variables. That is, you tentatively state the nature of the relationship between variables that you expect to uncover with your research. The tentative statement that you offer concerning the relationship between your variables of interest is called a *hypothesis*. It is important that any hypothesis you develop be testable with empirical research.

As an example of formulating a hypothesis, consider the issue of the relationship between talking on a cell phone and walking After your preliminary observations, you might formulate the following hypothesis: A person is more likely to enter a dangerous situation when talking on a cell phone than when not talking on a cell phone.

Notice that the hypothesis links two variables (talking or not talking on a cell phone and entering dangerous situations) by a statement indicating the expected rela-tionship between them. In this case, the relationship expected is that talking on a cell phone will increase errors on a simulated walking task. Research hypotheses often take the form of a statement of how changes in the value of one variable (talking or not talking on a cell phone) will affect the value of the other variable (number of danger-ous situations entered).

*Further Observing and Experimenting*      When Cialdini (1994) talked about "trap-ping" effects, he was referring to the process of designing empirical research studies to isolate the relationship between the variables chosen for study. Up to the point of developing a hypothesis, the scientific method does not differ markedly from other methods of acquiring knowledge. At this point, all you have done is to identify a prob-lem to study and develop a hypothesis based on some initial observation. The scientific method, however, does not stop here. The third step in the scientific method marks the point at which the scientific method differs from other methods of inquiry. Unlike the other methods of inquiry, the scientific method demands that further observations be carried out to test the validity of any hypotheses that you develop. In other words, "a-trapping we shall go."

What exactly is meant by "making further observations"? The answer to this question is what the scientific method is all about. After formulating your hypothesis, you design a research study to test the relationship that you proposed. This study can take a variety of forms. It could be a *correlational study* in which you measure two or more variables and look for a relationship between them (see Chapter 4), a *quasi-experimental study* in which you take advantage of some naturally occurring event or preexisting conditions, or an *experiment* in which you systematically manipulate a variable and look for changes in the value of another that occur as a result (see Chapters 10–12).

In this case, you decide to design an experiment in which you systematically manipulate whether a person talks on a cell phone and observe the number of errors made on a simulated walking task.

*Refining and Retesting Explanations*   The final step in the scientific method is the process of refinement and retesting. As an example of this process, imagine that you found that individuals are more likely to bump into things while texting on a cell phone. Having obtained this result, you would probably want to explore the phenomenon further: Is texting more distracting than doing something else (e.g., conversing) while walking? A refined research hypothesis might take the following form: A pedestrian will be more likely to enter a dangerous situation while texting than when talking with others in a live conversation.

This process of generating new, more specific hypotheses in the light of previous results illustrates the *refinement process.* Often, confirming a hypothesis with a research study leads to other hypotheses that expand on the relationships discovered, explore the limits of the phenomenon under study, or examine the causes for the relationship observed.

As you become more familiar with the process of conducting research, you will find that not all research studies produce affirmative results. That is, sometimes your research does not confirm your hypothesis. What do you do then? In some cases, you might completely discard your original hypothesis. In other cases, however, you might revise and retest your hypothesis. In the latter instance, you are using a strategy known as *retesting.* Keep in mind that any revised or refined hypothesis must be tested as rigorously as was the original hypothesis.

The scientific method requires a great deal of time making careful observations. Sometimes your observations don't confirm your hypothesis. Is the scientific method worth all the extra effort? In fact, the ability to discover that a relationship does *not* exist makes the scientific method the powerful tool that it is. By repeatedly checking and rechecking hypotheses in the ruthless arena of empirical testing, the scientist learns which ideas are worthy and which belong on the trash heap. No other method incorporates such a powerful check on the validity of its conclusions.

Finally, it is worth noting that the scientific method should not be construed as a rigid series of stages that *must* be followed, and in the same order, for all research situations (Gibbs & Lawson, 1992). As you become more familiar with the research process and your own research, you will undoubtedly find that the scientific method is a highly flexible template that you will apply to address and answer a wide range of research questions. More than anything, the scientific method will become a way of seeing the world and approaching research questions. It will allow you to explore behavior from a scientific perspective and work toward developing scientific explanations for the behaviors you observe.

## The Scientific Method at Work: Using a Cell Phone While Walking

Throughout this chapter, we've used the issue of the safety of cell phone use while walking to illustrate how you might go about developing, testing, and refining a research hypothesis. As you may have suspected, the question has actually been the subject of scientific research, and we thought it might be helpful for you to see how an actual research study on this topic was carried out. The study that we chose for our example was conducted by Katherine Byington and David Schwebel (2013).

Byington and Schwebel (2013) exposed their participants to a virtual environment (VE) comprising a 180-degree view of busy street and accompanying sounds of birds and traffic. Participants were asked to step off a "curb" when they felt it safe to cross the street, and as they did so, an avatar resembling themselves began to cross the street at a speed matched to participants' natural walking speed. If a participant stepped off the curb at the wrong time, the avatar might be hit or nearly hit by a passing vehicle.

Participants were exposed repeatedly to two conditions. In one condition they attempted to cross the virtual street without distraction. In the other, they attempted to cross the street while answering e-mailed questions that required them to do some Internet searching to find the answers. Byington and Schwebel (2013) summarized their results as follows:

> While distracted in the VE, participants looked to the left and right less before crossing, spent a greater percentage of time looking away from the road, took longer to initiate crossing when a safe gap was available, and were hit or almost hit by oncoming vehicles more often. They also waited longer to cross and missed more safe opportunities to cross.

The Byington and Schwebel study thus offers scientific support for our previous speculation that texting or otherwise interacting with the Internet on a cell phone increases the dangers inherent in crossing a busy street.

## QUESTIONS TO PONDER

1. What are the defining characteristics and weaknesses of the method of authority and the rational method?

2. How are the method of authority and rational method used in science?

3. What are the steps involved in the scientific method?

4. Why is the scientific method preferred in science?

## The Steps of the Research Process

Scientists in the field of psychology adhere to the scientific method as the principal method for acquiring information about behavior. This is true whether the psychologist is a *clinical psychologist* evaluating the effectiveness of a new therapy technique or an *experimental psychologist* investigating the variables that affect memory. Of course, researchers in psychology adopt a wide variety of techniques in their quest for scientific knowledge.

From the inception of a research idea to the final report of results, the research process has several crucial steps. These steps are outlined in Figure 1-2. At each step, you must make one or more important decision that will influence the direction of your research. Let's explore each of these steps and some of the decisions you must make.

*Developing a Research Idea and Hypothesis*    The first step in the research process is to identify an issue that you want to study. There are many sources of research ideas (e.g., observing everyday behavior or reading scientific journals). Once you have identified a behavior to study, you must then state a research question in terms that will allow others to test it empirically. Many students of research have trouble at this point. Students seem to have little trouble identifying interesting, broadly defined behaviors to study (e.g., "I want to study memory"), but they have trouble isolating crucial variables that need to be explored.

Applying the scientific method requires you to state clearly the relationships that you expect to emerge in a research study. In other words, you must be able to formulate a precise, testable hypothesis. As noted in Figure 1-2, hypothesis development involves **deductive reasoning**, which involves deriving a specific hypothesis (in this case) from general ideas. For example, during your literature review, you may have come across information on why walking while texting on a cell phone leads to decreased performance. Using the information you found, you might deduce that one variable (the complexity of a texting task) causes changes in a second (the ability to move through an environment). The specific statement you develop connecting these two variables is your hypothesis.

*Choosing a Research Design*    Once you have narrowed your research question and developed a testable hypothesis, you must next decide on a research design to test it. As discussed in later chapters, a variety of options is available to you. Other important decisions at this point include where to conduct your study (in the laboratory or in the field) and how you are going to measure the behavior of interest.

*Choosing Subjects*    Your next decision concerns your research subjects. There are two options available to you: human participants or animal subjects. Whichever you choose, you must decide how to obtain your subjects and how they will be handled in your study. You also must be concerned with treating your subjects in an ethical manner.

*Deciding on What to Observe and Appropriate Measures*    Your next step is to decide the behavior you want to observe. This will be determined by the topic or issue that you have chosen to study. For example, if you were interested in the issue of the effects of distraction on walking ability you need a measure of walking ability. After choosing what to observe, you must next decide on the most appropriate way to

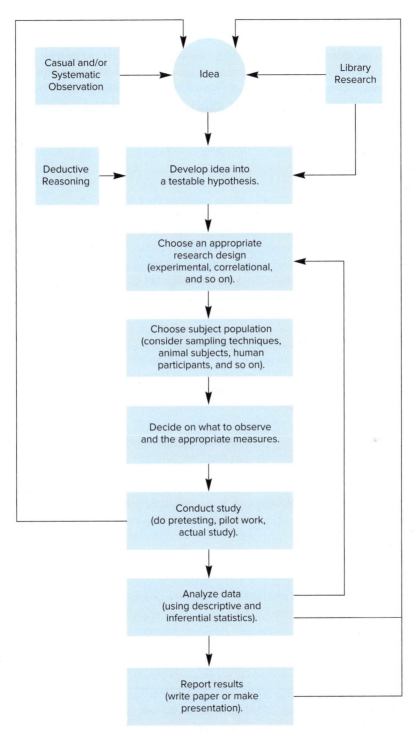

**FIGURE 1-2**   The research process. Arrows show the sequence of steps, along with feedback pathways.

measure the behavior of interest. For example, should you use a measure used in previous research or develop a new one?

With the preliminary decisions out of the way, you must consider a host of practical issues (equipment needs, preparation of materials, etc.). You might find it necessary to conduct a miniature version of your study, called a **pilot study**, to be sure your chosen procedures and materials work the way that you think they will.

*Conducting Your Study*     Now you actually have your participants take part in your study. You observe and measure their behavior. Data are formally recorded for later analysis.

*Analyzing Your Results*     After you have collected your data, you must summarize and analyze them. The analysis process involves a number of decisions. You can analyze your data in several ways, and some types of data are better analyzed with one method than with another. In most cases, you will probably calculate some descriptive statistics that provide a "nutshell" description of your data (such as averages and standard deviations) and inferential statistics that assess the reliability of your data (such as a *t test*).

*Reporting Your Results*     After analyzing your data, you are nearing the final steps in the research process. You are now ready to prepare a report of your research. If your results were reliable and sufficiently important, you may want to publish them. Consequently, you would prepare a formal paper, usually in American Psychological Association (APA) style, and submit it to a journal for review. You also might decide to present your paper at a scientific meeting, in which case you prepare a brief abstract of your research for review.

*Starting the Whole Process Over Again*     Your final report of your research is usually not the final step in your research. You may have achieved closure on (finished and analyzed) one research project. However, the results from your first study may raise more questions. These questions often serve as the seeds for a new study. In fact, you may want to replicate an interesting finding within the context of a new study. This possibility is represented in Figure 1-2 by the arrow connecting "Report results" with "Idea."

## QUESTIONS TO PONDER

1. What are the steps involved in the research process?
2. What important decisions must be made at each step of the research process?

## SUMMARY

Although we are constantly trying to explain the behavior that we see around us, commonsense explanations of behavior often are too simplistic, situation specific, and frequently based on hearsay, conjecture, anecdote, or other unreliable sources. Scientific explanations are based on carefully made observations of behavior, rigorously tested against alternative explanations, and developed to provide the most general account that is applicable over a variety of situations. For these reasons, scientific explanations tend to be more valid and general than those provided by common sense.

The goal of the science of psychology is to build an organized body of knowledge about its subject matter and to develop explanations for phenomena within its domain. It is important to distinguish between a true science, protoscience, nonscience, and pseudoscience because the quality of the information obtained depends on how it is acquired. The principal method used in a true science to build an organized body of knowledge and develop scientific explanations is research. Research involves three steps: identifying a phenomenon to study, discovering information about that phenomenon, and developing explanations for the phenomenon. A useful analogy is to think of science as a hunting trip. First, you scout where you are going to hunt for prey (analogous to identifying a phenomenon to study). Second, you go hunting to trap your prey (analogous to discovering information and developing explanations).

Explanations for behavior also are provided by beliefs. Explanations provided by belief differ from scientific explanations in that they are considered absolutely true, whereas scientific explanations are always considered tentative. Consequently, when evidence conflicts with an explanation based on belief, the evidence is questioned. When evidence conflicts with a scientific explanation, the explanation is questioned. Although beliefs can provide answers to virtually any question, the scientific method can address only those questions that can be answered through observation.

Even explanations that sound scientific may fail because relationships are often inferred from observable events. The danger always exists that inferences are incorrect, despite being based on empirical data. An explanation also may fail if you do not use independent measures of the explanatory concept and the behavior to be explained. In such cases, you have a pseudoexplanation, which is only a new label for behavior. Finally, an explanation may fail because new, reliable evidence emerges that contradicts the explanation.

There are many ways to acquire knowledge about behavior. With the method of authority, you acquire information from sources that you perceive to be expert on your topic of interest and use the information to develop an explanation for behavior. With the rational method, you deduce explanations from other sources of information. Although the method of authority and the rational method play important roles in the early stages of science, they are not acceptable methods for acquiring scientific knowledge. The scientific method is the only method accepted for the acquisition of scientific knowledge.

The four major steps of the scientific method are (1) observation of a phenomenon, (2) formation of tentative explanations or statements of cause and effect, (3) further observation or experimentation to rule out alternative explanations (or both), and (4) retesting and refinement of the explanations. The scientific method is also an attitude or a way of viewing the world. The scientist frames problems in terms of the scientific method.

The scientific method is translated into action by the research process. When performing research, you first choose a technique. Regardless of the technique chosen, research must follow the guidelines of the scientific method. The science of psychology is highly complex and diverse, and the goals of research vary from individual to individual. Some researchers, who are mainly interested in solving real-world problems, conduct applied research. Other scientists, mainly those interested in evaluating theoretical problems, conduct basic research. Even though basic and applied research are different to some extent, considerable overlap does exist. Some basic research problems have real-world applications, and some applied problems have some basic research undertones.

The research process involves a sequence of steps. At each step, important decisions affect the course of research and how you analyze and interpret data. The steps in the research process are (1) develop a research idea into a testable hypothesis, (2) choose a research design, (3) choose a subject or participant population, (4) decide on what to observe and appropriate measures, (5) obtain subjects or participants for the study and conduct the study, (6) analyze results, and (7) report results. Often the results of research raise a host of new research ideas, which starts the whole research process over again.

## KEY TERMS

| | |
|---|---|
| science | belief-based explanation |
| scientist | pseudoexplanation |
| basic research | circular explanation or tautology |
| applied research | method of authority |
| confirmation bias | rational method |
| protoscience | scientific method |
| pseudoscience | variable |
| scientific explanation | deductive reasoning |
| parsimonious explanation | pilot study |
| commonsense explanations | |

## CHAPTER 2

# Developing and Evaluating Theories of Behavior

A major goal of any science is to develop valid, general explanations for the phenomena within its field of inquiry. Thus, a considerable portion of the research effort in psychology focuses on the development and testing of theories: proposed explanations for observed psychological phenomena. Because so many research studies are designed for the purpose of testing and evaluating the merits of one or another theory, it is important to have a solid understanding of what theories are, how they are developed, and how to go about evaluating them against a number of criteria before turning our attention to the nuts and bolts of the research process in the next chapter. We begin by defining "theory" and distinguishing it from some related terms.

## WHAT IS A THEORY?

In everyday discourse we tend to use the word *theory* rather loosely, to describe everything from well-tested explanations for some event to simple guesses that seem consistent with whatever information we happen to possess. Unfortunately, such loose usage has promoted a fundamental misunderstanding of the term as it is used in science. In particular, those nonscientists who criticize Darwin's theory of evolution by natural selection have asserted that this explanation for the diversity of life on this planet is "just a theory," as if it were a mere hunch or guess, no better or worse than anyone else's explanation. Based on this understanding of the meaning of the word "theory" as used in science, some have advocated teaching explanations such as intelligent design as alternatives to Darwin's, as if all have an equal scientific footing. In response to this and other misunderstandings, the U.S. National Academy of Sciences (2013) published a set of definitions for several terms that commonly appear in discussions of evolutionary theory and related topics. In this section, and those immediately following, we have adopted those definitions.

According to the U.S. Academy of Sciences (2013), a **theory** is "a plausible or scientifically acceptable, well-substantiated explanation of some aspect of the natural world; an organized system of accepted knowledge that applies in a variety of circumstances to explain a specific set of phenomena and predict the characteristics of as yet unobserved phenomena." That's a lengthy definition, so let's examine it part by part.

To begin with, a theory is an explanation; moreover, it is an explanation of some aspect of the *natural* world. That restriction means only observable, confirmable phenomena fall within the sphere of a scientific theory. Furthermore, a theory is plausible or scientifically acceptable—the explanation follows logically from reasonable assumptions, given our current state of knowledge.

According to the definition, a theory is also well substantiated, which means the theory successfully accounts for known phenomena and has correctly predicted the outcomes of new observations. A theory is also said to represent an organized system of accepted knowledge. Its assumptions must be consistent with well-established facts and must organize their relationships in a plausible, logical way.

The final part of the definition relates to the generality of the theory and its predictive abilities: It applies in a variety of circumstances to predict a specific set of phenomena and predicts the characteristics of as yet unobserved phenomena. For example, Darwin's theory applies whether we are talking about the evolution of microbes, plants, or animals living in a wide variety of environments and across an enormous span of time. It predicts a specific set of phenomena (e.g., the effects of predation and the physical separation of the members of a species into different populations). It has successfully predicted the characteristics of phenomena that were unknown at the time Darwin proposed it (e.g., the genetic similarities and differences between and across species).

Rigorous theory-building has been most successful in fields such as physics and chemistry, where it is possible to isolate small portions of the systems under investigation and gain strong control over the relevant variables. It has proven immensely more difficult to develop similarly rigorous theories in fields that involve highly complex interacting systems that often cannot be broken down for study into simpler systems. We're talking, of course, of intact biological systems such as the ones we deal with in psychology, sociology, anthropology, education, and related fields. Even so, developing good, predictive theories in these fields remains a central goal.

Colloquial use of the term *theory* leads to confusion over what a theory really is. You can also find confusion within the scientific community over the term. Even in scientific writing, *theory, hypothesis, law,* and *model* often are used interchangeably. Nevertheless, these terms can be distinguished, as described in the next sections.

## Theory Versus Hypothesis

Students often confuse theory with hypothesis, and even professionals sometimes use these terms interchangeably. This is understandable because scientific hypotheses and theories share certain characteristics in common. According to the U.S. National Academy of Sciences (2013), a **hypothesis** is "a tentative explanation for an observation, phenomenon, or scientific problem that can be tested by further investigation. Scientific hypotheses must be posed in a form that allows them to be rejected." Thus, hypotheses and theories both provide *tentative* explanations for observations, and both must be *testable*—capable of being rejected if predictions based on them fail to be confirmed. Nevertheless, they differ in important ways.

First, unlike theories, hypotheses are not well substantiated. They are more like educated guesses to be tested than well-supported explanations. Second, hypotheses are more limited in scope than theories. They propose that certain variables relate to one another in specific ways under a particular set of conditions. In contrast, theories represent "an organized body of knowledge that applies in a variety of circumstances." Third, hypotheses are relatively simple: They do not involve a complex set of assumptions and logical relationships as theories usually do.

Perhaps too often, the term *hypothesis* is used as a synonym for prediction, as in "I hypothesize that my new therapy for posttraumatic stress disorder will be more effective than the standard one." That's a prediction, not a hypothesis. It states the expected result but does not explain why that result is expected.

An example may help to clarify the distinction between hypothesis and theory. Darwin's theory of evolution describes a mechanism through which living organisms change over time, eventually leading to the emergence of new species. This theory proposes three principles: variation, natural selection, and the reproduction of the selected characteristics. Individuals within a species vary to some degree in their characteristics (variation); within a given environment, those individuals with certain variations are more likely to survive and successfully reproduce (natural selection); and the offspring of the survivors resemble their parents (reproduction of selected characteristics). In combination, these three principles offer a powerful explanation for how species change over time, the emergence of new species, and the extinction of others, in organisms ranging from viruses to humans. This broad scope qualifies Darwin's proposal as a theory.

We can use Darwin's theory to develop a specific hypothesis to explain the glorious tail-plumage of peacocks, which they show off in front of any available peahen during the mating season. Based on Darwin's theory, one could hypothesize that the peacock's impressive plumage is a product of natural selection or, to put it another way, that having such plumage is adaptive in the male, despite the fact that it requires energy to produce and carry about and that it probably makes the peacock stand out to natural predators as well as to the peahen. To test this hypothesis, one could set up an experiment in which, say, peacocks' tail-feathers were trimmed, and compare the mating success of these birds to that of other males whose feathers were not altered. Based on our hypothesis, we would predict that males with the trimmed feathers would prove less successful at mating.

Whereas Darwin's theory has broad scope, the hypothesis just presented applies to a specific question about a particular characteristic of a male of a single species. The hypothesis is testable in that it leads to specific predictions that can be supported or refuted by the proposed experimental observations.

A study similar to the one described was actually conducted, although on widowbirds (whose tails are extremely long). Extending the tail beyond its natural length increased the male's mating success (Andersson, 1982). Marion Petrie (1994) subsequently demonstrated that mating success in peacocks depended on the number of "eyes" (conspicuous circles), among other factors, displayed by the tail-feathers.

## Theory Versus Law

A theory that has been substantially verified is sometimes called a law. However, most laws do not derive from theories in this way. A **law** is an empirically verified, quantitative relationship between two or more variables. A nice example from the field of animal learning is the *matching law,* which was proposed by Richard Herrnstein (1970) to describe how pigeons divide their keypecks between two response keys associated with two different variable-interval schedules of reinforcement. According to the matching law, the relative rate of responding on a key (the percentage of responses directed to that key per unit of time) will match the relative rate of reinforcement (the percentage of reinforcers delivered on the schedule associated with that key per unit of time). The matching law has been found to hold under a variety of conditions beyond those for which it was originally formulated and even has been shown to describe the proportion of shots taken by basketball players from beyond the three-point line (Vollmer & Bourret, 2000) and the relative ratio of passing plays to rushing plays in football (Reed, Critchfield, & Martins, 2006).

Sometimes laws idealize real-world relationships—for example, Boyle's law, which relates change in temperature to change in pressure of a confined ideal gas. Because there are no ideal gases, the relationship described by Boyle's law is not directly observable. However, as a description of the behavior of real gases, it holds well enough for most purposes. To an approximation, it represents a verified empirical relationship.

Some sources describe laws as highly verified theories. However, such empirical laws are not highly verified theories. They are well-established relationships that must be explained by theory. The matching law, for example, merely describes how behavior is allocated among alternatives; it does not *explain* why matching occurs. For that, you need a theory. To explain matching, Herrnstein and Prelec (1992) proposed that an individual repeatedly samples the ratio of responses to reinforcements associated with each option and responds by moving toward the more favorable alternative—a process they termed "melioration." (Melioration theory is but one of several proposed theories of matching the scientific community is currently evaluating.)

Laws ideally should express their relationships mathematically, but mathematically expressed laws are rare in psychology and related disciplines owing to the difficulty of controlling extraneous variables that can obscure and distort the relationships. More common are laws stating the general nature of the supposedly lawful relationship. The economic laws of supply and demand, for example, state only that rising prices for a good increase the supply of that good and decrease the demand for it. They do not state *how much* a given increase in price will increase supply or decrease demand. However, the laws of supply and demand are still capable of yielding useful predictions, despite their lack of quantitative precision. Considered together, they imply that in the long run, the price of a commodity will move toward a stable equilibrium value at which supply roughly matches demand.

## Theory Versus Model

Like *theory,* the term *model* can refer to a range of concepts. In some cases, it is simply used as a synonym for *theory.* However, in most cases **model** refers to a specific implementation of a more general theoretical view. For example, the Rescorla–Wagner model of classical conditioning formalizes a more general associative theory of conditioning (Rescorla & Wagner, 1972). This model specifies how the associative strength of a conditional stimulus (CS) is to be calculated following each of a series of trials in which the CS is presented alone or in conjunction with other stimuli. Where the general associative theory simply states that the strength of the stimulus will increase each time that the CS is paired with an unconditional stimulus (US), the Rescorla–Wagner model supplies a set of assumptions that mathematically specifies how characteristics of the stimuli interact on each trial to produce observed changes in response strength.

Rescorla and Wagner (1972) made it clear when they presented their model that the assumptions were simply starting points. For example, they assumed that the associative strength of a compound stimulus (two or more stimuli presented together) would equal the sum of the strengths of the individual stimuli. If the learning curves resulting from this assumption proved not to fit the curves obtained from experiment, then the assumption would be modified.

Rescorla and Wagner (1972) could have chosen to try several rules for combining stimulus strengths. Each variation would represent a somewhat different model of classical conditioning although all would derive from a common associative view of the conditioning process.

In a related sense, a model can represent an application of a general theory to a specific situation. In the case of the Rescorla–Wagner model, the assumptions of the model can be applied to generate predictions for reinforcement of a simple CS, for reinforcement of a compound CS, for inhibitory conditioning, for extinction, and for discrimination learning (to name a few). The assumptions of the model remain the same across all these cases, but the set of equations required in order to make the predictions changes from case to case. You might then say that each set of equations represents a different model: a model of simple conditioning, a model of compound conditioning, a model of differential conditioning, and so on. However, all the models would share the same assumptions of the Rescorla–Wagner model of conditioning.

*Computer Modeling*    Theories in psychology most commonly take the form of a set of verbal statements that describe their basic assumptions and the ways in which the various entities of the theory interact to produce behavior. Unfortunately, predictions based on such theories must be derived by verbally tracing a chain of events from a set of initial conditions to the ultimate result, a difficult process to carry out successfully in an even moderately complex theory and one that may be impossible if the theory involves entities that mutually influence one another. Because of these difficulties, scientists may occasionally disagree about what a given theory predicts under given circumstances.

One way to avoid such problems is to cast specific implementations of the theory in the form of a computer model. A *computer model* is a set of program statements that define the variables to be considered and the ways in which their values will change over the course of time or trials. The process of creating a model forces you to be specific: to state precisely what variables are involved, what their initial values or states will be, and how the variables will interact. Developing a computer model offers several advantages:

1.  The attempt to build a computer model may reveal inconsistencies, unspoken assumptions, or other defects in the theory and thus can help bring to light problems in the theory that otherwise might go unnoticed.

2. Having a computer model eliminates ambiguity; you can determine exactly what the model assumes by examining the code.

3. A properly implemented computer model will show what is to be expected under specified conditions. These predictions may be difficult or impossible to derive correctly by verbally tracing out the implications of the theory.

4. The behavior of the model under simulated conditions can be compared with the behavior of real people or animals under actual conditions to determine whether the model behaves realistically. Discrepancies reveal where the model has problems and may suggest how the model can be improved.

5. Competing theories can be evaluated by building computer models based on each and then determining which model does a better job of accounting for observed phenomena.

An interesting example of computer modeling is provided by Josef Nerb and Hans Spada (2001). Nerb and Spada were interested in explaining the relationship between cognitive, emotional, and behavioral responses to environmental disasters. More specifically, they were interested in investigating the relationship between media portrayals of single-event environmental disasters and cognitive, emotional, and behavioral responses to them. They developed a computer model called Intuitive Thinking in Environmental Risk Appraisal, or ITERA for short. The ITERA model was designed to make predictions about the cognitive appraisals made about environmental disasters as well as the emotions and behavioral tendencies generated in response to the disasters. By inputting data into the model relating to several variables, one can make predictions about cognitive, emotional, and behavioral outcomes. Those predictions could then be tested empirically to verify the validity of the computer model.

Let's see how the model works. Nerb and Spada (2001) extracted crucial pieces of information from media reports of environmental disasters that related to elements of the ITERA model. This information was systematically varied and entered as variables into the model. For example, one piece of information referred to damage done by the disaster. This was entered into the model as "given," "not given," or "unknown." The same protocol was followed for other variables (e.g., extent to which the events surrounding the disaster were controllable). By systematically entering one or more variables into the model, predictions about cognitive, emotional, and behavioral responses can be made. The computer model predicts that if information is entered indicating that the events leading to the disaster were controllable, anger should be a stronger emotion than sadness, and boycott behavior should be preferred over providing help. In contrast, the model predicts that if the disaster was uncontrollable, the dominant emotion should be sadness, and the dominant behavioral tendency would be to offer help.

Nerb and Spada (2001) tested this prediction in an experiment in which participants read a fictitious but realistic newspaper account of a tanker running aground in the North Sea, spilling oil into the sea. There were three versions of the newspaper article. In one version, participants were told that "the tanker did not fulfill safety guidelines, and the damage could have been avoided." In a second version, participants read that "the tanker did fulfill safety guidelines, and the damage could not have been avoided." In the third condition, no information was provided about safety guidelines or whether the damage could have been avoided. The results from the experiment were compared to the predictions made by the ITERA computer model. Nerb and Spada found that the model correctly predicted emotional and behavioral outcomes for the controllable condition (safety guidelines not followed and the damage could have been avoided). Consistent with the model's prediction, the dominant emotion reported by participants was anger, and the favored behavioral response was a boycott. However, the model did not correctly predict outcomes for an uncontrollable event (guidelines followed and damage was unavoidable). In this condition, sadness and helping did not dominate.

## Mechanistic Explanations Versus Functional Explanations

Theories provide explanations for observed phenomena, but not all explanations are alike. When evaluating a theory, you should carefully note whether the explanations provided are mechanistic or functional. A **mechanistic explanation** describes the mechanism (physical components) and the chain of cause and effect through which conditions act on the mechanism to produce its behavior; it describes *how* something works. In contrast, a **functional explanation** describes an attribute of something (such as physical attractiveness) in terms of its function—that is, what it does (e.g., in women, beauty signals reproductive health, according to evolutionary psychologists); it describes *why* the attribute or system exists.

Mechanistic explanations tell you how a system works without necessarily telling you why it does what it does; functional explanations refer to the purpose or goal of a given attribute or system without describing how those purposes or goals are achieved. A full understanding requires both types of explanation.

Although you can usually determine a mechanism's function once you know how it works, the converse is not true. Knowing what a system does gives only hints as to the underlying mechanism through which its functions are carried out. Consider, the buttons on your television's remote control. You can quickly determine their functions by trying them out—this one turns on the power, that one changes the volume, the next one changes the channel. However, without some knowledge of electronics, you may have no idea how a certain button accomplishes its function—and even with that knowledge, there may be dozens of different circuits (mechanisms) that can do the job. Knowing *what* a button does in no way tells you *how* it does it.

Given the choice between a mechanistic explanation and a functional one, you should prefer the mechanistic one. Unfortunately, arriving at the correct mechanism underlying a given bit of human or animal behavior often may not be possible given our current understanding of the brain. For example, we currently have no firm idea how memories are stored in the brain and subsequently accessed (although there has been plenty of speculation). Yet we do have a fair understanding of many functional properties of the brain mechanism or mechanisms involved. Given this knowledge, it is possible to construct a theory of choice among alternatives not currently present that simply *assumes* a memory with certain properties, without getting into the details of mechanism.

## QUESTIONS TO PONDER

1. What is the definition of a theory?
2. How does a theory differ from a hypothesis, a law, and a model?
3. What is a computer model, and what are the advantages of designing one?
4. How do mechanistic and functional theories differ? Which type is better, and why?


## CLASSIFYING THEORIES

Theories can be classified along several dimensions. Three important ones are (1) quantitative or qualitative aspect, (2) level of description, and (3) scope (or domain) of the theory. In light of these distinctions, we've organized our discussion by posing three questions that you can ask about any theory:

1. Is the theory quantitative or qualitative?
2. At what level of description does the theory operate?
3. What is the theory's domain?

### Is the Theory Quantitative or Qualitative?

The first dimension along which a theory can be classified is whether the theory is quantitative or qualitative. Here we describe the characteristics of each type.

*Quantitative Theory*    A **quantitative theory** defines the relationships between its variables and constants in a set of mathematical formulas. Given specific numerical inputs, the quantitative theory generates specific numerical outputs. The relationships thus described then can be tested by setting up the specified conditions and observing whether the outputs take on the specified values (within the error of measurement).

Norman Anderson's (1968) information integration theory provides a nice example of a quantitative theory in psychology. Anderson's theory attempts to explain how diverse sources of information are integrated into an overall impression. The theory proposes that each item of information used in an impression formation task is assigned both a weight and scale value. The weights and scale values are then combined according to the following formula:

$$J = \Sigma(w_i s_i)/\Sigma w_i$$

where $w_i$ is the weight assigned to each item of information and $s_i$ is the scale value assigned to each item of information. The formula states that in forming an overall impression, you in effect multiply the weight of each source of information by its scale value, add all these products together, and then divide the result by the sum of all the weights. (The theory does not assume that you carry out these mathematical operations in your head, but that your brain does something equivalent to that unconsciously.) Thus, your final judgment ($J$) about a stimulus (e.g., whether you describe a person as warm or cold, caring or uncaring, honest or dishonest) will be the result of a mathematical combination of the weights and scale values assigned to each piece of information.

*Qualitative Theory*   A **qualitative theory** is any theory that is not quantitative. Qualitative theories tend to be stated in verbal rather than mathematical terms. These theories state which variables are important and, loosely, how those variables interact.

The relationships described by qualitative theories may be quantitative, but if so, the quantities will be measured on no higher than an ordinal scale (as rankings, such as predicting that anxiety will increase, without specifying by how much). A theory of drug addiction may state that craving for the drug will increase with the time since the last administration and that this craving will be intensified by emotional stress. Note the predictions of the theory specify only ordinal relationships. They state craving will be greater under some conditions than under others, but they do not state by how much.

A good example of a qualitative theory in psychology is a theory of language acquisition by Noam Chomsky (1965). This theory states that a child acquires language by analyzing the language that he or she hears. The language heard by the child is processed, according to Chomsky, and the rules of language are extracted. The child then formulates hypotheses about how language works and tests those hypotheses against reality. No attempt is made in the theory to quantify the parameters of language acquisition. Instead, the theory specifies verbally the important variables that contribute to language acquisition.

## At What Level of Description Does the Theory Operate?

The second dimension along which theories may be categorized is according to the level of description the theory provides. Two goals of science are to describe and explain phenomena within its domain. A theory may address itself to the first goal (description), whereas another may address itself to the second (explanation). So some theories are primarily designed to describe a phenomenon whereas others attempt to explain relationships among variables that control a phenomenon. The following sections differentiate theories that deal with phenomena at different levels: descriptive, analogical, and fundamental.

*Descriptive Theories*   At the lowest level, a theory may simply describe how certain variables are related without providing an explanation for the relationship. A theory that merely describes a relationship is termed a **descriptive theory.**

An example of a descriptive theory is Wilhelm Wundt's systematic theory of the structure of consciousness. Wundt, as you probably know, is credited with being the founder of scientific psychology. His empirical and theoretical work centered on describing the structure of consciousness. Wundt (1897) maintained that consciousness is made up of *psychical elements* (sensations, feelings, and volition). He stated that all examples of consciousness are made up of these three basic building blocks. When the psychical elements combined, they formed *psychical compounds.* Wundt focused on describing the structure of consciousness and how complex conscious events could be broken down into their component parts.

Most descriptive theories are simply proposed generalizations from observation. For example, arousal theory states that task performance increases with arousal up to some optimal arousal value and then deteriorates with further increases in arousal. The proposed relationship thus follows an inverted U-shaped function. Arousal and task performance are both classes of variables that can be operationally defined a number of ways. Arousal and task performance are general concepts rather than specific variables. The proposed relationship is thus not directly observable but must be inferred from observing many specific variables representative of each concept. Note also that the theory describes the relationship but offers no real explanation for it.

Descriptive theories provide only the weakest form of explanation. If you discover being in elevators makes you nervous, then you could explain your current high level of anxiety by noting that you are standing in an elevator. But such an explanation does not tell you *why* elevators have the effect on you that they do.

*Analogical Theories*    At the next level is an **analogical theory**, which explains a relationship through analogy. Such theories borrow from well-understood models (usually of physical systems) by suggesting that the system to be explained behaves in a fashion similar to that described by the well-understood model.

To develop an analogical theory, you equate each variable in the physical system with a variable in the behavioral system to be modeled. You then plug in values for the new variables and apply the rules of the original theory in order to generate predictions.

An example of an analogical theory was provided by Konrad Lorenz (1950). Lorenz wanted to explain some relationships that he had observed between the occurrence of a specific behavioral pattern (called a *fixed-action pattern,* or FAP), a triggering stimulus (called a *sign* or *releaser stimulus*), and the time since the last occurrence of the FAP. For example, chickens scan the ground and then direct pecks at any seeds they find there. In this example, the visual characteristics of the seeds act as a releaser stimulus, and the directed pecking at the seeds is the FAP. Lorenz had observed that the FAP could be elicited more easily by a sign stimulus as the time increased since the last appearance of the FAP. In fact, with enough time, the behavior became so primed that it sometimes occurred in the absence of any identifiable sign stimulus. However, if the behavior had just occurred, the sign stimulus usually could not elicit the FAP again.

Let's return to the chicken example. At first, chickens peck only at seeds. However, with increasing hunger, they begin to peck at stimuli that only remotely resemble seeds, like pencil marks on a piece of paper. With further deprivation, they even peck at a blank paper.

To explain this relationship, Lorenz imagined that the motivation to perform the FAP was like the pressure of water at the bottom of a tank that was being continuously filled (see Figure 2-1). As time went on, the water in the tank became deeper and the pressure greater. Lorenz pictured a pressure-sensitive valve at the bottom of the tank. This valve could be opened by depressing a lever, but the pressure required to open it became less as the pressure inside the tank rose. In Lorenz's conception, the lever was normally "pressed" by the appearance of the sign stimulus.

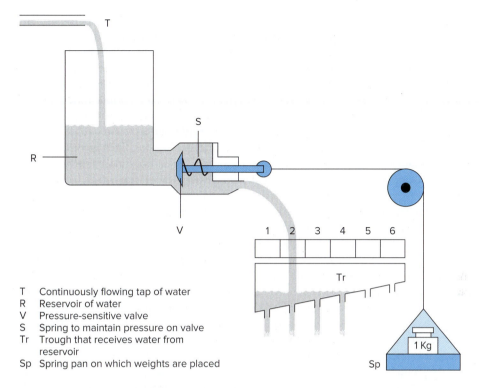

T   Continuously flowing tap of water
R   Reservoir of water
V   Pressure-sensitive valve
S   Spring to maintain pressure on valve
Tr  Trough that receives water from
    reservoir
Sp  Spring pan on which weights are placed

**FIGURE 2-1**   Lorenz's hydraulic model of motivation
Source: Lorenz, K. (1950). The comparative method in studying innate behavior patterns. *In Physiological Mechanisms of Animal Behavior: Symposium of the Society for Experimental Biology in Great Britian, No. 4,* 221–268.

Notice the analogies in Lorenz's model. Motivation to perform the FAP is analogous to water pressure. Engaging in the FAP is analogous to water rushing out the open valve, and perception of the sign stimulus is analogous to pressing the lever to open the valve.

Now put the model into action. Motivation to perform the FAP builds as time passes (the tank fills). If a sign stimulus appears after the tank has partially filled, the valve opens and the FAP occurs. However, if the sign stimulus does not occur for a long time, the tank overfills and the pressure triggers the valve to open spontaneously (the FAP occurs without the sign stimulus). Finally, if the FAP has just occurred (the valve has just opened), there is no motivation to perform the FAP (the tank is empty), and the sign stimulus is ineffective. The model thus nicely accounts for the observed facts.

Lorenz's hydraulic model of motivation eventually gave way to more sophisticated theories when new data revealed its limitations. In general, analogical theories can be pushed only so far. At some point, the analogy breaks down. After all, motivation is *not* quite the same thing as water pressure in a tank and may vary in ways quite unexpected for water pressure. Nevertheless, analogical theories can provide conceptual organization for the data and may predict relationships that otherwise would be unexpected.

*Fundamental Theories*    At the highest level are theories that are created to explain phenomena within a particular area of research but do not depend on analogy to provide their basic structures. Instead, they propose a new structure that directly relates the variables and constants of the system. This structure includes entities and processes not directly observable but invented to account for the observed relationships. Thus, these entities and processes go beyond descriptive theories, which simply describe relationships among observable variables. Because these theories have no accepted name, we'll call this type of theory a **fundamental theory** to distinguish them from the more superficial descriptive and analogical types. Such theories seek to model an underlying reality that produces the observed relationships among variables. In this sense, they propose a more fundamental description of reality than the analogical theory.

Although psychological theories abound, fundamental theories are disturbingly rare in psychology. Part of the reason for this rarity is that psychology is still a relatively new science, but this is probably only a small part. Mostly this rarity is because of the complexity of the system being studied and because of the extreme difficulty in controlling the relevant variables well enough to clearly reveal the true relationships among them (or even to measure them properly). The physicist can expect every electron to behave exactly like every other. The psychologist cannot even hope that his or her subjects will be this interchangeable. Nevertheless, some attempts at fundamental theorizing have been made. One of the most famous fundamental theories is *cognitive dissonance theory* proposed by Festinger (1957).

According to the theory, dissonance is the fundamental process in cognitive dissonance theory. Whenever two (or more) attitudes or behaviors are inconsistent, a negative psychological state called *cognitive dissonance* is aroused. The arousal of dissonance motivates the individual to reduce dissonance. This can be done by changing behavior or by changing attitudes. Festinger's theory thus described how dissonance leads to behavioral or attitude change.

Another example of fundamental theory in psychology is the Scalar Expectancy Theory (SET) proposed by John Gibbon (1977) to account for the patterns of responding that develop under various schedules of reinforcement. The central idea of Gibbon's theory is that well-trained subjects are able to estimate time to reinforcement by means of a "scalar timing" process. With scalar timing, the subject can adjust to changes in the time constant of a schedule by simply rescaling the estimated time distribution to fit the new constant. Estimates of time to reinforcement (together with the size and attractiveness of the reinforcer) determine the "expectancy" of reward, which in turn determines the probability of a response through a well-defined mechanism. Gibbon described how the assumption of scalar timing produces a better fit to data from a variety of paradigms than do other assumptions (such as timing based on a Poisson process).

## What Is the Theory's Domain?

The third dimension along which theories differ is **domain**, or *scope*. This dimension concerns the range of situations to which the theory may be legitimately applied. A theory with a wide scope can be applied to a wider range of situations than can a theory with a more limited scope.

Gibbon's (1977) Scalar Expectancy Theory is an example of a theory with a relatively limited scope. It provided an explanation for behavioral patterns that emerge under a wide variety of reinforcement schedules, but it did not attempt to account for other factors that could affect behavior. Cognitive consistency theory, such as Festinger's (1957) theory of cognitive dissonance, is an example of a theory with a wider scope. It has been applied beyond attitude change (for which it was developed) to help explain motivational processes in other contexts.

The chances of dealing adequately with a range of phenomena are better for a small area of behavior than they are for a large area. On the negative side, however, concepts invented to deal with one area may have no relationship to those invented to deal with others, even though the behaviors may be mediated by partly overlapping (or even identical) mechanisms.

## QUESTIONS TO PONDER

1. What are the defining characteristics of quantitative and qualitative theories?

2. What is a descriptive theory?

3. What is an analogical theory?

4. What is a fundamental theory?

5. How do descriptive, analogical, and fundamental theories differ? Which is preferred and why?

## ROLES OF THEORY IN SCIENCE

Theories have several roles to play in science. These roles include providing an understanding of the phenomena for which they account, providing a basis for prediction, and guiding the direction of research.

### Understanding

At the highest level, theories represent a particular way to understand the phenomena with which they deal. To the degree that a theory models an underlying reality, this understanding can be deep and powerful. For example, Jean Piaget's (1952) theory of development provided a deep insight into the thought processes of children and helped us better understand how these processes change with age and experience. Piaget provided a broad description of the behaviors that are characteristic of children at various ages. Within the theory, he also proposed mechanisms (organization, adaptation, and equilibration) to explain how development takes place.

### Prediction

Even when theories do not provide a fundamental insight into the mechanisms of a behaving system (as descriptive theories do not), they at least can provide a way to predict the behavior of the system under different values of its controlling variables.

The descriptive theory will specify which variables need to be considered and how they interact to determine the behavior to be explained. If it is a good theory, the predictions will match the empirical outcome with a reasonable degree of precision.

A good example of how a theory can generate testable predictions comes from *social impact theory* proposed by Bibb Latané (1981). Social impact theory is intended to explain the process of social influence (e.g., conformity and obedience). According to the theory, the amount of influence obtained is dependent upon the interaction of three factors: the strength of an influence source ($S$), the immediacy of an influence source ($I$), and the number of influence sources ($N$). The relationship between influence and these three variables is summed up with this simple formula:

$$\text{Influence} = f(S \times I \times N)$$

One prediction made by the theory is that the relationship between the number of sources and the amount of influence obtained is nonlinear. That is, after a certain number of sources, influence should not increase significantly and should "level off." The prediction made from social impact theory is consistent with the results obtained from empirical research findings on the relationship between the size of a majority and conformity.

## Organizing and Interpreting Research Results

A theory can provide a sound framework for organizing and interpreting research results. For example, the results of an experiment designed to test Piaget's theory will be organized within the existing structure of confirmatory and disconfirmatory results. This organization is preferable to having a loose conglomeration of results on a topic.

In addition to being organized by theory, research results can be interpreted in the light of a theory. This is true even if your research was not specifically designed to test a particular theory. For example, results of a study of decision making may be interpreted in the light of cognitive dissonance theory even though you did not specifically set out to test dissonance theory.

## Generating Research

Finally, theories are valuable because they often provide ideas for new research. This is known as the *heuristic value* of a theory. The heuristic value of a theory is often independent of its validity. A theory can have heuristic value even when it is not supported by subsequent empirical research. Such a theory may implicate certain variables in a particular phenomenon, variables that had not been previously suspected of being important. Researchers may then design experiments or collect observations to examine the role of these variables. Often such variables turn out to be significant although the theory that emphasized them eventually may be proved wrong.

A theory specifies the variables that need to be examined and the conditions under which they are to be observed—and may even state how they are to be measured. It provides a framework within which certain research questions make sense and others become irrelevant or even nonsensical. Franz Gall's phrenology provides an example of how a theory guides research and determines which questions will be considered important. Gall was a 19th-century surgeon who was convinced that a person's abilities, traits, and personality were determined by specific areas of the cerebral cortex. Gall believed if a part of the brain were highly developed, a person would have a higher degree of the particular trait or ability associated with that area than if that same part of the brain were less highly developed. In addition, Gall reasoned, the more highly developed area would require more volume of cortex. Consequently, the part of the skull covering this area would bulge outward and create a "bump" on the person's head (Fancher, 1979).

In the context of Gall's theory, the important research problems were to identify which parts of the cortex represented which traits or abilities and to relate individual differences in the topography of the skull (its characteristic bumps and valleys) to personality variables. Researchers developed special instruments to measure the skull and devoted thousands of hours to making measurements and collecting profiles of mental abilities and personality traits.

Phrenology never gained acceptance within the scientific community and was severely damaged by evidence (provided by Pierre Flourens and other of Gall's contemporaries) showing rather conclusively that at least some of the brain areas identified as the seat of a particular trait had entirely different functions (Fancher, 1979). With the discrediting of phrenology, interest in measuring the skull and in correlating these measurements with traits and abilities went with it.

Phrenology provided a framework for research within which certain problems and questions became important. When this view was displaced, much of the work conducted under it became irrelevant. This loss of relevance is a serious concern. If data collected under a particular theory become worthless when the theory dies, then researchers working within a particular framework face the possibility that in the future, their efforts will be viewed as wasted.

This possibility has led some researchers to suggest that perhaps theories should be avoided, at least in the early stages of research. Speaking at a time when the Hull–Spence learning theory was still a force within the psychology of learning, B. F. Skinner (1949) asked in his presidential address to the Midwestern Psychological Association, "Are theories of learning necessary?" In this address, Skinner disputed the claim that theories are necessary to organize and guide research. Research should be guided, Skinner said, not by theory but by the search for functional relationships and for orderly changes in data that follow the manipulation of effective independent variables. Such clearly established relationships have enduring value. These relationships become the data with which any adequate theory must deal.

Skinner's point has a great deal of merit, and it is discussed later in this chapter. However, for now you should understand the importance of theory—that it is not useless or, even worse, wasteful. Even theories that are eventually overthrown do provide a standard against which to judge new developments. New developments that do not fit the existing theory become anomalies, and anomalies generate further research in an effort to show they result from measurement error or some other problem unrelated to the content of the theory. The accumulation of serious anomalies can destroy a theory. In the process, however, the intense focus on the problem areas may bring new insights and rapid progress within the field. Because anomalies are unexpected findings, they exist only in the context of expectation—expectation provided by theory. Thus, even in failing, a theory can have heuristic value.

## CHARACTERISTICS OF A GOOD THEORY

In the history of psychology, many theories have been advanced to explain behavioral phenomena. Some of these theories have stood the test of time, whereas others have fallen by the wayside. Whether or not a theory endures depends on several factors, including the following.

### Ability to Account for Data

To be of any value, a theory must account for most of the existing data within its domain. Note that the amount of data is "most" rather than "all" because at least some of the data may in fact be unreliable. A theory can be excused for failing to account for erroneous data. However, a theory that fails to account for well-established facts within its domain is in serious trouble. The phrase "within its domain" is crucial. If the theory is designed to explain the habituation of responses, it can hardly be criticized for its failure to account for schizophrenia. Such an account clearly would be beyond the scope of the theory.

### Explanatory Relevance

A theory also must meet the criterion of *explanatory relevance* (Hempel, 1966). That is, the explanation for a phenomenon provided by a theory must offer good grounds for believing that the phenomenon would occur under the specified conditions. If a theory meets this criterion, you should find yourself saying, "Ah, but of course! That was indeed to be expected under the circumstances!" (Hempel, 1966). If someone were to suggest that the rough sleep you had last night was caused by the color of your socks, you would probably reject this theory on the grounds that it lacks explanatory relevance. There is simply no good reason to believe that wearing a particular color of socks would affect your sleep. To be adequate, the theory must define some logical link between socks and sleep.

### Testability

A condition that every *scientific* theory must meet is *testability*. A theory is testable if it is capable of failing some empirical test. That is, the theory specifies outcomes under particular conditions, and if these outcomes do not occur, then the theory is rejected.

The criterion of testability is a major problem for many aspects of Freud's psychodynamic theory of personality. Freud's theory provides explanations for a number of personality traits and disorders, but it is too complex and loosely specified to make specific, testable predictions. For example, if a person is observed to be stingy and obstinate, Freudian theory points to unsuccessful resolution of the anal stage of psychosexual development. Yet diametrically opposite traits also can be accounted for with the same explanation. There is no mechanism within the theory to specify which will develop in any particular case. When a theory can provide a seemingly reasonable explanation no matter what the outcome of an observation, you are probably dealing with an untestable theory.

### Prediction of Novel Events

A good theory should predict new phenomena. Within its domain, a good theory should predict phenomena beyond those for which the theory was originally designed.

Strictly speaking, such predicted phenomena do not have to be new in the sense of not yet observed. Rather, they must be new in the sense that they were not taken into account in the formulation of the theory.

As an example, consider the Rescorla–Wagner model of classical conditioning we described previously in the chapter. The model predicts that when two fully conditioned stimuli are presented together, the resulting compound CS initially will evoke an even stronger response than either single stimulus presented alone, a phenomenon now called "overexpectation." Furthermore, the model predicted that further pairings of the compound CS with the unconditioned stimulus would cause the conditioned response to weaken—a surprising result given that such a "reinforcement" process normally would be expected to strengthen, not weaken, the response. Appropriate tests confirmed both of these predictions.

## Parsimony

The medieval English philosopher William of Ockham popularized an important principle stated by Aristotle. Aristotle's principle states, "Entities must not be multiplied beyond what is necessary" (Ockham's Razor, n.d.). Ockham's refinement of this principle is now called *Ockham's Razor* and states that a problem should be stated in the simplest possible terms and explained with the fewest postulates possible. Today we know this as the *law of parsimony*. Simply put, a theory should account for phenomena within its domain in the simplest terms possible and with the fewest assumptions. If there are two competing theories concerning a behavior, the one that explains the behavior in the simplest terms is preferred under the law of parsimony.

Many theories in psychology fit this requirement very well. Modern theories of memory, attribution processes, development, and motivation all adhere to this principle. However, the history of science in general, and psychology in particular, is littered with theories that were crushed under their own weight of complexity.

For example, the collapse of interest in the Hull–Spence theory of learning occurred primarily because the theory had been modified so many times to account for anomalous data (and had in the process gained so many ad hoc assumptions) that it was no longer parsimonious. Researchers could not bring themselves to believe that learning could be *that* complicated.

## QUESTIONS TO PONDER

1. What roles do theories play in science? Describe each role in detail.
2. What are the defining characteristics of a "good" theory? Describe each characteristic in detail.

## STRATEGIES FOR TESTING THEORIES

A major theme developed in the preceding sections is that a good scientific theory must be testable with empirical methods. In fact, the final step in the business of theory construction is to subject the propositions of your theory to rigorous empirical scrutiny.

## Following a Confirmational Strategy

A theory is usually tested by identifying implications of the theory for a specific situation not yet examined and then setting up the situation and observing whether the predicted effects occur. If the predicted effects are observed, the theory is said to be supported by the results, and your confidence in the theory increases. If the predicted effects do not occur, then the theory is not supported, and your confidence in it weakens.

When you test the implications of a theory in this way, you are following what is called a **confirmational strategy** (i.e., a strategy of looking for confirmation of the theory's predictions). A positive outcome supports the theory.

Looking for confirmation is an important part of theory testing, but it does have an important limitation. Although the theory must find confirmation if it is to survive (too many failures would kill it), you can find confirmation until doomsday, and the theory may still be wrong.

Spurious confirmations are particularly likely to happen when the prediction only loosely specifies an outcome. For example, in an experiment with two groups, if a theory predicts that group A will score higher on the dependent measure than group B, only three outcomes are possible at this level of precision: A may be greater than B, B may be greater than A, or A and B may be equal. Thus, the theory has about a 1-in-3 chance of being supported by a lucky coincidence.

Such coincidental support becomes less likely as the predictions of the theory become more precise. For example, if the theory predicts that group A will score 25, plus or minus 2, points higher than group B, it is fairly unlikely that a difference in this direction and within this range will occur by coincidence. Because of this relationship, confirmation of a theory's predictions has a much greater impact on your confidence in the theory when the predictions are precisely stated than when they are loosely stated.

## Following a Disconfirmational Strategy

Even when a theory's predictions are relatively precise, many alternative theories could potentially be constructed that would make the same predictions within the stated margin of error. Because of this fact, following a confirmational strategy is not enough. To test a theory requires more than simply finding out if its predictions are confirmed. You also must determine whether outcomes *not* expected, according to the theory, do or do not occur.

This strategy follows this form: If A is true (the theory is correct), then B will not be true (a certain outcome will not occur); thus, if B is true (the outcome does happen), then A is false (the theory is erroneous). Because a positive result will *disconfirm* (rather than confirm) the prediction, this way of testing a theory is called a **disconfirmational strategy**.

## Using Confirmational and Disconfirmational Strategies Together

Adequately testing a theory requires using both confirmational and disconfirmational strategies. Usually, you will pursue a confirmational strategy when a theory is fresh and relatively untested. The object during this phase of testing is to determine whether the theory can predict or explain the phenomena within its domain with reasonable precision.

If the theory survives these tests, you will eventually want to pursue a disconfirmational strategy. The objective during this phase of testing is to determine whether outcomes that are unexpected from the point of view of the theory nevertheless happen. If unexpected outcomes do occur, it means that the theory is, at best, incomplete. It will have to be developed further so that it can account for the previously unexpected outcome, or it will have to be replaced by a better theory.

## Using Strong Inference

The usual picture of progress in science is that theories are subjected to testing and then gradually modified as the need arises. The theory evolves through a succession of tests and modifications until it can handle all extant data with a high degree of precision. This view of science has been challenged by Thomas Kuhn (1970). According to Kuhn, the history of science reveals that most theories continue to be defended and elaborated by their supporters even after convincing evidence to the contrary has been amassed. People who have spent their professional careers developing a theoretical view have too much invested to give up the view. When a more adequate view appears, the supporters of the old view find ways to rationalize the failures of their view and the successes of the new one. Kuhn concluded that the new view takes hold only after the supporters of the old view actually die off or retire from the profession. Then a new generation of researchers without investment in either theory objectively evaluates the evidence and makes its choice.

Commitment to a theoretical position well beyond the point at which it is objectively no longer viable is wasteful of time, money, and talent. Years may be spent evaluating and defending a view, with nothing to show for the investment. According to John Platt (1964), this trap can be avoided. Platt stated that the way to progress in science is to develop several alternative explanations for a phenomenon. Each of these alternatives should give rise to testable predictions. To test the alternatives, you try to devise experiments in which their outcomes can support either one or a few alternatives while ruling out the others.

When the initial experiment has been conducted, some of the alternatives will have been ruled out. You then design the next experiment to decide among the remaining alternatives. You continue this process until only one alternative remains. Platt (1964) called this process **strong inference**.

Strong inference can work only if the alternative explanations generate well-defined predictions. In biochemistry (the field that Platt, 1964, uses to exemplify the method), strong inference is a viable procedure because of the degree of control that scientists have over variables and the precision of their measures. The procedure tends to break down when the necessary degree of control is absent (so that the data become equivocal) or when the alternatives do not specify outcomes with sufficient precision to discriminate them. Unfortunately, in most areas of psychology, the degree of control is not sufficient, and the theories (usually loosely stated verbalizations) generally predict little more than the fact that one group mean will be different from another.

Nevertheless, Platt's (1964) approach can often be applied to test specific assumptions within the context of a particular view. In this case, applying strong inference means developing alternative models of the theory and then identifying areas in which clear differences emerge in predicted outcomes. The appropriate test then can be performed to decide which assumptions to discard and which to submit to further testing.

If several theories have been applied to the same set of phenomena and if these theories have been specified in sufficient detail to make predictions possible, you also may be able to use the method of strong inference if the theories make opposing predictions for a particular situation. The outcome of the experiment, if it is clear, will lend support to one or more of the theories while damaging others. This procedure is much more efficient than separately testing each theory, and you should adopt it wherever possible.

You now should have clear ideas about how to recognize, develop, and test adequate theories. However, an important question remains to be addressed: Should research be directed primarily toward testing theories or toward discovering empirical relationships?

## QUESTIONS TO PONDER

1. What is meant by confirmation and disconfirmation of a theory?
2. How are theories tested?
3. What is the difference between a confirmational and a disconfirmational strategy? How are they used to test a theory?
4. What is strong interference, and how is it used to test a theory?

## THEORY-DRIVEN VERSUS DATA-DRIVEN RESEARCH

At one time in the not-too-distant history of psychology, research efforts in one field centered on developing a theory of learning. This theory would organize and explain data obtained from many experiments involving white laboratory rats running down straight alleys, learning discrimination tasks, and finding their ways through mazes. Ultimately, this was to be a mathematical theory, complete with equations relating theoretical entities to each other and to observable variables.

The task of developing such a theory was taken up by Clark Hull at Iowa State University and by Hull's student, Kenneth Spence. Hull's approach to theory development was to follow the "hypothetico-deductive method," which consisted of adopting specific assumptions about the processes involved in learning, deriving predictions, submitting these predictions to experimental test, and then (as required) modifying one or more assumptions in the light of new evidence. Applied at a time when very few data were in fact available, the method was remarkably successful in producing an account that handled the relevant observations. This initial success galvanized researchers in the field, and soon it seemed that nearly everyone was conducting experiments to test the Hull–Spence theory.

The new data quickly revealed discrepancies between prediction and outcome. Some researchers, such as Edward Tolman, rejected some of the key assumptions of the Hull–Spence theory and proposed alternative views. However, they were never able to develop their positions completely enough to provide a really viable theory of equivalent scope and testability. Besides, every time that Tolman and others would find an outcome incompatible with the Hull–Spence view, Hull and Spence would find a way to modify the theory in such a way that it would now account for the new data. The theory evolved with each new challenge.

These were exciting times for researchers in the field of learning. The development of a truly powerful, grand theory of learning seemed just around the corner. Then, gradually, things began to come apart. Hull died in 1952. Even before his death, discontent was beginning to set in, and even the continued efforts of Spence were not enough to hold researchers' interest in the theory.

Interest in the Hull–Spence theory collapsed for a number of reasons. Probably the most significant reason was that it had simply become too complex, with too many assumptions, and variables whose values had to be extracted from the very data that the theory was meant to explain. Like the Ptolemaic theory of planetary motion, the system could predict nearly any observation (after the fact) once the right constants were plugged in—but it had lost much of its true predictive power, its parsimony, and its elegance.

With the loss of interest in the Hull–Spence theory went the relevance of much of the research that had been conducted to test it. Particularly vulnerable were those experiments that manipulated some set of variables in a complex fashion in order to check on some implication of the theory. These experiments demonstrated no clear functional relationship among simple variables, and the results were therefore of little interest except within the context of the theory. Viewed outside this context, the research seemed to have been a waste of time and effort.

It was a tough lesson for many researchers. Much of the time and effort spent theorizing, tracing implications of the theory, developing experimental tests, and conducting observations was lost. This experience raises several questions concerning the use of theory in psychology. Should you attempt to develop theories? If you should develop theories, at what point should you begin? Should you focus your research efforts on testing the theories that you do develop?

The answer to the first question is definitely yes; you should attempt to develop theories. The history of science is littered with failed theories: the Ptolemaic system of astronomy, the phlogiston theory of heat, Gall's phrenology—the list goes on. In each case, much of the theorizing and testing became irrelevant when the theory was discarded. However, in each case, the attempt to grapple with the observations (particularly the anomalous ones) eventually led to the development of a more adequate theory. In this sense, the earlier efforts were not wasted.

Furthermore, it is the business of science to organize the available observations and to provide a framework within which the observations can be understood. At some point, theories must be developed if psychology is to progress.

The real question is not whether you should develop theories but when. The major problem with the Hull–Spence theory is probably that it was premature. The attempt was made to develop a theory of broad scope before there was an adequate empirical database on which to formulate it. As a result, the requirements of the theory were not sufficiently constrained. The assumptions had to be repeatedly modified as new data became available, making some tests obsolete even before they could be published.

To avoid this problem, a theory that is more than a simple hypothesis should await the development of an adequate observational base. A sufficient number of well-established phenomena and functional relationships should be available to guide theory development and demonstrate the power of the resulting formulation.

To what extent should you focus your research efforts on testing the theories that you develop? There is no general agreement on the answer to this question. For one side of the issue, consider the letter written to *Science* by Bernard Forscher (1963) entitled "Chaos in the Brickyard."

Forscher's (1963) letter presented an allegory in which scientists were compared to builders of brick edifices. The bricks were facts (observations), and the edifices were theories. According to Forscher's story, at one time the builders made their own bricks. This was a slow process, and the demand for bricks was always ahead of the supply. Still, the bricks were made to order, guided in their manufacture by a blueprint called a *theory* or *hypothesis*.

To speed the process, a new trade of brickmaking was developed, with the brickmakers producing bricks according to specifications given by the builders. With time, however, the brickmakers became obsessed with making bricks and began to create them without direction from the builders. When reminded that the goal was to create edifices not bricks the brickmakers replied that when enough bricks had been made, the builders could select the ones they needed.

Thus, it came to pass that the land was flooded with bricks. For the builders, constructing an edifice became impossible. They had to examine hundreds of bricks to find a suitable one, and it was difficult to find a clear spot of ground on which to build. Worst of all, little effort was made to maintain the distinction between an edifice and a pile of bricks.

Forscher's message was that experimentation conducted without the guidance of theory produces a significant amount of irrelevant information that is likely to obscure the important observations. From the infinite number of potential observations you could make, you need to select just those observations that will contribute most to progress in understanding. Theory provides one rationale for making that selection.

However, theory does not provide the only guide to choosing what observations to make. Observation also can be guided by the systematic exploration of functional relationships within a well-defined domain. This empirical approach was forcefully defended by B. F. Skinner in his 1949 address to the Midwestern Psychological Association.

Much of the research conducted in psychology has followed this program. A systematic study of memory by Ebbinghaus (1885/1964), and the work that followed it, provides a case in point. Ebbinghaus invented a nearly meaningless unit to memorize (the consonant–vowel–consonant, or CVC, trigram) and several methods to measure the strength of memory for the CVCs. He then systematically explored the effects of many variables in a series of parametric experiments. These variables included the amount of practice, spacing of practice, length of the retention interval, and serial position of the CVC within the list. The resulting functional relationships between these variables and retention were subsequently shown to be highly reliable phenomena.

The data from such observations provide the reliable phenomena that any subsequently developed theory must explain. As Skinner (1949) and others have indicated, these data stand independent of any particular theoretical view. Thus, if an experiment is designed to clearly illuminate simple functional relationships among variables— even when the experiment is conducted mainly for the purpose of testing theory—then the data will retain their value even if the theory is later discarded.

What conclusions can you draw from this discussion? First, the choice of observations to make can be guided both by theory and by a plan of systematic exploration. Second, guidance by theory is more likely to be of value when sufficient observations already have been conducted to construct a reasonably powerful theory. Third, even when theory testing is the major goal of the research, designing the study to illuminate simple functional relationships among the variables ensures that the resulting observations will continue to have value beyond the usefulness of the theory.

Chapter 1 indicated that a science is an organized and systematic way of acquiring knowledge. Science is best advanced when results from research endeavors can be organized within some kind of framework. In many cases, results from both basic and applied research can be understood best when organized within a theory. However, keep in mind that not all research *must* be organized within a theoretical framework. Some purely applied research, for example, may best be organized with other research that also was geared toward the solution of a specific problem. Nevertheless, theory plays a central role in advancing science.

## QUESTIONS TO PONDER

1. How do theory-driven research and data-driven research differ?
2. What are the relative advantages and disadvantages of theory-driven and data-driven research?

## SUMMARY

A theory is a partially verified statement concerning the relationship among variables. A theory usually consists of a set of interrelated propositions and corollaries that specify how variables relate to the phenomena to be explained. *Hypothesis, law,* and *model* are all terms that are often used as synonyms for *theory.* There are, however, important differences among them. A *hypothesis* is a specific statement about a relationship that is subjected to direct empirical test. A *law* is a relationship that has received substantial support and is not usually subject to disconfirmation as theories are. A *model* is a specific implementation of a more general theoretical perspective. Models therefore usually have a more limited domain than do theories.

Computer models test the implications of a theory by encoding the theory as a series of program statements, supplying a set of initial conditions, and then observing how the model behaves. Such models remove ambiguity in the specific application of a theory and can reveal predictions of the theory that cannot be deduced by mere verbal reasoning. The behavior of the model under simulated conditions can be compared with the actual behavior of people or animals to determine whether the model behaves correctly, and alternative models can be compared to determine which does a better job of modeling actual behavior under given conditions.

Explanations provided by theories may be mechanistic or functional. Mechanistic explanations describe the physical components of a system and their connections (mechanism) whereas functional explanations describe only what the system does (function). Because function can be deduced from mechanism but mechanism cannot be uniquely deduced from function, you should prefer mechanistic theories over functional ones.

Theories vary along at least three dimensions. First, theories may be quantitative or qualitative. Quantitative theories express relationships among variables in mathematical terms. Anderson's integration theory and the Rescorla–Wagner model of classical conditioning are examples of quantitative theories. Qualitative theories verbally express relationships among variables. No attempt is made to mathematically specify the nature of the relationships. Piaget's theory of cognitive development is an example of a qualitative theory. Second, theories differ according to level of analysis. At the lowest level, descriptive theories simply seek to describe a phenomenon. At the next level, analogical theories try to explain phenomena by drawing parallels between known systems and the phenomenon of interest. At the highest level, fundamental theories represent new ways of explaining a phenomenon. These theories tend to provide a more fundamental look at a phenomenon than do descriptive or analogical theories. Third, theories differ according to domain. A theory with a large domain accounts for more phenomena than does a theory with a more limited domain.

Theories play an important role in science. They help us to understand a phenomenon better, allow us to predict relationships, help us to organize and interpret our data, and help generate new research. This latter role is often independent of the correctness of the theory. Some theories, even though they are not correct, have led to important research and new discoveries that greatly advance science.

A theory must meet certain criteria before it can be accepted as a good theory. It must be able to account for most of the data within its domain. A theory that does not do this is of little value. A good theory also must meet the criterion of explanatory relevance, which means that it must offer good grounds for believing that the phenomenon would occur under the specified conditions. Crucially, the propositions stated in and the predictions made by a theory must be testable with empirical methods. Theories that are not testable, such as Freudian psychodynamics, cannot be classified as valid scientific theories. A theory also must be able to account for novel events within its domain. Finally, it should be parsimonious. That is, it should explain a phenomenon with the fewest number of propositions possible.

Theories that are subjected to empirical tests can be confirmed or disconfirmed. Confirmation of a theory means that you have more confidence in it than before confirmation. Unfortunately, it is logically impossible to prove that a theory is absolutely correct. Theories that are disconfirmed may be modified or discarded entirely although many disconfirmed theories are adhered to for a variety of reasons.

In the course of testing a theory, various strategies can be used. Strong inference involves developing testable alternative explanations for a phenomenon and subjecting them simultaneously to an empirical test. The empirical test should be one that will unambiguously show which alternative is best. One way to test a theory is to use a confirmational strategy. That is, you design tests that will confirm the predictions made by the theory under test. When predictions are confirmed, then your confidence in the theory increases. Unfortunately, you may find confirming evidence even though the theory is wrong. Another approach is to adopt a disconfirmational strategy. In this case, you look for evidence that does not support the predictions made by a theory. Often the best strategy to adopt is to use both confirmational and disconfirmational strategies together.

Finally, a controversy exists over the role that a theory should play in driving research. Some scientists believe that research should be data driven, whereas others believe that research should be theory driven. Strong arguments have been made for each position, and no simple solution to the controversy exists.

## KEY TERMS

theory

hypothesis

law

model

mechanistic explanation

functional explanation

quantitative theory

qualitative theory

descriptive theory

analogical theory

fundamental theory

domain

confirmational strategy

disconfirmational strategy

strong inference

# Getting Ideas for Research

As a student who is just becoming acquainted with the research process, you are probably wondering just how to come up with good ideas for research. It may seem to you that, by this point in the history of psychology, every interesting research question must already have been asked and answered. Nothing could be further from the truth! Each year hundreds of novel research studies are published in scores of psychology journals. Or perhaps you do have some rather general idea of a topic that you'd like to explore but don't know how to convert that idea into something specific that you could actually carry out.

Once you learn how to go about it, finding a research topic and developing it into an executable project becomes relatively easy—you just have to know where and how to look. In fact, you may be surprised to find that your biggest problem is deciding which of several interesting research ideas you should pursue first. To help you reach that point, in the first part of this chapter we identify a number of sources of research ideas and offer some guidelines for developing good research questions.

Although finding and developing a research idea is usually the first step in the research process, the ultimate goal of that process, as noted in Chapter 1, is to develop valid explanations for behavior. These explanations may be limited in scope (e.g., an explanation of why a certain autistic child keeps banging his head against the wall) or comprehensive (e.g., a system that explains the fundamental mechanisms of learning). Of course, any single study will have only a limited purpose, such as to test a particular hypothesis, to identify how certain variables are related, or simply to describe what behaviors occur under given conditions. Yet each properly conceived and executed study contributes new information—perhaps, for example, by identifying new behaviors for which explanations will be needed or by ruling out certain alternative explanations. Ultimately, this information shapes the formulation of new explanations or tests the adequacy of existing ones.

In this chapter, we pursue two separate but related topics. First, we explore how to get research ideas and how to develop them into viable, testable research questions. Second, we describe the tools available to you to search the scientific literature on your topic.

## SOURCES OF RESEARCH IDEAS

The sources of research ideas are virtually endless. They range from casual observation to systematic research. However, they can be seen as falling into three broad categories: experience, theory, and applied issues.

### Experience

Your everyday experience and observations of what goes on around you are rich sources of research ideas. Some of these observations may be unsystematic and informal. For example, after reading a newspaper article about a terrorist attack, you may begin to wonder how people who have to live with terrorism every day cope. Subsidiary questions might also come to your mind, such as: Do men and women cope differently with terrorism? Do adults adjust better than children? General questions like these can be translated into viable research questions. Other observations may be more systematic and formal. For example, after reading a journal article for a class, you may begin to formulate a set of questions raised by the article. These too could serve as the foundation of a viable research study.

*Unsystematic Observation*   One of the most potent sources of research ideas is curiosity about the causes or determinants of commonplace, everyday behavior. You make a helpful suggestion to a friend, and she angrily rebukes you. Why? Perhaps she just found out she did not get the job that she wanted badly. Is this the cause, or is it something else? Or you study all week for an important exam, and the test results show you did very well. Although initially you feel good, the emotion soon passes, and you find yourself falling into a deep depression. What caused this seemingly strange shift in your emotions? Such observations can provide the basis for a research project.

Casual observation of animal behavior also can lead to research ideas. Behaviors such as starlings staging a mass attack on a soaring hawk, a squirrel dropping an acorn on your head, and the antics of a pet all raise questions about why those behaviors occur—questions that can be the basis of a research idea. For example, Niko Tinbergen's (1951) well-known research on territorial defense and courtship behavior in the three-spined stickleback (a minnow-sized fish that inhabits European streams) began when Tinbergen happened to observe some odd behavior in a small group of sticklebacks that he kept in an aquarium near a window. During breeding season, the males' underbellies turn bright red and the males construct a nest on the bottom of the stream. They then defend the territory around the nest from intrusion by other male sticklebacks. One day as a Dutch mail truck passed by the window, Tinbergen watched in astonishment as the male sticklebacks rushed to the surface of the water nearest the window in an apparent attempt to attack the red truck and drive it away. Because mail trucks are not normally a part of a stickleback's environment, Tinbergen wondered whether the males' red underbellies might be the normal trigger for attack by other males. This was the catalyst for a carefully designed research project aimed at answering this question. (See Chapter 4 for more information about this research.)

Unsystematic observation sometimes is a good way to discover a general research idea. Given your casual observations, you may decide to study a particular issue. For example, your questions about coping with terrorism may lead you to some general questions about the factors that cause terrorism. You may decide to focus your research on one or two variables that you believe may be important. For example, you could focus your research on the attitudes that underlie terrorism and how religion and terrorism relate.

You also can get research ideas just by paying attention in your classes. In many classes, your professors undoubtedly use research examples to illustrate points. As you listen to or read about these research examples, you may be able to think of some interesting research questions. For example, you might ask whether those results apply equally to men and women or to Western as well as non-Western cultures. You might also wonder if the results from a study conducted 30 years ago are still valid today. You may find that with a little follow-up digging through published research, many questions remain unanswered.

Casual observations are only a starting point. You still must transform your casual observations into a form that you can test empirically. Rarely will you be able to infer the causes of observed behavior from your casual observations. You can infer such causes only through a careful and systematic study of the behavior of interest.

*Systematic Observation*   Systematic observation of behavior is another powerful source of research ideas. In contrast to casual observation, systematic observation is planned. You decide what you are going to observe, how you are going to observe it, and how you will record your observations. Your own systematic observations of real-world behavior can provide the basis for a research idea. Consider the work of Jean Piaget (1952). Piaget spent many an hour systematically observing the behavior of his own children at home and other children on playgrounds. These observations helped lay the foundation for his comprehensive theory of cognitive development.

It is important to note that Piaget did not make his observations in a vacuum. Instead, he approached a situation with some ideas in mind about the nature of children's thought processes. As he observed children's behavior, he began developing hypotheses that he tested in further research.

A second valuable source of systematic observation is published research reports. Instead of observing behavior firsthand, you read about other firsthand observations from researchers. Published research offers an almost limitless source of systematic observations of both human and animal behavior made under well-defined conditions. Although such research answers many questions, it typically raises more than it answers. Are the results reliable? Would the same thing happen if participants with different characteristics were used? What is the shape of the function relating the variables under study? Would you obtain the same results if the dependent measure were defined differently? These questions and others like them provide a rich source of research ideas.

You can also get research ideas by asking, under what other conditions does an observed behavior occur? As an example let's examine an experiment by Stavrinos, Byington, and Schwebel (2011) on distracted walking. Stavrinos et al. found that talking on a cell phone made walking more risky. Is this increased risk unique to having a real conversation on a cell phone? Or, would other types of distraction do the same? In a second study, Stavrinos et al. had participants engage in a naturalistic conversation, perform a spatial task (describe the layout of where they live), or perform a mathematical task (count backward from 101 by threes) while they walked through the virtual traffic world. Stavrinos et al. found an increase in risky behaviors in all three distraction conditions. So, there is nothing unique about an actual phone conversation that makes walking more risky. Any distraction increases risk.

Another potent, systematic source of research ideas is your own previous or ongoing research. Unexpected observations made during the course of a project (e.g., a result that contradicts expectations) or the need to test the generality of a finding can be the basis for further research. As you examine your data, you may see unexpected relationships or trends emerging. These trends may be interesting enough to warrant a new study.

For example, my (Bordens) research colleague and I conducted an experiment on the effect of the number of plaintiffs in a civil trial on damage awards. In our original experiment (Horowitz & Bordens, 1988), we found that as the size of the plaintiff population increased so did damage awards. This finding then led us to wonder what number of plaintiffs yields the highest award. In follow-up experiments, we found that the critical number of plaintiffs was four.

In this example, we found something interesting (increasing the size of the plaintiff population leads to higher damage awards), which led to another interesting question (what is the critical number?). In the same way, you can get research ideas from your own research.

It is important to note that this particular source of research ideas usually is not immediately available to the scientific community. Other researchers may not become aware of your findings until you publish or present them. Consequently, you and your close colleagues may be the only ones who can benefit from this potentially rich source of research ideas.

Finally, you may be able to get some research ideas by perusing research projects being run on the Internet. At any given time there may be many different psychological research projects being conducted there. These include nonexperimental studies such as surveys, as well as experimental studies. You can find a wide variety of such studies on the Hanover College Psychology Department's *Psychological Research on the Net* website (at the time of this writing, http://psych.hanover.edu/research/exponnet.html). This website lists psychological studies broken down into categories (e.g., social psychology, cognition, and personality). You can take part in these studies, and you may get some good ideas for your own research based on your participation.

## QUESTIONS TO PONDER

1. How can experience help you come up with research ideas?

2. How can unsystematic observation help you develop research ideas?

3. How can systematic observation help you develop research ideas?

## Theory

As defined in Chapter 2, a *theory* is a set of assumptions about the causes of behavior and rules that specify how those causes act. Designed to account for known relationships among given variables and behavior, theories can also be a rich source of research ideas.

Theories can provide ideas for research in two ways. First, theories allow you to predict what should happen under conditions not previously observed. You can design your research study to test those predictions. A nice example is the "overexpectation" phenomenon predicted by the Rescorla–Wagner theory of classical conditioning (Rescorla & Wagner, 1972).

In classical conditioning, a neutral stimulus is followed repeatedly by an "unconditional" stimulus (US) that triggers a strong innate response. As these pairings continue over a series of trials, a response develops to the originally neutral stimulus. For example, a dog does not naturally salivate to the sound of a tone (thus, a tone is neutral stimulus with respect to salivation), whereas it does naturally salivate when meat powder is placed in its mouth (thus, meat powder is a US). When meat powder follows the tone across a series of tone presentations, the tone gradually acquires the power to elicit salivation. The tone is now a "conditional stimulus" (CS) that elicits a "conditional response" (CR). As trials continue, conditioning eventually reaches a peak strength beyond which no further increase occurs no matter how many times the CS and US are paired.

But what would happen if you fully conditioned the *same* response (e.g., salivation) to two dissimilar stimuli (e.g., a light and a tone) and then formed a new "compound" CS by presenting them together as a unit? Figure 3-1 displays the predictions of the Rescorla–Wagner theory.

The graph begins at left with both individual CSs fully conditioned at 100% response strength (lower curve). Combining them to form the compound CS (upper curve) yields a stimulus that is predicted to have a response strength *greater than* the level normally possible (here, 200%)! This is the predicted "overexpectation" effect.

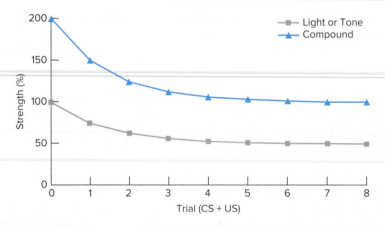

**FIGURE 3-1**   Overexpectation effects predicted by Rescorla–Wagner. At start, strength of response to tone + light compound (top) exceeds that of fully conditioned individual elements (bottom). Further conditioning trials causes a paradoxical reduction in these strengths.

But there's more: Pairing a CS with a US normally would be expected to increase the strength of the CR (unless the CS is fully conditioned), but here, as the compound CS and US continues to be paired, the strengths of the compound CS and of its component stimuli are predicted to *decrease*—yet another bizarre and unexpected result! Nevertheless, a number of studies have in general confirmed these predictions (e.g., Rescorla, 1999).

The second way that theory can generate research ideas arises when two or more alternative theories account for the same initial observations. This situation may provide a fascinating opportunity to pit the different interpretations against one another. If the alternatives are rigorously specified and mutually exclusive, they may lead to different predictions about what will be observed under a new set of conditions. In this case, a single experiment or observation may be enough to provide strong support for one alternative over another.

## Applied Issues

Often research ideas arise from the need to solve practical problems. Chapter 1 distinguished between basic and applied research. Applied research is problem oriented whereas basic research is aimed toward building basic knowledge about phenomena. You might design an applied research study to develop interventions to help people cope with terrorism. Of course, before you can design any intervention, you must first know something about how people react to terrorism. It may be that you have to use different intervention programs depending on individuals' unique characteristics.

A study by Moshe Zeidner (2006) investigated how Israeli men and women reacted to the chronic threat of terrorism. Male and female Israelis living in and around Haifa (in northern Israel) completed several measures designed to determine how they coped with the chronic threat of terrorism. Participants completed a battery of measures that included four categories of variables: (1) terror stress (measuring reactions to continued political violence and conflict), (2) personal variables (experience of negative emotion and degree of control over events), (3) coping processes (strategies used to cope with terrorism), and (4) stress reactions (symptoms experienced). Zeidner collected his data between April and June 2002, which was at the height of the Palestinian al-Aqsa Intifada. Zeidner's results were that men and women had different responses to the threat of terrorism. As shown in Figure 3-2, Israeli women experienced much higher levels of terror-related stress than men experienced and reported feeling more threatened by terrorism than men. Further, men indicated slightly more perceived control over the situation than did women. Women reported using more emotion-focused (e.g., denial, behavioral and mental disengagement, and alcohol/drug use) and problem-focused (e.g., positive reinterpretation and social support) behavior than men.

A wealth of other practical problems lend themselves to similar research solutions. For example, finding an effective way to get people to practice safe sex or finding an effective diet that people will follow might require a systematic evaluation of several proposed solutions to identify those that lead to success. Applied research also might identify the most effective therapy for depression or develop a work environment that leads to the highest levels of productivity and job satisfaction. Thus, a need to solve a practical problem can be a rich source of research ideas.

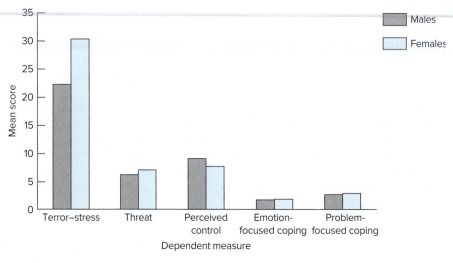

**FIGURE 3-2**    Gender differences in coping with chronic terrorism.
SOURCE: Zeidner, 2006.

## QUESTIONS TO PONDER

1. In what two ways can a theory help you develop research ideas?

2. How can applied issues suggest research ideas to you?

## DEVELOPING GOOD RESEARCH QUESTIONS

Coming up with a creative and unique general research question based on experience, theory, or application is not sufficient in science. After coming up with an inspired idea, you must translate that idea into a good research question that can be tested empirically. This section describes how to identify good research questions and suggests what kinds of questions are likely to be important.

### Asking Answerable Questions

The first step in developing a workable research project is to ask the kind of question that you can answer with the scientific method. Not all questions can. Here are a few questions that cannot be answered by scientific means: Does God exist? Why is there suffering in the world? Are there human abilities that cannot be measured? How many angels can stand on the head of a pin? Is embryonic stem cell research moral or immoral?

*Asking Empirical Questions*    The preceding questions are not answerable by scientific means because you can't find the answers through objective observation. To be objective a question must meet three criteria. First, you must be able to make the observations under precisely defined conditions. Second, your observations must be reproducible when those same conditions are present again. Third, your observations must be confirmable by others.

A question you can answer with objective observation is called an **empirical question.** Here are some examples of empirical questions: Do males and females cope differently with terrorism? Do men and women prefer different characteristics in potential mates? Does a deprived early environment result in lower intelligence? Is punishment an effective tool in socializing children? You can answer all of these questions through appropriately designed and executed research. Unlike the first set of questions, the second set identifies variables that you can define in terms of observable characteristics. For example, the question of whether males and females cope differently with terrorism asks about the relationship between two observable variables: gender and coping skills.

Some questions seem to be empirical but are formulated too broadly to make appropriate observations. Consider the following example of such a question: Do children raised in a permissive atmosphere lack self-discipline as adults? Before you can answer this question, a number of preliminary questions must be addressed. What exactly is a permissive atmosphere? How do you measure permissiveness? Precisely what does it mean to lack self-discipline, and how do we determine when self-discipline is present or absent? Until you can specify exactly what these terms mean and how to measure the variables they represent, you cannot answer the original question.

*Operationally Defining Variables*   One way to give precise meaning to the terms that you use is to provide an operational definition for each variable you are using. An **operational definition** involves defining a variable in terms of the operations required to measure it. Defining variables operationally allows you to measure precisely the variables that you include in your study and to determine whether a relationship exists between them. For example, you could operationally define "permissive parenting" in terms of the frequency that parents discipline their children for bad behavior. You could operationally define "lack of self-discipline" in an adult as the number of reprimands a person receives at work for late or sloppy work. With these precise definitions, you are now in a position to conduct a study to see if increased parental permissiveness is related to decreased adult self-discipline in the hypothesized way.

Although defining variables operationally is generally a good thing, there is a downside. Operational definitions restrict the generality of answers obtained. Permissive parenting, for example, is no longer addressed in general but as particular behaviors defined as permissive. Self-discipline is no longer addressed in general but in the context of specific behaviors said to indicate self-discipline. Other ways of measuring the two variables may yield a different answer to the question. Nevertheless, without using operational definitions, the question cannot be answered meaningfully.

To summarize, to conduct meaningful research you must choose a question that you can answer through scientific means. You must then operationally define your variables carefully so that you are working with precise definitions. When you have formulated your empirically testable question, you then proceed to the next step in the research process.

## Asking Important Questions

Developing answerable questions is not enough. They also should be important questions. Researching a question imposes demands on your time, financial resources, and the institution's available space. Researching a question makes demands on the available population of human participants or animal subjects. You should not expend these resources to answer trivial questions. However, whether a question is important is often difficult to determine. It is certainly possible to obtain valuable information in the course of answering an apparently unimportant question. Some questions that once seemed important to answer now appear trivial. Some rough guidelines will help in identifying important questions.

A question is probably important if answering it will clarify relationships among variables known to affect the behavior under study. For example, knowing that memory tends to deteriorate with time since learning, you would want to establish the rate of deterioration as a function of time. You would want to identify how the amount of initial practice, overlearning, previous learning, activity during the retention interval, and other such factors combine to determine the rate of forgetting under specified conditions.

A question is probably important if the answer can support only one of several competing models or theoretical views. As noted in Chapter 2, developing and testing such questions is at the heart of the scientific method. The answers to such questions allow you to "home in" on a proper interpretation of the data. (We discuss this technique later in the chapter.) On the negative side, if the theories undergoing testing are later discarded, research designed to test them may become irrelevant unless the findings demonstrate clear empirical relationships that other theories must explain.

A question is probably important if its answer leads to obvious practical application. (However, the lack of obvious practical application does *not* render the question automatically unimportant!) Researchers have conducted much research to identify working conditions that maximize productivity and job satisfaction or to screen drugs for potential effectiveness in controlling psychosis. Few would argue that the answers to these problems are unimportant.

In contrast, a question is probably unimportant if its answer is already firmly established. *Firmly established* means that different scientists have replicated (duplicated) a research finding and agree that the finding does occur under the stated conditions. Unless you can identify serious deficiencies in the methods used to establish those answers, performing the research again is likely to be a waste of time.

A question is probably unimportant if the variables under scrutiny are known to have small effects on the behavior of interest and if these effects are of no theoretical interest. A question is also probably unimportant if there is no a priori reason to believe that the variables in question are causally related. Research aimed at determining whether the temperature of a room affects memory recall for faces may turn out to have surprising and useful results. However, without a reason to expect a relationship, such research amounts to a "fishing expedition" that is unlikely to pay off. Your time would be better spent pursuing more promising leads.

When you have identified your research idea, the next step is to develop it to the point at which you can specify testable hypotheses and define the specific methods to be used to test these hypotheses. You accomplish this step by identifying and familiarizing yourself with research already conducted in your area of interest, an activity called "reviewing the literature." We show you how to review the literature and evaluate research reports in the following section.

## QUESTIONS TO PONDER

1. What are the characteristics of an empirical question?
2. Why is it necessary to define your terms operationally?
3. What makes a research question important, and why should you ask important questions?

## DEVELOPING RESEARCH IDEAS: REVIEWING THE LITERATURE

One of the most important preliminary steps in the research process is doing a thorough review of the scientific literature on the topic that you have identified for study. This is true whether you begin only with a vague idea of a research project or with a well-developed research plan. In this section, we discuss the tools, techniques, and knowledge that will enable you to identify, read, and evaluate published information on your research topic. In addition, we discuss the process of scientific peer review and describe how this process affects the content and quality of published scientific findings.

### Reasons for Reviewing the Scientific Literature

A **literature review** is the process of locating, obtaining, reading, and evaluating the research literature in your area of interest. Perhaps the most important reason for conducting a literature review is to avoid needless duplication of effort. No matter what topic you choose, chances are that someone has already done research on it. By becoming familiar with that area through a literature review, you can avoid "reinventing the wheel."

Another reason for conducting a literature review is that your specific research question may have already been addressed and answered. If so, then conducting your research as originally planned would be a waste of time. This does not mean, however, that you must start over from scratch. To the contrary, your literature review may reveal other questions (perhaps more interesting) that remain to be answered. By familiarizing yourself with existing research and theory in an area, you can revise your research project to explore some of these newly identified questions.

Another reason for reviewing the literature applies to the design phase of your research. Designing a study involves several decisions as to what variables to include and how to measure them, what materials or apparatus to use, what procedures to use, and so on. Published research provides you with a rich resource for addressing these important design questions. You may find, for example, that you can use established procedures and existing materials.

Reviewing the literature also keeps you up to date on current empirical or theoretical controversies in a particular research area. As science progresses, new ideas develop concerning age-old behavioral issues. For example, there is a debate concerning the motives for altruistic behavior. Some argue that empathy (a concern for the victim) motivates altruism and others argue that egoism (self-satisfaction) motivates altruism. Such controversies not only provide a rich source of research ideas but also give direction to specific research hypotheses and designs.

## Sources of Research Information

Sources of information about a topic range in quality from the high levels found in the scholarly books and journals of a discipline to the low levels found in the supermarket tabloids of the sensationalist press. Although information presented in the tabloids may arouse your curiosity and suggest a topic for scientific research, you cannot count on that information to be accurate or even true. Popular writing found in magazines such as *Time* may provide more reliable information gleaned from scientific sources, but the information presented generally lacks the detail that would allow you to determine much beyond the major conclusions offered. More substantive writing aimed at a better-educated reader generally provides more details about the methods used to gather the information but still omits important details and may not mention alternative interpretations or other evidence for or against the conclusions presented. You can only count on scholarly sources to provide the level of detail and thoroughness needed for a competent scientific review. Table 3-1, which is based on an analysis provided by the Cornell University Library (2015), identifies four types of periodicals and compares them on a number of important features. You can use this table to help you determine whether a publication is scholarly or not.

## QUESTIONS TO PONDER

1. Why should you review the literature on your topic before you begin to design your study?

2. What are the differences between the different types of periodicals, and on which should you rely most heavily (and why)?

Sources of research findings include books, scholarly journals, conventions and professional meetings, and others such as personal communications and certain pages on the Internet. In the following sections we review a few things you should know about these sources.

*Primary Versus Secondary Sources*    Sources containing research information are classified according to whether a source is primary or secondary. A **primary source** is one containing the full research report, including all details necessary to duplicate the study. A primary source includes descriptions of the rationale of the study, its participants or subjects, materials or apparatus, procedure, results, and references. A **secondary source** is one that summarizes information from primary sources (such as presenting the basic findings). Secondary sources of research include review papers

**TABLE 3-1  Comparison of Four Types of Published Periodicals**

| SCHOLARLY | SUBSTANTIVE NEWS/ GENERAL INTEREST | POPULAR | SENSATIONAL |
|---|---|---|---|
| Sober, serious look with graphs and tables | Attractive appearance, usually with photographs | Often have a slick, attractive appearance with many photographs | Often in newspaper format |
| Reference citations always provided | Sources are sometimes cited | Sources are rarely, if ever, cited | References to sources are often obscure |
| Written by a scholar in the field or someone who has done research in the field | Articles written by members of editorial staff, scholar, or free-lance writer | Written by a wide range of authors who may or may not have expertise in an area | Written by a variety of authors |
| Language of the discipline, assuming a scholarly background of the reader | Language geared to educated audience, but no specialty assumed | Written in simple language with short articles geared to audience with minimal education | Elementary, inflammatory language geared to a gullible audience |
| Report original research | Do not report original research, report *on* research in format geared to a general audience | Research may be mentioned, but it may come from an obscure source | Support may come from pseudoscientific sources |
| Many, but not all, published by professional organizations | Published by commercial publishers or individuals, but some from professional organizations | Published commercially with the intent to entertain the reader, sell products, or promote a viewpoint | Commercially published to arouse curiosity and play to popular superstition. Use flashy, astonishing headlines |
| Examples: *Journal of Personality and Social Psychology; Child Development, Journal of Experimental Psychology* | Examples: *National Geographic, Scientific American, New York Times, Christian Science Monitor* | Examples: *Time, Parents, Reader's Digest* | Examples: *National Enquirer, Globe, Star, Weekly World News* |

and theoretical articles that briefly describe studies and results, as well as descriptions of research found in textbooks, popular magazines, newspaper articles, television programs, films, or lectures. Another type of secondary source is a meta-analysis. In a meta-analysis, a researcher statistically combines or compares the results from research in a particular area to determine which variables are important contributors to behavior. (We discuss meta-analysis in Chapter 8.)

Distinguishing primary from secondary sources is important. Students often rely too heavily on secondary sources, perhaps because it can be a daunting task to read a primary source research report. The language can be technical, and the statistical tests reported can be intimidating. However, with some experience and perseverance, you can get through and understand primary source materials.

Another reason that students may rely heavily on secondary sources is to "save time." After all, someone else has already read and summarized the research, so why not save time and use the summary? This sounds good but can lead to trouble. The author of a secondary source may describe or interpret research results incorrectly or simply view data from a single (and perhaps narrow) theoretical perspective. In addition, secondary sources do not usually present detailed descriptions of methods used in the cited studies. You must know the details of the methods used in a study before you can evaluate its quality and importance. The only way to obtain such detailed information is to read the primary source.

Relying heavily on secondary sources can be dangerous because you cannot be sure that the information in a secondary source is complete and accurate. For example, one of the most widely cited studies in introductory psychology textbooks is John Watson and Rosalie Rayner's (1920) "Little Albert" study. In this study, Watson and Rayner conditioned a child (Albert) to show a fear response to a white rat. They also reported that Albert's fear generalized to other white, furry objects. In a review of how accurately Watson and Rayner's study was portrayed in textbooks, Griggs (2014) found that the study was inaccurately presented in textbooks, especially with respect to the generalization results. Similarly, Treadway and McCloskey (1987) found that many secondary sources misrepresented the methods and results of a classic memory experiment conducted by Allport and Postman (1945). These representations led researchers—and sometimes courts—to draw incorrect inferences concerning the role of racial bias in eyewitness accuracy. To avoid this trap, obtain and read the original report.

Secondary sources do have value, which lies in the summaries, presentations, and integrations of results from related research studies. The secondary source provides an excellent starting point for your literature search. Additionally, an up-to-date review paper or meta-analysis includes a reference section from which you can generate a list of primary sources. However, you should not consider a secondary source as a substitute for the primary source.

You may need to use a secondary source if the primary source it refers to is not available. If you must do so, always stay aware of the possible problems. In addition, cite the secondary source in your research report, not the primary one that you were unable to obtain.

To summarize, use secondary sources as a starting point in your literature search. Avoid overreliance on secondary sources and make every effort to obtain the primary sources of interest to you. Only by reading the primary source can you critically evaluate a study and determine whether the reported results are reliable and important. Finally, do not rely on a single secondary source. The author of a review article may not have completely reviewed the literature. Always augment the information obtained from a secondary source with a thorough literature search of your own.

*Books*   You are probably most familiar with general textbooks (such as those covering introductory psychology) or texts covering content areas (such as motivation and emotion, abnormal psychology, social psychology, personality, or cognitive psychology). Other books may contain more detailed information about your research topic. Specialized professional texts present the results of programmatic research conducted by the author over a period of years. These specialized texts may cover research previously published in journals, as well as findings not presented elsewhere. Edited anthologies present a series of articles on related topics, each written by a different set of authors. Some anthologies are collections of articles previously published separately; others present articles written especially for the occasion. Either kind of text may present reviews of the literature, theoretical articles, articles dealing with methodological issues, or original research.

Anthologies are useful because they assemble papers that the editor believes are important in a given area. However, be cautious when reading an anthology. The editor may be biased in judgment on which articles to include. Also, be sure to check the original publication date of articles in an anthology. Even if the publication date of the anthology is recent, it may contain outdated (sometimes classic) articles.

Texts or anthologies are most valuable in the early stages of the literature search. Often you can use the references from these books to track down relevant articles. You may have to treat books (especially textbooks) as secondary sources. Whenever you use a textbook as a source, make an effort to obtain a copy of the primary source cited in the textbook.

The articles in an anthology may be original works and thus can be treated as primary sources—provided that they have been reproduced exactly, not edited for the anthology. Be careful about relying on a chapter reproduced from a book. Isolating a single chapter from the original book can be misleading. In other chapters from the same book, the original author might elaborate on points made in the reproduced chapter. You could miss important points if you do not read the original work.

Whereas some books present original research, others provide only summaries. For example, if you were studying the development of intelligence, you could use Piaget's *The Origins of Intelligence in Children* (1952) as a good original source. However, a book such as *Piaget's Theory of Cognitive Development* by Wadsworth (1971)—a primer on Piaget's theory—should be treated as a secondary source in which you may find references for Piaget's original work.

Whatever route you choose, keep in mind one important factor. Even though you may have used an original work such as Piaget's (1952), problems with using it as a principal source may still exist. Books (especially by noted authors) may not undergo as rigorous a review as works published in scientific journals. You cannot be assured of the quality of any original research reported in the book. In addition, you would be well advised to seek out recent research on the issues covered in a book. Was Piaget correct when he speculated in his book about the origins of intelligence? Research published since his book came out may bear on this question. A review of the recent research would help you evaluate Piaget's theory and contributions.

## QUESTIONS TO PONDER

1. What is the difference between a primary and a secondary source, and why should you not rely too heavily on secondary sources?

2. What are the advantages and disadvantages to using various types of books as sources?

*Scholarly Journals*    Although textbooks are valuable, the information they contain tends to be somewhat dated. By the time a scientific finding makes its way into a text, it could already have been around for several years. For current research and theories regarding a subject, researchers turn to scholarly journals. Like popular magazines, journals appear periodically over the year in monthly, bimonthly, or quarterly issues. Some journals focus on detailed research reports (although occasionally a theoretical or methodological article may appear). These research reports are the most important primary sources. Other journals deal with reviews of the literature, issues in methodology, or theoretical views.

Keep in mind that not all journals are created equal. You must consider the source. When you submit your work to a **refereed journal,** it is reviewed, usually by two (or more) reviewers, to determine whether the paper merits publication. Other, **nonrefereed journals** do not have such a review process; the articles may be published in the order in which they were received or according to some fee that the author must pay. The review process is intended to ensure that high-quality articles appear in the journal. Although problems do occur with the review procedures, you can have greater confidence in an article from a refereed journal than in one from a nonrefereed journal.

A problem you are more likely to encounter in a nonrefereed journal than in a refereed journal is information that is sketchy and incomplete (Mayo & LaFrance, 1977). If information is incomplete, you may not be able to determine the significance of the article. Rely more heavily on articles published in high-quality, refereed journals than on articles in lower-quality, nonrefereed journals.

How can you determine whether a journal is refereed or nonrefereed? Search the Internet for the journal and check the editorial policy or submission guidelines for authors included on the journal's website. If you have a printed issue of the journal at hand, check the inside front or rear cover for a statement of the journal's review policy.

You can assess the quality of a scholarly journal in several ways. First, you can consult *Journals in Psychology,* published by the APA. This publication lists journals alphabetically and gives their manuscript acceptance rates. Top journals in a field have low acceptance rates (15% or less), whereas lesser journals have higher acceptance rates. Second, you can consult the *Journal Citations Report* available online from Thomson Reuters. Journals are ranked within category by their *impact factor,* which is a measure of "the frequency with which the 'average article' in a journal [was] cited in a particular year . . ." (Institute for Scientific Information [ISI], 1988, p. 10A). Third, you can consult the *Social Science Citations Index (SSCI).* One section of this publication lists journals by category (e.g., psychology) and subcategory (social psychology, experimental psychology, etc.). Fourth, you can use the online resource, the SCImago Journal & Country Rank (SJR, http://www.scimagojr.com/journalrank.php). The SJR ranks both journals and their countries of origin for quality. You can search by subject area (e.g., psychology) and subarea (e.g., social psychology) or search for a specific journal. Finally, you can use the method of authority discussed in Chapter 1. Ask your professors which journals in their fields of specialty are of highest and lowest quality.

## QUESTIONS TO PONDER

1. Why are scholarly journals the preferred sources for research information?

2. What is the difference between a nonrefereed and a refereed journal? Which is more trustworthy (and why)?

3. How do you assess the quality of a scholarly journal?

*Conventions and Professional Meetings*    Books and journals are not the only sources of research findings, nor are they necessarily the most current. Behavioral scientists who want the most up-to-date information about research in their areas attend psychological conventions. If you attended one of these conventions, you would find a number of **paper sessions** covering different areas of research. Paper sessions are usually simultaneously conducted in different rooms and follow one another throughout the day (much as classes do on campus). At these sessions, researchers present their research, usually within a 15- to 20-minute time period.

Paper sessions are not the best way to convey details of methodology. The written report is far superior for that purpose. At a convention, the author of a paper typically has only 15 minutes to describe his or her research. In that short time, the author must often omit some details of methodology.

Another popular format for convention presentations is the **poster session.** In this format, the presenter prepares a poster that is displayed on a bulletin board. The poster includes an introduction to the topic and method, results, discussion, and reference sections, and the presenter is usually there to discuss the research with you and answer any questions. This forum allows the author to provide more details than would be practical in a paper session and allows you to speak directly to the researcher about the research. Many good research ideas can emerge from such encounters.

Attending a paper or poster session has two distinct advantages over reading a journal article. First, the information is from the very frontiers of research. The findings presented may not appear in print for many months (or even years), if ever. Attending a paper session exposes you to newly conducted research that might otherwise be unavailable to you. Second, it provides an opportunity to meet other researchers in your field and to discuss ideas, clarify methodology, or seek assistance. These contacts could prove valuable in the future.

One drawback to paper and poster sessions at a convention is that a convention can be expensive to attend. In most instances, conventions are located in cities other than where you live. This means you must pay for travel, lodging, and food. Fortunately, you can gain some of the benefits of going to a conference by obtaining a copy of the program. By reading the abstracts of the papers, you can identify those papers of interest and glean something of the findings. If you want more information, you can then write or call the author. Many professional organizations provide full programs online. Visit one or more of the websites for these organizations (e.g., Eastern Psychological Association, Midwestern Psychological Association, and the Society for Psychological Science) to see if online versions of programs are available.

*Other Sources of Research Information*    Personal replies to your inquiries fall under the heading of **personal communications** and are yet another source of research information. Projects completed under the auspices of a grant or an agency often result in the production of a *technical report,* which can be obtained through the agency. In addition, dissertations and theses completed by graduate students as part of their degree requirements are placed on file in the libraries of the university at which the work was done. You can find abstracts describing these studies in *Dissertation Abstracts International,* a reference work indexed in many electronic databases. For a fee, the abstracting service will send you a copy of the complete manuscript on paper or as a PDF digital file.

Websites on the Internet are yet another potential source of research information, including limited access to scientific sources discussed earlier such as articles published in scientific journals. In addition, many laboratories doing scientific research maintain websites on which they discuss research currently under way, post lists of references to research papers coming out of the laboratory (and sometimes downloadable copies of those papers), and even may offer videos or computer simulations that you can view. Other websites not providing direct access to scientific material should be treated as secondary sources. Wikipedia, for example, covers a huge number of topics, including those of a scientific nature. Articles summarizing scientific findings or presenting theoretical views can provide a good overview of a given research topic, but keep in mind that these are not peer-reviewed and may reflect strong biases on the part of the writer.

To judge the quality of material found on the Internet, Purdue University's OWL website suggests evaluating Internet sources according to four categories: authorship (e.g., Is an author clearly indicated?), accuracy of the information (e.g., Is the information current and are sources provided?), the goals of the website (e.g., Is it informative, persuasive, or intended to advertise?), and access (e.g., How did you find the site, and are there links to other reputable sites?). Use caution if you cannot determine the quality of a resource found on the Internet.

The Internet also offers services that will allow you to search for and obtain full-text versions of articles from a variety of publications (some scholarly and some not). We discuss these in the next section.

## QUESTIONS TO PONDER

1. How can professional conferences provide you with information about research?

2. How can Internet resources be used to track down research information?

3. How do you assess the quality of information found on the Internet?

## SEARCHING THE SCIENTIFIC LITERATURE

With so many potential sources of information, how can you quickly and efficiently locate sources that are directly relevant to your research topic? Fortunately, you have available to you a number of powerful tools to help you do just that. In this section, we describe a number of electronic databases and specialized search engines that you can use to turn up relevant sources and, in the case of journal articles, even obtain a copy of the article. Next, we briefly take you through the process, using for our example a search of the PsycINFO database using the EBSCOhost search engine. Finally, we describe a "basic strategy" for identifying virtually all the published articles that are relevant to your research topic.

### Research Tools

University libraries subscribe to a number of search engines and associated electronic databases that allow you to search for information sources quickly and easily. Some databases cover a broad range of sources from a variety of disciplines; others specialize in sources pertinent to specific disciplines such as medicine, psychology, or philosophy. In psychology, for example, the American Psychological Association (APA) offers two relevant databases: PsycINFO and PsycARTICLES. We now briefly describe these and a few other databases you may find useful when looking for scientific research in psychology.

*PsycINFO and PsycARTICLES*    **PsycINFO** indexes journals, books, dissertations, and other sources relevant to psychology. More than 2,500 journals are covered, dating back as far as 1872. Some of the sources turned up in a search include a link to the article itself. By clicking on that link, you can download a copy of the article in HTML or PDF format. Most sources do not include such a link, however. To obtain the source, you may have to locate it in the library or request it through your library's document delivery service.

**PsycARTICLES** indexes articles appearing in selected journals published by the APA, the Canadian Psychological Association, and a few other publishers. The advantage of using PsycARTICLES rather than PsycINFO is that sources turned up by PsycARTICLES are available for immediate download. However, a search using PsycARTICLES is likely to turn up fewer sources owing to its more limited journal coverage.

The APA's PsycINFO and PsycARTICLES databases are accessible through a number of search engines, including those provided by DIMDI, EBSCO, Ovid Technologies, and ProQuest, as well as through the APA's own search engine, PsycNET. PsycNET offers an advantage over these other search engines in that it is specifically designed for searches of psychological research content and is closely integrated with the APA's *Thesaurus of Psychological Index Terms*. You can use the *Thesaurus* to identify keywords and phrases relevant to your topic as well as identify broader or narrower terms that you can use to expand or restrict your search.

*PubMed*    If your research topic has a medical or biological component, consider doing a search using the PubMed database. According to the PubMed website,

"PubMed comprises more than 26 million citations for biomedical literature from MEDLINE, life science journals, and online books. Citations may include links to full-text content from PubMed Central and publisher web sites." Some areas of research within psychology also focus on biological or medical questions, so a search using PsycINFO or PsycARTICLES may also turn up relevant sources.

*The Web of Science*    The Web of Science website provides subscription access to two databases: Science Citations Index (SCI) and Social Science Citations Index (SSCI). Both databases index articles relevant to psychology, although the coverage of sources is different. As you might guess, SCI covers sources with a more biological focus, whereas SSCI covers those with a more social or clinical focus.

If you have identified an older article on your topic, you can use SCI or SSCI to identify more recent sources that cited your older article. This allows you to efficiently bridge the gap between your article and current research on your topic. You can then use the references found in these newer sources to locate yet other relevant sources.

*JSTOR*    Another tool you may find useful is JSTOR, a search engine and associated database that indexes journals from a wide range of fields (e.g., sociology, philosophy, anthropology, and political science). JSTOR provides access to abstracts and allows you to download a full version of an article (you can limit your search to full-text sources) free of charge in a number of different formats. JSTOR may not be the best choice for searching specific topics in psychology, but used as a supplement to other databases, it may turn up articles that give a different perspective on your topic. From this broader perspective, you may gain some additional ideas about research that needs to be done.

*Google Scholar and Microsoft Academic Search*    Both Google and Microsoft offer free web searches of academic sources (Google Scholar and Microsoft Academic Search). These employ the familiar Google or Bing search engines, but with databases restricted to academic content. Searches using these products may turn up sources relevant to your topic, including books, journal articles, and websites. In some cases, you even can download a PDF file of an article or view pages from a relevant book. These sources provide a starting point for your literature search, but should not be counted on to turn up all relevant sources as coverage may be quite limited.

*Journal or Author-Associated Websites*    Many scientific papers are available for download from the journal publisher's website. Usually you can view the table of contents of the current issue and sometimes of past issues. Browsing the most recent issues of journals that publish in your area of interest can reveal some of the most recent publications. Selected articles may be available for download free of charge, but if you are not a subscriber, you may have to pay a hefty fee to obtain others. You may be able to avoid paying the fee, however. Some library database subscriptions allow legitimate users (such as students and faculty) to download articles from certain publishers without charge, as is the case when searching via PsycARTICLES. Alternatively, the author(s) of the paper may have made a free PDF available on their own website. Finally, you may be able to use your library's document delivery service to request a copy. Usually such requests are handled with a day or two, and your article delivered to you via email.

## QUESTIONS TO PONDER

1. The American Psychological Association maintains two electronic databases of journal articles and other published sources that cover topics related to Psychology: PsycINFO and PsycARTICLES. How do they differ?

2. What database should you search if your topic has a strong biological or medical component?

3. You have located an older article on your topic. What two databases can you use to identify more recent articles that cited your older one?

4. What sources can you use to locate a downloadable copy of a given research paper?

## Conducting an Electronic Database Search

Search engines developed by different providers offer somewhat different user interfaces through which you interact with the engine. We do not have space here to review them all; however, to give you a feel for the search process, we describe a search conducted using EBSCO's EBSCOhost search engine and the PsycINFO database.

Figure 3-3 shows the EBSCOhost screen as it appeared during a search we conducted using the keyword phrase "short term memory loss" that was entered in the first

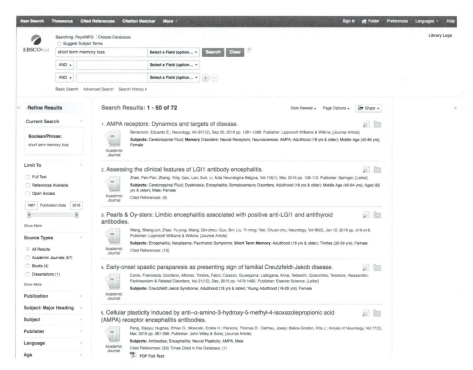

**FIGURE 3-3**    Searching PsycINFO using EBSCOhost.
SOURCE: Reprinted by permission of EBSCO Information Services.

search box. Immediately above this box are the words "Searching PsycINFO," identifying the database currently selected for searching. By clicking on the words "Choose Databases," you bring up a list of databases from which to choose. You can select one or more of these by clicking on the checkbox next to each option. For example, if you were searching for sources on a topic with both psychological and medical or biological aspects, you might want to select both PsycINFO and PubMed.

Immediately to the right of the search box in which we entered the key phrase "short term memory loss" is a button labeled "Select a Field (optional)." Use this button to limit the search to a particular field within the source's citation. For example, if you wanted to search for publications by a certain author, you could select "Author" from the menu that appears when you click the button and enter the author's name in the search box next to it. If you do not choose a field, the engine defaults to a search of the entire citation, including such things as the title and the contents of the abstract.

You can enter additional search terms in the other boxes and choose how the search terms in the different boxes will be combined: AND to locate any source that includes terms from both boxes, OR to locate sources that contain terms from either box, and NOT to find sources that match terms in the top box but do not match the terms in the second.

When entering terms in the search boxes, EBSCOhost may pop up a submenu suggesting additional terms you could use to narrow your search. When searching the PsycINFO or PsycARTICLES databases, you can also access key terms found in the *Thesaurus of Psychological Index Terms*. You can access the *Thesaurus* by clicking the tab that appears along the top of the EBSCOhost screen (see Figure 3-3).

As shown in Figure 3-3, our search turned up 122 sources, the first two of which are shown. By clicking on the title of the source, you bring up another page (not shown) containing the article's abstract and other information. You can read the abstract to determine whether the source is relevant to your topic.

Appearing immediately beneath the first source listed is a button labeled "Find It." Clicking on this button will cause the search engine to look for a location from which you may be able to download a copy of the paper, although you may have to pay a fee for the privilege. Alternatively, you may be able to obtain a free copy by taking advantage of your library's document delivery service. Requested journal articles typically will be e-mailed to you within a day or two; books that the library must obtain through interlibrary loan will take longer to arrive, and you will then have to go to the library to check them out.

The second source listed in Figure 3-3 sports two buttons in addition to the "Find It" button. If these are present (as here), you can obtain a copy of the article in HTML or PDF format simply by clicking on one of these buttons. Because we searched using PsycINFO, many of the sources turned up did not include these buttons as these appeared in publications not affiliated with the APA.

You do not necessarily need to obtain a copy of an article in order to identify the references cited in it. As shown in Figure 3-3, the second source listed includes a link to "56 Cited References" that are indexed in PsycINFO. Likewise, you can obtain the references cited in an article through the Web of Science search engine during a search of the SCI or SSCI databases.

## A Note of Caution When Searching an Electronic Database

Electronic search engines can save you considerable time and effort when searching a database. However, a search is only as good as the keywords you enter. The computer is incredibly fast and obedient and, unfortunately, pretty stupid. It will do only what you tell it to do. It cannot think for itself and figure out what you really want when you enter your search terms. It will find *every* reference that includes your keywords. You may find, much to your annoyance, that the terms are used more broadly in the indexed material than you anticipated. If, for example, you entered the keyword "age" (as in age-ed) to find research on a topic concerning the elderly, you might be shocked to find that the search turned up every study that gave the age ranges of the participants (e.g., "participants *aged* 12–14 years"). If this happens, use the online thesaurus (if available) to help you identify more useful keywords.

Another word of caution: With easy access to full-text versions of journal articles, you may be tempted to cut and paste portions of articles verbatim and use them in your course papers. *This is entirely inappropriate and may result in a low or failing grade in the course.* For now, it is sufficient to say that what you present in your writing must be presented in your own words with appropriate citations and references to works you use. Be careful how you use material from electronic versions of articles you find. We discuss the issues of plagiarism and lazy writing in Chapter 16. You may want to read ahead and review that material now so you can avoid problems with plagiarism and lazy writing.

## The Basic Strategy for Conducting a Thorough Search

Articles published in scientific journals or books carefully cite the sources of ideas or research findings that the authors use to support arguments, justify conclusions, and so on. The references for these citations appear in a reference section or bibliography that appears at the end of the article. Typically, these references will include earlier published work on the same topic as the article in hand.

To conduct a thorough search of the scientific literature—one that will turn up nearly every published article relating to your topic—there is a "basic strategy" you can follow:

1. Obtain one or more relevant articles.

2. Examine the reference section or bibliography of each article to identify older sources relating to your topic.

3. Repeat steps 1 and 2 until you are no longer finding any additional relevant articles.

4. Identify more recently published sources that cited the sources you have already identified.

5. Repeat steps 1 and 2 with these sources to "fill in" any gap between these newer sources and the ones previously obtained.

The basic strategy just described has two limitations. First, you must have a relevant article with which to begin your search. Second, you must have a way to identify more recent sources that cited the ones you identified in steps 1 through 3.

Overcoming the first limitation can be as easy as doing a quick web search using appropriate keywords. Such a search generally turns up a large number of sources of varying quality, but as noted earlier, among these results sometimes appear research published in scientific books and journals, as well as secondary sources (such as Wikipedia) that include relevant references. If available to you, you could also use one of the specialized search engines to search databases such as PsycINFO for relevant articles.

Given that you have identified an older source that is directly relevant to your topic, you have a couple of options for locating more recent sources. If you have access to the Web of Science search engine, you can search the Science Citations Index and Social Science Citations Index to identify published sources that have cited your article. Many of these will be directly relevant to your research topic. You can then obtain those articles and use their reference sections to fill in the gaps. Some journal websites and search engines identify sources that cite a given article and may even provide links to those articles where you can read the abstract and, in some cases, obtain a copy of the article itself.

## Searching for Books and Other Library Materials

Many libraries have installed electronic databases indexing the books and journals housed in the library. These systems are similar to other databases such as EBSCOhost and allow you to search for materials by author, title, subject, and keywords. Because libraries generally provide access to these databases via the web, you are not limited to searching just your own library. Try searching the web using the search phrase "university libraries databases." This will take you to a list of links to university libraries that you can search. Or, you can type in the name of a specific library (e.g., Purdue University Library) to search that library's holdings.

## QUESTIONS TO PONDER

1. When searching the literature using PsycINFO, what should you do if your search returns a huge number of articles? What should you do if it returns too few?

2. When using PsycINFO, what tool is available find search terms to either broaden or narrow your search?

3. Libraries maintain electronic databases of the materials in their collections. How can you access the electronic "card catalogs" of libraries distant from your location?

## READING A RESEARCH REPORT

Scientific papers fall into different categories depending on the nature of their content: literature reviews, theoretical articles, papers on research methodology or statistical analysis, and reports of original research. The formats of these papers vary with the category, although they share certain elements in common, such as the formatting of title pages, abstracts, and references. However, most of the papers you will acquire during a search of the literature on your topic will be journal articles presenting original research. In this section, we describe the sections and subsections of a typical research paper, as specified by the *Style Manual of the American Psychological Association*—hereafter referred to as "APA style"—and offer guidelines for the critical reading of each part.

## Reading the Literature Critically

When reading a journal article, think of yourself as a consumer of research. Apply the same skills to deciding whether you are going to "buy" a piece of research as you would when deciding whether to buy any other product. Critically reading and analyzing research literature (or any source of information for that matter) involves two steps: an initial appraisal and a careful analysis of content (Cornell University Library, 2015).

The *initial* appraisal involves evaluating the following (Cornell University Library, 2015):

- Author
- Date of publication
- Edition or revision
- Publisher
- Title of the journal

When evaluating the author, you should look at his or her credentials, including institutional affiliation and past experience in the area. It is important to consider the author and the author's institutional affiliation because not all research findings are reported in scholarly journals. Some research is disseminated through "research centers" and other organizations. By evaluating the author and the institution, you can make an assessment of any potential biases. For example, a study that comes from an organization with a political agenda may not present facts in a correct or unbiased fashion. The main author of a research report from such an organization might not even be academically qualified or trained to conduct research and correctly interpret findings. One way you can check on the author is to see if the author's work has been cited by others in the same area. Important works by respected authors are often cited by other researchers.

Look at the date of the publication to see if the source is current or potentially out of date. In some areas (e.g., neuroscience), new discoveries are made almost daily and may make older research out of date and obsolete. Try to find the most up-to-date sources that you can. It might be worth checking journal websites for the most up-to-date articles. Many journals now publish "Internet first" articles on important topics, which are available before they appear in the journal. When evaluating a book, determine if the copy you have is the most recent edition. If it is not, find the most recent edition because it will have been updated with the most current information available at the date of publication. Also, note the publisher for both books and journals. Some books are published by companies (sometimes called "vanity presses") that require authors to pay for publication of their works. Books published in this way may not undergo a careful scholarly review prior to publication. Generally, books published by university publishers will be scholarly, as will books published by well-recognized publishing houses (e.g., Lawrence Erlbaum Associates). Although this is no guarantee of quality, a book from a reputable publisher will usually be of high quality. The same goes for journals. As indicated earlier, some journals are peer reviewed and some are not. Try to use peer-reviewed journals whenever possible. Finally, look at the title of the publication that you are thinking of using. This will help you determine if the publication is scholarly or not. There is no hard-and-fast rule of thumb to tell you if a publication is scholarly. Use the guidelines in Table 3-1 to determine the nature of the publication.

The second step is to evaluate the content of the published material. Evaluating the content of an article published in a scholarly psychological journal involves a careful reading and analysis of the different parts of the article (outlined in Table 3-2). In the next sections, we explore how to critically analyze each section of an APA-style journal article.

## QUESTIONS TO PONDER

1. Why is it important to read a research report critically?
2. What initial appraisals should you make of an article that you are going to read?

Assume that you have obtained a copy of a research report. Knowing what you will find in it can save you time in locating specific kinds of information. The information contained in the report reflects the purposes for which it was written. These purposes include (1) arguing the need for doing the research, (2) showing how the research addresses that need, (3) clearly describing the methods used so that others can duplicate them, (4) presenting the findings of the research, and (5) integrating the findings with previous knowledge, including previous research findings and theories.

Consider the components of a typical research report and how they fulfill these purposes. Although the format of an article may vary from journal to journal, most research articles include the standard sections shown in Table 3-2. Sometimes sections are combined (e.g., results and discussion) or a section is added (e.g., design). Generally, however, research articles in psychological journals follow the outline shown in Table 3-2. Below we explore how to critically analyze each section of an APA-style journal article.

---

**TABLE 3-2    Parts of an APA-Style Article**

Abstract
Introduction
Method
    Participants or subjects
    Apparatus or materials
    Procedure
Results
Discussion
References

*Evaluating the Introduction*     When reading the introduction to a paper, determine whether or not the author has adequately reviewed the relevant literature. Were any important papers neglected? Does the author support any assertions with reference citations? In addition, ask yourself the following:

1. Has the author correctly represented the results from previous research? Sometimes when authors summarize previous research, they make errors or select only findings consistent with their ideas. Also, as already noted, authors may have a theoretical orientation that may bias their summary of existing research findings. If you are suspicious, look up the original sources and evaluate them for yourself. Also, you should determine if the author has cited the most up-to-date materials. Reliance on older material may not give you an accurate picture of the current research or theory in an area.

2. Does the author clearly state the purposes of the study and the nature of the problem under study?

3. Do the hypotheses logically follow from the discussion in the introduction?

4. Are the hypotheses clearly stated and, more important, are they testable?

*Evaluating the Method Section*     The method section describes precisely how the study was carried out. You might think of this section as a "cookbook," or a set of directions, for conducting the study. It usually contains subsections including *participants* or *subjects* (describing the nature of the subject sample used), *materials* or *apparatus* (describing any equipment or other materials used), and *procedure* (describing precisely how the study was carried out). You should spend considerable time evaluating the method section because sound methodology is crucial to whether the findings are valid. When reading the method section of an article, evaluate the following:

1. Who served as participants in the study? How were the participants selected (randomly, through a subject pool, etc.)? Were the participants all of one race, gender, or ethnic background? If so, this could limit the generality of the results (the degree to which the results apply beyond the parameters of the study). For example, if only male participants were used, a legitimate question is whether the results would apply as well to females. Also, look at the size of the sample. Were enough participants included to allow an adequate test of any hypotheses stated in the introduction?

2. Does the design of the study allow an adequate test of the hypotheses stated in the introduction? For example, do the levels of the independent variables allow an adequate test of the hypotheses? Is information provided about the reliability and validity of any measures used?

3. Are there any flaws in materials or procedures used that might affect the validity of the study? A good way to assess this is to map out the design (discussed next) of the study and evaluate it against the stated purpose of the study.

To better understand the design of an experiment you may want to "map out" the study. You can do this by drawing a grid or grids representing the design. For example,

**FIGURE 3-4**   Graphical display of an experimental design.

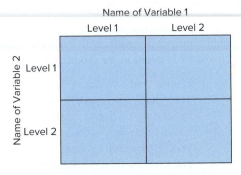

if you were reading about an experiment on stereotype threat which included two independent variables, a map of the experiment would look like the one shown in Figure 3-4. In Figure 3-4, the name of variable 1 (e.g., Stereotype threat condition) would go on top with the names of the two levels (e.g., Threat and No threat) underneath above each row. The name of variable 2 (e.g., Test anxiety assessment) would go on the side next to the names of the two levels to the left of each row (e.g., Before and After). Each box, or cell, on the figure represents a unique combination of variables 1 and 2. Of course, more complex designs would require more complex maps. However, the general strategy of mapping out designs, especially complex ones, can help you better conceptualize what was done in an experiment.

## QUESTIONS TO PONDER

1. What should you evaluate when reading the introduction to an APA-style paper?
2. What should you look for when evaluating the method section of an APA-style paper?

*Evaluating the Results Section*   The results section presents the data of the study, usually in summary form (means, standard deviations, correlations, etc.), along with the results from any inferential statistical tests applied to the data (e.g., a *t* test or analysis of variance). When evaluating the results section, look for the following:

1. Which effects are statistically significant? Note which effects were significant and whether those effects are consistent with the hypotheses stated in the introduction.[1]
2. Are the differences reported large or small? Look at the means (or other measures of center) being compared and note how much difference emerged.

---

[1]Some journals now actively discourage the publication of *p-values* in favor of confidence intervals, which are more informative. Confidence intervals indicate not only average differences between conditions, but also the degree of overlap in the scores.

Note the effect size, if given. Effect size tells you how big a difference is relative to the overall variability in the scores. You may find that, although an effect is statistically significant, it is small. A small effect may be meaningful from a theoretical perspective but of little practical value.

3. Were the appropriate statistics used?

4. Do the text, tables, and figures match? Sometimes errors occur in the preparation of tables and figures, so be sure to check for accuracy. Also, check to see if the author's description of the relationships depicted in any tables or figures matches what is shown.

5. If data are presented numerically in tables or in the text of the article, you should graph those results. This is especially important when complex relationships are reported among variables.

If statistics are not reported, determine whether the author has correctly described the relationships among the variables and has indicated how reliability was assessed.

*Evaluating the Discussion Section*    In the discussion section, you will find the author's interpretations of the results. The discussion section usually begins with a summary of the major findings of the study, followed by the author's interpretations of the data and a synthesis of the findings with previous research and theory. You also may find a discussion of any limitations of the study. When evaluating the discussion section, here are a few things to look for:

1. Do the author's conclusions follow from the results reported? Sometimes authors overstep the bounds of the results and draw unwarranted conclusions.

2. Does the author offer speculations concerning the results? In the discussion section, the author is free to speculate on the meaning of the results and on any applications. Carefully evaluate the discussion section and separate author speculations from conclusions supported directly by the results. Evaluate whether the author strays too far from the data when speculating about the implications of the results.

3. How well do the findings of the study mesh with previous research and existing theory? Are the results consistent with previous research, or are they unique? If the study is the only one that has found a certain effect (if other research has failed to find the effect or found just the opposite effect), be skeptical about the results.

4. Does the author suggest directions for future research in the area? That is, does the author indicate other variables that might affect the behavior studied and suggest new studies to test the effects of these variables?

*References*    The final section of an article is usually the reference section (a few articles include appendixes as well) in which the author lists all the references cited in the body of the paper. Complete references are provided. You can use these to find other research on your topic.

1. What information should you evaluate in the results section of an APA-style paper?

2. What information should you evaluate in the discussion section of an APA-style paper?

## FACTORS AFFECTING THE QUALITY OF A SOURCE OF RESEARCH INFORMATION

One thing to keep in mind when selecting a source of information about a particular area of research is that not all books, journals, or convention presentations are created equal. Some sources of information publish original research whereas others may only summarize the findings of a study. The criteria that journals use for accepting a manuscript determine which manuscripts will be accepted or rejected for publication, leading potentially to a bias in the content of the journal. Additionally, although most publications use a peer-review process to ensure the quality of the works published, some do not. In this section, we explore these issues and show how they relate to your literature review.

### Publication Practices

When you conduct a literature review, one question should come to mind in considering a research area as a whole: Do the articles that you are reading provide a fair and accurate picture of the state of the research in the field? Figure 3-5 shows the general process that a manuscript undergoes when it is submitted for publication. Although it is true that journals generally provide a good comprehensive view of the research within their scope, there may be research that never makes it into the hallowed pages of scientific journals because of the publication practices adopted by scholarly journals.

When a manuscript is submitted for consideration to a scholarly journal, editors and reviewers guide their evaluations of the manuscript by a set of largely unwritten rules. These include whether the results reported meet conventionally accepted levels of statistical significance, whether the findings are consistent with other findings in the area, and whether the contribution of the research to the area is significant. The policies adopted by the current editor also could affect the chances of a manuscript being accepted for publication. We examine these publication practices and their possible effects on the published literature next.

### Statistical Significance

Data collected in psychological research are usually subjected to a statistical analysis in order to determine the probability that chance and chance alone would have resulted in effects as large as or larger than those actually observed. If this probability is sufficiently low (e.g., less than .05, or 1 chance in 20), it is deemed unlikely that chance alone was

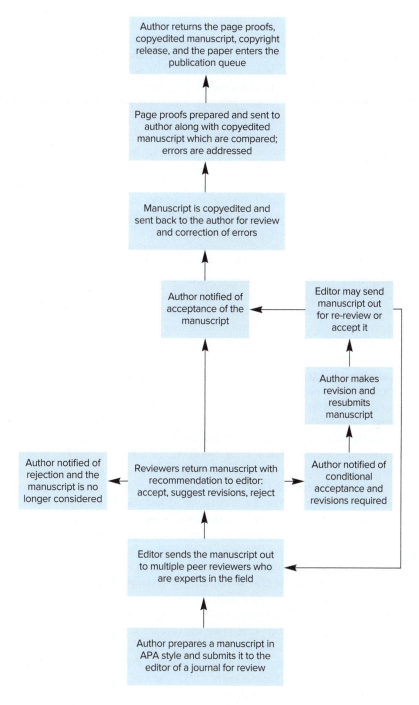

**FIGURE 3-5**   Diagram of the editorial review process.

responsible for the observed effect, and the effect is said to be *statistically significant.* (See Chapter 14 for a more detailed discussion of statistical significance testing.) The criterion probability used to determine statistical significance, called *alpha,* determines how often effects that are just chance differences end up being declared statistically significant. Thus, if alpha is .05, a chance effect will be declared statistically significant, on average, 5 times in 100 tests. In most journals, editors are reluctant to accept papers in which results fail to achieve the accepted minimum alpha level of .05. The reason, of course, is that such results stand a relatively high chance of being due to random factors rather than to the variable whose possible effect was being assessed in the study. Researchers are aware of the requirement for statistical significance and therefore usually do not report the results of studies that fail to meet it. It is worth noting here that there is a nascent movement to abandon statistical significance as a criterion for publication (Siegfried, 2015). For example, in 2015 the journal *Basic and Applied Social Psychology* changed its editorial policy so that *p*-values will no longer be published.

If the investigator is convinced that an effect is there, despite the lack of statistical significance, he or she may elect to repeat the study while using better controls or different parameters. Nothing is inherently wrong with such a strategy. If the effect is there, better control over extraneous variables and selection of more favorable parameters are likely to reveal it. If the effect is *not* there, however, repeated attempts to demonstrate the effect eventually lead to obtaining statistically significant results by chance. Through probability pyramiding (see Chapter 14), the likelihood that this will happen is much greater than the stated alpha level would suggest.

The failures to obtain significant results generally wind up in someone's file drawer, forgotten and buried. In most cases, only those attempts that were successful in obtaining significant results are submitted for publication. Yet, because of probability pyramiding, the published results are more likely to have been significant because of chance than the stated alpha would lead us to believe. This effect is known as the **file drawer phenomenon** (Rosenthal, 1979, 1984). To the extent that the file drawer phenomenon operates, published findings as a group may be less reliable than they seem.

The problem of negative findings is serious. The failure to obtain an expected relationship can be as important for understanding and for advancement of theory as confirmation. Yet this information is difficult to disseminate to the scientific community. Laboratories may independently and needlessly duplicate each other's negative findings simply because they are unaware of each other's negative results.

To combat the file drawer phenomenon and certain other sources of bias, some researchers and journal editors have advocated the "pre-registration" of scientific studies (see, e.g., Gonzales & Cunningham, 2015). Pre-registration involves submitting the design and methodology of a proposed study to an appropriate journal prior to actually conducting the study. Reviewers determine whether the study is properly designed to answer the questions it poses; if approved, then the results of the study will be accepted for publication (barring other complications) whether they are positive or negative. According to Gonzales and Cunningham (2015), several journals of the American Psychological Association were in the process of developing a pre-registration option for submitters. However, not everyone is convinced that pre-registration is a good idea (e.g., Scott, 2013), and it remains to be seen whether the potential advantages of the practice will outweigh its significant disadvantages.

## QUESTIONS TO PONDER

1. How do publication practices affect the articles that ultimately get published in journals?

2. What role does statistical significance play in determining what gets published in a journal?

3. What is the file drawer phenomenon and how does it relate to published research?

## Consistency with Previous Knowledge

Another criterion used to assess a research paper's acceptability is the consistency of its findings with previous knowledge. Most findings are expected to build on the existing structure of knowledge in the field, that is, to add new information, to demonstrate the applicability of known principles in new areas, and to show the limits of conditions within which a phenomenon holds. Findings that do not make sense within the currently accepted framework are suspect.

When the currently accepted framework has deep support, then such anomalous findings call into question the study that generated them rather than the framework itself. Reviewers and editors are likely to give the paper an especially critical appraisal in an attempt to identify faults in the logic and implementation of the design that may have led to the anomalous results. Ultimately, some reason may be found for rejecting the paper.

An excellent example in which this process operated was the initial work by Garcia and Koelling (1966) on learned taste aversions. Garcia and Koelling exposed thirsty rats to a solution of water that had been given a flavor unfamiliar to the rats. Some of the rats were then injected with lithium chloride, and the rest of the group was given a placebo injection of saline solution. The rats injected with lithium chloride became ill from the injection about 6 hours later. The rats were allowed to recover and then were given a choice between drinking plain water or the flavored water. Rats injected with the saline solution showed no preference between the two, but rats injected with lithium chloride avoided the novel flavor.

From this evidence, Garcia and Koelling (1966) concluded that the rats injected with lithium chloride had formed, in a single "trial," an association between the novel flavor and the illness. In other words, classical conditioning had occurred between a conditioned stimulus (the flavor) and an unconditioned stimulus (the illness) across a 6-hour interstimulus interval.

This was a striking finding. Classical conditioning had been extensively researched by Pavlov and others. It was well known that interstimulus intervals beyond a few *minutes* were completely ineffective in establishing a conditioned response, even when hundreds of trials were conducted. To reviewers and editors looking at Garcia and Koelling's (1966) manuscript, something was fishy. Garcia and Koelling's finding was a fluke, or some unreported aspect of methodology was introducing a confounding factor. The results simply couldn't be correct. The paper was repeatedly rejected by reviewers.

It was not until others heard of Garcia and Koelling's (1966) findings "through the grapevine" and successfully replicated their results that the phenomenon of learned taste aversions gained credibility among reviewers. Only then did papers on the topic begin to be accepted in the established refereed journals. Once accepted, Garcia and Koelling's discovery and other similarly anomalous findings became the basis for new theories concerning the nature and limits of laws of learning (see, e.g., Seligman & Hager, 1972). Hence, in refusing to publish Garcia and Koelling's findings, reviewers and editors delayed progress, but ultimately the new findings surfaced to challenge established thinking.

Editors and reviewers are thus in a tough position. To function effectively, they must be conservative in accepting papers that report anomalous findings. Yet they must be open-minded enough to avoid simply assuming that such findings *must* result from methodological flaws. Later in this chapter, we examine just how successful editors and reviewers have been at maintaining this balance.

## Significance of the Contribution

When determining whether to accept or reject a paper for publication, editors and reviewers must assess the degree to which the findings described in the paper contribute to the advancement of knowledge. At one time, papers were considered acceptable even if they reported only a single experiment involving simply an experimental and a control group. A researcher could publish a number of papers in a relatively short time, but each contributed little new information.

Today, journals usually insist that a paper report a series of experiments or at least a parametric study involving several levels of two or more variables. For example, a paper might report a first experiment that demonstrates a relationship between two variables. Several follow-up experiments might then appear that trace the effective range of the independent variable and test various alternative explanations for the relationship. Such a paper provides a fair amount of information about the phenomenon under investigation and, in pursuing the phenomenon through several experiments, also demonstrates the phenomenon's reliability through immediate systematic replication.

Although these are important advantages, insisting on multiple experiments or studies within a paper also can have a negative side. Although the study provides more information, the information contained in the study cannot see the light of day until the entire series of experiments or observations has been completed. The resulting paper is more time-consuming to review and evaluate. Reviewers have more opportunities to find defects that may require modification of the manuscript. The result is delay in getting out what may be an important finding to the scientific community.

## Editorial Policy

Editorial policy is yet another factor that can influence what appears in journals. Frequently, an area of research becomes "hot," resulting in a flood of articles in the area. Researchers latch on to a particular research area (e.g., eyewitness identification, day care in early infancy) and investigate it, sometimes to the exclusion of other important research areas. When this happens, a journal editor may take steps to ensure that more variety appears in a journal. For example, research on eyewitness identification became a hot topic in the area of psychology and law. Interest reached its peak in the 1980s, and the premier journal in the area, *Law and Human Behavior,* published a large number of articles on this topic—perhaps too large a number. In 1986 Michael Saks took over as editor of the journal. He made it clear that he was going to give preference to manuscripts dealing with issues other than eyewitness identification.

Editorial policy also can show itself if the editor enters an unintended bias into the review system. The editor is the one who decides whether a paper will be sent out for review and, ultimately, if it will be published. If the editor has a bias—say, toward a particular theory—that editor may be unwilling to publish articles that do not support that theory. We discuss this issue in the next section.

## QUESTIONS TO PONDER

1. How can consistency with previous knowledge affect whether a paper gets published in a journal?

2. How does the significance of a contribution influence an editor's decision to publish a paper in a journal?

3. How can editorial policy affect whether a paper gets published in a journal?

## Peer Review

Some sources of information (including books, journal articles, and convention proceedings) use a **peer-review** process. This means that the materials to be published or presented are reviewed by experts in the area that the material covers. These experts receive a copy of the materials and do a thorough review of the content.

There are three functions of the peer-review process (Resnik & Elmore, 2016). First is to provide advice to an editor whether to accept or reject a paper for publication. The editor of the journal can either accept (outright or with revisions) or reject the manuscript. Second, through the peer-review process, authors receive feedback, which allows them to make changes and improvements to a paper. Third, through interaction with reviewers and editors, authors can learn to do better science and better writing.

Peer review is a time-honored tradition in science as a way to ensure quality and provide feedback to authors. Most authors receiving feedback from the process (73.8%) believe that they received useful feedback, and a large majority (75.6%) believe that reviews provided a firm basis for an editor's decision (Shattell, Chinn, Thomas, & Cowling III., 2010). However, peer review is far from perfect. In one study, for example, authors reported several "ethical" problems with the peer-review process. As shown in Figure 3-6, 61.8% of authors reported incompetent reviews, 50.5% reported a biased review, and 22.7% reported that reviewers required them to cite the reviewer's research. Remember, although peer review helps to ensure quality, it does not guarantee it. Conversely, you may find some gems in nonrefereed journals. The reason for this seeming lack of consistency has to do with problems in the peer-review process.

*Problems with Peer Review*    As we noted, when you send a manuscript to a refereed journal, the editor will send your manuscript to expert reviewers (usually two) who will carefully evaluate your paper. In some cases, peer review is anonymous, and in

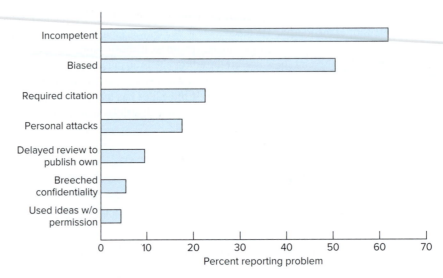

**FIGURE 3-6**    Problems with peer review reported by authors.
SOURCE: Resnik, Gutierrez-Ford, and Peddada, 2008.

others it is not. Individual journals determine their peer-review policies, and some choose to use anonymous peer review. Anonymous peer review might be necessary, but it does have its problems. Although you hope that your colleagues in research are honest and fair in their appraisals of your work, someone with a personal dislike for you or your ideas could sabotage your efforts. Even in the absence of malice, the reviewer may judge your manuscript unfairly because of a lack of knowledge, a bias against your general approach to research, or misreading.

Suls and Martin (2009) suggest that there are several problems with traditional peer review in the social sciences that may make the process unfair or biased. Suls and Martin point out that even though reviewers are supposed to be "experts," reviewers may lack expertise relating to the methods and issues within a field. Even if a reviewer is a true expert, he or she may be a direct competitor of the author of an article, coloring that reviewer's evaluation. Suls and Martin also suggest that using anonymous reviewers might encourage reviewers to be overly critical of a paper due to lack of accountability. Reviewers may also see their role as "gatekeeper" and be overly harsh and critical especially for articles with controversial content. Suls and Martin also note that a frequent criticism of peer review is that papers from well-established authors are treated more leniently than papers from lesser-known authors. The result is that papers from well-known authors have a better chance of being published, even if the work is of lower quality. Yet another problem with peer review is low levels of agreement between reviewers of the same paper (Suls & Martin, 2009).

The extent to which such factors operate within the peer-review system has been the subject of research and debate. For example, Mahoney (1977) investigated the influence of several properties of a research manuscript on its acceptance for publication by reviewers. With the approval of the editor, Mahoney sent manuscripts describing a fictitious experiment to 75 reviewers working for the *Journal of Applied Behavior Analysis*.

Five randomly constituted groups of reviewers received different versions of the manuscript that varied according to their results and interpretations of those results. Mahoney found that the paper was consistently rated higher if its results supported the reviewer's theoretical bias and lower if they did not. How the results were interpreted had little impact. Similarly, the recommendation to accept or reject the paper for publication was strongly influenced by the direction of the data. If the data supported the reviewer's theoretical leanings, the reviewer usually recommended acceptance. If the data argued against those leanings, the reviewer usually recommended rejection or major revision.

Mahoney's (1977) findings showed that results favorable or unfavorable to the reviewer's point of view affect how the reviewer receives the manuscript. If the results are favorable, the reviewer is likely to believe that the results are valid and that the methodology was adequate. If the results are unfavorable, however, the reviewer is likely to believe that the study must be defective. The reviewer will search diligently for flaws in the design or execution of the study and use even minor problems as reasons for rejection.

Partly because of such sources of bias, estimates of inter-reviewer reliability in the social sciences have tended to be low. Fiske and Fogg (1990) examined 402 reviews of 153 papers and found almost no agreement among reviewers, not because the reviewers overtly disagreed but because the reviewers found different aspects of the papers to criticize. It was as if they had read different papers! Lindsey (1978), in his book *The Scientific Publication System in Social Science,* notes that empirical studies have consistently found reliabilities of around .25 (the correlation between reviewer judgments). Whether both reviewers will agree that your paper is publishable is thus very nearly a chance affair.

Other research shows there may be an own-country bias in the review process. Lutz Bornmann and Hans-Dieter Daniel (2009) examined a number of factors that related to a reviewer's decision to accept or reject a manuscript in a German-language international chemistry journal. The journal required its reviewers to provide a host of information about themselves, which Bornmann and Daniel related to a number of manuscript characteristics. Among their findings was that a manuscript was more likely to be accepted by a reviewer if the authors and/or the reviewers had a German institutional affiliation and that ratings were most favorable if both the reviewer and author were German. Bornmann and Daniel also found that although scientific impact was an important factor in determining ultimate acceptance of rejection of a manuscript, a manuscript had a greater chance of being accepted if it had scientific impact and if all of the authors were at German institutions.

Gender also appears to relate to the review process. With respect to the gender of the reviewer, the evidence is mixed. Two studies using different methods (Mutz, Bornmann, & Daniel, 2012; Borsuk et al., 2009) found that female reviewers tend to be more critical than male reviewers. Mutz, Bornmann, and Daniels found that grant applications were more likely to be recommended for funding by an all-male panel of reviewers than by an all-female panel or one with gender parity. However, another study (Grod et al., 2008) found that males recommended rejection of manuscripts more frequently than females. The difference in the findings of these studies may relate to the samples used, the task required, and the type of material to be reviewed. What we can conclude at this point is that gender does relate to the outcome of peer review in some way.

How about the gender of the author? Is there any systematic bias against male or female authors? Commentators have been concerned that there may be a systematic bias against female authors in the peer-review process. However, evidence suggests that there is no systematic bias against female authors (Marsh, Bornmann, Mutz, Daniel, & O'Mara, 2009). For example, Herbert Marsh and his colleagues conducted a meta-analysis (a study that statistically compares results of a number of studies on a given topic) of the literature on the relationship between author gender and the peer review process for grant applications. They found no evidence for a bias against women in the peer review process. In fact, they found a slight pro-woman author bias. Robyn Borsuk and her colleagues (2009) also found no evidence for a bias against women authors in review of a manuscript.

The unreliability of the peer-review system was highlighted by a study conducted by Peters and Ceci (1982). Peters and Ceci identified 12 *published* articles that had appeared in different major psychology journals. Each article was authored by at least one individual from a "prestige" institution and had appeared between 18 and 32 months earlier. The names of the original authors and their institutional affiliations were removed and replaced by fictitious names and affiliations. In addition, the titles, abstracts, and introductions were cosmetically altered (without changing the content) to reduce the chances that the articles would be recognized. Retyped as manuscripts, the articles were then resubmitted *to the same journals that had originally published them* (and in most cases, to the same editor).

The results were dramatic. Only 3 of the 12 articles were identified as resubmissions and rejected for this reason. The remaining 9 were undetected. Of those 9, *8 were rejected for publication.* Even more amazing, in every case both reviewers agreed and the editor concurred.

Because the articles had appeared before, the reviewers might have rejected the papers because they remembered the earlier data (although not the articles themselves) and thus viewed the information they contained as contributing nothing new. If this were the case, however, no hint of this was given in the reasons cited by the reviewers. According to Peters and Ceci (1982), the reasons given for rejecting the papers usually concerned major flaws in the methodology. Thus, papers that had already been accepted into the archival literature only months earlier were subsequently seen as too methodologically flawed to merit publication.

Peters and Ceci (1982) offer two possible reasons for the new attitude toward the papers. The change in authorship and affiliation from prestigious to unknown may have had a negative influence on the evaluation. Or, because of the approximately 80% rejection rate, peer review may have been so unreliable that the chances of getting positive evaluations were just too low to expect acceptance the second time. This latter view assumes that getting a positive evaluation is essentially a matter of chance for manuscripts that cannot be rejected out of hand for obvious fatal flaws. Whether either or both possibilities are true, the implication is that acceptance of your paper (given that it is reasonably good) depends to a large extent on factors that are not under your control.

Can anything be done to improve the peer-review process? A number of commentators have offered suggestions to improve the process. Cooper (2009), for example, suggests a training program for reviewers. She points out that at the present time, reviewers receive little, if any, formal training. One way to do this is to include graduate students as co-reviewers during their graduate training (Cooper, 2009). Cooper also suggests that increasing accountability can help improve the process. According to Cooper, this could be accomplished by allowing authors to provide feedback on the review process and/or allowing an appeal process for authors. Another thing that could improve the review process is to relieve the burden on reviewers by reducing the number of manuscripts they review (Cooper, 2009). According to Cooper, editors could reject more obviously poor papers before sending them out for review or solicit fewer reviews for each paper submitted.

Despite the problems associated with the peer-review process, it does work pretty well. Although peer review is no guarantee that all things published are of impeccable quality, it does provide a measure of confidence that what you read is valid and reliable.

## QUESTIONS TO PONDER

1. What is peer review, and what are the major problems associated with the practice?

2. How can the peer-review process affect the likelihood that a paper will be published in a journal?

3. What evidence is there that the peer-review process affects publication practices?

### Values Reflected in Research

Another thing you need to take into account when evaluating research is whether values have influenced the research hypotheses tested and how results are interpreted. Values may flow from an entire field of science or from individual authors. For example, currently there is discussion about the ideological bias in social psychology. The majority of social psychologists identify themselves as politically liberal on a number of issues. In one study (Inbar & Lammers, 2012), only 5.5% of social psychologists described themselves as "moderate" and even fewer (3.9%) as "conservative" on social issues. The percentage identifying in various ideological categories varied according to the issue evaluated. For example more social psychologists describe themselves as moderate or conservative (compared to social issues) on economic (18.9% and 17.9%, respectively) and foreign policy (21% and 10.3%, respectively). Inbar and Lammers also found that moderates and conservatives were more likely to have experienced a hostile climate in the science than liberals. Ominously, the more liberal social psychologists were, the more willing they indicated they would be to discriminate against a conservative social psychologist (e.g., in hiring, publication and grant decisions).

The bottom line is that scientists are human beings and have their own attitudes, values, and biases that may be reflected in science. These values sometimes show up in published research, potentially reducing the its validity. When general cultural values, political agendas, and personal values of the researcher are introduced into the research process, it can affect the validity and generality of science. For example, Duarte and colleagues (2014) indicate that ideological values in social psychology can result in three negative consequences for the science. First, the values becoming embedded in the theory and methods of the science, resulting in research questions being approached from only one point of view. Second, researchers might focus only on issues that validate the dominant ideology, while ignoring those that do not. Third, the behaviors and motives of members of the nondominant ideology might be mischaracterized. So, although we would like to think of research as "value free" and objective, some philosophers of science suggest that research cannot easily be separated from a set of values dominating a culture or a person (Longino, 1990).

Values can influence science in other ways as well. Helen Longino (1990), for example, lists five nonmutually exclusive categories of these influences (p. 86):

1. *Practices.* Values can influence the practice of science, which affects the integrity of the knowledge gained by the scientific method.

2. *Questions.* Values can determine which questions are addressed and which are ignored about a given phenomenon.

3. *Data.* Values can affect how data are interpreted. Value-laden terms can affect how research data are described. Values also can determine which data are selected for analysis and the decision concerning which phenomena are to be studied in the first place.

4. *Specific assumptions.* Values influence the basic assumptions that scientists make concerning the phenomena that they study. This may cause a scientist to make inferences in specific areas of study.

5. *Global assumptions.* Values can affect the nature of the global assumptions that scientists make that can affect the nature and character of the research conducted in an entire area.

Similarly, David Myers (2008) indicates a number of ways that values can affect science. First, scientists often come from a common culture and share a set of beliefs about the world, which may go unchallenged. These unchallenged beliefs become resistant to change, and anyone from outside who challenges them is viewed with suspicion and their ideas given little weight. Because of this, new ideas and research issues may not be accepted. Second, values may be expressed as value judgments concerning the best way to live one's life (Myers, 2008). Myers gives the example of Abraham Maslow's concept of self-actualization as a person who is autonomous and mystical. That concept was based on Maslow's personal values and may have been different had Maslow had different personal values. Third, values can influence how we conceptualize behavior or scientific phenomena. For example, if a study finds that authoritarian people are more likely to endorse "unethical" positions, values can influence what a researcher considers "unethical" (Duarte et al., 2015). Or, if unethical is defined in terms of not taking a liberal or conservative view of what is unethical, then values are directly reflected in how that construct is defined and measured (Duarte et al., 2015). Third, Myers (2008) states that values can affect how we label behavior or psychological phenomena. The classic example is that one person's "terrorist" is another person's "freedom fighter" (Myers, 2008).

*How Values Influence What and How Scientists Study*    Cultural values can be seen operating on science. For example, in the United States, researchers interested in conformity effects have focused on the role of the majority in influencing the minority.

This probably filters down from the American political system in which the "majority rules." In Europe where there are parliamentary democracies, minority viewpoints are often taken into account when political coalitions are formed. As a consequence, much of the research on how a minority can influence a majority came out of European psychological laboratories.

Feminist scholars point out that assumptions about gender can influence how research questions are formulated (Unger & Crawford, 1992). For example, research on the effects of early infant day care on children is usually couched in negative terms concerning how maternal employment may adversely affect a child's development. Rarely are such questions phrased in terms of the potential positive outcomes (Unger & Crawford, 1992).

Unger and Crawford (1992) also point out that gender may play a role in the manner in which research hypotheses are tested. They suggest, for example, that focusing on quantitative data (representing behavior with numerical values) may be biased against female research participants. They suggest that research also should be done that focuses on qualitative data. Such a focus would lead to a richer understanding of the motives underlying behavior. They also point out that research designs are not value neutral. Overreliance on rigid, laboratory experimentation, according to Unger and Crawford, divorces social behavior from its normal social context. They suggest using more field-oriented techniques. They do not advocate, however, abandoning experimental techniques.

What you read in scientific journals and in the media is filtered through a system in which reviewers and editors—and their values—determine what gets published or widely disseminated. We have already seen how agreement with a reviewer's point of view increases the likelihood that a manuscript will be accepted. Journal and media editors serve as *gatekeepers*, determining what research will be published (Crane, 1967). On another level, what may be *allowed* to be disseminated may depend on biases of editors and those within the scientific community as a whole. In this way, editors affect those who read journals, society as a whole, and authors by limiting what is disseminated (Hojat, Gonnella, & Caelleigh, 2003). This problem becomes most serious when scientific, political, or personal agendas systematically suppress research on one side of an issue. Let's look at a couple of examples of how this works.

Between 2004 and 2006, NASA scientist James E. Hanson alleged that his research and conclusions on the causes of climate change were systematically suppressed by political appointees with NASA. As a result, the public was allegedly exposed to a biased view of global climate change. In response to the allegations, the Inspector General of NASA initiated an investigation. Based on this investigation, the Inspector General concluded, "the NASA Headquarters Office of Public Affairs managed the topic of climate change in a manner that reduced, marginalized, or mischaracterized climate change science made available to the general public through those particular media over which the Office of Public Affairs had control" (Winters, 2008, p. 1). The Inspector General's report indicated that NASA officials used a number of tactics to minimize the impact of certain research findings. These included denying access to media, adding statements concerning uncertainty, timing release of research so that it had minimal impact, and releasing unfavorable information to lesser news outlets. Practices like this may lead to a one-sided presentation of scientific findings, where those who subscribe to the accepted view are more likely to have their results published or disseminated in the media. In fact, a survey by Naiomi Oreskes (2004) of 928 published papers on the causes of climate change provides evidence for this. Oreskes found that 75% of the published papers agreed with the prevailing views of the causes of climate change, and the other 25% took no mention (e.g., dealt with methodological or other issues).

The gatekeepers of science sometimes send clear messages to scientists about what is appropriate subject matter for study. In addition, negative personal and professional consequences may befall scientists who try to publish research that is perceived to fly in the face of what is conventionally acceptable. Consider the case of Mark Regenerus. Regenerus published a study questioning the equivalence of "gay parenting" and traditional parenting (by heterosexual parents), which is the widely accepted "truth" in this research area. After his article was published, Regenerus was the target of much vitriol by the scientific community and by the public at large. He was accused by colleagues of damaging the image of the University of Texas, was the target of an investigation into his research integrity, and was the target of a complaint to the Texas Attorney General (Ferguson, 2012). The very public excoriation of Regenerus sends a clear message to other researchers who might dare to challenge the prevailing view in science: don't do it (Ferguson, 2012).

*Interpreting Behavior*     Scientists do not merely "read" what is out there in nature. Rather, scientists interpret what they observe (Myers, 2008). One's personal biases and cultural values may exert a strong influence over how a particular behavior is interpreted. For example, a conservative scientist may favor a biological explanation for aggression whereas a more liberal one may favor a societal explanation. In such cases, the values of the researcher provide an overarching view of the world that biases his or her interpretations of a behavioral event.

*Moving from What Is to What Ought to Be*     Values also can creep into science when scientists go beyond describing and explaining relationships and begin to speculate on what ought to be (Myers, 1999). That is, scientists allow values to creep into the research process when they endeavor to define what is "right" or "normal" based on research findings. On another level, this influence of values also is seen when researchers conduct research to influence the course of political and social events. Some feminist scholars, for example, suggest that we should not only acknowledge that values enter into science but also use them to evaluate all aspects of the research process (Unger, 1983). According to this view, science should be used to foster social change and challenge existing power structures (Peplau & Conrad, 1989).

Making sense of research requires that you be aware of the biases and other sources of error that afflict research. Given the ubiquitous nature of these sources, it is not surprising that research findings within a given area often appear contradictory.

*Combating Values and Ideological Homogeneity in Science.*     Is there anything we can do to address the problems of values and ideological bias in science? Fortunately, there is. Although we may never be able to eliminate these influences, we may be able to reduce them. In the context of ideological homogeneity, Roy Baumeister (2015)

| TABLE 3-3   Areas in Which Ideological Bias in Science Can Be Addressed | | |
|---|---|---|
| **ORGANIZATIONAL RESPONSES** | **PROFESSIONAL RESPONSES** | **RESEARCH PRACTICES** |
| Formulate anti-discrimination policies relating to ideological diversity. | Raise awareness by acknowledging the presence of ideological bias. | Be aware of double standards that result in harsher criticism of conservative than liberal ideas and findings. |
| Implement a "climate study" to evaluate experiences of members of nondominant ideology groups. | Solicit and welcome feedback from nonliberal students. | Support "adversarial" collaborations by encouraging researchers with differing views to collaborate on research. |
| Conduct studies of the barriers to nonliberal students. | Expand diversity statements and policies to include ideology and diversity of thought. | Place more emphasis on getting science right and establish norms for handling when scientific claims are shown to be incorrect. |
| Expand the number of nonliberal reviewers. | | |
| Develop strategies to recruit, hire and retain nonliberal students and professionals. | | |

SOURCE: Duarte et al., 2015.

suggests that we can attenuate the influence of a particular ideological bias by becoming aware of our own biases and how they might be affecting the course of research. One strategy he suggests is to try to think about an issue from a perspective different from your own. So, if you believe that differences between racial groups are due to environmental factors, you should address the issue from a biological perspective. Duarte et al. (2015) suggest that there are three areas in which ideological bias can be addressed. These, along with their examples, are shown in Table 3-3. Although these suggestions were proposed in the context of ideological homogeneity, they may also apply to reducing other forms of value-related bias in science.

## DEVELOPING HYPOTHESES

Your library research and critical reading have now put you on the threshold of the next major step in the research process: developing your idea into a testable hypothesis. This hypothesis, as we pointed out in Chapter 1, will be a tentative statement relating two (or more) variables that you are interested in studying. Your hypothesis should flow logically from the sources of information used to develop your research question. That is, given what you already know from previous research (either your own or what you read in the journals), you should be able to make a tentative statement about how your variables of interest relate to one another.

Hypothesis development is an important step in the research process because it will drive your later decisions concerning the variables to be manipulated and measured in your study. Because a poorly conceived research hypothesis may lead to invalid results, take considerable care when stating your hypothesis.

As an example, imagine that your general research question centers on the relationship between aging and memory. You have spent several hours in the library using PsycINFO to find relevant research articles. You have found several articles showing that older adults show poorer memory performance on tasks such as learning nonsense syllables, learning lists of words, and recognizing pictures. However, you find very little on age differences in the ability to recall details of a complex event such as a crime. Based on what you found about age differences in memory from your literature review, you strongly suspect that older adults will not recall the details of a complex event as well as younger adults.

Thus far, you have a general research question that centers on age differences in the ability to recall details of a complex event. You have identified two variables to study: participant age and memory for a complex event. Your next step is to translate your suspicion about the relationship between these two variables into a testable research hypothesis. You might, for example, develop the following hypothesis:

> Older adults are expected to recall fewer details of a complex event correctly than younger adults.

Notice that you have taken the two variables from your general research question and have linked them with a specific statement concerning the expected relationship between them. This is the essence of distilling a general research question into a testable hypothesis.

Once you have developed your hypothesis, your next task is to decide how to test it. You must make a variety of important decisions concerning how to conduct your study. The next chapter explores the major issues you will face during the preliminary stages of planning your study.

## QUESTIONS TO PONDER

1. How do values affect the research process?
2. How do you develop hypotheses for research?

## SUMMARY

Sources of research ideas include experience (unsystematic observation and systematic observation), theory, and the need to solve a practical problem. Unsystematic observation includes casual observation of both human and animal behavior. Systematic observation includes carefully planned personal observations, published research reports, and your own previous or ongoing research. Theory is a set of assumptions about the causes of a phenomenon and the rules that specify how causes act; predictions made by theory can provide testable research hypotheses. The need to solve a real-world, applied issue can also be a rich source of research ideas.

Developing good research questions begins by asking questions that are answerable through objective observations. Such questions are said to be empirical. Before a question can be answered through objective observation, its terms must be supplied with operational definitions. An operational definition defines a variable in terms of the operations required to measure it. Operationally defined variables can be measured precisely but may lack generality. You must also strive to answer the "right" questions. There are some questions (e.g., "Is abortion moral or immoral?") that are not addressable with scientific, empirical observation. You must develop questions that lend themselves to scientific scrutiny.

Good research questions should address important issues. A research question is probably important if (1) answering it will clarify relationships among variables known to affect the behavioral system under study, (2) the answer can support only one of several competing hypotheses, or (3) the answer leads to obvious practical applications. A research question is probably unimportant if (1) its answer is already firmly established; (2) the variables under scrutiny are known to have small, theoretically uninteresting effects; or (3) there is no a priori reason to believe the variables in question are causally related.

After developing your research idea, you need to conduct a careful review of the literature in your area of interest. Conducting a careful literature review can prevent you from carrying out a study that has already been done, can identify questions that need to be answered, and can help you get ideas for designing your study.

Research information can be found in several different types of sources. The best source of information is a scholarly source, such as a journal. This type of source centers on research and theory in a given area. Another source is a substantial publication containing information that rests on a solid base of research findings. A popular publication, intended for the general population, may have articles relevant to your topic of study. However, you will not find original sources or reference citations in these publications. Finally, a sensational publication is intended to arouse curiosity or emotion. Typically, information from such a source cannot be trusted.

Scholarly information can be found in books and journals, at conventions and meetings of professional associations, and through other sources such as the Internet. Books come in a variety of forms, including original works, anthologies, and textbooks. Some books contain original material whereas others have secondhand material. Books are a useful source of information, but they may be unreviewed or out of date. Scholarly journals provide articles on current theory and research. Some journals are refereed (the articles undergo prepublication peer review) whereas others are nonrefereed (there is no prepublication review). Generally, articles in refereed journals are preferred over those in nonrefereed journals. The most up-to-date information is presented at professional conventions and meetings. You also can find research information on the Internet through sources such as EBSCOhost.

The basic strategy to follow in reviewing the literature is (1) find a relevant review article, (2) use the references in the article to find other relevant articles, and (3) use one of the many literature search tools to locate more recent articles. We identified a number of electronic tools to help you find articles relevant to your research topic, such as EBSCOhost, the Web of Science, and associated databases.

Research reports follow a standard format that includes an abstract, introduction, method section, results section, discussion section, and references. Each section has a specific purpose. When you read a research report, read it critically, asking questions about the soundness of the reasoning in the introduction, the adequacy of the methods to test the hypothesis, and how well the data were analyzed and interpreted. A good rule of thumb to follow when reading critically is to be skeptical of everything you read.

Publication practices are one source of bias in scientific findings. Criteria for publication of a manuscript in a scientific journal include statistical significance of the results, consistency of results with previous findings, and editorial policy. Each of these can affect which manuscripts are eventually accepted for publication. The result is that published articles are only those that meet subjective, and somewhat strict, publication criteria.

The peer-review process is intended to ensure the quality of the product in scientific journals. Peer review involves an editor of a journal sending your manuscript to two (perhaps more) experts in your research field. The reviewers are expected to read your work and pass judgment. Unfortunately, peer reviewers are affected by personal bias. For example, reviewers are more likely to find fault with a manuscript if the reported results do not agree with their personal views on the issue studied.

Values also can enter the research process and affect the process of research, the types of questions asked, how data are interpreted, and the types of assumptions made about phenomena under study. Values also can enter into science when scientists translate their findings into what "ought to be." Although many scientists believe that values should not be allowed to creep into research, others believe that values should be acknowledged and used to evaluate all aspects of science. There are ways that one can combat values creeping into science. For example, one can think about an issue from a perspective that is different from one's own.

Your literature review and careful, critical reading of the sources you found lead you to the next step in the research process: developing a testable hypothesis. This is an important step in your research because your hypothesis will influence later decisions about which variables to measure or manipulate. Developing a research hypothesis involves taking your general research question and translating them into a statement that clearly specifies the expected relationships among variables.

## KEY TERMS

| | |
|---|---|
| empirical question | paper session |
| operational definition | poster session |
| literature review | personal communications |
| primary source | PsycINFO |
| secondary source | PsycARTICLES |
| refereed journal | file drawer phenomenon |
| nonrefereed journal | peer review |

# Choosing a Research Design

After spending long hours reading and digesting the literature in a particular research area, you have isolated a behavior that needs further investigation. You have identified some potentially important variables and probably have become familiar with the methods commonly used to measure that behavior. You may even have developed some possible explanations for the relationships that you have identified through your reading and personal experience. You are now ready to choose a research design that will allow you to evaluate the relationships that you suspect exist.

Choosing an appropriate research design is crucially important to the success of your project. The decisions you make at this stage of the research process do much to determine the quality of the conclusions you can draw from your research results. This chapter identifies the problems you must face when choosing a research design, introduces the major types of research design, and describes how each type attempts to solve (or at least cope with) these problems.

## FUNCTIONS OF A RESEARCH DESIGN

Scientific studies tend to focus on one or the other of two major activities. The first activity consists of *exploratory data collection and analysis,* which has two aims. One aim is classifying behaviors in a given research area. For example, social psychologists interested in studying aggression might classify aggression into several categories (e.g., hostile aggression, instrumental aggression, sanctioned aggression). The other aim is to identify the variables involved in explaining the behavior of interest. For example, anger might be an important variable leading to aggression. Having identified anger and aggression as potentially important variables, a scientist will investigate their relationship.

Exploring variables relevant to behavior is typical of the early stages of research in an area and is the "scouting" process we discussed in Chapter 1. The second major activity is *hypothesis testing*. Hypothesis testing consists of forming tentative explanations for behavior and then testing those tentative explanations. For example, you might hypothesize that anger causes an increase in aggressive behavior. You then set out to test this hypothesis. Developing testable explanations allows you to predict the relationships you should or should not observe if the explanation is correct. Hypothesis testing usually begins after you have collected enough information about the behavior to begin developing supportable explanations. This is essentially the "trapping" process described in Chapter 1.

## CAUSAL VERSUS CORRELATIONAL RELATIONSHIPS

The relationships you identify in these activities fall into two broad categories: causal and correlational. In a **causal relationship**, one variable directly or indirectly influences another. In other words, changes in the value of one variable directly or indirectly cause changes in the value of a second. For example, if you accidentally drop a brick on your toe, the impact of the brick will probably set off a chain of events (stimulation of pain receptors in your toe, avalanche of neural impulses traveling up your leg to the spinal cord and from there to your brain, registration of pain in your brain, involuntary scream). Although there are several intervening steps between the impact of the brick on your toe and the scream, it would be proper in this case to conclude that dropping the brick on your toe *causes* you to scream. This is because it is possible to trace an unbroken chain of physical influence running from the initial event (impact of brick on toe) to the final result (scream).

Causal relationships can be unidirectional, in which case variable A influences variable B but not vice versa. The impact of the brick (A) may produce a scream (B), but screaming (B) does not cause the impact of the brick on your toe (A). They also can be bidirectional, in which case each variable influences the other. Everything else being equal, reducing the amount of exercise a person gets leads to weight gain. Because of the increased effort involved, heavier people tend to exercise less. Thus, exercise influences body weight, and body weight influences exercise. Even more complex causal relationships exist, and teasing them out may require considerable ingenuity on the part of the investigator. In each case, however, one can identify a set of physical influences that ties the variables together.

Simply observing that changes in one variable tend to be associated with changes in another is not enough to establish that the relationship between them is a causal one. In a **correlational relationship**, changes in one variable accompany changes in another, but the proper tests have not been conducted to show that either variable actually causes changes in the other. Thus, all that is known is that a relationship between them exists. When changes in one variable tend to be accompanied by specific changes in another, the two variables are said to *covary*. However, such covariation does not necessarily mean that either variable exerts a causal influence on the other (although it may). The number of baseball games and the number of mosquitoes tend to covary (both increase in the spring and decrease in the fall), yet you would not conclude that mosquitoes cause baseball games or vice versa.

When you first begin to develop explanations for a given behavior, knowledge of observed relationships can serve as an important guide even though you may not yet know which relationships are causal. You simply make your best guess and then develop your explanation based on the causal relationships that you think exist. The validity of your explanation will then depend in part on whether the proposed causal relationships turn out, on closer examination, to be in fact causal. Distinguishing between causal and correlational relationships is thus an important part of the research process, particularly in the hypothesis-testing phase.

Your ability to identify causal relationships and to distinguish causal from correlational relationships varies with the degree of control that you have over the variables under study. The next sections describe two broad types of research design: correlational and experimental. Both approaches allow you to identify relationships among variables, but they differ in the degree of control exerted over variables and in the ability to identify causal relationships. We begin with correlational research.

## QUESTIONS TO PONDER

1. What are exploratory data collection and analysis and hypothesis testing? What is involved in each?

2. How are correlational and causal relationships similar, and how are they different?

3. Can a causal relationship be bidirectional? Explain and give an example.

## CORRELATIONAL RESEARCH

In **correlational research**, your main interest is to determine whether two (or more) variables covary and, if so, to establish the directions, magnitudes, and forms of the observed relationships. The strategy involves developing measures of the variables of interest and collecting your data.

Correlational research belongs to a broader category called *nonexperimental* research, which also includes designs not specifically aimed at identifying relationships between variables. The latter type of research, for example, might seek to determine the average values and typical spread of scores on certain variables (e.g., grade point average and SAT scores) in a given population (e.g., applicants for admission to a particular university). Strictly speaking, such a study would be nonexperimental but not correlational. Our discussion here focuses on those nonexperimental methods used to identify and characterize relationships.

Correlational research involves observing the values of two or more variables and determining what relationships exist between them. In correlational research, you make no attempt to manipulate variables but observe them "as is." For example, imagine that you wished to determine the nature of the relationship, if any, between pretest anxiety and test performance in introductory psychology students on campus. On test day, you have each student rate his or her own level of pretest anxiety and, after the test results are in, you determine the test performances of those same students. Your data consist of two scores for each student: self-rated anxiety level and test score. You analyze your data to determine the relationship (if any) between these variables. Note that both anxiety level and test score are observed as found in each student.

In some types of correlational research, you compare the average value of some variable across preformed groups of individuals where membership in a group depends on characteristics or circumstances of the participant (such as political party affiliation, eye color, handedness, occupation, economic level, or age). For example, you might compare Democrats to Republicans on attitudes toward education. Such a study would qualify as correlational research because group membership (whether Democrat or Republican) was determined by the participants' choice of party and was not in the hands of the researcher. You can only measure party affiliation; you cannot change a person's party affiliation in your study.

Establishing that a correlational relationship exists between two variables makes it possible to predict from the value of one variable the probable value of the other variable. For example, if you know that college grade point average (GPA) is correlated with Scholastic Assessment Test (SAT) scores, then you can use a student's SAT score to predict (within limits) the student's college GPA.

When you use correlational relationships for prediction, the variable used to predict is called the *predictor variable,* and the variable whose value is being predicted is called the *criterion variable.* Whether the linkage between these variables is causal remains an open question.

## An Example of Correlational Research: Playing Violent Video Games and Being a Bully

It is well known that exposure to violent video games is related to increases in certain forms of aggression. One type of aggression that social scientists have focused on is "bullying." The American Psychological Association (2016) defines bullying as "a form of aggressive behavior in which someone intentionally and repeatedly causes another person injury or discomfort" (paragraph 1). In "cyberbullying," bullying takes place on electronic media. Being the victim of cyberbullying is associated with a range of negative outcomes including stress, anxiety, and depression (Kowalski, Giumetti, Schroeder, & Lattanner, 2014).

Researchers have been studying the factors that contribute to being a bully and being a victim of bullying. One study investigated the relationship between exposure to violent online video games and cyberbullying among Chinese adolescents (Lam, Cheng, & Liu, 2013). Lam et al. had Chinese high school students (ages 13–18) complete a health survey, including scales measuring cyberbullying (being a bully) and cyberbullying victimization. Lam et al. also included a number of questions about the students' Internet use, including measures of exposure to violent online video games. According to their findings, the more an adolescent was exposed to violent online video games, the more likely it was that he or she would be a bully or both a bully *and* a victim of bullying.

*Assessing the Lam et al. Study*   What qualifies the study by Lam et al. as a correlational study? Both exposure to violent online video games and bullying status were simply measured. The researchers made no attempt manipulate variables in order to observe any potential effects of those variables. For example, they did not expose some participants to violent video games and others to nonviolent games and then measure bullying.

## Behavior Causation and the Correlational Approach

Given the results obtained by the Lam et al. (2013) study, you might be tempted to conclude that increased exposure to or playing of violent video games *causes* bullying. However, this conclusion that a causal relationship exists is inappropriate even though the relationship appears compelling. Two obstacles stand in the way of drawing clear causal inferences from correlational data: the third-variable problem and the directionality problem.

*The Third-Variable Problem*    To establish a causal relationship between two variables, you must be able to demonstrate that variation in one of the observed variables could only be due to the influence of the other observed variable. In the example, you want to know whether increased exposure to violent video games *causes* increased bullying. However, it is possible that the observed increase in bullying in the Lam et al. study was actually due to another, unmeasured variable. Perhaps adolescents who play a lot of online video games also have parents who use a great deal of physical punishment. If so, it may be that this increased use of physical punishment—and not the playing of violent video games—is the actual cause for the increased bullying observed.

The possibility that correlational relationships may result from the action of an unobserved "third variable" is called the **third-variable problem**. This unobserved variable may influence both of the observed variables (e.g., playing violent video games and bullying), causing them to vary together even though no direct relationship exists between them. The two observed variables thus may be strongly correlated even though neither variable causes changes in the other.

To resolve the third-variable problem, you must examine the effects of each potential third variable to determine whether it does, in fact, account for the observed relationship. Techniques to evaluate and statistically control the effects of such variables are available (see Chapter 15).

*The Directionality Problem*    A second reason why it is hazardous to draw causal inferences from correlational data is that, even when a direct causal relationship exists, the direction of causality is sometimes difficult to determine. This difficulty is known as the **directionality problem**.

In our example, we want to conclude that playing violent video games causes bullying. This causal connection seems to make intuitive sense. However, one could also argue just as well that bullies enjoy violence and, therefore, prefer to play more violent video games than nonbullies. With a purely correlational study, there is no way to determine unambiguously which way the causal arrow points.

## Why Use Correlational Research?

Given the problems of interpreting the results of correlational research, you may wonder why you would want to use this approach. However, correlational research has a variety of applications, and there are many reasons to consider using it. In this section, we discuss three situations in which a correlational approach makes good sense.

*Gathering Data in the Early Stages of Research*    During the initial, exploratory stage of a research project, the correlational approach's ability to identify potential causal relationships can provide a rich source of hypotheses that later may be tested experimentally. Consider the following example.

Niko Tinbergen (1951) became interested in the behavior of the three-spined stickleback, a fish that inhabits the bottoms of sandy streams in Europe. Observing sticklebacks in their natural habitat, Tinbergen found that, during the spring, the male stickleback claims a small area of a streambed and builds a cylindrically shaped nest at its center. At the same time, the male's underbelly changes from the usual dull color to a bright red, and the male begins to drive other males from the territory surrounding the nest. Female sticklebacks lack this coloration and are not driven away by the males.

These initial observations were purely correlational and as such do not allow one to draw firm conclusions with respect to cause and effect. The observations showed that the defending male's behavior toward an intruding stickleback is correlated with the intruder's physical characteristics, but which characteristics actually determine whether or not an attack will occur? Certainly many cues, such as the male's red coloration, his shape, or even perhaps his odor, could be responsible. However, these cues always appeared and disappeared together (along with the fish to which they belonged). So there was no way, through correlational study alone, to determine whether the red coloration was the actual cause of the defensive behavior or merely an ineffective correlate.

To disentangle these variables, Tinbergen (1951) turned to the experimental approach. He set up an artificial stream in his laboratory and brought in several male sticklebacks. The fish soon adapted to the new surroundings, setting up territories and building nests. Tinbergen then constructed a number of models designed to mimic several characteristics of male sticklebacks. These models ranged from one that faithfully duplicated the appearance (but not the smell) of a real stickleback to one that was just a gray disk (Figure 4-1). Some of the models included red coloration, and some did not.

When the realistic model with a red underbelly was waved past a male stickleback in the artificial stream, the male immediately tried to drive it away. Odor obviously was not necessary to elicit defensive behavior. However, Tinbergen (1951) soon discovered that almost any model with red color elicited the response. The only requirements were that the model include an eyespot near the top and that the red color appear below the eyespot.

By manipulating factors such as color and shape, Tinbergen (1951) could experimentally identify the factors that were necessary to elicit the behavior. The earlier, correlational research conducted in a naturalistic (and therefore poorly controlled) setting had paved the way for the more definitive research that followed.

*Inability to Manipulate Variables*    In an experimental design, variables are manipulated to determine their effects on other variables. A second reason for choosing a

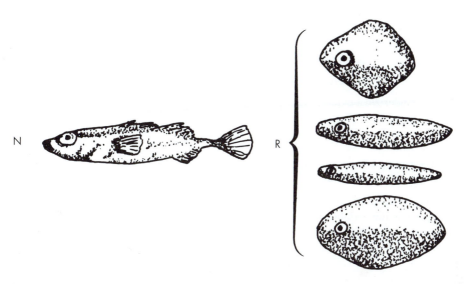

**FIGURE 4-1**  Stimuli used by Tinbergen to follow up on initial observations made in the field: N, neutral underbelly; R, red underbelly.
SOURCE: Tinbergen, N. *The Study of Instinct*, Figure 20, page 28. Oxford, UK: Clarendon Press, 1969.

correlational design over an experimental one is that manipulating the variables of interest may be impossible or unethical (see Chapter 7 for a discussion of ethics). For example, imagine that you were interested in determining whether psychopathic personality develops when a child is raised by cold, uncaring parents. To establish a clear causal connection between the parents' behavior toward the child and psychopathic personality, you would have to conduct an experiment in which the parents' behavior was manipulated by assigning infants at random to be raised by either normal parents or cold, uncaring ones. However, this experiment would be impossible to carry out (who would allow their child to participate in such an experiment?) and, because of its potential for inflicting serious harm on the child, unethical as well. In such cases, a correlational design may be the only practical and ethical option.

*Relating Naturally Occurring Variables*  A third situation in which you may choose a correlational research design over an experimental design is one in which you want to see how naturally occurring variables relate in the real world. For example, imagine you are interested in whether individuals are more susceptible to suffering from posttraumatic stress disorder (PTSD) after different traumatic events (e.g., a severe hurricane or a flood). You could address this problem with a correlational study. You could compare the number of PTSD symptoms a person experiences after a hurricane to those experienced after a flood. Of course, you cannot manipulate weather conditions; you can only measure them. You have to wait until a hurricane or flood occurs to include that variable in your study. Results of such a study might be valuable in predicting reactions to different types of traumatic events. These results could then help to design different treatment methods for the effects of those different events.

## QUESTIONS TO PONDER

1. What are the defining features of correlational research?
2. Why is it inappropriate to draw causal inferences from correlational data?
3. Under what conditions is correlational research preferred over experimental research?

## EXPERIMENTAL RESEARCH

Unlike correlational research, experimental research incorporates a high degree of control over the variables of your study. This control, if used properly, permits you to establish causal relationships among your variables. This section describes the defining characteristics of experimental research and explains how these characteristics enable us to identify causal relationships in data.

### Characteristics of Experimental Research

**Experimental research** has two defining characteristics: manipulation of one or more independent variables and control over extraneous variables. Be sure that you understand these concepts, described as follows, because they are central to understanding experimental research.

*Manipulation of Independent Variables*    An **independent variable** is a variable whose values are chosen and set by the experimenter. (Another way to look at it is that the value of the independent variable is independent of the participant's behavior.) We call these set values the *levels* of the independent variable. For example, imagine you want to determine how sleep deprivation affects a person's ability to recall previously memorized material. To examine this relationship, you might assign participants to one of three groups defined by the number of hours of sleep deprivation: 0 hours (rested), 24 hours, and 48 hours. These three amounts would constitute the three levels of sleep deprivation, your independent variable. Notice how this strategy differs from addressing this question in a correlational study in which you would simply *measure* how much sleep a participant received and then test memory.

To *manipulate* your independent variable, you must expose your participants to at least two levels of that variable. The specific conditions associated with each level are called the **treatments** of the experiment. Depending on the design of your experiment, the independent variable may be manipulated by exposing a different group of participants to each treatment or by exposing each participant to all the treatments in sequence. By manipulating the independent variable, you hope to show that changes in the level of the independent variable *cause* changes in the behavior being recorded.

The variable whose value you observe and measure in experimental designs is called the **dependent variable** (or *dependent measure*). If a causal relationship exists, then the value of the dependent variable depends, at least to some extent, on the level of the independent variable. (Its value also depends on other factors such as participant characteristics.) Another way to think about the dependent variable is that its value depends on the behavior of the participant, rather than being set by the experimenter.

Manipulating an independent variable can be as simple as exposing one group of participants to some treatment (e.g., distracting noises) and another group of participants to the absence of the treatment (no distracting noise). In this most basic of experimental designs, the group receiving the treatment is called the **experimental group** and the other group the **control group**. The control group is treated exactly like the experimental group except that it is not exposed to the experimental treatment. The performance of the participants in the control group provides a baseline of behavior against which the behavior of the participants in the experimental groups is compared.

Although all experiments present at least two levels of the independent variable, many do not include a no-treatment control group. A clinical study, for example, might compare a standard therapy with a new, experimental therapy of unknown effectiveness. Administering the standard therapy to the control group ensures that even the participants who do not receive the experimental treatment do not go untreated for their disorder. In both cases, the behavior of participants in the control group provides a baseline against which to compare the behavior of participants in the experimental group.

More complex experiments can be conducted using more levels of the independent variable, several independent variables, and several dependent variables. You also can choose to expose a single group, or even a single participant, to several levels of an independent variable. These experimental designs are discussed in Chapters 10 and 12.

*Control over Extraneous Variables*    The second characteristic of experimental research is control over extraneous variables. **Extraneous variables** are those that may affect the behavior you wish to investigate but are not of interest for the present experiment. For example, you may be interested in determining how well a new anxiety therapy (experimental group), compared to an existing therapy (control group), affects test anxiety in anxious students. If some of your participants show up for the experiment drunk, their degree of intoxication becomes an extraneous variable. This would be especially problematic if more drunk students ended up in one group than in the other.

If allowed to vary on their own, extraneous variables can produce uncontrolled changes in the value of the dependent variable, with two rather nasty possible consequences. First, uncontrolled variability may make it difficult or impossible to detect any effects of the independent variable. (In our example, the effects of the therapy could be hidden by the effects of the alcohol.) Second, uncontrolled variability may produce chance differences in behavior across the levels of the independent variable. These differences could make it appear as though the independent variable produced effects when it did not (the therapy would appear to work even though the real effect came from the alcohol). To identify clear causal relationships between your indepen-dent and dependent variables, you must control the effects of extraneous variables.

You have two ways to control these effects. The first way is to *hold extraneous variables constant.* If these variables do not vary over the course of your experiment, they cannot cause uncontrolled variation in your dependent variable. In the anxiety therapy experiment, for example, you might want to make sure that all your participants are sober (or at least intoxicated to the same degree). In fact, to the degree possible, you would want to make sure that all treatments are *exactly* alike, except for the level of the independent variable.

The second way to deal with extraneous variables is to *randomize their effects across treatments*. This technique deals with the effects of extraneous variables that cannot be held constant or, for reasons that will be explained later, should not be held constant. In an experiment assessing the effect of sleep deprivation on memory, for example, it may not be possible to ensure that all your participants have had identical amounts of sleep deprivation (some may have slept better than others the day before your experiment began) or that their recall abilities are equivalent. The idea is to distribute the effects of these differences across treatments in such a way that they tend to even out and thus cannot be mistaken for effects of the independent variable.

For statistical reasons, one of the better ways to accomplish this goal is to use random assignment of subjects to treatments. With **random assignment**, you assign participants to treatments randomly by means of a table of random numbers or a computer's random number generator. Random assignment does not *guarantee* that the effects of extraneous variables will be distributed evenly across treatments, but it usually works reasonably well; better yet, it allows you to use inferential statistics to evaluate the probability with which chance alone could have produced differences in performance across treatments at least as large as those actually observed in your experiment. (We discuss the logic underlying inferential statistics in Chapter 14.) Other techniques to deal with uncontrolled extraneous variables are also available. We describe these in later chapters that cover specific design options.

However it is done, control over extraneous variables is crucial to establishing clear causal relationships between your variables. By controlling variables that might affect your dependent variable, you rule them out as possible alternative explanations for your results.

## An Example of Experimental Research: Violent Video Games and Aggression

As an illustration of experimental research, consider a study by Hollingdale and Greitemeyer (2014) investigating the relationship between playing a violent video game and behaving aggressively. Hollingdale and Greitmeyer randomly assigned participants to play either a violent or nonviolent video game either online or offline while alone in a room. Participants used the same game console whether they played the game online or offline. The measure of aggression (one commonly used in this kind of research) was the number of grams of hot sauce added to water for another person to drink in a supposedly unrelated taste test. Participants who played the violent video game added more hot sauce for the taster than those who played the nonviolent video game, especially if the game were played online rather than offline.

*Assessing the Hollingdale and Greitemeyer Experiment*    Have you identified the features of the Hollingdale and Greitemeyer (2014) experiment that qualify it as a true experiment? If you have not done so yet, do it now before you read the next paragraphs. A crucial element of every true experiment is the manipulation of at least one independent variable. What were the independent variables in the Hollingdale and Greitemeyer study? If you said that the independent variables were the type of game played (violent or nonviolent) and how the game was played (online or offline), you are correct. Note that the values of the independent variable to which a given participant was exposed (violent or nonviolent game, online or offline) were assigned by the experimenters; the participant did not choose which type of game to play nor the condition under which the game was played.

A second crucial element in an experiment is measuring a dependent variable. Can you identify the dependent variable in Hollingdale and Greitemeyer's experiment? If you said that the amount of hot sauce a participant added to the water was the dependent variable, you are correct. Notice that Hollingdale and Greitemeyer were looking for changes in the value of the dependent variable that were caused by changes in the value of the independent variable.

A third crucial element of an experiment is control over extraneous variables. Were extraneous variables controlled in the Hollingdale and Greitemeyer (2014) experiment and, if so, how? The answer to the first part of this question is yes, using both methods described earlier. First, several extraneous variables were held constant across treatments. All participants played the game on the same game console and all played the game while alone in the room. Second, the participants were assigned to their treatments randomly, not according to some behavior or characteristic of the participants. This design ensured that any remaining uncontrolled differences in the participants would tend to be distributed evenly across the treatments. As a result, the investigators could be reasonably sure that any effects observed were caused by differences in treatment and not by extraneous variables.

## Strengths and Limitations of the Experimental Approach

The great strength of the experimental approach is its ability to identify and describe causal relationships. This ability is not shared by the correlational approach. Whereas the correlational approach can tell you only that changes in the value of one variable tend to accompany changes in the value of a second variable, the experimental approach can tell you whether changes in one variable (the independent variable) actually caused changes in the other (the dependent variable).

Despite its power to identify causal relationships, the experimental approach has limitations that restrict its use under certain conditions. The most serious limitation is that you cannot use the experimental method if you cannot manipulate your hypothesized causal variables. For example, studies of personality disorders must use correlational approaches to identify possible causal relationships. Exposing people to various nasty conditions in order to identify which of those conditions cause personality disorders is not ethical.

A second limitation of the experimental approach entails the tight control over extraneous factors required to clearly reveal the effects of the independent variable. Such control tends to reduce your ability to apply your findings to situations that differ from the conditions of your original experiment. A rather unpleasant trade-off exists in experimental research: As you increase the degree of control you exert over extraneous variables (and thus your ability to establish causal relationships), you decrease your ability to generalize your findings beyond the conditions assessed in your experiment.

## Experiments Versus Demonstrations

One kind of research design resembles an experiment but lacks one of the crucial features of a true experiment: an independent variable. This design, called a **demonstration**, exposes a group of subjects to one (and only one) treatment condition. Remember, a true experiment requires exposing subjects to at least two treatments. Whereas a true experiment shows the effect of manipulating an independent variable, a demonstration simply shows what happens under a specified set of conditions. To conduct a demonstration, you simply expose a single group to a particular treatment and measure the resulting behavior.

Demonstrations can be useful because they show that, under such-and-such conditions, *this* happens and not *that*. However, demonstrations are not experiments and thus do not show causal relationships. This fact is sometimes overlooked as the following example shows.

In his book *Subliminal Seduction* (1973), Wilson Bryan Key reported a study in which the participants looked at a Gilbey's Gin advertisement that allegedly had subliminal sexual messages embedded within it. The most prominent subliminal message was the word "SEX" spelled out in the bottom three ice cubes in the glass to the right of a bottle of gin (Key, 1973).

Key (1973) reported that the ad was tested "with over a thousand subjects" (the details of the study were not given). According to Key, 62% of the male and female participants reported feelings of sexual arousal in response to the ad. Key concluded that the subliminal messages led to sexual arousal. Key asserted that advertisers capitalize on these subliminal messages to get you to buy their products.

Are you convinced of the power of subliminal messages by this demonstration? If you said you are not convinced, good for you! The fact that 62% of the participants reported arousal is *not* evidence that the subliminal messages caused the arousal, no matter how many participated. All you know from this demonstration is that under the conditions tested, the advertisement evoked reports of arousal in a fair proportion of the participants. You do not learn the cause.

In fact, several plausible alternatives can be offered to the explanation that the arousal was caused by subliminal perception. For example, an advertisement for alcohol may lead participants to recall how they feel when under the influence or may conjure up images of having fun at a party. As the demonstration was reported, you cannot tell which of the potential explanations is valid. What would you have to do to fully test whether subliminal messages (such as the ones in the Gilbey's Gin ad) actually lead to sexual arousal? Give this question some thought before continuing.

To test whether subliminal messages caused the arousal, you need to add a control group and randomly assign participants to groups. Participants in this control group would see the same Gilbey's Gin ad but without the subliminal messages. If 62% of the participants in the "subliminal" group were aroused but only 10% in the control group were aroused, then you could reasonably conclude that the subliminal messages caused the arousal. A different conclusion would be drawn if 62% of the participants in *both* groups reported arousal. In this case, you would have to conclude that the subliminal messages were ineffective. The fact that the ad leads to reports of sexual arousal (as shown by the demonstration) would have to be explained by some other factor. By the way, most of the controlled, scientific research on subliminal perception shows little or no effect of subliminal messages on behavior.

## QUESTIONS TO PONDER

1. What are the characteristics of experimental research?
2. What is the relationship between an independent and a dependent variable in an experiment?
3. How do extraneous variables affect your research?
4. What can be done to control extraneous variables?
5. How does a demonstration differ from a true experiment?
6. What is the value of doing a demonstration?

## INTERNAL AND EXTERNAL VALIDITY

Whether the general design of your study is experimental or correlational, you need to consider carefully two important but often conflicting attributes of any design: internal and external validity. In this section, we define these concepts and briefly discuss the factors that you should consider relating to internal and external validity when choosing a research design.

### Internal Validity

Much of your research will be aimed at testing the hypotheses you developed long before you collected any data. The ability of your research design to adequately test your hypotheses is known as its **internal validity** (Campbell & Stanley, 1963). Essentially, internal validity is the ability of your design to test the hypothesis that it was designed to test.

In an experiment, this means showing that variation in the independent variable, and only the independent variable, caused the observed variation in the dependent variable. In a correlational study, it means showing that changes in the value of your criterion variable relate solely to changes in the value of your predictor variable and not to changes in other, extraneous variables that may have varied along with your predictor variable.

Internal validity is threatened to the extent that extraneous variables can provide alternative explanations for the findings of a study, or as Huck and Sandler (1979) called them, *rival hypotheses*. As an example, imagine that an instructor wants to know whether a new teaching method works better than the traditional method used with students in an introductory psychology course. The instructor decides to answer this question by using the new method to teach her morning section of introductory psychology and using the traditional method to teach her afternoon section. Both sections will use the same text, cover the same material, and receive the same tests. The effectiveness of the two methods will be assessed by comparing the average scores achieved on the test by the two sections. Now, imagine that the instructor conducts the study and finds that the section receiving the new method receives a substantially higher average grade than the section receiving the traditional method. She concludes that the new method is definitely better for teaching introductory psychology. Is she justified in drawing this conclusion?

The answer, as you probably suspected, is no. Several rival hypotheses cannot be eliminated by the study, explanations at least as credible as the instructor's. Consider the following rival hypotheses:

1. The morning students did better because they were "fresher" than the afternoon students.

2. The morning students did better because their instructor was "fresher" in the morning than in the afternoon.

3. The instructor expected the new method to work better and thus was more enthusiastic when using the new method than when using the old one.

4. Students who registered for the morning class were more motivated to do well in the course than those who registered for the afternoon class.

These rival hypotheses do not exhaust the possibilities; perhaps you can think of others. Because the study was not designed to rule out these alternatives, there is no way to know whether the observed difference between the two sections in student performance was due to the difference in teaching methods, instructor enthusiasm, alertness of the students, or other factors whose levels differed across the sections. Whenever two or more variables combine in such a way that their effects cannot be separated, a **confounding** of those variables has occurred. In the teaching study, teaching method is confounded by all those variables just listed and more. Such a study lacks internal validity.

Confounding, although always a matter of concern, does not necessarily present a serious threat to internal validity. Confounding is less problematic when the confounding variable is known to have little or no effect on the dependent or criterion variable or when its known effect can be taken into account in the analysis. For example, in the teaching study, it may be possible to eliminate concern about the difference in class meeting times by comparing classes that meet at different times but use the same teaching method. Such data may show that meeting time has only a small effect that can be ignored. If meeting time had a larger effect, you could arrange your study of teaching method so that the effect of meeting time would tend to make the new teaching method appear worse than the standard one, thus biasing the results against your hypothesis. If your results still favored the new teaching method, that outcome would have occurred despite the confounding rather than because of it. Thus, a study may include confounding and still maintain a fair degree of internal validity if the effects of the confounding variable in the situation under scrutiny are known.

This is fortunate because it is often impossible to eliminate all sources of confounding in a study. For example, the instructor in our example might have attempted to eliminate confounding by having students randomly assigned to two sections meeting simultaneously. This would certainly eliminate those sources of confounding related to any difference in the time at which the sections met, but now it would be impossible for the instructor to teach both classes. If a second instructor is recruited to teach one of the sections using the standard method, this introduces a new source of confounding in that the two instructors may not be equivalent in a number of ways that could affect class performance. Often the best that can be done is to substitute what you believe to be less serious threats to internal validity for the more serious ones.

*Threats to Internal Validity*    Confounding variables occur in both experimental and correlational designs, but they are far more likely to be a problem in the latter, in which tight control over extraneous variables is usually lacking. Campbell and Stanley (1963) identify seven general sources of confounding that may affect internal validity: history, maturation, testing, instrumentation, statistical regression, biased selection of subjects, and experimental mortality (summarized in Table 4-1).

*History* may confound studies in which multiple observations are taken over time. Specific events may occur between observations that affect the results. For example, a study of the effectiveness of an advertising campaign against drunk driving might measure the number of arrests for drunk driving immediately before and after the campaign. If the police institute a crackdown on drunk driving at the same time that the advertisements air, this event will destroy the internal validity of your study.

**TABLE 4-1    Factors Affecting Internal Validity**

| FACTOR | DESCRIPTION |
| --- | --- |
| History | Specific events other than the treatment occur between observations |
| Maturation | Performance changes due to age or fatigue confound the effect of treatment |
| Testing | Testing prior to the treatment changes how subjects respond in posttreatment testing |
| Instrumentation | Unobserved changes in observer criteria or instrument calibration confound the effect of the treatment |
| Statistical regression | Subjects selected for treatment on the basis of their extreme scores tend to move closer to the mean on retesting |
| Biased selection of subjects | Groups of subjects exposed to different treatments are not equivalent prior to treatment |
| Experimental mortality | Differential loss of subjects from the groups of a study results in nonequivalent groups |

*Maturation* refers to the effect of age or fatigue. Performance changes observed over time due to these factors may confound those due to the variables being studied. You might, for example, assess performance on a proofreading task before and after some experimental manipulation. Decreased performance on the second proofreading assessment may be due to fatigue rather than to any effect of your manipulation.

*Testing* effects occur when a pretest sensitizes participants to what you are investigating in your study. As a consequence, they may respond differently on a posttreatment measure than if no pretest were given. For example, if you measure participants' racial attitudes and then manipulate race in an experiment on person perception, participants may respond to the treatment differently than if no such pretest of racial attitudes was given.

In *instrumentation,* confounding may be introduced by unobserved changes in criteria used by observers or in instrument calibration. If observers change what counts as "verbal aggression" when scoring behavior under two experimental conditions, any apparent difference between those conditions in verbal aggression could be due as much to the changed criterion as to any effect of the independent variable. Similarly, if an instrument used to record activity of rats in a cage becomes more (or less) sensitive over time, it becomes impossible to tell whether activity is really changing or just the ability of the instrument to detect activity.

*Statistical regression* threatens internal validity when participants have been selected based on extreme scores on some measure. When measured again, scores will tend to be closer to the average in the population. Thus, if students are targeted for a special reading program based on their unusually low reading test scores, they will tend to do better, on average, on retesting even if the reading program has no effect.

*Biased selection of subjects* threatens internal validity because subjects may differ initially in ways that affect their scores on the dependent measure. Any influence of the independent variable on scores cannot be separated from the effect of the preexisting bias. This problem typically arises when researchers use preexisting groups in their studies rather than assigning subjects to groups at random. For example, the effect of a program designed to improve worker job satisfaction might be evaluated by administering the program to workers at one factory (experimental group) and then comparing the level of job satisfaction of those workers to that of workers at another factory where the program was not given (control group). If workers given the job satisfaction program indicate more satisfaction with their jobs, is it due to the program or to preexisting differences between the two groups? There is no way to tell.

Finally, *experimental mortality* refers to the differential loss of participants from groups in a study. For example, imagine that some people drop out of a study because of frustration with the task. A group exposed to difficult conditions is more likely to lose its frustration-intolerant participants than one exposed to less difficult conditions. Any differences between the groups in performance may be due as much to the resulting difference in participants as to any difference in conditions.

*Enhancing Internal Validity*    The time to be concerned with internal validity is during the design phase of your study. During this phase, you should carefully plan which variables will be manipulated or observed and recorded, identify any plausible rival hypotheses not eliminated in your initial design, and redesign so as to eliminate those that seriously threaten internal validity. Discovering problems with internal validity after you have run your study is too late. A poorly designed study cannot be fixed later on.

## External Validity

A study has **external validity** to the degree that its results can be extended (generalized) beyond the limited research setting and sample in which they were obtained. A common complaint about research using white rats or college students and conducted under the artificial conditions of the laboratory is that it may tell us little about how white rats and college sophomores (let alone animals or people in general) behave under the conditions imposed on them in the much richer arena of the real world.

The idea seems to be that all studies *should* be conducted in such a way that the findings can be generalized immediately to real-world situations and to larger populations. However, as Mook (1983) noted, it is a fallacy to assume "that the purpose of collecting data in the laboratory is to predict real-life behavior in the real world" (p. 381). Mook pointed out that much of the research conducted in the laboratory is designed to determine one of the following:

1. Whether something *can* happen, rather than whether it typically *does* happen.

2. Whether something we specify *ought* to happen (according to some hypothesis) under specific conditions in the lab *does* happen there under those conditions.

3. What happens under conditions not encountered in the real world.

In each of these cases, the objective is to gain insight into the underlying mechanisms of behavior rather than to discover relationships that apply under normal conditions in the real world. It is this understanding that generalizes to everyday life, not the specific findings themselves.

*Threats to External Validity*    In Chapter 1, we distinguished between basic research, which is aimed at developing a better understanding of the underlying mechanisms of behavior, and applied research, which is aimed at developing information that can be directly applied to solve real-world problems. The question of external validity may be less relevant in basic research settings that seek theoretical reasons to determine what will happen under conditions not usually found in natural settings or that examine fundamental processes expected to operate under a wide variety of conditions. The degree of external validity of a study becomes more relevant when the findings are expected to be applied directly to real-world settings. In such studies, external validity is affected by several factors. Using highly controlled laboratory settings (as opposed to naturalistic settings) is one such factor. Data obtained from a tightly controlled laboratory may not generalize to more naturalistic situations in which behavior occurs. Other factors that affect external validity, as discussed by Campbell and Stanley (1963), are listed and briefly described in Table 4-2. Many of these threats to external validity are discussed in later chapters, along with the appropriate research design.

How does research in psychology fare with respect to external validity? A few studies suggest that it fares pretty well. For example, Craig Anderson, James Lindsay, and Brad Bushman (1999) compared the results from laboratory studies and field

**TABLE 4-2    Factors Affecting External Validity**

| FACTOR | DESCRIPTION |
|---|---|
| Reactive testing | Occurs when a pretest affects participants' reaction to an experimental variable, making those participants' responses unrepresentative of the general population |
| Interactions between participant selection biases and the independent variable | Effects observed may apply only to the participants included in the study, especially if they are unique to a group (such as college sophomores rather than a cross section of adults) |
| Reactive effects of experimental arrangements | Refers to the effects of highly artificial experimental situations used in some research and the participant's knowledge that he or she is a research participant |
| Multiple treatment interference | Occurs when participants are exposed to multiple experimental treatments in which exposure to early treatments affects responses to later treatments |

studies (a study done in a participant's natural environment) that were published in a number of social psychological journals. Anderson et al. found a strong correlation ($r = .73$) between the outcomes of research conducted in the laboratory and in the field. More recently, Gregory Mitchell (2012) also found a strong correlation between laboratory and field studies conducted in a number of subfields in psychology (correlations ranged from .53 to .89). The strongest correlations were found for industrial/organizational psychology ($r = .89$) and personality psychology ($r = .83$). The field with the lowest level of external validity was developmental psychology ($r = -.82$). Finally, laboratory studies that produced strong effects were more likely to match results from the field than were those that produced weaker effects.

What about animal research? How well do results from research with animals generalize to human populations? As we point out in Chapter 10, many behavioral findings generalize quite well from animal to human research (e.g., conditioning). A good degree of generality also appears in other research areas such as genetics and medical research (Baker, 2011; Regenberg et al., 2009). Monya Baker noted that the relationships between genetic factors and disease found in animals often match well with findings in humans. Similarly, Regenberg et al. suggest that animal models are useful in understanding human outcomes in the field of regenerative medicine. However, Regenberg et al. point to several obstacles that may call into question how well animal research generalizes to human regenerative medicine. These include anatomical differences between species, neurological differences, and differences in how clinical trial experiments are done with animal and human samples. Baker suggests that animal models may have about an 80% concordance with human outcomes, which may be sufficient to warrant clinical trials in humans.

## Internal Versus External Validity

Although you should strive to achieve a high degree of both internal and external validity in your research, in practice you will find that the steps you take to increase one type of validity tend to decrease the other. For example, a tightly controlled laboratory experiment affords you a relatively high degree of internal validity. Your findings, however, may not generalize to other samples and situations; thus, external validity may be reduced. Often, the best that you can do is reach a compromise on the relative amounts of internal and external validity in your research.

Whether internal or external validity is more important depends on your reasons for conducting the research. If you are most interested in testing a theoretical position (as is often the case in basic research), you might be more concerned with internal than external validity and hence conduct a tightly controlled laboratory experiment. However, if you are more concerned with applying your results to a real-world problem (as in applied research), you might take steps to increase the external validity while attempting to maintain a reasonable degree of internal validity. These issues need to be considered at the time when you design your study.

As just mentioned, the setting in which you conduct your research strongly influences the internal and external validity of your results. The kinds of setting available and the issues that you should consider when choosing a research setting are the topics that we take up next.

## QUESTIONS TO PONDER

1. What is internal validity, and why is it important?
2. What factors threaten internal validity?
3. How do confounding variables threaten internal validity, and how can they be avoided?
4. What is external validity, and when is it important to have high levels of external validity?
5. How do internal and external validity relate to one another?

## RESEARCH SETTINGS

In addition to deciding on the design of your research, you also must decide on the setting in which you conduct your research. Your choice of setting is affected by the potential costs of the setting, its convenience, ethical considerations, and the research question you are addressing.

The two research settings open for psychological research are the laboratory and the field. For this discussion, the term *laboratory* is used in a broad sense. A laboratory is any research setting that is artificial relative to the setting in which the behavior naturally occurs. This definition is not limited to a special room with special equipment for research. A laboratory can be a formal lab, but it also can be a classroom, a room in the library, or a room in the student union building. In contrast, the *field* is the setting in which the behavior under study naturally occurs.

Your decision concerning the setting for your research is an important one, so you must be familiar with the relative advantages and disadvantages of each.

## The Laboratory Setting

If you choose to conduct your research in a *laboratory setting,* you gain important control over the variables that could affect your results. The degree of control depends on the nature of the laboratory setting. For example, if you are interested in animal learning, you can structure the setting to eliminate virtually all extraneous variables that could affect the course of learning. This is what Ivan Pavlov did in his investigations of classical conditioning. Pavlov exposed dogs to his experimental conditions while the dogs stood in a sound-shielded room. The shielded room permitted Pavlov to investigate the impact of the experimental stimuli free from any interfering sounds. Like Pavlov, you can control important variables within the laboratory that could affect the outcome of your research.

Complete control over extraneous variables may not be possible in all laboratory settings. For example, if you were administering your study to a large group of students in a psychology class, you could not control all the variables as well as you might wish (students may arrive late, or disruptions may occur in the hallway). For the most part, the laboratory affords more control over the research situation than does the field.

*Simulation: Re-creating the World in the Laboratory*    When you choose the laboratory as your research setting, you gain control over extraneous variables that could affect the value of your dependent variable. However, you make a trade-off when choosing the laboratory. Although you gain better control over variables, your results may lose some generality (the ability to apply your results beyond your specific laboratory conditions). If you are concerned with the ability to generalize your results, as well as with controlling extraneous variables, consider using a **simulation**. In a simulation, you attempt to re-create (as closely as possible) a real-world situation in the laboratory. A carefully designed and executed simulation may increase the generality of results. Because this strategy has been used with increasing frequency lately, a detailed discussion is in order.

You may decide for a variety of reasons to simulate rather than conduct research in the real world. You may choose simulation because the behavior of interest could not be studied ethically in the real world. For example, creating a panic situation in order to study the ensuing behavior is unethical. Bode and Codling (2013) avoided this problem by studying panic in a simulated environment—a virtual room containing a crowd of people and offering only two exits. To establish a familiar route, Bode and Codling had participants practice leaving the virtual room via one of the exits. The researchers varied the distribution of others trying to exit the room (equally or unequally distributed between the two exists) and the motivation to exit. In one condition, participants were simply told to exit the room. In the second, they were told to exit the room before a time shown on the screen was up. This second condition was intended to simulate getting out of a crowded room under stress. Bode and Codling found that under stress, participants preferred a familiar route, even if that route was clogged with others. They did not do so when stress was absent.

Often researchers choose to simulate for practical reasons. A simulation may be used because studying a behavior under its naturally occurring conditions is expensive and time consuming. By simulating in the laboratory, the researcher also gains the advantage of retaining control over variables while studying the behavior under relatively realistic conditions.

For a simulation to improve the generality of laboratory-based research, it must be properly designed. Observe the actual situation and study it carefully (Winkel & Sasanoff, 1970). Identify the crucial elements and then try to reproduce them in the laboratory. The more realistic the simulation, the greater are the chances that the results will be applicable to the simulated real-world phenomenon.

To summarize, the laboratory approach to research has the advantage of allowing you to control variables and thus to isolate the effects of the variables under study. However, in gaining such control over variables, you lose a degree of generality of results. Using simulations that are high in experimental realism may improve the ability to generalize laboratory results in the real world.

## The Field Setting

*Field research* is research conducted outside the laboratory in the participants' natural environment (the "field"). In this section, we briefly discuss conducting experiments in the field. However, most field research employs nonexperimental (correlational) methods such as naturalistic observation or survey designs. (We discuss these nonexperimental methods in Chapters 8 and 9.)

*The Field Experiment*    A *field experiment* is an experiment conducted in the participant's natural environment. In a field experiment (as in a laboratory experiment), you manipulate independent variables and measure a dependent variable. You decide which variables to manipulate, how to manipulate them, and when to manipulate them. Essentially, the field experiment has all the qualities of the laboratory experiment except that the research is conducted in the real world rather than in the artificial laboratory setting.

As an example, consider a field experiment conducted by George Schreer, Saundra Smith, and Kirsten Thomas (2009) on whether Black and White customers in "upscale" shops are treated differently. In a store selling expensive sunglasses, Schreer et al. had either a Black or White "customer" (who was working for the researchers) approach a White salesperson and ask to have the security tag removed from a pair of sunglasses so that he or she could try them on. The customer then walked to the closest mirror and examined him- or herself in the mirror for 1 minute. Observers in the store (one Black and one White) recorded three behaviors: whether or not the salesperson removed the tag, how much the salesperson followed the customer (1 = no following to 5 = shadows the customer), and the degree to which the salesperson stared at the customer (1 = no staring to 5 = looks over repeatedly or maintains stare for more than 4 seconds). Schreer et al. found that in all cases, the salespersons removed the security tag from the sunglasses. However, they followed and stared at the Black customer significantly more than the White customer. This study suggests that "shopping while Black" (where Black customers are treated with greater suspicion than White customers) may be a real problem. Of course, more research of this type would be necessary before we can increase our confidence in this conclusion.

The Schreer et al. field experiment has all of the features of a true experiment. An independent variable was manipulated (the race of the customer) and dependent variables were measured (willingness to remove the security tag, following, and staring). Because this was an experiment, a causal inference can be drawn between the race of the customer and signs of prejudicial behavior.

*Advantages and Disadvantages of the Field Experiment*    As with the laboratory experiment, the field experiment has its advantages and disadvantages. Because the research is conducted in the real world, one important advantage is that the results easily can be generalized to the real world (i.e., high external validity). An important disadvantage is that you have little control over potential confounding variables (i.e., you have low internal validity). In the Schreer et al. (2009) field experiment, for example, the researchers could not control the number of customers who were in the store at the time of the experiment. Differing numbers of other customers in the store could differently affect the salesperson's reactions to the experimental customer. Additionally, the researchers could not prevent the observers from knowing whether the customer was Black or White. The observers might interpret a salesperson's behavior differently knowing that the customer was Black versus White. Extraneous variables such as these can obscure or distort the effects of the independent variables manipulated in field experiments.

## A Look Ahead

At this point, you have been introduced to the broad issues that you should consider when choosing a research design, the basic design options available to you, and the strengths and weaknesses of each choice. Before you are ready to conduct your first study, you also will need to know how to measure your variables; what methods of observation are available; how to conduct systematic, reliable, and objective observations; how to choose participants and deal with them ethically; how to minimize participant and experimenter biases; and many other details concerning specific research designs. In the next chapter, we consider how to go about making systematic, scientifically valid observations.

## QUESTIONS TO PONDER

1. What is a simulation, and why would you use one?
2. What are the defining features of laboratory and field research?
3. What are the relative advantages and disadvantages of laboratory and field research?

## SUMMARY

Some of the most important decisions that you will make about your research concern its basic design and the setting in which it will be conducted. Research designs serve one or both of two major functions: (1) exploratory data collection and analysis (to identify new phenomena and relationships) and (2) hypothesis testing (to check the adequacy of proposed explanations). In the latter case, it is particularly important to distinguish causal from correlational relationships between variables. The relationship is causal if one variable directly or indirectly influences the other. The relationship is correlational if the two variables simply change values together (covary) and may or may not influence one another.

Two basic designs are available for determining relationships between variables: correlational designs and experimental designs. Correlational research involves collecting data on two or more variables across subjects or time periods. The states of the variables are simply observed or measured "as is" and not manipulated. Participants enter a correlational study already "assigned" to values of the variables of interest by nature or circumstances. Correlational designs can establish the existence of relationships between the observed variables and determine the direction of the relationships. However, two problems prevent such designs from determining whether the relationships are causal. The third-variable problem arises because of the possibility that a third, unmeasured variable influences both observed variables in such a way as to produce the correlation between them. The directionality problem arises because, even if two variables are causally related, correlational designs cannot determine in which direction the causal arrow points.

Despite its limitations, correlational research is useful on several accounts. It provides a good method for identifying potential causal relationships during the early stages of a research project, can be used to identify relationships when the variables of interest cannot or should not be manipulated, and can show how variables relate to one another in the real world outside the laboratory. Such relationships can be used to make predictions even when the reasons for the correlation are unknown. A variable in a correlational relationship that is used to make predictions is termed a *predictor variable,* and a variable whose value is being predicted is termed a *criterion variable.*

Experimental designs provide strong control over variables and allow you to establish whether variables are causally related. The defining characteristics of experimental research are (1) manipulation of an independent variable and (2) control over extraneous variables. Independent variables are manipulated by exposing subjects to different values or levels and then assessing differences in the participants' behavior across the levels. The observed behavior constitutes the dependent variable of the study. Extraneous variables are controlled by holding them constant, if possible, or by randomizing their effects across the levels of the independent variable.

The simplest experimental designs involve two groups of participants. The experimental group receives the experimental treatment; the control group is treated identically except that it does not receive the treatment. More complex designs may include more levels of the independent variable, more independent variables, or more dependent variables.

Although experiments can identify causal relationships, in some situations they cannot or should not be used. Variables may be impossible to manipulate, or it may be unethical to do so. In addition, tight control over extraneous variables may limit the generality of the results.

A demonstration is a type of nonexperimental design that resembles an experiment but lacks manipulation of an independent variable. It is useful for showing what sorts of behaviors occur under specific conditions, but it cannot identify relationships among variables.

Two important characteristics of any design are its internal and external validity. Internal validity is the ability of a design to test what it was intended to test. Results from designs low in internal validity are likely to be unreliable. A serious threat to internal validity comes from confounding. Confounding exists in a design when two variables are linked in such a way that the effects of one cannot be separated from the effects of the other. External validity is the ability of a design to produce results that apply beyond the sample and situation within which the data were collected. Results from designs low in external validity have little generality when applied directly to real-world situations. However, not all research is designed for such application; non-applied studies need not possess high external validity.

After deciding on a research design, you must then decide on a setting for your research. You can conduct your research in the laboratory or in the field. The laboratory setting affords you almost total control over your variables. You can tightly control extraneous variables that might confound your results. Laboratory studies, however, tend to have a degree of artificiality. You cannot be sure that the results you obtain in the laboratory apply to real-world behavior. Simulation is a technique in which you seek to re-create the setting in which the behavior naturally occurs.

Field research is conducted in your participants' natural environment. Although this setting allows you to generalize your results to the real world, you lose control over extraneous variables. Field experiments therefore tend to have high external validity but relatively low internal validity.

## KEY TERMS

| | |
|---|---|
| causal relationship | experimental group |
| correlational relationship | control group |
| correlational research | extraneous variable |
| third-variable problem | random assignment |
| directionality problem | demonstration |
| experimental research | internal validity |
| independent variable | confounding |
| treatments | external validity |
| dependent variable | simulation |

# Making Systematic Observations

T he everyday observations we make (the weather is hot and humid today; Martha is unusually grouchy; I'm feeling grouchy, too) are generally unsystematic, informal, and made haphazardly, without a plan. In contrast, scientific observations are systematic: What will be observed, how the observations will be made, and when the observations will be made are all carefully planned in advance.

Information recorded in this systematic way becomes the data of your study. Your conclusions come from these data, so it is important that you understand how your choice of variables to observe, methods of measurement, and conditions of observation affect the conclusions you can legitimately draw. This chapter provides the information you need to make these choices intelligently.

## DECIDING WHAT TO OBSERVE

In Chapters 3 and 4, we discussed how to obtain and develop a research idea and how to select a general strategy to attack the questions your research idea raises. After you select a specific question to investigate, you must decide exactly what to observe. Most research situations offer many ways to address a single question.

As one example, assume you want to study the relationship between weather and mood. Your general research question involves how the weather relates to a person's mood. You must decide what specific observations to make. First, you must specify what you mean by *weather*. *Weather* can be defined in terms of a number of specific variables, such as barometric pressure, air temperature and humidity, amount of sunlight, and the type and amount of precipitation. You may want to measure and record all these variables, or you may want to define *weather* in terms of some combination of these variables. For instance, you could dichotomize weather into two general categories: gloomy (cloudy or foggy, humid, low barometric pressure) and zesty (sunny, dry, high barometric pressure).

You also must decide how to index the moods of your participants. Again, a number of possibilities exist. You may choose to have participants rate their own moods, perhaps by using the Mood Adjective Check List (Nowlis & Green, 1957, cited in Walster, Walster, & Berscheid, 1978), or you may decide to gauge the moods of your participants through observation of mood-related behaviors. In this example, you have translated your general research idea into action by selecting particular observations to make. Note that the same general variables (weather, mood) can be defined and measured in a number of ways. As discussed in Chapter 3, the specific way that you choose to measure a variable becomes the *operational definition* of that variable within the context of your study. How you choose to operationalize a variable, and thus to observe and measure it, affects how you will later analyze your data and determines what conclusions you can draw from that analysis. So, you should carefully consider what variables to observe and manipulate and how to operationally define them.

## CHOOSING SPECIFIC VARIABLES FOR YOUR STUDY

Assuming that you have decided on a general research topic, a number of factors may influence your choice of specific variables to observe and manipulate. Some of them are research tradition, theory, availability of new techniques, and availability of equipment.

### Research Tradition

If your topic follows up on previous research in a particular area, the variables you choose to observe may be the same as those previously studied. In particular, you may choose to study the same dependent variables while manipulating new independent variables. For example, research on operant conditioning typically focuses on how various factors affect the rate of lever pressing (in rats) or key pecking (in pigeons). In experiments on cognitive processing, reaction times are frequently recorded to determine how long a hypothesized process requires to complete. In social psychology, the Implicit Associations Test (IAT) has become a standard measure of nonconscious processes. Using these traditional measures allows you to compare the results of different manipulations across experiments.

### Theory

Your decision about what to observe may depend on a particular theoretical point of view. For example, you may choose to observe behaviors that are seen as important from a certain theoretical perspective. If these behaviors (or other variables) have been used in previous research, you probably should use the measures already developed for them. However, the theory may suggest looking at behaviors not previously observed, in which case you may need to develop your own measures.

## Availability of New Techniques

Sometimes a variable cannot be investigated because there is no suitable way to measure it. In this case, the development of new techniques may open the way to observation and experimentation. You may want to use the new measure simply to explore its potential for answering your research question. As an example, consider the development of positron emission tomography (PET), a technique allowing researchers to visualize the level of activity of parts of a person's brain. A scanner picks up positrons (positively charged electrical particles) emitted by radioactively labeled glucose, which is being absorbed by neurons of the cerebral cortex to fuel their metabolic activity. More active neurons absorb more glucose and therefore emit more positrons. A computer translates the rates of positron emission in various regions of the cortex into a color-coded image of the cortex on the computer's display screen. By keeping track of changes in the colors, an observer can determine the ongoing pattern of neural activity.

This technology has enabled researchers to observe which parts of the cortex are most active during a variety of cognitive tasks. For example, using PET technology, Hakan Fischer, Jesper Anderson, Thoms Furmark, Gustav Wik, and Mats Fredrikson (2002) found increased metabolic activity in the right medial gyrus of the prefrontal cortex when an individual was presented with a fear-inducing stimulus. No such activity was found when an individual was presented with a nonfear control stimulus. Thus, using PET scan technology, Fischer et al. could confirm the role of the prefrontal cortex in mediating fear responses.

## Availability of Equipment

You are always tempted to adopt measures for which you already are equipped. For example, if you have invested in an operant chamber equipped with a lever and feeder, you may find it easier to continue your studies of operant conditioning by using this equipment rather than starting from scratch. Perhaps this equipment makes it trivially easy to collect data on response frequency (number of lever presses per minute) but does not readily yield information about response duration (amount of time the lever is depressed) or response force (amount of pressure exerted on the lever). You may decide that measuring response frequency will be adequate to answer your research question, particularly if previous research has successfully used this measure.

If the chosen measures provide reasonable answers to your research questions, this decision is not wrong. Problems arise when the measure really is not appropriate or adequate for the question being investigated but is chosen anyway on the basis of mere convenience. If you have chosen a particular measure simply because it is readily available or convenient, you should ask yourself whether it really *is* the best measure for your question.

In some cases, it may be necessary to use a measure that closely matches what people do in the real world. This refers to the *ecological validity* of a measure (Neisser, 1976), which we will discuss in more detail later in this chapter. For now, it is worth noting that you may have to take into account how well your measure matches up with the real-world experiences of people in the situation you are studying. For example, in a great majority of criminal trials, juries are required to make a guilty/not guilty decision.

They do not rate guilt on a rating scale. Therefore, to preserve ecological validity in a jury decision-making study, you would include a guilty/not guilty measure.

The decision of how to observe the behavior and other variables of your study requires that you select appropriate measures of these variables. In the next section, we examine some issues that you need to consider when choosing measures of your variables.

## QUESTION TO PONDER

1. What factors should you consider when deciding what to observe in a study?

## CHOOSING YOUR MEASURES

Whether your research design is experimental or correlational, your study will involve measuring the values of those variables included in the design. Yet there are many ways in which a given variable can be measured, and some may prove better for your purposes than others. In this section, we describe several important characteristics of a measure that you should consider before adopting it for your study, including its reliability, its accuracy, its validity, and the level of measurement it represents. We then discuss two additional factors that affect the adequacy of a dependent measure: its sensitivity and its susceptibility to range effects. Next, we take up the problem of tailoring your measures to your research participants. Measures must be adapted to the special situations posed (for example, by the testing of young children). Finally, we identify and describe several types of behavioral measure commonly used in psychological research.

### Reliability of a Measure

The **reliability** of a measure concerns its ability to produce similar results when repeated measurements are made under identical conditions. Imagine weighing yourself several times in quick succession using an ordinary bathroom scale. You expect to see the same body weight appear on the scale each time, but if the scale is cheap or worn, the numbers may vary by 1 or 2 pounds, or even worse. The more variability that you observe, the less reliable is the measure. Procedures used to assess reliability differ depending on the type of measure, as discussed next.

*Reliability of a Physical Measure*    You assess the reliability of measures of physical variables such as height and weight by repeatedly measuring a fixed quantity of the variable and using the observed variation in measured value to derive the *precision* of the measure, which represents the range of variation to be expected on repeated measurement. For example, the precision of weighings produced by a given bathroom scale might be reported as ±1.2 pounds. A more precise measurement has a smaller range of variation.

*Reliability of Population Estimates*    For measures of opinion, attitude, and similar psychological variables, in which the problem is to estimate the average value of the variable in a given population based on a sample drawn from that population, the precision of the estimate (its likely variation from sample to sample) is called the *margin of error*. The results of a poll of registered voters asking whether the voter favors or opposes stronger legislation on gun control might be reported as "41% favor stronger legislation, 54% are against it, and 5% are unsure, with a margin of error of ±3%."

*Reliability of Judgments or Ratings by Multiple Observers*     When the measure being made consists of judgments or ratings of multiple observers, you can establish the degree of agreement among observers by using a statistical measure of *interrater reliability*. (We describe ways to assess interrater reliability in Chapter 6.)

*Reliability of Psychological Tests or Measures*     Assessing the reliability of measures of psychological variables such as intelligence, introversion/extraversion, anxiety level, mood, and so on poses a special difficulty in that these variables tend to change naturally over time. By the time you repeat a measurement of, say, mood or anxiety level, the underlying quantity being measured in the individual may have changed. If so, the measure will appear to be unreliable even though the changes in measured value reflect real changes in the variable. In addition, for various reasons, it is often not possible to administer psychological assessment devices to the same individuals a sufficient number of times to determine the reliability of the measure. Thus, an alternative strategy is needed for assessing the reliability of these measures.

The basic strategy for assessing the reliability of psychological measures is to administer the assessment twice to a large group of individuals and then determine the correlation (Pearson $r$) between the scores on the first and second administrations. The higher the correlation, the greater the reliability. A test is considered to have high reliability if $r$ is .95 or higher. (See Chapter 13 for a discussion of the Pearson $r$ statistic.) You can choose among several methods for assessing the reliability of a psychological test, each with a different set of advantages and drawbacks. These include the test–retest, parallel-forms, and split-half reliability assessments.

To assess **test–retest reliability**, you administer the same test twice, separated by a relatively long interval of time, to the same individuals. To the extent that the test is reliable, scores on the two administrations of the test will be strongly positively correlated.

Because you administer the same test twice, any changes in scores cannot be due to differences in question wording or the use of nonequivalent items. However, this advantage must be weighed against two disadvantages. First, if, on second administration, participants simply recall how they answered the items on first administration, the test may appear to be more reliable than it actually is. Second, participants may change between administrations of the test. Although changes in test scores may accurately reflect this difference, they can make the test appear less reliable than it actually is. For these reasons, the test–retest method is best for assessing stable characteristics of individuals such as intelligence. The variable being assessed by the test is unlikely to change much between administrations, and administrations can be spaced far enough apart that participants are unlikely to remember much about their previous responses to the test.

You can avoid the problem of remembering previous responses by assessing a **parallel-forms reliability** (or *alternate-forms reliability*). This is the same as test–retest reliability except that the form of the test used on first administration is replaced on second administration by a parallel form. A parallel form contains items supposedly equivalent to those found in the original form. These assess the same knowledge, skills, and so on but use somewhat different questions or problems—which eliminates the possibility that on second administration the participant was simply recalling his or her answer on the previous occasion. However, if the items of the parallel form are not truly equivalent, differences in test performance due to this nonequivalence may reduce the apparent reliability of the test. In addition, the parallel-forms method still suffers from the possibility that the quantity measured may have changed since first administration, thus making the test appear less reliable than it really is.

You can avoid the problem caused by changes between administrations in the quantity being measured by choosing the **split-half reliability** method. Here, the two parallel forms of the test are intermingled in a single test and administered together in one sitting. The responses to the two forms are then separated and scored individually. Because both forms are administered simultaneously, the quantity being measured has no time to change. However, the need to use alternate forms in the two halves introduces the same problem found in the parallel-forms method, that of ensuring that the two forms are in fact equivalent.

These methods for assessing the reliability of a psychological test apply equally well to assessing the reliability of a questionnaire designed for distribution in a survey. (For a discussion of these methods in the context of survey design, see Chapter 9.)

## Accuracy of a Measure

The term **accuracy** describes a measure that produces results that agree with a known standard. For example, a bathroom scale is accurate if it indicates 50 pounds when a standard 50-pound weight is placed on it, 100 pounds when a standard 100-pound weight is placed on it, and so on. A thermometer calibrated in degrees Celsius (C) is accurate if it reads 0 degrees when tested in a slurry of ice and 100 degrees when placed in boiling water (both tested under sea-level air pressure). A counter is accurate if the number of events counted equals the actual number of events that occurred.

Determining accuracy is hampered by lack of precision. Your measurement may not agree with the known standard each time that you make it. However, the measurement may still be accurate in the sense that the value observed agrees with the standard *on average.* Thus, you can determine accuracy by measuring the standard a large number of times and computing the average; the measure is accurate if the average value equals the value of the standard. Any difference between this average value and the standard value is termed *bias.* Bias can be overcome either by adjusting the measuring instrument to eliminate it or, if this is not possible, by mathematically removing the bias from the measured value.

Although a somewhat unreliable measure may be accurate *on average,* any *single* measurement in such a case will tend to deviate from the actual value by some amount. When a value is reported as being "accurate to within ±0.1 centimeter," this means that measured values will tend to fall within 0.1 cm of the true value. Thus, the precision of the measure limits the accuracy (probable closeness to the true value) of a single measurement. However, the converse is not true. A measurement can be precise (repeatable within narrow limits) and yet wildly inaccurate. For example, a thermometer whose glass has slipped with respect to the scale behind it may yield the same value in ice water within ±0.1 °C, yet give an average value of 23 degrees instead of the correct 0 degrees.

In psychological measurement, standards are rare and, therefore, the accuracy of a measure cannot be assessed. This does not mean that you should ignore accuracy issues altogether. For example, no standard introvert exists against which to assess the accuracy of a measure of introversion/extraversion (a personality variable). In such cases, test scores may be *standardized* by statistical methods to have a specified average value in a given population and a specified amount of variability. You can find an extensive discussion of these methods and other issues related to psychological testing in Cohen, Swerdlik, and Sturman (2013).

## Validity of a Measure

In the previous chapter, we introduced the concepts of internal and external validity, which are attributes of a research design. In this section, we discuss other forms of validity that apply to measures. The **validity** of a *measure* is the extent to which it measures what you intend it to measure. Imagine you decided you could measure a person's general intelligence by placing a tape measure around that person's skull at the level of the forehead, on the theory that larger skulls house larger brains and that larger brains produce higher intelligence. Most of us would agree that the tape measure can provide a valid measure of *skull circumference,* but used in this way, is it a valid measure of intelligence? This question was actually investigated. Near the end of the 19th century, the so-called science of phrenology enjoyed a brief popularity. Phrenologists believed that by carefully measuring the cranium of a person they could learn something about that person's personality, aptitudes, and, yes, general intelligence. They were wrong. For one thing, over the normal range of variation (excluding pathological cases such as microcephaly) the correlations between brain size and intelligence are very small. In fact, the largest brain on record belonged to a mildly retarded person, and several of the leading thinkers of the day turned out to have disappointingly small brains. Thus, measures of brain size turned out not to be the most valid indicator of intelligence (Fancher, 1979).

You should always be concerned about the validity of any measure, but in psychology the topic comes up most often when discussing tests designed to measure psychological attributes. In this context, several types of validity have been defined, each requiring a somewhat different operation to establish. Here we briefly discuss three: face validity, content validity, and criterion-related validity. (For more information on test validity, see Chapter 9.)

**Face validity** describes how well a measurement instrument (e.g., a test of intelligence) appears to measure (judging by its appearance) what it was designed to measure. For instance, a test of mathematical ability would have face validity if it contained math problems. Face validity is a weak form of validity in that an instrument may lack face validity and yet, by other criteria, measure what it is intended to measure. Nevertheless, having good face validity may be important. If those who take the test do not perceive the test as valid, they may develop a negative attitude about its usefulness (Cohen et al., 2013).

**Content validity** has to do with how adequately the content of a test samples the knowledge, skills, or behaviors that the test is intended to measure. For example, a final exam for a course would have content validity if it adequately sampled the material taught in the course. An employment test would have content validity if it adequately sampled from the larger set of job-related skills. Finally, a test designed to measure "assertiveness" would have content validity to the extent that it adequately sampled from the population of all behaviors that would be judged as "assertive" (Cohen et al., 2013).

**Criterion-related validity** reflects how adequately a test score can be used to infer an individual's value on some *criterion* measure. To determine the test's criterion-related validity, you compare the values inferred from the test to the criterion values actually observed. Criterion-related validity includes two subtypes. You assess **concurrent validity** if the scores on your test and the criterion are collected at about the same time. For example, you might establish the concurrent validity of a new, 10-minute, paper-and-pencil test of intelligence by administering it and the Stanford–Binet (an established test of intelligence) at about the same time and demonstrating that the scores on the two tests correlate strongly. You assess **predictive validity** by comparing the scores on your test with the value of a criterion measure observed at a later time. A high correlation between these measures indicates good predictive validity. Predictive validity indicates the ability of a test to predict some future behavior. For example, the Scholastic Assessment Test (SAT), given in high school, does a good job of predicting future college performance (as shown by its high correlation with the latter) and thus has predictive validity.

Finally, **construct validity** applies when a test is designed to measure a *construct*, which is a variable, not directly observable, that has been developed to explain behavior on the basis of some theory. Examples of constructs include such variables as "intelligence," "self-esteem," and "achievement motivation." To demonstrate the construct validity of a measure, you must demonstrate that those who score high or low on the measure behave as predicted by the theory. For example, those who receive low (high) scores on an intelligence test should behave the way people of low (high) intelligence would be expected to behave, as predicted by the theory of intelligence on which the construct was based.

Just as a measure can be reliable but inaccurate, it also can be reliable but invalid. The phrenologists whom we discussed earlier developed large calipers and other precision instruments to make the task of measurement reliable. By using these instruments properly, they were able to collect highly reliable measurements of cranial shapes and sizes. Unfortunately, the phrenologists chose to interpret these measurements as indicators of the magnitudes of various mental characteristics such as memory, personality, intelligence, and criminality. Of course, cranial size and shape actually provide no such information. Despite being highly reliable, the phrenologists' measures were not valid indicators of mental characteristics.

Although a measure can be reliable but invalid, the converse is not true. If a measure is unreliable, it is not a valid gauge of anything except the amount of random error in the measuring instrument.

## Acceptance as an Established Measure

In our weather and mood example, the Mood Adjective Check List was one possible measure of participants' moods. This established measure has been used in previous research. Using established measures is advantageous because the reliability and the validity of the measure are known.

Although you do not have to spend precious time validating an established measure, it may not be suitable for addressing your research questions. A case in which the established measure was *not* appropriate comes from the literature on jury decision making. Early research on the factors that affect jury decision making required participants to sentence a defendant (e.g., see Landy & Aronson, 1969), and several subsequent studies also used this measure. Because jurors are not empowered to sentence a defendant (except in death penalty cases and a few other cases in some jurisdictions), the established measure lacked realism. Later research attempted to correct this problem by having participants evaluate the guilt of the defendant either on rating scales or as a dichotomous (two-value) guilty/not guilty verdict.

An alternative to using established measures is to develop your own. This alternative has the advantage of freeing you from previous dogma and theory. In fact, a successful new measure may shed new light on an old phenomenon. However, you should evaluate its reliability and validity. This may mean testing reliability and validity before you use your new measure in your research. Alternatively, you can use your measure in your research and demonstrate its reliability and validity based on your results. A danger with this latter strategy is that if the measure has problems with reliability or validity, the results of your research will be questionable. Because demonstrating the validity, reliability, and accuracy of a new measure can be time consuming and expensive, using measures that are already available (especially if you are new to a research area) is advisable.

## QUESTIONS TO PONDER

1. What is the reliability of a measure?
2. How does the concept of reliability apply to different types of measures?
3. What is meant by the accuracy of a measure?
4. How do the reliability and accuracy of a measure affect the generality of the results of a study?
5. What is the validity of a measure?
6. What are the ways you can assess the validity of a measure?
7. What is the relationship between the reliability and validity of a measure?

## Scale of Measurement

The phrase *scale of measurement* usually refers to the units in which a variable is measured: centimeters, seconds, IQ points, and so on. However, this phrase also can refer to the *type* of scale represented by a given set of units. Stevens (1946) identified four basic scales, which can be arranged in order of information provided about the values along the scale. These are the nominal, ordinal, interval, and ratio scales. Stevens argued that the type of scale along which a given variable is measured determines the kinds of statistical analyses that can be applied to the data. Because some kinds of statistical analysis are more informative and sensitive than others, it is important that you carefully consider the scale of measurement when evaluating the suitability of a given variable for your study. You should learn the characteristics of each scale and be able to identify the type of scale a given variable represents.

*Nominal Scales*     At the lowest level of measurement, a variable may simply define a set of cases or types that are qualitatively different. For example, sex may be male or female. According to one scheme, a person's personality may be classified as introverted or extraverted. Variables whose values differ in quality and not quantity are said to fall along a **nominal scale**. In a nominal scale, the values have different names (in fact, the term *nominal* refers to name), but no ordering of the values is implied. For example, to say that male is higher or lower in value than female makes no sense. They are simply different.

Sometimes the qualitative values of a nominal-scale variable are identified by numbers (typically for the purpose of computer analysis). For example, three candidates for political office—Smith, Jones, and Brown—might be assigned the numbers 0, 1, and 2, respectively. If the assignment of numbers to the different qualitative values is arbitrary and does not imply any quantitative ordering of the values, then the results of certain mathematical calculations on these numbers will be meaningless.

To see that this is true, imagine that you determine how many voters voted for Smith, for Jones, and for Brown in a recent election and identify each candidate by a number as indicated earlier. You compute the average vote, which turns out to be 1.5. What does it mean to say that the average vote was 1.5? Does it mean that the average voter favored a candidate who was halfway between Jones (candidate 1) and Brown (candidate 2)? That seems doubtful. Moreover, had you assigned different numbers to the three candidates (say, Brown = 0, Smith = 1, and Jones = 2), you would have obtained a different average.

Although it makes no sense to apply mathematical operations to nominal values (even when these values are represented by numbers), you *can* count the number of cases (observations) falling into each nominal category and apply mathematical operations to those counts. So, you could count the number of voters who cast their ballots for Smith, Brown, and Jones and see which candidate garnered the most or least number of votes. Such counts fall along a ratio scale (discussed later).

*Ordinal Scales*     At the next level of measurement are variables measured along an **ordinal scale**. The different values of a variable in an ordinal scale not only have different names (as in the nominal scale) but also can be ranked according to quantity. For instance, a participant's self-esteem may be scored along an ordinal scale as low, moderate, or high. However, the distance between low and moderate and between moderate and high is not known. All you can say for sure is that moderate is greater than low and high is greater than moderate. Because you do not know the actual amount of difference between ordinal values, mathematical operations such as addition, subtraction, multiplication, and division (which assume that the quantitative distance between values is known) are likely to produce misleading results. For example, if three teams are ranked first, second, and third, the difference in ranking between first and second and between second and third are both 1.0. This implies that the teams are equally spaced in terms of performance. However, it may be the case that the first- and second-place teams are almost neck-and-neck and both performing far above the third-place team.

*Interval and Ratio Scales*    If the spacing between values along the scale is known, then the scale is either an **interval scale** or a **ratio scale**. In either case, you know that one unit is larger or smaller than another, as well as by how much.

The two types of scale differ as follows. A ratio scale has a zero point that literally indicates the absence of the quantity being measured. An interval scale has a zero point that does *not* indicate the absence of the quantity. With interval scales, the position of the zero point is established on the basis of convenience, but its position is purely arbitrary.

The Celsius scale for temperature is an interval scale. Its zero point does not really indicate the absence of all temperature. Zero on the Celsius scale is the temperature at which ice melts—a convenient, easy-to-determine value. Although this temperature may seem cold to you, things can get much colder. In contrast, the Kelvin scale for temperature is a ratio scale. Its zero point is the temperature at which all heat is absent. You simply can't get any colder.

In psychological research, when you measure the number of responses on a lever in an operant chamber, you are using a ratio scale. Zero responses means literally that there are no responses. Other examples of psychological research data measured on a ratio scale are the number of items recalled in a memory experiment, the number of errors made in a signal-detection experiment, and the time required to respond in a reaction-time experiment. Again, zero on these scales indicates an absence of the quantity measured. In contrast, if you have participants rate how much they like something on a scale from 0 to 10, you are using an interval scale. In this case, a rating of zero does not necessarily mean the total absence of liking.

For practical purposes, an important difference between interval and ratio scales concerns the kinds of mathematical operations that you can legitimately apply to the data. Both scales allow you to determine by how much the various data points *differ*. For example, if one participant makes 30 responses and a second makes 15 responses, you can confidently state that there is a 15-response difference between participants. If the data are measured on a ratio scale (as in this example), you can also correctly state that one participant made half as many responses as the other (i.e., you can divide one quantity by the other to form a ratio). Making ratio comparisons makes little sense when data are scaled on an interval scale. Consider the IQ scale of intelligence, which is an interval scale. If one person has an IQ of 70 and another an IQ of 140, saying that the person with the 140 IQ is twice as intelligent as the person with the 70 IQ is nonsense. The reason is that even a person scoring zero on the test may have some degree of intelligence.

## Variables and Scales of Measurement

The four basic scales of measurement identified by Stevens (1946) help clarify the level of information conveyed by the numbers that result from measuring some variable. However, they should be viewed only as rough guides to aid in thinking about the numbers. Not all measures fall precisely into one or the other scale category; for example, many psychological measures do not seem to fall along a scale of precisely equal intervals, as required of an interval-scale measure, yet the distances between values along the scale are known with greater precision than would be implied by the mere rank ordering of an ordinal scale. Researchers usually analyze such measures as if they had full interval-scale properties. Furthermore, it is possible to construct alternatives or additions to the basic scales. For example, Mosteller and Tukey (1977) offer an alternative classification that includes seven categories: amounts, counts, counted fractions (ratios with a fixed base, such as "8 out of 10 doctors"), names (categories with no particular order), ranks, grades (categories with a natural order), and balances. This scheme is based on the nature of the values rather than on what logical or mathematical operations legitimately can be performed on them.

Despite these caveats, Stevens's (1946) four basic scales do at least highlight the information content of a set of numbers representing some particular variable as measured. In the next section, we discuss several factors that you should consider when deciding on a scale of measurement to adopt for some variable to be included in your study.

## Choosing a Scale of Measurement

You should consider at least three factors when choosing a scale of measurement for a given variable: the information yielded, the statistical measures you would like to apply to the data, and (if you expect to apply your results directly to natural settings), the ecological validity of the measure.

*Information Yielded*   One way to think about the four scales of measurement described is in terms of the amount of information each provides. The nominal scale provides the least amount of information: All you know is that the values differ in *quality*. The ordinal scale adds crude information about *quantity* (you can rank the order of the values). The interval scale refines the measurement of quantity by indicating how much the values *differ*. Finally, the ratio scale indicates precisely how much of the quantity exists. When possible, you should adopt the scale that provides the most information.

*Statistical Tests*   As noted, Stevens (1946) argues that the basic scale of measurement of a variable determines the kinds of statistics that can be applied to the analysis of your data. Typically, the statistics for nominal and ordinal data are less powerful (i.e., less sensitive to relationships among variables) than are the statistics used for interval or ratio data. (See Chapter 14 for a more detailed discussion of the power of a statistical test.) On a practical level, this means you are less likely to detect a statistically significant relationship among variables when using a nominal or an ordinal scale of measurement.

Many statisticians believe this view is overly restrictive. They suggest that the numbers resulting from measurement are just numbers and that a statistical analysis does not "care" how the numbers were derived or where they came from (e.g., see Velleman & Wilkinson, 1993). To illustrate this viewpoint, Lord (1953) tells a story about football jerseys being sold to the football team on campus. Each jersey displayed a number. When used to identify which jersey belongs to whom, the numbers serve only as names; they might just as well be letters when used for this purpose, and thus they represent a nominal scale of measurement. However, according to the story, after quite a number of jerseys had been sold, the members of the freshman team became quite unhappy when the sophomore team began laughing at them because the freshman players' jerseys all had low numbers. The freshman players suspected a trick was being played on them, so they asked a statistician to investigate. The statistician immediately computed the mean (average) jersey number for the freshman players for all the jerseys that had been in the store's original inventory. The freshman students were indeed getting more than their fair share of low numbers, and the probability that this would have occurred purely by chance was so low as to be essentially zero.

To compute the means, the statistician used the jersey numbers as quantities along an interval scale of measurement as if larger numbers indicated larger amounts of some variable. Indeed, both freshmen and sophomores were behaving as if the numbers represented something like social status, with low numbers corresponding to low status and high numbers corresponding to high status. In fact, the analysis in terms of means was meant to discover whether the jersey numbers were systematically assigned according to class rank rather than being arbitrarily assigned substitutes for the player's names, as would normally be the case for nominally scaled values.

As Lord's story makes clear, the scale of measurement that applies to a number depends on how the number is to be interpreted when the data are analyzed. This interpretation determines what sorts of analyses can be applied legitimately to the data. If the numbers were interpreted as nominal-scale values, for example, then it would not be legitimate to perform analyses based on the means of those numbers.

*Ecological Validity*   The discussion thus far would indicate that you should use ratio or interval scales whenever possible in order to maximize the amount of information contained in the data. However, as we noted earlier, your research question may limit your choice of a measurement scale. If you are planning to conduct applied research, for example, you may be forced to use a certain scale even if that scale is one of the less informative ones. Consider the following example.

One author of this book (Bordens, 1984) conducted a study of the factors that influence the decision to accept a plea bargain. In this study, participants were told to play the role of either an innocent or a guilty defendant. They then were given information concerning the likelihood of conviction at trial and the sentences that would be received on conviction at trial or after a plea bargain.

In this situation, the most realistic dependent measure is a simple "acceptance–rejection" of the plea bargain. Real defendants in plea bargaining must make such a choice, so a dichotomous accept–reject measure was used even though it employs a less informative (dichotomous) scale of measurement (nominal). Sometimes you must compromise your desire for a sensitive measurement scale so that you will have an ecologically valid dependent measure (Neisser, 1976). A dependent measure has *ecological validity* if it reflects what people must do in real-life situations.

Adopting a more limited (nominal, ordinal, dichotomous) scale for your measure (even if it results in an ecologically valid measure) has two problems: The amount of information is limited, and the statistical tests that can be applied are less powerful. If you need to adopt a more limited measure to preserve ecological validity, you may be able to circumvent the limitations of scale by using special techniques.

One technique is to include an interval or ratio scale in your study along with your nominal or ordinal measure. Before you analyze your data, you can create a *composite scale* from these measures. A composite scale is one that combines the features of more than one scale.

In the plea-bargaining study, Bordens (1984) included both a nominal dichotomous accept–reject measure and an interval scale (participants rated how firm their decisions were on a scale ranging from 0 to 10). A composite scale was created from these two scales by adding 11 points to the firmness score of participants who rejected the plea bargain and subtracting from 10 the firmness scores of participants who accepted the plea bargain. The resulting scale (0 to 21) provided a continuous measure of degree of firmness of a participant's decision to accept or reject a plea bargain (0 was *firmly accept,* and 21 was *firmly reject* the plea bargain). The composite scale was reported along with the dichotomous accept–reject measure. The composite scale revealed some subtle effects of the independent variables that were not apparent with the dichotomous measure.

Another strategy you can use when you feel that a dichotomous scale is important is to arrange an interval scale so that a dichotomous decision is also required. For example, Horowitz, Bordens, and Feldman (1980) developed a scale that preserved some of the qualities of an interval scale while yielding dichotomous data. To assess the guilt or innocence of a defendant in a simulated criminal trial, Horowitz et al. used the 6-point, bracketed scale illustrated in Figure 5-1. Notice that points 1 through 3 are bracketed as a not-guilty verdict and points 4 through 6 are bracketed as a guilty verdict. The points on the scale were labeled so that participants could also rate the degree to which the evidence proved either guilt or innocence. This scale forced participants to decide that the defendant was either guilty or innocent while yielding a more sensitive measure of the effects of the independent variables.

**FIGURE 5-1**   A bracketed 6-point scale.
SOURCE: Horowitz, Bordens, and Feldman, 1980.

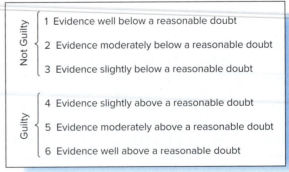

## QUESTIONS TO PONDER

1. What are the defining characteristics of Stevens's four scales of measurement? Do all measures fall neatly into one of the four categories?

2. What factors affect your choice of a scale of measurement?

3. What is ecological validity, and why should you be concerned about it?

## Adequacy of a Dependent Measure

You might find that a carefully planned dependent measure looks better on paper than it works in practice. Two potential problems involve the sensitivity of the dependent measure and range effects.

*Sensitivity of the Dependent Measure*     Some measures of a dependent variable may be insensitive to the effect of a manipulation, whereas other measures under the same conditions definitely show an effect, as was clearly demonstrated to one author of this book (Abbott) in a study designed to investigate the role of the cerebral cortex in the expression of fear. Normal laboratory rats and rats whose cortexes had been surgically removed immediately after birth were exposed to three brief (0.5-second), relatively mild foot shocks in an operant chamber, where they were observed for several minutes. During the observation period, fear of the chamber cues was assessed by recording the number of 2-second intervals during which the rats "froze" (remained immobile). The normal rats froze during most of the observation period (as is typical), but no freezing was observed in the decorticate rats.

If only observations of freezing had been collected, the experimenter would have concluded from these data that the shocks had absolutely no effect on the post shock behaviors of the decorticate rats. However, unsystematic observations made during the course of the experiment revealed that, far from being unaffected by the shock, the behaviors of the decorticate rats changed radically. Even with almost no freezing, exploratory activity (which had been going on strongly prior to shock) all but ceased following the shocks and was replaced by a tentative stretch-and-quickly-withdraw behavior. Although frequently observed prior to shock, standing on the hind legs alone was all but absent following shock.

Unfortunately, these behaviors were not carefully defined and systematically recorded. The experimenter could refer only to impressions of behavioral change rather than to hard data. To determine the precise effect of the shocks on decorticate behaviors, the experiment must be run again, with the dichotomously scaled freezing measure replaced by a ratio-scaled continuous measure of behavioral activity, and the incidence of other behaviors (such as rearing) must be recorded.

In this case, the measure of freezing was insensitive to the subtle changes in behavior brought about by the independent variable. This was the case despite the fact that the measure had proven effective in other experiments. Unsystematic observations carried out during the course of the experiment can provide a useful check on the adequacy of your measure and may reveal defects as they did here. Although you may have to redesign and rerun your study, your understanding of the phenomenon under investigation will benefit.

*Range Effects*    In addition to worrying about the sensitivity of your dependent variable, you need to be concerned with what are commonly called range effects. **Range effects** occur when the values of a variable have an upper or lower limit, which is encountered during the course of the observation. Range effects come in two types: floor effects and ceiling effects. As you might expect from the names, floor effects occur when the variable reaches its lowest possible value, whereas ceiling effects occur when the variable reaches its highest possible value.

The problems that range effects can cause are subtle and pernicious (harmful). They are subtle in that you don't always know that you have encountered them. Range effects are pernicious in that their consequences are hard to deal with after the fact and may require a redesign of the study. Consider the following example.

Assume that you have decided to study the effect of retention interval on memory for fruit and vegetable words (you happen to be fond of salads). You settle on a set of retention intervals that span 10 to 100 minutes in 10-minute increments, and you decide to measure retention by having participants attempt to pick out the correct word from a list of 10 items. The retention score for each participant is the percentage of correct choices in 10 trials.

You vary the retention interval across trials and get a retention score for each interval. To your surprise, you find absolutely no effect of retention interval; averaged across participants, retention is about 95% at each interval!

Fortunately, you are aware of the potential for range effects in your data and stop to examine the scores more closely before concluding that retention interval has no effect on memory for fruit and vegetable words. Looking at the scores of each participant, you realize that 19 out of 20 participants have scored perfectly at every interval. Could the retention task be too easy?

It is possible that differences in retention might have been detected if the task were more demanding. Perhaps there *is* an effect of retention interval on memory. In this case, however, even at the longest interval, memory was still good enough to score 100% correct on the retention task. Because 100% was the upper limit of your measure, showing any better retention at shorter intervals was impossible. You have encountered a ceiling effect.

Range effects affect your data in two distinct ways: First, by limiting the values of your highest (or lowest) data points, range effects decrease the differences among your treatment means, perhaps to the extent that no statistically reliable differences will surface between them. Second, range effects reduce the variability of scores within the affected treatments is reduced. Because many commonly used inferential statistics use the variability of scores within the treatments to estimate variability due to random causes, these statistics tend to give misleading results when range effects are present. They underestimate the probability of the observed differences in treatments arising through chance alone. (See Chapter 14 for a discussion of inferential statistics and how they work.)

Because range effects distort your data both in central tendency and in variability, do your best to avoid them. Previous research often provides a guide, but on some occasions you may need to determine appropriate methods by trial and error.

## Tailoring Your Measures to Your Research Participants

As another aspect to designing appropriate measures, you must consider the capabilities of your research participants. If you are working with young children or mentally impaired adults, you must tailor your measure to their level of understanding. It makes little sense to use a complicated rating scale with complex instructions if your participants have limited mental capacities.

One way to tailor the dependent measure to your participants is to represent your measures graphically. For example, instead of using a rating scale to measure a preference among young children (perhaps for a toy), you could use a more concrete measure. The child could be asked to give you a number of blocks, blow up a balloon, or vary the space between two objects to indicate the degree of preference. Another technique used with children is to adapt rating scales to a visual format. For instance, a scale for children to rate pain uses a series of six cartoon faces with varying expressions (Wong & Baker, 1988). Children point to the face that best reflects the level of pain they are experiencing. This scale is shown in Figure 5-2. Creative measurement techniques also may be needed when dealing with intellectually impaired or very old adults.

Some good examples of creative measurement techniques are those developed to study infant development. With preverbal infants, you have the problem that the participants of your study cannot understand verbal instructions or respond to measures as would an older child or an adult. Consequently, researchers of infant behavior have developed techniques to indirectly test the capabilities of the infant. Popular techniques used with preverbal infants include habituation, preference testing, and discrimination learning. The *habituation technique* capitalizes on the fact that even infants get bored with repeatedly presented stimuli. For example, in a study of the ability to discriminate shapes, you might repeatedly present the infant with a square until the infant no longer looks at the stimulus. You would then present a new stimulus (a circle). If the infant looked at the circle, you could infer that the infant could tell the difference between the two stimuli.

Alternatively, you could investigate the same problem with the *preference technique.* Here you present the two stimuli simultaneously. If the infant looks at one stimulus more than the other, you can infer that the infant can distinguish them.

**FIGURE 5-2** The Wong–Baker faces pain rating scale.
SOURCE: Reprinted by permission of the Wong–Baker FACES Foundation, Oklahoma City, Oklahoma.

In *discrimination learning,* you attempt to train different behaviors to the different stimuli (e.g., suck on an instrumented pacifier when a square is present, but not when a circle is present). Differential rates of responding suggest the capacity to discriminate.

The need to tailor a measure to your participants is not limited to children and impaired adults. Even adults of normal intelligence may have difficulty responding to your measures. Remember that your participants are probably naive to the research jargon with which you are familiar. For example, they may not understand what you mean when you say that increasing numbers on a scale represent an increase in whatever is being studied. Whenever you suspect that your participants may misunderstand how to use the measure, make a special effort to clearly describe it. Figure 5-3 shows how a scale from 0 to 10 can be presented graphically. Notice how the arrow increases in width as the numbers increase. Such a visual presentation may help participants understand that a 7 means they feel more strongly and a 4 less so.

Regardless of the measure chosen, pretest it to ensure that it is appropriate for your participants. During the pretest, you may find that your measure must be modified to fit the needs of your research; such modifications can then be made before you invest large amounts of time and effort in your actual study. You could also search the literature to see if the reliability and validity of such a measure has been established. For instance, Maria Ferreira-Valente, José Pais-Ribeiro, and Mark Jensen (2011) found that the pain faces scale is a valid measure of pain, although it was a bit less sensitive than other measures.

## QUESTIONS TO PONDER

1. What is meant by the adequacy of a dependent measure?
2. What is meant by the sensitivity of a dependent measure, and why should you be concerned about it?
3. What are range effects, and why should you be concerned about them?
4. When should you consider tailoring your dependent measures to the needs of your research participants?
5. How can you tailor your dependent measures? (Give examples.)

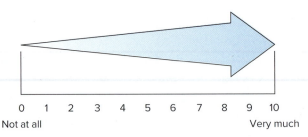

**FIGURE 5-3** How to format a rating scale to reinforce the idea that increasing numbers represent an increasing amount of some characteristic.

## Types of Dependent Variables and How to Use Them

Now that we have covered some of the basics of measurement and scaling, we can examine the types of dependent variables in psychological research and their uses. The following sections describe four types of dependent measures: behavioral measures, physiological measures, self-report measures, and implicit measures.

*Behavioral Measures*     Although the number of dependent variables is potentially vast, those used in behavioral research do tend to fall into a few basic categories. One type of dependent measure is a **behavioral measure**. When using a behavioral measure, you record the actual behavior of your subjects. In a study of helping behavior, for example, you might expose participants to different treatments (such as having a male or a female experimenter drop some packages) and then take note of the behavior of your participants (such as whether or not a participant helps).

One behavioral measure is *frequency*. To determine the frequency of a behavior, you count the number of occurrences over some specified period. For example, Goldiamond (1965) calculated the frequency of stuttering in a behavior modification study. Participants read pages of text, and Goldiamond counted the instances of stuttering across successive pages. Goldiamond found that the rate of stuttering declined during periods in which stuttering was punished with bursts of loud noise. Frequency counts also can be made over successive time periods.

Another behavioral measure is *latency*. Here you measure the amount of time it takes for subjects to respond to some stimulus. In the helping experiment described earlier, you could have measured how long it took participants to offer help in addition to whether or not participants helped. Any measure of reaction time is a latency measure.

In some types of research, *number of errors* might be an appropriate behavioral measure, which can be used with a well-defined "correct" response. Learning experiments often record number of errors as a function of the number of learning trials.

Behavioral measures are fine indicators of overt behavior. However, with a behavioral measure, you may not be able to collect data dealing with the underlying causes of behavior. To gain insight into the factors that underlie behavior, you often must follow up behavioral measures with other measures.

*Physiological Measures*     A second type of dependent variable is a **physiological measure**. This type of measure typically requires special equipment designed to monitor the participant's bodily functions. Such measures include heart rate, respiration rate, electrical activity of the brain, electrodermal activity, and blood pressure, among others.

A good example of the application of physiological measures is found in research on sleep. In the sleep laboratory, physiological responses such as brain activity (measured with an electroencephalogram, or EEG), heart rate, respiration rate, and eye movements are recorded. This research has shown that the activities of the brain and body change cyclically over the course of a night's sleep.

Modern brain-imaging techniques such as positron emission tomography (PET) and functional magnetic resonance imaging (fMRI) have opened a new window into the dynamic activity of the brain during various kinds of mental tasks and have high-lighted differences in brain functioning between normal individuals and those diagnosed with mental disorders such as schizophrenia.

The physiological measures just described are all noninvasive and do not harm the participant. Invasive measures, which sometimes do inflict a degree of harm, usually require the use of animals. For example, a physiological psychologist may implant an electrode into a rat's brain in order to record the activity of particular brain cells while the animal learns to perform a new behavior. Changes in brain-cell activity during learning constitute the dependent variable.

Physiological measures provide you with fairly accurate information about such things as the state of arousal within the participant's body. A drawback to this type of measure is that you often must infer psychological states from physiological states. As noted in Chapter 1, whenever you make inferences, you run the risk of drawing incorrect conclusions.

*Self-Report Measures*    A third method commonly used to assess behavior is the **self-report measure**. Self-report measures take a variety of forms. One common form is the *rating scale*. In a study of jury decision making, for example, participants could rate the degree of guilt on a scale ranging from 0 to 10. A popular method in attitude assessment is *Likert scaling*. Participants are provided with statements (e.g., "Nuclear power plants are dangerous") and are asked to indicate the degree to which they agree or disagree with the statement on a 5-point scale ranging from 1 (strongly disagree) to 5 (strongly agree). (See Chapter 9 for more information on rating scales.)

Rating scales are but one method of quantifying a dependent variable. Another method is **Q-sort methodology**, a qualitative measurement technique that involves establishing evaluative categories and sorting items into those categories. The method, pioneered by William Stephenson in 1935, is a technique for exploring subjectivity in a wide variety of situations (Brown, 1996). For instance, if you were interested in having participants evaluate poems representing different literary styles, you could have them read short poems printed on index cards and sort them into seven evaluative categories: dislike very much, dislike somewhat, dislike slightly, neutral, like slightly, like somewhat, and like very much. You would then analyze the data from each participant to determine whether any significant patterns exist (e.g., a general liking for Haiku and a general disliking for blank verse). This can be accomplished with specialized Q-sort correlational and factor analytic techniques (see Brown, 1996, for an example). You can also enter Q-sort data into a standard analysis of variance to explore main effects and interactions among variables.

Self-report measures are highly versatile and relatively easy to use. You can ask participants to evaluate how they are feeling at the present time. In the jury decision example, participants would provide an evaluation of the defendant's guilt immediately after exposure to a trial. In other cases, you may ask participants to reflect on past experiences and evaluate those experiences. This is referred to as a *retrospective verbal report* (Sheridan, 1979). In still other cases, you may ask for a *prospective verbal report* (Sheridan, 1979). Here you ask participants to speculate on how they *would* react in a certain future situation.

Although self-reports are popular and relatively easy to use, they do suffer from reliability and validity problems. When using the retrospective verbal report, you must be aware of the possibility that the measure is somewhat invalid. You cannot really be sure that the participant is giving an accurate assessment of prior behaviors. The participant may be giving you a report or reconstruction of how he or she felt about the behavior you are studying rather than a true account of what happened. The report provided by the participant could be clouded by events that intervened between the original event and the present report. Validity is lowered to the extent that this report is at variance with the actual behavior. Similarly, prospective verbal reports require a participant to speculate about future behavior. In this case, you cannot be sure that what the participant says he or she will do is what he or she actually does. For these reasons, a self-report measure should be used along with another measure whenever possible.

Another problem with self-report measures is that you cannot be sure that participants are telling the truth. Participants have a tendency to project themselves in a socially desirable manner. In a study of racial prejudice using a Likert-scaling technique, for example, participants may not be willing to admit that they have prejudicial attitudes. In fact, research in social psychology has found that self-reports of attitudes (especially on sensitive topics) often do not accurately reflect actual attitudes. You can detect responses that project social desirability by including questions that, if the participant agrees (or disagrees) with them, indicate self-effacement—such as "I have never had a bad thought about a member of a racial minority." If a participant says he or she has *never* had such a thought, he or she is probably responding in a socially desirable way.

*Implicit Measures*    A dependent measure that has become increasingly popular in social psychology to measure attitudes and prejudice is an *implicit measure,* which is not under direct conscious control. For example, a person who is prejudiced may not admit to being prejudiced on a self-report measure. However, the person may show an emotional reaction to a person of a given race. An experiment by Correll, Park, Judd, and Wittenbrink (2002), in which participants playing a video game had to decide instantaneously whether to shoot or not shoot a potentially armed suspect, used an implicit measure of prejudice: the difference in likelihood that a Black or White suspect would be shot.

The most popular measure of implicit attitudes is the **Implicit Association Test (IAT)** developed by Greenwald, McGhee, and Schwartz (1998). In the IAT, you are presented with a set of words or images that you classify into groups (e.g., good/bad; Muslim/other person) as quickly as you can. The theory behind the measure is that you will more quickly associate positive characteristics (e.g., smart and happy) with members of a social group you like than with members of a social group you dislike. Because stimuli are presented rapidly and you are instructed to respond as rapidly as possible, your responses are generally outside your conscious control. Studies using this measure often find that even those who say they are not prejudiced show a preference for one group over another on the IAT. (You can try out the IAT for yourself online at https://implicit.harvard.edu/implicit/.)

## QUESTIONS TO PONDER

1. What are defining characteristics of the four types of dependent variables?

2. What are the advantages and disadvantages of each?

3. What is Q-sort methodology, and when is it used?

4. What do implicit measures reveal?

## CHOOSING WHEN TO OBSERVE

After you have chosen what to observe and how to measure it, you need to decide when you will make your observations. In laboratory research, experimental sessions generally are *when* you would observe. However, even within experimental sessions, you must still decide when observations are to be made.

As with the other aspects of your design, *when* you observe may be determined by established practices. For example, if previous research has proven the adequacy of a time-sampling procedure (you make observations at 10-minute intervals during the session), then making continuous observations may be safely abandoned in favor of the less demanding technique.

Your decision of when to observe may have to take into account the resources you have at your disposal, particularly if the required observations must be made frequently or over long periods of time. For example, in the "freezing" experiment described earlier, an enormous amount of time would be required to code freezing behavior across consecutive 2-second intervals of time during an experimental session that lasted 5 hours, especially if observing a large number of subjects. In such cases, you may be able to adopt a sampling strategy and make occasional observations at randomly chosen intervals during the session. Averaged over a number of subjects, such observations could provide a representative picture of changes across time.

An even better solution than the sampling strategy is to automate the observations. For example, Robert Leaton and George Borszcz of Dartmouth College describe a way to automatically record the freezing behavior of rats (Leaton & Borszcz, 1985). They suspended the observation chamber between stiff springs. A bar magnet affixed to the chamber moved slightly up or down whenever the rat made the slightest move, generating an electric current in a coil of wire through which the magnet passed. When the rat froze, movement ceased and the current disappeared. A computer counted the passing intervals of time and scored each interval for the presence or absence of movement. With the apparatus used by Leaton and Borszcz, it was possible to continuously observe the freezing behavior during sessions of any desired length.

Of course, it is important to show that any device provides a good measure of the variable before you adopt the measure. One good measure of success is the degree to which the new measurements agree with measurements done "the old-fashioned way." In the case of the automated freezing measure, Leaton and Borszcz (1985) demonstrated that the automatic readings correlate highly with personal observations. (Did you recognize this as an example of concurrent validity?) Techniques for automating your experiment are discussed in more detail later in the chapter.

# THE REACTIVE NATURE OF PSYCHOLOGICAL MEASUREMENT

One advantage that physicists and chemists have over psychologists when it comes to conducting research is that the "subjects" of physical and chemical experiments (e.g., balls rolling down inclined planes) pay absolutely no attention to the fact that they are participants in an experiment. They behave as they ordinarily do in nature. The subjects (rats, pigeons) and participants (college students, human adults) of psychological research do pay attention to their status as such and may modify their behavior as a result of their perceptions. This "reactive" nature of subjects and participants must be considered when designing and assessing psychological research. This section describes the kinds of reactions, the situations that sometimes give rise to them, and the things you can do to minimize (or at least assess) their impact on your data. A discussion of research with human participants begins this section, followed by a discussion of research with animal subjects.

## Reactivity in Research with Human Participants

Assume for the moment that you have defined your population of participants and are now ready to acquire your participants and run your experiment. You plan to have volunteers sign up and come to your laboratory for your experiment. What can you expect from these creatures we call human participants?

Understand that the psychological experiment is a social situation. You as the experimenter are in a position of power over the participant. Your participant enters this situation with a social history that may affect how he or she responds to your manipulations. Assuming that the participant is a passive recipient of your experimental manipulations is a mistake. The participant is a living, thinking human being who will generate personal interpretations of your experiment and behave based on these interpretations. In short, the participant is a reactive creature. The behavior you observe in your participants may not be representative of normal behavior because of these reactions.

To help you understand the reactions of research participants to your experiment, imagine you have volunteered for a psychological experiment for the first time. As you sit waiting to be called for the experiment, you imagine what the experiment will be like. Perhaps you have just discussed Milgram's obedience research in your psychology class or saw a documentary about it on television and are wondering if you are going to be given electric shocks or if the researcher is going to be honest with you. You wonder if you are going to be told the experiment is about one thing when it is actually about something else.

At last, the experimenter comes out of the laboratory and says she is ready for you. You are led into a room with a white tile floor, white walls, a stainless steel sink in the corner, some ominous-looking equipment in another corner, and rather harsh fluorescent lighting. The experimenter apologizes for the cold surroundings and says that she is a graduate student and had to settle for a former animal lab to run her master's thesis research. (Do you believe her?) You take a look around the room and muster enough courage to ask whether you are going to be shocked. The experimenter chuckles and assures you that the experiment deals with memory for abstract pictures. She then begins to read you the instructions. At that moment, some workers begin to hammer out in the hall. (Is this part of the experiment?) Again, the experimenter apologizes. She explains that they are installing a new air-conditioning system in that wing of the building. You think you detect a hint of a smile on her face. You don't believe her. You have decided that the experimenter is really trying to test how well you can perform a memory task under distracting conditions. You decide to "show the experimenter" that you can do well despite her obvious attempt to trick you. The experimenter runs you through the experiment. Of course, you try your hardest to get all the items right.

After you have completed the memory test, the experimenter asks you whether you have any questions. You smugly tell her that you saw through her obvious deception and worked even harder to get the items correct. After all, you weren't born yesterday! To this the experimenter incredulously assures you that the noise was not part of the experiment and tells you that she will have to throw out your data.

*Demand Characteristics*    Consider the psychological experiment in the light of this example. As stated, human participants in a psychological experiment do not passively respond to what you may expose them to. On entering the laboratory, your participants probably assesses you and the laboratory (Adair, 1973). Given these assessments, participants begin to draw inferences concerning what the experiment is about and how they will be expected to respond.

Cues inadvertently provided by the researcher or research context concerning the purposes of a study or the behavior expected from participants are referred to as **demand characteristics**. Participants gain information about the experiment from these demand characteristics. Consequently, they may attend to cues that are irrelevant to the experiment at hand. With information obtained from the demand characteristics, the participant begins to formulate hypotheses about the nature of the experiment (such as "The experiment is measuring my ability to perform under adverse conditions") and begins to behave in a manner consistent with those hypotheses. Problems occur when the participant's hypotheses differ from the intended purpose of the experiment; Adair (1973) refers to this class of demand characteristic as *performance cues.*

A second class of demand characteristics centers on the participant. **Role attitude cues** are unintended cues in an experiment that suggest to the participants how they are expected to behave. They may signal participants that a *change* in attitude is needed in order to conform to their new role as research participants (Adair, 1973, p. 24).

*Preexisting* attitudes can also influence how participants respond to the experimental manipulation. Adair lists the following three categories of predisposing attitudes of participants: the cooperative attitude, the defensive or apprehensive attitude, and the negative attitude.

The *cooperative attitude* is characterized by a strong desire to please the experimenter. According to Adair, volunteering for an experiment "seals a contract between the experimenter and the participant, fostering cooperative behavior" (1973, p. 26). Reasons for the cooperative attitude include desires to help science, please the experimenter, perform as well as possible, and be positively evaluated by others.

Several demonstrations of the impact of this positive attitude on the outcome of an experiment have been made. For example, Orne (1962) demonstrated that participants will engage in a boring, repetitive task for hours to please the experimenter. Participants were provided 2,000 sheets of paper (on which were columns of numbers to add) and a stack of index cards (on which instructions were printed). They were instructed to select the first card (which told the participants to add the numbers on the page) and then to select the next card. The next card told the participants to tear the completed sheet into pieces (not fewer than 32) and then select another sheet and add the numbers. The cycle of adding numbers and tearing sheets continued for as long as a participant was willing to go on.

If you were a participant in this experiment, what would you do? You may have said, "I'd do it for a few times and then quit." In fact, quite the opposite happened: Participants continued to do the task for hours. Evidently, participants perceived the test as one of endurance. The participants' cooperative attitude in this example interacted with the demand characteristics to produce some rather bizarre behavior. This "good participant" effect was also shown in an experiment by Goldstein, Rosnow, Goodstadt, and Suls (1972).

Some participants enter the laboratory worried about what will happen to them and have an *apprehensive attitude.* One of us (Bordens) was conducting an experiment on jury decision making, and several participants, on entering the lab, asked if they were going to be shocked. This apprehension may stem from the participants' perception of the experimenter as someone who will be evaluating the participants' behavior (Adair, 1973). The apprehensive attitude also has been shown to affect the research outcome, especially in the areas of compliance and attitude change (Adair, 1973).

Some participants come to the laboratory with a *negative attitude.* Even though most participants are either positive or defensive (Adair, 1973), some participants come to the lab to try to ruin the experiment. This attitude was most prevalent when participants were *required* to serve in experiments. Required participation made many participants angry. The present rules against forced participation may reduce the frequency of negative attitudes. However, you cannot rule out the possibility that some participants will be highly negative toward the experiment and experimenter.

*Events Outside the Laboratory*   In addition to demand characteristics and participants' attitudes, evidence also indicates that events outside the laboratory can affect research. For example, Greene and Loftus (1984) conducted an experiment on jury decision making in which eyewitness testimony was being studied. Around the time that the experiment was conducted and in the same city, a celebrated case of mistaken identification was being unmasked. Knowledge of that case was reflected in the data. Participants tested while the case was in the news were more skeptical of the eyewitness testimony than participants who were tested later.

The lesson from this story is that participants are not passive responders to the experiment. The experiment is a social situation in which the interaction between participant attitudes and the experimental context may affect the outcome of the experiment. As a researcher, you must be aware of demand characteristics and take steps to avoid them—or at least to assess their impact. As with other participant-related problems, demand characteristics, participant attitudes, previous research experience, and exposure to everyday life can affect both internal and external validity.

*Experimenter Bias*    The participant is not the only potential source of bias in the psychological experiment. The experimenter can sometimes unintentionally affect the outcome of the experiment. The case of "Clever Hans" provides a classic example.

More than a century ago, German mathematics teacher Wilhelm von Osten astounded the world by demonstrating that his horse Hans apparently could solve mathematical problems (see Figure 5-4). Hans was given a problem either verbally or in writing, and the horse responded by repeatedly clopping his hoof, stopping only when he had reached the correct answer. Through numerous public demonstrations of his astounding abilities, "Clever Hans" (as the horse came to be known) gained worldwide fame.

Von Osten claimed that Hans' mathematical prowess (not to mention his ability to understand the problems when presented verbally) emerged from a rigorous training program to which von Osten had subjected the horse. Others were skeptical of this claim, and in 1904, a special commission was formed to determine whether von Osten might actually have trained Hans to respond to hidden gestures or other cues that would signal when to stop clopping. However, careful observation by the committee (which included a circus trainer, among others) failed to disclose any such signs being employed. Still, the commission had only ruled out any *intentional* trickery on von Osten's part. Was it possible that Hans had learned to respond to *unintentional* cues unconsciously provided by his questioners?

Not long after the commission finished its work, psychologist Oskar Pfungst conducted a series of experimental tests on Hans designed to answer to this question

Das lesende und rechnende Pferd, mit seinem Lehrer HERRN von OSTEN (Berlin)

**FIGURE 5-4**    Wilhelm von Osten with his horse, Hans.
Source: © Mary Evans Picture Library / Alamy Stock Photo.

definitively (Pfungst, 1911). Pfungst established that Hans was able to give the correct answer only if the *questioner* knew the answer. Furthermore, careful observations of von Osten in action revealed that he was indeed unintentionally cueing the horse when to start clopping and when to stop. Von Osten tended to lean forward slightly after presenting a question, and Hans had learned to start clopping when this happened. Von Osten unconsciously leaned slightly backward when the correct answer was reached, which the horse had learned to use as a signal to stop. These movements were so slight that neither von Osten nor the members of the commission had noticed them. As proof that he had identified the proper cues, Stumpf demonstrated that he could get Hans to start and stop simply by standing in front of Hans and making the same slight motions von Osten had made (Pfungst, 1911). Despite this, von Osten himself remained unconvinced and continued to believe in Hans' cognitive abilities.

You might think that researchers today would not be taken in by the "Clever Hans" phenomenon, but you would be wrong. There is a procedure known as *facilitated communication* being touted as a way to allow severely impaired persons to communicate with others in ways and at levels previously believed to be impossible. The procedure involves a "facilitator" physically helping an impaired person communicate by supporting the impaired person's hand while the impaired person supposedly guides his or her finger to different symbols on a board or screen. But is facilitated communication a real phenomenon or another example of the Clever Hans phenomenon? Let's find out.

Barbara Montee, Raymond Miltenberger, and David Wittrock (1995) conducted an experiment to test the validity of facilitated communication. Seven client–facilitator dyads participated in this experiment. The experiment was conducted in the client–facilitator pairs' normal setting (e.g., day-care center) at the usual time of day. The pairs completed several facilitated communication tasks involving describing an activity or naming a picture. The independent variable was the information provided to the facilitators prior to the facilitated communication session. In one condition (the known condition), the facilitator was informed about the activity that the client had engaged in or the picture that the client had been shown. In another condition (the unknown condition), the facilitator was not informed about the activity or picture. In the final condition (the false feedback condition), the facilitator was given incorrect information about the activity or picture. The dependent variable was whether, using facilitated communication, the client correctly described the activity or named the picture.

The results of this experiment were rather dramatic and are shown in Table 5-1. As you can see, the client's ability to describe the activity or name the picture was almost totally dependent upon whether the facilitator had accurate information about the nature of the activity or picture. Just as Hans could not solve his math problems when von Osten did not know the answer, so the clients in this experiment could not respond correctly unless the facilitators knew the answers.

In both the Clever Hans and facilitated communication situations, there was a common problem known as **experimenter bias** (Rosenthal, 1976). Experimenter bias creeps in when the behavior of the experimenter influences the results of the experiment. This influence serves to confound the effect of your independent

**TABLE 5-1    Mean Number of Correct Responses Made in the Montee, Miltenberger, and Wittrock (1995) Experiment on Facilitated Communication**

| | INFORMATION CONDITION | | |
| --- | --- | --- | --- |
| *TASK* | *Known* | *Unknown* | *False* |
| Picture naming | 75 | 0 | 1.8 |
| Activity identification | 87 | 0 | 0 |

variable, making it impossible to determine which of the two was responsible for any observed differences in performance on the dependent measure. Experimenter bias flows from at least two sources: expectancy effects and treating various experimental groups differently, so as to produce results consistent with the preexperimental hypotheses.

**Expectancy effects** emerge when a researcher's preconceived ideas about how participants should behave are subtly communicated to subjects and, in turn, affect the participants' behavior. Rosenthal (1976) reports a perception experiment in which the independent variable was the information provided to students acting as experimenters. Some students were told that, according to previous ratings, their participants should perform well. Others were told that the participants would probably perform poorly. The student experimenters also were told they would be paid twice as much if the results confirmed the prior expectations. Rosenthal reports that establishing the expectancy led to different behavior on the part of the participants in the two experimental groups. Rosenthal points out that such expectancy effects may be a problem in not only experimental research but also survey research and clinical studies. In demonstrations of facilitated communication, facilitators expected their severely impaired clients to communicate by spelling out words using the supported hand, but unwittingly guided their clients' hands to spell out their own ideas.

A second source of experimenter bias occurs when the experimenter unwittingly treats participants in the different experimental groups in such a way as to confirm the hypothesis being tested. For example, the experimenter might speak more distinctly when presenting verbal stimuli to a group that is expected to perform best on a test of verbal memory.

These two sources of experimenter bias threaten both internal and external validity. If your behavior becomes a source of systematic bias or error, then you cannot be sure that the independent variable caused the observed changes in the dependent variable. External validity is threatened because the data obtained may be idiosyncratic to your particular influence.

Because experimenter bias can pose such a serious threat to internal and external validity, you must take steps to reduce the bias. You can do this by using a *blind technique*. In the **single-blind technique**, the experimenter does not know which treatment a subject has been assigned to. For example, in an experiment on the effect of children watching violent television on aggression, children could be randomly assigned to watch either violent cartoons or nonviolent cartoons. The measure of aggression could be the number of aggressive acts a child engages in during free play on the playground. In a single-blind experiment, the observers watching the children do not know the condition to which the children were assigned.

In the **double-blind technique**, neither the experimenter nor the participants know at the time of testing which treatments the participants are receiving. If you were interested in testing the effects of a particular drug on learning abilities, for example, you would give some participants the active drug and some a placebo (perhaps an injection of saline solution). The participants would not know which treatment was being administered, thus reducing the possibility that the participants' expectations about the drug would affect the results. Furthermore, you would have an assistant mix the drugs and label them arbitrarily with some code, such as "A" and "B." As the experimenter, you would not be told which was the active drug and which was the placebo until after the experiment was completed and the data were analyzed. Thus, neither you nor the participant would know at the time of testing which treatment the participant was receiving. Neither your expectations nor the participants' could systematically bias the results.

Another method for reducing experimenter bias is to *automate* the experiment as much as possible. In a memory experiment, you could present your stimulus items and time their presentations accurately using a personal computer. The interval between stimulus presentations would be held constant, avoiding the possibility that you might present the stimuli more rapidly to one group than to the other. You also could automate the instructions by using a recorded version of the instructions. All participants would thus be exposed to the same instructions. (Automation is more fully discussed later in this chapter.)

Other potential sources of experimenter bias include the sex, personality, and previous experience of the experimenter. It is beyond the scope of this book to explore all the potential experimenter effects. See *Experimenter Effects in Behavioral Research* (Rosenthal, 1976) for a complete treatment of this topic.

## Reactivity in Research with Animal Subjects

The section on using human participants in research pointed out that the behavior of participants can be affected by the behavior of the experimenter and by demand characteristics. Similar effects can be found with animal subjects. For example, Rosenthal (1976) reports research in which experimenter expectancy influenced the rate at which animals learned to navigate a maze. Participants serving as experimenters were told that the rats they would be teaching to run a maze were either very bright (would learn the maze quickly with few errors) or very dull (would have trouble learning the maze). The animals were actually assigned at random to the experimenters. Rosenthal found that the animals in the "bright" condition learned more quickly than the animals in the "dull" condition. The differing expectations of the student experimenters led them to treat their rats differently, and these differences in treatment led to changes in the behaviors of the rats.

Use blind techniques to avoid these and other sources of experimenter bias in animal research. For example, in a study in which a drug is to be administered, the person making the observations of the animal's behavior should not know which subjects received the drug and which received the placebo.

Remember that demand characteristics are cues that subjects use to guide behavior within an experiment. Although animals will not be sensitive to demand characteristics in the same way that human participants are, some features of your experiment may inadvertently affect your subject's behavior. For instance, you may be interested in how a rat's learning capacity is affected by receiving electric shocks just before the opportunity to work for food. If you do not clean the experimental chamber thoroughly after each animal is tested, the animals may respond to the odor cues from the previous animal. These odor cues may affect the current animal's behavior differently, depending on whether or not the previous animal had received a shock. You must remember that, much like the human participant, the animal subject is an active processor of information. Your animals sense cues that are not intended to be a part of the experiment and may behave accordingly. Ultimately, the internal validity of your experiment may be threatened by the effects of these cues.

## QUESTIONS TO PONDER

1. How can the act of measurement affect your subjects' responses?
2. What are role attitude cues, and how might they affect the results of your study?
3. What are demand characteristics, and how can they affect the results of your study?
4. What is experimenter bias, and how can it affect the results of your study?
5. What measures can be taken to deal with reactivity in research?

## AUTOMATING YOUR EXPERIMENTS

We have seen how psychological research presents many opportunities for outside, uncontrolled variables to affect your results. Fortunately, you can eliminate or reduce the effects of these variables by automating your studies. With the advent of relatively inexpensive personal computers has come an explosion in the number of studies that are automated. Automation involves having a computer present the various levels of your independent variables and/or collect the data on your dependent variables. Computer automation is available for both nonexperimental (e.g., questionnaires and surveys) and experimental research.

One advantage of automation is that you can eliminate some sources of experimenter bias. For example, you can have all instructions and stimuli presented by a computer. This eliminates the human factor from these elements of your research and, consequently, any biasing effects that could result from experimenters treating participants in different conditions differently. In addition, automation can save time. Automated equipment allows you to run subjects even if you cannot be present. This is most useful in animal research in which subjects can be left unattended in the testing apparatus. In this case, you simply start the testing program and then return at the end of the session to record the data and return the subjects to their home cages.

Automation has other advantages as well. Automated measurements tend to be more accurate and less variable because they are not subject to the vagaries of human judgment. An automated system is not likely to miss an important event because it was daydreaming at the moment or distracted by an aching back; nor is such a system likely to misperceive what actually happened because of expectations about what will happen (eliminating this source of experimenter bias).

Conversely, automation can cause you to miss important details. The changes in behavior shown by the nonfreezing decorticate rats might not have been detected had the automated freezing measure of Leaton and Borszcz (1985) been in use. Even when all your measurements are automated, you should observe your subjects occasionally. What you learn from these observations may provide fruitful explanations for changes detected by your automated variables and may give you new ideas to test.

If you use computers to conduct your research, remember that the computer performs many of the more tedious tasks involved in your research quickly and accurately but always does what you tell it to do (even if you make a mistake). Your automated experiment will only be as good as your program. Whether you use commercially available software or programs that you write yourself, you must be intimately familiar with the commercial software or with the computer language that you will be using and know how to interface your computer with your equipment.

## DETECTING AND CORRECTING PROBLEMS

No matter how carefully you plan your study, problems almost inevitably crop up when you begin to execute it. Two methods you can use to minimize these problems and ensure the usefulness of the data you collect are conducting a pilot study and adding manipulation checks.

### Conducting a Pilot Study

A **pilot study** is a small-scale version of a study used to establish procedures, materials, and parameters to be used in the full study. Frequently, it is a study that began life as a serious piece of research but went wrong somewhere along the way. The decorticate rat study became a pilot study for this reason. However, many pilot studies are designed from the ground up as pilot studies, intended to provide useful information that can be used when the "real" study gets under way.

Pilot studies can save tremendous amounts of time and money if done properly. Perhaps you intend to conduct a large study involving several hundred participants in order to determine which of two methods of teaching works best in introductory psychology. As part of the study, you intend to hand out a large questionnaire to the students in several introductory psychology classes. Conducting a small pilot study (in which you hand out the questionnaire to students in only a couple of classes) may turn up inadequacies in your formulation of questions, inadequacies that lead to confusion or misinterpretation. Finding these problems *before* you train instructors in the two teaching methods, have them teach a full term, and then collect the questionnaires from 2,000 students is certainly preferable to finding the problems afterward.

Pilot studies can help you clarify instructions, determine appropriate levels of independent variables (to avoid range effects), determine the reliability and validity of your observational methods, and work the bugs out of your procedures. They also can give you practice in conducting your study so that you make fewer mistakes when you "do it for real." For these reasons, pilot studies are often valuable.

You should also be aware of some negative aspects of pilot studies. Pilot studies require time to conduct and may entail some expenditure of supplies. Where animals are involved, their use for pilot work may be questioned by the local animal care and use committee (particularly if the procedures involve surgery, stressful stimulation, or deprivation). In these cases, you may want to use the best available information to determine procedures and to try to get it right the first time around. Then only if you guess wrong will the study become a pilot study.

## Adding Manipulation Checks

In addition to the dependent measures of the behavior under study, you should include manipulation checks. A **manipulation check** simply tests whether or not your independent variables had the intended effects on your participants. They allow you to determine if the participants in your study perceived your experiment in the manner in which you intended. For example, if you were investigating the impact of a person's attractiveness on how his or her work is evaluated, you might have participants evaluate an essay attributed to either an attractive or unattractive author. This could be done by attaching a photograph of an attractive or unattractive person to an author profile accompanying the essay. As a manipulation check, you could have participants rate the attractiveness of the author on a rating scale.

Manipulation checks also provide you with information that may be useful later when interpreting your data. If your experiment yielded results you did not expect, it may be that participants interpreted your independent variable differently from the way you thought they would. Without manipulation checks, you may not be able to properly interpret surprising effects. Manipulation checks may permit you to determine why an independent variable failed to produce an effect. For example, they may show that you did not effectively manipulate your independent variable.

A set of measures closely related to manipulation checks are those asking participants to report their perceptions of the entire experiment. Factors to be evaluated might include their perceptions of the experimenter, what they believed to be the true purpose of the experiment, the impact of any deception, and any other factors you think are important. Like manipulation checks, these measures help you interpret your results and establish the generality of your data. If you find that participants perceived your experiment as you intended, you are in a better position to argue that your results are valid and perhaps apply beyond the laboratory.

## QUESTIONS TO PONDER

1. What is a pilot study, and why should you conduct one?
2. What are manipulation checks, and why should you include them in your study?

## SUMMARY

In contrast to casual, everyday observations, scientific observations are systematic. Systematic observation involves making decisions about what, how, and when to make observations. Observations of behavior are made under controlled conditions using operational definitions of the variables of interest.

When choosing variables for your study, you should be guided in your choice by research tradition in the area of study, theory, the availability of new techniques or measures, and the limits imposed by the equipment available to you. In addition, you need to be concerned with the characteristics of the measure, including its reliability, its validity, and the level of measurement it represents. A measure is reliable to the extent that repeated measurements of the same quantity yield similar values. For measures of physical variables, reliability is indexed by the precision of the measure, and for population estimates, by the margin of error. The reliability of the judgments of multiple observers is indexed by a statistical measure of interrater reliability. The reliability of psychological tests can be determined in a variety of ways, yielding test–retest, parallel-forms, or split-half reliabilities. A measure is accurate if the numbers it yields agree with a known standard. Accuracy is not a characteristic of most psychological measures because there are no agreed-upon standards for them. A measure is valid to the extent that it measures what it is intended to measure. Several types of validity assessment exist for psychological tests, including face validity, content validity, construct validity, and criterion-related validity. The latter takes two forms, called concurrent validity and predictive validity.

One aspect of systematic observation is developing dependent measures. Your data can be scaled along one of four scales of measurement: nominal, ordinal, interval, and ratio. Nominal and ordinal scales provide less information than do interval and ratio scales, so use an interval or ratio scale whenever possible. You cannot use an interval or ratio scale in all cases because some research questions demand that a nominal or ordinal scale be used. Your choice of measurement scale should be guided by the needs of your research question. When a less informational scale must be used to preserve ecological validity, you can preserve information by creating a composite scale from a nominal and interval scale. This will help you to "recover" information not yielded by a nominal scale.

Beyond choosing a scale of measurement, you must also decide how to design and collect your dependent measures. Your measures must be appropriate for your subject population. Consequently, you may have to be creative when you design your measures. You may count number of responses, which is a ratio scale. You can use interval scales in a variety of research applications. You must decide how to format these scales, how to present them to subjects, and how to develop clear and concise instructions for their uses.

In some research, your measure of behavior may be limited by range effects. That is, there may be an upper and lower limit imposed on your measure by the behavior of interest. For example, rats can run just so fast in a maze. Range effects become a problem when the behavior quickly reaches its upper or lower limit. In such cases, you may not detect a difference between two groups because of ceiling or floor effects. It is a good idea to conduct pilot studies to test your measures before investing the time and energy in your study. During the pilot study, you may find that your measures need to be modified.

There are four types of dependent variables you can use in your research: behavioral measures, physiological measures, self-report measures, and implicit measures. Behavioral measures include direct measures of behavior such as number of responses made or the number of errors made. Physiological measures involve measuring some biological change (e.g., heart rate, respiration rate, or brain activity). Physiological measures can be noninvasive (e.g., a PET scan) or invasive (e.g., implanting an electrode in a rat's brain). Self-report measures have participants report on their own behavior and can be prospective (speculate on future behavior) or retrospective (report on past behavior). One special form of a self-report method is the Q-sort method in which participants classify stimuli into categories. Implicit measures measure unconscious reactions to stimuli and are used to tap into attitudes that individuals may not admit to overtly.

Observation in psychological research differs from observation in the physical sciences because the psychologist deals with living organisms. The participants in an experiment are reactive; they may respond to more in the experimental situation than the manipulated variables. Participants bring to the experiment unique histories and attitudes that may affect the outcome of your experiment.

Demand characteristics can be a problem in behavioral research. Participants pick up on cues from the experimenter and research context. These cues may affect the participant's behavior. Furthermore, the experimenter must be careful not to inadvertently affect the participants. Experimenter effects can be avoided by using blind techniques or automating your experiment or both. Automation can be done by recording instructions and by applying computers to control your experiment.

Before conducting a study, it is a good idea to do a pilot study, which is a small-scale version of your study used to test the effectiveness of your materials, procedures, and other parameters. You can identify and correct problems before investing time and effort in your main study. It is also a good idea to include manipulation checks. These are measures specifically designed to determine how participants perceived the variables of your study. This information can help you to interpret your results and identify problems that may have emerged in your study.

## KEY TERMS

| | |
|---|---|
| reliability | split-half reliability |
| test–retest reliability | accuracy |
| parallel-forms reliability | validity |

face validity

content validity

criterion-related validity

concurrent validity

predictive validity

construct validity

nominal scale

ordinal scale

interval scale

ratio scale

range effects

behavioral measure

physiological measure

self-report measure

Q-sort methodology

Implicit Association Test (IAT)

demand characteristics

role attitude cues

experimenter bias

expectancy effects

single-blind technique

double-blind technique

pilot study

manipulation check

# 6

## *CHAPTER*

# Choosing and Using Research Subjects

So far in the research process, you have made several important decisions. You have decided on a topic for your research; have taken a broad idea and honed it into a tight, testable research hypothesis. You also have made some important decisions about whether to conduct a correlational or experimental study and how to measure or manipulate your variables. Your next decision involves who will participate in your research study.

A number of important questions must be addressed when choosing subjects for psychological research. Should you use human participants or animal subjects?[1] How will you acquire your sample? What ethical guidelines must you follow when using human participants or animal subjects (see Chapter 7)? If you choose human participants, what is your sample going to look like (age, race, gender, ethnicity, etc.)? If you choose to use animals, where will you get them? What are the implications of choosing one species or strain of a species over another? We explore these and other questions in this chapter. The principles discussed in this chapter apply equally to experimental and nonexperimental research. However, there are additional subject-related issues to consider if your study uses survey methodology. We discuss these issues in Chapter 9, along with other issues concerning survey research methodology.

## GENERAL CONSIDERATIONS

As we have already noted, choosing and using subjects in psychological research requires you to confront several important questions and make several important decisions. The nature of your research may

---

[1] When discussing those who serve in psychological research, we refer to humans as *participants* and to animals as *subjects*. We also use the term *subjects* when the discussion could apply to either humans or nonhumans (e.g., between-subjects design). The American Psychological Association (APA, 2001) adopted these conventions, so we will follow them throughout this book in order to be consistent with APA usage.

drive some of those decisions. For example, if you are experimentally investigating the effects of brain lesions on learning abilities, you must use animal subjects. If you are interested in determining the best persuasion technique to get people to quit smoking, you must use human participants. However, you may investigate many research areas using either animals or humans (such as operant conditioning, memory, or perception). In these cases, your choice of animals versus humans may depend on the needs of your particular experiment. However, regardless of whether you choose humans or animals, you must consider issues such as ethics, how the subjects will react to your experimental procedure, and the degree of generality of your results.

## Populations and Samples

Imagine you are interested in investigating the effect of a new computer-based teaching technique on how well eighth-graders learn mathematics. Would it be feasible to include *every* eighth-grader in the world in your experiment? Obviously not, but what is the alternative? You may have thought to yourself, "I will have to choose *some* eighth-graders for the experiment." If this is what you thought, you are considering an important distinction in research methodology: populations versus samples.

In the hypothetical experiment, you could not hope to include all eighth-graders. "All eighth-graders" constitutes the **population** under study. Because it is usually not possible to study an entire population, you must be content to study a sample of that population. A **sample** is a small subgroup chosen from the larger population. Figure 6-1 illustrates the relationship between populations and samples.

Often, researchers find it necessary to define a *subpopulation* for study. In your imaginary study, cost or other factors may limit you to studying a certain region of the country. Your subpopulation might consist of eighth-graders from a particular city, town, or district. Furthermore, you might limit yourself to studying certain eighth-grade classes (especially if the school district is too large to allow you to study every class). In this case, you are further dividing your subpopulation. In effect, rather than studying an entire population, you are studying only a small segment of that population.

You can define a population in many ways. For example, if you were interested in how prejudiced attitudes develop in young children, you could define the population as those children enrolled in day-care centers and early elementary school grades. If you were interested in jury decision making, you could define the population as registered voters who are eligible for jury duty. In any case, you may need to limit the nature of the subject population and sample because of special needs of the research.

## QUESTIONS TO PONDER

1. How does the nature of your research affect whether you use human participants or animal subjects in your research?
2. What is the difference between a population and a sample?

Population

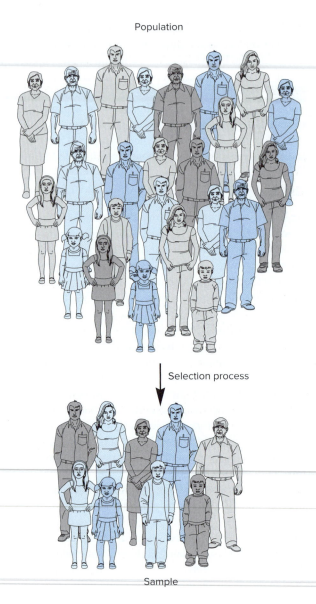

Selection process

Sample

**FIGURE 6-1**    Relationship between population and sample. A sample is a subset of individuals selected from a larger population.

## Sampling and Generalization

An important goal of many research studies is to apply the results, based on a sample of individuals, to the larger population from which the individuals were drawn. You do not want the results from your study of the new teaching techniques to apply only to those eighth-graders who participated in the study. Rather, you want your results to apply to all eighth-graders. **Generalization** is the ability to apply findings from a sample to a larger population. In Chapter 4, we noted that studies whose findings can be applied across a variety of research settings and subject populations possess a high degree of *external validity*. Thus, the ability to generalize findings to a larger population contributes to the external validity of a study.

If the results of a study are to generalize to the intended population, you must be careful when you select your sample. The optimal procedure is to identify the population and then draw a **random sample** of individuals from that population. In a random sample, every person in the population has an equal chance of being chosen for the study. (Chapter 9 on using survey research explores the various methods that you can use to acquire a random sample.) A true random sample allows for the highest level of generality from research to real life.

## Nonrandom Sampling

Unfortunately, in psychological research we rarely meet the ideal of having a random sample from the population. In practice, most psychological studies use a **nonrandom sample**, usually of individuals from highly specialized subpopulation such as college students. In fact, McNemar (1946) characterized psychology as the "science of college sophomores." Higbee, Millard, and Folkman (1982) reported that a majority of studies in social psychology published in the 1970s relied on college students for participants. This may have been true for a long time in psychology. However, the landscape may be changing.

We conducted a content analysis of a random sample of articles from the 2006 (volume 90, five articles per issue) volume of the *Journal of Personality and Social Psychology* (the premier journal in social psychology). The analysis found that 80% of the studies reported using college students exclusively. A similar analysis of articles from 2015 (volume 108) revealed that only 46.3% were using college students nearly a decade later. Why the change?

Our content analysis revealed that a number of studies using noncollege participants recruited using a crowdsourcing website known as *Amazon Mechanical Turk* (AMT). In 2010, social science researchers started using the service to recruit participants for research. The workers on AMT perform a variety of tasks, including participation in research, for minimal compensation (Paolacci & Chandler, 2014). They hail from more than 190 countries, although the greatest numbers come from the United States and India.

AMT provides an easily accessed pool of research participants from a diverse range of backgrounds and demographics. This easy access has allowed researchers to move from relying heavily on college students to using a more diverse pool of participants. However, workers on AMT are not representative of the general population. For example, they are more educated, younger, less often employed, and more politically liberal than the general population (Paolacci & Chandler, 2014). And, as noted earlier, they are paid for participation (as are some other participants in research). Do these differences translate into different outcomes for research? Bartneck, Duenser, Moltchanova, and Zawieska (2015) compared the results of studies recruiting participants from AMT, other online sources, and college subject pools. Participants completed a questionnaire on which they evaluated different facial expressions of emotion shown on LEGO figurines. Bartneck et al. found that the AMT participants differed from the other methods (which did not differ) on around 15% to 20% of the facial evaluations. Because the differences were small, Bartneck et al. suggested that the differences had little practical significance. In another study, AMT was found not to differ from other recruitment techniques on a psycholinguistic task (Enochson & Culbertson, 2015). Additionally, a number (but not all) of classic psychological effects (e.g., the Stroop effect, visual perception) have been successfully replicated using online methods using AMT recruitment (Crump, McDonnell, & Gureckis, 2013).

Like other recruitment methods, AMT has drawbacks. For example, nothing prevents AMT workers from participating in a number of highly similar experiments. Such experiences may affect how they perform in your study (Chandler, Mueller, & Paolacci, 2014). Despite such drawbacks, it appears that AMT can provide a viable alternative to college campus recruitment. The fact that the *Journal of Personality and Social Psychology* accepts research using AMT bodes well for the tool.

Using college students as participants in psychological research is likely to remain popular, even with the availability of AMT. Psychological research uses college students because most psychological research is conducted by college professors. For them, college students form a readily available pool of potential research participants. In fact, many psychology departments set up a subject pool, usually comprising introductory psychology students, to provide participants for psychological studies. They are an easily tapped captive pool of individuals.

Sampling from a relatively small subject pool is much easier than drawing a random sample from the general population and greatly reduces the time and financial costs of doing research. However, using such a nonrandom sample may reduce the external validity of your results. Participants making up a convenience sample differ from the general population in a number of ways (such as in age or socioeconomic status) that may limit your ability to apply your results to the larger population beyond college.

## QUESTIONS TO PONDER

1. What is random sampling, and how does it relate to generality of findings?

2. What is nonrandom sampling, and what problems does it pose for research?

*Nonrandom Sampling and Internet Research*    Studies being conducted on the Internet provide further examples of nonrandom sampling. Participants are volunteers who choose whether to fill out online questionnaires or participate in experiments posted to the web. These participants are individuals who know how to use computers, have access to them, know enough about the Internet to find the studies, and volunteer to participate in them. These characteristics may not be true of many in the general population. However, proponents of Internet-based research argue that similar problems exist when using traditional subject pools, such as those from which college students are drawn. Proponents of Internet research suggest that proper participant recruitment techniques (using postings to various news groups, discussion groups, list servers, and websites) are analogous to recruiting participants from a traditional subject pool. Proponents argue that proper recruitment for Internet studies may lead to a broader sample of participants geographically and demographically than do traditional subject pools.

So where do things stand on the Internet sampling issue? John Krantz and Reeshad Dalal (2000) suggest that there are two ways to establish the validity of web-based research. First, you can compare results from studies (surveys and experiments) done on the web to results from parallel studies done using more traditional methods. Second, you can evaluate the results from web-based research to see if they conform to theoretical predictions. Krantz and Dalal conclude that, for the most part, research (survey and experimental studies) conducted via the Internet produces results that are highly similar to those from research done with more conventional methods.

The limited amount of research comparing traditional surveys and web surveys bears this out (Hamby, Sugarman, & Boney-McCoy, 2006; Huang, 2005; Riva, Teruzzi, & Anolli, 2003). For example, Riva et al. compared the results from an attitude survey administered via the Internet with those from the same survey administered using a paper-and-pencil format. They found no major differences between the two methods. They conclude that, given careful attention to sampling, reliability, and validity issues, the Internet can produce results that mirror those from traditional surveys.

A study by Bethell, Fiorillo, Lansky, Hendryx, and Knickman (2004) confirms this. Bethell et al. administered a questionnaire on quality of health care either online or by telephone. The data obtained from the telephone and online surveys were compared to each other and to general population data. Bethell et al. found that the sample for the online survey matched closely the sample of the general population. There was some overrepresentation of respondents in the 45 to 64 age group and some underrepresentation in the 18 to 24 age group. Both the telephone and online surveys underrepresented non-White populations, respondents with less than a high school education, and respondents with annual incomes above $75,000. Despite these differences, Bethell et al. conclude that the telephone and online samples were representative of the general population. Furthermore, the results obtained from the online survey did not differ significantly from those obtained from existing surveys on the U.S. health care system.

Although there are striking parallels between the results of Internet and non-Internet studies, this does not mean that all web-based findings match findings using other methods (Krantz & Dalal, 2000). For example, Michael Link and Ali Mokdad (2005) compared mail, telephone, and web-survey methods. The survey measured participants' level of alcohol consumption. They found that the web survey generated a lower response rate (15.4%) than the telephone survey (40.1%) or mail survey (43.6%). They also found that web-survey respondents in all demographic categories were more likely to report heavy drinking (five or more drinks in a day) than telephone respondents. Link and Mokdad suggest that the higher reported rates of heavy drinking among web respondents may be due to nonresponse bias.

Clearly, more research is needed on this issue. Overall, the research in this area suggests that the Internet provides a powerful tool for researchers that may have fewer liabilities than critics allege. However, the method may be more problematic when you are asking about sensitive issues such as alcohol consumption.

*Nonrandom Sampling and Animal Subjects*    Nonrandom sampling is not restricted to research using human participants. In fact, it is almost standard procedure for research using animal subjects. Laboratory animals are usually ordered for a given study from a single supplier and typically consist of animals of the same species, strain, sex, and age (indeed, many of them may be littermates). A group of 30 female Sprague–Dawley laboratory rats, all 90 days old and obtained from the same supplier, can hardly be considered a random sample of all female laboratory rats, let alone rats in general. In some cases, even supposedly minor differences in strain have been found to alter the results. For example, Helmstetter and Fanselow (1987) showed that the opiate blocker naloxone was effective in suppressing conditioned analgesia (reduced sensitivity to pain) under certain conditions in the Long–Evans strain of laboratory rat but not in the Sprague–Dawley strain. Those who believed that their research on the effects of this drug would generalize from the strain of rat they had selected for testing to laboratory rats in general turned out to be mistaken. However, this problem may be mitigated somewhat if different laboratories attempt to follow up on initial reports but employ animals of different species, strain, sex, or age, or even similar animals from a different supplier. If the original findings are restricted to a given species, strain, sex, age, or supplier, they will fail to replicate in laboratories in which these factors differ. In fact, Helmstetter and Fanselow's study was prompted by such a replication failure.

## Is Random Sampling Always Necessary?

The highest level of generality will flow from research using a true random sample. However, is it necessary for all kinds of research to have high levels of generality (external validity)? As we noted in Chapter 4, perhaps not. Random sampling is especially necessary when you want to apply your findings directly to a population (Mook, 1983; Stanovich, 1986). Political polls, for example, have such a requirement. Pollsters want to predict accurately the percentage of voters who will vote for candidate A or B. That is, pollsters try to predict a specific behavior (e.g., voting) in a specific set of circumstances (Stanovich, 1986). Mook (1983), however, suggests that most research in psychology does not have a specific-to-specific application. In fact, the goal of most psychological research is to predict from the general level (e.g., a theory) to the specific (specific behavior; Stanovich, 1986). Most findings from psychological research are applied *indirectly* through theories and models (Stanovich, 1986). According to Stanovich, many applications of psychological research operate indirectly through the impact of their theories, thus making random samples less of a concern.

Factors other than the nature of the sample that affect the generality of your results include the realism of the research setting and the way in which you manipulate the independent variables. Other sampling considerations most relevant to nonexperimental research are discussed in Chapters 8 and 9.

## QUESTIONS TO PONDER

1. How does nonrandom sampling apply to Internet research?
2. What does research tell us about sampling issues relating to Internet research?
3. How does nonrandom sampling apply to animal research?
4. In what types of research might random sampling be less important?

## ACQUIRING HUMAN PARTICIPANTS FOR RESEARCH

Whether your research is experimental or nonexperimental, you must consider three factors when acquiring participants for your research: You must consider (1) the setting in which your research will take place, (2) any special needs of your particular research, and (3) any institutional, departmental, and ethical policies and guidelines governing the use of participants in research.

### The Research Setting

Chapter 4 distinguished between laboratory and field research. In field research, you conduct your research in the participant's natural environment, whereas in laboratory research you bring your participants into a laboratory environment of your creation. Acquiring participants for laboratory research differs from acquiring them for field research.

*Laboratory Research*    If you choose to conduct your research in a laboratory setting, there are two principal ways of acquiring participants. First, you can solicit volunteers from whatever participant population is available. For example, you could recruit participants from your university library or lounge area. These participants would serve on a voluntary basis. (As we indicate later in this chapter, voluntary participation has both positive and negative consequences for your research.) Second, you can use a subject pool if one exists. Individuals in the subject pool may be required to participate in a certain number of studies (with an alternative to the research option provided). If you adopt this strategy, you must make sure that your recruitment procedures do not coerce folks into participating. Even when using a subject pool, participation in a research study must be voluntary.

*Field Research*    Field research requires you to select your participants while they are in their natural environment. How you acquire your participants for field research depends on the nature of your study. For example, if you are conducting a survey, you would use one of the survey sampling techniques discussed in Chapter 9 to acquire a sample of participants. Essentially, these techniques involve selecting a participant from a population, contacting that person, and having him or her complete your questionnaire.

If you were running a field experiment, you could use one of two methods for acquiring participants, again depending on the nature and needs of your study. Some field experiments are actually carried out much like laboratory experiments except that you take your "show" (equipment, assistants, measuring devices, etc.) on the road and set up in the participant's natural environment. This is what Sheina Orbell and Martin Hagger (2006) did in a field experiment investigating how adults respond to persuasive messages about the effects of diabetes.

Participants were recruited by having researchers do home visits in a particular town. Participants were invited to take part in a study of their attitudes about taking part in a diabetes screening program and were asked to complete a questionnaire about participation in such a program. In this experiment, participants were randomly assigned to one of two versions of a persuasive appeal. One paragraph of the instructions for the questionnaire pointed out the positive and negative consequences of participating in the screening program. The main independent variable was the "time frame" for the positive and negative aspects of participation. In one condition, the positive aspects were said to be long term (participating in screening gives people peace of mind for years to come) and the negative consequences short term (undergoing unpleasant procedures immediately). In the other condition, the positive consequences were cast as short term ("getting immediate peace of mind" about their health) and the negative consequences in the long term (worrying about taking medicine for their whole lives).

In this type of field experiment, the researchers maintain about as much control over participant selection and assignment as they would if the experiment were conducted in the laboratory. However, the researchers are at the mercy of whoever happens to be at home on any given day.

In another type of field experiment, you set up a situation and wait for participants to happen along. A field experiment reported by Michael Shohat and Jochen Musch (2003) conducted in Germany illustrates this strategy. Shohat and Musch were interested in studying ethnic discrimination. They set up auctions on eBay to sell DVDs, and manipulated the ethnicity of the seller. On one eBay listing, the seller had a Turkish username. On another, the seller had a German username. The researchers recorded the number of hits on each listing as well as the average price paid for the DVDs. In this kind of field experiment, you have less control over who participates in your research. Whoever happens to sign in to eBay at a particular time and search for DVDs would be potential participants.

## The Needs of Your Research

Special needs of your research may affect how you acquire participants. In some cases, you may have to screen potential participants for certain characteristics (such as gender, age, or personality characteristics). For example, in a jury study, you might screen participants for their level of authoritarianism and include only authoritarians in your research. Bear in mind that doing this affects the external validity of your findings. The results you obtain with participants who score high in authoritarianism may not apply to those who show lower levels of authoritarianism.

As another example, you may need children of certain ages for a developmental study of intelligence. Acquiring a sample of children for your research is a bit more involved than acquiring a sample of adults. You must obtain permission from the child's parent or guardian, as well as from the child him- or herself. In practice, some parents may not want their children to participate. This again raises issues of external validity. Your sample of children of parents who agree to allow participation may differ from the general population of children.

## Institutional Policies and Ethical Guidelines

All psychological research involving human participants must comply with the ethical guidelines set out by the American Psychological Association (APA) and with federal and state laws regulating such research. (We discuss these requirements in the next chapter.) Institutions have their own rules concerning how human participants can be recruited and used in research. Although these rules must conform to relevant ethical codes and laws, there is considerable latitude when it comes to setting up subject pools. During the planning stages of your research, you should familiarize yourself with the federal and state laws concerning research using human participants, as well as the policies of the institution in which you are conducting your research. You may even have to take an online course before you are allowed to use human participants or animal subjects in your research.

## QUESTIONS TO PONDER

1. How does the setting for your research affect participant recruitment?
2. How do the needs of your research influence participant recruitment?
3. How do institutional policies and ethical considerations affect participant recruitment?

## VOLUNTARY PARTICIPATION AND VALIDITY

Participants must voluntarily agree to be in your research. This raises an important question: Are volunteer participants representative of the general population? Individuals who choose to participate in research undoubtedly differ those who do not. This difference is known as **volunteer bias**. In this section we identify factors that affect the decision to volunteer and then discuss how volunteer bias may affect internal and external validity.

### Factors That Affect the Decision to Volunteer

Two categories of factors affect a prospective participant's decision to volunteer: characteristics of the participant and situational factors. We explore each of these next.

*Participant-Related Characteristics*    Rosenthal and Rosnow (1975) provide the most comprehensive study of the characteristics of the volunteer subject in their book *The Volunteer Subject.* Table 6-1 lists several characteristics that distinguish volunteers from nonvolunteers.

Volunteer bias is a particular problem when dealing with sensitive behaviors (e.g., sexual behavior or substance abuse) or great deal of stress (e.g., a study of prison life). Based on a review of the literature, Boynton (2003) concluded that women were less likely to volunteer for research on sexual behavior than men and were more likely than men to refuse to answer certain questions about sexuality. Generally, individuals who are comfortable with sexuality are more likely to volunteer for this type of research than those who are less comfortable (Boynton, 2003). A similar finding was obtained by Nirenberg et al. (1991), who compared alcoholics who volunteered to participate in a study on sexual functioning and behavior with alcoholics who declined to participate. Volunteers expressed greater interest in sex, less satisfaction with sex, higher rates of premature ejaculation, and more concern over sexual functioning than

---

**TABLE 6-1    Characteristics of People Who Volunteer for Research**

Volunteers are more highly educated than nonvolunteers.[a]

Volunteers are of a higher social class than nonvolunteers.

Volunteers have higher intelligence in general, but not when volunteering for atypical research (such as hypnosis, sex research).[a]

Volunteers have a higher need for approval than nonvolunteers.[a]

Volunteers are more social than nonvolunteers.[a]

Volunteers are more "arousal seeking" than nonvolunteers (especially when the research involves stress).[a]

Volunteers for sex research are more unconventional than nonvolunteers.[a]

Females are more likely to volunteer than males, except where the research involves physical or emotional stress.[a]

Volunteers are less authoritarian than nonvolunteers.[a]

Jews are more likely to volunteer than Protestants; however, Protestants are more likely to volunteer than Catholics.[a]

Volunteers are less conforming than nonvolunteers, except where the volunteers are female and the research is clinically oriented.[a]

Volunteers are more field dependent (rely heavily on environmental cues) than nonvolunteers.[b]

Volunteers are more willing to endure higher levels of stress in an experiment than nonvolunteers.[c]

Volunteers are more agreeable and open to new experience than nonvolunteers.[d]

Volunteers are lower in neuroticism and higher in conscientiousness than nonvolunteers.[e]

SOURCES: [a]Rosenthal and Rosnow, 1975; [b]Cooperman, 1980; [c]Saunders, 1980; [d]Marcus and Schütz, 2005; [e]Lönnqvist et al., 2006.

nonvolunteers. Additionally, volunteers used substance-abuse counseling more often and had higher rates of drug use. On the other hand, Mandel, Weiner, Kaplan, Pelcovitz, and Labruna (2000) found few differences between volunteer and nonvolunteer samples of abused families. In fact, Mandel et al. report that there were far more similarities than dissimilarities between the volunteers and nonvolunteers. A similar problem may exist for research on substance abuse (Reynolds, Tarter, & Kirisci, 2004) and alcoholism (Taylor, Obitz, & Reich, 1985). Additionally, Thomas Carnahan and Sam McFarland (2007) found that participants who volunteered for a "psychological study on prison life" differed significantly from those who volunteered for what was described simply as a "psychological study." We explore this study in more depth later in this chapter.

In a study of the willingness of medical doctors to participate in a study in which data on them would be collected by postgraduate directors, Callahan, Hojat, and Gonnella (2007) found that volunteers differed from nonvolunteers on a number of dimensions. Volunteers performed better in and after medical school and scored better on medical licensing exams. Additionally, women and members of ethnic minority groups were less likely to volunteer. These studies tell us that the individuals who make up a volunteer sample may differ in important ways from those who do not volunteer. You may need to take this into account when assessing research outcomes.

Where does all of this leave us? It is clear that under some circumstances volunteers and nonvolunteers differ. These differences may translate into lower external validity for findings based on volunteer participant samples. The best advice we can give is to be aware of the potential for volunteer bias and take it into account when interpreting your results.

*Situational Factors*    In addition to participant characteristics, situational factors may affect a person's decision to volunteer for behavioral research. Table 6-2 shows a number of situational characteristics that can affect a person's decision to volunteer for a study.

As with the participant-related factors, the operation of the situational factors may be complex. For example, people are generally less disposed to volunteer for

**TABLE 6-2    Situational Factors Affecting the Decision to Volunteer**

Interesting topic being researched and high potential for being favorably evaluated

Important topic being investigated

Incentives for participation offered

Amount of stress involved in a study

Characteristics of the person asking for participation

Perception that participation is normative

Personal acquaintance with recruiter

Public commitment to volunteering

SOURCE: Rosenthal and Rosnow, 1975.

experiments that involve stress or aversive situations. According to Rosenthal and Rosnow (1975), the personal characteristics of the potential participant and the nature of the incentives offered may mediate the decision to volunteer for this type of research. Also, stable personal characteristics may mediate the impact of offering material rewards for participation in research.

The general conclusion from the research of Rosenthal and Rosnow (1975) is that several participant-related and situational characteristics affect an individual's decision about volunteering for a particular research study. Such a decision may be influenced by a variety of factors that interact with one another. In any case, it is apparent that volunteering is not a simple random process. Certain types of people are disposed to volunteer generally and others for certain specific types of research.

The nature of the stimuli used in a study also affects the likelihood of volunteering. For example, Gaither, Sellbom, and Meier (2003) had men and women fill out a questionnaire asking them whether they would be willing to participate in research in which a variety of different sexually explicit images were to be judged. Gaither et al. found that men were more likely than women to volunteer for research involving viewing images of heterosexual sexual behavior, nude women, and female homosexual sexual behavior. Women were more likely than men to volunteer for research involving viewing images of nude men and male homosexual sexual behavior. Gaither et al. also found that regardless of gender, those willing to volunteer for this type of research were higher in sexual and nonsexual sensation seeking.

Finally, media coverage may relate to willingness to volunteer. Gary Mans and Christopher Stream (2006) investigated the relationship between the amount and nature of media coverage and volunteering for medical research. Mans and Stream found that the greater the *positive* media coverage of a study, the more willing people are to volunteer (although the converse was not true). There was no relationship between the *amount* of media coverage and willingness to volunteer, however.

## QUESTIONS TO PONDER

1. What is the volunteer bias and why is it important to consider in your research?

2. How do volunteers and nonvolunteers differ in terms of personality and other characteristics?

3. What are some of the situational factors that affect a participant's decision to volunteer?

### Volunteerism and Internal Validity

Ideally, you want to establish that variation in your independent variable *causes* observed variation in your dependent variable. However, variables related to voluntary participation may, quite subtly, cause variation in your dependent variable. If you conclude that the variation in your independent variable caused the observed effects, you may be mistaken. Thus, volunteerism may affect "inferred causality" (Rosenthal & Rosnow, 1975), which closely relates to internal validity.

Rosenthal and Rosnow (1975) conducted a series of experiments investigating the impact of volunteering on inferred causality within the context of an attitude change experiment. In the first experiment, 42 undergraduate women (20 of whom had previously indicated their willingness to volunteer for a study) were given an attitude questionnaire concerning fraternities on college campuses. A week later, the experimenters randomly assigned some participants to a profraternity communication, others to an antifraternity communication, and still others to no persuasive communication. The participants were then given a measure of their attitudes toward fraternities.

Although the persuasive communication changed attitudes more than the other types, the volunteers were more affected by the antifraternity communication than were nonvolunteers, as shown in Figure 6-2. A tentative explanation offered by Rosenthal and Rosnow (1975) for this effect centered on the higher need for approval among volunteers than nonvolunteers. Volunteers tended to see the experimenter as being antifraternity (although only slightly). Apparently, the volunteers were more motivated to please the experimenter than were the nonvolunteers. The desire to please the experimenter, not the content of the persuasive measure, may have caused the observed attitude change. The results of this experiment show that variables relating to voluntary participation may cloud any causal inferences you draw about the relationship between your independent and dependent variables. Rosenthal and Rosnow conclude that "subjects' reactions to a persuasive communication can be largely predicted from their original willingness to participate in the research" (1975, p. 155). According to Rosenthal and Rosnow, the volunteers' predisposition to comply with demand characteristics of the experiment indicates that volunteerism serves as a "motivation mediator" and may affect the internal validity of an experiment.

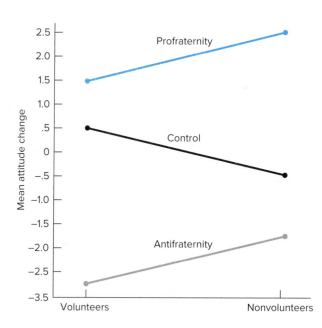

**FIGURE 6-2**  Attitude change as a function of type of message and volunteerism.
SOURCE: Rosenthal and Rosnow, 1975.

## Volunteerism and External Validity

Ideally, we would like the results of our research to generalize beyond our sample. Volunteerism may affect our ability to generalize, thus reducing external validity. If volunteer participants have unique characteristics, your findings may apply only to participants with those characteristics.

There is evidence that individuals who volunteer for certain types of research differ from nonvolunteers. For example, Davis et al. (1999) found that individuals high on a measure of empathy were more likely to volunteer for a sympathy-arousing activity than those lower in empathy. In another study, Carnahan and McFarland (2007) investigated whether individuals who volunteered for a "study of prison life" (such as the Stanford prison study described in detail later in this chapter) differed from those who volunteered for an otherwise identically described study omitting the reference to "prison life." Carnahan and McFarland found that individuals who volunteered for the prison life study were higher on aggressiveness, right wing authoritarianism (a measure of submissiveness to authority), Machiavellianism (a tendency to manipulate others), narcissism (a need for power and negative responses to threats to self-esteem), and social dominance (the desire for one's group to dominate others) than those who volunteered for a "psychological study." Additionally, those who volunteered for the "psychological study" were higher on empathy and altruism. In another study, women who were willing to volunteer for a study of sexual arousal to viewing erotic materials using a vaginal measure of arousal were more likely to have experienced sexual trauma and had fewer objections to viewing erotic material than nonvolunteers (Wolchik, Spencer, & Lisi, 1983). Among introductory psychology students offered extra credit for research participation, volunteers were higher in academic ability than nonvolunteers (Padilla-Walker, Zamboanga, Thompson, & Schmersal, 2005). Finally, volunteers and nonvolunteers react differently to persuasive communications using fear (Horowitz, 1969). As shown in Figure 6-3, volunteers showed more attitude change in response to a high-fear communication than did the nonvolunteers. However, little difference emerged between volunteers and nonvolunteers in a low-fear condition.

The results of these studies suggest that using volunteer participants may yield results that do not generalize to the general population. For example, the results from

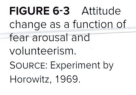

**FIGURE 6-3** Attitude change as a function of fear arousal and volunteerism.
SOURCE: Experiment by Horowitz, 1969.

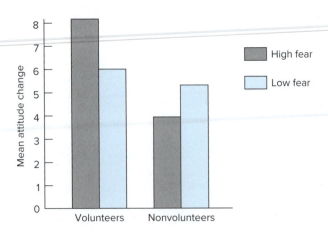

Carnahan and McFarland's (2007) study suggest that how participants in the original Stanford prison study (e.g., participants randomly assigned to be guards acting cruelly) responded may not represent how people in general would respond in such a situation. The reaction observed in that study may be limited to those who are predisposed to react cruelly. Similarly, findings relating to how women respond to erotica may not apply to all women. In both examples, the special characteristics of the volunteers limits the generality of the findings.

## Remedies for Volunteerism

Are there any remedies for the "volunteerism" problem? Rosenthal and Rosnow (1975, pp. 198–199) list the following actions you can take to reduce the bias inherent in the recruitment of volunteers:

1. Make the appeal for participants as interesting as possible, keeping in mind the nature of the target population.

2. Make the appeal as nonthreatening as possible so that potential volunteers will not be "put off" by unwarranted fears of unfavorable evaluation.

3. Explicitly state the theoretical and practical importance of the research for which volunteering is requested.

4. Explicitly state in what way the target population is particularly relevant to the research being conducted and the responsibility of the potential volunteers to participate in research that has the potential for benefiting others.

5. When possible, potential volunteers should be offered not only pay for participation but also small courtesy gifts simply for taking the time to consider whether they will want to participate.

6. Have the request for volunteering made by a person of status as high as possible and preferably by a woman.

7. When possible, avoid research tasks that may be psychologically or biologically stressful.

8. When possible, communicate the normative nature of the volunteering response.

9. After a target population has been defined, make an effort to have someone known to that population make an appeal for volunteers. The request for volunteers itself may be more successful if a personalized appeal is made.

10. For situations in which volunteering is regarded by the target population as normative, conditions of public commitment to volunteer may be more successful. If nonvolunteering is regarded as normative, conditions of private commitment may be more successful.

## QUESTIONS TO PONDER

1. How does the volunteer bias relate to internal and external validity?

2. What are some of the remedies for the problem of volunteer bias?

## RESEARCH USING DECEPTION

Imagine you are riding a bus home from school. All of a sudden someone from the back of the bus staggers past you and falls down, hitting his head. You notice a small trickle of blood running down the side of the victim's mouth. You are both alarmed and concerned about the victim, but you don't get up to help. However, you see several others are going to the victim's aid. At that point, a person at the front of the bus stands up and informs you that you were all participants in a psychological experiment on helping behavior. You have just been a participant in an experiment using deception. How would you feel about this situation? Would you be relieved that the "victim" was not really hurt? Would you be angry that the researchers included you in their experiment without your knowing about it?

In most cases, psychological research involves fully informing participants of the purposes and nature of an experiment. Participants in research on basic processes such as perception and memory are usually informed beforehand of what the experiment will involve. However, in some cases, full disclosure of the nature and purpose of your study would invalidate your research findings. When you either actively mislead participants or purposely withhold information from the participant, you are using **deception**. Although the use of deception in research declined (Sieber, Iannuzzo, & Rodriguez, 1995) between 1969 and 1995, it is still used for some research applications. However, using deception is very controversial, with opponents and proponents on both sides of the issue (Pittinger, 2002).

Why use deception? There are two main reasons (Hertwig & Ortmann, 2008). First, deception allows you to create interesting situations that are not likely to occur naturally and then study the reactions of individuals who experience them (Hertwig & Ortmann, 2008). This is what you experienced in our hypothetical helping study previously mentioned. It is much more efficient to create an emergency situation (a person falling down on a bus) than it is to wait around for one to occur on its own. Second, there are certain aspects of behavior that can only be studied if a person is caught off guard (Hertwig & Ortmann, 2008). Again, this second factor was evident in the example that opened this section. Proponents of deception argue that if you told people beforehand that an actor was going to fall down in front of them, they would behave differently than if the same situation were presented without the prior information.

In the sections that follow, we discuss how deception is used, its effects on research participants, and possible remedies to the problems inherent in using deception in research.

### Research Deception in Context

Deception in research has a long history, especially in social psychology. Although the frequency with which deception has been used has fluctuated since the 1970s, its rate of use in published studies remains within a 30% to 35% range (Kimmel, Smith, & Klein, 2011). Using deception in research raises a number of issues, some methodological and others ethical. (We cover research ethics in Chapter 7.)

One way to evaluate the propriety of research deception is to conduct a cost–benefit analysis, in which the needs of the participant, the needs of the research, and the potential contributions of the research findings are weighed against each other (Kimmel et al., 2011). If the greater weight comes down on the side of the researcher, then the deception is justified. However, Kimmel et al. suggest that a pure cost–benefit analysis may not be wholly adequate to assess the ethics of using deception. Instead, they suggest approaching the issue from a "social contract theory" perspective. In brief, *social contract theory* states that in a social interaction (such as an experiment) one party (e.g., the participant) consensually gives up some of his or her rights to another party who has power (e.g., the experimenter).

How does this theory apply to deception in research? According to Kimmel et al., prior to participation a researcher and participant should come to some agreement that is acceptable to the participant and the researcher about how research should be conducted. This approach would pose no problem for research that does not include deception. However, research in which deception is necessary would require agreement by the participant that as long as human dignity is maintained, some deception might be necessary (Kimmel et al., 2011). Based on their social contract approach, Kimmel et al. list several "principles" that, if followed, make deception ethically permissible:

1. Research deception is used as a last resort when no other method of study is available.

2. The scope of informed consent is widened, and participants are informed that deception might be used.

3. Researchers make an effort to predict vulnerabilities of participants when designing studies and when obtaining informed consent to participate.

4. Researchers never use research practices that they would not use on themselves or would refuse to accept.

5. Research participants act in good faith in any studies they agree to participate in.

## Types of Research Deception

Deception may take a variety of forms. Arellano-Galdamas (1972, cited in Schuler, 1982) distinguishes between active and passive deception. *Active deception* includes the following behavior (Schuler, 1982, p. 79):

1. Misrepresenting the purposes of the research.

2. Making false statements as to the identity of the researcher.

3. Making false promises to the participants.

4. Violating a promise to keep the participant anonymous.

5. Providing misleading explanations of equipment and procedures.

6. Using pseudosubjects (people who pose as participants but work for the experimenter).

7. Making false diagnoses and other reports.

8. Using false interaction.

9. Using placebos and secret administration of drugs.

10. Providing misleading settings for the investigations and corresponding behavior by the experimenter.

*Passive deception* includes the following (Schuler, 1982, p. 79):

1. Unrecognized conditioning.

2. Provocation and secret recording of negatively evaluated behavior.

3. Concealed observation.

4. Unrecognized participant observation.

5. Use of projective techniques and other personality tests.

The forms of deception just discussed fall into the category of intentional deception (Baumrind, 1985), in which you have a specific intent to deceive a participant. In contrast, *nonintentional deception* involves *not* fully disclosing details of a study, *not* fully informing participants what a study involves, and misunderstanding (Kimmel et al., 2011). Kimmel et al. point out that it is not always possible or desirable to fully inform participants about all features and details of a study, even if such disclosure might lead a potential participant to refuse participation in your study.

## Problems Involved in Using Deception

Although deception is a popular research tactic (especially in social psychology), some researchers consider it inappropriate (Kelman, 1967). In fact, deception does pose a number of problems for both the participant and the experimenter. For example, research suggests that once deceived, participants may react differently from nondeceived participants in a subsequent experiment (Silverman, Shulman, & Weisenthal, 1970).

Deception may also influence whether a person would be willing to volunteer for future research. Generally, research participants have a negative view of deception and indicate that they would be less likely to participate in a subsequent study if they were deceived in an earlier one (Blatchley & O'Brien, 2007). Participants in Blatchley and O'Brien's study also indicated that the more frequently deception was seen as part of psychological research, the less likely they would be to participate in a subsequent study. Blatchley and O'Brien concluded that frequent use of deception in research results in negative attitudes toward research and toward psychology as a whole, resulting in a "reputational spillover effect" (p. 527).

Despite the evidence for a reputational spillover effect, the news about using deception is not all bad. Deception does not always lead to negative outcomes for participants (Boynton, Portnoy, & Johnson, 2013). Boynton et al. found that participants were far more upset by unprofessional behavior on the part of the experimenter than by being deceived. There are situations in which research participants understand the need for deception. For example, Aguinis and Henle (2001) investigated potential research participants' reactions to a technique called the "bogus pipeline." This technique assesses attitudes by hooking up participants to a machine they believe will tell a researcher whether they are telling the truth about their attitudes. The catch is that the machine does nothing. However, research has found that the bogus pipeline procedure elicits more accurate measures of attitudes than conventional questionnaires. Participants in Aguinis and Henle's study were given a summary of a published article that used the bogus pipeline to assess attitudes and were then asked several questions about the technique. Aguinis and Henle found that even though their respondents believed that the participants in the study would react negatively to the deception involved in the bogus pipeline, they saw the technique as a valuable tool for getting truthful information and believed that the benefits derived from the technique outweighed the costs.

Another problem with deception is that the participant has been exposed to an elaborate hoax. Most research participants are not expecting to be deceived in an experiment (Blatchley & O'Brien, 2007). Being deceived in an experiment may violate an assumed trust between the participant and the researcher. As a consequence, a participant who has been deceived may feel betrayed and duped by the experimenter. The participant may experience a loss of self-esteem or develop a negative attitude toward research. According to Holmes (1976a), the researcher's responsibility is to "dehoax" the participant after the experiment.

Yet another problem may arise from deception research if, during the course of the experiment, participants find out something disturbing about themselves. Holmes (1976b) maintains that the researcher has the responsibility to desensitize participants concerning their own behaviors.

Stanley Milgram's (1963, 1974) classic obedience research illustrates these problems of deception research. Briefly, Milgram led participants to believe they were participating in an experiment investigating the effects of punishment on learning. The participant was told to deliver an electric shock to the "learner" each time the learner made an error. The shock intensity was to be increased following each delivery of shock. In reality, the assignment of individuals to the role of "teacher" or "learner" was prearranged (the "learner" was a confederate of the researcher), and no real shocks were being delivered by the participants. The true purpose of the research was to test the participant's obedience to an authority figure (the experimenter) who insisted that the participant continue with the procedure whenever the participant protested.

Milgram's research relied heavily on deception. Participants were deceived into believing that the experiment was about learning and that they were actually delivering painful electric shocks to another person. The problem of hoaxing is evident in this experiment. Participants also were induced to behave in a highly unacceptable manner. The participant may have found out that he or she was "the type of person who would intentionally hurt another," an obvious threat to the participant's self-concept. To be fair, Milgram did extensively debrief his participants to help reduce the impact of the experimental manipulations. (Debriefing is discussed later in the chapter.) However, some social psychologists (e.g., Baumrind, 1964) maintain that the experiment was still unethical.

Ethical treatment of participants requires that you inform participants of the nature and purpose of the research before they participate. Does deception on the part of the researcher constitute unethical behavior? According to the APA ethical principles (2002), deception may be used only if the experimenter can justify the use of deception based on the study's scientific, educational, or applied value; if alternative procedures that do not use deception are not available; and if the participants are provided with an explanation for the deception as soon as possible. The APA code of ethics thus allows researchers to use deception but only under restricted conditions.

## QUESTIONS TO PONDER

1. What is deception, and why is it used in research?
2. What are the different types of research deception?
3. What are the problems created by using deception?

### Solutions to the Problem of Deception

Obviously, deception may result in ethical and practical problems for your research. To avoid these problems, researchers have suggested some solutions. These range from eliminating deception completely and substituting an alternative method called *role playing* to retaining deception but adopting methods to soften its impact.

*Role Playing*    As an alternative to deception, critics have suggested using **role playing**. In role playing, participants are fully informed about the nature of the research and are asked to act as though they were subjected to a particular treatment condition. The technique thus relies on a participant's ability to assume and play out a given role.

Some studies demonstrate that participants *can* become immersed in a role and act accordingly. The famous Stanford prison study is one such example. In that study, participants were randomly assigned to the role of either prisoners or guards in a simulated prison. Observations were made of the interactions between the "guards" and their "prisoners" (Haney, Banks, & Zimbardo, 1973). Participants were able to play out their roles even though they were fully aware of the experimental nature of the situation. Similarly, Janis and Mann (1965) directly tested the impact of emotional role playing by having participants assume the role of a dying cancer patient. Other, non-role-playing participants did not assume the role but were exposed to the same information as the role-playing participants. Participants in the role-playing condition showed more attitudinal and behavioral changes than participants in the non-role-playing control group.

Participants are thus *capable* of assuming a role. The next question is whether the data obtained from role-playing participants are equivalent to the data generated from deception methods.

Opponents of role playing have likened the practice of role playing to "the days of prescientific techniques when intuition and consensus took the place of data" (Freedman, 1969, p. 100). They contend that participants fully informed of the nature and purposes of research will produce results qualitatively different from those produced from uninformed participants.

Resnick and Schwartz (1973) provide support for this view. In a simple verbal conditioning experiment (statements that use "I" or "we" were reinforced), some participants were fully informed of the reinforcement manipulation whereas others were not. The results showed that the uninformed participants displayed the usual learning curve (using more "I–we" statements in the reinforcement condition). In contrast, the fully informed volunteers showed a decline in the rate of "I–we" statements. Thus, informed and uninformed participants behaved differently. Other research (Horowitz & Rothschild, 1970) has provided additional evidence that role-playing techniques are not equivalent to deception methods.

The use of deception raises questions of both ethics and sound methodology. Role playing has not been the panacea for the problems of deception research. For this reason, deception continues to be used in psychological research (most often in social psychological research). Given that you may decide to use deception in your research, are there any steps that you can take to deal with the ethical questions about deception and reduce the impact of deception on participants? The answer to this question is a qualified yes.

*Obtaining Prior Consent to Be Deceived*     Campbell (1969) suggests that participants in a subject pool be told at the beginning of the semester that some experiments in which they may participate might involve deception. They could be provided with an explanation of the need for deception at that time. Gamson, Fireman, and Rytina (1982) devised an additional ingenious method for the securing of informed consent to be deceived. Participants were contacted and asked to indicate the types of research in which they would be willing to participate. Included in the list was research in which the participants were not fully informed. With this strategy, you might choose only those participants who agree to be deceived. Of course, choosing only the agreeable participants may contribute to sampling error and affect external validity.

Another strategy would be to include a "prior authorization" for deception in an informed consent form. On such a form, participants are told that in order to obtain valid results, researchers sometimes do not provide completely accurate descriptions of experiments and that such practices are approved by ethics committees (Martin & Katz, 2010). A study by Andrea Martin and Joel Katz (2010) demonstrates that this strategy does not significantly affect the outcome of an experiment (on pain tolerance) and that participants prefer a consent form that includes prior authorization for deception. Therefore, this might offer a good solution to the problem of using deception in research.

*Debriefing*     Even if you can quell your conscience about the ethical aspects of deception by obtaining prior consent to deceive, you are still obligated to your participants to inform them of the deception as soon as possible after the research. A technique commonly used to do this is **debriefing**.

During a debriefing session, you inform your participants about the nature of the deception used and why the deception was necessary. Because knowledge of having been deceived may lead to bad feelings on the part of the participant, one goal of the debriefing session should be to restore the participant's trust and self-esteem. You want the participant to leave the experiment feeling good about the research experience and less suspicious of other research.

Research shows that debriefing has become more frequent in research (Ullman & Jackson, 1982). Ullman and Jackson showed that only 12% of studies published in two major social psychology journals reported using debriefing in 1964. In contrast, 47%

were found to have used debriefing in 1980. Clearly, researchers are becoming sensitive to the problems of deception research and have begun to use debriefing more.

But is debriefing effective? Research on this issue has yielded conflicting results. Walster, Berscheid, Abrahams, and Aronson (1967) found that the effects of deception persisted even after debriefing. In contrast, Boynton, Portnoy, and Johnson (2013) found that debriefing was effective in removing the negative effects of deception and unprofessional experimenter behavior. Additionally, Smith and Richardson (1983) report that debriefing was successful in removing negative feelings about deception research. They conclude that effective debriefing not only can reverse the ill effects of deception but also can help make participants who felt harmed by research become more positive about the research experience.

In an experiment by Nicholas Epley and Chuck Huff (1998), participants served in a replication of a deception experiment. During the first experimental session, participants completed several tasks, including completion of a self-efficacy scale and a task requiring them to read short essays and answer questions about them. Half of the participants were given positive feedback about their performance on the essay task, and half were given negative feedback. At the end of the first session, half of the participants received full debriefing that explained the deception (false feedback). The remaining participants were partially debriefed, not including a description of the deception. In two subsequent sessions, participants completed several measures, some of which were the same measures completed in the first session.

Epley and Huff (1998) found that participants generally reported positive reactions to being in the experiment, regardless of whether they received full or partial debriefing. However, participants who were fully debriefed indicated greater suspicion concerning future experiments than those who were only partially debriefed. The suspicion over future research persisted and actually gained strength over three months. Generally, participants did not have strong negative reactions to being in a deception experiment. Apparently, deception is not as costly and negative to research participants as previously believed (Epley & Huff, 1998).

A possible resolution to this conflict in results emerges from an evaluation of different debriefing techniques. Smith and Richardson (1983) point out that "effective" debriefing can reverse the negative feelings associated with deception. But what constitutes "effective" debriefing?

An answer to this question can be found in a study reported by Ross, Lepper, and Hubbard (1975). This study found that the effects of false feedback about task performance persevered beyond debriefing. When participants were presented with "outcome" debriefing (which merely pointed out the deception and justified it), the effects of deception persevered. In contrast, if participants were told that sometimes the effects of experimental manipulations persist after the experiment is over, the debriefing was more successful.

There is another component you can add to standard outcome debriefing that can increase its effectiveness. Cathy McFarland, Adeline Cheam, and Roger Buehler (2007) report that in addition to informing participants that the test results provided by experimenters are false, participants should be informed that the test itself was bogus. When participants were told of the bogus nature of the test during debriefing, perseverance effects were reduced markedly. Oczak and Niedźwieńska (2007) tested the effectiveness of an even more extensive debriefing procedure. In the expanded debriefing, the mechanisms used in the debriefing were explained and participants were given practice detecting and countering deception. The extended debriefing procedure, according to Oczak and Niedźwieńska, allows participants to effectively recognize and cope with future attempts to deceive them. When the expanded debriefing was compared to a standard debriefing procedure, Oczak and Niedźwieńska found that participants exposed to the expanded procedure reported a more positive mood and a more positive attitude toward research than those exposed to the standard procedure. These two studies suggest that expanding debriefing to address deception more effectively can remove negative effects of deception and help counter negative attitudes toward research.

Although no easy answers to the problems generated by using deception can be found, some insight on how to soften the effects of deceptive strategies might help solve the problems. First, carefully consider the ethical implications of deception before using it. You, the researcher, are ultimately responsible for treating your participants ethically. If deception is necessary, you should take steps both to dehoax and to desensitize participants through debriefing (Holmes, 1976a, 1976b). The debriefing session should be conducted as soon as possible after the experimental manipulations and should include

1. A full disclosure of the purposes of the experiment.

2. A complete description of the deception used and a thorough explanation of why the deception was necessary.

3. A discussion of the problem of perseverance of the effects of the experimental manipulations.

4. A convincing argument for the necessity of the deception. You also should convince the participant that the research is scientifically important and has potential applications.

During debriefing, be as sincere with the participants as possible. The participant has already been "duped" in your experiment. The last thing that the participant needs is an experimenter who behaves in a condescending manner during debriefing (Aronson & Carlsmith, 1968). Despite the deception used, make the participant recognize that he or she was an important part of the research.

One final question about debriefing: Will the participant believe your debriefing? That is, will the person who has already been deceived believe the experimenter's assertions made during debriefing? Holmes (1976a) points out that there is no guarantee that the participants will believe the experimenter during debriefing. According to Holmes, participants may feel that they are being set up for another deception. The researcher may need to take drastic measures to ensure that the participant leaves the experiment believing the debriefing. Holmes (1976a) suggests the following options:

1. Use demonstrations for the participant. For example, the participant could be shown that the experimenter never saw the participant's actual responses (this would be effective when false feedback is given) or that the equipment used to monitor the participant was fake.

2. Allow the participants to observe a subsequent experimental session showing another participant receiving the deception.

3. Give participants an active role in the research. For example, the participant could help the experimenter run a subsequent experimental session.

Complete and honest debriefing is designed to make the participant feel more comfortable about deceptive research practices. Whereas this goal may be accomplished to some degree, the integrity of your research may be compromised. If your participants tell other prospective participants about your experiment (especially in cases in which deception is used), subsequent data may be invalid. Consequently, it's a good idea to ask participants not to discuss with anyone else the nature of your experiment. Point out to the participants that any disclosure of the deception or any other information about your experiment will invalidate your results. Your goal should be to have your participant understand and agree that not disclosing information about your experiment is important. Finally, there may be situations in which it is ethically permissible to forgo debriefing when deception is used (Sommers & Miller, 2013). Sommers and Miller suggest the following three conditions under which not debriefing after deception is ethically justified: (1) when debriefing would contaminate the subject pool, (2) if participants will be harmed by disclosures made during debriefing, and (3) when experimental conditions make debriefing overly onerous or impractical (e.g., in a field experiment). If you are contemplating not using debriefing after deception, it is likely that you will have to justify this procedure to an Institutional Review Board, which screens research projects for adherence to ethical standards (see Chapter 7).

Debriefing is not used exclusively for research using deception. In fact, it is good, ethical research practice to debrief participants after *any* experiment. During such a debriefing session, the participants should be given a full explanation of the methods used in the experiment, the purpose of the experiment, and any results available. Of course, you should also give participants honest answers to any questions they may have.

How do participants respond to being in research and debriefing? A survey of research participants by Janet Brody, John Gluck, and Alfredo Aragon (2000) found that only 32% of research participants surveyed found their research experience completely positive. Participants' reports indicated that the debriefing they received varied in quality, quantity, and format. However, survey respondents reported the most positive debriefing experiences when they were given a thorough explanation of the study in which they had participated and when they were given a detailed account of how the research is broadly relevant. Respondents' biggest complaint about debriefing was that the debriefing was unclear or provided insufficient information.

To summarize, deception raises serious questions about ethical treatment of participants in psychological research. In the absence of alternative techniques, you may find yourself in the position of having to use deception. Strive to maintain the dignity of the participant by using effective debriefing techniques. However, do not be lulled into believing that you can use ethically questionable research techniques just because you include debriefing (Schuler, 1982).

## QUESTIONS TO PONDER

1. What is the status of role playing as an alternative to deception?

2. How can you obtain prior consent to be deceived?

3. What is debriefing and how can it be made most effective?

4. What steps can you take to reduce the impact of deception on participants?

## CONSIDERATIONS WHEN USING ANIMALS AS SUBJECTS IN RESEARCH

Psychological research is not limited to research with human participants. There is a rich history of using animals as research subjects dating back to the turn of the 20th century. Generally, there is considerable support among psychologists for using animals as subjects in research (Plous, 1996). Plous reports that 80% of respondents to a survey either supported or strongly supported using animals in research. Support for animal research was weakest for research that involved suffering, pain, or death of the animals, even if the research was described as having scientific merit and institutional support. Interestingly, respondents were more accepting of animal research involving pain or death for rats or pigeons than for primates or dogs. Additionally, there is greater support for animal medical research than for animal research directed toward theory testing, cosmetics-safety testing, or agricultural issues (Wuensch & Poteat, 1998). Finally, men tend to be more accepting of animal research than women (Gabriel, Rutledge, & Barkley, 2012; Wuensch & Poteat, 1998).

Research using animals must conform to strict federal and local regulations and to ethical guidelines set out by the APA. We discuss these requirements in Chapter 7.

The final section of this chapter considers some factors that become relevant if you decide to use animals as your research subjects.

### Contributions of Research Using Animal Subjects

Animal research has played a prominent role in the development of theories in psychology and in the solution of applied problems. For example, Pavlov discovered the principles of classical conditioning by using animal subjects (dogs). Thorndike laid the groundwork for modern operant conditioning by using cats as subjects. B. F. Skinner developed the principles of modern operant conditioning by using rats and pigeons as subjects.

Snowdon (1983) points out several areas in which research using animal subjects has contributed significantly to knowledge about behavior. For example, animal research has helped explain the variability in behavior across species. This is important because understanding the variability across animal species may help explain the variability in behavior across humans. Also, research using animals has led to the development of animal models of human psychopathology. Such models may help explain the causes of human mental illness and facilitate the development of effective treatments. Animal research also has contributed significantly to explaining how the brain works and how basic psychological processes (such as learning and memory) operate.

## Choosing Which Animal to Use

Animals used in psychological research include (but are not limited to) chimpanzees and gorillas (language-acquisition research), monkeys (attachment-formation research), cats (learning, memory, physiology), dogs (learning, memory), fish (learning), pigeons (learning), and rats and mice (learning, memory, physiology). Of these, the laboratory rat and the pigeon are by far the most popular. The choice of which animal to use depends on several factors. Certain research questions may mandate the use of a particular species of animal. For example, you would probably use chimpanzees or gorillas if you were interested in investigating the nature of language and cognition in nonhuman subjects. In addition, using the same type of animal used in a previous experiment allows you to relate your findings to those previously obtained without having to worry about generalizing across animals.

Your choice of animals also will depend in part on the facilities at your particular institution. Many institutions are not equipped to handle primates or, for that matter, any large animal. You may be limited to using smaller animals such as rats, mice, or birds. Even if you do have the facilities to support the larger animals, your choice may be limited by the availability of certain animals (chimpanzees and monkeys are difficult to obtain). Finally, cost also may be a factor as animals bred for research can be quite expensive.

## QUESTIONS TO PONDER

1. What are the general considerations concerning using animals in research?
2. What roles has animal research played in psychology?
3. What factors enter into your decision about which animals to use in your research?

## Why Use Animals?

You might choose to use animals in your research for many reasons. One reason is that some procedures can be used on animals that cannot be used on humans. Research investigating how different parts of the brain influence behavior often uses surgical techniques such as lesions, ablation, and cannula surgery. These procedures obviously cannot be conducted on humans.

As an example, suppose you were interested in studying how lesions to the hypothalamus affect motivation. You probably would not find many humans willing to volunteer for research that involves destroying a part of the brain! Animal subjects are the only available choice for research of this type. Similarly, even if there are areas of research that can be studied with humans (such as examining the effects of stress on learning), you may not be able to expose humans to extremely high levels of an independent variable. Again, animals would be the choice for subjects in research in which the independent variable cannot be manipulated adequately within the guidelines for the ethical treatment of human participants.

In addition to these reasons for choosing animals, animals allow you greater control over environmental conditions (both within the experiment and in the living conditions of the animal). Such control may be necessary to ensure internal validity. By controlling the environment, you can eliminate extraneous, possibly confounding, variables. By using animals, you also have control over the genetic or biological characteristics of your subjects. If you wanted to replicate an experiment that used Long–Evans rats, you could acquire your animals from the same source that supplied them to the author of the original study. Finally, animal subjects are convenient.

## How to Acquire Animals for Research

After you have decided to use animals and have chosen which animals you are going to use, your next step is to acquire the animals. Two methods for acquiring animals are acceptable. First, your institution may maintain a breeding colony. Second, you may use one of the many reliable and reputable breeding farms that specialize in raising animals for research.

Each method has advantages and disadvantages. The onsite colony is convenient, but the usefulness of these animals may be limited. The conditions under which they were bred and housed may cause them to react in idiosyncratic ways to experimental manipulations. Thus, you cannot be sure that the results you produce with onsite animals will be the same as the results that would be obtained had you used animals from a breeding farm.

One advantage to using animals from a breeding farm is that you can be reasonably sure of the history of the animals. These farms specialize in breeding animals for research purposes. The animals are bred and housed under controlled conditions, ensuring a degree of uniformity across the animals. However, animals of the same strain obtained from different breeding farms may differ significantly. For example, Sprague–Dawley rats obtained from different breeders may differ in subtle characteristics such as reactivity to stimuli. These differences may affect the results of some experiments.

## Generality of Animal Research Data

One criticism of animal research is that the results may not generalize to humans or even to other animal species. This criticism has at its core a basic assumption: All psychological research must be applicable to humans. However, psychology is not concerned only with human behavior. Many research psychologists are interested in exploring the parameters of animal behavior, with little or no eye toward making statements about human behavior.

Much animal research does in fact generalize to humans. The basic laws of classical and operant conditioning, which were discovered through animal research, have been found to apply to human behavior. Figure 6-4 shows a comparison between two extinction curves. Panel (a) shows a typical extinction curve generated by an animal in an operant chamber after reinforcement of a response has been withdrawn. Panel (b) shows the extinction curve generated when a parent stops reinforcing a child's crying

**FIGURE 6-4** Comparison of extinction curves: (a) a rat's lever-pressing behavior and (b) a child's crying at bedtime.
Source: Williams, C. D. The elimination of tantrum behavior by extinction procedures. *Journal of Abnormal and Social Psychology*, 59, 269. Copyright 1959 by American Psychological Association.

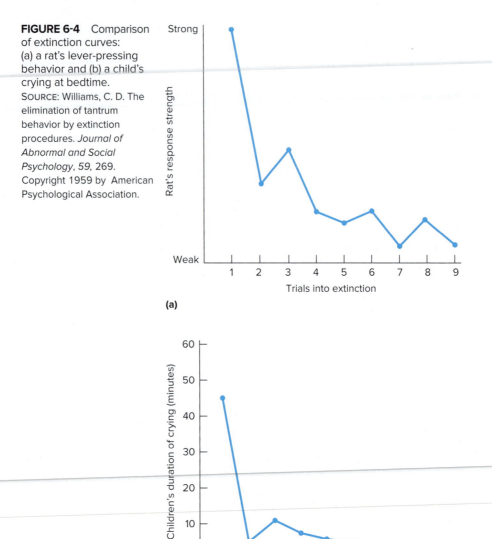

(a)

(b)

at bedtime (Williams, 1959). Notice the similarities. Other examples also can be cited. The effects of alcohol on prenatal development have been studied extensively with rats and mice. The pattern of malformations found in the animal research is highly similar to the pattern observed in the offspring of alcoholic mothers.

Although results from animal studies often do generalize to humans, such generalization should always be done with caution, as the following example illustrates. In the 1950s, many pregnant women (mainly in Sweden) took the drug thalidomide to help reduce morning sickness. Some of the mothers who took thalidomide gave birth to children with a gross physical defect called *phocomelia.* A child with this defect might be born without legs and have feet attached directly to the lower body. Tests were conducted on rats to determine whether thalidomide was the cause for the malformations. No abnormalities were found among the rats. However, the malformations were found when animals more closely related to humans (monkeys) were used.

Of course, whether results obtained with animal subjects can be applied to humans is an empirical question that can be answered through further research—if the findings have relevance to human behavior, then so much the better. Even if they do not, we gain a better understanding of the factors that differentiate humans from other animals and of the limits to our behavioral laws.

## QUESTIONS TO PONDER

1. What arguments can you make for using animals in research?
2. How do you acquire animals for research?
3. What are the main arguments surrounding the generality of animal research data?

## The Animal Rights Movement

Humans have been using animals in research for thousands of years. In fact, we can trace the use of animals in research to when medical science emerged (Baumans, 2004). Baumans points out that using animals for medical research goes all the way back to ancient Greek philosophers such as Aristotle and the Roman physician Galen. After a lull in animal research in the Middle Ages, animal experimentation again became popular during the Renaissance. Trends in the 20th century show that animal research increased sharply between the early 1900s and the 1960s, peaking in 1970 (Baumans, 2004). Baumans reports a small reduction in animal research from its peak to the end of the 20th century. By far, mice and rats make up the majority of animals used in research, accounting for 77% of animals used in research in England (Baumans, 2004) and around 90% in the United States (Shanks, 2003).

Despite the long history of using animals in research, concern has been expressed about using animals in this capacity. Concern over using animals in research stretches back to the early days of using animals (Baumans, 2004). Modern public and political concern over using animals in research can be traced back to the 1874 meeting of the British Medical Association (Matfield, 2002). At the meeting, using a dog as a subject, a doctor demonstrated how an epileptic seizure could be induced with a drug. After the demonstration, some members of the audience protested against using the dog in such a capacity (Matfield, 2002). Organizations to protect animals against cruel treatment, such as the Humane Society and the American Society for the Prevention of Cruelty to Animals (ASPCA) have existed for many years. For example, the ASPCA also dates back to 1874.

The concern over treatment of animals in a variety of areas (farming, research, etc.) has become more visible. People have begun to question seriously the use of animals in research. Many people have taken the position that the role of the animal in research should be reduced. Some have even advocated completely banning the use of animals as subjects in research. For example, there is a movement afoot to ban invasive research using chimpanzees in the United States. Opponents maintain that such research is both unnecessary and cruel (Wadman, 2011).

It is important to understand that this issue has potentially serious consequences beyond the moral questions surrounding using animals as research subjects (Shanks, 2003). A majority of research using animals in research is biomedical research (e.g., drug research and testing new medical treatments), which has implications for human health, well-being, and life. A significant reduction in such research may have long-term health consequences for humans. The degree of reduction being advocated varies from a total ban on using animals to simply ensuring that researchers treat their animals ethically.

We can summarize the public and policy debate over using animals in research to two major questions: Is animal research cruel, and is animal research necessary? (Matfield, 2002). Mark Matfield points out that the necessity issue embodies three main points. First, are there viable alternatives to animal research? Second, do results from animal research generalize sufficiently to humans to make it worthwhile? Third, is animal research necessary in general? The remainder of this chapter is devoted to exploring the issues surrounding the arguments made against using animals in research. The intention of this discussion is to present the arguments made by both sides and then analyze them critically. The final judgment about the role of animals in research is left to you.

## Animal Research Issues

Singer (1975, 2002), in a book devoted exclusively to the treatment of animals, raises several objections to using animals in a variety of capacities (from research subjects to food). This discussion is limited to the issue of using animals in research. It is important to understand Singer's main thesis. Singer (2002) does not maintain that animals and humans are equal in an absolute sense. He does argue, however, that animals and humans are entitled to equal consideration; that differences exist between animals and humans does not justify treating animals in a way that causes suffering. For Singer, the capacity to experience suffering and happiness is central to giving animals equal consideration with humans. Singer (2002) states that it is "speciesist" to give consideration to the pain and suffering of humans but not to animals. According to Singer, avoiding speciesism requires an allowance that "all beings who are similar in all relevant aspects have a similar right to life" (Singer, 2002, p. 19). It makes no sense to him that mere membership in the human species grants this right and deprives animals of it.

Within this general philosophical framework, Singer, (1975, 2002) maintains that animals should not be used in research that causes them to suffer. Singer (1975) further argues that "most animal studies published are trivial anyway" (p. 227). To support his point, Singer provides a litany of research examples that subjected animals to sometimes painful procedures. Included in this list are the classic studies by Harry Harlow on attachment in infant monkeys and Martin Seligman on learned helplessness. According to Singer, the suffering of the animals was not justified given the trivial nature of the research question and results. Consider an example that Singer (2002) provides (a critical analysis of Singer's assertions follows):

> I reported on an experiment performed at Bowling Green University in Ohio by P. Badia and two colleagues, and published in 1973. In that experiment ten rats were tested in sessions that were six hours long, during which frequent shock was "at all times unavoidable and inescapable." The rats could press either of two levers within the test chamber in order to receive a warning of a coming shock. The experimenters concluded that the rats did prefer to be warned of a shock. In 1984 the same experiment was still being carried out. Because someone had suggested that the previous experiment could have been "methodologically unsound," P. Badia, this time with B. Abbott of Indiana University, placed ten rats in electrified chambers, subjecting them again to six-hour shock sessions. . . . The experimenters found, once again, that the rats preferred shock that was signaled, even if it resulted in their receiving more shocks. (Source: Singer, P., (2002). *Animal Liberation*. New York: HarperCollins Publishers, 2002.)

These and several other summaries like them are included in Singer's book to point out the trivial nature of the research results obtained at the expense of animal suffering. If you had read only Singer's book, you would probably come away with the feeling that "everyone already knows that rats will prefer a warning." We can criticize Singer on at least three grounds concerning the brief research summaries.

First, each of the summaries referred to research that was taken out of the theoretical, empirical, or applied context in which the research was originally conducted. By isolating a study from its scientific context, Singer made the research appear trivial. You could take just about any piece of research and trivialize it by removing it from its context. In fact, Badia's studies (summarized in the preceding excerpts) provided important information about how organisms react to stress. To gain a full understanding of the purposes of research, you *must* read the original paper (as pointed out in Chapter 3). In the introduction to the paper, the author will surely provide the theoretical context and potential importance of the research.

Second, Singer leaves the strong impression that each study of a series merely replicates the ones before it, without contributing anything new to our understanding of the phenomenon under investigation or to its generality across different procedures and contexts. For example, in the paragraph just quoted reviewing the follow-up study by Badia and Abbott (1984), Singer begins by asserting that "the *same* research was still being conducted" (emphasis ours). In fact, scientific understanding of a phenomenon typically progresses by the gradual elimination of rival explanations over a long series of experiments designed for that purpose and by demonstrations that a phenomenon is not an artifact of a particular method of study.

Third, Singer's presentation of the research strongly suggests that the research was unnecessary because the findings were already obvious and known. Singer committed what social psychologists call the "I-knew-it-all-along phenomenon" (Myers, 1999). The "I-knew-it-all-along phenomenon" refers to the fact that when you hear about some research results, you have the tendency to believe that you already knew that the reported relationship exists. Several researchers (Slovic & Fischoff, 1977; Wood, 1979) have shown that when individuals are asked to predict the outcome of research *before* they hear the results, they fail. However, when the results are known, they are not surprised. You can demonstrate this for yourself with the following experiment, suggested by Bolt and Myers (1983).

Choose 10 participants for this demonstration. Provide half of them with the following statement:

> Social psychologists have found that the adage "Out of sight, out of mind" is valid.

Provide the other half with this statement:

> Social psychologists have found that the adage "Absence makes the heart grow fonder" is valid.

Ask participants to indicate whether they are surprised by the finding. You should find that your participants are not surprised by the finding reported to them. Next, have participants write a brief paragraph explaining why they believe that the statement is true. You should find that, in addition to believing that the statement is true, participants will be able to justify the reported finding.

The point of this exercise is that when you are told about the results of research, they often seem obvious. Singer played on this tendency (probably inadvertently) when he presented results from animal studies and then implied that "we knew it all along." In fact, before the research was done, we probably did *not* know it all along. The research reported by Singer made valuable contributions to science. Taking it out of context and suggesting that the results were obvious leads to the illusion that the research was trivial.

Not all the points made by Singer are invalid. In fact, researchers should treat their animals in a humane fashion. However, you must consider the cost–benefit ratio when evaluating animal research. Is the cost to the subject outweighed by the benefits of the research? Some people within the animal rights movement place a high value on the cost factor and a low value on the benefit factor. You must consider the benefits of the research that you plan to do on several levels: theoretical, empirical, and applied. In many cases, the benefits derived from the research outweigh the costs to the subjects. You should remember, however, that it is not always immediately obvious what the benefits of a particular line of research might be. It may take several years and a number of studies to be conducted before the benefit of research emerges.

Although controversy over the use of animals in research still exists, a majority of people support animal research. Public opinion of animal research is generally favorable, especially if it is done under the right conditions (Swami, Furnham, & Christopher, 2008). According to a 2005 Hart poll released by the Foundation for Biomedical Research (2005), 76% of Americans polled believed that animal research was important, with 40% indicating it contributed a great deal. Only 14% believed that animal research contributed very little or not at all (Foundation for Biomedical Research, 2005). In the poll, 56% believed that current regulations are sufficient to protect animals used in research. In a 2010 Gallup poll, 59% of Americans indicated that medical research using animals is morally acceptable, and 34% indicated that it was morally unacceptable (Saad, 2010). A poll done in the United Kingdom indicated that 85% of respondents found animal research conditionally acceptable, and 55% found it acceptable under any circumstances (Ipsos MORI, 2014). Thus, support for animal research remains high. There also appear to be some differences across nationalities and between genders. For example, Swami, Furnham, and Christopher (2008) found that Americans held more positive attitudes toward animal research and less concern for animal welfare than individuals from Great Britain. They also found that women were more strongly against animal research than were men.

Another characteristic relating to attitudes toward using animals in research is a belief in the animal mind. Persons subscribing to this belief hold that animals are self-aware, are capable of complex thought, and experience emotions. They are more opposed to animal research than others. In fact, belief in the animal mind is a stronger predictor of attitudes about using animals in research than are other personal characteristics (Ormandy, & Schuppli, 2014). Acceptance of animal research also relates to a host of other factors. For example, people are less likely to support animal research that is invasive or uses genetically modified animals. Additionally, vegetarians, people familiar with animal welfare issues, and activists are less likely to support animal research (Ormandy, Schuppli, & Weary, 2013).

The tensions between animal rights activists and researchers have also moderated. A study by Plous (1998) compared attitude changes of animal rights activists between 1990 and 1996. Plous reports that in 1990 a majority of animal rights activists believed that using animals in research was the most important issue facing the animal rights movement. A similar survey of activists done in 1996 revealed that a majority of activists believed that the use of animals in agriculture was the number-one issue facing the animal rights movement. Further, respondents to the 1996 survey advocated less radical methods for dealing with animals used in research. For example, fewer respondents (compared to the 1990 survey) advocated break-ins at laboratories using animals as a method of controlling the use of animals in research. In fact, most respondents in 1996 advocated more dialogue between activists and animal researchers.

Understand that those who advocate for animal rights are not bad people. Quite the contrary, individuals who advocate animal rights typically have a genuine interest in protecting the welfare of animals. In fact, such individuals have a high level of moral reasoning (Block, 2003), have positive attitudes concerning animal welfare (Signal & Taylor, 2006), hold romantic views of the environment (Kruse, 1999), and even have dreams with more animal characters than the general population (Lewis, 2008). Animal rights advocates have raised awareness of how animals are treated in research and brought about changes in animal welfare laws (Wolfensohn & Maguire, 2010).

Having said this, we should note that some extreme animal rights activists resort to radical tactics. For example, on November 14, 2004, members of the Animal Liberation Front (ALF) broke into the psychology department's animal laboratory at the University of Iowa. According to their press release, they "liberated" 88 mice and 313 rats. According to university officials, the ALF activists also destroyed up to 30 computers and poured acid on equipment. University of Iowa President David Skorton testified before Congress that the break-in caused about $450,000 in damage (GazetteOnline, 2005). Such tactics may have an effect on researchers. For example, a survey of researchers who use animals in research found that around 30% of researchers in the United States have been affected or know someone affected by extreme animal rights activists. However, only a small number (less than 10%) report changing their research tactics (Cressy, 2011). It may be a while before common ground can be found.

## ALTERNATIVES TO ANIMALS IN RESEARCH: IN VITRO METHODS AND COMPUTER SIMULATION

Animal rights activists point out that viable alternatives to using living animals in research (known as in vivo methods) exist, two of which are in vitro methods and computer simulations. These methods are more applicable to biological and medical research than to behavioral research. *In vitro* (which means "in glass") *methods* substitute isolated living tissue cultures for whole, living animals. Experiments using this method have been performed to test the toxicity and mutagenicity of various chemicals and drugs on living tissue. *Computer simulations* also have been suggested as an alternative to using living organisms in research. In a computer simulation study, a mathematical model of the process to be simulated is programmed into the computer. Parameters and data concerning variables fed into a computer then indicate what patterns of behavior would develop according to the model. A recently developed technology called *organ-on-a-chip* shows promise for the area of drug testing. In this technology, living organic tissue is combined with computer chips in such a way that the reactions of living tissues to various substances (e.g., drugs) can be assessed. As this technology develops, it may help reduce or eliminate the use of animals in drug-testing research. However, organ-on-a-chip technology is still in its developing stage, and it remains to be seen whether it will live up to its expectations.

Several problems with in vitro, organ-on-a-chip, and computer simulation methods preclude them from being substitutes for psychological research on living organisms. In drug studies, for example, in vitro methods may be adequate in the early stages of testing. However, the only way to determine the drug's effects on behavior is to test the drug on living, behaving animals. At present, the behavioral or psychological effects of these chemical agents cannot be predicted by the reactions of tissue samples or the results of computer simulations. Behavioral systems are simply too complex for that. Would you feel confident taking a new tranquilizer that had only been tested on tissues in a petri dish?

The effects of environmental variables and manipulations of the brain also cannot be studied using in vitro methods. It is necessary to have a living organism. For example, if you were interested in determining how a particular part of the brain affects aggression, you could not study this problem with an in vitro method. You would need an intact organism (such as a rat) in order to systematically manipulate the brain and observe behavioral changes.

A different problem arises with computer simulation. You need enough information to write the simulation, and this information can only be obtained by observing and testing live, intact animals. Even when a model has been developed, behavioral research on animals is necessary to determine whether the model correctly predicts behavior. Far from eliminating the need for animals in behavioral research, developing and testing computer simulations actually increases this need.

In short, there are really no viable alternatives to using animals in behavioral research. Ultimately, it is up to you to be sure that the techniques you use do not cause the animals undue suffering. Always be aware of your responsibility to treat your animal subjects ethically and humanely.

## QUESTIONS TO PONDER

1. What basic arguments do animal rights activists make concerning the use of animals in research?
2. What are Singer's criticisms of animal research?
3. What arguments can be made against Singer's views of animal research?
4. What evidence can you cite that the animal rights controversy might be settling down, or perhaps not settling down?
5. What alternatives have been proposed to using animals in research and why do some of them not apply to behavioral sciences?

## SUMMARY

After you have developed your research idea into a testable hypothesis and settled on a research design, your next step is to recruit participants or subjects for your study. Before you can proceed with your study, however, it must be evaluated for ethical issues. A review board will determine if your research protocol adheres to accepted ethical guidelines. Before you begin your research there are several issues you must consider when using human participants or animal subjects in your research. One important general consideration is the sample you will use in your research. It is not practical to include all members of a given population (e.g., third-grade children, college students) in your research. Instead you select a smaller sample of the population to include in your research.

One goal is to generalize the findings from your sample used in your study to the larger population. This is most effectively accomplished when you have a random sample of participants in your study, meaning that each individual in the population has an equal chance of being selected for inclusion in your sample. The reality of psychological research is that the ideal of a random sample is rarely achieved. Instead, nonrandom samples are used because they are convenient. In many psychological studies college students are used because they comprise the subject pools at many universities. Nonrandom samples are also common in studies conducted on the Internet and in animal research. Using subjects obtained through nonrandom sampling may limit the generality of your results. However, there are situations in which random sampling may not be necessary.

Regardless of the type of research you conduct using human participants, you must consider three factors: the setting in which your research will take place (field or laboratory), any special needs of your particular research (e.g., needing participants with certain personality characteristics), and any institutional, departmental, and ethical policies and guidelines governing the use of participants in research.

The requirement of voluntary participation and full disclosure of the methods of your research may lead to problems. For example, individuals who volunteer have been found to differ from nonvolunteers in several ways. This volunteer bias represents a threat to both internal and external validity. It can be counteracted to some extent by careful participant recruitment procedures. In cases in which you must use a deceptive technique, take special care to ensure that your participants leave your experiment in the proper frame of mind. You can accomplish this through using role playing or using effective debriefing techniques. At all times, however, you must remain cognizant of the problems with deception even if debriefing is used.

A large amount of psychological research uses animal subjects. Animals are preferred to humans in situations in which experimental manipulations are unethical for use with humans. In recent decades, the animal rights movement has evolved to challenge the use of animals in research. Animal rights advocates push for restricting the use of animals in research and call for ethical treatment. However, if you use animal subjects, you are still bound by a strict ethical code. Animals must be treated humanely. It is to your advantage to treat your animals ethically because research shows that mistreated animals may yield data that are invalid.

Alternatives to using animals in research have been proposed, including the use of in vitro testing and computer simulation. These alternatives, unfortunately, are not viable for behavioral research in which the goal is to understand the influences of variables on the behavior of the intact, living animals.

## KEY TERMS

| | |
|---|---|
| population | volunteer bias |
| sample | deception |
| generalization | role playing |
| random sample | debriefing |
| nonrandom sample | |

# Understanding Ethical Issues in the Research Process

As characterized in Chapter 1, the research process involves a regularized progression of getting and developing research ideas, choosing a research design, deciding on a subject population to use, conducting your study, analyzing data, and reporting results. Central to research in the social sciences in general and psychology in particular is the inclusion of living organisms as research subjects.

Using living organisms, whether human or animal, in research imposes upon you an obligation to treat those organisms in a humane, respectful, and ethical manner. In this chapter, we review various aspects of ethics as they apply to the research process. We explore the ethical issues that apply to research using human participants, including a brief history of the evolution of the ethical principles that guide research with human participants. We also explore the ethical principles that apply to using animal subjects in research. Finally, we explore another issue of research ethics: your obligation as a researcher to approach your science ethically and honestly.

## ETHICAL RESEARCH PRACTICE WITH HUMAN PARTICIPANTS

In the early years of psychological research, researchers were pretty much left on their own to conduct their research. They decided when, how, and with whom research would be conducted. Little, if any, attention was paid to ethical issues. Researchers were responsible for making their own determinations about ethical research practice. Unfortunately, this led to some experiments that would most likely be considered unethical by today's standards. Let's look at a couple of examples.

### John Watson and Little Albert

John Watson was the founder of the behaviorist school of psychology. According to behaviorism, psychologists should only study

199

observable stimuli (S) and observable responses (R). One of Watson's studies attempted to determine if emotional responses could be learned. He and his graduate student Rosalie Rayner conducted a study in which a young child (whom they called Albert) was exposed to a white rat. Albert initially showed no negative response to the white rat. Next, Watson and Rayner (1920) presented Albert with the white rat followed by a loud noise produced by striking a steel bar with a hammer behind Albert. After several instances in which the white rat and clanging of the steel bar were presented jointly, Watson and Rayner tested Albert's reaction to the white rat alone. Here is what they found:

> Rat alone. The instant the rat was shown the baby began to cry. Almost instantly he turned sharply to the left, fell over on left side, raised himself on all fours and began to crawl away so rapidly that he was caught with difficulty before reaching the edge of the table. (p. 5)

Watson and Rayner (1920) continued their study by testing Albert's reactions to a number of other stimuli (a white rabbit, some toy blocks, and a fur coat) and found that Albert showed a negative reaction to stimuli that were similar to the white rat (the rabbit or fur coat), but not toward other stimuli (the blocks). They concluded that Albert's negative conditioned emotional response had transferred to the other similar stimuli. Finally, Watson and Rayner wanted to study "detachment" of the conditioned emotional response to the white rat. That is, they wanted to see if they could eliminate or reduce the negative emotional response that they had conditioned into Albert. Unfortunately, Albert's mother (who worked at the hospital where the experiment was being conducted) left the hospital, taking Albert with her. Watson and Rayner never got to reverse the conditioning process in their lab.

***Ethical Issues Raised by the Watson and Rayner Study***    As viewed from a modern perspective, Watson and Rayner's study raises a number of ethical concerns. First, Watson and Rayner make no mention of whether Albert's mother granted permission to use Albert in their study. Current research practice, as we explain later in this chapter, requires obtaining **informed consent**, a process that involves informing a participant about research and obtaining consent to participate in it. In Albert's case, his mother should have been informed of the nature of the procedure to which Albert was to be exposed and given the opportunity to provide or withhold her informed consent to Albert's participation. Second, one can legitimately question whether it is ethical to condition fear into an 11-month-old child. What short-term and/or long-term consequences could the conditioning process have had on Albert's behavior and well-being? Third, Watson and Rayner had no opportunity to reverse the effects of the conditioning process because Albert's mother removed him from the hospital. It would be incumbent upon any modern researcher to remove any ill effects of the experimental manipulations.

## Is It Fear or Is It Anger?

For many years, psychologists have wondered about the physiological underpinnings of emotions. Does each emotion have its own, unique physiological response? Or do all emotions share a common physiological response? An experiment conducted by Albert Ax (1953) sought to address these questions. Ax obtained physiological data from participants who were induced to experience the emotions of fear and anger. It is how Ax induced the fear that might raise some ethics eyebrows.

Participants were told that they were taking part in an experiment to study the physiological differences between people with and without hypertension. Ax hooked participants up to a shock generator and gave them a series of mild electric shocks that did not cause any pain. Ax then instructed the participant to indicate when the shock first could be felt. When the participant reported feeling the shock, the experimenter expressed surprise and proceeded to check the wiring on the shock generator. While checking the wiring, the experimenter secretly pressed a switch that caused the shock generator to spew sparks near the participant. At this point, the experimenter, in an alarmed voice, said that there was a "dangerous high voltage short circuit" (Ax, 1953, p. 435). After 5 minutes, the experimenter removed the wire from the participant's finger, telling the participant that there was no longer any danger.

*Ethical Issues Raised by Ax's Study*    How would you have felt if you had been in Ax's experiment and been subjected to the fear-inducing procedure? Would you have felt that your life was in danger or that you could be seriously harmed? Of course, in Ax's procedure, participants were not actually in any danger. The sparking and reactions from the technician were all staged, but the participant did not know that. The biggest ethical question surrounding Ax's procedure is the use of deception. Whenever you tell your participants something that is false (or withhold information), you are using deception. Is it ethical to lie to people in the name of science? Should there have been full disclosure of the procedure for inducing fear before the experiment? These are questions that must be addressed when you consider using a deceptive research procedure. In fact, deception is addressed by the ethical guidelines of the American Psychological Association (APA), which we discuss later in the chapter.

## Putting Ethical Considerations in Context

The Watson and Rayner and the Ax studies illustrate some of the ethical issues that arise when you do research. Currently there are numerous rules, regulations, and guidelines regarding research ethics that you must follow. You must present your research protocol for review of ethical issues *before* you can conduct your research. Your proposal is reviewed to make sure that the safety, well-being, dignity, and rights of your participants are protected.

The rules that define ethical research practice did not emerge overnight. Instead, they evolved slowly over a number of years and in reaction to various ethical issues that emerged along the way. In the next section, we review the evolution of the present-day ethical guidelines that apply to research using human participants. In a later section, we explore the ethical guidelines that apply to research with animal subjects.

## QUESTIONS TO PONDER

1. What ethical issues does Watson and Rayner's "Little Albert" study raise?

2. What ethical issues does Ax's experiment raise?

3. What could you do to address some of the ethical issues raised in the two studies reviewed?

## The Evolution of Ethical Principles for Research with Human Participants

In 1954, W. Edgar Vinacke wrote a letter to the editor of the *American Psychologist* (the official journal of the APA) taking psychologists to task for a lack of concern over the welfare of their research participants. In his letter, Vinacke pointed out that the psychological researcher frequently misinforms participants (as in Ax's study) or exposes them to painful or embarrassing conditions (as in Watson and Rayner's study), often without revealing the nature and purpose of the study.

Although Vinacke's concerns were well founded and represented some of the earliest criticisms of research practice among psychologists, the concern over ethical treatment of research participants predates Vinacke's letter by several years. The APA established a committee in 1938 to consider the issue of ethics within psychological research (Schuler, 1982).

The current concern over ethical treatment of research participants can be traced to the post–World War II Nuremberg war crimes trials. Many of the ethical principles eventually adopted by the APA in 1951 are rooted in what is now called the Nuremberg Code.

## The Nuremberg Code

The evolution of modern ethical codes for research can be traced to the end of World War II. At the Nazi death camp Auschwitz, "medical" experiments were conducted on some of the inmates. For example, an SS doctor at Auschwitz named Josef Mengele selected inmates at "the ramp" for either immediate extermination or incarceration. Some of those spared (most notably, twins) served as participants in a variety of experiments, often in the name of eugenics, aimed at proving the existence of a master race or "improving" the genetic stock of such a race. Mass sterilization procedures (without anesthesia) were tried out on inmates in an attempt to find the most efficient way to reduce the population of "inferior races."

In these and other experiments, the inmates were unwilling participants. They certainly did not give their free consent to be participants in this cruel research. After the war, when the Nazi atrocities became known, some of those responsible were tried at Nuremberg for their crimes; a majority of the doctors so tried were convicted. Out of the trials came the **Nuremberg Code**, which laid the groundwork for many of the current ethical standards for psychological and medical research.

There were 10 points to the Nuremberg Code (you can read them online at https://history.nih.gov/research/downloads/nuremberg.pdf), including the stipulation that participation in research be voluntary and the assertion that participants have the right to know the nature, purposes, and duration of the research. The 10 points of the Nuremberg Code were subsequently embodied in the ethical standards adopted by the APA and by the U.S. Department of Health and Human Services (HHS).

## The Declaration of Helsinki

Another major step in the evolution of ethical codes came in 1964 when the **Declaration of Helsinki** was adopted by the World Medical Association. Although the Declaration of Helsinki specifically addressed medical research, it also applies to research in the social sciences. For example, as in medical research, social science researchers are obligated to protect the health, welfare, and dignity of research participants. Another basic principle states that all medical research must conform to accepted scientific principles and be based on knowledge of relevant scientific literature. The declaration also states that research must be reviewed by an independent group of individuals who will ensure that the research protocol adheres to accepted ethical standards. As we will see later, all of these principles are embodied in the code of ethics adopted by the APA.

## The Belmont Report

The **Belmont Report** was issued in 1979 and further delineated ethical research practice with human participants (Cohen, Bankert, & Cooper, 2005). The Belmont Report presents three basic principles of ethical treatment of human participants underlying all medical and behavioral research: respect for persons, beneficence, and justice (Belmont Report, 1979). Several of the principles elaborated here have been incorporated into ethical codes developed by professional organizations, including the American Psychological Association.

1. **Respect for persons**. Respect for persons involves two components. First, research participants must be treated as individuals who are capable of making their own decisions. Second, persons with diminished autonomy or capacity deserve protection. On a practical level, this provision requires that research participants enter into participation voluntarily and be fully informed.

2. **Beneficence**. Ethical research also requires the researcher to protect the well-being of participants. Beneficence includes two components: to do no harm to participants and to maximize benefits while minimizing harm.

3. **Justice**. The principle of justice states that both the researcher and the participant should share the costs and potential benefits of the research. The principle of justice also prohibits using participant populations simply because they are readily available, are convenient, and may have difficulty refusing participation in research.

## QUESTIONS TO PONDER

1. What is the Nuremberg Code, and how does it relate to current ethical guidelines?
2. What did the Declaration of Helsinki add to the Nuremberg Code?
3. What are the three principles laid out in the Belmont Report?

## APA Ethical Guidelines

The APA began preparing its ethical guidelines in 1947. Complaints from members of the APA served as the impetus for looking into the establishment of ethical guidelines for researchers. The first ethical code of the APA was accepted in 1953 (Schuler, 1982). Since their original publication in 1953, the APA guidelines have been revised several times, most recently in 2002, which took effect in June 2003. The APA's **Ethical Principles of Psychologists and Code of Conduct 2002** is a comprehensive document specifying the ethical responsibilities of psychologists and researchers. The Code of Conduct was amended in 2010 and 2016. The amendments clarified what to do if the APA Code conflicts with law or organizational demands. You can find the amended code at http://www.apa.org/ethics/code/index.aspx. The document is too long to present in its entirety. Table 7-1 presents the most recent version of the guidelines for using human participants in research. The APA (1973) also established a set of ethical guidelines for research in which children are used as participants. If you are going to use children as participants, you should familiarize yourself with those guidelines.

## Government Regulations

The period spanning the early 1940s through the late 1950s was one in which researchers became increasingly concerned with the ethical treatment of research participants. This was true for researchers in psychology as well as in the medical profession. However, despite the Nuremberg Code, Helsinki Declaration, Belmont Report, and APA ethical guidelines, research abuses continued. The greater sensitivity about ethics and the newly drafted guidelines did not ensure that research was carried out in an ethical manner, as the next example clearly shows.

The director of medicine at the Jewish Chronic Disease Hospital in Brooklyn, New York, approved the injection of live cancer cells into two chronically ill patients in July 1963. The patients were unaware of the procedure, which was designed to test the ability of the patients' bodies to reject foreign cells (Katz, 1972). Predictably, the discovery of this ethical violation of the patients' rights raised quite a controversy.

Because of abuses similar to the Jewish Chronic Disease Hospital case, the U.S. government addressed the issue of ethical treatment of human participants in research. The result of this involvement was the establishment of the HHS guidelines for the "protection of human subjects" (U.S. Department of Health and Human Services, 2009). These guidelines specify which categories of research must be reviewed by an institutional review board, and the rules under which review board approval shall be granted. You can find the HHS guidelines at http://www.hhs.gov/ohrp/regulations-and-policy/regulations/45-cfr-46/index.html.

**TABLE 7-1   Summary of the 2002 APA Ethical Principles That Apply to Human Research Participants**

1. Research proposals submitted to Institutional Review Boards shall contain accurate information. Upon approval researchers shall conduct their research within the approved protocol.

2. When informed consent is required, informed consent shall include: (1) the purpose of the research, expected duration, and procedures; (2) their right to decline to participate and to withdraw from the research once participation has begun; (3) the foreseeable consequences of declining or withdrawing; (4) reasonably foreseeable factors that may be expected to influence their willingness to participate such as potential risks, discomfort, or adverse effects; (5) any prospective research benefits; (6) limits of confidentiality; (7) incentives for participation; and (8) whom to contact for questions about the research and research participants' rights. They provide opportunity for the prospective participants to ask questions and receive answers.

3. When intervention research is conducted that includes experimental treatments, participants shall be informed at the outset of the research of (1) the experimental nature of the treatment; (2) the services that will or will not be available to the control group(s) if appropriate; (3) the means by which assignment to treatment and control groups will be made; (4) available treatment alternatives if an individual does not wish to participate in the research or wishes to withdraw once a study has begun; and (5) compensation for or monetary costs of participating including, if appropriate, whether reimbursement from the participant or a third-party payor will be sought.

4. Informed consent shall be obtained when voices or images are recorded as data unless (1) the research consists solely of naturalistic observations in public places, and it is not anticipated that the recording will be used in a manner that could cause personal identification or harm, or (2) the research design includes deception, and consent for the use of the recording is obtained during debriefing.

5. When psychologists conduct research with clients/patients, students, or subordinates as participants, psychologists take steps to protect the prospective participants from adverse consequences of declining or withdrawing from participation. When research participation is a course requirement or an opportunity for extra credit, the prospective participant is given the choice of equitable alternative activities.

6. Informed consent may be dispensed with only (1) where research would not reasonably be assumed to create distress or harm and involves (a) the study of normal educational practices, curricula, or classroom management methods conducted in educational settings; (b) only anonymous questionnaires, naturalistic observations, or archival research for which disclosure of responses would not place participants at risk of criminal or civil liability or damage their financial standing, employability, or reputation, and confidentiality is protected; or (c) the study of factors related to job or organization effectiveness conducted in organizational settings for which there is no risk to participants' employability, and confidentiality is protected or (2) where otherwise permitted by law or federal or institutional regulations.

TABLE 7-1   **Summary of the 2002 APA Ethical Principles That Apply to Human Research Participants** *(continued)*

7. Psychologists make reasonable efforts to avoid offering excessive or inappropriate financial or other inducements for research participation when such inducements are likely to coerce participation. When offering professional services as an inducement for research participation, psychologists clarify the nature of the services, as well as the risks, obligations, and limitations.

8. Deception in research shall be used only if they have determined that the use of deceptive techniques is justified by the study's significant prospective scientific, educational, or applied value and that effective nondeceptive alternative procedures are not feasible. Deception is not used if the research is reasonably expected to cause physical pain or several emotional distress. Psychologists explain any deception that is an integral feature of the design and conduct of an experiment to participants as early as is feasible, preferably at the conclusion of their participation, but no later than at the conclusion of the data collection, and permit participants to withdraw their data.

9. (a) Psychologists offer participants a prompt opportunity to obtain appropriate information about the nature, results, and conclusions of the research, and they take reasonable steps to correct any misconceptions that participants may have of which the psychologists are aware. (b) If scientific or humane values justify delaying or withholding this information, psychologists take reasonable measures to reduce the risk of harm. (c) When psychologists become aware that research procedures have harmed a participant, they take reasonable steps to minimize the harm.

SOURCE: American Psychological Association. Ethical principles of psychologists and code of conduct. Copyright 2002 by American Psychological Association. Retrieved from: http://www.apa.org/ethics/code2002.html.

There are also guidelines that apply to using children as research participants. The U.S. Department of Health and Human Services (2009) regulations for research with human participants states that unless the research involving children is exempt under the code, the assent of the child must be obtained. This means that the child must be informed about the study and must give his or her permission for participation. If the child is not old enough to give such assent, then permission must be obtained from one or both parents. Permission from one parent is sufficient if the research poses no more than minimal risk or has a direct potential benefit to the child participant. Permission from both parents is required if there is greater than minimal risk and there is no direct benefit to the child participant.

The federal regulations covering the use of human research participants and the APA code of ethics are both intended to safeguard the health and welfare of child research participants. However, ethical issues arise even in cases in which all regulations and codes are followed. Take the case of memory-implantation research conducted with children. In a typical experiment, an event that never happened will be implanted in a child's memory. The purpose of this type of research is to discover the extent to which memories can be implanted in children. Douglas Herrmann and Carol Yoder (1998) have raised some serious ethical issues concerning this type of research. They point out that children and adults may respond very differently to the deception involved in implanted-memory research. They argue further that children may not fully understand the nature of the deception being used and may be participating only under parental permission. Herrmann and Yoder suggest that at the time parental permission is sought, it is not possible to fully inform parents of the potential risks because those risks are not fully understood. They called upon researchers in this area to rethink the ethics of the implanted-memory procedure with children.

On the other side of the argument, Stephen Ceci, Maggie Bruck, and Elizabeth Loftus (1998), while agreeing that it is important to protect the welfare of child participants, state that many of the risks that Herrmann and Yoder wrote about were either inflated or nonexistent. In addition, one must also balance the potential risk to the individual child against the potential benefits that come from systematic research (Ornstein & Gordon, 1998). However, Ornstein and Gordon point out that it is essential for researchers to follow up with parents to make sure that child participants do not experience negative side effects because of their participation in a memory-implantation study. They also suggest that careful screening of children (for psychopathology and self-esteem) be conducted before allowing a child to participate.

As you can see, issues surrounding using children as research participants are complex. There is no simple answer to the question of whether children should be allowed to participate in psychological experiments. Certainly, it is important to protect the welfare of children who take part in research. However, discontinuing an important line of research with potential benefits to society would be "throwing the baby out with the bathwater."

Of course, it is possible to balance the costs and benefits of research using children and conduct such research in an ethically acceptable way. The Ethical Research Involving Children (ERIC) project (2013) has a useful compendium that can help you better understand ethical issues posed by research with children and make sure that your research addresses these issues (http://childethics.com/wp-content/uploads/2013/10/ERIC-compendium-approved-digital-web.pdf).

## QUESTIONS TO PONDER

1. What are the main points of the APA code of research ethics?
2. What guidelines were instituted by the Department of Health and Human Services, and why were they necessary?
3. What are the ethical issues raised by using children as research participants?

## Internet Research and Ethical Research Practice

How well do ethical guidelines developed for offline research apply to research conducted on the Internet? In some cases, ethical guidelines transfer quite well. Some Internet research involves a potential participant going to a website and choosing a study to participate in. As in an offline study, the participants will be given a full description of the study, an informed-consent form, and an opportunity to withdraw from the study. They will also receive information on how to obtain follow-up information. This category of research poses no more ethical concerns than offline research.

Not covered well by existing ethical guidelines is research using social media, chat rooms, forums and communities, and e-mail groups. For example, entering an online forum to study the interactions among the participants raises two ethical issues. First, how do you obtain informed consent from the participants? Second, how do you protect the privacy and confidentiality of research participants online? Should participants who agree to remain in the forum be assigned pseudonyms to protect their identities?

To address key ethical issues posed by Internet research, the Association of Internet Researchers (AoIR) has developed a set of guidelines that are rooted strongly in the documents such as the Belmont Report and the Helsinki Declaration. These guidelines are "bottom-up" principles; that is, they address ethical issues based on the nature and needs of specific research studies rather than on philosophically driven ethical arguments (Lomborg, 2013). Table 7-2 summarizes the main ethical principles developed by the AoIR (Markham & Buchanan, 2012).

*Informed-Consent Issues*    Resolving the issue of informed consent would seem a simple matter: Just have willing participants sign an electronic version of a consent form. However, this procedure may not work well when studying people in chat rooms (Jones, 1994). Robert Jones suggests that it may be unethical to exclude individuals from a chat room (especially if it is one that people join to get help for some condition) if they refuse to take part in the research study. One solution would be to allow everyone to participate but exclude responses from those who refuse to be in the study. Jones, however, questions whether this is feasible and whether it is possible to ensure the anonymity and privacy of nonparticipants.

**TABLE 7-2    Principles for Ethical Internet Research Practice**

The more vulnerable the target of the research, the greater is the obligation of the researcher to protect the target of the research.

Because "harm" is defined contextually, decisions about ethical issues are best approached through the application of practical judgment relating to the specific situation.

Because all digital information at some point involves individual persons, consideration of principles related to research on human subjects may be necessary even if it is not immediately apparent how and where participants are involved in the research.

When making decisions about the ethics of Internet research, the rights of the participants must be balanced against the social benefits of the research and the rights of the researcher to conduct research.

Ethical issues must be addressed at every stage of the research process, including designing the study, conducting the study, and disseminating the results.

Because making ethical decisions is a deliberative process, the Internet researcher should consult others when making these decisions, including other researchers, review boards, and published research.

SOURCE: http://aoir.org/reports/ethics2.pdf.

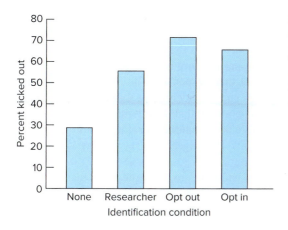

**FIGURE 7-1** Influence of researcher identification method on the percentage of times that the researcher is kicked out of an online chat room.
SOURCE: Hudson and Bruckman, 2004.

How might chat room participants respond to being part of a research study? James Hudson and Amy Bruckman (2004) investigated this question, and the results were not pretty. Hudson and Bruckman entered more than 500 chat rooms under one of four conditions. In the first condition, they did not identify themselves as researchers conducting a study. In the second condition, they entered the chat room and identified themselves as researchers studying language use in chat room discussions. In the third condition, they entered the chat room, identified themselves as researchers, and gave chat room participants the option of privately opting out of the study. The fourth condition was identical to the third except that chat room participants were given an opportunity to privately opt into the study.

As shown in Figure 7-1, the researchers were more likely to be kicked out of a chat room when they identified themselves as researchers. It didn't matter which introduction they used. Additionally, they found that they were more likely to be kicked out of small chat rooms than large ones. Hudson and Bruckman (2004) note that for every increase of 13 chat room members, the likelihood of being kicked out was halved. As the number of moderators in a chat room increased, so did the likelihood of being kicked out. Hudson and Bruckman's results indicate that in general chat room members do not like being studied. This can pose serious problems for Internet researchers who must obtain informed consent from potential research participants.

Chat rooms and online discussion forums are not the only Internet media where informed consent is an issue. In recent years, there has been an explosion in the use of social media such as Facebook. People with Facebook accounts post all kinds of personal information, links, photographs, and other information on their pages. Is the information posted there "public," and thus fair game for researchers to study, or is informed consent needed from page owners? The answer to this question is more complex than meets the eye. Perhaps one could argue that information posted on a public-access Facebook page can be studied without informed consent. However, what about information or materials posted by others (e.g., via a newsfeed) on a friend's Facebook page? This third-party consent issue has not been widely considered by researchers and institutional review boards (IRB Advisor, 2011). The moral to the story is that you must be careful when studying material posted on a social media site. What may appear to be public information may not always be.

*Anonymity and Confidentiality*    Regardless of the research environment you choose, you must be concerned with maintaining the anonymity of your participants and the confidentiality of their responses. *Anonymity* means that you must assure your participants that they cannot be identified as participants in your study. *Confidentiality* means that you guarantee the security of their responses. The Internet environment poses challenges concerning anonymity and confidentiality that are not present in offline research. David Pittenger (2003) points out that the Internet, by its very nature, is a very public medium. The public nature of the Internet poses a serious threat to the privacy of Internet research participants (Pittenger, 2003). Pittenger raises two concerns.

The first concern is a technical one and refers to the protections that are available in the software programs used by researchers. These programs vary in their ability to secure unauthorized access by computer hackers. You must be reasonably sure that hackers will not gain access to participants' responses. Additionally, if data are housed on a publicly owned computer, the data may be vulnerable to exposure by existing freedom of information laws (Pittenger, 2003). You are ethically bound to protect the confidentiality of participants' responses. You can do this by using appropriate hardware and software and by keeping data stored on a portable storage device like an external hard drive or a USB drive. If you use Amazon Mechanical Turk (see Chapter 6) to recruit participants, safeguarding data is easier because each participant is assigned a unique, anonymous identification number. Of course, you should inform potential participants of the possibility of data disclosure.

The second concern is over the ethical responsibilities of researchers who insinuate themselves into online groups (e.g., chat rooms and communities) without identifying themselves as researchers. You, as the researcher, must be mindful of whether the group that you are studying is a public or private group (Pittenger, 2003). Entering a private group poses special ethical concerns for your research. Research on participants in public groups may pose fewer concerns. Pittenger offers three arguments for considering the Internet equivalent to a public place like a shopping mall.

1. Internet use is now so common that users should understand that it does not afford privacy.

2. A person can easily maintain anonymity by using a pseudonym that cannot be traced back to reveal the user's identity.

3. The exchange of information in open, public Internet forums does not fall under the heading of research that requires informed consent and can be legitimately studied as long as there is no potential harm to participants.

Of course, such arguments would not apply to forums or groups advertised as being "confidential" or as having limited access. Internet groups created for people with medical conditions (e.g., AIDS) or other afflictions (e.g., alcoholism) often include these provisions. Doing research on such groups requires a stricter research protocol including full disclosure and informed consent.

Pittenger (2003) suggests the following guidelines for ethical research on Internet groups:

1. Learn about and respect the rules of the Internet group you are going to study. Find out if the group is an open, public one or a closed, private one.

2. Edit any data collected. Comb through the data and eliminate any names or pseudonyms that may lead to participant identification. You should also eliminate any references to the name of the group being studied.

3. Use multiple groups. You might consider studying several groups devoted to the same topic or issue (e.g., several groups for alcoholics). In addition to increasing the generality of your results, this technique adds another layer of protection to participant privacy.

In any research environment, it may be necessary to guarantee participants' anonymity. This means you assure participants that they will not be identified in any way and that their names will not be associated with their responses. Online studies have anonymity issues that are not present in offline research. For example, if you use e-mail addresses to contact potential participants, you may not be able to guarantee anonymity (Keller & Lee, 2003). Logs of e-mail traffic may be maintained on e-mail and other servers. If others have access to these logs, anonymity can be compromised. One solution to this problem is to use e-mail stripping software that removes identifying information from the e-mails. Or you might employ online services that allow you to set up temporary "ghost" e-mail accounts that hide one's actual e-mail address.

Maintaining anonymity may be especially problematic if a participant uses a work e-mail account to respond (Keller & Lee, 2003). Employer-supplied e-mail accounts belong to the employer and not the employee. This is especially important if your participants are government employees. Current regulations in the United States require that certain categories of e-mails be archived and made part of the national record. These archived e-mails may be obtained by an interested party via the Freedom of Information Act. Consequently, the participant's employer or others may be able to gain access to any e-mails related to your research and thus compromise anonymity. Because of these issues, you should warn participants not to use work e-mail accounts when responding.

*Deception in Internet Research*    The APA ethical guidelines permit deceptive research under certain conditions. In and of itself, deception does not automatically qualify research as unethical. However, you must be especially careful to protect the dignity of research participants if you use deception. When deception is used, you have an obligation to debrief your participants and dehoax them (see Chapter 6). *Debriefing* means that you explain the methods used in your study, including any deception. *Dehoaxing* means that you convince participants that the deception was necessary and take steps to reverse any ill effects of being deceived. Pittenger (2003) suggests that debriefing and dehoaxing may be more difficult in Internet research. If, for example, participants leave a group before the end of a session or study, it may be difficult to track them down for debriefing and dehoaxing. Pittenger suggests creating a separate Internet group or "enclave" where participants can go for debriefing and dehoaxing.

## QUESTIONS TO PONDER

1. What special ethical concerns face you if you conduct your research on the Internet?

2. What are the issues involved in obtaining informed consent in Internet research?

3. What are the issues surrounding anonymity and confidentiality in Internet research?

4. What steps can be taken to protect Internet participants' anonymity?

5. What special issues are presented by using deception in Internet research?

## Ethical Guidelines, Your Research, and the Institutional Review Board

Now that you are familiar with the ethical principles for research with human participants, can you now proceed with your research? In days gone by, you could have done just that. Currently, you will most likely be required to complete an ethics training course. Many institutions require all individuals involved in research to pass a training course on ethical treatment of research participants. One popular online training course is the Collaborative Institutional Training Initiative (CITI) from the University of Miami. The CITI training course has versions for principal investigators and research assistants. Before you can conduct research with human participants, you may have to pass one of these courses. You should check with your institution to determine if such training is necessary.

After you successfully complete a training course, you will most likely have to submit a research proposal to an **institutional review board (IRB)** for review. If you are affiliated with any institution that receives federal funding and your research does not fall into an exempted category, you must have your research screened for ethical treatment of participants before you can begin to conduct your research. The role of the IRB is to ensure that you adhere to established ethical guidelines.

Submitting your research to the IRB for review involves drafting a proposal. The form of that proposal varies from institution to institution. However, to evaluate your proposal an IRB requires certain information. Information will be needed concerning how participants will be acquired, procedures for obtaining informed consent, experimental procedures, potential risks to the participants, and plans for following up your research with reports to participants. Depending on the nature of your research, you may be required to submit a draft of an informed-consent form outlining to your participants the nature of the study. Additional sections would be added to the consent form if your research participants will be paid, may sustain injury, or will incur any additional expenses (e.g., transportation costs and research-related supplies). Each institution, however, may have additional requirements for what must be included in an informed-consent form. Additionally, requirements for informed-consent forms may change frequently within an institution. Before using any consent form, you should consult your IRB and ensure that your form complies with its requirements.

You may see these preliminary steps as unnecessary and, at times, a bother. After all, aren't you (the researcher) competent to determine whether participants are being treated ethically? Although you may be qualified to evaluate the ethics of your experiment, you still have a vested interest in your research. Such a vested interest may blind you to some ethical implications of your research.

The IRB is important because it allows a group of individuals who do not have a vested interest in your research to screen your study. The IRB review and approval provides protection for you, your participants, and the sponsoring institution. If you choose to ignore the recommendations of the IRB, you may be assuming legal liability for any harm that comes to people as a result of participation in your research. Additionally, after receiving initial approval, you most likely will have to file annual reports to the IRB on the progress of your research. You will have to do these continuing reviews until you finish your research and the IRB protocol is closed. Some journals now require that you submit your IRB proposal and approval before they send your paper out for review or publication (Hamilton & Stichler, 2015). In the long run, the extra time and effort needed to prepare the IRB proposal is in the best interests of the sponsoring institution, the participant, and you.

One factor that both the IRB and the researcher must assess is the risk–benefit ratio of doing research. Research may involve some degree of risk to participants, ranging from minimal to very high. This risk might involve psychological and/or physical harm to the participants. For example, a participant in an experiment on the effects of stress on learning might be subjected to stimuli that create high-level stress. It is possible the participants might be harmed psychologically by such high levels of stress. The researcher and the IRB must determine if the benefits of the research (new techniques for handling stress discovered, new knowledge about the effects of stress, etc.) outweigh the potential risks to the participant. In the event that high-risk research is approved by the IRB, the researcher will be required to take steps to deal with any harmful side effects of participation in such research. For example, you may have to give participants the opportunity to speak to a counselor if they have an adverse reaction to your study.

A few final notes on the role of the IRB are in order. Many researchers view the IRB as an annoyance and an impediment to their research (Fiske, 2009). In a survey of clinical psychology researchers and IRB members, 33% of researchers felt that IRB review hindered research on innovative therapies, while only 4% of IRB members felt this way. This despite the fact that large majorities of both groups held that IRB review helps protect participants and provides a good ethical review (Stryjewski, Kalish, Silverman, & Lehmann, 2015). Additionally, there is evidence that IRB review adds to the costs of doing research. IRB review leads to delay in conducting research and may result in inconsistent review and in IRB decisions that are inconsistent with federal guidelines (Silberman & Kahn, 2011). Some commentators believe that IRBs have been overstepping their original mission and passing judgment on the morality of certain research proposals. They suggest that this "mission creep" may be causing some researchers to avoid doing research on topics they believe an IRB would not approve (Sontag, 2012).

Despite these liabilities, an IRB serves an important function. It ensures that your research conforms to accepted ethical principles and protects you from liability in case a participant suffers harm in your study. Susan Fiske (2009) states that IRBs work well when they adhere to two principles. First, they must act to protect human research participants against harm and unethical treatment. Second, they serve to promote research by adequately training IRB staff and researchers concerning the IRB's function. Improving communication between researchers and IRB members is also part of this second function. With improved communication the review process can be viewed more as a collaborative process than one where the IRB mandates certain rules and procedures.

## QUESTIONS TO PONDER

1. What role does an institutional review board (IRB) play in the research process?
2. Why is IRB review important?
3. What are the IRB's two roles?
4. What are the advantages and disadvantages of IRB review?

## ETHICAL CONSIDERATIONS WHEN USING ANIMAL SUBJECTS

You might be thinking to yourself, at this point, that with all of the rules and regulations governing the use of human research participants, you will circumvent them by doing your research using animals. After all, animals aren't people and probably won't have the same restrictive ethical rules and guidelines applying to them. Think again! If you choose to use animals in your research, you will have to adhere to a set of ethical guidelines that are just as comprehensive as those covering research with humans.

It is certainly true that you can carry out experiments with animals that are not ethically permissible with human participants. For example, you may do physiological research on the brain that involves systematically destroying parts of the brain. Such research, of course, would not be possible with human participants. We doubt that anyone would willingly give informed consent to have parts of the brain destroyed in the name of science. However, such techniques can (and have) been used with animal subjects.

Does this mean that if you use animals in your research you have a free hand to do anything you please? The answer is no. If you use animals in research, you are bound by a code of ethics, just as when you use human participants. This ethical code specifies how animals may be treated, housed, and disposed of after use. Table 7-3 summarizes the APA (2012) Ethical Code for the Care and Use of Animal Subjects. If you are going to use animals in your research, you must review the entire code (http://www.apa.org/science/leadership/care/care-animal-guidelines.pdf). The U.S. Department of Agriculture, National Agricultural Library (2013) has a set of guidelines for using animals in research that is very similar to the APA Code (information on these guidelines can be found at https://www.nal.usda.gov/awic/animal-welfare-act).

These guidelines make it clear that if you use animals in your research you must follow all applicable laws and closely supervise all procedures involving animals, including procedures carried out by laboratory assistants. They also make clear your responsibility to minimize discomfort, illness, and pain of the animals and to use painful procedures only if alternatives are not available.

**TABLE 7-3    2012 APA Ethical Code for the Care and Use of Animal Subjects**

| PRINCIPLE | SUMMARY |
|---|---|
| Justification of the Research | Research should be undertaken with a clear scientific purpose, which justifies the use of nonhuman animals. The researcher should be familiar with relevant literature and determine if there are alternatives to using animals. No research shall be conducted without review, and the researcher shall monitor the welfare of animals throughout the research. |
| Personnel | Personnel involved in doing research with animals must be familiar with the APA Code and conform to the Animal Welfare Act. Personnel must be familiar with the normal behavior of animal subjects to detect any abnormal conditions. All personnel must be trained in the methods used and the care and welfare of the animals used. |
| Care and Housing of Laboratory Animals | The researcher is responsible for the maintenance and welfare of animal subjects. All relevant laws and guidelines concerning housing of animals must be followed. All procedures used must be reviewed by a review board to ensure they are safe and humane. Animals must be provided with humane care and healthful conditions in any facilities of an institution. |
| Acquisition of Laboratory Animals | Animals not bred at the research facility must be obtained lawfully, and adequate care must be given during transport. Animals taken from the wild must be trapped humanely and lawfully. Endangered species must be obtained with proper permits and be treated humanely. |
| Experimental Procedures | Humane treatment must be considered when designing and conducting research. Observational and noninvasive procedures are acceptable. When possible, procedures must be chosen that minimize discomfort to the animals. Procedures involving aversive stimulation must be justified and reviewed. Surgical procedures require sanitary conditions and steps to reduce the suffering of animals. Euthanasia must be done humanely. |
| Field Research | Field research that might disrupt fragile ecosystems must undergo careful review. Researchers should disturb populations as little as possible and respect all property rights of others. |
| Educational Use of Nonhuman Animals | Animals may be used in classroom exercises and demonstrations, but must undergo ethical review. Considerations should be given to using nonanimal alternatives. |

SOURCE: *Guidelines for Ethical Conduct in the Care and Use of Non-Human Animals in Research*. Washington, DC, Copyright 2012 by American Psychological Association.

## The Institutional Animal Care and Use Committee

Just as proposals for research using human participants must be reviewed and approved by an IRB before the research can be conducted, so proposals for research using animal subjects must be reviewed and approved by an **institutional animal care and use committee (IACUC)**. According to the *Guide for the Care and Use of Laboratory Animals* (National Research Council, 2011), committee membership should include the following:

- A doctor of veterinary medicine, who is certified . . . or has training or experience in laboratory animal science and medicine or in the use of the species in question.

- At least one practicing scientist experienced in research involving animals.

- At least one member who is not a scientist selected from inside or outside the institution.

- At least one public member to represent general community interests in the proper care and use of animals. Public members should not be laboratory animal users, be affiliated with the institution, or be members of the immediate family of a person who is affiliated with the institution.

In addition to the IACUC, an institution using animals in research must also have an attending veterinarian. The attending veterinarian is empowered to ensure the health and welfare of the animals used in research. The attending veterinarian oversees all aspects of animals in research, including husbandry and housing (National Research Council, 2011).

In practice, such committees are usually larger than this minimum. In colleges and universities, it is common to find representatives from departments that do *not* use animals in their research or teaching, as well as from those that do, and at least one student representative. The Purdue Animal Care and Use Committee (PACUC) at Purdue University includes more than 30 members and has a full-time staff, including specialists in laboratory animal science and veterinary medicine.

The use of animal subjects for research or teaching is regulated by the federal government, which mandates oversight by the IACUC and by the U.S. Department of Agriculture, as well as by various state and local agencies. The strict requirements for institutional care and use of animals under federal jurisdiction are given in the *Guide for the Care and Use of Laboratory Animals* (National Research Council, 2011). (You can find this publication online at http://grants.nih.gov/grants/olaw/Guide-for-the-Care-and-Use-of-Laboratory-Animals.pdf.)

Before you begin conducting your research using animal subjects, you should familiarize yourself with the principles for the care and use of animals and design your research accordingly. Before you can begin testing, you must submit a research protocol to your IACUC, describing what animals you plan to use in your research, how you plan to use them, and justifying your decisions concerning the species and number of animals to be used and the specifics of your procedure. Only when your protocol has been formally approved by the IACUC will you be permitted to obtain your animals.

Finally, keep in mind that ethical treatment of animals is in your best interest as a researcher. Ample evidence shows that mistreatment of animals (such as rough handling or housing them under stressful conditions) leads to physiological changes (e.g., housing animals under crowded conditions leads to changes in the adrenal glands). These physiological changes may interact with your experimental manipulations, perhaps damaging the external validity of your results. Proper care and handling of your subjects helps you obtain reliable and generalizable results. Thus, it is to your benefit to treat animal subjects properly.

## Cost–Benefit Assessment: Should the Research Be Done?

Even though a study is designed to conform to ethical standards for the use of animal subjects—giving proper care and housing, avoiding unnecessary pain or hardship, and so on—this does not automatically mean that the study should be done. Your decision to go ahead with the study should be based on a critical evaluation of the cost of the study to the subjects weighed against its potential benefits, otherwise known as the *cost–benefit ratio*. Cost to the subjects includes such factors as the stressfulness of the procedures and the likely degree of discomfort or suffering that the subjects may experience as a result of the study's procedures. The potential benefits of the study include the study's possible contribution to knowledge about the determinants of behavior, its ability to discriminate among competing theoretical views, or its possible applied value in the real world.

Conducting an unbiased evaluation is not easy. Having designed the study, you have a certain vested interest in carrying it out and must guard against this bias. Yet if you reject a study because its potential findings do not have obvious practical application, you may be tossing out research that would have provided key insights necessary for the development of such applications. The history of science is littered with research findings whose immense value was not recognized at the time they were announced.

Despite these difficulties, in most cases it is possible to come up with a reasonable assessment of the potential cost–benefit ratio of your study. For example, imagine you have designed a study to evaluate the antianxiety effect of a certain drug (paramethyl-doublefloop). You have no particular reason to believe that it has any effect on anxiety; in fact, its chemical structure argues against such an effect. However, you have a sample of the drug, and you're curious. Your subjects (rats) will have to endure a procedure involving water deprivation and exposure to foot shock in order for you to assess the effect of the drug. Given that the cost in stress and discomfort to the rats is not balanced against any credible rationale for conducting the study, you should shelve the study.

## QUESTIONS TO PONDER

1. What are the ethical guidelines you must follow when using animal subjects?

2. What is the composition of the institutional animal care and use committee, and why is review important?

3. How does a cost–benefit analysis enter into one's decision to conduct a study using animal subjects?

## TREATING SCIENCE ETHICALLY

Thus far, we have made a case for you to treat your human participants or animal subjects ethically and in a manner consistent with all relevant professional and government regulations. However, your responsibility to be an ethical researcher does not end with how you treat your participants or subjects. You also have an obligation to treat your science ethically and with integrity. This is stated clearly in Section C (Integrity) of the ethical code of the APA: Psychologists seek to promote accuracy, honesty, and truthfulness in the science, teaching, and practice of psychology. In these activities psychologists do not steal, cheat, or engage in fraud, subterfuge, or intentional misrepresentation of fact (APA, 2002).

This ethical principle should not be taken lightly. Fraudulent or otherwise dishonest research practices can erode the public's confidence in scientific findings. It can also lead to potentially harmful outcomes for others. Take the 2011 case of Dutch social psychologist Diederik Stapel. Stapel became noteworthy for his innovative research on stereotyping and prejudice. In one study, for example, Stapel found that individuals in a dirty, smelly environment were more likely than those in a clean environment to discriminate against another person. Stapel quickly rose in the ranks of social psychology and was regarded as one of its up-and-coming stars. Unfortunately, many of Stapel's studies were based on fraudulent, fabricated data.

Stapel and his graduate students designed experiments to test various hypotheses. However, when it came time to collect the data, Stapel took over, claiming he had networks he could tap into for participants. Eventually, he produced a data set that was fraudulent (Callaway, 2011). Stapel's research fraud continued until three graduate students noticed a number of inconsistencies in Stapel's published research. They took their concerns to the department chair, who launched an investigation (Callaway, 2011). Eventually, Stapel was dismissed from Tilburg University, and criminal charges were pursued against him.

Stapel's fraud had wide-ranging consequences. When stories like Stapel's are disseminated, the public loses confidence in the social sciences (and science in general). As a result of his dishonesty, there are now several articles in the literature that are fraudulent and misleading, thus polluting the body of knowledge in social psychology. His dishonesty may also affect negatively the reputations of his graduate students and co-authors on the published papers (who had nothing to do with Stapel's fraud).

The preceding example illustrates how the process of science can be subverted by a dishonest scientist. Expectations of a researcher also can affect the outcome of a study. The case of Diederik Stapel reveals an important truth about research in the social and behavioral sciences: It is a very human affair. The research process benefits from all the good qualities of human researchers: ingenuity, dedication, hard work, a desire to discover the truth, and so on. However, as in any human endeavor, the more negative qualities of human researchers also may creep into the research process. Thus, ambition, self-promotion, ego, the need to secure and keep a job, and the desire to obtain scarce grant money may tempt a researcher to falsify research findings. Assuming the role of a scientist does not guarantee that a person checks his or her ambitions, flaws, desires, and needs at the laboratory door (Broad & Wade, 1983).

Research fraud has implications far beyond the integrity of science. It can also have real and detrimental effects on a person's health and well-being. Take the example of research by Andrew Wakefield and his colleagues (1998) that linked the measles, mumps, and rubella vaccine (MMR) to an increase in the rate of autism. Wakefield et al. reported that autism in children could be traced to their having received the MMR vaccine. Based upon Wakefield et al.'s study, a number of celebrities took up the cause to ban the MMR vaccine. As you might expect, this raised a firestorm of controversy. Failure to get the MMR vaccine raises the rates of the diseases the vaccine protects against. In fact, a major outbreak of measles in 2008 and 2009 was attributed to children not getting the MMR vaccine (Eggerston, 2010). The Wakefield et al. study later was found to be ethically questionable and fraudulent. Evidence showed that Wakefield et al. were highly selective in choosing children for their study, had altered the children's medical histories, and had received funding for the research from a law firm representing parents who were suing the makers of the MMR vaccines (Godlee, Smith, & Marcovitch, 2011; Eggerston, 2010). In 2010, *The Lancet* (the journal that originally published the article) retracted it. Unfortunately, the retraction did not quell the drive to ban the MMR vaccine (Eggerston, 2010).

Misconceptions based on fraudulent research make their way into the mainstream of culture and are difficult to root out. For example, in 2016 Robert DeNiro listed a film named *Vaxxed* in his prestigious *Tribeca Film Festival*. The film was based largely on the discredited vaccination findings and directed by Andrew Wakefield, the discredited scientist. Fortunately, DeNiro pulled the film at the last minute over concerns with the validity of its content. The lesson, however, is clear. Fraudulent research, even when publically discredited, may still influence people and have serious consequences.

Research fraud touches all types of research, from the social sciences to medical sciences. The U.S. **Office of Research Integrity (ORI)** is an office within the U.S. Department of Health and Human Services that oversees the integrity of the research process. The ORI documents and investigates cases of research misconduct in science, including psychological research. For example, a 2006 case involving a former psychology graduate student at UCLA found that she had "engaged in scientific misconduct by falsifying or fabricating data and statistical results for up to nine pilot studies on the impact of vulnerability on decision making from fall 2000 to winter 2002 as a basis for her doctoral thesis research" (Office of Research Integrity, 2006). The falsified data were used in a manuscript submitted to the journal *Psychological Science* and in a National Institutes of Mental Health grant proposal.

## QUESTIONS TO PONDER

1. What does the APA ethical code say about research integrity?

2. Why should we be concerned with research fraud?

3. What is the ORI and what does it do?

## What Constitutes Misconduct in Research?

The ORI (2016) defines three categories of research misconduct:

1. Data fabrication: Making up data or results and recording or reporting on them.

2. Falsification: Manipulating research materials, equipment, or processes, or changing or omitting data or results such that the research is not accurately represented in the research record.

3. Plagiarism: The appropriation of another person's ideas, processes, results, or words without giving appropriate credit.

According to the ORI (2016), honest errors and differences of scientific opinion do not constitute research misconsduct.

Perhaps the most harmful, but rare, form of research fraud is the outright fabrication of data (Broad & Wade, 1983), as was the case for Diederik Stapel. A scientist may fabricate an entire set of data based on an experiment that might never have been run or replace actual data with false data. Other forms of fraud in research include altering data to make them "look better" or fit with a theory, selecting only the best data for publication, and publishing stolen or plagiarized work (Broad & Wade, 1983). Altering or otherwise manipulating data in order to achieve statistical significance (e.g., selectively dropping data from an analysis without noting that this was done or without offering an appropriate justification) also would constitute research fraud.

Broad and Wade (1983) also suggest that using the *least-publishable-unit rule,* which involves getting several small publications out of a single experiment (as opposed to publishing one large paper), might be considered dishonest. Research fraud can occur if scientists sabotage each other's work. Claiming credit for work done by others also could be considered fraud. If, for example, a student conceptualizes, designs, and carries out a study but a professor takes senior author status on the publication, this would be considered fraud. It is also dishonest to attach your name to research that you had little to do with, just to pad your résumé. Some articles may have as many as 10 or more authors. Each of the junior authors may have had some minor input (such as suggesting that Wistar rats be used rather than Long–Evans rats). However, that minor input may not warrant authorship credit. Finally, plagiarism, in which a researcher uses another person's work or ideas without proper acknowledgment, is also a form of research fraud.

## The Prevalence of Research Misconduct

The editor of *Science* once stated that 99.9999% of scientific papers are truthful and accurate (Bell, 1992). However, in 2015 the U.S. ORI found misconduct in 14 out of 31 cases it closed (K. Partin, personal communication, April 4, 2016). A survey by Geggie (2001) of medical consultants in England found that 55.7% of respondents reported witnessing some form of research misconduct firsthand. Additionally, 5.7% reported engaging in misconduct themselves, and 18% indicated that they would consider engaging in misconduct in the future or were unsure about whether they would engage in research misconduct. A study of papers actually retracted from medical journals found that 26.5% of published papers were retracted due to fraud (Steen, 2011).

So, the numbers don't seem to be huge. However, critics suggest that it is not possible to exactly quantify research fraud (Bell, 1992). For one thing, fraud may not be reported, even if it is detected. In addition, in one survey (cited in Bell, 1992), many researchers who suspected that a colleague was falsifying data did not report it. Fraud may also go unreported because the liabilities associated with "blowing the whistle" can be quite severe. Whistle-blowers may be vilified, their credibility called into question, or even be fired for "doing the right thing." Thus, the relatively few celebrated cases of fraud reported may be only the tip of the iceberg.

No matter how low the actual rate of fraud in science turns out to be, even a few cases can have a damaging effect on the credibility of science and scientists (Broad & Wade, 1983). Erosion of the credibility of science undermines the public's confidence in the results that flow from scientific research. In the long run, this works to the detriment of individuals and of society.

## Explanations for Research Misconduct

Why would a scientist perpetrate a fraud? There are many reasons. Fraud may be perpetrated for personal recognition. Publishing an article in a prestigious journal is a boost to one's self-esteem. Personal pressure for such self-esteem and recognition from others can motivate a person to falsify data or commit some other form of research fraud. Some commentators believe this was one motivation for Diederik Stapel's extensive research fraud (Dutch News, 2012).

The pursuit of money is a major factor in fraudulent research (Bell, 1992). Doing research on a large scale takes quite a bit of money, and researchers are generally not wealthy and cannot fund their own research. Nor can financially strapped universities or hospitals provide the level of funding needed for many research projects. Consequently, researchers must look to funding agencies such as the National Science Foundation, the National Institute of Mental Health, or some other available funding source. The budgets for these agencies are typically limited with respect to the number of applications that can be accepted for funding. Consequently, competition for research funding becomes intense. In addition, it is generally easier to obtain grant money if you have a good track record of publications. The pressure for obtaining scarce grant money can lead a person to falsify data in order to "produce" and be in a good position to get more funding. Moreover, at some universities, obtaining grants is used as an index of one's worth and may even be a requirement of retaining one's job. This can add additional pressure toward committing research fraud.

Another reason for fraud in research relates to the tenure process within the academic environment. A new faculty member usually has 5 years to "prove" him- or herself. During this 5-year probationary period, the faculty member is expected to publish some given quantity of research articles. At high-power, research-oriented universities, the number of publications required may be large, creating a strong "publish or perish" atmosphere. This atmosphere seems to have grown stronger over the past 40 years. When James D. Watson (Nobel Prize winner with Francis Crick for his discovery of the DNA double helix) was a candidate for tenure and promotion at Harvard University in 1958, he had 18 publications. By 1982, 50 publications were required for the same promotion (Broad & Wade, 1983). This need to publish as many papers as possible in a relatively short period of time can lead to outright fraud and/or vita (résumé) padding using the least-publishable-unit rule. Diederik Stapel himself cited this pressure to publish as a reason for his research fraud (Dutch News, 2012). Finally, fraud in research can arise from scientific "elitism" (Broad & Wade, 1983). Sometimes we see fraud committed by some of the biggest names in science because their elite standing in the scientific community shields their work from careful scrutiny.

### Detecting and Dealing with Research Misconduct

Before one can effectively deal with research fraud, one has to detect it. Detecting research fraud may not be a simple matter. It may require sharp-eyed researchers, reviewers, or assistants to notice something is not quite right with some aspect of the research process. This was how Stapel's fraud was uncovered. Fraud can also be detected using the peer review process or through replication of results (Morrison, 1990). Another method is to develop methods to detect the indicators of fraud. For example, Markowitz and Hancock (2014) compared published papers by Stapel that were confirmed to be genuine with those that were fraudulent. In the fraudulent papers, Staple used more terms relating to methods, investigation, and certainty. His fraudulent writings also displayed telltale signs of deception found in other deceptive writings, such as a lower level of descriptive detail.

Another way to detect fraud in research is to search for signs of it in the data. Uri Simonsohn of the University of Pennsylvania developed a statistical method to detect fraudulent data and used it to uncover the research fraud committed by consumer psychologist Dirk Smeesters of Erasmus University, Netherlands (Enserink, 2012). Simonsohn's (2013) method involves analyzing the means and standard deviations from published papers by a given author to see if they are statistically too similar. Although this technique can be useful in detecting fraud, Simonsohn notes that it is easier to detect fraud using raw data. Consequently, he advocates for posting raw data publically.

Bell (1992) points out that science has three general methods for guarding against research fraud: the grant-review process, the peer-review process for publication, and replication of results. Bell points out that, unfortunately, none of these is effective in detecting fraud. Editors may be disinclined to publish papers that are critical of other researchers, let alone that make accusations of fraud (Bell, 1992). In addition, replication of experiments is expensive and time consuming and unlikely to occur across labs (Bell, 1992). Even if a finding cannot be replicated, that does not necessarily mean fraud has occurred.

One way to deal with research fraud is to train students in the ethics of the research process. Students should learn, early in their academic careers, that ethical research practice requires scientific integrity and that research fraud is unethical. Unfortunately, students often are not taught this lesson very well. Michael Kalichman and Paul Friedman (1992) conducted a survey of biomedical science trainees and found that only 24% indicated that they had received training in scientific ethics. Additionally, 15% said that they would be willing to alter or manipulate data in order to get a grant or a publication. Geggie (2001) found that only 17% of respondents had received any training in research ethics. A study reported by David Wright, Sandra Titus, and Jered Cornelison (2008) paints an even bleaker picture. These researchers reviewed cases between 1990 and 2004 in which the ORI had found research misconduct by research trainees (graduate students, lab assistants, and postdoctoral fellows) to see if their mentors had monitored their work. Wright et al. found that the mentors failed to review raw data in 73% of the cases and set no standards in 62% of the cases. In 53% of the cases, the relationship between the mentors and trainees was stressful. Mentors were doing very little to reduce the likelihood of research fraud.

The ORI offers the Responsible Conduct of Research (RCR) program, which is designed to educate scientists about research misconduct. This program includes educational experiences centering on issues such as research misconduct, responsible authorship, and peer review. Educational materials for this program can be found at http://ori.hhs.gov/general-resources-0. Another ORI education effort is an RCR exposition. At the exposition, various "vendors" can showcase their programs and products designed to reduce research misconduct. Finally, the ORI has a simulation exercise called "The Lab" that presents a misconduct scenario and then allows the user to go back and assume the roles of various people in the scenario in order to explore how the misconduct could have been avoided. You can take part in The Lab at http://ori.hhs.gov/thelab.

Jane Steinberg (2002) indicates that another safeguard against fraud is to make it clear to scientists and assistants that they will be caught if they commit scientific fraud. Steinberg suggests that researchers check data often and openly in front of those who collect and analyze the data. Questions should be asked about any suspicious marks on datasheets or changes/corrections made to the data.

Probably the best guard against fraud in science is to imbue researchers during the training process with the idea that ethical research means being honest. This process should begin as early as possible. Steinberg (2002) suggests that teaching about research fraud should begin in psychology students' research methods courses. She recommends that students be presented with cases of research fraud. Those cases should be discussed and evaluated carefully. Students should learn the implications of research fraud for researchers themselves, their field of study, and the credibility of science (Steinberg, 2002). The short-term consequences (loss of a job, expulsion from school, etc.) and long-term consequences (harm to innocent individuals because of false results, damage to the credibility of science, etc.) should be communicated clearly to researchers during their education and training.

Another strategy suggested by Steinberg (2002) is to contact research participants after they have participated in a study to see if they actually participated. Participants should be asked (if they actually met with the person running the study) whether they met eligibility requirements, if they knew the person running the study beforehand, and if the study ran for the appropriate amount of time. Similar steps can be taken with animal subjects by carefully scrutinizing animal use records and laboratory notes (Steinberg, 2002).

Journals can do their part to guard against research fraud. Cate et al. (2013) suggest the following steps that journals can take to help fight research fraud:

1. *Strengthen the culture of integrity in research teams*: Researchers and supervisors can stress the importance of research integrity within their research teams.

2. *Require multiple authors to confirm the completeness and accuracy of datasets*: A statement from one or more co-authors should be obtained indicating that they have examined and confirmed that no data manipulation has occurred.

3. *Provide reviewers the opportunity to review datasets*: Authors should submit raw data along with their manuscript so that reviewers can examine the data.

4. *Require an independent researcher to review raw data*: A researcher who was not involved in the authors' research should review data before a manuscript is submitted for review.

5. *Remove the publication bias against null results*: A journal should encourage the publication of null results based on methodologically sound studies. This may discourage the practice of manipulating data so that hypotheses are confirmed.

When fraud does occur, scientists should be encouraged to blow the whistle when they have strong proof that fraud took place. The Office of Research Integrity (2013) suggests that whistleblowers are a crucial component in the fight against misconduct in science. The ORI recommends that before making an allegation of research fraud, the whistleblower become familiar with the policies of the institution, learn what to include in a report, and find out to whom the report should be given. The whistleblower also should find out about protection against retaliation and about the role that he or she will play after the report is made. The ORI (1995) states that institutions are obligated to protect whistleblowers from retaliation in accordance with U.S. law.

The ORI has developed a "Whistleblower Bill of Rights" (Office of Research Integrity, n.d.). Among the rights enumerated are the rights to lawfully report research misconduct; to be free from retaliation; to fair, impartial, and objective investigation methods; and to have their role acknowledged promptly when misconduct has been confirmed. The ORI underscores the need for institutions to protect whistleblowers from negative consequences.

A survey commissioned by the ORI (Research Triangle Institute, 1995) found that 30.9% of whistleblowers studied reported no negative consequences for their actions. However, 27.9% reported at least one negative consequence, and 41.2% reported multiple negative outcomes. Those negative outcomes included being pressured to drop the charges (42.6%), being hit with a countercomplaint (40%), being ostracized by coworkers (25%), or being fired or not receiving tenure (23.6%). Thus, the climate for whistleblowers is quite hostile. For example, Stephen Bruening based a recommendation that retarded children be treated with stimulants (most research and practice suggested using tranquilizers) on years of fraudulent data. Robert Sprague exposed Bruening's fraud and was subjected to pressure from members of the University of Pittsburgh administration not to pursue his allegations against Bruening. Sprague was even threatened with a lawsuit.

Finally, a researcher must determine whether fraud has actually occurred. In some cases, this may be relatively easy. If a scientist knows for a fact that a particular study reported in a journal was never done, fraud can be alleged with confidence. In other cases, fraud may be detected by noticing strange patterns in the data reported. This is essentially what happened in the case of Cyril Burt, whose research had found strong correlations between the intelligence test scores of identical twins. Some researchers noted that some of Burt's correlations remained invariant from study to study even though the numbers of participants on which the correlations were based changed. This, and the fact that an assistant whom Burt claimed helped him could not be found, served as the foundation of what seemed like a strong case against Burt based on circumstantial evidence.

Burt's posthumous reputation has been ruined and his work discredited. However, Joynson (1989) has reevaluated the Burt case and has provided convincing alternative explanations for the oddities in Burt's data. Joynson maintains that Burt did not deliberately perpetrate a fraud on science and that Burt's name should be cleared. Even if Burt did not commit fraud, he was willing to misrepresent his data and recycle old text (Butler & Petrulis, 1999). On the other hand, there are those who contend that the evidence shows that Burt was guilty of fraud beyond any reasonable doubt (Tucker, 1997).

## QUESTIONS TO PONDER

1. What constitutes research misconduct, and why does it occur?
2. How prevalent is research misconduct?
3. How can research misconduct be dealt with?

## SUMMARY

After you have developed your research idea into a testable hypothesis and settled on a research design, your next step is to recruit participants or subjects for your study. Before you can proceed with your study, however, it must be evaluated for ethical issues. A review board will determine if your research protocol adheres to accepted ethical guidelines.

You must consider the ethics of your research when human participants are chosen for study. Concern over the ethical treatment of participants can be traced back to the Nuremberg trials after World War II. During those trials, medical experiments conducted on inmates in concentration camps came to light. Because of the treatment of individuals in those experiments, the Nuremberg Code was developed to govern experiments with humans. The Declaration of Helsinki expanded on the concepts embodied in the Nuremberg Code and specified a set of ethical principles governing medical research.

The Belmont Report defined three basic principles that apply to all research with human participants. *Respect for persons* states that research participants should be autonomous and allowed to make their own decisions and that participants with limited autonomy deserve special treatment. *Beneficence* states that research participants must have their well-being protected. Beneficence embodies two elements: do no harm and maximize benefits while minimizing harm. *Justice* divides the burdens and benefits equally between the researcher and participant. Many of the ethical rules and guidelines that researchers follow flow from these three principles. The Council for International Organizations of Medical Sciences is an international nongovernmental organization that expanded on the Declaration of Helsinki and the Belmont Report.

The APA developed a code of ethics for treatment of human participants in research that is based on the Nuremberg Code. This is the Ethical Principles of Psychologists and Code of Conduct 2002. Ethical treatment of participants in an experiment requires voluntary participation, informed consent, the right to withdraw, the right to obtain results, and the right to confidentiality (among others).

Because of continued concern over ethical treatment of human research participants and some high-profile cases of research that were ethically questionable, the U.S. Department of Health and Human Services issued its own set of guidelines for research using human participants. These guidelines apply to all research with human participants except for some research that meets certain criteria. The guidelines mandate committee review and approval of research and mandate special protections for vulnerable populations.

The Internet has provided a rich venue for researchers. Some research falls easily under established ethical guidelines. However, other research (e.g., participant observation of chat rooms) poses special ethical questions. These special ethical questions fall into three areas: obtaining informed consent, maintaining privacy and confidentiality of participants, and using deception in Internet research.

The institutional review board (IRB) is a committee that screens research proposals using humans as participants to ensure that the participants are treated ethically. When a research proposal is submitted to the IRB, it normally includes a description of how participants will be acquired, procedures for obtaining informed consent, experimental procedures, potential risks to the participants, and plans for following up the research with reports to participants. Depending on the nature of your research, you may be required to submit a draft of an informed-consent form outlining to your participants the nature of the study. IRB review is important because it allows a group of individuals with no vested interest in your research to ensure that ethical guidelines are followed.

A fair amount of psychological research uses animal subjects. Animals are preferred to humans in situations in which experimental manipulations are unethical for use with humans. However, if you use animal subjects, you are still bound by an ethical code. Animals must be treated humanely. Any research proposing to use animals as subjects must be reviewed by an institutional animal care and use committee (IACUC). The IACUC includes, among others, a veterinarian, a scientist experienced in animal research, and an interested member of the public. There are also federal, state, and local regulations that govern the use of animals in research that must be followed. It is to your advantage to treat your animals ethically because research shows that mistreated animals may yield data that are invalid. Even if your proposal for animal research meets ethical requirements, you still must do a cost–benefit analysis to determine if the study is worth doing.

In addition to treating human participants and animal subjects ethically, you are obligated to treat your science ethically. This means that you should "seek to promote accuracy, honesty, and truthfulness in the science, teaching, and practice of psychology." This admonition from the APA should be taken seriously. Fraudulent, dishonest research has the potential to harm research participants and the credibility of scientists and science in general. Fraud in science is a problem that damages the credibility of science and its findings. Although it is rare, fraud does occur. Fraud includes outright fabrication of data, altering data to look better, selecting only the best data for publication, using the least publishable rule, and taking credit for another's work. Motivation to commit fraud may stem from the desire to publish in prestigious journals, pressure to obtain scarce research funding, pressure to obtain publications necessary for tenure, and scientific elitism. The best way to deal with fraud in research is to train scientists so that they understand the importance of honesty in research.

## KEY TERMS

informed consent

Nuremberg Code

Declaration of Helsinki

Belmont Report

respect for persons

beneficence

justice

Ethical Principles of Psychologists and Code of Conduct 2002

institutional review board (IRB)

institutional animal care and use committee (IACUC)

Office of Research Integrity (ORI)

# 8

## CHAPTER

# Doing Nonexperimental Research

In this chapter, we introduce you to several nonexperimental (correlational) research designs and to observational techniques often associated with them. Although all research is observational (in the sense that variables are observed and recorded), the research designs described in this chapter are purely observational in two senses: (1) They are correlational designs and thus do not involve manipulating independent variables, and (2) all use trained researchers to observe subject's behaviors.

## MAKING AND ASSESSING DIRECT OBSERVATIONS

We begin by describing how to make and assess direct behavioral observations. Although we discuss these techniques in the context of nonexperimental research, bear in mind that they also can be used when conducting experimental research.

When designing an observational study, the first step is to develop behavioral categories.

### Developing Behavioral Categories

**Behavioral categories** (also referred to as *coding schemes* or, in animal research, as *ethograms*) include both the general and specific classes of behavior you are interested in observing. Each category must be operationally defined. For example, Underwood, Scott, Galperin, Bjornstad, and Sexton (2004, p. 1545) defined the following behavioral categories for a study of social exclusion of a "new" child by a pair of friends:

*Verbal social exclusion:* Gossiping, planning to exclude the peer, emphasizing the friendship and the peer's outsider status, and whispering.

*Verbal aggression:* Mockery, sarcasm, and openly critical comments.

*Verbal assertion:* Saying "shhh!" to the peer, telling the peer to stop cheating or to stop bragging, or disputing the peer's comments.

Developing behavioral categories can be a simple or formidable task. Defining categories of physical activity (such as running or talking) is a relatively simple affair; defining categories of social behavior can be comparatively difficult. This is because coding socially based behaviors may involve cultural traditions that are not agreed on (e.g., coding certain speech as "obscene") (Bakeman & Gottman, 1997).

Your behavioral categories operationally define what behaviors are recorded during observation periods. It is important to define clear, mutually exclusive categories. Your observers should not be left wondering what category a particular behavior falls into. Ill-defined, ambiguous, or overlapping categories lead to recording errors and results that are difficult to interpret.

To develop clear, well-defined categories, begin with a clear idea about the hypotheses your study will be investigating. Clearly defined hypotheses help narrow your behavioral categories to those that are central to your research questions. Also, keep your behavioral categories as simple as possible (Bakeman & Gottman, 1997) and stay focused on your research objectives. Avoid the temptation to accomplish too much within a single study.

One way to develop behavioral categories is to make informal, preliminary observations of your subjects under the conditions that will prevail during your study. During these preliminary observation periods, become familiar with the behaviors exhibited by your subjects, and construct as complete a list of them as you can. Later, you can condense these behaviors into fewer categories, if necessary.

Another way to develop behavioral categories is to conduct a literature search to determine how other researchers in your field define behavioral categories in research situations similar to yours. You might even find an article in which the researchers used categories that are nearly perfect for your study. Adapting someone else's categories for your own use in an acceptable practice. In fact, standardizing on categories used in previous research will enhance the comparability of your data with data previously reported.

Even if you do find an article with what appear to be the perfect categories, make some preliminary observations to assure the categories fit your research needs. Take the time necessary to develop your categories carefully. In the long run, it is easier to adjust things before you begin your study than to worry about how to analyze data that were collected using poorly defined categories.

## Quantifying Behavior in an Observational Study

As with any other type of measure, direct behavioral observation requires that you develop ways to quantify the behaviors under observation. Methods used to quantify behavior include the frequency method, the duration method, and the intervals method (Badia & Runyon, 1982).

*Frequency Method*   You record the number of times a particular behavior occurs within a time period. This number is the frequency of the behavior. For example, Underwood et al. (2004) counted the number of statements the children made that were socially exclusive, aggressive, or assertive.

*Duration Method*    Your interest is in how long a particular behavior lasts. For example, you could record the duration of each verbally aggressive act displayed by children during a game-playing session. You can use the duration method along with the frequency method. In this case, you record both the frequency of occurrence of a behavior (e.g., the number of verbally aggressive acts) and its duration (e.g., how long a verbally aggressive act lasts).

*Intervals Method*    You divide your observation period into discrete time intervals and then record whether a behavior occurs within each interval. For instance, you might record whether an act of verbal exclusion occurs during successive 10-second time periods. Your intervals should be short enough that only one instance of a behavior can occur during an interval.

## Recording Single Events or Behavior Sequences

Researchers doing observational studies have long recorded single events occurring within some identifiable observation period. Bakeman and Gottman (1997) advocate looking at *behavior sequences* rather than at isolated behavioral events. Consider an observational study of language development in which you record the number of times a parent uses language to correct a child's behavior. Although such data may be informative, a better strategy might be to record those same behaviors sequentially, noting which instances of language normally follow one another. Is a harsh reprimand more likely to follow destructive behavior than nondestructive behavior? Recording such behavior sequences provides a more complete picture of complex social behaviors and the transitions between them.

Although recording behavior sequences requires more effort than recording single events, the richness of the resulting data may be well worth the effort. You can find more information about this method in Bakeman and Gottman (1997), *Observing Interaction: An Introduction to Sequential Analysis.* For a more advanced treatment, see Gottman and Roy (2008).

## Making Your Observations Live or from Recordings

You can conduct your behavioral observations in real time or video-record the activities of interest and base your observations on what you observe in these recordings. Although situations exist in which live observations are the only practical option, recording the action has significant advantages that make it the best choice. First, because you have a permanent record, you can review your subjects' behavior several times, perhaps picking up nuances you might have missed in a live observation. You could also use the recording to identify behavior sequences or to recode the behaviors in terms of other variables not initially chosen (e.g., duration). Second, you can have multiple observers watch the recording independently and then compare their evaluations of behavior. (Although you can use multiple observers for live observations, it may be disruptive to your subjects to have several observers watching.) Finally, you may be able to hide a camera more easily than you can hide yourself. The hidden camera may be less disruptive of your subjects' behavior than an observer.

## Coding the Behaviors

Whether you make your observations live or work from a recording, you will need a system for coding the behaviors you observe. One option is to develop a paper-and-pencil coding form similar to the one shown in Figure 8-1, which was developed for observations of children in day care using the intervals method. Your observers would use the form to code the behavior observed during each successive 10-second interval.

Another coding method involves the use of an audio recorder. Observers of live or recorded behavior watch the ongoing behavior stream and make notes by speaking into the recorder.

**FIGURE 8-1**   Example of a paper-and-pencil coding sheet for an observational study using event sampling.

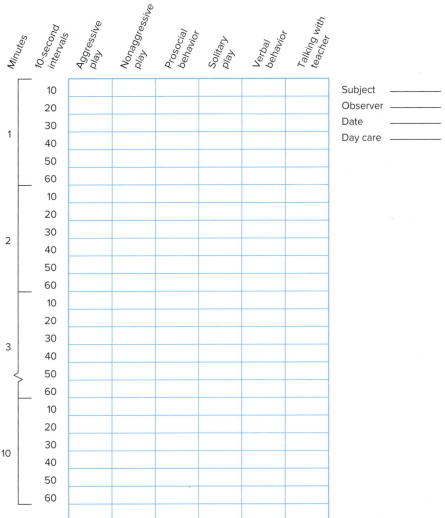

Paper-and-pencil coding largely has been replaced by applications running on personal computers and hand-held digital devices. The researcher can determine the behavioral categories to be coded and the type of data to be collected. Where convenient, these devices and their associated applications also may be used to digitally record live behavior sessions for later analysis.

During coding (whether done live or from a recording), your observers indicate the current ongoing behavior by touching the appropriate label being displayed on the device's touchscreen or by pressing a key assigned to that behavior on the keyboard. The device keeps track of the times at which each behavioral category is registered. The application analyzes this record to determine such things as the category of behavior coded in successive intervals (similar to the coding-sheet example), the duration of each bout of behavior, and the frequency with which the behavior occurred during the session.

Which of these coding methods is best depends on the nature of your study and limitations inherent in the situation. You can use paper-and-pencil coding sheets in just about any situation. They are quiet, cheap, and if properly constructed, efficient. However, if you require your observers to make extensive notes (not just checking behavioral categories), the task may become too complex and time consuming, especially if behaviors occur in rapid succession. In such cases, consider having your observers use audio recorders. Your observers will be able to speak into the recorder faster than they could make written notes. They also can keep their eyes on the subjects *while* making their notes. A disadvantage is that observers speaking into a recording device may disturb your subjects. Consequently, use this technique only when your observers are out of earshot of your subjects. Digital devices running behavior coding applications offer the greatest flexibility in terms of the information that can be extracted from the observational record, eliminate the need to manually transcribe the data for computer analysis, and may reduce coding errors relative to coding on paper and pencil. Phillips, Mudford, Zeleny, and Elliffe (2014) assessed the accuracy and precision of coding using paper-and-pencil, computer keyboard, or touchscreen and found that coding via touchscreen was superior to these other two methods.

## Coping with Complexity: Sampling Strategies

Imagine you are conducting a study of preschool children. You sit in an observation room equipped with a one-way mirror and begin to observe the children in the classroom on the other side of the mirror. It doesn't take you long to realize that something is wrong. Your participants are running around in small groups, scurrying here and there. You cannot possibly observe all the children at once. Dejectedly, you leave the preschool and return home to work out an effective observation strategy.

This vignette illustrates an important fact about behavioral observation: Having clearly defined behavioral categories and adequate quantification methods does not guarantee that your observational techniques will work. Naturally occurring behavior is often complex and fast paced. To make effective observations, you may need to use special techniques to deal with the rate at which the behaviors you wish to observe occur.

One solution to the problem, noted previously, is to video-record the behaviors for later observation and analysis. During playback, you can slow the action as necessary. You also can repeat the playback as often as needed to code the behaviors.

Another solution is to sample the behaviors under observation rather than attempt to record every occurrence. Three sampling techniques from which to choose are time sampling, individual sampling, and event sampling (Conrad & Maul, 1981).

*Time Sampling*    You scan the group for a specific period of time (e.g., 30 seconds) and then record the observed behaviors for the next period (e.g., another 30 seconds). You alternate between periods of observation and recording as long as necessary. Time sampling is most appropriate when the behavior occurs continuously rather than in short bursts spaced over time and when you are observing large groups of subjects engaged in complex interactions. This technique involves making rather detailed records of your observations rather than simply coding predefined behaviors into categories.

*Individual Sampling*    You select a single subject for observation over a given time period (e.g., 10 minutes) and record the observed behavior. Over successive time periods, repeat your observations for other individuals in the observed group. Individual sampling is most appropriate when you want to preserve the organization of an individual's behavior over time rather than simply noting how often particular behaviors occur.

*Event Sampling*    You observe only one behavior (e.g., sharing behavior) and record all instances of that behavior. Event sampling is most useful when you can clearly define one behavior of interest and focus on that one behavior.

## QUESTIONS TO PONDER

1. What are the defining characteristics of observational research?
2. How are behavioral categories that are used in observational research developed?
3. What are the techniques used to make behavioral observations in observational research?
4. What is the distinction between recording single acts and behavior sequences?
5. What are the sampling techniques used to handle complexity when making behavioral observations?

## Establishing the Accuracy and Reliability of Your Observations

Assume that you have adequately defined the behavior you want to observe, developed a coding scheme, and worked out how you are going to conduct your observations. You go into the field and make your observations. You apparently have covered every possible base and believe that your observations are accurate and reliable. But are they? Your personal biases and expectations may have affected how you recorded the behavior observed. As with any measurement technique, when you conduct direct behavioral observations, you should make an effort to establish their accuracy and reliability.

Unfortunately, it can be difficult to establish the accuracy of direct behavioral observations because establishing accuracy requires having an accepted standard against which to compare an observer's performance. If the observational session has been recorded, you could review the recorded behavior and compare it to the observer's coding. Judging the accuracy of these judgments will be easy for some behaviors (e.g., how many times a child got up from her chair), but for others, the interpretation may be more difficult. In those cases, the best one may be able to do is to look for consensus—do two or more observers agree as to how a given instance of behavior should be coded? Although you cannot be sure that the judgment is accurate, consensus at least indicates that your observers are sorting behaviors into categories in the same way. Poor agreement indicates that your observers require more training in the use of those categories or that the categories themselves need to be revised or better defined.

Theoretically, if you use well-trained observers and well-defined behavior categories, there should be a minimum of disagreement. However, disagreement is likely to arise despite your best efforts. Observers invariably differ in how they see and interpret behavior. Something as simple as a different angle of view can cause a disagreement. Disagreement also may arise if you have not clearly defined your behavioral categories.

Observer agreement reflects not only the possible accuracy of observers' coding but also its reliability. Observations are unreliable to the extent that judgments differ. For this reason, agreement is often described as a measure of **interrater reliability**—the degree to which two or more observers agree in their classification or quantification of behavior. Bakeman and Gottman (1997) identify three reasons to check for interrater reliability. First, establishing interrater reliability helps ensure that your observers are accurate and that you can reproduce your procedures. Second, you can check to see that your observers meet some standard of reliability that you have established. Third, you can detect any problems and correct them with additional observer training.

In this section, we discuss three measures of interrater reliability, including two based on agreement and one based on correlation. We begin with percent agreement.

*Percent Agreement*    If you have nominal behavioral categories (i.e., differing only in kind and not quantity), you could use *percent agreement* as your measure of interrater reliability. If you had two observers, this method involves counting the number of times your observers agreed, dividing this number by the total number of observations, and multiplying by 100. For example, if your observers agreed on 8 of 10 observations, percent agreement would be 80%.

Percent agreement can be extended to cases involving more than two observers by computing percent agreement for each possible pair of observers and averaging the result. Also, although originally designed for nominal-scale data (unordered categories), percent agreement has been applied to ordinal data (categories ordered by quantity) such as ratings on a Likert scale (e.g., strongly disapprove, disapprove, neutral, approve, strongly approve). However, in such cases percent agreement is likely to understate the true degree of agreement because observers may differ only slightly in the ratings they assign but consistently change their ratings in the same direction across observations (Mitchell, 1979). You can reduce this problem somewhat by using a looser definition of agreement. For instance, you could say that your observers agree if they choose the same or adjacent ratings.

Although simple to calculate, percent agreement has a drawback: It gives you only a raw level of agreement. Some agreement between observers is to be expected based on chance alone. Percent agreement makes no provision for estimating the extent to which the agreement observed may have occurred by chance. Furthermore, behaviors that occur with very high or low frequency may have extremely high levels of chance agreement. In those cases, percent agreement overstates the true level of interrater agreement (Mitchell, 1979).

*Cohen's Kappa*     A more popular method of assessing interrater reliability than percent agreement is **Cohen's Kappa (K)**. Like percent agreement, Cohen's Kappa provides a measure of agreement between two observers coding on a nominal scale. Unlike percent agreement, it assesses the observed level of agreement relative to the level of agreement that would be expected by chance (Bakeman & Gottman, 1997). To use this method, you need to determine (1) the proportion of actual agreement between observers (actual agreement) and (2) the proportion of agreement you would expect by chance (expected agreement). Use these two values in the following formula (Bakeman & Gottman, 1997):

$$K = \frac{P_o - P_c}{1 - P_c}$$

where $P_o$ is the observed proportion of actual agreement and $P_c$ is the proportion of agreement expected by chance. Generally, a Cohen's Kappa value of .7 or greater indicates acceptable interrater reliability (Bakeman & Gottman, 1997).

Suppose you conducted a study of the relationship between the number of hours that an infant spends in day care and later attachment security. (Attachment security reflects how protected a child feels by the caregivers and how confident the child feels that an absent caregiver will return.) As your measure of attachment security, you have two observers watch a mother and her child for a 20-minute period. The coding scheme here is simple. All your observers are required to do is code the child's behavior as indicative of either a "secure attachment" or an "insecure attachment" within each of 20 one-minute observation periods. Sample coding sheets are shown in Figure 8-2. A mark in a cell indicates that the behavior of the child fell into that category.

The first step in computing Cohen's Kappa is to tabulate in a *confusion matrix* the frequencies of agreements and disagreements between observers (Bakeman & Gottman, 1997), as shown in Figure 8-3. The numbers on the diagonal represent agreements, and the numbers off the diagonal represent disagreements. The numbers along the right edge and bottom of the matrix represent the row and column totals and the total number of observations.

The next step is compute the value of Cohen's Kappa. First, determine the proportion of actual agreement by summing the values along the diagonal and dividing by the total number of observations:

$$P_o = \frac{16 + 3}{20} = .95$$

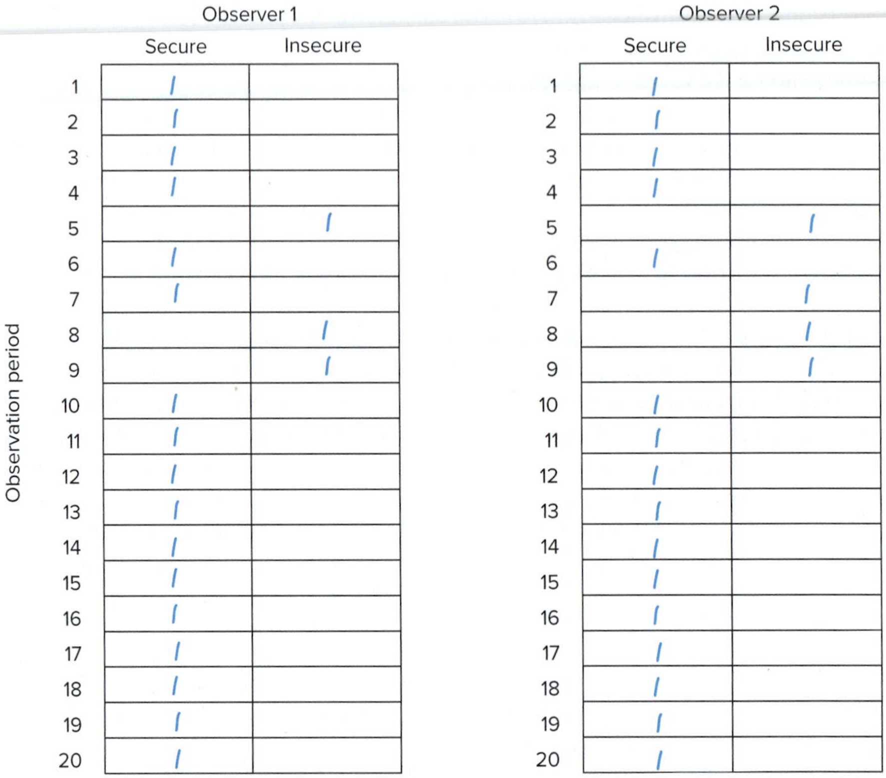

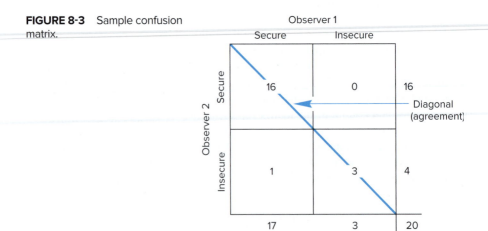

**FIGURE 8-2**    Sample coding sheets for two observers counting "secure" and "insecure" behavior instances.

**FIGURE 8-3**    Sample confusion matrix.

Next, find the proportion of expected agreement by multiplying corresponding row and column totals and dividing by the number of observations squared (Bakeman & Gottman, 1997):

$$P_c = \frac{(17 \times 16) + (3 \times 4)}{20^2} = .71$$

Finally, enter these numbers into the formula for Cohen's Kappa:

$$K = \frac{.95 - .71}{1 - .71} = .83$$

Although Cohen's Kappa was designed to take chance agreement into account, John Uebersax (2016) has argued that the correction for chance is based on an incorrect model of how observers behave and that, in fact, it is unnecessary. (See Uebersax, 2016, for details.) At present, however, the issue remains unsettled, and Cohen's Kappa remains the most popular measure of interobserver agreement.

*Pearson's Product-Moment Correlation*  Pearson's product-moment correlation coefficient, or Pearson $r$ (see Chapter 13), provides a convenient alternative to Cohen's Kappa for measuring interrater agreement. Table 8-1 shows the frequency of aggressive behavior among members of a hypothetical monkey colony over five 2-minute observation periods as coded by two observers. If your observers agree, Pearson $r$ will be strong and positive. For example, Pearson $r$ for the data shown in Table 8-1 is .90. This strong correlation (the maximum possible is 1.00) indicates substantial agreement. After calculating Pearson $r$, you can easily determine its statistical significance (see Chapter 13), an advantage over Cohen's Kappa.

You must be cautious when using Pearson $r$ to assess interrater agreement. Two sets of numbers can be highly correlated even when observers disagree markedly. This situation occurs when the *magnitudes* of the recorded scores increase and decrease similarly across observations by the two observers but differ in absolute value. For example, assume observer 1 recorded 1, 2, 3, 4, and 5 and observer 2 recorded 6, 7, 8, 9, and 10 over the same intervals. These numbers are perfectly correlated ($r = 1.00$), yet the two observers never agreed on the actual numbers to record. You can check for this problem by comparing the means and standard deviations of

**TABLE 8-1  Hypothetical Monkey Aggression Data Collected by Two Observers**

| FREQUENCY OF AGGRESSIVE BEHAVIOR | | |
| --- | --- | --- |
| *Observation Period* | *Observer 1* | *Observer 2* |
| One | 6 | 7 |
| Two | 2 | 4 |
| Three | 1 | 0 |
| Four | 5 | 7 |
| Five | 3 | 2 |

**TABLE 8-2   Hypothetical Data for an Intraclass Correlation Coefficient to Test Interrater Reliability**

| PARTICIPANT | RATER 1 | RATER 2 |
|:---:|:---:|:---:|
| 1 | 8 | 10 |
| 2 | 6 | 5 |
| 3 | 2 | 2 |
| 4 | 7 | 7 |
| 5 | 5 | 5 |
| 6 | 6 | 9 |
| 7 | 1 | 1 |
| 8 | 6 | 6 |
| 9 | 7 | 8 |
| 10 | 8 | 7 |

the two sets of scores. If they are similar and Pearson $r$ is high, you can safely assume that your observers agree.

*Intraclass Correlation Coefficient (ICC)*   You can use the **intraclass correlation coefficient ($r_I$)** to assess reliability if your observations are scaled on an interval or ratio scale of measurement. For example, you could use the ICC if you had observers count the frequency of aggressive behavior, which is a ratio-scaled measure. The ICC uses an analysis-of-variance approach to assess reliability. To compute an ICC, first construct a two-way table in which the columns represent observers' ratings (one column for each observer) and the rows represent participants (each row has the data from one participant), as shown in Table 8-2. The formula for calculating $r_I$ uses the mean squares ($MS$) components from the analysis of variance: the mean square within subjects ($MS_W$) and mean square between subjects ($MS_B$). The formula used to calculate $r_I$ suggested by Shrout and Fleiss (1979) is

$$r_I = \frac{MS_B - MS_W}{MS_B + (k - 1)(MS_W)}$$

where $k$ is the number of raters. For the data shown in Table 8-2, we have

$$r_I = \frac{14.6056 - .3833}{14.6056 + (2 - 1)(.3833)} = .95$$

ICC analysis is a flexible, powerful tool for evaluating interrater reliability. See Shrout and Fleiss (1979) and McGraw and Wong (1996) for in-depth discussions of ICC.

*Dealing with Data from Multiple Observers*    When multiple observers disagree, what should you do? If you have a high level of agreement, you can average across observers. For example, in Table 8-1, you can average across observers within each observation period to get a mean, or $M$ [for the first period, $M = (6 + 7)/2 = 6.5$], and then obtain an overall average across observation periods. This gives you the average aggression shown during the observation period.

Another common method is to have observers meet and resolve any discrepancies. This method is practical when you have recorded the behavior electronically and can review it. Yet another method is to designate one of the observers as the "main observer" and the other as the "secondary observer." Make this designation before you begin your observations. The observations from the "main observer" then serve as the numbers used in any data analyses. You use the observations from the "secondary observer" to establish reliability.

## Sources of Bias in Observational Research

Because observational research is a human endeavor, a degree of bias may contaminate the observations. One source of bias that can easily be avoided is observer bias. *Observer bias* occurs when your observers know the goals of a study or the hypotheses you are testing and their observations are influenced by this information. For example, suppose you have hypothesized that males will show more interpersonal aggression than females and have told your observers of this hypothesis. Your observers see a male child roughly take a toy away from another child and later see a female child do the same. Because of observer bias, your observers may code the male child's behavior, but not the female child's behavior, as aggressive. This is the same problem discussed in Chapter 5 as experimenter bias, and the solution is the same: Use a *blind observer*. A blind observer is one who is unaware of the hypotheses being tested. (For more details about blind techniques, see Chapter 5.)

Another source of bias in observational research arises when observers interpret what they see rather than simply record behavior. We have all seen nature specials on television in which a researcher is observing animals in the wild (e.g., chimpanzees). Too often, those researchers infer intentions behind the behaviors they observe. When one chimp prods another with a stick, for example, the researcher may record the behavior as a "playful, mischievous attack."

The problem with such inferences is that we simply do not know whether they are correct. We tend to interpret animals' behaviors and motives based on how we humans feel and behave. However, the animal's motivations and emotions may in fact be very different from ours. Stick to what is immediately apparent from the observation. If you have preserved the actual behavior in your records rather than your interpretation of the behavior, you can always provide an interpretation later. If new evidence suggests a different interpretation, you will have the original behavioral observations available to reinterpret.

When your subjects are people, you should still do your best to record behaviors rather than your interpretations of those behaviors. Piaget showed that inferences concerning the motivation and knowledge of children are often wrong, and the same is probably true of inferences about adults. Once again, if your data preserve the behavior rather than your interpretations of the behavior, you can always reinterpret your data later if required by new evidence.

## Quantitative and Qualitative Approaches to Data Collection

When making your observations and recording behavior, you can use two approaches to recording behavior. Counting and otherwise quantifying behavior yield **quantitative data**, which are expressed numerically. The main advantage of quantitative data is that a wide range of statistical tests is available for analyzing these data. Using a *quantitative approach* to study client reactions to a new form of psychotherapy, you might have therapy clients rate how they feel about their therapy on rating scales, or you might count the number of times that a certain thing was mentioned (such as the warmth of the experimenter). In both instances, your data will be numbers that can be mathematically manipulated and analyzed with available descriptive and inferential statistics.

In some instances, you might consider collecting **qualitative data**. Qualitative data consist of written records of observed behavior that you analyze qualitatively. No numbers are generated on rating scales nor are there counts of behavior. Using a *qualitative approach* to study client reactions to a new therapy technique, you could interview clients and then review the interview protocols to extract themes that emerged via the interviews (e.g., clients' impressions of the language used during the therapy). Because the data are qualitative, you cannot apply standard descriptive and inferential statistics to your data. In fact, analysis of qualitative data poses special problems for researchers. Usually, there are large amounts of raw data to deal with, and you will need specialized computer programs to analyze qualitative verbal information.

Depending on your research situation, you may collect only quantitative data, only qualitative data, or, as many studies do, a combination of the two. In the sections that follow, which introduce various nonexperimental methods, we present a mix of examples illustrating both quantitative and qualitative approaches.

## QUESTIONS TO PONDER

1. Why should you evaluate interrater reliability?
2. What are the techniques used to evaluate interrater reliability, and when would each be used?
3. How do you deal with data from multiple observers?
4. What are the sources of bias in observational research, and how can the bias be reduced?
5. What is the difference between quantitative and qualitative data?
6. What are the problems inherent in collecting qualitative data?

## NONEXPERIMENTAL RESEARCH DESIGNS

Now that you know how to develop and use direct behavioral measures, it is time to become familiar with several nonexperimental approaches to data collection. Keep in mind that in each of these designs you can apply any of the aforementioned observational methods to collect your data.

## Naturalistic Observation

**Naturalistic observation** involves observing your subjects in their natural environments without making any attempt to control or manipulate variables. For example, you might observe chimpanzees in their African habitat, children in a day-care center, shoppers in a mall, or participants in a court proceeding. In all these cases, you would avoid making any changes in the situation that might affect the natural, ongoing behaviors of your subjects.

*Making Unobtrusive Observations*   Although you may not intend it, the mere act of observing may disturb the behavior of your subjects. Such disturbances may reduce the internal or external validity of your observations. To prevent this difficulty, you should make *unobtrusive observations*—observations that do not alter the natural behaviors of your subjects.

Putting this requirement into practice may involve the use of special equipment. When studying the nesting habits of a particular species of birds, for example, you may have to build a blind (an enclosure that shields you from the view of your subjects) from which to make your observations. When studying social interactions among preschool children in a day-care center, you may have to make your observations from behind a one-way mirror. In either case, you want to prevent your subjects from knowing that they are being observed.

Unfortunately, it is not always possible to remain hidden. For example, you may need to be closer to your subjects than a blind or observation room allows. In such cases, a widely used technique is to habituate your subjects to your presence (a fancy way of saying "letting your subjects get used to you") before you begin making your observations. Habituating subjects involves gradually introducing yourself to the environment of your subjects. Eventually, your subjects will view your presence as normal and ignore you. If you were interested in observing children in a day-care center, for example, you might begin by sitting quietly away from the children (perhaps in a far corner of the room) until the children no longer paid attention to you. Gradually, you would move closer to the children, allowing them to habituate to your presence at each step before moving closer.

Habituation may be necessary even if you are going to videotape behavior for later analysis. The presence of a video camera in a room will attract attention at first. Allowing your subjects to habituate to the camera before you begin your observations will help reduce the camera's disruptive effects. Fortunately, modern video cameras have gotten smaller and smaller, making them less obtrusive.

You also can make observations unobtrusively by abandoning direct observations of behavior in favor of *indirect measures*. For example, to study recycling behavior you could look through recycling bins or trash to gauge the extent to which your participants recycle and determine the types of materials they recycle. In this case, participants do not know that their behavior is being observed (unless you get caught snooping through their trash and recycling material).

*Advantages and Disadvantages of Naturalistic Observation*   Naturalistic observation gives you insight into how behavior occurs in the real world. The observations you make are not tainted by an artificial laboratory setting, and therefore you can be reasonably sure that your observations are representative of naturally occurring behavior. In other words, properly conducted naturalistic observation has extremely high external validity.

Because naturalistic observation allows you only to describe the observed behavior, you cannot use this technique to investigate the underlying *causes* of those behaviors. In addition, naturalistic observation can be time consuming and expensive. Unlike some types of observation in which subjects in effect record their own data, naturalistic observation requires you to be there, engaged in observation, during the entire data-collecting period, which may last hours, days, or longer. Also, getting to the natural habitat of your subjects may not be easy. In some cases (such as observing chimpanzee behavior in the wild, as Jane Goodall did), naturalistic observation requires traveling great distances to reach the habitat of your subjects.

*An Example of Naturalistic Observation: Communication Among the Elderly*   As an example of naturalistic observation consider a study of communication patterns among elderly patients with aphasia (loss of speech functions) resulting from a stroke, conducted by Brownyn Davidson, Linda Worall, and Louise Hickson (2003). In this study, participant-observers made observations of communication during patients' everyday activities. (We discuss participant observation later in the section on ethnography.) Davidson et al. instructed the participant-observers not to initiate any communication with the patients but to make limited responses when addressed by patients. Observations were also made of healthy older adults.

Each patient was observed for 8 hours over three randomly determined time periods within a week. Davidson et al. (2003) had observers code a number of communication behaviors, including conversations, greetings, talking to pets, talking on the telephone, writing/word processing, and storytelling. Davidson et al. found that patients' conversations were most likely to occur at home or in some social group. They also found that aphasic and healthy elderly adults engaged in communication on a range of topics that were similar to those of healthy elderly adults. The main difference between the aphasic and elderly adults was that aphasics engaged in quantitatively less communication than healthy elderly adults. Finally, aphasics were far less likely to engage in storytelling than healthy elderly adults.

## Ethnography

In **ethnography**, a researcher becomes immersed in the behavioral or social system being studied (Berg, 2009). The technique is used primarily to study and describe the functioning of cultures through a study of social interactions and expressions between people and groups (Berg, 2009). Like an investigative reporter or undercover police officer, you insinuate yourself within a group and study the social structures and interaction patterns of that group from within. Your role as a researcher is to make careful observations and record the social structure of the group that you are studying.

Ethnography is a time-tested research technique that has been popular, especially in the field of anthropology. However, it is also used in sociological and psychological studies of various behavior systems. For example, ethnography is used to study client and therapist perceptions of marital therapy (Smith, Sells, & Clevenger, 1994), the learning of aggressive behaviors in different cultures (e.g., Fry, 1992), the assassination of John F. Kennedy (Trujillo, 1993), the sudden death of loved ones (Ellis, 1993), and even the consumer-based subculture of modern bikers who ride Harley-Davidson motorcycles (Schouten & McAlexander, 1995). In most cases, you conduct ethnographic research in field settings, which makes the ethnographer a field researcher.

As with any research method, ethnography takes a systematic approach to the topics and systems for which it is used. Berg (2009) describes the process of conducting ethnographic research in detail. According to Berg, an ethnographer faces several issues with this type of research. We explore these next.

*Observing as a Participant or Nonparticipant*     One decision that you will have to make early on is whether to conduct your observations using **participant observation**, in which you act as a functioning member of the group, or using **nonparticipant observation**, in which you observe as a nonmember. In addition, you will have to decide whether to conduct your observations overtly (the group members know that you are conducting research on the group) or covertly (unobtrusive observation). When done overtly, both participant and nonparticipant observation carry the possibility of subject reactivity; as we noted in Chapter 5, group members who know they are being observed may behave differently than they otherwise would, thus threatening external validity. This problem becomes more serious with participant observation in which you interact with your participants.

You can minimize this problem by training participant-observers not to interfere with the natural process of the group being studied or by using observers who are blind to the purposes of the study. Alternatively, if you must use participant observation, you could always become a passive participant. As such, you would keep your contributions to the group to a minimum so that you would not significantly alter the natural flow of behavior. Your main role would be to observe and record what is going on. Finally, if possible, you could become a nonparticipant-observer and avoid interacting with the group altogether.

You can reduce or remove the problem of reactivity by choosing to observe covertly. Nonparticipant covert observation is essentially naturalistic observation. Because your subjects do not know they are being observed, their behavior will be natural. Becoming a covert participant entails joining the group to be observed without disclosing your status as a researcher—again, your subjects will behave naturally in your presence. Additionally, by using covert entry, you may be able to gain access to information that would not be available if you used an overt entry strategy.

When using covert entry, you still need to be concerned about your presence disrupting the normal flow of the social interactions within the group. Your presence as a member-participant may influence how the group functions.

The practice of covertly infiltrating a group carries with it ethical liabilities. Because your subjects are not aware that they are being studied, they cannot give informed consent to participate. As discussed in Chapter 7, such violations may be acceptable if your results promise to make a significant contribution to the understanding of behavior. Thus, before deciding on covert entry, you must weigh the potential benefit of your research against the potential costs to the participants. You should adopt a covert entry strategy only if you and your institutional review board agree that the potential benefits outweigh the potential costs.

*Gaining Access to a Field Setting*    Your first task when conducting ethnographic research is to gain access to the group or organization you wish to study. In some cases, this would be easy. For example, if you wanted to conduct an ethnographic study of mall shoppers during the Christmas shopping season, you would only need to situate yourself in a mall and record the behaviors and verbalizations of shoppers. Being a public place, the mall offers free and unlimited access. In other cases, settings are more difficult to access. To conduct an ethnographic study of the police subculture, for example, you probably would need to obtain the permission of the police commissioner, various high-ranking police officers, and perhaps the rank-and-file police officers. Only then would you have access to police stations, squad cars, patrols, and so on. Access to the meeting places of elite groups (e.g., country clubs) also may be difficult because such groups often establish barriers and obstacles (such as membership requirements and restrictive guest access) to limit who has access to the facilities (Berg, 2009).

*Gaining Entry into the Group*    Gaining access to the research setting often requires gaining entry into the group you plan to study. A popular strategy is *case and approach* (Berg, 2009). In this strategy, you first "case" the group, much as a criminal cases a bank before robbing it. That is, you try to find information about the group, such as its social structure, its hierarchy of authority (if any), and its rituals and routines. Such foreknowledge makes it easier to enter the group and function effectively once inside. Berg suggests starting your search in the local library. Here you may find valuable information in newspapers, magazines, and other information sources. You also might check the Internet; many groups maintain websites that provide literature about themselves. Social networking sites such as Twitter or Instagram may also provide information.

To enter the group, you may have to bargain with the members to establish your role and your boundaries (Berg, 2009). You also may find that you need to get past *gatekeepers* who serve as formal or informal protectors of the group. Getting past gatekeepers may require some negotiation and mediation (Berg, 2009). If you can cast your research in a favorable light, you may facilitate your entry into the group. For example, in an ethnographic study of prisoners in a county jail, the gatekeepers are the warden and high-ranking enforcement officials. Your chances of gaining entry into the prison population will be greater if you can convince those officials of the potential benefits of your study.

Another strategy for gaining entry into a group is to use *guides* and *informants* (Berg, 2009). These are members of the group (e.g., model inmates and correction officers) who can help convince the gatekeepers that your aims are legitimate and your study is worthwhile.

Although these techniques for gaining entry into a group are effective, they raise some ethical issues. The targets of your observations may not know they are being studied, so participants cannot give informed consent. However, recall from Chapter 7 that under certain conditions an institutional review board (IRB) may approve a study that does not include informed consent. You need to consider the ethical implications of your ethnographic research and justify to an IRB the need to suspend the requirement for informed consent.

*Becoming Invisible*    Once inside the group, your presence may alter the behavior of your participants or the operation of the social system you are studying. Berg (2009) suggests several strategies for making yourself "invisible." If you are using an overt entry strategy, you could join in the routines and rituals of your participants, or you could foster good relations with your participants. You also could choose to enter covertly, masking your role as researcher. Whichever strategy you use, there are dangers to making yourself invisible (Berg, 2009). For example, if you use covert entry, there is the danger that your identity will be discovered, which would shatter any credibility you may have had.

*Making Observations and Recording Data*    The essence of ethnography is to keep a careful record of what transpires within the group being studied. The various recording techniques discussed previously can be applied to ethnography. You could, for example, make copious notes during critical interactions. If you were riding along with police officers, you could make notes of what is said and done during routine traffic stops. When such overt note taking is not possible (especially if you have decided to use covert entry into a group), you could instead keep scraps of paper or index cards and jot down thoughts you will expand later (Berg, 2009). You also could use voice-activated audio recorders or other recording devices. Another strategy involves waiting until the end of the day when you are alone to record your observations. One drawback to this latter strategy is that you are relying on your memory for your field notes. Over the course of the day, you may forget some details or distort others.

*Analyzing Ethnographic Data*    If you take a purely qualitative approach, your data do not take the form of numbers (e.g., the number of times that a police officer threatens a suspect with arrest) but rather the form of narrative field notes from which themes and ideas are to be extracted. The first step in analyzing ethnographic data is to do an initial reading of your field notes to identify any themes and hypotheses, perhaps with an eye toward identifying themes and hypotheses overlooked (Berg, 2009). You also would systematically extract any major topics, issues, or themes present in your field records (Berg, 2009). The second step in analyzing ethnographic data is to code any systematic patterns in your notes and consider doing an in-depth content analysis (as discussed later in this chapter). Of course, this analysis strategy would be strengthened by using multiple, independent coders and content analyzers.

*An Example of Ethnography: Rationalizing Smoking*    Despite the well-known dangers of smoking, millions of people around the world continue to smoke or begin smoking each year. Smokers are exposed to warnings about smoking (in public service advertisements, in messages on packs of cigars and cigarettes, and via the news media) and have been socially marginalized (e.g., relegated to smoking in designated areas only, away from nonsmokers). Despite all of this, smoking remains popular. How do people who smoke reconcile the hazards and social stigma associated with smoking and their continued smoking? One way is to rationalize. For example, smokers may come up with a list of advantages to smoking (e.g., weight control or a calming effect) to justify their decision to smoke. An ethnographic study conducted by Alan DeSantis (2003) investigated how smokers rationalized their decision to continue smoking.

DeSantis (2003) conducted his ethnographic study on cigar smokers who met regularly at a popular cigar shop in Kentucky. The study was conducted over a 3-year period (1997–2000). DeSantis used participant observation as his principal method of data collection. Cigar shop patrons were aware that DeSantis was a researcher. Before he began his study, DeSantis became a regular at the cigar shop, which allowed him to be "both a friend and a researcher with unlimited access to the shop's rituals, conversations, self-disclosures, arguments, parties and weekend outings" (p. 435). DeSantis was able to make firsthand observations of the cigar patrons' professional and private lives. He even became the drummer in the cigar shop's rock 'n' roll band! DeSantis, however, was very careful not to get so close to his participants that his observations and conclusions were compromised.

DeSantis (2003) made observations an average of 2 days per week (2 hours per visit) over the 3-year period of the study, using three procedures to collect data. First, he made extensive field notes in a notebook, to which the participants quickly habituated. Second, audio recordings were made of more extensive interactions and analyzed later. Third, DeSantis made extensive postencounter field notes. That is, after an observation at the shop, he would make extensive detailed notes of the observation session.

DeSantis (2003) found that the cigar store patrons developed five rationalizations for their smoking. These five rationalizations recurred throughout the period of observation. The five recurring rationalizations are as follows:

1. Things done in moderation won't hurt you.

2. Cigar smoking is actually beneficial to one's health through stress reduction.

3. Cigars are not as bad as cigarettes.

4. Research linking cigar smoking to health consequences is flawed and therefore invalid.

5. Other hazards in life are far more dangerous than cigar smoking.

DeSantis (2003) provided qualitative data to support each rationalization. These data were actual statements made by the cigar smokers. For example, in support of the moderation argument, one patron noted that "if I smoked cigars constantly, seven days a week, had one in my mouth all the time, I would worry about it. But on most Sundays, I will not smoke at all" (p. 447). In support of the health benefits rationalization a patron said, "I am kind of a hyper guy anyway. I need something to cool me down. That is probably why I smoke" (p. 449). And, in support of the flawed research rationalization another patron said, "What they tell you today is good for you, will kill you tomorrow. I have seen too many reversals over the years" (p. 454).

DeSantis's (2003) ethnographic analysis of the rationalizations of the cigar smokers is purely qualitative. Each rationalization and the evidence to support it are described in purely verbal terms. Nowhere in our brief description of the study are any numbers, percentages, or other statistics mentioned. For example, DeSantis did not count the number of statements made in support of the "flawed research" rationalization. Instead, he provided actual quotations from the cigar smokers to support the existence of this rationalization. The ethnographic analysis provided is purely *descriptive* in nature. That is, we cannot explain *why* an individual buys into a particular rationalization.

Although DeSantis (2003) made no quantitative analyses of his data, there is nothing about ethnography that precludes at least some quantification. For example, DeSantis might have reported on the average number of cigars that patrons smoked each week. The questions that you are interested in addressing should drive your decision concerning the mix of qualitative and quantitative analyses you will use in your study.

*Experimental Ethnography*    Our inclusion of ethnography in this chapter on nonexperimental designs might lead you to believe that it is limited to nonexperimental, observational research studies. Although ethnography traditionally has been used in the nonexperimental realm, the method can also be incorporated into experimental research that collects quantitative data. The blending of ethnographic methods within an experimental study is called *experimental ethnography* (Sherman & Strang, 2004). According to Lawrence Sherman and Heather Strang, qualitative methods of data collection can be incorporated into experimental designs that collect quantitative data. They argue that collecting ethnographic data along with measuring behavior numerically (and calculating averages) can provide a richer picture of how variables actually operate than does collecting numerical data alone. See Sherman and Strang's paper for a discussion about the advantages and disadvantages of including ethnographic data in experiments.

## QUESTIONS TO PONDER

1. Define naturalistic observation and unobtrusive observation. How are they used to study behavior?

2. What are some of the advantages and disadvantages of naturalistic observation?

3. What is ethnography, and what are the issues facing a field ethnographer?

4. How are ethnographic data recorded and analyzed?

## Sociometry

**Sociometry** involves identifying and measuring interpersonal relationships within a group (Berg, 2009). Sociometry has been applied to the systematic study of friendship patterns among children (e.g., Vandell & Hembree, 1994) and peer assessments of teenagers solicited to deal drugs (Weinfurt & Bush, 1995), as well as other social networks and work relationships (Berg, 2009).

To conduct a sociometric study, you have research participants evaluate each other along some dimension. For example, if you were interested in studying friendship patterns among third-grade students, you could have the students identify those in the class who are their friends and those who are not their friends. You could obtain similar sociometric ratings in a study of relationships among adults in a workplace.

You can use sociometry as the sole research tool to map interpersonal relationships—for example, to map friendship choices among five people in a club. (You might have each of the five people rank the three individuals they like best.)

**FIGURE 8-4**   Example of a sociometric scoring sheet.

| Person choosing | Person chosen |  |  |  |  |
|---|---|---|---|---|---|
|  | A | B | C | D | E |
| A |  | 1 |  | 3 | 2 |
| B | 1 |  | 2 |  | 3 |
| C | 1 | 2 |  | 3 |  |
| D |  | 1 | 2 |  | 3 |
| E | 2 | 1 |  | 3 |  |

Figure 8-4 shows some hypothetical data from such a study. The individuals being chosen appear along the top; those doing the choosing along the side. For instance, person A chose person B as her first choice, person E as her second, and person D as her third. Based on the data in Figure 8-4, you could graphically represent the pattern of friendship choices on a **sociogram**. Figure 8-5 displays an example sociogram.

You can include sociometric ratings within a wider study as one of many measures. For example, you could use the sociometric ratings just presented in a study of whether sociometric status within a group relates to leadership roles. If there is a relationship between friendship choices and leadership roles, you would expect person B to emerge as a club leader.

*An Example of Sociometry: Peer Rejection and Gender Identity*   Evidence shows that if a child is rejected by his or her peer group, it can have an effect on the child's social and emotional development, as well as on his or her academic performance. There are many reasons a child might be rejected by his or her peer group. For instance, children who are highly aggressive are more likely to be rejected than their nonaggressive peers.

**FIGURE 8-5**   Sociogram based on the data from Figure 8-4.

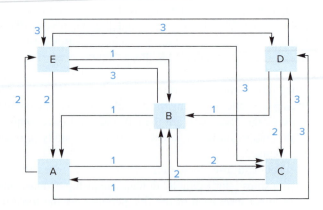

Is it possible that a child could be rejected based on his or her gender identity? A sociometric study by Madeline Wallien, Rene Veenstra, Baudewijnte Kreukels, and Peggy Cohen-Kettenis (2010) sought to answer this question.

Wallien et al. identified 44 children who were referred to a gender identity clinic for gender identity disorder (now called "gender dysphoria"). They also recruited 523 classmates of the gender identity–disordered children. Each child nominated other children in the class as either someone who was liked or disliked. Children also nominated others for how frequently they were bullied by others and how often they bullied others (and how the bullying took place). Wallien et al. looked at the patterns of the nominations made by the children to determine if gender identity–disordered children showed a pattern of friendships that differed from that of the non-disordered children.

Wallien et al. found that compared to non-disordered boys, gender-disordered boys were more likely to be nominated as a friend by female classmates than by male classmates. They also found that identity-disordered boys were more likely to be rejected by their non-disordered classmates. There was no difference between the dis-ordered and non-disordered boys on the bullying measures. A similar pattern was found for the gender-disordered girls. They were more likely to be nominated as a friend by male classmates than by female classmates. Additionally, as was the case for boys, gender-disordered girls were more likely to be rejected by female than by male classmates. No difference was found between the disordered and non-disordered girls on the bullying measures.

## The Case History

In some instances, your research needs may require you to study in depth a single case or just a few cases. The **case history** is a descriptive technique in which you observe and report on a single case (or a few cases). A case is the object of study, such as the development of a certain disease in a given individual.

The case history method has a long history in psychology and has many uses. For instance, a case history can be used to describe the typical development of a disease or the symptoms of a new disorder. In 1861, Paul Broca reported a case history of a 51-year-old patient who died at the Bicêtre hospital in France. Broca noted that when the patient (whom he called "Tan") was admitted to the hospital at the age of 21, he had already substantially lost his capacity to speak. In fact, he would usually respond to a question with one-syllable answers, most often with the word "tan" (thus, Broca's name for him). Tan was capable of understanding what was said to him, but he could not reply. Other than the speech problem, Tan was relatively healthy. However, over the course of his hospital stay, Tan's health gradually deteriorated to the point where he was losing control over the right side of his body. After Tan died, Broca examined Tan's brain and found a syphilitic lesion in the left frontal lobe. Broca reported that "the frontal lobe of the left hemisphere was soft over a great part of its extent; the convolutions of the orbital region, although atrophied, preserved their shape; most of the other frontal convolutions were entirely destroyed. The result of this destruction of the cerebral substance was a large cavity, capable of holding a chicken egg and filled with serous fluid" (Broca, 1861, p. 237).

Broca's case study of Tan became one of the most important findings in physiological psychology. Broca concluded that Tan's speech impairment was due to the lesion in the left frontal lobe and that the progressive damage to his brain eventually caused Tan to lose motor function on the right side of his body. Today we know that the area described by Broca (now called Broca's area) is essential to the articulation of spoken language.

Although a case history can be useful, it does not qualify as an experimental design. In fact, a case history is a special application of a demonstration (see Chapter 4). Because you do not manipulate independent variables, you cannot determine the causes of the behavior observed in your case history. You can, of course, speculate about such causes. You can even compare theories by interpreting cases from different perspectives, but you cannot state with any certainty which perspective is superior.

## Archival Research

**Archival research** is a nonexperimental strategy that involves studying existing records. These records can be historical accounts of events, census data, court records, police crime reports, published research articles, medical records, social media information, or any other archived information. A relatively new archival research technique is *record review*, in which you use specialized information extraction techniques to extract specific data from existing text-based records, such as medical records (Meystre, Savava, Kipper-Schuler, & Hurdle, 2008). We discuss information extraction in the following section on content analysis.

When planning archival research, you should have specific research questions in mind. You may find that the archived material contains an overwhelming amount of information. You need to be able to focus on specific aspects of the material. You can do so only if you know what you are looking for, which depends on having clearly defined and focused research hypotheses. In addition, all the factors pertaining to observational research (developing categories, coding sheets, multiple raters, etc.) apply to archival research.

An important practical matter to consider is your need to gain access to the archived material. This may not be easy. Sometimes the records you are interested in are not available to the general public. You may need to obtain special permission to gain access to the archives. In other cases, archival information may be available in libraries or on a computerized database (e.g., the Prosecutor's Management Information System, or PROMIS). Even in these cases, you may have to do some homework to find out how to access them.

Another practical matter is the completeness of the records. After gaining access to the archives, you may find that some of the information you wanted is unavailable. For example, if you were interested in studying court records, you might find that some information, such as background information on the defendant, is confidential and unavailable to you. In short, archived material may not be complete enough for your purposes. You may need to use multiple sources.

Like the case history method, archival research is purely descriptive. You may be able to identify some interesting trends or correlations based on your archival research. However, you cannot establish causal relationships.

*An Example of Archival Research: Does Residential Treatment Make Troubled Children Better or Worse?*    Each year, hundreds of children and adolescents are treated for conduct disorders in residential treatment centers. A child is checked into the facility and will be housed with other children who have similar conduct disorders. The goal of residential treatment is to reduce the child's maladaptive behavior related to the conduct disorder. However, is it possible that housing troubled children with other troubled children might make a conduct disorder worse rather than better? This question was investigated in an archival study conducted by Jonathan Huefner and Jay Ringle (2012), who used archival records at a residential treatment center to determine the effects of such treatment on conduct disorder behaviors.

Huefner and Ringle studied 1,438 records for first-time admissions to a residential treatment center in the Midwest. They used information on conduct disorder behaviors from the daily incident reports (DIRs), which are records of all incidents (e.g., aggressive behavior). They also determined the number of other troubled children who were housed along with the target subject, which provided a measure of negative peer density (NPD). Data were also collected on the length of a child's stay in the facility and a measure of the level of experience of the staff and educators at the facility.

Huefner and Ringle (2012) analyzed their data to determine if any of the variables measured (NPD, teacher experience, length of stay) related significantly to the rate of conduct disorder behaviors in the DIRs. They found that NPD was not significantly related to maladaptive behaviors among troubled youth. That is, the concern that troubled children's behavior might get worse because of being housed with other troubled youths may be unfounded. They did find, however, that maladaptive behavior was related to length of stay in a facility and to the level of training of staff and educators. The longer a child stayed in a facility, the lower was the rate of maladaptive behaviors. Similarly, fewer maladaptive behaviors were found when the staff and educators in the facility had more experience.

## Content Analysis

Use **content analysis** when you want to analyze a written or spoken record (or other meaningful matter) for the occurrence of specific categories or events (such as pauses in a speech), items (such as negative comments), or behavior (such as factual information offered during group discussion). Because it is difficult to content-analyze such materials in real time, you normally use archival sources for a content analysis. For example, if you wanted to content-analyze the answers given by two political candidates during a debate, it would be nearly impossible to do the analysis while the debate is going on. Instead, you would record the debate and use the resulting footage for your analysis. There are times, however, when you do a content analysis in real time. An example is a content analysis of court proceedings. Observers may actually sit in the courtroom and perform the content analysis.

Content analyses have been conducted on a wide range of materials such as mock juror deliberations (Horowitz, 1985), the content of television dramas (Greenberg, 1980), and the content of children's literature (Davis, 1984). In fact, the possible applications of content analysis are limited only by the imagination of the researcher (Holsti, 1969).

A relatively recent source of material for content analysis is the Internet, which offers a vast array of sources such as social networking sites (e.g., Twitter, Instagram), discussion lists, and online forums. Because the textual content of these sources is already stored in computer-readable files, such materials have the advantage that they can be submitted directly to specialized computer programs designed to perform content analysis. (See Krippendorff, 2004, for a thorough presentation of content analysis.)

Even though a content analysis seems rather simple to do, it can become as complex as any other research technique. You should perform content analysis within the context of a clearly developed research idea, including specific hypotheses and a sound research design. All factors that must be considered for observational research (except that of remaining unobtrusive) apply to a content analysis. You must clearly define your response categories and develop a method for quantifying behavior. In essence, content analysis is an observational technique. However, in content analysis, your unit of analysis is some written, visual, or spoken record rather than the behavior of participants.

*Defining Characteristics of Content Analysis*    Holsti (1969) points out that proper content analysis entails three defining characteristics. First, your content analysis should be objective. Each step of a content analysis should be guided by an explicit, clear set of rules or procedures. You should decide on the rules by which information will be acquired, categorized, and quantified and then adhere to those rules. You want to eliminate any subjective influence of the analyst.

Second, your content analysis should be systematic. Assign information to categories according to whatever rules you developed and then include as much information as possible in your analysis. For example, if you are doing a content analysis of a body of literature on a particular issue (such as racial attitudes), include articles that are *not* in favor of your position as well as those that are. A content analysis of literature is only as good as the literature search behind it.

Third, your content analysis should have generality. That is, your findings should fit within a theoretical, empirical, or applied context. Disconnected facts generated from a content analysis are of little value (Holsti, 1969).

*Performing Content Analysis*    To ensure that you acquire valid data for your content analysis, you must carefully define the response categories. According to Holsti (1969), your categories should reflect the purposes of the research, be exhaustive, be mutually exclusive, be independent, and be derived from one classification system.

The first requirement is the most important (Holsti, 1969): clear operational definitions of terms. Your categories must be clearly defined and remain focused on the research question outlined in your hypothesis. Unclear or poorly defined categories are difficult to use. The categories should be defined with sufficient precision to allow precise categorization.

Determining what your categories should be and how you should classify information within them is sometimes difficult. Reviewing related research in which a content analysis was used can help you develop and clearly define your categories. You can then add, delete, or expand categories to fit your specific research needs.

Before you begin to develop categories, read (or listen to) the materials to be analyzed. This will familiarize you with the material, help you develop categories, and help you avoid any surprises. That is, you will be less likely to encounter any information that does not fit into any category. Avoid making up categories as you go along.

After developing your categories, decide on a unit of analysis. The *recording unit* (Holsti, 1969) is the element of the material that you are going to record. The recording unit can be a word (or words), sentences, phrases, themes, and so on. Your recording unit should be relevant to your research question. Also, Holsti points out that defining a recording unit sometimes may not be enough. For example, if you were analyzing content of a jury deliberation, recording the frequency with which the word *defendant* (the recording unit) was used might not be sufficient. You might also have to note the *context unit*, or context within which the word was used (Holsti, 1969). Such a context unit gives meaning to the recording unit and may help later when you interpret the data. For example, you might record the number of times the word *defendant* was used along with the word *guilty*.

Another factor to consider when performing a content analysis is who will do the analysis. Observer bias can be a problem if the person performing the content analysis knows the hypotheses of the study or has a particular point of view. In such an instance, your results could be affected by your observer's biases. To avoid this problem, you should use a "blind" observer to do your ratings, one who does not know the purpose of your study. Also, avoid using observers who have strong feelings or characteristics that could bias the results. If you use more than one observer (and you should), you must evaluate interrater reliability.

The validity of your content analysis will depend on the materials analyzed. Make every effort to obtain relevant materials, be they books, films, or television shows. Unfortunately, it is often infeasible to analyze all materials. For example, a content analysis of all children's books is impossible. In such cases, obtain a sample of materials that is representative of the larger population of materials. A content analysis of a biased sample (e.g., only children's books written to be nonsexist) may produce biased results.

The results of a content analysis may be interesting in and of themselves. You may discover something interesting concerning the topic under study. Such was the case with Greenberg's (1980) content analysis of prime-time television shows aired during the fall of 1977. Greenberg found that Blacks were portrayed more often as having low-status jobs and athletic physiques compared with Whites.

*Limitations of Content Analysis*    Content analysis can be a useful technique to help you understand behavior, but keep in mind that it is purely descriptive. It cannot establish causal relationships among variables. Another limitation of content analysis is that its results may be invalidated over time. For example, Greenberg's (1980) findings about how Blacks are portrayed on television are no longer valid. Currently, Blacks are more likely to be portrayed in higher-status roles (doctors, lawyers, etc.) than in the past. Of course, whether such changes have occurred can be assessed with an updated content analysis!

*An Example of Content Analysis: Are the News Media Biased?*    It is not uncommon to hear individuals from both ends of the political spectrum claim that the news media are biased. Conservatives claim a widespread "liberal bias" in specific news outlets, whereas liberals claim a conservative bias. There is ample evidence that biases do exist in the traditional news media. However, is there a similar bias in Internet outlets? If there is, does it more commonly favor one side of the political spectrum than the other?

These questions were addressed in a content analysis reported by Eric Hehman, Elana Graber, Lindsay Hoffman, and Samuel Gaertner (2012). The main hypothesis was that media outlets portray a president more favorably if the president's political positions are similar to those of the media outlet.

In this content analysis, Hehman et al. (2012) analyzed the pictures of two presidents (George W. Bush and Barack Obama) that accompanied Internet news stories on several online news outlets, two identified with the political left (The Huffington Post and MSNBC.com) and two identified with the political right (Townhall.com and FOX. com). Fourteen research assistants who were blind to the purposes of the study collected 50 images of the two presidents from the websites. A different set of research assistants, who did not know the sources of the images, rated the pictures along the dimensions of competence and warmth.

Hehman et al.'s results supported their hypothesis (see Figure 8-6). Pictures portraying the two presidents from the media outlets sharing their views were rated more favorably on both dimensions than those from media outlets with opposing views.

*Information Extraction*    **Information extraction** is an advanced content analysis procedure using specialized information extraction techniques to study large databases such as medical records and e-books (Meystre et al., 2008). Traditional content analysis typically requires a great deal of time and effort to review and collect data. With the advent of huge electronic databases, traditional methods of content analysis have become less and less attractive to researchers (Wueest, Clematide, Bünzli, Laupper, & Frey, 2011).

Information extraction techniques have been developed to make collection of data from large databases easier and more reliable (Wueest et al., 2011). Information extraction involves using specific words, expressions, and numeric values (e.g., Social Security numbers) when analyzing archived records. Searches are highly rule-driven, with specific categories of information sought after (Manne & Fatima, 2011; Meystre et al., 2008). Techniques are also available to extract information from video streams (Pazouki & Rahmati, 2009).

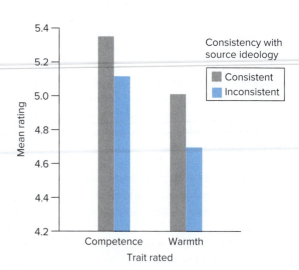

**FIGURE 8-6**   Ratings of competence and warmth as a function of consistency between a president's and website's political ideology.
SOURCE: Hehman et al., 2012.

When using information extraction, you are engaging in extensive *text data mining* of some written archival materials (Manne & Fatima, 2011). Just as physical mining extracts a specific mineral (e.g., gold) from the earth, informational data mining extracts specific patterns of information from an unstructured source. Systematic data extraction transforms the unstructured archival source into a more structured format that is easier to analyze (Manne & Fatima, 2011). Textual information from the source being analyzed is extracted with natural language processing (NLP), which essentially employs computer artificial intelligence technology to extract meaning from human languages (Meystre et al., 2008). Text mining involves three steps: information retrieval (i.e., finding relevant materials to be mined), information extraction (identifying specific information from the materials found), and data mining (finding meaningful associations among the units of information extracted) (Meystre et al., 2008). Meystre et al. suggest preprocessing the data to clean them up before starting to extract the data. For example, the text base can be spell-checked to eliminate spelling errors that can contribute to mining errors.

As an example of information extraction from a large database, consider a study by Bruno Wueest, Simon Clematide, Alexandria Bünzli, Daniel Laupper, and Timotheos Frey (2011). Wueest et al. investigated how different political parties in Switzerland stood on various political issues (e.g., the economy, social issues). Their information extraction study involved data mining the coverage of political parties by a major Swiss newspaper from 2003 to 2007. In their analysis, Wueest et al. used a natural language processing method that identified relationships between a political figure and a political issue. This involved breaking each sentence of a news article into its basic semantic structure. Once this was done, Wueest et al. constructed maps of how political parties related to various political issues. On the one hand, they found that the "Liberal Party" (left wing) emphasized economic issues (through explaining their budgetary rigor and liberal views on economics) while avoiding issues such as opposition to immigration. On the other hand, the "Swiss People's Party" (right wing) placed more emphasis on anti-immigration policies. All parties in the analysis were concerned with a host of issues such as welfare.

Although the techniques involved in information extraction have been around for a number of years, their application in the social sciences has been limited (Wueest et al., 2011). One reason for this is that information extraction systems are difficult to develop and, once developed, may not generalize well from one research area to another (Calif, Mooney, & Cohn, 2004). Consequently, information extraction may require you to do a great deal of background reading in order to select those methods that best apply to your research situation.

## QUESTIONS TO PONDER

1. What is sociometry, and when is it used?

2. How are the case history and archival research used?

3. What is content analysis, and what steps are taken when using it?

4. What is information extraction, and in what research situations would you consider using it?

## META-ANALYSIS: A TOOL FOR COMPARING RESULTS ACROSS STUDIES

Imagine you are a researcher investigating the relationship between attitudes and memory. Specifically, you have been investigating whether or not participants recall more attitude-consistent information than attitude-inconsistent information. After conducting several empirical investigations, you decide that a published literature review is needed to summarize and integrate the findings in the area. Consequently, you decide to conduct a literature review and to write a review article.

One strategy for this task is to conduct a traditional literature review. With this strategy, you read the relevant research in your area and then write an article. In your review, you may choose to summarize the major methods used to research the attitude-memory link, report the results of the major studies found, and draw conclusions about the variables that affect the relationship of interest.

In the traditional literature review, you summarize what you find and draw conclusions about the state of knowledge in a given area. For example, you might conclude that a certain variable is important (such as the length of a persuasive communication to which an individual is exposed) whereas others are less important (such as whether learning was incidental or intentional). However, the conclusions you draw are mostly subjective. The possibility exists that your subjective conclusion may not accurately reflect the strengths of the relationships examined in your review.

You can avoid this possibility by adding a meta-analysis to your traditional review. A **meta-analysis** is a set of statistical procedures that allow you to combine or compare results from different studies. Because you are making use of existing literature, meta-analysis is a form of archival research. When you conduct a meta-analysis, you find and analyze existing research (published and even unpublished) so you can make statistically guided decisions about the strength of the observed effects of independent variables and the reliability of results across studies. You can also do a meta-analysis of existing meta-analyses. This technique is known as a *second-order meta-analysis* (Hunter & Schmidt, 2004). In this technique, you find as many topic-relevant meta-analyses as possible and do a meta-analysis of their results.

To conduct a meta-analysis, you must follow three steps: (1) identify relevant variables, (2) locate relevant research to review, and (3) conduct the meta-analysis proper.

### Step 1: Identifying Relevant Variables

Before you can hope to conduct a meta-analysis, you must identify the variables to be analyzed. This may sound easy enough. However, you will find that in practice it is somewhat difficult, especially in a research area in which there is a wide body of research. Generally, the rules that apply to developing testable research questions (see Chapter 2) also apply to meta-analysis. It is not enough to say, "I want to do a meta-analysis of the memory literature." Such a broad, general analysis would be extremely difficult to do. The same is true even in less extensive research areas.

Your research question must be sufficiently focused to allow for a reasonable meta-analysis. The unit of analysis in a meta-analysis should be the impact of variable $X$ on variable $Y$ (Rosenthal, 1984). Therefore, focus only on those variables that relate to your

---

**TABLE 8-3    Sample of Factors to Include When Meta-Analyzing Literature**

Full reference citation

Names and addresses of authors

Sex of experimenter

Sex of subjects used in each experiment

Characteristics of subject sample (such as how obtained, number)

Task required of subjects and other details about the dependent variable

Design of the study (including any unusual features)

Control groups and procedures included to reduce confounding

Results from statistical tests that bear directly on the issue being considered in the meta-analysis (effect sizes, values of inferential statistics, *p* values)

SOURCE: Rosenthal, 1984.

---

specific question. For example, you might choose to meta-analyze the impact of imagery on memory. Here you are limiting yourself to a small segment of the memory literature.

After you have narrowed the scope of your analysis, you must decide what variables to record (such as sex of subject, independent variables) as you review each study. Your decision will be driven by your research question. Table 8-3 provides a list of information that might be included in a meta-analysis. For each study to be included in your meta-analysis, you should record the relevant variables, the full reference citation, and the nature of the subject sample and procedure (Rosenthal, 1984).

The heart of meta-analysis is the statistical combination of results across studies. Consequently, you also must record information about the findings from the results sections of the papers you review, including the values of any statistics given (e.g., *t*s and *F*s) and the associated *p* values (such as .05, .01). Later these values will be used as the *scores* in your meta-analysis. Collect data that help you evaluate your specific research questions. You do not have to record the results from overall analyses of variance (ANOVAs). Focus instead on the results of statistical tests that evaluate the specific relationships among the variables of interest (Rosenthal, 1984).

## Step 2: Locating Relevant Research to Review

One of the most important steps in a meta-analysis is locating relevant research to review. In meta-analysis, you want to draw conclusions about the potency of a set of variables in a particular research area. To accomplish this end, you must thoroughly search the literature. Chapter 3 described how to perform a literature search, so the topic is not examined here.

Recall the previously discussed *file drawer phenomenon* (Chapter 3) in which studies that do not achieve statistically reliable findings fail to reach publication (Rosenthal, 1979, 1984). The problem posed by the file drawer phenomenon is potentially serious for meta-analysis because it results in a biased sample. This bias inflates the probability of making a Type I error (concluding that a variable has an effect when it does not).

Studies that failed to be published because the investigated variables did not show statistically significant effects are not available to include in the meta-analysis.

There are two ways of dealing with the file drawer phenomenon. First, you can attempt to uncover those studies that never reach print. You can do this by identifying as many researchers as possible in the research area that you are covering. You then send each researcher a questionnaire, asking if any unpublished research on the issue of interest exists. You also could do a search of online journals that publish studies that produce null results such as the *Journal of Articles in Support of the Null Hypothesis* (www.jasnh.com/). Second, Rosenthal (1979, 1984) suggests estimating the extent of the impact of the file drawer phenomenon on your analysis. This is done by determining the number of studies that must be in the file drawer before serious biasing takes place, a procedure known as a "fail-safe" analysis. For example, if you determine (based on your analysis) that at least 3,000 studies must be in the file drawer before seriously biasing your results, you can be reasonably sure that the file drawer phenomenon is not a source of bias.

Rosenthal (1979, 1984) provided a method for computing the fail-safe number, but this method has been criticized by Rosenberg (2005) as being unweighted and "not based on the framework in which most meta-analyses are performed" (p. 264). He has proposed an alternative method said to correct these deficiencies (see Rosenberg, 2005).

## Step 3: Conducting the Meta-Analysis

When you have located relevant literature and collected your data, you are ready to apply one of the many available meta-analytic statistical techniques. Table 8-4 displays meta-analytic techniques that you can apply to the situation in which you have two studies. The first technique shows that you can compare studies. This comparison is made when you want to determine whether two studies produce significantly different effects. Essentially, doing a meta-analysis comparing studies is analogous to conducting an experiment using human or animal subjects. In the case of meta-analysis, each data point represents the results from a study rather than a subject's response. The second technique shows that you also can combine studies to determine the average effect of a variable across studies. Looking at the columns, you can evaluate studies by comparing or combining either the *p* values from significance testing or effect sizes (Rosenthal, 1984).

Comparing effect sizes of two studies is more desirable than simply looking at *p* values (Rosenthal, 1984). This is because effect sizes provide a better indication of the degree of impact of a variable than *p* values do. (Remember, all the *p* value tells you is the likelihood of making a Type I error.) Use *p* values when the information needed to analyze effect sizes is not included in the studies reviewed.

## Drawbacks to Meta-Analysis

Meta-analysis can be a powerful tool to evaluate results across studies. Even though many researchers have embraced the concept of meta-analysis, others question its usefulness on several grounds. This section explores some of the drawbacks to meta-analysis and presents some of the solutions suggested to overcome those drawbacks.

*Assessing the Quality of the Research Reviewed*    Chapter 3 pointed out that not all journals are created equal. The quality of the research found in a journal depends on its

**TABLE 8-4   Meta-Analytic Techniques for Comparing and Combining Two Studies**

| TECHNIQUE | COMMENTS |
|---|---|
| *Comparing Studies* | Used to determine if two studies produce significantly different results. |
| Significance testing | Record $p$ values from research and convert them to exact $p$ values (such as a finding reported at $p > .05$ may actually be $p = .036$). Used when information is not available to allow for evaluation of effect sizes. |
| Effect size estimation | Record values of inferential statistics (such as $F$ or $t$) along with associated degrees of freedom. Estimate effect sizes from these statistics. Preferred over significance testing. |
| *Combining Studies* | Used when you want to determine the potency of a variable across studies. |
| Significance testing | Can be used after comparing studies to arrive at an overall estimate of the probability of obtaining the two $p$ values under the null hypothesis (of no causal relationship between the analyzed variables). |
| Effect size estimation | Can be used after comparing studies to evaluate the average impact across studies of an independent variable on the dependent variable. |

SOURCE: Rosenthal, 1984.

editorial policy. Some journals have rigorous publication standards; others may not. This means that the quality of published research may vary considerably from journal to journal.

One problem facing the meta-analyst is how to deal with uneven quality of research. Should an article published in a nonrefereed journal be given as much weight as an article published in a refereed journal? Unfortunately, there is no simple answer to this question. Rosenthal (1984) suggests weighting articles according to quality.

There is no agreement as to the dimensions along which research should be weighted. The refereed–nonrefereed dimension is one possibility. You should exercise caution with this dimension because whether or not a journal is refereed is not a reliable indicator of the quality of published research. Research in a new area, using new methods, is sometimes rejected from refereed journals even though it is methodologically sound and of high quality. Similarly, publication in a refereed journal helps to ensure that the research is of high quality but does not guarantee it.

A second dimension along which research could be weighted is according to the soundness of methodology, regardless of journal quality. Rosenthal (1984) suggests having several experts on methodology rate each study for its quality (perhaps on a 0 to 10 scale). Quality ratings would be made twice: once after reading the method section alone and once after reading the method and results sections together (Rosenthal, 1984). The ratings would then be checked for interrater reliability and used to weight the degree of contribution of each study to the meta-analysis.

### Combining and Comparing Studies Using Different Methods

A frequent criticism of meta-analysis is that it is difficult to understand how studies with widely varying materials, measures, and methods can be compared. This is commonly referred to as the "apples-versus-oranges argument" (Glass, 1978).

Although common, this criticism of meta-analysis is not valid. Rosenthal (1984) and Glass (1978) suggest that comparing results from different studies is no different from averaging across heterogeneous subjects in an ordinary experiment. If you are willing to accept averaging across subjects, you can also accept averaging across heterogeneous studies (Glass, 1978; Rosenthal, 1984).

The core issue is not whether averaging should be done across heterogeneous studies but whether or not differing methods are related to different effect sizes. In this vein, Rosenthal (1984) points out that when a subject variable becomes a problem in research, you often "block" on that subject variable to determine how it relates to the differences that emerge. Similarly, if methodological differences appear to be related to the outcome of research, studies in a meta-analysis could be blocked on methodology (Rosenthal, 1984) to determine its effects.

### Practical Problems

The task facing a meta-analyst is a formidable one. Experiments on the same issue may use widely different methods and statistical techniques. Also, some studies may not provide the necessary information to conduct a meta-analysis. For example, Roberts (1985) was able to include only 38 studies in his meta-analysis of the attitude-memory relationship. Some studies had to be eliminated because sufficient information was not provided. Also, Roberts reports that when an article said that $F$ was less than 1 (as articles often do), he assigned $F$ a value of zero. The problem of insufficient or imprecise information (along with the file drawer problem) may result in a nonrepresentative sample of research being included in your meta-analysis. Admittedly, the bias may be small, but it nevertheless may exist.

### Do the Results of Meta-Analysis Differ from Those of Traditional Reviews?

Do traditional reviews produce results that differ qualitatively from those of a meta-analysis? To answer this question, Cooper and Rosenthal (1980) directly compared the two methods. Graduate students and professors were randomly assigned to conduct either a meta-analysis or a traditional review of seven articles dealing with the impact of the gender of the subject on persistence on a task. Two of the studies showed that females were more persistent than males; the remainder either presented no statistical data or showed no significant effect.

Participants using the meta-analysis were more likely to conclude that gender had and effect on persistence than were participants using the traditional method. Moreover, participants doing the traditional review believed that the effect of gender on persistence was smaller than did those doing the meta-analysis. Overall, 68% of the meta-analysts were prepared to conclude that gender had an effect on persistence whereas only 27% of participants using the traditional method were so inclined. In statistical terms, the meta-analysts were more willing than the traditional reviewers to reject the null hypothesis that gender had no effect, so using meta-analysis to evaluate research may lead to a reduction in Type II decision errors, concluding that a variable has no effect when it does have one (Cooper & Rosenthal, 1980).

Cooper and Rosenthal (1980) also report that there were no differences between meta-analysis and traditional review groups in their abilities to evaluate the methodology of the studies reviewed. Also, there was no difference between the two groups in their recommendations about future research in the area. Most participants believed that research in the area should continue.

Finally, it is worth noting that using the statistical approach inherent in meta-analysis applies the same research strategy as doing statistical analyses of data from traditional experiments. When we obtain results of an experiment, we don't just look at ("eyeball") the data to see if any patterns or relationships exist. Instead, in most instances (there are some exceptions that we discuss in Chapter 12), we apply statistical analyses to evaluate whether relationships exist. By the same token, it can be argued that it is better to apply a statistical analysis to the results of different studies to determine whether significant relationships exist than to eyeball the studies and speculate about possible relationships.

## QUESTIONS TO PONDER

1. What is meta-analysis, and what steps are involved in using it?
2. What are some of the issues facing you if you decide to do a meta-analysis?

## SUMMARY

In some situations, conducting an experiment may not be possible or desirable. In the early stages of research or when you are interested in studying naturally occurring behaviors of your subjects, a nonexperimental approach may be best.

Observational research involves observing and recording the behaviors of your subjects. This can be accomplished either in the field or in the lab and can use human participants or animal subjects. Although observational research sounds easy to conduct, as much preparation goes into an observational study as into any other study. Before making observations of behavior, you must clearly define the behaviors to be observed, develop observation techniques that do not interfere with the behaviors of your subjects, and work out a method of quantifying and recording behavior.

The frequency, duration, and intervals methods are three widely accepted ways to quantify behavior in an observational study. In the frequency method, you count the number of occurrences of a behavior within a specified period of time. In the duration method, you measure how long a behavior lasted. In the intervals method, you break your observation period into small time intervals and record whether or not a behavior occurred within each.

After you have decided how to quantify behavior, you must make some decisions about how to record your observations. Paper-and-pencil data-recording sheets provide a simple and, in most cases, adequate means of recording behavior. In some situations (such as when the behavior being observed is fast paced), you should consider using electronic recorders rather than a paper-and-pencil method. Using a recorder allows observers to keep their eyes on subjects while making notes about behavior.

In addition to developing a method for quantifying behavior, you must decide on how and when to make observations. Sometimes it is not possible to watch and record behaviors simultaneously because behavior may occur quickly and be highly complex. In such situations, you could use time sampling or individual sampling or automate your observations by using a video recorder.

In observational research, you should use multiple observers. When multiple observers are used, you must evaluate the degree of interrater reliability. This can be done using either percent agreement, Cohen's Kappa, intraclass correlation, or Pearson $r$. A Cohen's Kappa of .70 or greater or a statistically significant Pearson $r$ of around .90 or greater suggests an acceptable level of interrater reliability.

Nonexperimental techniques include naturalistic observation, ethnography, case study, archival research, and content analysis. In naturalistic observation, you make careful, unobtrusive observations of subjects in their natural environment so that you do not alter their natural behavior. In cases in which you cannot remain unobtrusive, there are steps you can take to habituate your participants to your presence.

Ethnography involves getting immersed in a behavioral or social system to be studied. The technique is best used to study and describe the operation of groups and the social interactions that take place within those groups. An ethnographic study can be run as a participant observation (in which the researcher actually becomes a member of the group) or as nonparticipant observation (in which the researcher is a nonparticipating observer). Ethnograpic techniques can be blended with experimental designs in experimental ethnography.

Sociometry involves identifying and measuring interpersonal relationships within a group. Research participants evaluate each other along some socially relevant dimension (e.g., friendship), and patterns of those ratings are analyzed to characterize the social structure of the group. The results of a sociometric analysis can be plotted on a sociogram, which graphically represents the social connections among participants. Sociometry can be used as a stand-alone research technique or as a measure within a wider study.

When using the case history approach, you analyze an interesting case that illustrates some empirical or theoretical point. Alternatively, you may compare and contrast two or more cases in order to illustrate such points. Archival research makes use of existing records. You examine those records and extract data to answer specific research questions.

Content analysis involves analyzing a written or spoken record (or other content) for the occurrence of specific categories of events or behaviors. As with any observational technique, you must develop behavior categories. During content analysis, you note and analyze recording and context units. A specialized form of content analysis in which language processing software is used to analyze large databases of information is known as *information extraction*.

Meta-analysis is a family of statistical techniques that can help you evaluate results from a number of studies in a given research area. In contrast to a traditional literature review (in which subjective evaluations rule), meta-analysis involves statistically combining the results from a number of studies. Meta-analytic techniques tend to be more objective than traditional literature review techniques.

The three steps involved in conducting a meta-analysis are (1) identifying relevant variables to study, (2) locating relevant research to review, and (3) actually doing the meta-analysis (comparing or combining results across studies). Although meta-analysis has advantages over traditional literature reviews, there are some drawbacks. First, it is sometimes difficult to evaluate the quality of the research reviewed. Second, studies in a research area may use vastly different methods, making comparison of results suspect. Third, the information in published articles may be incomplete, eliminating potentially important studies from the analysis.

## KEY TERMS

behavioral categories

interrater reliability

Cohen's Kappa ($K$)

intraclass correlation coefficient ($r_I$)

quantitative data

qualitative data

naturalistic observation

ethnography

participant observation

nonparticipant observation

sociometry

sociogram

case history

archival research

content analysis

information extraction

meta-analysis

# Doing Survey Research

G ordon Allport (1954) characterized an attitude as "probably the most distinctive and indispensable concept in contemporary social psychology" (p. 43). Since Allport's assessment, attitudes have transcended social psychology to become important in our everyday lives. We are surrounded by issues related to attitudes and their measurement. Pollsters and politicians are constantly measuring and trying to change our attitudes about a wide range of issues (such as abortion, the war on terrorism, and tax cuts). How and where we obtain information on these issues are also changing.

The election of Barack Obama in 2008 as president of the United States marked a change in how Americans obtained information about political candidates. According to a 2009 survey conducted by the Pew Research Center, 74% of Internet users relied on the Internet to participate in or get information about the presidential election. More interestingly, there was a major increase in the percentage of adults in general as well as Internet users who obtain political news over the Internet.

As the 2009 Pew survey shows, technology is becoming increasingly important in election politics. In 2012, another Pew survey showed that voters were no longer tied to their laptops to obtain political information; many were now using cell phone technology to stay abreast of the presidential campaign. According to the survey, 27% of registered voters—Republicans and Democrats alike—reported using their cell phone to stay current on election-specific and general political issues. However, the survey also found that liberals were slightly more likely than conservatives to use their smartphones for political purposes. Figure 9-1 summarizes the various uses to which voters put their smartphones with respect to the presidential election. As you can see, a sizable percentage of voters used their smartphones to read others' political posts and post their own thoughts on social media websites and to fact-check information they encountered. A 2014 Pew survey showed yet another trend in smartphone use for political purposes. From 2010 to 2014, the percentage of registered voters using

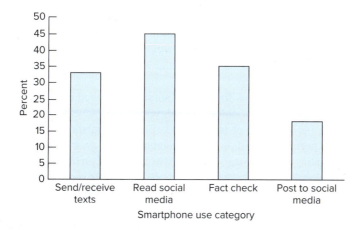

**FIGURE 9-1**    Ways in which cell phones were used for political information.
SOURCE: Smith Aaron, and Maeve Duggan, "The State of the 2012 Election—Mobile Politics"
October 3, 2012, Washington, DC: Pew Research Center, 2012.

their phones to follow politicians increased from 6% to 18%. The increases were found for Republicans, Democrats, and Independents.

Surveys are a widely used research technique. You may have participated in a survey yourself, or (perhaps more likely) you may have been the recipient of survey results. If you have answered a few questions from a local political party during election time, you have participated in a survey. Even those annoying questions on warranty registration cards that come with most products qualify as a survey of sorts. You are typically asked about your age, income, interests, magazines to which you subscribe, and so on. If you answered those questions and mailed back the card, you took part in a survey.

Even if you rarely participate in surveys, you are still likely to have encountered survey results. Political polls designed to gauge people's attitudes on key issues and candidates come out almost daily during election time. Polls about the U.S. president's approval rating, wars, and health care issues come out several times over the course of a year.

Because survey research is highly visible, you should understand the "ins and outs" of this important research technique. If you plan to use a survey technique in your own research, you should know about proper questionnaire construction, administration techniques, sampling techniques, and data analysis. Even if you never use survey techniques, understanding something about them will help you make sense out of the surveys that you are exposed to every day.

## SURVEY RESEARCH

Before we discuss survey techniques, note the difference between the *field survey* and the observational techniques described in Chapter 8. In both naturalistic observation and participant observation, you observe behaviors and make copious notes about them. You do not administer any measures to your participants. Consequently, you can only speculate about the motives, attitudes, and beliefs underlying the observed behaviors. In a field survey, you directly question your participants about their behavior (past, present, or future) and their underlying attitudes, beliefs, and intentions. From the data collected, you can draw inferences about the factors underlying behavior.

The inferences you can draw from a field survey are limited by the fact that you do not manipulate independent variables. Instead, you acquire several (perhaps hundreds of) measures of the behaviors of interest. This purely correlational research strategy usually does not permit you to draw causal inferences from your data (see Chapter 4). For example, finding that political conservatism is a good predictor of voter choices does not justify concluding that political conservatism *causes* voter choices.

Instead, you use the field survey to evaluate specific attitudes such as those concerning issues surrounding energy policy, political candidates, or economic issues. You also can use the field survey to evaluate behaviors. For example, you could design a questionnaire to determine which household products people use.

Surveys also have another important use: predicting behavior. Political polls often seek to predict behavior. Attitudes about political candidates are assessed, and then projections are made about subsequent voter behavior.

When you conduct survey research, you must ensure that your participants are treated ethically. One major ethical issue concerns whether and how you will maintain the *anonymity* of your participants and the *confidentiality* of their responses. Maintaining anonymity means that you guarantee there will be no way for the participants' names to be associated with their answers. This might be accomplished by instructing participants to mail back their questionnaires and informed-consent forms separately. No coding scheme would be used that would allow you to match up individual participants and their questionnaires. However, sometimes you may wish to code the questionnaires and informed-consent forms so that you can match them up later. You might do this, for example, if a participant has second thoughts about participating after the questionnaire has been returned. If so and you have promised your participants that their responses will remain anonymous, you must take steps to ensure that only authorized personnel associated with the research project can gain access to the code and only for the stated purpose.

Maintaining confidentiality means that you do not disclose any data in individual form, even if you know which participants filled out which questionnaires. If you promise your participants that their responses will remain confidential, ethical practice dictates that you report only aggregate results.

## QUESTIONS TO PONDER

1. What are some of the applications of survey research?
2. Why is it important to know about survey methods, even if you do not intend to conduct surveys?
3. How does a field survey differ from other observational methods?
4. What are anonymity and confidentiality, and why are they important?

# DESIGNING YOUR QUESTIONNAIRE

The first step in designing a questionnaire is to clearly define the topic of your study. A clear, concise definition of what you are studying will yield results that can be interpreted unambiguously. Results from surveys that do not clearly define the topic area may be confusing. It is also important to have clear, precise operational definitions for the attitudes or behaviors being studied. Behaviors and attitudes that are not defined precisely also may yield results that are confusing and difficult to interpret.

Having a clearly defined topic has another important advantage: It keeps your questionnaire focused on the behavior or attitude chosen for study (Moser & Kalton, 1972). You should avoid the temptation to do too much in a single survey. Tackling too much in a single survey leads to an inordinately long questionnaire that may confuse or overburden your participants. It also may make it more difficult for you to summarize and analyze your data (Moser & Kalton, 1972). Your questionnaire should include a broad enough range of questions so that you can thoroughly assess behavior but not so broad as to lose focus and become confusing. Your questionnaire should elicit the responses you are most interested in without much extraneous information.

The type of information gathered on a questionnaire depends on its purpose. However, most questionnaires include items designed to assess the characteristics of the participants, such as age, sex, marital status, occupation, income, and education. Such characteristics are called *demographics.* Demographics are often used as *predictor variables* during analysis of the data to determine whether participant characteristics correlate with or predict responses to other items in the survey. Other, nondemographic items also can be included to provide predictor variables. For example, attitudes toward abortion might be used to predict voter preference. In this case, attitude toward abortion would be used as a predictor variable.

In addition to demographics and predictor variables, you will have items designed to assess the behavior of interest. For example, if you were interested in predicting voter preference, you would include an item or items on your questionnaire specifically to measure voter preference (e.g., asking participants to indicate candidate preferences). That item, or a combination of several items, would constitute the *criterion variable.*

The questions to which your participants will respond are the heart of your questionnaire. Take great care to develop questions that are clear, to the point, and relevant to the aims of your research. The time spent in this early phase of your research will pay dividends later. Well-constructed items are easier to summarize, analyze, and interpret than poorly constructed ones. Before designing your questionnaire or writing questions, you should put yourself in a respondent's state of mind (Dillman, Christian, & Smyth, 2014). This means you should try to imagine how everything about your questionnaire will appear to your respondents. For example, you should consider how the respondent will navigate through your questionnaire and whether he or she will be able to understand your questions. Dillman et al. state that doing this will allow you to avoid a situation in which the questionnaire you think is perfect will not be completed by your respondents. The next section introduces several popular item formats and offers suggestions for writing good questionnaire items.

## Writing Questionnaire Items

Writing effective questionnaire items that obtain the information you want requires care and skill. You cannot simply sit down, write several questions, and use those first-draft questions on your final questionnaire. Writing questionnaire items involves writing and rewriting items until they are clear and succinct. In fact, having written your items and assembled your questionnaire, you should administer it to a pilot group of participants matching your main sample in order to ensure that the items are reliable and valid. You can save yourself a great deal of time and effort by looking at questions used on existing surveys and adapting them for your survey. You can also review the literature or consult experts for this purpose (Sinkowitz-Cochran, 2013).

Before you begin writing your questions, you should first identify the main concepts you wish to measure. This ensures that the questions you eventually write address those concepts. You can start this process by writing down a clear set of research questions and objectives (Dillman et al., 2014). Once you have done this, you can then start crafting your questions. When writing questionnaire items, you may choose among several popular types. Here we discuss the open-ended, restricted, partially open-ended, and rating-scale item types.

*Open-Ended Items*    **Open-ended items** allow the participant to respond in his or her own words. The following example might appear in a survey like the Pew cell phone use survey:

**How often did you use your cell phone to get political news for the 2016 presidential election?**

In response to this question, the respondent writes an answer to the question in the space provided immediately below. There are three types of open-ended questions (Dillman et al., 2014). In a *descriptive open-ended question,* you ask for a narrative answer concerning a topic. In a *numerical response open-ended question,* you ask about frequencies or amounts of what you are interested in. The preceding example is a numerical open-ended question. In a *list of items open-ended question,* you ask for a list relating to what you are interested in. For example, you could ask your respondents to list the specific types of political information they obtained using their cell phones. It is important that you specify which type of information you want in the stem of your open-ended questions (Dillman et al., 2014).

An advantage of an open-ended question is that the information you get may be more complete and accurate than the information obtained with a restricted item (discussed next). There are, however, also drawbacks to open-ended items. For example, respondents may not understand exactly what you are looking for or may inadvertently omit some answers. Thus, participants may fail to provide the needed information. Another drawback to the open-ended item is that it can make summarizing your data difficult. Essentially, you must perform a content analysis on open-ended answers. All of the methods and rules that we discussed in Chapter 8 would come into play. It may be tempting to interpret open-ended responses rather than just summarize them, running the risk of misclassifying the answers.

*Restricted Items*     **Restricted items** (also called *closed-ended items*) provide a limited number of specific response alternatives. A restricted item with ordered alternatives lists these alternatives in a logical order, as shown in the following example:

> **How often did you use your cell phone to get political information during the 2016 presidential election campaign?**
>
> __ Very often
>
> __ Sometimes
>
> __ Not too often
>
> __ Never

Note how the alternatives for this question go from very often to never. Participants would respond by checking the blank space to the left of the desired answer. However, other methods for recording choices can be used with restricted items. For example, you could use a number to the right of each alternative and have participants circle the numbers corresponding to their choices.

Use unordered alternatives whenever there is no logical basis for choosing a given order, as shown in this example:

> **Do you think that the political information you obtained using your cell phone during the 2016 presidential election campaign was generally accurate or inaccurate?**
>
> __ Accurate
>
> __ Inaccurate
>
> __ Neither
>
> __ Don't know

Because there is no inherent order to the alternatives, other orders would serve just as well. For example, you just as easily could have put "Inaccurate" before "Accurate."

By offering only specific response alternatives, restricted items control the participant's range of responses. The responses made to restricted items are therefore easier to summarize and analyze than the responses made to open-ended items. However, the information you obtain from a restricted item is not as rich as the information from an open-ended item. Participants cannot qualify or otherwise elaborate on their responses. Also, you may fail to include an alternative that correctly describes the participant's opinion, thus forcing the participant to choose an alternative that does not really fit.

There are a few general guidelines you should follow when writing restricted items (Dillman et al., 2014). First, if you are asking either/or questions, you should include both the positive and negative poles in your question. For example, if you are asking whether the respondent favors or opposes using cell phones to get political information, the stem of your question should include both of these words (Do you favor or oppose using cell phones to get political information?). Second, if you use a list of items from which respondents choose, be sure to include all possible options. In a question asking about where respondents get political information on their cell phones, if you leave out Twitter or Instagram, you are missing a major source of such information. Third, be sure that items on a list are mutually exclusive. Fourth, if you are asking respondents to rank alternatives, keep the list relatively short. Dillman et al. offer a number of other guidelines you should familiarize yourself with when writing restricted items.

*Partially Open-Ended Items*    **Partially open-ended items** resemble restricted items but provide an additional, "other" category and an opportunity to give an answer not listed among the specific alternatives, as shown in this example:

**How did you most use your cell phone during the 2016 presidential election campaign?**

____Send a political text

____Receive a political text

____Read another person's political views on social media

____Post my political views on social media

____Fact-check information I encountered

____Other (Specify)_____

Dillman (2000) offers several suggestions for formatting restricted and partially open-ended items. First, use a boldface font for the stem of a question and a normal font for response category labels (as we have done in the previous examples). This helps respondents separate the question from the response categories that follow. Second, make any special instructions intended to clarify a question a part of the question itself. Third, put check boxes, blank spaces, or numbers in a consistent position throughout your questionnaire (e.g., to the left of the response alternatives). Fourth, place all alternatives in a single column. Other tips offered by Dillman (2000) for constructing and formatting questionnaire items are summarized in Table 9-1.

*Rating Scales*    A variation on the restricted item uses a rating scale rather than response alternatives. A rating scale provides a graded response to a question:

**How much confidence do you have that the political information you obtained using your cell phone during the 2016 presidential campaign was accurate?**

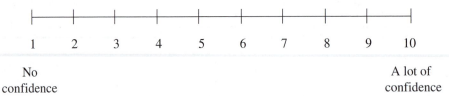

| 1 | 2 | 3 | 4 | 5 | 6 | 7 | 8 | 9 | 10 |

No
confidence

A lot of
confidence

There is no set number of points a rating scale must have. A rating scale can have as few as 3 and as many as 100 points. However, rating scales commonly do not exceed 10 points. A 10-point scale has enough points to allow a wide range of choice while

**TABLE 9-1  Suggestions for Writing Good Survey Items**

| SUGGESTION | EXAMPLE |
|---|---|
| Use simple rather than complex words. | Use "work" rather than "employment." |
| Make the stem of a question as short and easy to understand as possible, but use complete sentences. | "Would you like to study in America?" |
| Avoid vague questions in favor of more precise ones. | Use "How many years have you lived in your current house?" rather than "Years in your house." |
| Avoid asking for too much information. Respondents may not have an answer readily available. | Use a list of ordered alternatives rather than an open-ended question when asking how often the respondent does something. |
| Avoid "check all that apply" questions. | Instead of "check all that apply," list each item separately and have respondent indicate liking/disliking for each. |
| Avoid questions that ask for more than one thing. | Instead of asking "Would you like to study and then live in America?" ask "Would you like to study in America?" and "Would you like to live in America?" separately. |
| Soften the impact of potentially sensitive questions. | Instead of asking "Have you ever stolen anything?" ask "Have you ever taken anything without paying for it?" |

SOURCE: Dillman, 2000.

not overburdening the participant. Scales with fewer than 10 points also are used frequently, but you should not go below 5 points. Many participants may not want to use the extreme values on a scale. Consequently, if you have a 5-point scale and the participant excludes the end points, you really have only three usable points. Scales ranging from 7 to 10 points leave several points for the participants to choose among, even if participants do avoid the extreme values.

You also must decide how to label your scale. Figure 9-2 shows three ways you might do this. In panel (a), only the end points are labeled. In this case, the participant is told the upper and lower limits of the scale. Such labeled points are called *anchors* because they keep the participant's interpretation of the scale values from drifting.

With only the end points anchored, the participant must interpret the meaning of the rest of the points. In Figure 9-2(b), all points are labeled. The participant knows exactly what each point means and consequently may provide more accurate information. In Figure 9-2(c), the scale is labeled at the end points and at the midpoint. This scale provides three anchors for the participant—a reasonable compromise between labeling only the end points and labeling all the points.

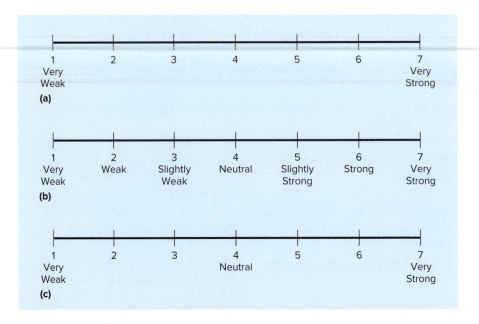

**FIGURE 9-2**    Three ways of labeling a rating scale: (a) end points only, (b) each point labeled, and (c) end points and midpoint labeled.

You may be wondering if the formatting of your scale affects responses. Recent research suggests that it does. Bert Weijters, Elke Cabooter, and Niels Schillewaert (2010) conducted an experiment on the formatting of rating scales in which they systematically varied the number of points indicated along the scale (4 to 7) and whether each point was labeled or only the endpoints. These variables affected participants' responses on all three dependent measures used in the study. For example, Weijters et al. found that labeling all points on a scale (versus only the endpoints) resulted in a greater tendency to agree with a statement, a reduction in extreme responses, and more errors on reversed items (where a low value means agreement on one version of an item and a high value means agreement on another version).

How respondents respond to a questionnaire item is also affected by the numbers on your scale. Norbert Schwarz, Bärbel Knäuper, Hans-J Hippler, Elisabeth Noel-Neumann, and Leslie Clark (1991) had participants rate how successful they felt in their lives on two forms of rating scale. One form used a 0 (Not at all successful) to 10 (Very successful) rating scale, whereas the other used a −5 (Not at all successful) to +5 (Very successful) rating scale. Schwarz et al. found that more participants (34%) used the center range of values on the 0 to 10 scale than on the −5 to +5 scale (13%). It may be that participants were reluctant to assign themselves a negative value on the −5 to +5 scale (Schwarz et al., 1991).

The nature of the labels you attach to the rating points along your scale can also affect your results. For example, Grace French-Lazovik and Curtis Gibson (1984) found that rating scales anchored with more positive labels (e.g., 1 = Exceptional, 2 = Very good, 3 = Good, 4 = Satisfactory, 5 = Unsatisfactory) yielded lower teaching evaluations than a scale with more traditional labeling (5 = Very effective, 4 = Above average, 3 = Average, 2 = Below average, 1 = Very ineffective). Additionally, it is important that the labels you place on your rating scale are consistent with the wording of the question being evaluated. A mismatch between question and scale labels may lead your respondents to ignore your labels and respond based on what they think you mean. This can lower the reliability of your questionnaire (Lam & Kolic, 2008).

Nearly all rating scales found in psychological research present alternatives equally spaced along the scale. In some cases, however, this scale format may not be best for what you are trying to measure. For example, if you are measuring the likelihood that a relatively rare event will occur (e.g., occurrence of a hurricane like Katrina or Sandy), it might make more sense to give the lower end of your rating scale a finer scaling format than the remainder of the scale. When you adopt this rating strategy, you are using a *stretched rating scale.* A stretched rating scale gives your respondents the opportunity to make finer judgments at the low-probability end of the scale (Knäuper, Stich, Yugo, & Tate, 2008). Individuals tend to overestimate the frequency of rare events; the stretched scale compensates for this by shifting responses to the lower end of the scale (Knäuper et al., 2008). Unfortunately, it also may set up a demand characteristic to respond on the finer end of the scale (Knäuper et al., 2008), thereby reducing the validity of the measurement.

In the previous examples, participants respond by checking or circling the scale value that best represents their judgments. Alternative ways to format your scale give participants more flexibility in their responses. In the *visual analog scale* (VAS), respondents place a mark along a continuous scale to indicate their choice. Figure 9-3 shows an example in which only the end points are anchored. To quantify the responses, you use a ruler to measure from an end point to the participant's mark. Your scale is then expressed in terms of inches or centimeters, and the resulting numbers are treated just like the numbers on a numbered scale.

Another variation on the rating scale is the *Likert scale,* which is widely used in attitude measurement research. A Likert scale provides a series of statements to which participants can indicate degrees of agreement or disagreement. Figure 9-4 shows two examples of formatting a Likert-scale item. In the first example, the attitude statement is followed by five blank spaces labeled from "Strongly Agree" to "Strongly Disagree." The participant simply checks the space that best reflects the degree of agreement or disagreement with each statement. The second example provides consecutive numbers rather than blank spaces and includes descriptive anchors only at the ends. Participants are instructed to circle the number that best reflects how

**FIGURE 9-3** Rating scale formatted with no numbers. End points are labeled, and respondents place marks on the line to indicate their responses.

Most political information on the Internet is accurate.

| Strongly Agree | Agree | Neutral | Disagree | Strongly Disagree |
|:---:|:---:|:---:|:---:|:---:|
| _____ | _____ | _____ | _____ | _____ |

(a)

Most political information on the Internet is accurate.

| Strongly Agree | | | | Strongly Disagree |
|:---:|:---:|:---:|:---:|:---:|
| 1 | 2 | 3 | 4 | 5 |

(b)

**FIGURE 9-4**    Samples showing Likert scales: (a) a standard Likert item on which the participant places a check in the blank under the statement that best reflects how he or she feels; (b) a five-point Likert scale using numbers that the participant circles.

much they agree or disagree with each statement. (For further information on Likert scaling, see Edwards, 1953).

A final note on rating scales is in order. Although rating scales have been presented in the context of survey research, be aware that rating scales are widely used in experimental research as well. Adapting rating scales to your particular research needs is a relatively simple affair. Anytime your research calls for rating scales, you can apply the suggestions presented here.

## QUESTIONS TO PONDER

1. What are the steps involved in designing a questionnaire?
2. How do open-ended and restricted items differ, and what are the advantages and disadvantages of each?
3. What are the ways in which questionnaire items can be formatted?
4. What are some of the factors that you should pay attention to when constructing questionnaire items?
5. How do you design effective rating scales?

### Assembling Your Questionnaire

If your questionnaire is to be effective, its items must be organized into a coherent, visually pleasing format. This process involves paying attention to the order in which the items are included and to the way in which they are presented.

Dillman (2000) and Moser and Kalton (1972) agree that demographic items should *not* be presented first on the questionnaire. These questions, although easy to complete, may lead participants to believe that the questionnaire is boring. Dillman emphasizes the importance of the first question on a questionnaire. A good first question should be interesting and engaging so that the respondent will be motivated to continue. According to Dillman, the first question should apply to everybody completing the questionnaire, be easy so that it takes only a few seconds to answer, and be interesting. Of course, these rules are not carved in stone. If your research needs require a certain question to be presented first, that consideration should take precedence (Dillman, 2000).

Your questionnaire should have continuity; that is, related items should be presented together. This keeps your participant's attention on one issue at a time rather than jumping from issue to issue. Your questionnaire will have greater continuity if related items are grouped. An organized questionnaire is much easier and more enjoyable for the participant to complete, factors that may increase the completion rate. Continuity also means that groups of related questions should be logically ordered. Your questionnaire should read like a book. Avoid the temptation to skip around from topic to topic in an attempt to hold the attention of the participant. Rather, strive to build "cognitive ties" between related groups of items (Dillman, 2000).

The order in which questions are included on a questionnaire has been shown to affect the responses of participants. For example, McFarland (1981) presented questions on a questionnaire ordered in two ways. Some participants answered a general question before specific questions, whereas others answered the specific questions first. McFarland found that participants expressed more interest in politics and religion when the specific questions were asked first than when the general questions were asked first. Sigelman (1981) found that question order affected whether or not participants expressed an opinion (about the popularity of the president), but only if the participants were poorly educated. Hence, question order may play a greater role for some participants than for others. Carefully consider your sample and the chosen topic when deciding on the order in which questions are asked.

The placement of items asking for sensitive information (such as sexual preferences or illegal behavior) is an important factor. Dillman (2000) suggests placing objectionable questions after less objectionable ones, perhaps even at the end of the questionnaire. Once your participants are committed to answering your questions, they may be more willing to answer some sensitive questions. Additionally, a question may not seem as objectionable after the respondent has answered previous items than if the objectionable item is placed earlier in the questionnaire (Dillman, 2000). You also should pay attention to the way that each page of your questionnaire is set up. There should be a logical "navigational path" (Dillman, 2000) that your respondent can follow. This path should lead the respondent through the questionnaire as if he or she were reading a book.

One way to accomplish this is to use appropriate graphics (e.g., arrows and other symbols) to guide respondents through the questionnaire. In fact, Dillman talks about two "languages" of a questionnaire. One language is verbal and relates to how your questions are worded. The other language is graphical and relates to the symbols and graphics used to guide respondents through the items on your questionnaire. Symbols and graphics can be used to separate groups of items, direct respondents where to go in the event of a certain answer (e.g., "If you answered 'No' to item 5, skip to item 7" could be accompanied by an arrow pointing to item 7), or direct respondents to certain pages on the questionnaire. Dillman suggests the following three steps for integrating the verbal and graphical languages into an effective questionnaire:

1. Design a navigational path directing respondents to read all the information on a page.

2. Create effective visual navigational guides to help respondents stay on the navigational path.

3. Develop alternate navigational guides to help with situations where the normal navigational guide will be interrupted (e.g., skipping items or sections).

## QUESTIONS TO PONDER

1. Why is the first question on a questionnaire so important?

2. What does it mean that a questionnaire should have continuity? Why is continuity important?

3. What is a questionnaire's navigational path, and why is it important?

## ADMINISTERING YOUR QUESTIONNAIRE

After you develop your questionnaire, you must decide how to administer it. You could mail your questionnaire to your participants, deliver your questionnaire via e-mail or post it on the Internet, telephone participants to ask the questions directly, administer your questionnaire to a large group at once, conduct face-to-face interviews, or use a mixed-mode technique combining survey methods. Each method has advantages and disadvantages and makes its own special demands.

### Mail Surveys

In a **mail survey**, you mail your questionnaire directly to your participants. They complete and return the questionnaire at their leisure. This is a rather convenient method. All you need to do is put your questionnaires into addressed envelopes and mail them. However, a serious problem called **nonresponse bias** occurs when a large proportion of participants fail to complete and return your questionnaire. If the participants who fail to return the questionnaire differ in significant ways from those who do return it, your survey may yield answers that do not represent the opinions of the intended population.

*Combating Nonresponse Bias*    To reduce nonresponse bias, you should develop strategies to increase your return rate. Dillman (2000) notes that the single most effective strategy for increasing response rate is to make multiple contacts with respondents. Dillman suggests making four contacts via mail. The first consists of a *prenotice letter* sent to the respondent a few days before the questionnaire is sent. The prenotice letter should inform the respondent that an important questionnaire will be coming in the mail in a few days. It also should inform the respondent what the survey is about and why the survey will be useful. The second mailing would deliver the questionnaire itself, accompanied by a cover letter. The cover letter should include the following elements in the order listed (Dillman, 2000): the specific request to complete the questionnaire, why the respondent was selected for the survey, the usefulness of the survey, a statement of confidentiality of the respondent's answers, an offer of a token of appreciation (if such an offer is to be made), an offer to answer questions, and a real signature.

The third mailing would take the form of a *thank you postcard* sent a few days or a week after the questionnaire was mailed. The postcard should thank the respondent for completing the questionnaire and remind the respondent to complete the questionnaire if not already done. The fourth contact provides a *replacement questionnaire,* sent 2 to 4 weeks after the original questionnaire and accompanied by a letter indicating that the original questionnaire had not been received. The letter also should urge the respondent to complete the replacement questionnaire and return it.

You may be able to increase your return rate somewhat by including a small token of your appreciation, such as a pen or pencil that the participant can keep. Some researchers include a small amount of money as an incentive to complete the questionnaire. As a rule, it is better to send the token along with the questionnaire rather than make the token contingent upon returning the questionnaire. One study found that 57% of respondents returned a survey questionnaire when promised $50 for its return whereas 64% returned the questionnaire when $1 was included with it (James & Bolstein, 1992). Benjamin Messer and Don Dillman (2011) found that response rates to a mail survey increased from 59% to 68% when a follow-up mailing that included a second monetary incentive ($5) and a new copy of the questionnaire was sent via Priority Mail. In this case, two incentives were better than one.

Ironically, smaller rewards seem to produce better results than larger ones (Kanuk & Berenson, 1975; Warner, Berman, Weyant, & Ciarlo, 1983). Dillman (2000) suggests that a $1 token is preferred because it is easy to mail and seems to produce the desired results. Finally, monetary incentives work better than tangible rewards (Church, 1993).

A few factors that do *not* significantly affect response rate include questionnaire length, personalization, promise of anonymity, and inclusion of a deadline (Kanuk & Berenson, 1975). (For reviews of the research supporting these findings, see Kanuk & Berenson, 1975, and Warner et al., 1983.)

## Internet Surveys

An increasingly popular method of administering questionnaires is to post them on the Internet. **Internet surveys** can be distributed via e-mail or listservs or posted on a website. Which method you use depends on the nature and purpose of your survey. E-mail surveys are easy to distribute but do not permit complex navigational designs (Dillman, 2000). Consequently, e-mail surveys are best for relatively short, simple questionnaires. Web-based surveys allow you to create and present more complex questionnaires that incorporate many of the design features discussed previously (Dillman, 2000). To aid you in the task of implementing a web-based survey, commercial software packages are available that allow you to design sophisticated questionnaires for posting on a website. There is significant advantage to using the Internet to conduct a survey or recruit participants: You can reach a large body of potential participants with relative ease. Data can be collected quickly and easily, resulting in a large data set.

With web surveys, as with mail surveys, nonresponse bias can be a problem, one that you can combat with prenotification. You can address the problem of nonresponse bias for web surveys by sending a short text message (which is more effective than an e-mail notice) to potential respondents (Bosnjak, Neubarth, Couper, Bandilla, & Kaczmirek, 2008). Among college populations, lottery incentives (in which respondents are entered into a lottery for prizes) can also increase response rates (Laguilles, Williams, & Saunders, 2011), but maybe not for other populations of respondents (Halpern et al., 2011; Roberts, Wilson, Roalfe, & Bridge, 2004). Additionally, it might be a good idea to use a female solicitor for your Internet survey, especially with a male target population (Keusch, 2012). Finally, a review of the literature on increasing response rates to web surveys, conducted by Paula Vicente and Elizabeth Reis (2010), suggests the following steps to increase response and completion rates in web surveys:

1. Present all of the questions on a single web page that allows respondents to scroll at will through the survey.

2. Provide a progress bar showing how much of the survey has been completed and how much remains.

3. Keep the survey as short as possible. Long surveys result in fewer completed surveys.

4. Use a few graphic elements in the survey. However, don't use too many because they may cause technical problems and distract respondents from the survey questions.

5. Have respondents use radio buttons rather than drop-down menus to indicate their responses.

There are also disadvantages to Internet surveys. As discussed in Chapter 6, a sample of respondents from the Internet may not be representative of the general population. According to a 2011 study by the U.S. Department of Commerce (2013), 71.7% of households had access to the Internet in the home. Further, households with younger residents and higher levels of education and income were more likely to have Internet access. Additionally, access was greater for Asians (82%) and Whites (76.2%) than Blacks (56.9%) or Hispanics (58.3%). Another disadvantage is that one must have the resources available to post a survey on the Internet. This requires computer space on a server and the ability to create the necessary web pages or the resources to pay someone to create your net survey for you.

Despite the potential for biased samples in Internet surveys, there is evidence that the results obtained from Internet surveys are equivalent to the results obtained from paper-and-pencil surveys. Alan De Beuckelear and Flip Lievens (2009) conducted a survey across 16 countries using both Internet and paper-and-pencil deliveries. The results showed that in all of the countries the Internet and paper-and-pencil surveys returned equivalent results. De Beuckelear and Lievens concluded that data collected with the two methods could be combined because the two methods produced such highly similar data. In another study, Christopher Fleming and Mark Bowden (2009) found that the sample demographics of an Internet and a mail survey on travel preferences did not differ significantly. Even if some differences are found between Internet surveys and more traditional methods, these differences may not translate into different conclusions being drawn from the resulting data (Stephenson & Crête, 2010).

In the studies just cited, the topics of the surveys were not sensitive or controversial. There is some evidence that the equivalence of Internet and conventional methods may not apply to more sensitive topics (DiNitto et al., 2009). DiNitto et al. conducted a survey over the Internet and by telephone asking men about sexual assault behaviors. The results showed that respondents in both types of survey reported sexual assault behavior. However, a wider variety of sexual assault behaviors were reported by respondents to the telephone survey.

So, where does this leave us? It would appear that Internet surveys may produce comparable results to other survey methods for nonsensitive issues. You can be reasonably confident that your Internet survey on such issues will yield data that are highly similar to data collected with more conventional methods. However, you must exercise more caution when surveying about sensitive behaviors. In the latter case, an Internet survey may produce results that differ from more conventional methods.

## Telephone Surveys

In a **telephone survey**, you contact participants by telephone rather than by mail or via the Internet. You can ask some questions more easily over the telephone than you can in written form. Telephone surveys can be done by having an interviewer ask respondents a series of questions or by interactive voice response (IVR). Telephone surveys using live interviewers have lost popularity as new technologies have become available. IVR surveys involve respondents using a touch-tone telephone to respond to a series of prerecorded questions. Modern IVR technologies also allow respondents to provide verbal answers in addition to numeric responses.

Telephone surveys may not be the best way to administer a questionnaire. The plethora of "junk calls" to which the population is exposed has given rise to a backlash against telephone intrusions. Laws have been passed on the state and federal level protecting people from unwanted calls, making it more difficult to reach prospective respondents. These laws, combined with caller ID and answering machines (which allow residents to screen their calls), make the telephone a less attractive medium for surveys now than in the past. In fact, research shows declining response and cooperation rates for telephone surveys from 1997 to 2003 (Keeter, Kennedy, Dimock, Best, & Craighill, 2006). This is partially due to the fact that as of 2008 only 70% of households have landlines and as we shall see below, including cell phone numbers presents its own problems.

## Group-Administered Surveys

Sometimes you may have at your disposal a large group of individuals to whom you can administer your questionnaire. In such a case, you design your questionnaire as you would for a mail survey but administer it to the assembled group. For example, you might distribute to a first-year college class a questionnaire on attitudes toward premarital sex. Using such a captive audience permits you to collect large amounts of data in a relatively short time. You do not have to worry about participants misplacing or forgetting about your questionnaire. You also may be able to reduce any volunteer bias, especially if you administer your questionnaire during a class period. People may participate because very little effort is required.

As usual, this method has some drawbacks. Participants may not treat the questionnaire as seriously when they fill it out as a group as when they fill it out alone. Also, you may not be able to ensure anonymity in the large group if you are asking for sensitive information. Participants may feel that other participants are looking at their answers. (You may be able to overcome this problem by giving adjacently seated participants alternate forms of the questionnaire.) Also, a few participants may express hostility about the questionnaire by purposely providing false information.

A final drawback to group administration concerns the participant's right to decline participation. A participant may feel pressure to participate in your survey. This pressure arises from the participant's observation that just about everyone else is participating. In essence, a conformity effect occurs because completing your survey becomes the norm defined by the behavior of your other participants. Make special efforts to reinforce the understanding that participants should not feel compelled to participate.

## Face-to-Face Interviews

Still another method for obtaining survey data is the **face-to-face interview**. In this method, you talk to each participant directly. This can be done in the participant's home or place of employment, in your office, or in any other suitable place. If you decide to use a face-to-face interview, keep several things in mind. First, decide whether to use a structured interview or an unstructured interview. In a *structured interview,* you ask prepared questions. This is similar to the telephone survey in that you prepare a questionnaire in advance and simply read the ordered questions to your participants. In the *unstructured interview,* you have a general idea about the issues to discuss. However, you do not have a predetermined sequence of questions.

An advantage of the structured interview is that all participants are asked the same questions in the same order. This eliminates fluctuations in the data that result from differences in when and how questions are asked. Responses from a structured interview are therefore easier to summarize and analyze. However, the structured interview tends to be inflexible. You may miss some important information by having a highly structured interview. The unstructured interview is superior in this respect. By asking general questions and having participants provide answers in their own words, you may gain more complete (although perhaps less accurate) information. However, responses from an unstructured interview may be more difficult to code and analyze later on. You can gain some advantages of each method by combining them in one interview. For example, begin the interview with a structured format by asking prepared questions; later in the interview, switch to an unstructured format.

Using the face-to-face interview strategy leads to a problem that is not present in mail or Internet surveys but is present to some extent in telephone surveys: The appearance and demeanor of the interviewer may affect the responses of the participants. Experimenter bias and demand characteristics become a problem. Subtle changes in the way in which an interviewer asks a question may elicit different answers. Also, your interviewer may not respond similarly to all participants (e.g., an interviewer may react differently to an attractive participant than to an unattractive one). This, too, can affect the results.

The best way to combat this problem is to use interviewers who have received extensive training in interview techniques. Interviewers must be trained to ask questions in the same way for each participant. They also must be trained not to emphasize any particular words in the stem of a question or in the response list. The questions should be read in a neutral manner. Also, try to anticipate any questions that participants may have and provide your interviewers with standardized responses. This can be accomplished by running a small pilot version of your survey before running the actual survey. During this pilot study, try out the interview procedure on a small sample of participants. (This can be done with just about anyone, such as friends, colleagues, or students.) Correct any problems that arise.

Another problem with the interview method is that the social context in which the interview takes place may affect a participant's responses. For example, in a survey of sexual attitudes known as the "Sex in America" survey (Michael, Gagnon, Laumann, & Kolata, 1994), some questions were asked during a face-to-face interview. Some participants were interviewed alone whereas others were interviewed with a spouse or other sex partner present. Having the sex partner present changed the responses to some questions. For example, when asked a question about the number of sex partners one had over the past year, 17% of the participants interviewed alone reported two or more. When interviewed with their sex partner present, only 5% said they had two or more sex partners. It would be most desirable to conduct the interviews in a standardized fashion with only the participant present.

## Mixed-Mode Surveys

In years gone by, surveys were conducted using only one method of obtaining respondents, such as a mail survey. However, recent changes in society and culture have made such unimethod techniques difficult to carry out. Don Dillman and Benjamin Messer (2010) suggest that changes in telephone technology and usage (e.g., fewer landlines, portable cell phone numbers, caller ID and answering machines, and increased reliance on e-mail over traditional mail) all have made obtaining respondents for traditional surveys difficult. To circumvent some of these issues, they suggest using a **mixed-mode survey** method, which employs more than one survey technique. For example, a survey can be distributed by both mail and the Internet. Research shows that using a mixed-mode survey technique in which both web and mail surveys are used can increase overall response rates. This is especially true when a follow-up postal mailing of the web-based questionnaire is sent via Priority Mail and accompanied by a second monetary incentive (Messer & Dillman, 2011).

Dillman and Messer (2010) point out both advantages and disadvantages of the mixed-mode method. On the positive side, a mixed-mode method can increase the "coverage" area for potential respondents, thus increasing the likelihood of reaching potential respondents. Using the mixed-mode method can also reduce nonresponse bias, because some respondents may be more willing to answer one form of survey (e.g., Internet) and others another (e.g., mail survey). Finally, mixed-mode surveys can help reduce costs. It is less costly to distribute an Internet survey, for example, than a mail survey. On the negative side, respondents may respond differently to the same question delivered in different modes.

## A Final Note on Survey Techniques

Although technology has opened up new methods for surveys, mail surveys remain popular. You might think with the movement away from traditional mail to electronic communication that it would be hard to get a representative sample using a traditional mail survey. This is not the case. Dillman, Christian, and Smyth (2014) provide evidence that it is possible to get response rates of greater than 75% using traditional mail with multiple contacts. As has been true in the past, the mail survey can reach large numbers of participants at a lower cost than either the telephone survey or the face-to-face interview (Warner et al., 1983). Mail surveys can also produce data that are less affected by social desirability effects (answering in a way that seems socially desirable). For these reasons, you might consider using a mail survey first.

After designing your questionnaire and choosing a method of administration, the next step is to assess the reliability and validity of your questionnaire. This is typically done by administering your questionnaire to a small but representative sample of participants. Based on the results, you may have to rework your questionnaire to meet acceptable levels of reliability and validity. In the next sections, we introduce you to the processes of evaluating the reliability and validity of your questionnaire.

## QUESTIONS TO PONDER

1. What are the different ways of administering a questionnaire?

2. What are the advantages and disadvantages of the different ways of administering a questionnaire?

3. What is nonresponse bias, and what can you do to combat it?

4. How do social desirability effects affect your decision about how to administer a questionnaire?

## ASSESSING THE RELIABILITY OF YOUR QUESTIONNAIRE

Constructing a questionnaire is typically not a one-shot deal. That is, you don't just sit down and write some questions and magically produce a high-quality questionnaire. Developing a quality questionnaire usually involves designing the questionnaire, administering it, and then evaluating it to see if it does the job.

One dimension you must pay attention to is the reliability of your questionnaire. In Chapter 5, we defined *reliability* as the ability of a measure to produce the same or highly similar results on repeated administrations. This definition extends to a questionnaire. If, on testing and retesting, your questionnaire produces highly similar results, you have a reliable instrument. In contrast, if the responses vary widely, your instrument is not reliable (Rogers, 1995).

In Chapter 5, we described two ways to assess the reliability of a measure: the test–retest method and the split-half method. In the next sections, we discuss the application of these two methods when assessing the reliability of a questionnaire.

## Assessing Reliability by Repeated Administration

Evaluating test–retest reliability is the oldest and conceptually simplest way of establishing the reliability of your questionnaire. You simply administer your questionnaire, allow some time to elapse, and then administer the questionnaire (or a parallel form of it) again to the same group of participants. Although this method is relatively simple to execute, you need to consider some issues before using it.

First, you must consider how long to wait between administrations of your questionnaire. An intertest interval that is too short may result in participants remembering your questions and the answers they gave. This could lead to an artificially high level of test–retest reliability. If, however, you wait too long, test–retest reliability may be artificially low. According to Tim Rogers (1995), the intertest interval should depend on the nature of the variables being measured, with an interval of a few weeks being sufficient for most applications. Rogers suggests that test–retest methods may be particularly problematic when applied to the following:

1. *Measuring ideas that fluctuate with time.* For example, an instrument to measure attitudes toward universal health care should not be evaluated with the test–retest method because attitudes on this topic seem to shift quickly.

2. *Issues for which individuals are likely to remember their answers on the first testing.*

3. *Questionnaires that are very long and boring.* The problem here is that participants may not be highly motivated to accurately complete an overly long questionnaire and therefore may give answers that reduce reliability.

Some of the problems inherent in using the *same* measure on multiple occasions can be avoided by using alternate or parallel forms of your questionnaire for retesting. As noted in Chapter 5, the type of reliability being assessed with this technique is known as parallel-forms reliability (Rogers, 1995).

For the parallel-forms method to work, the parallel forms of your questionnaire must be equivalent so that direct comparison is meaningful. According to Rogers (1995), parallel forms should have the same number of items and the same response format, cover the same issues with different items, be equally difficult, use the same instructions, and have the same time limits. In short, the parallel versions of a test must be as equivalent as possible (Rogers, 1995).

Although the parallel-forms method improves on the test–retest method, it does not solve all the problems associated with multiple testing. Using parallel forms does not eliminate the possibility that rapidly changing attitudes will result in low reliability. As with the test–retest method, such changes make the questionnaire appear less reliable than it actually is. In addition, practice effects may occur even when alternate forms are used (Rogers, 1995). Even though you use different questions on the parallel form, participants may respond similarly on the second test because they are familiar with your question format.

## Assessing Reliability with a Single Administration

Because of the problems associated with repeated testing, you might consider assessing reliability by means of a single administration of your questionnaire. As noted in Chapter 5, this approach involves splitting the questionnaire into equivalent halves and deriving a score for each half; the correlation between scores from the two halves is known as split-half reliability (Rogers, 1995). This technique works best when your survey is limited to a single specific area (e.g., sexual behavior) as opposed to multiple areas (sexual behavior and sexual attitudes).

Although the split-half method circumvents the problems associated with repeated testing, it introduces others. First, when you split a questionnaire, each score is based on a limited set of items, which can reduce reliability (Rogers, 1995). Consequently, the split-half method may underestimate reliability. Second, it is not clear how splitting should be done. If you simply do a first-half/second-half split, artificially low reliability may occur if the two halves of the form are not equivalent or if participants are less motivated to answer questions accurately on the second half of your questionnaire and therefore give inconsistent answers to your questions. One remedy for this is to use an odd–even split. In this case, you derive a score for the odd items and a score for the even items.

Perhaps the most desirable way to assess the split-half reliability of your questionnaire is to apply the Kuder–Richardson formula. This formula yields the average of all the split-half reliabilities that could be derived from splitting your questionnaire into two halves in every possible way. The resulting number (designated KR20) will lie between 0 and 1; the higher the number, the greater the reliability of your questionnaire. A KR20 of .75 indicates a "moderate" level of reliability (Rogers, 1995).

In cases in which your questionnaire uses a Likert format, a variation on the Kuder–Richardson formula known as *coefficient alpha* is used (Rogers, 1995). Like KR20, coefficient alpha is a score between 0 and 1, with higher numbers indicating greater reliability. Computation of this formula can be complex. For details, see a text on psychological testing (e.g., see Cohen, Swerdlik, & Sturman, 2013; Rogers, 1995).

## Increasing Reliability

Regardless of the method you use to assess reliability, there are steps you can take to increase the reliability of your questionnaire (Rogers, 1995):

1. Increase the number of items on your questionnaire. Generally, higher reliability is associated with increasing numbers of items. Of course, if your instrument becomes too long, participants may become angry, tired, or bored. You must weigh the benefits of increasing questionnaire length against possible liabilities.

2. Standardize administration procedures. Reliability will be enhanced if you treat all participants alike when administering your questionnaire. Make sure that timing procedures, lighting, ventilation, instructions to participants, and instructions to administrators are kept constant.

3. Score your questionnaire carefully. Scoring errors can reduce reliability.

4. Make sure that the items on your questionnaire are clear, well written, and appropriate for your sample (see our previous discussion on writing items).

## QUESTIONS TO PONDER

1. What is meant by the reliability of a questionnaire, and why is it important?

2. How do you assess reliability with repeated administrations?

3. How do you assess reliability with a single administration?

4. What steps can be taken to increase reliability?

## ASSESSING THE VALIDITY OF YOUR QUESTIONNAIRE

In Chapter 5, we discussed the validity of a measure and described several forms of validity that differ in their method of assessment: content validity, criterion-related validity, construct validity, and face validity. As with other measures, a questionnaire must have validity if it is to be useful; that is, it must measure what it is intended to measure. For example, if you are designing a questionnaire to assess political attitudes, the questions on your test should tap into political attitudes and not, say, religious attitudes.

Here we review content validity, construct validity, and criterion-related validity as applied to a questionnaire (Rogers, 1995). In a questionnaire, *content validity* assesses whether the questions cover the range of behaviors normally considered to be part of the dimension that you are assessing. To have content validity, your questionnaire on political attitudes should include items relevant to all the major issues relating to such attitudes (e.g., abortion, health care, the economy, and defense). The *construct validity* of a questionnaire can be established by showing that the questionnaire's results agree with predictions based on theory.

Establishing the *criterion-related validity* of a questionnaire involves correlating the questionnaire's results with those from another, established measure. There are two ways to do this. First, you can establish *concurrent validity* by correlating your questionnaire's results with those of another measure of the *same* dimension administered at the same time. In the case of your questionnaire on political attitudes, you would correlate its results with those of another, established measure of political attitudes. Second, you can establish *predictive validity* by correlating the questionnaire's results with some behavior that would be expected to occur, given the results. For example, your questionnaire on political attitudes would be shown to have predictive validity if the questionnaire's results correctly predicted election outcomes.

The validity of a questionnaire may be affected by a variety of factors. As noted earlier, how you define the behavior or attitude that you are measuring can affect validity. Validity also can be affected by the methods used to gather your data. In the "Sex in America" survey, some respondents were interviewed alone and others with someone else present. One cannot be sure that the responses given with another person present are an accurate reflection of one's sexual behavior (Stevenson, 1995). Generally, methodological flaws, poor conceptualization, and unclear questions can all contribute to lowered levels of validity.

## QUESTIONS TO PONDER

1. What is the validity of a questionnaire, and why is it important?
2. What are the different types of validity you should consider?
3. What factors can affect the validity of your questionnaire?

## ACQUIRING A SAMPLE FOR YOUR SURVEY

In Chapter 6, we distinguished between a population (all individuals in a well-defined group) and a sample (a smaller number of individuals selected from the population). Once you have designed and pretested your questionnaire, you then administer it to a group of participants. It is usually impractical to have everyone in the population (however that may be defined) complete your survey. Instead, you administer your questionnaire to a small sample of that population. The most widely used technique to acquire a sample for a survey is probability sampling. In **probability sampling**, each member of a population has a known probability of being in the sample. Ideally, each member of the population has an equal chance of being in your sample (Dattalo, 2008). The sampling techniques we discuss below are all probability sampling techniques.

Proper sampling is a crucial aspect of sound survey research methodology. Without proper sampling, you can't generalize your results to your target population (e.g., accurately predict voter behavior in an election). Three sampling-related issues you must consider are representativeness, sampling technique, and sample size.

### Representativeness

However you acquire your sample, it should be representative of the population of interest. A **representative sample** closely matches the characteristics of the population. Imagine that you have a bag containing 300 golf balls: 100 are white, 100 are orange, and 100 are yellow. You then select a sample of 30 golf balls. A representative sample would have 10 balls of each color. A sample having 25 white and 5 orange would not be representative (the ratio of colors does not approximate that of the population) and would constitute a nonrepresentative or **biased sample**.

The importance of representative sampling is shown by the failure of a political poll taken during the 1936 presidential election. In that election, Alf Landon was opposing Franklin Roosevelt. The editors of the *Literary Digest* (a now-defunct magazine) conducted a poll by using telephone directories and vehicle registration lists to draw their sample. The final sample consisted of nearly 10 million people! The results showed that Landon would beat Roosevelt by a landslide. Quite to the contrary, Roosevelt soundly defeated Landon. Why was the poll so wrong?

The problem stemmed from the method used to obtain the sample. Fewer people owned a car or telephone in the 1930s than do today. In fact, very few owned either. Those who did own a telephone or car tended to be relatively wealthy and Republican. Consequently, most of the participants polled favored the Republican candidate. Unfortunately for the *Literary Digest,* this sample did not represent the population of voters, and the prediction failed. How could the editors have been so stupid? In fact, they weren't stupid. Such sampling techniques had been used before and worked. It was only in that particular election (in which people were clearly split along party lines) that the problem emerged (Hooke, 1983).

The *Literary Digest* poll failed because it used a biased source (car registration and telephone listings). Whatever source you choose, you should make an effort to determine whether it includes members from all segments of the population in which you have an interest. A good way to overcome the problem of biased source lists is to use multiple lists. For example, you could use the telephone book *and* vehicle registration *and* voter registration lists to select your sample.

## Sampling Techniques

At the heart of all sampling techniques is the concept of *random sampling.* In random sampling, every member of the population has an equal chance of appearing in your sample. A participant is included in your sample (or not) based on chance alone. Sampling is typically done without replacement. Once an individual is chosen for your sample, he or she cannot be chosen a second time for that sample.

Random sampling eliminates the possibility that the sample is biased by the preferences of the person selecting the sample. In addition, random sampling affords some assurance that the sample does not bias itself. As an example of self-biasing, consider the following case. In 1976, Shere Hite published *The Hite Report: A Nationwide Study on Female Sexuality,* which was a survey of women's sexual attitudes and behaviors. Hite's sample was obtained by initially distributing questionnaires through national mailings to women's groups (the National Organization for Women, abortion rights groups, university women's centers, and others). Later, advertisements were placed in several magazines (the *Village Voice, Mademoiselle, Brides,* and *Ms.*) informing women where they could write for a copy of the questionnaire. Finally, the questionnaire was reprinted in *Oui* magazine in its entirety (253 women returned the questionnaire from *Oui*).

The question you should ask yourself at this point is, "Did Hite obtain a random sample of the population of women?" The answer is no. Hite's method had several problems. First, the memberships of the organizations that Hite contacted may not represent the population of women. For example, you cannot assume that members of NOW hold similar views, on the average, to those of the population of all women. Second, asking people through magazine ads to write in for questionnaires further biases the sample. Can you figure out why?

If you said that the people who write in for the questionnaires may be somehow different from those who do not, you are correct. Who would write in to obtain a questionnaire on sexuality? Obviously, women who have an interest in such an issue. In fact, Hite indicates that many of her participants expressed such an interest. One woman wrote, "I answered this questionnaire because I think the time is long overdue for women to speak out about their feelings about sex" (Hite, 1976, p. xxxii). As with the members of the women's organizations, you could question whether the women who wrote in for questionnaires are representative of all women. They probably are not.

When a sample is biased, the data obtained may not indicate the attitudes of the population as a whole. Hite concluded from her sample that women in this country were experiencing a "new sexuality." However, that new sexuality was limited to those women whose attitudes were similar to those who answered her questionnaires.

In 1983, Hite published *The Hite Report on Male Sexuality.* The method she used to gather data was similar to the one used in her earlier study of women. In this book, Hite responded to the criticisms of her method. She presented evidence that her sample of men was similar in age, religion, and education to the most recent census data. What was not clear, however, was whether the attitudes of the men who responded to her questionnaire were similar to those of the general population. As in the survey of women, the data obtained may not be representative of the population of men. Some evidence suggests they were not. Hite said that 72% of married men reported having had an extramarital affair. Is this an accurate estimate of the population or an estimate of a special subsection of the population? Apparently, it is the latter. Other surveys have found that about 25% of men report having had extramarital affairs.

The same problem is evident in polls and surveys sponsored by media outlets. It has become common for news outlets to pose questions to viewers and have them respond via the Internet (e.g., by texting). Sampling bias is evident in these surveys because only viewers of the show are likely to respond, and these may represent limited demographic groups (e.g., liberals or conservatives) that are not representative of the population at large. You should always be skeptical of these "nonscientific" (often labeled as such) polls or surveys.

The lesson of these examples is that you should make every effort to obtain a random sample. This may be difficult, especially if you are dealing with a sensitive topic. You could use some of the strategies previously suggested for reducing nonresponse bias (such as including a small reward or using follow-ups). If your sample turns out to be nonrandom and nonrepresentative, temper any conclusions you draw.

Using the proper sampling technique is one way to obtain a representative sample. Several techniques are available to you. Five of them (simple random sampling, stratified sampling, proportionate sampling, systematic sampling, and cluster sampling) are discussed next. These techniques are not mutually exclusive. Often researchers combine them to help ensure a representative sample of the population.

*Simple Random Sampling*    Randomly selecting a certain number of individuals from the population is a technique called **simple random sampling**. Remember the golf ball example? A simple random sample of 50 would involve dipping your hand into the bag 50 times, each time withdrawing a single ball. Figure 9-5 illustrates the simple random sampling strategy. From the population illustrated at the top of the figure, 10 participants are selected at random for inclusion in your survey.

In practice, selecting a random sample for a survey is more involved than pulling golf balls from a bag. Often it involves consulting a table of random numbers or using

Population

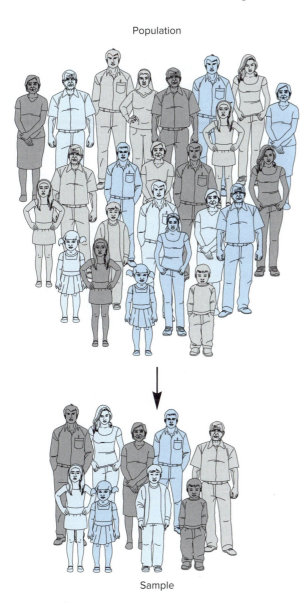

**FIGURE 9-5** Example of simple random sampling. The people at the top of the figure represent the population, and the people at the bottom represent the randomly selected sample.

Sample

a random number generator (available online). The numbers in such a table have been chosen at random and then subjected to a number of statistical tests to ensure that they have the expected properties of random numbers.

As an example of how to use a table of random numbers to select a random sample, imagine you are using the telephone book as a source list. Starting on any page of the random number table, close your eyes and drop your finger on the page. Open your eyes and read the number under your finger. Assume that the number is 235,035. Then go to page 235 in the telephone book and select the 35th name on that page. Repeat this process until you select all the participants constituting the sample.

A variant of random sampling that can be used when conducting a telephone survey is *random digit dialing* (Dillman, 2000). List all the exchanges in a particular area (the first three digits of the phone numbers, not including the area code). You then use the table of random numbers or a computer to select four-digit numbers (e.g., 5,891). The exchange plus the four-digit number provides the number to be called. (Any nonworking numbers are discarded.) This technique allows you to reach unlisted as well as listed numbers. The advent of modern electronic communication systems has created problems for random digit dialing. One problem is that an increasing number of people do not have landlines, especially younger people (Lavrakas, Shuttles, Steeh, & Fienberg, 2007). Some survey researchers, in fact, suggest that it no longer makes much sense to even sample landline users and sample only cell phone users. Fortunately, research suggests that cellular telephone databases currently available can produce an unbiased sample of survey respondents (Gundersen, Peters, Conner, Dayton, & Delnevo, 2014). If you do include cell phone users in a telephone survey, research shows that sending a short text message before calling can increase response rates (Dal Grande, Chittleborough, Campostrini, Dollard, & Taylor, 2016). Another problem is that some smartphone users may not even use their devices primarily as traditional telephones and use them for alternative forms of communication such as texting or social media (Gundersen et al., 2014). This problem is compounded by the fact that some people from some demographic groups may use their smartphones for this purpose more than others. For example, Blacks (85%) and Hispanics (87%) report using their smartphones more for texting than Whites (79%) (Pew Research Center, 2013). Because of these problems, you may have to take extra steps when using random digit dialing to ensure that you are obtaining a representative sample of potential respondents.

Research suggests that random digit dialing has been yielding lower and lower response rates over the past several years (Lavrakas, 2010), even when cell phones are targeted (Lavrakas et al., 2007). Consequently, survey researchers have been looking for an alternative way to deliver surveys. One such strategy is to use address-based sampling in which you use an existing U.S. Postal Service Computerized Delivery Sequence File (DFS) as your source for potential respondents. Preliminary research on this list has shown that the DFS is a viable technique for survey sampling (Brick, Williams, & Montaquila, 2011; Innacchione, 2011).

Even though random sampling reduces the possibility of systematic bias in your sample, it does not guarantee a representative sample. You could, quite at random, select participants who represent only a small segment of the population. In the golf ball example, you might select 50 orange golf balls. White and yellow golf balls, even though represented in the population, are not in your sample. One way to combat this problem is to select a large sample (such as 200 rather than just 50 balls). A large sample is more likely to represent all segments of the population than a small one. However, it does not *guarantee* that representation in your sample will be proportionate to representation in the population. You may end up with 90 white, 90 orange, and only 20 yellow golf balls in a sample of 200, although such a result is highly unlikely. In addition, as you increase sample size, you also increase the cost and time needed to complete the survey. Fortunately, more sophisticated techniques provide a random yet representative sample without requiring a large number of participants.

## QUESTIONS TO PONDER

1. What is a representative sample, and why is it important to have one for a survey?
2. What is a biased sample, and how can a biased sample affect your results?
3. What is a random sample, and why is it important to do random sampling?
4. What is simple random sampling?

*Stratified Sampling*    **Stratified sampling** provides one way to obtain a representative sample. You begin by dividing the population into segments, or *strata* (Kish, 1965). For example, you could divide the population of a particular town into Whites, Blacks, and Hispanics. Next, you select a separate random sample of equal size from each stratum. Because individuals are selected from each stratum, you guarantee that each segment of the population is represented in your sample. Figure 9-6 shows the stratified sampling strategy. Notice that the population has been divided into two segments (blue and gray figures). A random sample is then selected from each segment.

*Proportionate Sampling*    Simple stratified sampling ensures a degree of representativeness, but it may lead to a segment of the population being overrepresented in your sample. For example, consider a community of 5,000 that has 500 Hispanics, 1,500 Blacks, and 3,000 Whites. If you used a simple stratification technique in which you randomly selected 400 people from each stratum, Hispanics would be overrepresented in your sample relative to Blacks and Whites, and Blacks would be overrepresented relative to Whites. You could avoid this problem by using a variant of stratified sampling called **proportionate sampling**.

In proportionate sampling, the proportions of people in the population are reflected in your sample. In the population example, your sample would consist of 10% Hispanics (500/5,000 = 10%), 30% Blacks (1,500/5,000 = 30%), and 60% Whites (3,000/5,000 = 60%). So, if you draw a sample of 1,200, you would have 120 Hispanics, 360 Blacks, and 720 Whites. According to Kish (1965), this technique is the most popular method of sampling.

By the way, stratification and proportionate sampling can be done after a sample has been obtained (Kish, 1965). You randomly select from the participants who responded the number from each stratum needed to match the characteristics of the population.

*Systematic Sampling*    **Systematic sampling** is a popular technique that is often used in conjunction with stratified sampling (Kish, 1965). This technique involves sampling every *k*th element after a random start. Figure 9-7 illustrates the systematic sampling technique.

*Cluster Sampling*    In some cases, populations may be too large to allow cost-effective random sampling or even systematic sampling. You might be interested in surveying children in a large school district. To make sampling more manageable, you could identify naturally occurring groups of participants (clusters) and randomly select certain

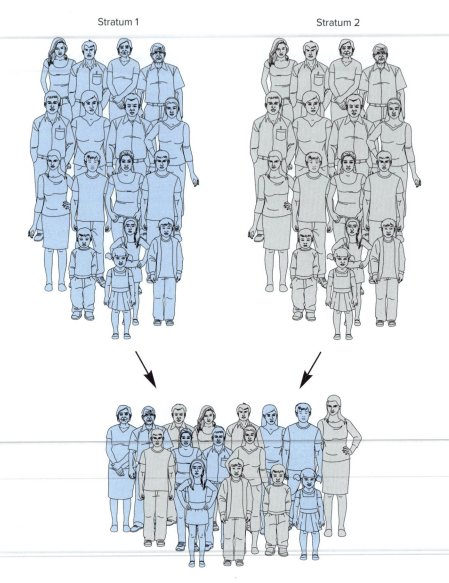

Stratum 1                                Stratum 2

**FIGURE 9-6**  Example of stratified sampling. The population is divided into two strata from which independent random samples are drawn.

clusters. For example, you could randomly select certain departments or classes from which to sample. Once the clusters have been selected, you would then survey all participants within the clusters. **Cluster sampling** differs from the other forms of sampling already discussed in that the basic sampling unit is a group of participants (the cluster) rather than the individual participant (Kish, 1965). Figure 9-8 illustrates cluster sampling. This figure shows how you select four groups from a larger pool of groups.

    An obvious advantage of cluster sampling is that it saves time. It is not always feasible to select random samples that focus on single elements (individuals, families, etc.). Cluster

| | |
|---|---|
| Richardson, E. | 555–6396* |
| Richardson, J. B. | 555–6789 |
| Richardson, L. R. | 555–2311 |
| Richardson, M. | 555–9902 |
| Richardson, V. | 555–7822* |
| Richeson, A. P. | 555–8211 |
| Richeson, T. | 555–3762 |
| Richey, B. B. | 555–9943 |
| Richey, C. L. | 555–1470* |
| Richey, G. J. | 555–8218 |
| Richhart, W. | 555–6539 |
| Richman, A. | 555–8902 |
| Richman, B. I. | 555–0076* |
| Richman, H. H. | 555–9215 |
| Richman, Z. L. | 555–1093 |
| Richmond, A. | 555–7634 |
| Richmond, B. B. | 555–7890* |
| Richmond, C. | 555–2609 |
| Rideman, L. | 555–7245 |
| Ritchey, A. K. | 555–6790 |

Each of the names with a star (*) would be included in your sample.

**FIGURE 9-7**  Example of systemic sampling. After a random start, every fifth name (indicated with an asterisk) is included in the sample.

sampling provides an acceptable, cost-effective method of acquiring a sample. On the negative side, cluster sampling does limit your sample to those participants found in the chosen clusters. If participants within clusters are fairly similar to one another but differ from those in other clusters, the sample will leave out important elements of the population. For example, clusters consisting of geographical areas of the United States (e.g., East, Midwest, South, Southwest, and West) may differ widely in political opinion. If only East and Midwest are selected for the sample, the opinions collected may not reflect the opinions of the country as a whole. Thus, cluster sampling does have drawbacks.

A variant of cluster sampling is **multistage sampling**. You begin by identifying large clusters and randomly selecting from among them (first stage). From the selected clusters, you then randomly select individual elements (rather than selecting all elements in the cluster). This method can be combined with stratification procedures to ensure a representative sample.

Other sophisticated sampling techniques are available to the survey researcher, but to explore them all would require a whole book. If you are interested in learning about these techniques, read Dattalo (2008) or Kish (1965).

## Random and Nonrandom Sampling Revisited

In Chapter 6, we distinguished between random sampling (in which each member of a population has an equal chance of being selected) and nonrandom sampling. Ideally,

**FIGURE 9-8** Example of cluster sampling. After randomly selecting subgroups of the population, all participants in each selected subgroup are surveyed.

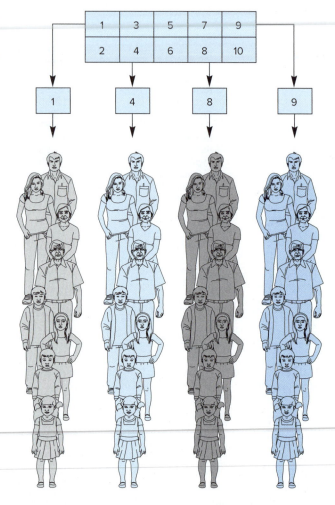

you would want to use some form of random sampling. This is especially true, as noted in Chapter 6, if you want to make specific predictions about specific behaviors. However, as a practical matter, it may not always be possible to use a true random sample. Instead, you may have to administer your questionnaire to an *availability sample* (convenience sample) of respondents you have easy access to (Dattalo, 2008). For example, you might use students at a particular university, which is a nonrandom sample of all university students. Similarly, surveys conducted via the Internet typically use nonrandom samples, consisting only of those with access the Internet who discover the survey and decide to complete it. Of course, using a nonrandom sample limits the generality of your results, and making specific predictions about behavior may not be possible. However, a nonrandom sample (as noted in Chapter 6) is perfectly acceptable for most research interests in psychology. If you use nonrandom sampling, you should include a discussion of possible limitations of your results in the discussion section of any report that you write.

## QUESTIONS TO PONDER

1. What are the various sampling techniques that represent modifications of simple random sampling?

2. Under what conditions would you use each of the sampling techniques discussed in this section?

3. What are the implications of using a nonrandom sample?

## Sample Size

One factor you must contend with if you perform a survey is the size of your sample. There are situations in which a large sample is essential. For example, a large sample is necessary if you anticipate a large number of uncontrolled variables or if your sample is to be subdivided (Dattalo, 2008). A small sample is acceptable in exploratory studies or when you have tight control over variables (Dattalo, 2008). The best advice concerning sample size is to select an *economic sample*—one that includes enough participants to ensure a valid survey and no more. You must take into account two factors when considering the size of the sample needed to ensure a valid survey: the amount of acceptable error and the expected magnitude of the population proportions.

The question of acceptable error arises because in most cases the composition of your sample will differ to some extent from that of the population. If you conduct a political poll on a sample of 1,500 registered voters and find that 62% of the *sample* favors Smith and 38% Jones, you would like to say that 62% of the *population* favors Smith. However, the proportion in the whole population might actually be 59% for Smith and 41% for Jones. In this case, the proportion you observed in your sample overestimate how many people favor Smith and underestimate how many people favor Jones. The extent to which the characteristics of your sample differ from those of the population is called **sampling error**.

In surveys, sampling error is estimated by the margin of error. In our political pole example, preference for Smith might be reported as 68 ±4 percent, where the ±4 percent is the margin of error. The size of the margin of error depends on a number of factors. One is the selected level of confidence. A 95% level of confidence means that the true population value will fall within the margin of error in 95 of 100 samples taken from the same population; thus you can be 95% confident that the population value lies within this range. You can choose a higher level of confidence (e.g., 99%) but the margin of error will be larger in order have this greater chance of overlapping the true population value. Another factor determining the margin of error is the size of your sample. As sample size increases, the margin of error diminishes. However, there is a law of diminishing returns at work here: as sample size increases, the amount by which the margin of error decreases gets smaller and smaller. Because of this, increasing your sample size beyond a certain level does not pay off. The small reduction in the margin of error is not worth the increased cost and time.

Computing the sample size required to obtain a given margin of error can be complex, depending on the sampling strategy used to collect the data. However, for our polling data involving the percentage of respondents favoring each political candidate and random sampling, the computations are fairly simple. You begin by guessing the population proportion, if you have previous information suggesting what it might be. If not, the conservative strategy is to use 0.5 (50%). Plug the estimated proportion ($P'$) into the following formula:

$$n' = \frac{z^2 P'(1 - P')}{ME^2}$$

If you are using the 95% level of confidence, $z = 1.96$; for the 99% level, $z = 2.58$. $ME$ is your desired margin of error. If you want the margin of error to be $\pm 4$ percent, then $ME = .04$. Plugging these numbers into the equation (assuming a 95% confidence level), we have

$$n' = \frac{1.96^2(.25)}{.04^2}$$

This works out to $n' = 600.25$ or 601. Thus, to obtain a margin of error of 4% at the 95% confidence level, you need 601 respondents in your sample.

The above formula is valid only if both $P'$ and $1 - P'$ are at least .10 (10%) and the population from which the sample was drawn is large. Currently the Survey Monkey website offers a sample size calculator (http://hamsterandwheel.com/grids/index2d.php) that takes population size into account. Simply specify your estimated population size, confidence level, and desired margin of error and the calculator spits out the required sample size.

For stratified sampling, determining sample size is more difficult than for simple random sampling. You must take into account the between-strata error (the variability in the scores of participants in different strata) and the within-strata error (the variability in the scores of participants within the same stratum). The formulas for computing sample size with the more sophisticated sampling techniques are complex. If you pursue survey research using these techniques, consult Moser and Kalton (1972), Crano and Brewer (1986), and Kish (1965).

## QUESTIONS TO PONDER

1. What is meant by an "economic sample"?

2. What is sampling error, and how do you know if you have an acceptable level?

3. What variables determine the sample size needed to obtain a given margin of error?

## SUMMARY

Survey research is used to evaluate the behavior (past, present, and future) and attitudes of a specified population. Survey research falls into the category of correlational research. Therefore, you cannot draw causal inferences about behavior from your survey data, no matter how compelling the data look. Surveys are used in a wide variety of situations. They can be used to research the marketability of a new product, to predict voter behavior, or to measure existing attitudes on a variety of issues.

The first step in a survey is to clearly define the goals of your research. Your questionnaire is then designed around those goals. You should have a reasonably focused goal for your survey. A questionnaire that tries to do too much may be confusing and burdensome to your participants. Keep your questionnaire focused on the central issues of your research.

Often a questionnaire is organized so that questions about your participants' characteristics (demographic items) and questions about the behavior or attitude of interest are included. The demographic items can later be used as predictor variables when you look for relationships among the variables that you measured.

Questionnaire items can be of several types. Open-ended questions allow your participants to answer in their own words. A major advantage of this type of question is the richness of the information obtained. A drawback is that responses are difficult to summarize and analyze. A restricted question provides response alternatives for participants to choose from. A variation on the restricted item is a rating scale on which participants circle a number reflecting how they feel. This type of item yields data that are easier to summarize and analyze. However, the responses made to restricted items are not as rich as those obtained with an open-ended item. A partially open-ended item gives participants not only clearly defined response alternatives but also a space to write in their own response category.

Once you have decided what types of items to include on your questionnaire, you must then actually write your questions. When writing items, you should avoid using overly complex words when simpler words will suffice. Your questions should be precise. Vague or overly complex wording yields inconsistent data. In addition, you should avoid using words that are biased or judgmental.

A questionnaire must be carefully structured. Questions should be presented in a logical order so that your questionnaire has continuity. Also, it is a good idea to place demographic items at the end. These questions tend to be boring, and participants may be turned off if you have demographic items at the beginning of your questionnaire. Sensitive questions should be placed toward the middle. Your participants may be more willing to answer such questions after answering several other, more innocuous questions. Sensitive items should be carefully worded. Your questionnaire should have a logical "navigational path." This path should lead the respondent through the questionnaire as if he or she were reading a book.

Constructing a questionnaire involves more than sitting down and writing a set of items. Developing a good questionnaire involves several steps, including assessing its reliability, or your questionnaire's ability to produce consistent results. One way to assess reliability is to administer your questionnaire (or parallel forms of the questionnaire) more than once. If the results are highly similar, the questionnaire is reliable. Another way to assess reliability is with a single administration of your questionnaire. The most common way to do this is to use a split-half method by which you divide your questionnaire in half (e.g., odd versus even items) and correlate the two halves. Two statistics used to evaluate split-half reliability are the Kuder–Richardson formula and coefficient alpha.

If you find low reliability, you can do several things to increase it. You can increase the number of items on your questionnaire, standardize administration procedures, make sure that you score questions carefully, and ensure that your items are clear, well written, and appropriate for your sample.

In addition to assessing reliability, you should evaluate the validity of your questionnaire. The term *validity* in this context refers to whether your questionnaire actually measures what you intend it to measure. There are three ways to assess validity. First, you can establish content validity by making sure that items on your questionnaire cover the full range of issues relevant to the phenomenon you are studying.

Second, criterion-related validity can be established by correlating the results from your questionnaire with one of established validity. Third, you can establish construct validity by establishing that the results from your questionnaire match well with predictions made by a theory. No one of these methods is best. Perhaps the best approach is to establish validity using more than one of the three methods.

Ways to administer your questionnaire are the mail survey, group administration, telephone survey, face-to-face interview, Internet survey, and the mixed-mode method. The mail survey is easiest. You simply mail your questionnaires and wait for a response. However, this method is plagued by nonresponse bias. Return rates can be increased with effective cover letters, follow-up reminders tailored to the nature of your participant population, and small rewards. In group administration, you bring a large group of participants together and administer your questionnaire to all of them at once. The advantage of group administration is that you can collect large amounts of data quickly. Surveys also can be conducted over the telephone. Questionnaires designed for telephone surveys should be relatively short, with clearly worded, short questions. Because your questions will be read to your participants, make sure that the person reading the questions speaks clearly and slowly. In an interview, you ask your questions to your participants in a face-to-face session. Interviews can be either structured (questions asked from a prepared questionnaire in a fixed order) or unstructured (each interview is different). You can conduct your survey on the Internet, which allows you to reach large numbers of potential respondents. Data can be collected quickly and easily via the Internet. However, the sample obtained from the Internet may not be representative, and you must have the equipment, resources, and knowledge necessary to post a questionnaire this way. Finally, you can use a mixed-mode method which combines different survey delivery methods.

One of the most crucial stages of survey research is acquiring a sample of participants. Because you want to make statements about how people think on an issue, be sure your sample represents the population. Biased samples lead to invalid data and ultimately to incorrect conclusions. Sampling techniques include simple random sampling (in which every respondent has an equal chance to participate in your survey) and stratified sampling (in which your population is broken into smaller segments and random samples are then drawn from those smaller segments). Other sampling techniques are proportionate sampling, multistage sampling, and cluster sampling. The sampling technique you use depends on the needs of your survey.

Whichever sampling technique you choose, you must consider the issue of sample size. Your sample should be large enough to be representative of the population, yet not too large. Try to acquire an economic sample that has just enough participants to adequately assess behavior or attitudes. Formulas are available for determining the size of the most economic sample that will produce a specified margin of error.

## KEY TERMS

| | |
|---|---|
| open-ended item | mail survey |
| restricted item | nonresponse bias |
| partially open-ended item | Internet survey |

telephone survey

face-to-face interview

mixed-mode survey

probability sampling

representative sample

biased sample

simple random sampling

stratified sampling

proportionate sampling

systematic sampling

cluster sampling

multistage sampling

sampling error

# Using Between-Subjects and Within-Subjects Experimental Designs

Correlational research designs identify potential causal relationships and often are used when potential causal variables cannot or should not be manipulated. However, correlational designs are simply not adequate for establishing causal relationships between variables.

When your goal is to establish causal relationships and you can manipulate variables, an experimental research design is used. By manipulating an independent variable while rigidly controlling extraneous factors, you can determine whether this manipulation causes changes in the value of the dependent variable.

## TYPES OF EXPERIMENTAL DESIGN

The simple logic of manipulating an independent variable and observing related changes in behavior is at the heart of every experimental design. However, to deal with the complexities of real-world research problems, researchers have developed a wide variety of experimental designs. We can simplify the situation somewhat by noting that experimental designs can be categorized into three basic types: between-subjects, within-subjects, and single-subject designs. In a **between-subjects design**, each treatment is administered to a different group of subjects. In a **within-subjects design**, a *single* group of subjects is exposed to *all* of the treatments, one treatment at a time. In both the between-subjects and within-subjects designs, data collected from subjects within a given treatment are averaged. Any effects of your independent variables will appear as differences in these treatment averages. A **single-subject design** is similar to the within-subjects design in that subjects are exposed to all treatments. The main difference from the within-subjects design is that you do not average data across subjects. Instead, you focus on changes in the behavior of a single subject (or a small number of individual subjects) under the different treatment conditions.

In this chapter, we discuss between-subjects and within-subjects designs. (Single-subject designs are discussed in Chapter 12.) The plan of this chapter is to discuss, first, the problem of error variance in experimental design and how it is handled. We then introduce single-factor between-subjects and within-subjects designs, designs that include only one independent variable. Finally, we explore between-subjects and within-subjects designs that include two or more independent variables.

## THE PROBLEM OF ERROR VARIANCE IN BETWEEN-SUBJECTS AND WITHIN-SUBJECTS DESIGNS

**Error variance** is the variability among scores caused by variables other than your independent variables (extraneous variables or subject-related variables such as age, gender, and personality). The problems posed by error variance are common to all three experimental designs. However, each design has its own way of dealing with error variance. In this chapter, we focus on how we deal with error variance in between-subjects and within-subjects designs. In Chapter 12, we discuss how error variance is handled in single-subject designs.

### Sources of Error Variance

In the real world, it is rarely possible to hold constant all the extraneous variables that could affect the value of your dependent variable. Subjects in your experiment differ in innumerable ways that could individually or collectively affect their scores on the dependent measure; in addition, the environmental conditions are not absolutely constant, and even the same subject will not be exactly the same from moment to moment. To the extent that these variations affect your dependent variable, they induce differences in scores that are not caused by your independent variable. That is, they produce error variance.

An example may help clarify this concept. In an experiment on the effects of THC (the active ingredient in marijuana) on a simulated air traffic–control task, one group is exposed to a dose of THC (the experimental group) and one is not (the control group). Within each group, all participants are exposed to the same level of the independent variable. Yet it is unlikely that all participants in a given group would turn in the same scores on the simulated air traffic–controller task. Participants differ in many ways that affect their performance. Some may be more resistant to THC, have better attention skills, or have greater perceptual abilities than others. The variation in scores produced by these uncontrolled variables is the error variance that we are discussing.

Table 10-1 shows the scores turned in by participants in this hypothetical experiment. The mean (average) scores for each group are presented at the bottom of the table. On average, the scores of the experimental group are lower than those the control group. What explains this difference? One possibility is that THC reduced the participants' scores on the dependent variable. However, given the variability in scores

TABLE 10-1  Scores from Hypothetical THC Experiment

PERFORMANCE ON DEPENDENT MEASURE

| | Control Group | Experimental Group |
|---|---|---|
| | 25 | 13 |
| | 24 | 19 |
| | 18 | 22 |
| | 29 | 18 |
| | 19 | 23 |
| Mean | 23 | 19 |

evident within each group, it seems plausible to suggest a second possibility: that the difference in the means reflects nothing more than error variance, that is, preexisting participant differences that did not quite balance out across the two conditions of the experiment. The problem is that you cannot tell, simply by looking at the means, which explanation is correct. The problem of error variance is therefore serious. It affects your ability to determine the effectiveness of your independent variable.

## QUESTIONS TO PONDER

1. In what two ways can you manipulate an independent variable?
2. How do between-subjects, within-subjects, and single-subject experiments differ?
3. What is error variance, and why does it create problems when trying to determine the influence of an independent variable on your dependent measure?

### Handling Error Variance

Fortunately, there are ways you can cope with the problem of error variance. You can take steps to reduce error variance, you can take steps to increase the effect of your independent variable, and you can randomize error variance across groups. Let's examine each of these strategies.

*Reducing Error Variance*    A principal way to deal with error variance in experimental research is to reduce it as much as possible. It is primarily for this reason that experiments are so often conducted in a laboratory environment, where the researcher can gain strict control over many of the extraneous variables that might otherwise cause error variance. One can test subjects under conditions that, to the extent possible, differ only in the levels of the independent variable to which the given subjects are exposed.

Although making test conditions as uniform as possible across treatments can help to reduce error variance, this strategy does not deal with error variance caused by subject differences. Subjects can differ on a large number of characteristics, some of which may have strong effects on your dependent variable. You can reduce this source of error variance by using subjects matched on characteristics you believe contribute to it. For example, you could use participants who are of the same age or educational level. Although this may reduce external validity, you can always relax the restrictions in a later experiment. The first priority is to obtain reliable results. A similar tactic is to match subjects across groups on some characteristic relating to the dependent variable in a matched-groups design or use the same subjects for all levels of your independent variable in a within-subjects design. (We discuss matching and using within-subjects designs later in this chapter.)

*Increasing the Effectiveness of Your Independent Variable*    Another way to deal with error variance is to select the correct levels of your independent variable for your experiment. A weak manipulation (e.g., too low a dose of THC) may have only a weak influence on your dependent variable, leaving the effect of your independent variable obscured by error variance. Of course, it is difficult to know beforehand just how to manipulate your independent variable. You can get some idea about the levels to include from previous research and by conducting a pilot study before you run your actual experiment. It is also important to select a dependent variable that is sensitive enough to detect the effects of your independent variable. Previous research or pilot work can help in this selection.

*Randomizing Error Variance Across Groups*    Regardless of the steps you take to minimize error variance, you can never eliminate it completely. In between-subjects designs, you can deal with remaining error variance by randomizing error variance across groups. This is accomplished through random assignment of subjects to your treatment conditions. As noted in Chapter 4, *random assignment* means that subjects are assigned to groups on a random basis so that each subject has an equal chance of appearing in any group of your experiment. Random assignment results in groups of subjects that, on average, tend to be highly similar on individual difference factors (e.g., intelligence and gender) that contribute to error variance. Furthermore, when subjects have been assigned to groups at random, you can employ *inferential statistics* to assess the probability with which error variance alone would produce between-group differences on your dependent measure at least as large as those you actually observed in your data. If this probability is low enough, the difference is declared to be *statistically significant*. This means that a difference this large is highly unlikely to have resulted from a failure of random assignment to equalize the groups on subject-related variables. Consequently, you can have more confidence that these differences are due to the effect of your independent variable. (See Chapter 14 for a detailed discussion of inferential statistics.)

## QUESTIONS TO PONDER

1. What steps can you take to deal with error variance in a between-subjects design?

2. How are inferential statistics used to evaluate the possibility that between-group differences on the dependent measure were *not* caused by the independent variable?


## BETWEEN-SUBJECTS DESIGNS

The time has come to examine the types of between-subjects designs available to you. We begin with single-factor designs, in which you manipulate only one independent variable.

### The Single-Factor Randomized-Groups Design

In single-factor randomized-groups designs, you assign your subjects at random to different groups. You then expose each group to a different level of your independent variable while otherwise treating them as alike as possible. There are two variants of the randomized-groups design: the randomized two-group design and the randomized multigroup design. We explore these designs next.

*The Randomized Two-Group Design*    If you randomly assign your subjects to two groups, expose the two groups to different levels of the independent variable, and take steps to hold extraneous variables constant, you are using a **randomized two-group design**. Figure 10-1 illustrates the basic steps to follow when conducting a randomized two-group experiment. Begin by sampling a group of subjects from the general population (top). Then, randomly assign the participants from this group into your two treatment groups. Next, expose the participants in each group to their treatments and record their responses. Compare the two means to determine whether they differ. Finally, submit the data to a statistical analysis to assess the reliability of any difference you find.

An experiment conducted by Jo-Ann Tsang (2006) provides an excellent example of an experiment using a randomized two-group design. Tsang was interested in investigating whether gratitude resulted in more prosocial behavior than mere positive emotion. Participants in Tsang's experiment were told that they would be playing a game in which they would be allocating resources to another participant in the study (in reality, there was no other participant). Participants were told further that the game would be played in three rounds. Resource allocations were made by writing down an amount of money to allocate to the fictitious participant on a slip of paper, which would be taken to the fictitious participant by the experimenter.

Tsang (2006) randomly assigned the real participants to one of two conditions. In the "favor condition," participants were told that their partner had allocated $9 of $10 to them and kept $1 for himself in the second round. They were also given a note

Sample

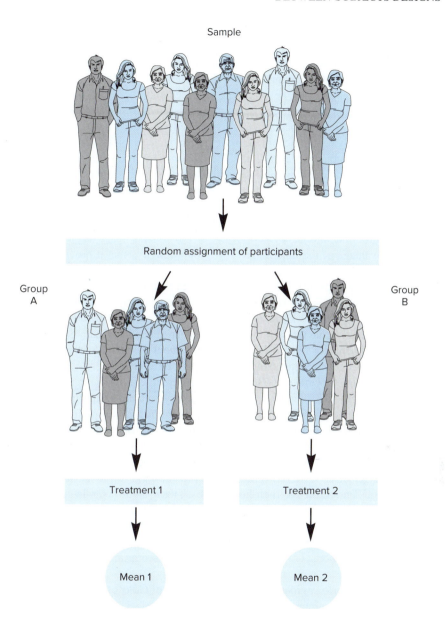

Random assignment of participants

Group
A

Group
B

Treatment 1

Treatment 2

Mean 1

Mean 2

**FIGURE 10-1**    The randomized two-group experimental design.

saying, "I saw that you did not get a lot in the last round—that must have been a bum-
mer" (Tsang, 2006, p. 142). In the "chance control condition," participants were told
that they had received the $9 by chance and that their partner had received $1 by
chance. No note accompanied the distribution information. The measure of prosocial
behavior directed at the fictitious participant was the amount of money that the real
participant allocated (out of $10) in Round 3. Tsang found that participants allocated

significantly more money to the fictitious other participant in the favor condition ($M = \$7.38$) than in the chance control condition ($M = \$5.84$).

The randomized two-group design is one of the simplest available, yet it has several advantages over other, more complex designs. First, it is simple to carry out. As was the case in Tsang's (2006) experiment, you need only two levels of your independent variable. Second, everything else being equal, it requires relatively few subjects. Tsang used only 40 participants in her experiment. An experiment with these few subjects is relatively economical in terms of time and materials. Third, no pretesting or categorization of subjects is necessary. The randomized-group design often is more than adequate to test your hypothesis, avoiding the need for a more complex matching design (see the section on matched-groups designs later in this chapter). Finally, statistical analysis of the resulting data is relatively simple. Indeed, some electronic calculators have the required statistics built into them, so you need only enter the data and press the appropriate button.

A disadvantage of the randomized two-group design is that it provides a limited amount of information about the effect of the independent variable. You learn only whether the two groups differed (on the average) in their responses to the independent variable under the two levels tested, in what direction, and by how much. In Tsang's (2006) experiment, all you know is that believing that someone gave you $9 of $10 increases prosocial behavior. But, how would other allocations (e.g., $6 out of $10) affect prosocial behavior? You do not learn much about the nature of the relationship, or *function,* relating the independent and dependent variables.

An experiment by Gold (1987) illustrates this point. Gold was interested in determining whether glucose (blood sugar) affects memory. In Gold's experiment, rats were individually placed on the white side of a rectangular box that was divided into a well-lit white compartment and a dimly lit black compartment. Because rats tend to prefer darkness over light, they quickly crossed into the black compartment, where they received a mild foot shock. Immediately after this experience, the rats were each injected with glucose. Different groups received different amounts of the glucose. The rats were then returned to their home cages. Twenty-four hours later, the animals were again placed in the white compartment and the amount of time they took to reenter the black compartment was recorded. The rats should have been hesitant to reenter to the extent that they remembered the shock they had received there on the previous day. Thus, greater amounts of delay to reenter should have reflected better memory for the shock.

Figure 10-2 shows, in idealized form, the results of Gold's (1987) experiment. In panel (a), the mean number of seconds to reenter the black compartment is plotted against glucose dose. Glucose did affect memory and in a dose-dependent manner. The function relating glucose dose to reentry time is shaped somewhat like an inverted U, with intermediate doses being more effective than higher or lower doses. Gold concluded that glucose can be used in some cases to improve memory (if it's not overdone).

Although Gold's (1987) experiment used several groups, imagine that Gold had used only two. Panel (b) shows what Gold's results would have looked like had he chosen to use only the two lowest glucose doses. Based on those two points, Gold would have concluded that an increase in glucose dose improves the association of

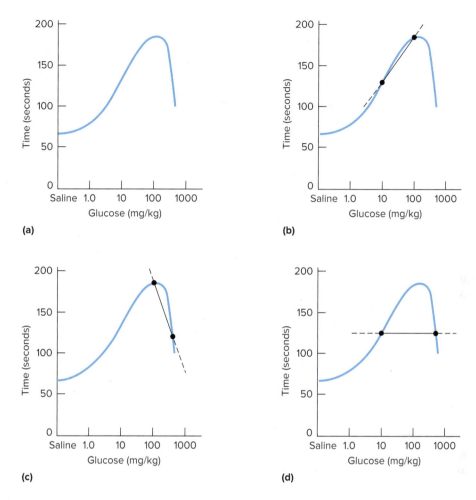

**FIGURE 10-2**    (a) Results of experiment relating glucose dosage to memory (as measured by the time required to enter a dark compartment); (b, c, and d) three functions based on Gold's data, showing lines estimated from various pairs of points.
SOURCE: Gold, Paul, E., Sweet Memories American Scientist Mar.–Apr. 1987, Sigma Xi, New Haven, CT: Sigma Xi, 1987.

shock with the dark compartment. Panel (c) shows what Gold's (1987) results would have looked like had he chosen to use only the two highest doses. Here, Gold's conclusion would have been that increasing the dose of glucose decreases the association of shock with the dark compartment. Finally, panel (d) shows Gold's (1987) results had he chosen only the highest and lowest doses. Gold would have concluded that glucose dose has no effect on the association of shock with the dark compartment.

If you were unaware of the inverted U-shaped function relating memory to glucose level, it might seem that these three experiments had yielded contradictory results. Furthermore, if you attempted to extrapolate the function beyond the two data points collected in a given experiment—dashed lines in panels (b), (c), and (d)—you would form an erroneous picture of the relationship.

This problem can be solved by conducting a series of two-group experiments in which different levels of the independent variable are chosen for each experiment. However, more efficient designs for sweeping out a functional relationship are available and will be examined later.

A second limitation of the randomized two-group design concerns its sensitivity to the effect of the independent variable. In cases in which subjects differ greatly on characteristics that influence their performances on the dependent measure, these variations may make it difficult to detect the effect of the independent variable. In such cases, the randomized two-group design may fail to detect a real effect of the independent variable.

Finally, when you are interested in investigating the limits of an effect, you will need to include more than two levels of your independent variable, as is done in a randomized multigroup design.

*The Randomized Multigroup Design*    One way to expand the randomized two-group design is to add one or more levels of the independent variable. You can of course include as many levels of your independent variable as needed to test your hypothesis. As we noted earlier, there are two ways to manipulate your independent variable: quantitatively or qualitatively. When you manipulate your independent variable quantitatively, you are using a **parametric design**. The term *parametric* refers to the systematic variation of the amount of the independent variable. Manipulating your independent variable qualitatively results in a **nonparametric design**.

A nice illustration of the single-factor, randomized, multigroup design comes from a field experiment conducted by Nicholas Guéguen (2015), who wanted to know what effect wearing high heels has on the attractiveness of women. The setting for the research was a small French town on the coast of Brittany. A 19-year-old female confederate of the experimenter stood in front of a store and asked 90 randomly chosen male passersby to complete a brief survey on gender equality. She was fashionably dressed in a black straight skirt, white long-sleeved shirt, black suit jacket, and black leather shoes. To be chosen, passersby had to be walking unaccompanied toward the confederate and appear to be between 25 and 50 years old.

The independent variable in the study was the heel-height of the confederate's shoes: flat, 5-cm high, or 9-cm high. Thus, there were three groups of participants, each exposed to a different heel height. The confederate switched shoes, in random order, after every 10 participants. The dependent variable was the percentage of participants who agreed to complete the survey. When the confederate wore flat heels, only 14 of 30, or 46.7%, agreed, but when she wore 5-cm heels, the numbers increased to 19 of 30, or 63.3 percent. Agreement reached 25 of 30, or 83.3%, when she wore the 9-cm heels. Statistical analysis revealed that agreement was significantly higher in the 9-cm-heels condition relative to the flat-heels condition. Guéguen concluded that wearing high heels increased the confederate's attractiveness, making the male participants more willing to complete the survey for her.

A variation on the single-factor multigroup design is one that includes multiple control groups. This design is used when a single control group is not adequate to rule out alternative explanations of your results, and it is known as the **multiple control group design**.

## QUESTIONS TO PONDER

1. How does a two-group, randomized design work?
2. What are some of the advantages and disadvantages of the two-group, randomized design?
3. How do parametric and nonparametric multigroup randomized designs differ?

### Matched-Groups Designs

In some cases, you know or suspect that some subject characteristics correlate strongly with the dependent variable. For instance, subjects often differ considerably in their reaction times to simple stimuli. If you were interested in studying the effect of stimulus complexity on reaction time, this large inherent variation in reaction time across your subjects could produce large amounts of error variance, swamping any effect of stimulus complexity and thus making even large differences in group means statistically unreliable. One way to deal with this problem is to use a matched-groups design.

A **matched-groups design** is one in which matched sets of subjects are distributed at random, one subject per group, into the groups of the experiment. Figure 10-3 illustrates this process. You begin by obtaining a sample of subjects (group at the top of the figure) from the larger population. Next, you assess the subjects on one or more characteristics that you believe exert an influence on the dependent measure and then group the subjects whose characteristics match. In a reaction-time experiment, for example, participants could be pretested for their simple reaction times and then grouped into pairs whose reaction times were similar. These pairs of participants are shown in the middle portion of Figure 10-3.

Having matched your participants, you then distribute them randomly across the experimental groups. In the reaction-time experiment, one participant of each pair is randomly assigned to one of the treatments (perhaps to a high-stimulus-complexity condition); the other participant then automatically goes into the other treatment (in this case, a low-stimulus-complexity condition). This assignment to treatments is shown in the bottom of Figure 10-3.

From here on, you conduct the experiment as in the randomized-groups design. You expose your participants to their respective levels of the independent variable and record the resulting data. Then you compare the data from the different groups to determine the effect of the independent variable.

*Logic of the Matched-Groups Design*    Because each of the matched subjects goes into a different group, the effect of the characteristic on which the subjects were matched gets distributed evenly across the treatments. As a result, this characteristic contributes little to the differences between group means. The effect of the error variance contributed by the characteristic has been minimized, making it more likely that any effect of the independent variable will be detected.

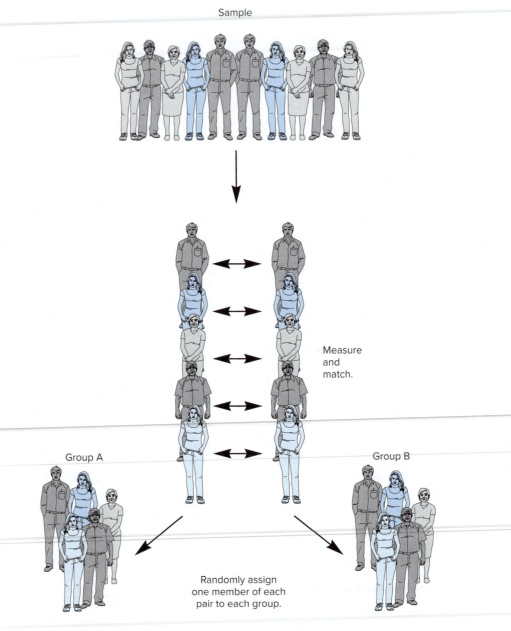

**FIGURE 10-3**    Matched-groups experimental design with two groups.

*Advantages and Disadvantages of the Matched-Groups Design*    The advantage of matching over random assignment is that it allows you to control subject variables that may otherwise obscure the effect of the independent variable under investigation. Where such variables exist, matching can increase the experiment's sensitivity to the effect of the independent variable (if such an effect is present). This is a potent advantage. You may be able to discover effects that you would otherwise miss. In addition, you may be able to demonstrate a given effect with fewer subjects, thus saving time and money. However, using a matched design is not without risks and disadvantages.

One risk involved in using a matched design concerns what happens if the matched characteristic does *not* have much effect on the dependent variable under the conditions of the study. Matched designs require you to use somewhat modified versions of the inferential statistics you would use in an unmatched, completely randomized design (see Chapter 14). These statistics for matched groups are somewhat less powerful than their unmatched equivalents. This means that they are less able to discriminate any effect of the independent variable from the effect of uncontrolled, extraneous variables.

If the matched characteristic has a *large* effect on the dependent variable, eliminating this effect from group differences will more than compensate for the reduced sensitivity of the statistic, resulting in a more sensitive experiment. However (and this is an important "however"), if the matched characteristic has *little or no effect* on the dependent variable, then matching will do no good. Worse, the loss of statistical power will *reduce* your ability to detect the effect of the independent variable. For this reason, use matching only when you have good reason to believe that the matching variable has a relatively strong effect on the dependent measure.

When using a matched design, you also must be sure that the instrument used to determine the match is valid and reliable. If you want to match on IQ, for example, be sure that the test you use to measure IQ is valid and reliable. Of course, for some characteristics, such as race, age, and sex, this is usually not a problem.

In other respects, matched-groups designs have the same advantages and disadvantages as randomized-groups designs. However, the requirement for pretesting and matching makes the matched design more demanding and time consuming than the randomized design. In addition, you may need to expand your subject pool if you cannot match up some of the subjects. This may be particularly troublesome if you are attempting to match subjects on more than one variable or if the subject pool is limited.

Any of the randomized-groups designs described in the previous sections of this chapter could be modified into a matched-groups design. The simplest case, described next, involves the two-group design.

*The Matched-Pairs Design*     The **matched-pairs design** is the matched-groups equivalent to the randomized two-group design. The hypothetical reaction time experiment described earlier uses a matched-pairs design. As with the randomized two-group design, the need for only two groups makes this approach relatively economical of time and subjects but does limit the amount of information you can obtain from the experiment.

*Matched-Multigroup Designs*     The same approach used in the matched-pairs design can be extended to other, more complex designs involving multiple levels of a single factor (single-factor, multigroup designs) or multiple factors (factorial designs). You use these matched-groups designs to gain control over subject-related variables that affect your dependent variable.

Using the matching strategy on these multigroup designs requires you to find a matched subject for every treatment group in your experiment. Thus, if your experiment included four treatment groups, you would need to find quadruplets of subjects having similar characteristics on the variables being matched. After matching subjects, you would distribute the subjects from each quadruplet randomly across your experimental groups.

As you might guess, matching becomes unwieldy if your design has more than about three groups because it becomes increasingly difficult to find three, four, or more subjects with equivalent scores on the variable or variables to be matched. In this case, a better approach might be to use a within-subjects design. The within-subjects design eliminates the need for measuring and matching subject variables, reduces the number of subjects required for the experiment, and yet provides the ultimate degree of matching—in effect, each subject is matched with himself or herself. Unfortunately, situations do occur in which the within-subjects design cannot or should not be used. In such cases, matching may be your best alternative.

## QUESTIONS TO PONDER

1. What is a matched-groups design, and when would you use one?
2. How does a matched-pairs design differ from a randomized two-group design?
3. What are some of the advantages and disadvantages of the matching strategy?

## WITHIN-SUBJECTS DESIGNS

In between-subjects designs, you randomly assign subjects to groups and then expose each group to a different, *single* experimental treatment. You measure each subject's performance on the dependent variable, calculate the average score for each group, and then compare the means to determine whether the independent variable or variables had any apparent influence on the dependent variable. You then subject the data to a statistical analysis to assess the reliability of your conclusions.

The within-subjects design follows the same basic strategy as the between-subjects design with one important difference. In the within-subjects design, each subject is exposed to all levels of your independent variable rather than being randomly assigned to one level. This strategy is shown in Figure 10-4 with a simple two-treatment experiment. Notice that each participant's performance is measured under treatment A and then again under treatment B. The design is called *within-subjects* because comparison of the treatment effects involves looking at changes in performance within each participant across treatments. Because participant behavior is measured repeatedly, the within-subjects design is also called a *repeated-measures design.*

Within-subjects designs are closely related to the matched-groups designs that we discussed in the previous section, in which subjects are first matched into sets on some characteristic (such as IQ score) and then members of each matched set are assigned at random, one to each treatment condition. You might think of a within-subjects design

Treatment A                    Treatment B

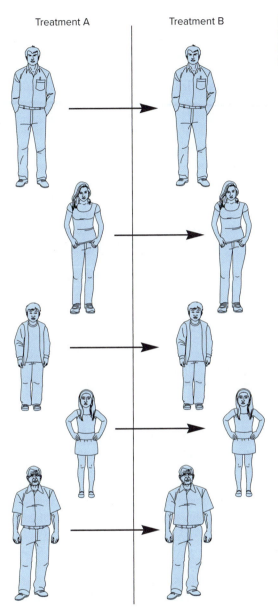

as providing the ultimate in matching because each participant in effect serves as his or her own matched partner across the treatments.

## An Example of a Within-Subjects Design: Does Caffeine Keep Us Going?

It is a ritual that is played out in many circumstances at various times: Something has to be done that requires burning the midnight oil (e.g., studying for a final exam or driving all night to your vacation destination). In such circumstances, we often turn to the most widely available stimulant: caffeine. Caffeine is commonly found in coffee and in a variety of caffeinated soft drinks. It is commonly believed that consuming such beverages will keep us awake and keep our cognitive wits sharp while we try to stay awake. But is this true? An experiment using a within-subjects design conducted by H. J. Smit and P. J. Rogers (2000) investigated this issue.

Participants in this experiment were 23 adult males and females. Each participant consumed a beverage containing 0, 12.5, 25, 50, or 100 mg of caffeine. What makes this experiment a within-subjects design is that each participant received all five dosages of caffeine. Each beverage was administered once per week and the order in which the beverages were consumed was counterbalanced; that is, different participants received the doses in a different order. Participants completed two measures of cognitive performance (a simple reaction-time measure and a more complex cognitive task) both before and after exposure to the caffeine. The results revealed a dose-response relationship between caffeine dosage and reaction time: higher doses produced faster reaction times. On the more complex cognitive task, increasing the dosage of caffeine led to better performance but only among participants who normally consume higher levels of caffeine.

## Advantages and Disadvantages of the Within-Subjects Design

Within-subjects designs offer some powerful advantages over the equivalent between-subjects designs if certain conditions can be met. They also introduce problems whose solution adds complexity to the basic designs, and they present other disadvantages as well. We begin by examining the advantages.

*Advantages of the Within-Subjects Design*    Previously in this chapter, we noted that scores *within* a treatment group differ for reasons having nothing to do with your independent variable. These differences arise from the effects of extraneous variables, which include relatively stable subject-related characteristics as well as fluctuations that change each subject's performance from moment to moment. Such error variance can be a serious problem because it may mask any effects of your independent variable. Recall that a major strategy for dealing with error variance in the between-subjects design is to randomly assign subjects to treatment groups and to apply statistical analysis to your data to estimate the probability with which chance alone might have produced the effect. When subject-related factors are large, they exert a strong influence on performance, resulting in levels of error variance that obscure the effect of your independent variable. Matching can help reduce this important source of error variance.

The within-subjects design pushes the logic of matching to the limit. Each subject is matched with other subjects who are virtual clones of each other, because they are in fact the same subject. All subject-related factors (such as age, weight, IQ, personality, religion, and gender) are literally identical across treatments. Thus, any performance differences across treatments cannot be due to error variance arising from such differences. The reduced error variance makes the within-subjects design is more powerful (i.e., more sensitive to the effects of your independent variable) than the equivalent between-subjects design. This increased power has two benefits. First, you are more likely to detect an effect of your independent variable. Second, you can use fewer subjects in your experiment. Consider that a four-group between-subjects design with 10 subjects per treatment would require 40 subjects. The equivalent within-subjects experiment would require only 10 subjects, representing a significant savings in time, materials, and money. In the Smit and Rogers (2000) study on caffeine, only 23 participants were required. Of course, you could always use more subjects in a within-subjects design if you needed even more power for your statistical analysis in order to detect the effect of a weak independent variable.

*Disadvantages of the Within-Subjects Design*     Although the within-subjects design has its advantages, it also has some important disadvantages, which may preclude its use in certain situations. One disadvantage is that a within-subjects design is more demanding on subjects because each subject must be exposed to every level of the experimental treatment. A complex design involving, say, nine treatments would require a great deal of time to complete. It may be difficult to find participants willing to take part in such an experiment. Those who do take part may become bored or fatigued after being in an experiment that might be several hours long. You can get around the problem of fatigue and boredom by administering only one or two treatments per session, spreading sessions out over some period of time. However, if you take this approach, you may lose some participants from the experiment because they fail to show up for the additional sessions.

Subject attrition also can occur if you make a mistake while administering one of your treatments (e.g., you read the wrong instructions), if you experience equipment failure, or if your subject dies. In each case, you have to throw out the data from the lost subjects and start over with their replacements.

A second and potentially more serious problem with the within-subjects design is its ability to produce carryover effects. **Carryover effects** occur when a treatment alters the behavior observed in a subsequent treatment. The previous treatment changes the subject, and those changes carry over into the subsequent treatment and alter how the subject performs in it. This upsets the "perfect match" of subject characteristics that the within-subjects design is supposed to provide.

As an illustration of carryover effects, imagine you are conducting an experiment to assess the effect of two kinds of practice (simple rehearsal and rehearsal plus imagery) on memory for lists of concrete nouns. Your participants first learn a list of nouns using simple rehearsal and then are tested for retention. Next the participants learn a second list of nouns, using rehearsal plus imagery, and are again tested. You find that participants correctly recalled more nouns when they used a rehearsal-plus-imagery technique than when they used rehearsal alone. However, you cannot confidently conclude that the former technique is superior to the latter.

The problem is that the rehearsal-alone treatment gave participants practice memorizing nouns. They may have done better in the rehearsal-plus-imagery treatment simply because they were more practiced at the task rather than because of any effect of imagery. The previous exposure to the rehearsal-alone treatment may have changed the way participants performed in the subsequent treatment.

Carryover effects can be a serious problem in any within-subjects design. Between-subjects designs do not suffer from carryover effects simply because there are no previous conditions from which effects can carry over. A matched-groups design may provide a reasonable compromise in those situations in which carryover is a serious problem but in which you want to retain the control over subject variables provided by a within-subjects design.

The problem of carryover in within-subjects designs has received plenty of attention from researchers, who have developed strategies to deal with it. The next section identifies potential sources of carryover. After that, we describe several design options that can help you deal with potential carryover effects.

## QUESTIONS TO PONDER

1. How does a within-subjects design differ from a between-subjects design?
2. What are the advantages of the within-subjects experimental design?
3. What are the disadvantages of the within-subjects experimental design?
4. How do carryover effects influence the interpretation of the results from a within-subjects experiment?

### Sources of Carryover

Carryover effects can arise from a number of sources, including the following:

- *Learning.* If a subject learns how to perform a task in the first treatment, performance is likely to be better if the same or similar tasks are used in subsequent treatments. For instance, rats given alternate sessions of reinforcement and extinction show faster acquisition of lever pressing across successive reinforcement sessions and more rapid return to baseline rates of responding across successive extinction sessions.

- *Fatigue.* If performance in earlier treatments leads to fatigue, then performance in later treatments may deteriorate. If measuring your dependent variable involves having participants squeeze against a strong spring device to determine their strength of grip, the participants are likely to tire if repeated testing takes place over a short period of time.

- *Habituation.* Under some conditions, repeated exposure to a stimulus leads to reduced responsiveness to that stimulus because the stimulus is becoming either more familiar or expected. This reduction is termed *habituation.* Your subjects may jump the first time you surprise them with a sudden loud noise, but they may not do so after repeated presentations of the noise.

- *Sensitization.* Sometimes exposure to one stimulus can cause subjects to respond more strongly to another stimulus. In a phenomenon called *potentiated startle,* a rat will show an exaggerated startle-response to a sudden noise if the rat has recently received a brief foot shock in the same situation.

- *Contrast.* A contrast effect may emerge when subjects can compare what they receive in one condition to what they receive in another condition. For example, if you pay your participants a relatively large amount for successful performance on one task and then pay them less in a subsequent task, they may feel underpaid in the second task. Consequently, they may work less than they otherwise might have.

- *Adaptation.* If subjects go through a period of adaptation (e.g., becoming adjusted to the dark), then earlier results may differ from later results because of the adaptive changes. Adaptive changes may increase responsiveness to a stimulus (e.g., sight gradually improves while you sit in a darkened theater) or decrease responsiveness (e.g., you readjust to the bright outdoor light as you leave the theater). Adaptation to a drug schedule is a common example. If adaptation to the drug causes a reduced response, the change is called *tolerance.*

### Dealing with Carryover Effects

You can deal with carryover effects in three ways: You can (1) use counterbalancing to even out carryover effects across treatments, (2) take steps to minimize carryover, and (3) separate carryover effects from treatment effects by making treatment order an independent variable.

*Counterbalancing*   In **counterbalancing**, you assign the various treatments of the experiment in a different order for different subjects. The goal is to distribute any carryover equally across treatments so that it does not produce differences in treatment means that could be mistaken for an effect of the independent variable. Smit and Rogers (2000) used this strategy in the experiment presented earlier. Each participant received the various caffeine doses in a different, counterbalanced order.

Two counterbalancing options are complete counterbalancing and partial counterbalancing. *Complete counterbalancing* provides every possible ordering of treatments and assigns at least one subject to each ordering. Table 10-2 shows an example of a completely counterbalanced single-factor design that includes three treatments. Six subjects are to be tested (identified as subjects $S_1$ through $S_6$), one for each possible ordering of treatments $T_1$, $T_2$, and $T_3$. Note that in a completely counterbalanced design, every treatment follows every other treatment equally often across subjects, and every treatment appears equally often in each position (first, second, etc.).

The minimum number of subjects required for complete counterbalancing is equal to the number of different orderings of the treatments: $k$ treatments have exactly $k!$ ($k$ factorial) orders, where $k! = k\,(k-1)(k-2)\cdots(1)$. For example, with three treatments (as in our example), the number of treatment orders is $3 \times 2 \times 1 = 6$. If you need to increase the number of subjects in order to improve statistical power, add the same number of additional subjects to each order so that the number of subjects receiving each order remains equal.

TABLE 10-2    **Counterbalanced Single-Factor Design with Three Treatments**

| | TREATMENTS | | |
|---|---|---|---|
| *Subjects* | $T_1$ | $T_2$ | $T_3$ |
| $S_1$ | 1 | 2 | 3 |
| $S_2$ | 1 | 3 | 2 |
| $S_3$ | 2 | 1 | 3 |
| $S_4$ | 2 | 3 | 1 |
| $S_5$ | 3 | 1 | 2 |
| $S_6$ | 3 | 2 | 1 |

Complete counterbalancing is practical for experiments with a small number of treatments, but this approach becomes increasingly burdensome as the number of treatments grows. For an experiment using only four treatments, the $4 \times 3 \times 2 \times 1 = 24$ possible treatment orders require at least 24 subjects to complete the counterbalancing. The economy of subjects that makes a within-subjects approach attractive erodes rapidly.

You can recover some of this economy by switching to *partial counterbalancing*, which includes only *some* of the possible treatment orders. The orders to be retained are chosen randomly from the total set with the restriction that each treatment appear equally often in each position. Table 10-3 displays all 24 possible orders for a four-treatment experiment, followed by a subset of 8 randomly selected orders that meet this criterion.

When you use partial counterbalancing, you assume that randomly chosen orders will randomly distribute carryover effects among the treatments. Although carryover effects may not balance out under such conditions, they usually will come close to doing so. Furthermore, the likelihood that treatments will differ because of carryover can be evaluated statistically and held to an acceptable level. If you choose to make the number of treatment orders in your partially counterbalanced design equal to the number of treatments, you can use a *Latin square design* to ensure that each treatment appears an equal number of times in each ordinal position. For more information on how to construct a Latin square design, see Edwards (1985). A handy Latin square generator is available as of this writing at http://hamsterandwheel.com/grids/index2d.php.

Counterbalancing (whether complete or partial) can be counted on to control carryover only if the carryover effects induced by different orders are of the same approximate magnitude. Consider the case of a simple two-treatment experiment shown in Table 10-4. This case has only two possible orders: $1 \rightarrow 2$ and $2 \rightarrow 1$. Assume that carryover from treatment 1 to treatment 2 increases the mean score of treatment 2 by 10 points and that carryover from treatment 2 to treatment 1 has a similar effect on the mean score of treatment 1. Table 10-4 shows the result for a completely counterbalanced design. Note that the two carryover effects, being equal, cancel out each other. When carryover effects are equivalent across orders, counterbalancing is effective.

**TABLE 10-3** Twenty-Four Possible Treatment Orders for a Four-Treatment Within-Subjects Design and a Randomly Selected Subset in Which Each Treatment Appears Equally Often in Each Position

| ENTIRE SET OF TREATMENT ORDERS | SELECTED SUBSET |
|---|---|
| 1. ABCD | 1. DABC |
| 2. ABDC | 2. ABCD |
| 3. ACBD | 3. CDAB |
| 4. ACDB | 4. BCDA |
| 5. ADBC | 5. DCBA |
| 6. ADCB | 6. ADCB |
| 7. BACD | 7. BADC |
| 8. BADC | 8. CBAD |
| 9. BCAD | |
| 10. BCDA | |
| 11. BDAC | |
| 12. BDCA | |
| 13. CABD | |
| 14. CADB | |
| 15. CBAD | |
| 16. CBDA | |
| 17. CDAB | |
| 18. CDBA | |
| 19. DABC | |
| 20. DACB | |
| 21. DBAC | |
| 22. DBCA | |
| 23. DCAB | |
| 24. DCBA | |

In contrast, when the magnitude of the carryover effect differs for different orders of treatment presentation, counterbalancing may be ineffective. Table 10-5 illustrates this problem, known as *differential carryover effects* (Keppel, 1982). In this example, the carryover from treatment 2 to treatment 1 averages 20 points—twice the carryover from treatment 1 to treatment 2. Thus, you have a treatment-by-position interaction. When this occurs, no amount of counterbalancing will eliminate the carryover effects (Keppel, 1982).

The most serious asymmetry in carryover effects occurs when a treatment produces *irreversible changes*. The classic type of irreversible change is that produced by a treatment such as brain lesioning. The effects of the operation, once present, cannot be undone. A somewhat less serious change may occur if subjects learn to perform a

**TABLE 10-4  Balancing of Order Effects in a Counterbalanced Two-Treatment Design**

| | TREATMENT | | |
|---|---|---|---|
| | *1* | *2* | |
| Actual treatment effect | 40 | 30 | (difference = 10) |
| Carryover effect (1→2) | | 10 | |
| Carryover effect (2→1) | 10 | — | |
| Observed treatment effect | 50 | 40 | (difference = 10) |

**TABLE 10-5  Failure of Order Effects to Balance Out in a Counterbalanced Two-Treatment Design**

| | TREATMENT | | |
|---|---|---|---|
| | *1* | *2* | |
| Actual treatment effect | 40 | 30 | (difference = 10) |
| Carryover effect (1–2) | | 10 | |
| Carryover effect (2–1) | 20 | — | |
| Observed treatment effect | 60 | 40 | (difference = 20) |

task in one treatment, and this learning then alters the way in which they perform in a subsequent treatment. It may not be possible to restore subjects to the "naive" state once they have learned the task. In either case, you would want to choose a between-subjects approach.

*Taking Steps to Minimize Carryover*   The second way to deal with carryover effects is to try to minimize or eliminate them. Of course, you would want to do this only if the carryover effects were not themselves the object of study. Minimizing carryover effects reduces error variance and increases the power of the design.

Carryover effects produced by learning are a common example. If you are not interested in the effect of learning per se, you may be able to pretrain your subjects before introducing your experimental treatments. Psychophysical experiments (testing such things as sensory thresholds) and experiments on human decision making often make use of such "practice sessions" to familiarize participants with the experimental tasks. The practice brings their performances up to desired levels, where they stabilize, and effectively eliminates changes caused by practice as a source of carryover.

Adaptation and habituation changes can be dealt with similarly. Before introducing the treatments, allowing time for subjects to adapt or habituate to the experimental conditions can eliminate carryover from these sources.

Another way to deal with habituation (if habituation is short term), adaptation, and fatigue is to allow breaks between the treatments. If sufficiently long, the breaks allow subjects to recover from any habituation, adaptation, or fatigue induced by the previous treatment.

*Making Treatment Order an Independent Variable*    A third way to deal with the problem of carryover is to make treatment order an independent variable. Your experimental design will expose different groups of subjects to different orderings of the treatments, just as in ordinary counterbalancing. However, you include a sufficient number of subjects in each group to permit statistical analysis of treatment order as a separate independent variable. For example, if you were going to conduct a one-factor experiment to compare the effect of two memorization strategies on recall, you could design the experiment to include the order of testing as a second independent variable. Figure 10-5 illustrates the resulting design, which now includes *two* independent variables. Called a *factorial design*, it requires a special type of analysis to separately evaluate the effect of each and is discussed later in this chapter (see "Factorial Designs: Designs with Two or More Independent Variables"). For now, it is enough to know that this design allows you to separate any carryover effects from the effect of your experimental treatment.

The main advantage of making order of treatments an independent variable is that you can measure the size of any carryover effects that may be present. You can then take these effects into account in future experiments. If you find that carryover is about equal in magnitude regardless of the order of treatments, for example, then you can be confident that counterbalancing will eliminate any carryover-induced bias.

In addition to identifying carryover effects, the strategy of making treatment order an independent variable provides a direct comparison of results obtained in the within-subjects design with those obtained in the logically equivalent between-subjects design. This comparison can be made because every treatment occurs first in at least one of the treatment orders. These "first exposures" provide the data for a purely between-subjects comparison in the absence of carryover effects.

Grice (1966) notes that between-subjects and within-subjects designs applied to the same variables do not always produce the same functional relationships. The reason is that subjects in the within-subjects experiment are able to make comparisons across treatments whereas those in the supposedly equivalent between-subjects

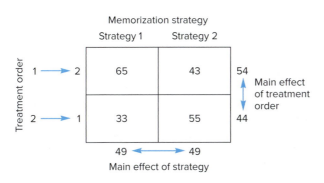

**FIGURE 10-5**   A design in which order of treatments is made an independent variable.

experiment are not. Imagine, for example, a study in which participants must rate the attractiveness of pictures on a 5-point scale. In one version of the study, different groups of participants see only one of the pictures. In another version, each participant views all the pictures. A particular picture may rate, say, 5 on the scale when viewed by itself. However, when seen in the context of the other pictures, the same picture may look better (or worse) in comparison and thus may produce a different rating. Such changes in response that arise from comparison, termed *contrast effects,* are possible only in the within-subjects version of the study.

The presence of such effects in some designs, but not in others, often can explain why studies manipulating the same variables sometimes yield different results.

Although making treatment order a factor in your experiment can provide important information about the size of carryover effects and can pinpoint the source of differences between findings obtained from within-subjects versus between-subjects experiments, the technique does have disadvantages. Every treatment order requires a separate group of subjects. These subjects must be tested under every treatment condition. The result is a complex, demanding experiment that is costly in terms of numbers of subjects and time to test them. Furthermore, these demands escalate rapidly as the number of treatments (and therefore number of treatment orders) increases. For these reasons, the approach is practical only with a small number of treatments.

## QUESTIONS TO PONDER

1. What are the sources of carryover effects in a within-subjects design?
2. Under what conditions will counterbalancing be effective or ineffective in dealing with carryover effects?
3. When do you use a Latin square design?
4. What strategies can be used to deal with carryover effects?

### When to Use a Within-Subjects Design

Given the problems created by the potential for carryover effects, the best strategy may be to avoid within-subjects designs. If you decide to do this, you have a lot of company. However, you should not let these difficulties prevent you from adopting the within-subjects design when it is clearly the best approach. The following are situations in which the within-subjects design may be the best—or even the only—available option.

*Subject Variables Correlated with the Dependent Variable*    You should strongly consider using a within-subjects design when subject differences contribute heavily to variation in the dependent variable. As an example, assume that you want to assess the effect of display complexity on target detection in a simulated air traffic–controller task. Your display simulates the computerized radar screen display seen in actual air traffic–control situations with aircraft (the targets) appearing as blips in motion across the screen. Your independent variable is the amount of information being displayed (the dots alone or dots plus transponder codes, altitude readings, etc.). Because this is a pilot study (no pun intended), you are using college sophomores as participants rather than real air traffic controllers.

Your student participants are likely to differ widely in their native ability to detect targets, regardless of the display complexity. If you were to conduct the experiment using a between-subjects design, this large variation in ability would contribute greatly to within-group error variance. As a consequence, the between-group differences would probably be obscured by these uncontrolled variations.

In this case, you could effectively eliminate the impact of subject differences by adopting a within-subjects design. Each participant is exposed to every level of display complexity. Because each participant's native ability at target detection remains essentially the same across all the treatment levels, the changes (if any) in target detection across treatments would clearly stand out. Of course, you would have to be reasonably sure that practice at the task does not contribute to success at target detection (or at least that the effect of such practice could be distributed evenly across treatments by using counterbalancing) before you decided to adopt the within-subjects approach. One way to eliminate practice as a source of confounding would be to include several practice sessions in which your participants became proficient enough at the task that little further improvement would be expected.

*Economizing on Subjects*    You also should consider using a within-subjects design when the number of available subjects is limited and carryover effects are absent (or can be minimized). If you were to use actual air traffic controllers in the previous study, for example, you probably would not have a large available group from which to sample. You probably would not be able to obtain enough participants for your study to achieve statistically reliable results using a between-subjects design. Using a within-subjects design would reduce the number of participants required for the study while preserving an acceptable degree of reliability.

*Assessing the Effects of Increasing Exposure on Behavior*    In cases in which you wish to assess changes in performance as a function of increasing exposure to the treatment conditions (measured as number of trials, passage of time, etc.), the within-subjects design is the only option (unless you have enough control to use a single-subject design—see Chapter 12). Designs that repeatedly sample the dependent variable across time or trials are frequently used in psychological research to examine the course of processes such as reinforcement, extinction, fatigue, and habituation. These changes occur as a function of earlier exposure to the experimental conditions and thus represent carryover effects. However, the carryover effects in these designs are the *object* of study rather than something to be eliminated by measures such as counterbalancing.

## Within-Subjects Versus Matched-Groups Designs

The within-subjects and matched-groups designs both deal with error variance by attempting to control subject-related factors. As we have seen, the two designs go about this in different ways. In the matched-groups design, you measure subject variables and match subjects accordingly, whereas in the within-subjects design, you use the same subjects in all treatments. Both designs take advantage of any correlations between subject variables and your dependent variable to improve power, and both use similar statistical analyses to take this correlation into account. However, if the correlation between those subject variables and the dependent variable is weak, a randomized-groups design will be more powerful. Thus, if you have reason to believe that the relationship between subject variables and your dependent variable is weak, use a randomized-groups design.

A matched-groups design would be a better choice than a within-subjects design if you are concerned that carryover effects will be a serious problem. Although you lose the economy of having fewer subjects, you avoid the possibility of carryover effects while preserving the power advantage made possible by matching.

## Types of Within-Subjects Designs

Just as with the between-subjects design, the within-subjects design is really a family of designs that incorporate the same basic structure. This section discusses several variations on the within-subjects design. These variations include the single-factor, multilevel within-subjects design (in both parametric and nonparametric versions); the multifactor within-subjects design; and multivariate within-subjects designs.

*The Single-Factor Two-Level Design*    The *single-factor two-level design* is the simplest form of within-subjects design and includes just two levels of a single independent variable. All subjects receive both levels of the variable, but half the subjects receive the treatments in one order and half in the opposite order. The scores within each treatment are then averaged (ignoring the order in which the treatments were given), and the two treatment means are compared.

*Single-Factor Multilevel Designs*    Just as with the between-subjects design, the within-subjects design can include more than two levels of the independent variable. In the *single-factor multilevel within-subjects design,* a single group of subjects is exposed to three or more levels of a single independent variable. If the independent variable is not a cumulative factor (such as practice), then the order of treatments is counterbalanced to prevent any carryover effects from confounding the effects of the treatments.

Table 10-6 shows the organization of a single-factor within-subjects design with four levels or treatments and eight subjects. In this example, subjects have been randomly assigned to eight different treatment orders with the restriction that each treatment appears equally often in each ordinal position. Each row indicates the ordinal position of each treatment for a given subject. Treatment orders were determined by constructing two Latin squares, one for each batch of four subjects.

Earlier, we distinguished among several types of single-factor between-subjects design, including parametric, nonparametric, and multiple control group versions. The same distinctions can be applied to within-subjects designs. Because the basic features of these designs have been described before, a separate section is not provided here for each type. Instead, a parametric within-subjects experiment will illustrate the single-factor multilevel within-subjects design. Peterson and Peterson (1959) conducted a now-classic study of memory processes. This study was designed to determine the effect of retention interval on memory for three-consonant trigrams (such as *JHK*). Retention intervals of 3, 6, 9, 12, 15, and 18 seconds were tested, with each participant receiving all the retention intervals and with order of intervals counterbalanced across participants.

To prevent them from rehearsing the trigram during the retention intervals, the participants were kept busy doing a demanding mental arithmetic task. Figure 10-6 shows the results. Probability of correct recall was found to decline sharply as the

**TABLE 10-6    Structure of a Counterbalanced Single-Factor Within-Subjects Design with Four Treatments**

| | TREATMENTS | | | |
|---|---|---|---|---|
| *Subjects* | $T_1$ | $T_2$ | $T_3$ | $T_4$ |
| $S_1$ | 4 | 1 | 2 | 3 |
| $S_2$ | 1 | 2 | 3 | 4 |
| $S_3$ | 3 | 4 | 1 | 2 |
| $S_4$ | 2 | 3 | 4 | 1 |
| $S_5$ | 4 | 3 | 2 | 1 |
| $S_6$ | 1 | 4 | 3 | 2 |
| $S_7$ | 2 | 1 | 4 | 3 |
| $S_8$ | 3 | 2 | 1 | 4 |

retention interval increased. This evidence provided strong support for the existence of short-term memory as a separate entity from long-term memory.

The Petersons' (1959) experiment could have been conducted using a between-subjects design. In this case, however, the use of the within-subjects design reduced the time and the number of participants required to complete the study. At the same time, this design prevented the sometimes large individual differences in recall performance from obscuring the effect of retention interval.

The results from a multilevel within-subjects design are interpreted much like the results from a multigroup between-subjects design. If the independent variable is quantitative (i.e., measured along an interval or ratio scale), as in the Peterson and Peterson (1959) study or as in designs in which trials or time is the independent variable, then the design is said to be *parametric* (just as with between-subjects designs). In that case, your primary interest in conducting the study may be to determine the form of the function relating the independent and dependent variables. However, if

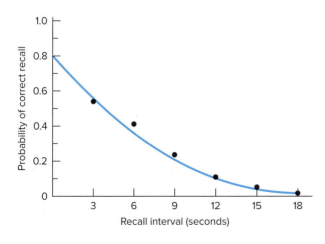

**FIGURE 10-6** Probability of correct recall as a function of retention interval.

SOURCE: Peterson, Lloyd, R., and Margaret Jean Peterson, "Short-Term Retention of Individual Items" *Journal of Experimental Psychology*, 58(3), 195. Washington, DC, Copyright 1959 by American Psychological Association.

your independent variable represented different categories (such as different types of drugs), then talking about functional relationships would be meaningless. In that case, you would want to compare the effects of the different treatments with each other and with those of any control conditions included in the design.

## QUESTIONS TO PONDER

1. Do between-subjects and within-subjects designs applied to the same variables always produce the same functional relationship? Why or why not?

2. When should you consider using a within-subjects design instead of a between-subjects design?

3. When should you consider using a matched-groups design rather than a within-subjects design?

4. How do single-factor and multifactor experimental design differ?

## FACTORIAL DESIGNS: DESIGNS WITH TWO OR MORE INDEPENDENT VARIABLES

Thus far, the discussion has considered designs involving only one independent variable being manipulated in an experiment. If you wanted to assess the effects of several independent variables on a given dependent variable, one solution would be to conduct a separate experiment for each independent variable of interest. Although this approach is sometimes used, you may be able to gain more information at less expense by using a **factorial design** that incorporates two or more independent variables in a single experiment.

In factorial designs, each independent variable is referred to as a *factor*. Factorial designs include at least two factors but may include more. Similarly, each factor will include at least two levels, but may include more. By convention, a two-factor design that includes two levels of factor A and three levels of factor B would be labeled a $2 \times 3$ factorial design. (As in lumber dimensions, the "$\times$" is read as "by," e.g., 2 by 3.) A three-factor design with three levels of each factor would be labeled a $3 \times 3 \times 3$ factorial design, and so on.

### An Example of a Factorial Design: Smoker's Recall of Fear-Appeal Imagery

There are countless advertisements urging you to avoid drugs, use your seatbelt, don't drink and drive, don't text and drive, and quit smoking. Most of these advertisements use a persuasion technique known as the fear appeal: They attempt to persuade you to do something by scaring you. Research shows that fear appeals can be effective as long as they are done right. But, how do they work? What do people focus on in these appeals? These questions were addressed in a study by Ethan Rayner, Stacey Baxter, and Jasmina Ilicic (2015). We use their experiment to illustrate a two-factor, between-subjects design.

Rayner et al. (2015) were interested in finding out how two variables relating to a fear appeal affected what the targets of the appeal remembered about the appeal.

The targets were smokers, and the appeal was aimed at convincing them to give up smoking. The first independent variable was the intensity of the fear aroused by the appeal (low or high), and the second was the fear type (social or physical). Rayner et al. used images obtained from the Internet to manipulate the two independent variables. The participants (a sample of 239 smokers from Australia) were each randomly assigned to one of the four experimental groups. After viewing an image and doing a 5-minute distractor task, participants were asked to recall as many details about the image they had viewed.

Before we discuss the findings, let's identify the experimental design. Different participants were randomly assigned to each condition in the experiment, so the design is between-subjects. Because it includes two independent variables (fear intensity and fear type), it is a two-factor between-subjects design. With two levels of each independent variable, the design is a 2 (low or high intensity fear) × 2 (fear of social or physical harm) between-subjects design.

## Main Effects and Interactions

On the surface, the Rayner et al. (2015) experiment appears horribly confounded because two independent variables have been allowed to vary at once. This is not the case, however. Because all possible combinations of the levels of the independent variables are represented, you can statistically separate the effects of the independent variables. In fact, the main advantage of a factorial design is that it allows you to separately assess the effect of each independent variable on the dependent variable. This separate effect is called a **main effect**. In the Rayner et al. (2015) experiment there are two possible main effects: fear intensity and fear type. You can also assess whether the effect of one independent variable changes across the levels of the other independent variable. This complex relationship is called an **interaction**.

*Main Effects*    Figure 10-7 illustrates how you compute the main effects of your independent variables. The two columns represent the two levels of fear type: social or physical. The two rows represent the two levels of fear intensity: low or high. The numbers inside each box are the mean number of images recalled by each group.

The two numbers at bottom are the means for social and physical fear types, averaged across the two levels of fear intensity. The difference between these two numbers (0.30 picture details recalled) is the main effect of fear type. The two numbers at right are the means for low and high fear intensity, averaged across the two levels of fear

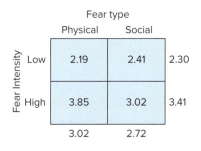

**FIGURE 10-7**   Organization of a 2 × 2 factorial design with cell means and row and column means.

SOURCE: Rayner, Baxter, and Ilicic (2015).

type. The difference between these two numbers (1.66 picture details recalled) is the main effect of fear intensity.

*Interactions*     An interaction is present when the effect of one independent variable varies over the levels of the other. Rayner et al. (2015) found that the type of fear significantly affected recall when fear intensity was high, but not when fear intensity was low. Figure 10-8 shows this interaction graphically. The colored line shows the effect of fear intensity for the two groups that were threatened with physical harm. The black line shows the effect of fear intensity for the two groups that were threatened with social harm. These lines are said to represent the simple main effects of fear intensity. In a two-factor design, a **simple main effect** represents the effect of one independent variable (e.g., fear intensity) at a given level of the other independent variable (e.g., fear type). In general, if the lines of the graph representing different levels of an independent variable are not parallel, an interaction may be present.

Figure 10-9 illustrates several ways that a 2 × 2 factorial experiment might come out. In panel (a), only factor A has a systematic effect on the dependent variable. In panel (b), only factor B has an effect. Panel (c) shows an interaction between factors A and B but no main effect of either factor due to the fact that the average value of each factor, collapsed over the other, is the same for each level. Both factors A and B affect the dependent variable, but their effects in this case show up only in the interaction. Panel (d) shows a main effect of both factors but no interaction (note the parallel lines).

## Factorial Within-Subjects Designs

In the factorial within-subjects design, each subject is exposed to every combination of levels of all the factors (independent variables).

An experiment conducted by Joshua Gowin, Alan Swann, F. Gerald Moeller, and Scott Lane (2010) illustrates the factorial within-subjects design. A well-known

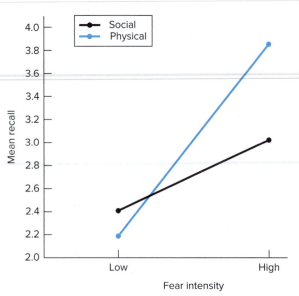

**FIGURE 10-8**  Interaction between fear type and fear intensity.
SOURCE: Rayner, Baxter, and Ilicic (2015).

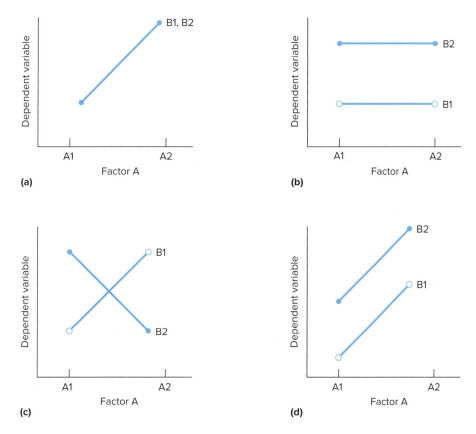

**FIGURE 10-9**  Some possible outcomes of a 2 × 2 factorial experiment (see text for description).

finding is that alcohol consumption increases aggression, perhaps by reducing the levels of the neurotransmitter serotonin in the brain. If so, then raising brain levels of serotonin after alcohol consumption should mitigate the effect of the alcohol on aggression. To evaluate this hypothesis, Gowin et al. conducted a 2 × 3 within-subjects experiment.

Participants were 11 social drinkers who completed the experiment over a period of 3 or 4 weeks. The first independent variable was the dose of zolmitriphan (an active drug known to increase brain serotonin). Participants received either 5 mg of the drug or 0 mg (placebo control). The second independent variable was the amount of alcohol consumed during a session. The dose of alcohol was varied between 0.0 g/kg (placebo control), 0.4 g/kg, and 0.8 g/kg. The measure of aggression (dependent variable) was the number of points the participant chose to subtract from a nonexistent confederate's score during a computerized game.

Every participant received all possible combinations of the levels of both independent variables over the course of the experiment, making it a completely within-subjects, factorial design. The order in which the levels of these two variables were given was counterbalanced to test for carryover effects.

The results revealed a significant interaction between alcohol dose and zolmitriphan dose. Specifically, aggression was lower at both alcohol doses when participants received zolmitriptan than when they received the placebo. (Zolmitriphan administered by itself had no effect on aggression.) The authors concluded that raising serotonin in the brain can reduce the effects of alcohol on aggression.

## QUESTIONS TO PONDER

1. What is a factorial design?
2. What are the advantages to using a factorial experimental design?
3. What is a main effect?
4. What is an interaction, and how does it differ from main effects?

### Higher-Order Factorial Designs

You can extend the simple two-factor, four-cell design to include any number of levels of a given factor and any number of factors. A factorial design including more than two independent variables is known as a **higher-order factorial design**. However, practical considerations limit the usefulness of these designs if you try to extend them too far. Two important problems concern the number of subjects required for the design and the complexity of potential interactions.

You should probably use at least five subjects per group for a reasonable ability to detect the effects of the independent variables. The number of required cells can be calculated by multiplying together the number of levels of each factor in the design. In a two-factor experiment with two levels of each independent variable, there would be four ($2 \times 2$) cells. If you were to conduct this study using 5 participants per group, you would need to recruit 20 participants. Adding a third two-level factor would produce a design that required eight ($2 \times 2 \times 2$) groups, or 40 ($5 \times 8$) participants. If each factor had three levels instead of two, you would need 27 ($3 \times 3 \times 3$) groups multiplied by 5, or 135 participants! And this estimate uses a *minimum* number of participants per group. It would be preferable to use more participants for statistical reliability, but could you afford the time and money required to run such an experiment? As you can see, extended factorial experiments get out of hand quickly.

The second problem with extended factorial designs concerns the number and complexity of the resulting interactions. With three factors, you get three main effects (one for each factor), three *two-way interactions* (factor A $\times$ factor B, factor A $\times$ factor C, and factor B $\times$ factor C), and a *three-way interaction* (factor A $\times$ factor B $\times$ factor C). The two-way interactions are each similar to the simple interaction found in the two-factor design. For example, the A $\times$ B interaction represents the interaction of factors A and B, averaged over the levels of factor C. However, what is the A $\times$ B $\times$ C interaction? This interaction occurs when the A $\times$ B *interaction* changes depending on the level of factor C! (Other interpretations are also possible.) Adding a fourth variable to your design adds further interactions, including the dreaded A $\times$ B $\times$ C $\times$ D four-way interaction, which few ordinary mortals can comprehend. Because data resulting from such designs are difficult to analyze and interpret (not to mention expensive because of the large subject requirement), most investigators limit factorial designs to no more than three factors.

In designs with three factors, the simple effects observed at each level of one of the factors consist of two-way interactions of the other two factors. You also could examine the simple effects of each combination of levels of two of the factors. Of course, the same logic can be applied to designs having more than three factors.

If you are willing to give up information about some of the higher-order interactions, you can include a relatively large number of factors and levels within factors while keeping the requirement for subjects within reasonable bounds. Describing the logic behind these designs and the analyses appropriate to them is beyond the scope of this book. If you are interested in looking into such designs, see the discussion of fractional replications of factorial designs in Edwards (1985, pp. 243–245) or Chapter 8 in Winer (1971).

## OTHER GROUP-BASED DESIGNS

This chapter presents a logical progression from the two-level design through the single-factor multilevel design and finally to the factorial design. This progression might lead you to believe that these are the only ways to conduct experiments. This is far from the truth.

Chapter 4 indicated that you should first develop your research questions and then choose your design. This rule applies when you are deciding how to conduct a between-subjects or within-subjects experiment. Situations occur in which a full factorial design is not the best design to test your hypotheses. After all, in a full factorial design, you examine every possible combination of the levels of your independent variables. In some research situations, this may be neither necessary nor desirable. For example, to address specific questions, you may need to add control groups or treatments to the basic factorial plan. Alternatively, some groups or treatments may not be possible (e.g., you may not be able to combine certain drugs).

Another creative design is the *fractional factorial design*. With this design you do not run a full factorial design with all levels of your independent variables crossed. Instead, you select only those levels of your independent variables that specifically test your hypotheses. This design allows you to evaluate a larger number of independent variables within a single design (Stolle, Robbennolt, Patry, & Penrod, 2002).

Designs such as these that do not follow one of the more standard design formats can help you address special questions or deal with unusual circumstances. However, the data that they provide sometimes require special statistical techniques to interpret properly. This may mean extra work in identifying the appropriate techniques and learning to apply them.

In short, the special versions of these designs may pose special problems for you. Nevertheless, you should make the effort. Choose the design that best addresses the questions that you want to answer. If your design does not address these questions, you may save some effort, but the effort you do make will be wasted.

## DESIGNS WITH TWO OR MORE DEPENDENT VARIABLES

Just as it is possible to include more than one independent variable in a design, it is also possible to include more than one dependent variable. Indeed, all the designs discussed thus far could be modified to include multiple dependent variables without changing their essential characters. Designs that include multiple dependent variables are termed *multivariate designs.* Those with single-dependent variables (such as previously discussed) are termed *univariate designs.* However, multivariate designs are not limited to experiments. Correlational research that simultaneously measures three or more variables is also termed *multivariate.* Chapter 15 covers multivariate designs in some detail, including experimental, correlational, and mixed strategies.

## QUESTIONS TO PONDER

1. What is a higher-order factorial design?
2. What are the advantages and disadvantages of a higher-order factorial design?
3. What are some of the other group-based designs?
4. How do designs with more than one dependent variable work?

## CONFOUNDING AND EXPERIMENTAL DESIGN

Chapter 4 defined a *confounding variable* as one that varies along with your independent variable. The presence of a confounding variable damages the internal validity of your experiment. Consequently, you may not be able to establish a causal relationship between your independent variable (or variables) and your dependent variable. One of the most important aspects of experimental design is to develop an experiment that is free of confounding variables.

Sometimes a source of confounding can be subtle and difficult to detect. Imagine that you are ready to run an experiment on the effect of drugs on discrimination learning. You are using rats as subjects. You order your rats, which are delivered in crates, each housing several animals. You begin to take the rats out of the crates and put them in individual cages in the colony room of your animal research facility. The first rats that you catch go in the first row of cages, and the remaining rats go in the second row. You decide to assign the rats in the first row to your experimental group and those in the second row to your control group. You run your experiment and find that the rats in the experimental group perform better than those in the control group and conclude that the drug improves performance. Is there another possible explanation? Unfortunately, there is. It could be that the rats in the experimental group were better at discrimination learning to start with. How can this be, you ask?

Remember how you assigned rats to their cages? You caught them and put them in two rows of cages. The rats that went in the first row were caught first. These rats were slower and easier to catch than those in the second row. It may be that these rats are more docile and easier to handle. It is possible that the more docile rats in the experimental group learned faster because they experienced less stress in your experiment than those in your control group. This, and not the drug that you administered, may have produced the observed difference. You could have avoided this problem by randomly assigning subjects to treatment conditions so that each subject, regardless of what row it was housed in, had an equal chance of appearing in either of your treatment groups.

Confounding also can occur if you are using human participants in an experiment that will take a long period of time to complete. You should be sure that your experimental treatments are spread out evenly over the entire period of the experiment. That is, be sure not to run all of your participants in one condition at the beginning of a semester and all the participants in another condition at the end. It could be that participants who volunteer for your experiment at the beginning of a semester differ in some important ways from those who volunteer later in a semester. By randomly assigning participants to treatment groups, you can avoid this problem.

Another source of confounding is *experimenter bias,* which we discussed in detail in Chapter 5. For example, if you assigned your participants to groups because you thought that certain participants would perform better in one group than in another, you introduced bias into your experiment as a confounding factor. To avoid this problem it would be best to use a blind or double-blind technique (see Chapter 5).

A major source of confounding occurs when your treatment conditions are not carefully conceived and, as a result, unintended variables are introduced whose values change in lockstep with those of the independent variable. The old "Pepsi Challenge" commercial, designed to test Pepsi against Coca-Cola, provides a classic example of this source of confounding. In the original version of the challenge, cups with Pepsi were always marked with an "M," and cups with Coca-Cola were marked with a "Q." The challenge showed that participants preferred the taste of Pepsi over Coca-Cola. However, when researchers from Coca-Cola tried to replicate the challenge, they found that participants chose the cup marked with an "M" even if both cups contained Coca-Cola (Huck & Sandler, 1979). Thus, in the original Pepsi Challenge, it is unclear whether participants were making their choice based on taste or on the letter used to mark the cup.

Avoiding this source of confounding requires paying attention to detail. In the Pepsi Challenge, the cups could have been left unmarked, or the letters could have been counterbalanced. Yet another approach would have been to have conducted a pilot study to determine whether a preference exists for certain letters over others.

The best way to avoid confounding in an experiment is to plan carefully how your independent variables are to be executed. Ask yourself whether there are potential alternative explanations for any effect that you may find. Is your independent variable the only factor that could affect the value of your dependent variable? Careful evaluation of your experimental design and variables and a good knowledge of the literature in your area will help you avoid confounding. Remember, results from a confounded experiment cannot be rehabilitated and are generally useless. Therefore, take care during the design stage of your experiment to eliminate confounding variables. This will ensure an experiment with the highest level of internal validity.

## QUESTIONS TO PONDER

1. How does a confounding variable affect the validity of your results?
2. How can confounding variables be eliminated?

## SUMMARY

Experimental designs can be classified as between-subjects, within-subjects, or single-subject designs. Between-subjects designs manipulate the independent variable by administering the different levels of the independent variable to different groups of subjects. Within-subjects designs administer the different levels of the independent variable at different times to a single group of subjects. Single-subject designs manipulate the independent variable as the within-subjects designs do but focus on the performances of single subjects rather than on the average performances of a group of subjects.

A key problem for any experimental design is the problem of error variance. Error variance consists of fluctuations in scores that have nothing to do with the effect of the independent variable. Error variance tends to obscure any causal relationship that may exist between your independent and dependent variables.

Several steps can be taken to reduce error variance. In any type of design, you can hold extraneous variables as constant as possible and manipulate your independent variable more strongly. In between-subjects designs, you also can randomize error variance across groups by assigning subjects to groups at random, thus tending to equalize the effect of error variance on mean performance across treatments. Alternatively, you can match subjects across treatments on characteristics that you believe may strongly affect the dependent variable, which will thus tend to eliminate any average differences in these characteristics across the treatments. In within-subjects designs, you can use the same subjects in each treatment and in effect match each subject with him- or herself and eliminate differences between subjects from the analysis. Whether you have used a randomized groups, matched-groups, or within-subjects design, you can then use inferential statistics to assess the probability with which random error variance by itself (in the absence of any effect of the independent variable) would have produced the observed differences in treatment means. If this probability is small, you can be reasonably confident that your independent variable is effective.

Between-subjects and within-subjects designs can be classified according to the number of levels of a single independent variable (two or more than two), the number of independent variables manipulated (single-factor or multifactor), the way in which subjects are assigned to treatments (random assignment, matching, or same subjects in every treatment), and the number of dependent variables (univariate or multivariate). If an independent variable takes on three or more quantitative values, the manipulation is described as parametric; otherwise, it is said to be nonparametric.

Designs may include multiple control groups or treatments to assess the impact of several potentially confounding factors. These additional conditions can be included in both parametric and nonparametric designs.

When subjects are assigned to groups at random, the design is termed a *randomized-groups design*. Such designs are best when subject characteristics do not contribute greatly to error variance. However, when subject characteristics strongly influence the dependent variable, you can reduce error variance created by these characteristics by using either a matched-groups design or a within-subjects design. This control over error variance can improve your chances of detecting any effects of your independent variable. However, compared with randomized-groups designs, matched-groups designs require the extra steps of testing and matching subjects. Both matched-groups and within-subjects designs use somewhat different inferential statistical tests to evaluate the data and may actually be less sensitive to the effects of the independent variable if matching or the use of the same subjects in each treatment does not succeed in reducing error variance. With matched-groups designs, it may be difficult to find enough matching subjects if the design includes several groups. With within-subjects designs, this problem is avoided, but the use of the same subjects in each treatment condition introduces the possibility of carryover, which occurs when exposure to one treatment condition changes how subjects behave in a subsequent treatment condition. Several methods are available for dealing with carryover, including counterbalancing (exposing subjects to treatments in different orders), taking steps to minimize carryover, and using a design that makes any carryover effect into an independent variable.

Two or more independent variables or factors may be manipulated simultaneously in a single experimental design. If each level of each factor is combined once with each level of every other factor, the design is called a factorial design. Each treatment in a factorial design represents a unique combination of the levels of the independent variables, and all possible combinations are represented. Factorial designs make it possible to assess in one experiment the main effect of each independent variable and any interactions among variables. The number of treatment cells required for a factorial design can be computed by multiplying together the number of levels of each factor manipulated.

Some questions are best addressed using designs other than the standard ones. For example, a basic between-subjects factorial design might be expanded to include control groups in order to make comparisons beyond those involving main effects and interactions. Although the statistical analyses required for these designs may be more difficult to define, do not let this difficulty prevent you from choosing the best design for the questions that you want to address.

Multivariate experimental designs include two or more dependent variables, in contrast to univariate designs, which include only one dependent variable.

Confounding occurs when the effects of uncontrolled extraneous variables cannot be separated from those of the intended independent variables. Nonrandom assignment (in between-subjects designs), carryover (in within-subjects designs), experimenter bias, and ill-conceived experimental conditions are sources of confounding. Steps such as random assignment, blind techniques, and careful assessment of experimental conditions and of potential alternative explanations should be taken to avoid potential confounding.

## KEY TERMS

| | |
|---|---|
| between-subjects design | matched-pairs design |
| within-subjects design | carryover effect |
| single-subject design | counterbalancing |
| error variance | factorial design |
| randomized two-group design | main effect |
| parametric design | interaction |
| nonparametric design | simple main effect |
| multiple control group design | higher-order factorial design |
| matched-groups design | |

# 11

## CHAPTER

# Using Specialized Research Designs

In Chapters 8, 9, and 10, we introduced you to a variety of research designs appropriate for nonexperimental and experimental research. Although these designs cover a wide range of conventional research situations, some research questions can be adequately addressed only by using a specialized design. In this chapter, we describe several designs in this category. These include combined between-subjects and within-subjects designs, combined experimental and correlational designs, pretest–posttest designs, quasi-experimental designs, and developmental designs.

## COMBINING BETWEEN-SUBJECTS AND WITHIN-SUBJECTS DESIGNS

It is possible (and at times desirable) to combine between-subjects and within-subjects manipulations in a single experiment. This section discusses two designs that combine between-subjects and within-subjects manipulations.

### The Mixed Design

A **mixed design** (also called a *split-plot design*) is a type of factorial design that combines between-subjects and within-subjects factors. The term *split plot* comes from agricultural research in which the design was first developed (it referred to a plot of land). A field was divided into several plots, and different plots received different levels of a given treatment (e.g., different pesticides). Each plot was then split into subplots, and each subplot received a different level of a second treatment (e.g., different fertilizers). Thus, each plot received all the levels of fertilizer, but only one level of pesticide. In psychological research, each "plot" is a group of subjects who all receive the same level of the between-subjects variable. Within a given plot, the subplots represent the different levels of the within-subjects variable to which all members of that group are exposed.

A mixed design allows you to assess the effects of variables that, because of irreversible effects or carryover, cannot be manipulated effectively within subjects. (These variables are manipulated between subjects.) A mixed design maintains the advantages of the within-subjects design for the remaining variables.

*An Example of a Mixed Design: Does Interpersonal Contact Reduce Stereotypes?*   Lindsay Cameron and Adam Rutland (2006) used a mixed design to determine whether contact between disabled and nondisabled children would reduce stereotyping of disabled children. It has long been known in social psychology that direct intergroup contact can be effective in reducing stereotypes and prejudice. Cameron and Rutland investigated the effects of indirect "extended" contact on stereotyping of and prejudice toward disabled children.

Nondisabled British schoolchildren between 5 and 10 years of age were randomly assigned to three extended-contact groups that were exposed to three different experimental conditions. All three groups heard a story depicting a friendship between a disabled child and a nondisabled child. In the neutral condition, the story minimized the categorization of the friends as disabled or nondisabled and provided no additional information about the characteristics of the two children. In the decategorization condition, the story included information about the children's individual characteristics (e.g., they were kind, liked chocolate, and enjoyed playing computer games). As in the neutral condition, the story minimized the categorization of the children as disabled or nondisabled. In the intergroup condition, the story emphasized that the disabled and the nondisabled child depicted in the story were typical of members of those groups. In all other ways, the story was identical to the version read in the decategorization condition. All participants were interviewed 1 week prior to the story intervention and again 1 week after. In these interviews, the participants' attitudes toward disabled children and their willingness to form a friendship with a disabled child were measured.

Figure 11-1 depicts the mixed design used by Cameron and Rutland (2006). The between-subjects factor is the extended-contact manipulation. Different participants were randomly assigned to each of the three extended-contact groups. The within-subjects factor was the time of measurement (before and after extended contact).

**FIGURE 11-1**   Design of Cameron and Rutland's (2006) mixed experiment. Extended contact condition (neutral, decategorization or intergroup) was the between-subjects factor, and time of interview (preintervention and postintervention) was the within-subjects factor.

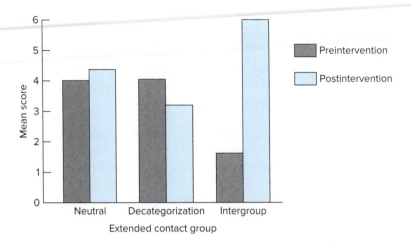

**FIGURE 11-2**   Bar chart showing an interaction between the extended-contact and time-of-measurement variables.
SOURCE: Cameron and Rutland, 2006.

All participants were assessed before the extended-contact manipulation and again after the manipulation.

Cameron and Rutland's (2006) study revealed a main effect of time of interview. Participants showed significantly more favorable attitudes toward the disabled after the intervention ($M = 4.38$) than before ($M = 3.24$). There was also an interaction between extended contact and time of the interview. This interaction is shown graphically in Figure 11-2. Cameron and Rutland report no significant difference between the first interview and the second interview for the neutral and decategorization groups but did find a significant effect for the intergroup group. As shown in Figure 11-2, attitudes toward the disabled were markedly more favorable after the intergroup extended contact than before it. Cameron and Rutland (2006) conclude that extended contact can be an effective tool in reducing children's prejudice directed toward disabled children.

## The Nested Design

Another design that combines within-subjects and between-subjects components is the nested design. In a **nested design**, different levels of a within-subjects independent variable are included under each level of a between-subjects factor. Figure 11-3 shows an example of a nested design. This example includes three levels of a between-subjects factor ($A_1$, $A_2$, and $A_3$). Under each of the levels of A are "nested" three levels of B. Notice that the levels of B found under different levels of A are *not* the same. For example, $B_1$, $B_2$, and $B_3$ appear under $A_1$ whereas $B_4$, $B_5$, and $B_6$ appear under $A_2$. Each level of factor A thus includes a within-subjects manipulation of factor B although the levels of B included in the manipulation differ with the A level.

Nested designs are more economical than factorial designs, in which each level of a factor is completely crossed with every level of every other factor. On the negative side, they do not yield as much information as factorial designs in that you cannot

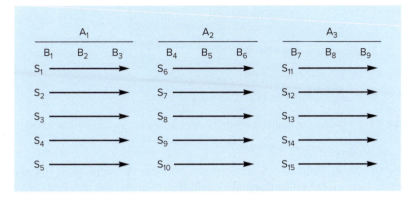

**FIGURE 11-3**    A nested design that has a within-subjects component.

evaluate certain interactions. However, there are situations in which a factorial design is simply not practical. In such cases, a nested design may give you the information you want. Here we discuss two types of nesting: nesting tasks and nesting groups of subjects.

*Nesting Tasks*    Nested designs are useful when you want to include more than one task under a level of an independent variable. For example, imagine that you are conducting an experiment on the effect of a safety campaign on the number of worker injuries. You want to establish that any positive effect of the campaign is not specific to one industry, so you include several companies in your study, representing different industries. However, each company has a different set of jobs. Company X provides jobs A, B, and C; company Y provides jobs D, E, and F; and company Z provides jobs G, H, and I. Thus, jobs are nested under the different companies. Figure 11-4 shows this design.

The major advantage of a nested design like the one shown in Figure 11-4 is that you increase the generality of your results. By demonstrating the effect of the safety campaign across many types of job within each company, you can be more certain that your effect is not limited to a particular type of job. However, the influences of job type and company (e.g., differences in corporate climate) on the effectiveness of the safety campaign are to some extent confounded in this design because the jobs nested under different companies are not strictly comparable.

| Company X | Company Y | Company Z |
|-----------|-----------|-----------|
| Job$_A$ | Job$_D$ | Job$_G$ |
| Job$_B$ | Job$_E$ | Job$_H$ |
| Job$_C$ | Job$_F$ | Job$_I$ |

**FIGURE 11-4**    A design with three jobs nested under each company. The jobs nested under each company are different.

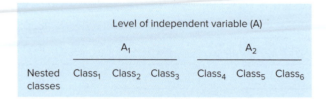

| Level of independent variable (A) | | | | | |
|---|---|---|---|---|---|
| $A_1$ | | | $A_2$ | | |
| Nested classes | Class$_1$ | Class$_2$ | Class$_3$ | Class$_4$ | Class$_5$ | Class$_6$ |

**FIGURE 11-5**   Groups of subjects nested under levels of the independent variable.

*Nesting Groups of Subjects*    A nested design also can be useful when you must test subjects in large groups rather than individually. For example, you may find it necessary to test participants during their regularly scheduled class hours. If you tested three classes under each of your experimental conditions, you would then have three classes nested under each level of your independent variable. Figure 11-5 illustrates this situation.

In this design, the classes are treated as the subjects, not the individual students. These classes would be randomly assigned to the experimental conditions, just as you would randomly assign participants to the experimental conditions in a between-subjects experiment. Random assignment tends to average out any differences between classes, making the experimental groups more nearly equivalent.

Nesting groups of subjects within levels of the independent variable should not be done if you can nest only one group under each level of your independent variable. In this case, your experiment is hopelessly confounded because you have no way of knowing whether the differences between groups of subjects across treatment levels occur because of your independent variable or because of something relating to the nested groups (Keppel, 1982).

In a between-subjects design, when you randomly assign individual subjects to conditions, you are essentially nesting subjects within treatments. Each group in a nested design can be viewed as a subject nested under a level of your independent variable. As long as you randomly assign groups of subjects to experimental conditions, nesting groups of subjects is legitimate.

## QUESTIONS TO PONDER

1. What is a mixed design, and when is it used?
2. What is a nested design, and when is it used?
3. What are the various types of nesting that can be done? Why would you use each?

## COMBINING EXPERIMENTAL AND CORRELATIONAL DESIGNS

Experimental designs have the strong advantage of allowing you to not only identify whether relationships exist between variables but also determine whether the relationships identified are causal ones. The strategy requires that you be able to manipulate the suspected causal variable (the independent variable), hold constant as many extraneous variables as possible, and randomize the effects of any remaining extraneous variables across treatments. Unfortunately, holding variables constant can reduce the generality of your findings (using only males as participants, for example, may yield results that do not generalize to females), whereas randomizing their effects across treatments can produce error variance that obscures the effects of your independent variables.

Fortunately, you often can deal with such problems effectively by using a design that combines experimental and correlational variables. In this section, we explore two ways to combine experimental and correlational variables: including a correlational variable as a covariate in an experimental design and including a quasi-independent variable.

## Including a Covariate in Your Experimental Design

When participants differ on some variable (such as IQ or reaction time), you can statistically control the effects of this variable by measuring the value of the variable for each participant along with the value of the dependent variable. This additional, correlational variable is called a **covariate**. The name derives from the fact that you expect the covariate to *covary* with the dependent variable. This will be the case if the covariate correlates directly with the dependent variable or with some unmeasured variable that correlates with the dependent variable.

By including a covariate in your experimental design, you can effectively subtract out the influence of the covariate (or any variable correlated with it) from the dependent variable. In this way you reduce error variance and improve the sensitivity of your experiment to the effect of your independent variable.

These designs are relatively easy to implement. Simply by collecting additional data on potentially relevant correlational variables, you can convert a standard experimental design into one that examines the impact of those variables on the relationship between the study's independent and dependent variables. For example, in an experiment on jury decision making, you might suspect that a participant's views on the death penalty might be related to his or her willingness to convict a defendant in a case not involving the death penalty. You could measure your participants' attitude toward the death penalty and then use that measure statistically as a covariate when analyzing your data.

Covariates typically take the form of continuous variables or of discrete variables having a relatively large number of levels. If the covariate in question is discrete and has relatively few levels, it may make more sense to treat it as a quasi-independent variable, as described next.

## Including Quasi-Independent Variables in an Experiment

A **quasi-independent variable** is a correlational variable that resembles an independent variable in an experiment. It is created by assigning subjects to groups according to some characteristic they possess (such as age, gender, or IQ), rather than using random assignment. For example, you might be interested in comparing the effectiveness of two types of incentive programs on sales by retail store clerks. You could include gender as a quasi-independent variable to determine whether male and female clerks tend to respond differently to the two programs.

Because subjects come into the experiment already assigned to their levels of the quasi-independent variable, it is always possible that any relationship discovered may be due to the action of some third, unmeasured variable that happens to correlate well with the quasi-independent variable. Even so, the knowledge that a relationship exists between the independent and quasi-independent variable (or a correlate of it) may be important.

Such combinations of both experimental and quasi-experimental variables often resemble the factorial designs described in Chapter 10. These combinations yield a main effect for each independent variable, a main effect for each quasi-independent variable, and one or more interactions. The interactions in such designs can be especially illuminating.

## An Example of a Combined Design: Is Coffee a Physical or Psychological Stimulant?

The morning ritual plays out in millions of homes across the world. The alarm clock rings, and you get out of bed and stumble bleary-eyed into the bathroom. You wash your face, take a shower, get dressed, and then head to the kitchen for your morning pick-me-up: a good strong cup of coffee. For many, the coffee serves as a quick way to get a jolt of energy before beginning the day. We all know that regular coffee contains caffeine, which is a stimulant. Theoretically, it should make us feel better and clear our heads in the morning.

One question that always crops up when discussing the effects of ingredients such as caffeine is whether these effects are due to a physical, pharmacological effect of the ingredient or to expectations about its effect. For caffeine, is it the physically stimulating effect of caffeine that provides the pick-me-up, or is it our belief that caffeine will stimulate us? An experiment conducted by Adam Oei and Laurence Hartley (2005) addressed this question.

Oei and Hartley (2005) approached this question experimentally by using a design that combined one correlational variable and two experimental variables. The correlational variable was whether participants expected that caffeine would stimulate them or believed that caffeine would not stimulate them. Having participants answer a question concerning their expectations about the effects of caffeine created this variable. Participants were *not* randomly assigned to levels of this variable. The two experimental variables were the type of coffee participants actually were given (caffeinated or decaffeinated) and the type they were led to believe they were given. The experimental variables were both manipulated within-subjects and counterbalanced using a Latin square design (see Chapter 10).

Participants came to a laboratory where the coffee was made right in front of them. The experimenters had four jars of coffee, two labeled "caffeinated coffee" and two labeled "decaffeinated coffee." One jar of each type was correctly labeled (e.g., caffeinated coffee in the caffeinated coffee jar), and the other was mislabeled (e.g., caffeinated coffee in the decaffeinated jar). This allowed Oei and Hartley (2005) to completely cross the beverage type with the information provided about the beverage type. Figure 11-6 shows the design of the experiment.

One hour after drinking the coffee, participants completed several tasks, including a signal-detection task. In this task, participants indicated across a series of trials whether or not an "x" appeared against a field of visual noise (dots) on a computer screen. One dependent measure was the number of correct detections, or "hits" (saying that an "x" was present when it actually was present).

Participants scored more hits after drinking caffeinated coffee than after drinking decaffeinated coffee, whether the coffee was correctly or incorrectly labeled. Almost identical results were obtained if participants merely *believed* they were drinking either the caffeinated or decaffeinated coffee, no matter which type of coffee they actually drank. However, in both cases, this effect was reliable only for those who believed that drinking a caffeinated beverage would affect them. Thus, there is support for the idea that your performance may be affected both by the physiological effects of caffeine and your expectation of its effects.

If you ignore the fact that participant expectation about caffeine is a correlational variable, then Oei and Hartley's (2005) design looks exactly like a $2 \times 2 \times 2$ mixed design (with participant expectancy as the between-subjects factor). This similarity extends even further as the results of the study would be analyzed exactly as those from the equivalent mixed factorial design. What differs is the interpretation.

Any significant effect of the *experimental* variables in the combined design can be interpreted to mean that the independent variable *caused* changes in the dependent variable. For example, Oei and Hartley (2005) found a main effect of beverage type on the number of hits made in the signal-detection task. More hits were made when caffeinated coffee was consumed than when decaffeinated coffee was consumed. You would be justified in concluding that the presence of caffeine *caused* an increase in hits. Any significant effect of the *correlational* variable in the study *cannot* be legitimately interpreted to indicate a causal relationship, no matter how tempting it may be to do so. Any correlation between two variables could result from the effect of a third, unmeasured variable that influences both variables. A significant effect of participant expectation on performance on the signal-detection task would indicate only that participant expectation about the effects of caffeine is related to performance on the signal-detection task but is not necessarily *causally* related.

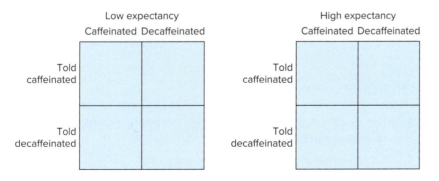

**FIGURE 11-6** Design of the Oei and Hartley (2005) combined experiment. The quasi-independent variable was participant expectancy (low or high) and the true independent variables were the actual beverage provided (caffeinated or decaffeinated) and the information provided about the beverage (told caffeinated or told decaffeinated).

*Advantages of Including a Quasi-Independent Variable*    Experimental designs that include a quasi-independent variable allow you to test the generality of your findings across the levels of the quasi-independent variable. In the example, Oei and Hartley (2005) were able to show that the effects of being told they were consuming caffeine did not generalize from participants who believed caffeine would stimulate them to those who did not hold this belief. These results also illustrate a second advantage of including a quasi-independent variable in your design. Had Oei and Hartley analyzed the data without regard to the participants' expectations, the effect of participants believing they had consumed caffeine might not have detected. Having included a quasi-independent variable in their design, Oei and Hartley were able to reduce error variance by segregating the data into groups of participants who responded in a similar fashion to the manipulation. In this way, the effect of this independent variable was made clearly visible.

*Disadvantages of Including a Quasi-Independent Variable*    The main disadvantage of including a quasi-independent variable in your design is that the results are frequently misinterpreted. Although paying lip service to the dictum "cause cannot be inferred from correlation," researchers too often discuss their results as if they had established causal links between their quasi-independent and dependent variables. This mistake is encouraged by the fact that quasi-independent variables look exactly like experimental variables in the statistical analysis of the data. In Oei and Hartley's (2005) experiment, you may wish to conclude that expecting caffeine to be a stimulant causes an increase in performance when a caffeinated beverage is consumed but does not for those who do not hold this belief. However, one could argue that feeling (or not feeling) stimulated by caffeine causes a person to believe that caffeine will be (or will not be) a stimulant. Because expectation was not experimentally manipulated, the causal status of this variable remains ambiguous.

Another disadvantage of these designs (although a minor one) is the extra effort sometimes required to obtain subjects differing in the required characteristics. Some quasi-experimental variables (such as anxiety level or IQ) require administration of a questionnaire or test before subjects can be classified. Adding quasi-experimental variables to an experimental design also increases the number of groups of subjects required and adds complexity to the analysis of the data.

## QUESTIONS TO PONDER

1. When should you consider using a design combining experimental and correlational variables?

2. What is a covariate, and when would you use one?

3. What is a quasi-independent variable, and when would you use one?

4. What are the advantages and disadvantages of including a quasi-independent variable in your research?

## QUASI-EXPERIMENTAL DESIGNS

Pure **quasi-experimental designs** are those that resemble experimental designs but use quasi-independent rather than true independent variables. In this section, we examine several types of quasi-experimental design, including time series designs, the equivalent time samples design, and the nonequivalent control group design.

### Time Series Designs

**Time series designs** collect a series of observations of behavior across time. The basic time series design is shown in Figure 11-7. In this design (Campbell & Stanley, 1963), you make several observations (O) of behavior over time prior to introducing your treatment ($O_1$ to $O_4$) and again after ($O_5$ to $O_8$). For example, you might measure children's school performance on a weekly basis for several weeks and then introduce a new teaching technique (the treatment). Following the introduction of the new teaching technique, you again measure school performance on a weekly basis. You then compare posttreatment to pretreatment performance. Here, treatment versus no treatment constitutes an independent variable, but there is no untreated control group that would allow you to assess whether any posttreatment changes in performance would have happened anyway if the treatment had not been introduced at that time.

*Interrupted Time Series Design*    A variation on the basic time series design is the **interrupted time series design** in which you chart changes in behavior as a function of some naturally occurring event (such as a natural disaster or the introduction of a new law) rather than manipulate an independent variable. In this design, the naturally occurring event is a quasi-independent variable. As with the other time series designs, you compare behavior prior to and after your subjects were exposed to the treatment.

   A study conducted by Sally Simpson, Leanna Bouffard, Joel Garner, and Laura Hickman (2006) provides a nice example of an interrupted time series design study. Simpson et al. were interested in whether a change in the domestic violence law in Maryland was related to changes in arrests made by police in cases of domestic violence. Simpson et al. used data collected by the state of Maryland on domestic violence before and after the 1994 change in the law. The researchers focused on statistics collected between 1991 (3 years before the new law went into effect) and 1997 (3 years after the law went into effect). The dependent variable was the likelihood that the police made an arrest when called to a domestic violence scene. The likelihood of police making an arrest increased significantly after the new law was enacted, with a major jump in arrests occurring around the time

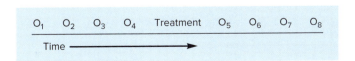

$O_1$    $O_2$    $O_3$    $O_4$    Treatment    $O_5$    $O_6$    $O_7$    $O_8$

Time ⟶

**FIGURE 11-7**   Basic time series design.

when the new law took effect. Overall, arrests were made in 27.3% of cases before the law went into effect and in 39.1% of cases after the law went into effect.

*Sources of Data for Time Series Studies*    The Simpson et al. (2006) study used archival data: arrest statistics from the "Battered Spouse Report" compiled by the state of Maryland. The inclusion of the quasi-independent (enactment of the new law) variable defined the study as a time series study.

Like the Simpson et al. (2006) report, many time series designs employ archival data. Fresh observations of your own are another potential source of data for such designs. In the example of the impact of a new teaching method on school performance, you could measure ongoing behavior (students' exam scores). In an interrupted time series design, if you know that an event is going to happen (such as the introduction of a new, school-mandated teaching method systemwide), you can make your observations prior to the introduction of the quasi-independent variable and continue observations afterward.

## Equivalent Time Samples Design

A quasi-experimental strategy related to the time series design is the **equivalent time samples design** (Campbell & Stanley, 1963). In this design, you administer and withdraw a treatment repeatedly. Figure 11-8 shows this design. Note that the treatment is introduced and then observations (O) are made. Next, observations are made without the treatment, followed by a repeat of this sequence. You could repeat the sequence (in any order appropriate to the research question) as many times as necessary. This design is most appropriate when the effects of the treatment are temporary or transient (Campbell & Stanley, 1963).

## Advantages and Disadvantages of Quasi Experiments

One advantage of quasi-experimental designs is that they allow you to evaluate the impact of a quasi-independent variable under naturally occurring conditions. Whether you manipulate the independent variable or simply take advantage of a naturally occurring event, you may be able to establish clear causal relationships among variables. However, quasi-experimental research does have drawbacks that affect the internal and external validity of your research.

One drawback is that you do not have control over potential confounding variables. Another variable that changed along with the variable of interest actually may have caused the observed effect. For example, when the speed limit on the nation's

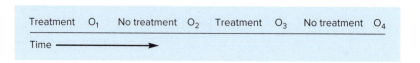

**FIGURE 11-8**   Equivalent time samples design.

highways was reduced to 55 mph in the 1970s, the accident and death rate noticeably decreased. The temptation is to conclude that driving more slowly caused a reduction in the accident rate.

Although this conclusion is the one that was drawn (and is probably true), other events occurred at the same time. The 55-mph speed limit was instituted during a gasoline shortage. In fact, people drove less and some states instituted "gasless Sundays" on which gasoline was not sold at all. The accident rate could have been reduced because fewer people were on the roads and because those who *were* on the roads drove less. Exercise caution when interpreting results from quasi experiments. Be careful to take into account any changes that may have accompanied changes in the variable of interest.

A second drawback to the quasi-experimental strategy also relates to your degree of control over variables. When using naturally occurring events as quasi-independent variables, you have no control over when the event will occur. For example, you have no control over when a law is changed or a new service is introduced. A research study of any kind requires significant preparation. In the absence of forewarning about an event, you may be caught off guard and not be able to adequately study the behaviors of interest prior to the change. In the case of a change in a law or introduction of a new service, keeping in touch with current events will provide you with enough advance warning to design a reasonably good quasi experiment. However, in other cases, you may not have such advance warning.

The major problems with the quasi experiment relate to issues of internal validity. Because the researcher has little or no control over the quasi-independent variable and other related variables, confounding variables will probably cloud any causal inferences drawn from the data collected. A partial solution to these problems is to include appropriate control groups in your quasi experiment. Campbell and Stanley (1963) suggest some quasi-experimental designs that include such control groups to evaluate the internal validity of your study. One of these is the nonequivalent control group design.

## Nonequivalent Control Group Design

In the **nonequivalent control group design**, you include a time series component along with a control group that is not exposed to the treatment. The essence of this design is that a comparable group of subjects is chosen and observed for the same period as the group for which the treatment is introduced. The control group is nonequivalent because it comes from a different community. Figure 11-9 illustrates this design.

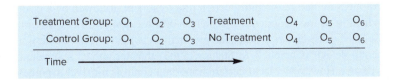

**FIGURE 11-9**  Nonequivalent control group design.

A study reported by Yun Hee Shin (1999) illustrates a multiple time series design with a nonequivalent control group. Shin investigated the impact of an outdoor walking exercise program on physical health and emotional well-being of elderly Korean women. A sample of women was recruited from an apartment complex for the elderly and enlisted in the walking program. The walking program consisted of a 5-minute warm-up period followed by 30 to 40 minutes of walking, 10 minutes of stretching, and a 5-minute cool-down period. The women in this group constituted the experimental group. A second sample of women recruited from another apartment complex for the elderly made up the control group and was not enlisted in an exercise program (participants in the control group were matched to the participants in the experimental group for age and activity level). Shin measured cardio-respiratory functioning, blood pressure, and resting pulse rate (among several other measures) in both groups before and after instituting the exercise program.

As shown in Figure 11-10, there are no significant differences between the experimental and control groups on three of the measures obtained before the exercise program began. However, as you can see, there are small but statistically significant differences between the groups after the exercise program. In all cases, physiological indicators were better for participants in the experimental group.

Although the nonequivalent control group design allows you to make comparisons that you ordinarily might not be able to make, there are some drawbacks to the design. First, the validity of the design will be compromised if your two groups differ on some important variable before the study begins (Campbell & Stanley, 1963). For example, living conditions in the apartment complex of participants in Shin's (1999) control group were worse than those in the complex of the experimental participants, and this could account for differences found. To minimize this problem, your groups must be matched as closely as possible prior to your study. Second, if either group is selected on the basis of extreme scores on the pretest, then any shift of scores from pretest to posttest toward the less extreme values may be due to regression toward the mean rather than to the effect of your treatment (Campbell & Stanley, 1963). For instance, if the members of the experimental group in Shin's study were selected because they were in poor health, any improvement might be due to a tendency for extreme scores to drift toward the average (regression to the mean) and not to the exercise program.

## PRETEST–POSTTEST DESIGNS

As the name suggests, a **pretest–posttest design** includes a pretest of participants on a dependent measure before the introduction of a treatment, followed by a posttest after the introduction of the treatment. The pretest–posttest design differs from the previously discussed quasi-experimental strategies in that the pretest–posttest design is a true experimental design (Campbell & Stanley, 1963) that resembles a standard within-subjects design. However, it lacks certain important controls for rival hypotheses.

Pretest–posttest designs are used to evaluate the effects of some change in the environment (including interventions such as drug treatment or psychotherapy) on

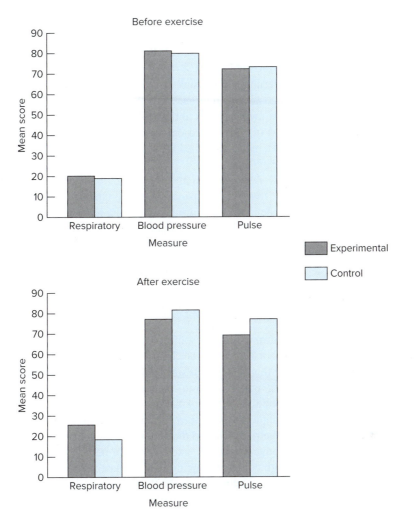

**FIGURE 11-10**   A nonequivalent control group study of the effects of exercise on the health of elderly women.
SOURCE: Shin (1999).

subsequent performance. You might employ a pretest–posttest design to assess the effect of changes in an educational environment (e.g., introduction of a new teaching method) or in the work environment (e.g., using work teams on an assembly line). The design can also be used to test the effects of an experimental manipulation on behavior. By using a pretest–posttest design, you can compare levels of performance before and after the introduction of your change.

It is well established that false memories of events can be implanted and can be as vivid as real memories. Can implanting a false memory generate an aversion to foods? Daniel Bernstein, Cara Laney, Erin Morris, and Elizabeth Loftus (2005) used a simple pretest–posttest design to find out.

In their experiment, participants completed a food history inventory (FHI) that asked them about their experiences with various foods when they were younger. Participants rated the likelihood that a food-related experience happened to them before age 10 (1 = definitely did not happen, 8 = definitely did happen). Embedded in the FHI were two items concerning getting sick after eating a hard-boiled egg or a dill pickle spear. A week later, participants returned to the laboratory and were given false feedback. They were told that their answers to the FHI indicated they had gotten sick after eating a particular food (a hard-boiled egg or a dill pickle). Participants then again completed the FHI and a measure of the kinds of foods they were likely to eat or not eat.

Comparing participants' responses on the first FHI to those on the second, Bernstein et al. (2005) found that telling a participant he or she had gotten sick on a particular food increased the belief that the event had actually happened. (Whether the food was hard-boiled eggs or dill pickles did not matter.) Furthermore, those who were told they had gotten sick from eggs were less likely to eat hard-boiled eggs, and those who were told they had gotten sick from dill pickles were less likely to eat dill pickles.

## Problems with the Pretest–Posttest Design

Evaluating changes in performance after some change of conditions would seem simple: Just measure a behavior, introduce the change, and then measure the behavior again. You should recognize this design as a simple within-subjects experiment with two levels: pretreatment and posttreatment. As with any within-subjects design, carryover effects may confound the effect of the manipulation. Giving your participants the pretest may change the way they perform after you introduce your manipulation—by drawing their attention to the behaviors you are assessing, providing practice on the test, introducing fatigue, and so on. Normally, you would control such carryover effects through counterbalancing. Unfortunately, you cannot counterbalance the pretest and posttest administrations (think about it!). Thus, a simple pretest–posttest design leads to problems with internal validity.

To ensure internal validity, you must include control groups. Campbell and Stanley (1963) discuss pretest–posttest designs extensively. According to Campbell and Stanley, the simplest practical pretest–posttest design should take the form of the diagram shown in Figure 11-11. This design includes two independent groups of participants. The treatment group receives your treatment (e.g., false feedback about getting sick after eating a food) between the pretest and posttest, whereas the control group does not (no false feedback).

**FIGURE 11-11** The simplest practical pretest–posttest design: A mixed design with pretest–posttest as the within-subjects factor and with treatment versus no treatment as the between-subjects factor.

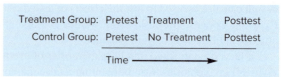

You may have recognized this design from earlier in the chapter: It is simply a mixed design with pretest–posttest as the within-subjects factor and treatment versus no treatment as the between-subjects factor. As such, you can use the design to determine the main effect of each factor and the interaction between them.

If the pretest affected performance on the posttest, you would expect to find a difference between pretest and posttest scores in *both* groups. The same could be said for the effects of any other events, unrelated to your treatment, that might occur between the pretest and posttest administrations: They would be expected to affect the two groups similarly. In contrast, if you found a difference between the pretest and posttest scores in the experimental group only, then you would be justified in concluding that your treatment, and not some other factor, produced the observed changes in performance.

Imagine you are interested in whether using computers in a second-grade class affects the children's knowledge of scientific principles. You obtain a sample of 100 second graders. You randomly assign 50 of them to a new teaching method involving computer-aided instruction. These participants constitute your experimental group; the remaining participants are your control group. You give a pretest of scientific principles to all 100 students and then provide computer-aided instruction to your experimental group (the control group continues to get the usual instruction). Finally, you give both groups your posttest.

Your experimental participants gain an average of 20 points from pretest to posttest whereas your control group gains only 2 points. You could then conclude that your new teaching method and not some other factor was responsible for the observed change. But what if both groups had shown the same 20-point gain? Would you reach the same conclusion? Of course not. You would have to conclude that the students improved at the same rate regardless of the teaching method used.

Campbell and Stanley (1963) point out that, for this design to qualify as a true experiment, participants must be randomly assigned to groups. You *could* use naturally formed groups in a pretest–posttest format, but then the between-subjects component would involve a quasi-independent variable and your conclusions regarding the effect of this variable would be weaker. For example, if you used different classes in your study of computer-aided instruction and found that the class receiving the computers showed a greater increase in performance from pretest to posttest, you could not conclude with confidence that the computers caused the difference. Perhaps they did, but it is also possible that the teacher of the experimental class simply did a better job of teaching.

Campbell and Stanley (1963) also point out that although the two-group pretest–posttest design ensures a degree of internal validity, it does not preclude problems with external validity. Your results may not generalize beyond the immediate research setting. Although this problem can affect any experiment, a particular problem of this design is that participants may be sensitized by the pretest, causing them to perform differently. Campbell and Stanley suggest two remedies to the problem.

## The Solomon Four-Group Design

The first remedy is to use the **Solomon four-group design**, as illustrated in Figure 11-12. Groups 1 and 2 are identical to those in the two-group design. The additional groups

**FIGURE 11-12** The Soloman four-group design.

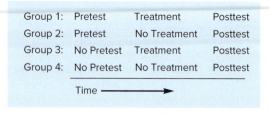

allow you to test for any possible sensitization effects of the pretest. Groups 3 (treatment and then posttest) and 4 (posttest alone) allow you to evaluate the impact of your treatment in the absence of a pretest. By comparing this effect to the impact of your treatment when a pretest is included, you can determine whether the pretest alters the effect of your treatment.

Tahira Probst (2003) used the Solomon four-group design to study the relationship between organizational restructuring (e.g., agency mergers and management reorganization) and various measures of employee reactions (e.g., perceived job security and emotional reactions). Participants in the study were employees of a midwestern state whose governor announced a restructuring plan for state agencies. The four groups in Probst's design (as shown in Figure 11-13) were employees affected by the reorganization who were pretested and posttested (Group 1), employees not affected by the reorganization who were pretested and posttested (Group 2), affected employees who were posttested but not pretested (Group 3), and unaffected employees who were posttested but not pretested (Group 4). For pretested participants, the pretest was given immediately before the announcement of the reorganization. The posttest was given to all participants 6 months after the announcement. Probst found that the reorganization plan had significant negative effects on employees' perceived job security, commitment to the agency, psychological well-being, and intentions to stay with the agency.

## Eliminating the Pretest

Campbell and Stanley's (1963) second remedy for pretest sensitization is simply to eliminate the pretest. Minus the pretest, this design reduces to a simple two-group experiment. The decision whether to eliminate the pretest depends on the question being asked. Situations may exist in which the pretest is needed to answer a research question completely. For example, you may want to know how much material students learn in a given course. However, because some students may come into a

**FIGURE 11-13** Design of a study using the Soloman four-group design.
SOURCE: Probst (2003).

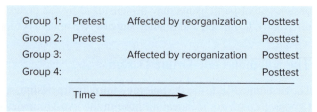

course already having some background in the subject, good performance on the final exam would not necessarily mean that the students had learned anything new. To eliminate this problem, you might administer a pretest on the first day of class over the same material to be assessed in the final exam. The results of this pretest would provide a baseline against which you could measure any change attributable to the course.

## QUESTIONS TO PONDER

1. What are the characteristics of the time series and equivalent time samples designs?

2. What are the advantages and disadvantages of quasi-experimental designs?

3. How are problems of internal validity addressed in quasi-experimental designs?

4. What is a nonequivalent control group design, and when would you use one?

5. What are the defining characteristics of the pretest–posttest design, and what are the design's strengths and weaknesses?

6. What is the Solomon four-group design, and why would you consider using it?

## DEVELOPMENTAL DESIGNS

If you were interested in evaluating changes in behavior that relate to changes in a person's chronological age, you would use one of the specialized *developmental designs* discussed in this section: the cross-sectional design, the longitudinal design, and the cohort-sequential design. These are special cases of quasi-experimental designs wherein the age of the participant serves as a quasi-independent variable. Because age cannot be assigned to participants randomly, it must be used either as a purely correlational variable or as a quasi-independent variable. Consequently, interpretations that you make from your data should not infer causal relationships between age and behavior change. We also should note that although we are presenting these designs as developmental designs, they often have applications outside of developmental psychology.

### The Cross-Sectional Design

In the **cross-sectional design**, you select several participants from each of a number of age groups. Figure 11-14 illustrates the general strategy of the cross-sectional design. In essence, you are creating groups based on the chronological ages of your participants *at the time of the study*. Different participants form each of the age groups.

Assume you are investigating developmental changes in intelligence across the life span (birth to death). Your hypothesis is that intelligence increases steadily during childhood and adolescence, levels off during early and middle adulthood, and declines in late adulthood. To evaluate this hypothesis with a cross-sectional design, you would obtain participants representing the different age groups elaborated in your hypothesis. You would then administer a standardized intelligence test (e.g., the Stanford–Binet) to each group and compare results across age groups.

An advantage of the cross-sectional design is that it permits you to obtain useful developmental data in a relatively short period. You do not have to follow the same participants for 10 years in order to assess age-related changes in behavior.

If you found data consistent with your hypothesis, what would you conclude? The purpose of the study was to draw conclusions about changes in intelligence

**FIGURE 11-14**   A cross-sectional developmental design.

across the life span. The observed decline in intelligence test scores would *seem* to indicate that intelligence deteriorates with age after middle adulthood. However, there is a serious problem with cross-sectional designs that may preclude drawing such conclusions: generation effects.

The term *generation effect* refers to the influence of generational differences in experience, which become confounded with the effects of age per se. This confounding threatens the internal validity of cross-sectional studies. Let's say that the participants in your late-adulthood group were 70 years old and participants in your early-adulthood group were 20 years old. Assume that your study was done in 2015. Simple subtraction shows that participants in the different groups not only were of different ages but also were born in different decades: the 70-year-olds in 1945 and the 20-year-olds in 1995.

The fact that participants in different age groups were born in different decades may provide an alternative explanation for the observed differences in intelligence scores, thus threatening the internal validity of your study. The educational opportunities available to those born in 1945 could have differed markedly from those available to participants born in 1995. The observed reduction in intelligence test scores for older participants may be due to poorer educational opportunity rather than to chronological age. Research indicates that the reduced intelligence test scores shown by older participants in cross-sectional studies were indeed attributable in part to a generation effect (Anastasi, 1976).

Generation effects are a major problem when you use a cross-sectional design to evaluate age-related changes in behavior of participants of quite disparate ages. The design may be more appropriate when the participants are closer in age. For example, you could use the design to evaluate the changes in the ability to solve verbal problems in children ranging in age from 2 to 6 years. These children would all be of the same generation.

## The Longitudinal Design

An alternative to the cross-sectional design, the **longitudinal design**, is illustrated in Figure 11-15. A single group of participants is followed over some time period. For example, you could obtain a group of participants and give them intelligence tests at 10-year intervals over a 50-year span.

*Generation Effects in Longitudinal Designs*      In one respect, the longitudinal design circumvents the problem of generation effects that plagues cross-sectional designs. Because you are studying people from the same age group, you need not worry about generational effects when drawing conclusions about *that* group. Even so, generation effects may still be of concern in the longitudinal design. Shaffer (1985) points out that longitudinal research has the problem of *cross-generational effects*. That is, the conclusion drawn from the longitudinal study of a particular generation may not apply to another generation.

Suppose a longitudinal study was begun in 1910 and carried out through 1940. Data were collected on attachment (the special bond between parent and child) and other developmental events. Would the conclusions derived from these data apply

**FIGURE 11-15** A longitudinal developmental design.

Time of measurement

1960    1970    1980    1990    2000    2010

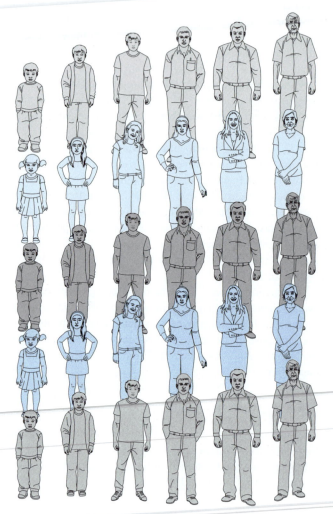

to the generation born in 1980? You cannot be sure. Changing attitudes toward child rearing, day care, breastfeeding, and so forth could invalidate the conclusions drawn from data accumulated during the period from 1910 to 1940. Thus, even though the longitudinal design provides important information about developmental trends, you must be careful when attempting to generalize from one generation to another.

Other problems you should consider when choosing a longitudinal design include subject mortality, testing effects, and the time needed to collect even small amounts of data.

*Subject Mortality*    The term *subject mortality* refers to the loss of subjects from the research over time. Participants may not complete a longitudinal study because they have moved (and don't notify you of their new address), lost interest in the study, find the study offensive, or have died. Animal subjects may pass away before the study ends.

Subject mortality reduces the external validity of a longitudinal study. This may not be a serious problem if subject mortality is due to factors such as moving or loss of interest. Loss of participants due to factors such as changes in address can be considered random in the sense that moving is as likely to happen to one participant as another. The problem may be more serious if participants drop out of a study because of the nature of the research (e.g., the methods are stressful or boring), because it creates a biased sample. Those participants who remain in the study (despite finding it offensive) may have special qualities that differentiate them from participants who quit for this reason. Because the loss of those participants biases the sample, the results may not apply to the general population.

Because subject mortality can bias the results of a longitudinal study, you should make every effort to evaluate why participants do not complete the study. Subject mortality may be more problematic with longitudinal research that spans a long period of time. The longer the period, the more difficult it is to keep track of participants.

*Multiple-Observation Effects*    In a longitudinal design, you make multiple observations of the same participants across time. This very procedure raises problems that may threaten the internal validity of your longitudinal research. Two factors related to multiple observations threaten internal validity.

First, improved performance on the tests over time may be related more to the participants' increasing experience with taking the tests than to changes related to age per se. For example, increases in intelligence scores with age may stem from the fact that participants develop a strategy for taking your test, not from age-related changes in cognitive abilities. Changes in performance due to repeated testing are a type of carryover effect (see Chapter 10 for additional information on carryover). The solution to the problem of carryover is relatively simple: On repeated testing, use alternate forms of the same test or use different tests that measure the same behavior.

The second problem that results from observing the same participants over time is that other factors tend to arise and become confounded with age (Applebaum & McCall, 1983). For example, if evaluations of behavior are made at 5-year intervals, it is not possible to say conclusively whether the changes observed were due to increased age or to some other factor not related to age. Campbell and Stanley (1963) call this a *history effect* that affects internal validity. An example may help to clarify this point.

Suppose you were interested in evaluating the strength of attachment between a parent and child. You choose a longitudinal design and evaluate attachment behaviors at 2-year intervals. You notice a change in attachment. Is the change caused by the fact that the child has grown older or by other factors such as a shift in attitudes toward children or increased use of day care (Applebaum & McCall, 1983)? It is difficult to know.

The longitudinal design suffers from a problem in which the prevailing attitudes at the time of behavior assessment may influence behavior as much as the change in chronological age. This problem is not as easily handled as is the problem of carryover. You might try to deal with it by including a large enough sample so that any effects of attitudes could be statistically controlled while you are evaluating age-related changes in behavior. However, such large samples of people who are willing to make a long-term commitment to a research project may be hard to find. Once found, those people may constitute a biased sample.

*Advantages of the Longitudinal Design*    Despite its disadvantages, the longitudinal design has an attractive quality. It permits you to see developmental changes clearly. You can witness those changes as they occur. This advantage may make the longitudinal design worth the rather large investment of time it takes to collect data.

Returning for the moment to the issue of changes in intelligence with age, longitudinal research indicates that intelligence for the most part changes very little with age. A few areas of intelligence, such as measures requiring reaction time or perceptual skills, do seem to decline with age. However, large declines seen with the cross-sectional design do not emerge in the longitudinal data.

## The Cohort-Sequential Design

A disadvantage of the cross-sectional and longitudinal designs is their relative inability to determine whether factors other than age are influencing the observed changes in behavior. The **cohort-sequential design**, described by Schaie (1965), combines the two developmental designs and lets you *evaluate* the degree of contribution made by factors such as generation effects. However, the cohort-sequential design does not *eliminate* generation effects. It simply lets you detect them and consider them when interpreting your data.

Figure 11-16 illustrates a cohort-sequential design. Notice that the design embodies the features of both the cross-sectional and longitudinal designs. Listed vertically along the left edge of Figure 11-16 is the year of birth. The participants making up one level of this variable (e.g., 1980) constitute a *cohort group*. Specifically, a cohort group consists of participants born at a specified time. In our example, there are three cohort groups: participants born in 1980 (cohort A), 1990 (cohort B), or 2000 (cohort C). These three cohort groups constitute the cross-sectional component when comparisons are made across cohort groups. Listed horizontally along the top edge of the figure is the time of measurement. The different measurement times constitute the longitudinal component when we look at a single cohort group across different times of measurement.

By comparing participants from different cohort groups of the same age (e.g., comparing the data from 10-year-olds across cohort groups), we can identify potential generation or cohort group effects. This design is thus useful for evaluating developmental changes in behavior while affording the capability to detect potentially important cohort effects. For a more detailed discussion of this and other developmental research designs, see Applebaum and McCall (1983).

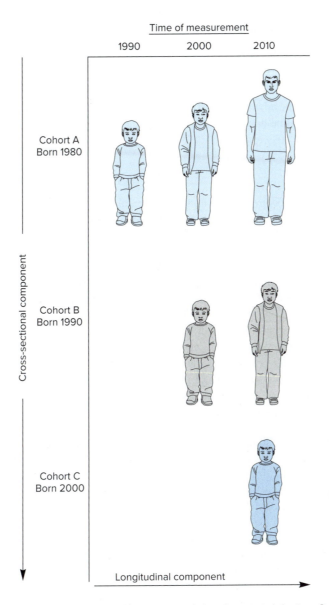

Time of measurement

1990     2000     2010

Cohort A
Born 1980

Cohort B
Born 1990

Cohort C
Born 2000

Cross-sectional component

Longitudinal component

**FIGURE 11-16** An example of cohort-sequential developmental design. Comparisons across time of measurement represent the longitudinal component, and comparisons across cohort groups represent the cross-sectional component of the design.

## QUESTIONS TO PONDER

1. What are the defining qualities of the cross-sectional developmental design?

2. What are the advantages and disadvantages of the cross-sectional developmental design?

3. What are the defining qualities of the longitudinal developmental design?

4. What are the advantages and disadvantages of the longitudinal developmental design?

5. What is a cohort-sequential design, and when would you use one?

6. What are the advantages and disadvantages of the cohort-sequential developmental design?

## SUMMARY

In cases in which a conventional nonexperimental or experimental design does not meet your research needs, you can use one of the various specialized designs available. The designs discussed in this chapter provide alternatives to conventional designs for specialized research situations.

The mixed design, also known as the split-plot design, combines a between-subjects and within-subjects design. This design allows you to assess the effects of variables that cannot be manipulated in a within-subjects manner due to irreversible carryover effects.

The nested design also combines between-subjects and within-subjects factors. There are two ways to implement a nested design. First, you can nest tasks under different levels of a between-subjects variable. This is useful when you want to include more than one task under a level of an independent variable (e.g., different lists of words to memorize). Second, you can nest groups of subjects under levels of a between-subjects independent variable. This is useful when you need to run subjects in large groups.

In some research situations, it is desirable to evaluate correlational variables and experimental variables at the same time. There are two ways in which you can add a correlational variable to an experimental design. First, you can include the correlational variable as a covariate. It is measured along with the dependent variable and then used to statistically "subtract out" the effect of the covariate from the dependent variable. Second, you can add the correlational variable as a quasi-independent variable. This variable resembles a true independent variable, but participants come already assigned to their particular level of the variable rather than being assigned to it at random by the experimenter.

Quasi-experimental designs are useful when true experimental designs do not apply to a research situation. They make use of naturally occurring events (such as a change in law or a disaster) as a quasi-independent variable. You do not randomly assign participants to conditions, and in some cases you may not have appropriate control groups. Typically, the quasi experiment suffers in the areas of both internal and external validity. You might consider using a quasi experiment employing the non-equivalent control group design to combat the problems of internal and external validity. However, you must take care when selecting groups for inclusion in this design so that validity is preserved.

Pretest–posttest designs are used when you want to evaluate the impact of some environmental change, such as a new company policy, or naturally occurring behavior, such as the productivity of the company's employees. Behavior is measured before and after the change. A major problem with this design is that participants may be sensitized by the pretest. The Solomon four-group design, a variation of the pretest–posttest design, allows you to test for pretest sensitization effects.

Developmental designs are correlational designs that examine changes in behavior that occur as a function of maturation and experience. The basic developmental designs are the longitudinal and cross-sectional designs. In a longitudinal study, a group of participants is followed over a period of time (weeks, months, or years). This design allows you to observe subtle changes in behavior but suffers from cross-generational problems, subject mortality, and high cost. In cross-sectional research, you study participants of different ages at the same time. This approach is less costly than the longitudinal design, but conceptual problems arise when a wide range exists between the youngest and oldest participants in your study. Generation effects may be a problem in this case. The cohort-sequential design, which combines elements of the longitudinal and cross-sectional designs, allows you to test for generation effects.

## KEY TERMS

| | |
|---|---|
| mixed design | equivalent time samples design |
| nested design | nonequivalent control group design |
| covariate | pretest–posttest design |
| quasi-independent variable | Solomon four-group design |
| quasi-experimental design | cross-sectional design |
| time series design | longitudinal design |
| interrupted time series design | cohort-sequential design |

# 12 *CHAPTER*

# Using Single-Subject Designs

The experimental designs described in the last two chapters require that one or more groups of subjects be exposed to the various treatments of the experiment. The data within each treatment are then averaged. The differences among the means are tested statistically to determine the probability that the observed differences could have arisen by chance through the operation of uncontrolled random factors. If this probability is acceptably low, the investigator concludes that the differences are reliable and attributes these differences to the effect of the independent variable.

This chapter presents a very different approach to conducting experimental research, one that focuses on the behavior of individual subjects. It does not depend on averaging across subjects to control the effects of random factors and therefore can be used with few or even only one subject. For this reason, the approach is often called the *single-subject* or *small-n* approach. If you have trouble with inferential statistics, you will be pleased to learn that this approach generally avoids them. This chapter describes the logic of the single-subject approach, indicates conditions under which the single-subject approach is appropriate or inappropriate, and identifies specific single-subject designs.

## A LITTLE HISTORY

A major goal of psychology is to understand human and animal behavior. Understanding a particular behavior means knowing what variables influence the behavior and what functional relationships exist between these variables and the behavior. To be useful to psychologists, this understanding must be applicable to individuals.

This emphasis on developing laws that can be applied to individuals dates back to psychology's beginnings as an experimental discipline in the latter half of the 19th century. The psychophysics of Ernst Weber and Gustav Fechner, the memory experiments of Herman

Ebbinghaus, the investigations of perceptual processes by the early Gestalt psychologists, and Wilhelm Wundt's examinations of "mental chronography," as well as the learning experiments of Edward L. Thorndike and Ivan Pavlov, all focused on the behaviors of individual subjects in an effort to understand psychological processes. An extreme example is provided by Ebbinghaus's research, which employed but a single participant—Ebbinghaus himself.

The pioneering experimentalists managed to identify important psychological phenomena, and the functional relationships they uncovered, by and large, have withstood later scrutiny. This was all accomplished without the benefit of inferential statistics, which had not yet been developed.

From the beginning, these early researchers recognized the problems created by apparently random variations in the behaviors of their subjects. One solution to these problems was to repeat the observations many times under a given set of conditions and then average across observations to provide a stable estimate of the "true" values. Although inferential statistics had not yet been developed, researchers knew that estimates based on means become more stable with increasing numbers of observations.

The focus on individual behavior naturally led investigators to adopt a type of within-subjects approach that differs from that described in Chapter 10. In the traditional within-subjects design outlined there, each subject is exposed once to each level of the independent variable, and then scores collected at each level are averaged across subjects. The method adopted by the early investigators exposed a single subject repeatedly to the different treatments and then averaged across exposures within each treatment. The result was a functional relationship between independent and dependent variables that applied (strictly speaking) to the one individual from whom the data were collected. Functional relationships from different individuals were then compared to determine the generality of the relationships.

Despite intersubject variability, the approach worked because of three factors. First, a large number of observations were collected from a single subject, thus allowing momentary fluctuations to average out. Second, to the extent possible, incidental factors that might contribute unwanted variability were rigidly controlled. For example, Ebbinghaus ate the same meal at the same time each day during the years he studied his own memory processes (Fancher, 1979). Third, the investigators focused their attentions on powerful variables whose effects could be detected easily against the remaining background of uncontrolled variability.

Of course, certain problems could not be attacked with this approach. These problems involved treatments that produced irreversible changes in subject behavior, exerted very weak effects on the dependent variable, or employed dependent variables that could not be stabilized through rigid control of experimental conditions. Such problems required an approach that could extract the relatively weak signal of the independent variable from the noisy background of uncontrolled variation. Inferential statistics were developed for these cases.

The application of statistical techniques to the study of individual differences was pioneered by Sir Frances Galton (a cousin of Charles Darwin) in the late 1800s. The first correlational statistic was developed by Karl Pearson under the guidance of Galton and laid the groundwork for the application of statistical techniques to other problems in psychology.

The next major step in the evolution of the statistical revolution came in the 1920s and 1930s when Sir Ronald Fisher and other statisticians developed the rationale of inferential statistics to provide some of the first statistical tests. Soon researchers in psychology recognized that these statistical techniques provided powerful tools for dealing with uncontrolled variability. Inferential statistics were adopted, and the single-subject approach waned in popularity. By 1950 it was virtually impossible to publish research in a respectable psychological journal unless the data had been subjected to an appropriate statistical test and judged by that test to be reliable.

Meanwhile, some die-hard researchers persisted in using the old nonstatistical, single-subject approach. Most prominent among these was B. F. Skinner. Focusing his efforts on the effects of environmental stimuli on the motor behavior of rats and pigeons, Skinner developed a highly controlled laboratory environment to observe and record selected behaviors of his subjects. Electromechanical equipment (such as clocks, relays, and switches) was used to gain precise control of environmental stimuli, to program the experimental contingencies, and to define and record the behavioral responses. Skinner and his students continued the tradition of observing and analyzing the behavior of individual subjects. In the process, they developed several methodological refinements that extended the power and usefulness of the single-subject approach.

Unfortunately for Skinner and his followers, their unwillingness to use inferential statistics to establish the reliability of their findings made it increasingly difficult for them to get their results published. In 1958, they attacked this problem by establishing their own journal, the *Journal of the Experimental Analysis of Behavior* (*JEAB*). Eventually, researchers using the single-subject approach were able to convince others of the validity of the method. Today the approach is widely accepted, and experiments using it are being published in many other psychology journals. Because the method specifically focuses on changes in the behavior of the single subject, it has gained widespread acceptance in applied situations in which it has been used to assess the effectiveness of behavioral change programs and therapies in the treatment of individuals.

In 1968, the publisher of *JEAB* launched a second journal, the *Journal of Applied Behavior Analysis* (*JABA*), to publish single-subject research on applied problems. This research provides empirical support for the effectiveness of behavioral management techniques employed by practitioners of applied behavior analysis. Since then, *JABA* has been joined by a number of other journals focusing on behavior analysis, such as *The Behavior Analyst,* which began publishing in 1978.

As this brief review indicates, single-subject designs have a long and respectable history and have emerged again into acceptance after being temporarily eclipsed by group-based designs.

## BASELINE, DYNAMIC, AND DISCRETE TRIALS DESIGNS

Although single-subject designs come in a variety of forms, all these forms can be categorized into one of three basic types: baseline designs (developed primarily by B. F. Skinner and his followers), what we will call *dynamic* designs, and discrete trials designs (the type used most often by early researchers). Today when researchers refer to "single-subject designs," they usually mean baseline designs. Dynamic designs, which are closely related to baseline designs, are less common but becoming more popular as researchers focus on understanding the dynamics (moment-by-moment changes over time) of behavior. Discrete trials designs are still in use, especially in areas such as psychophysics in which the emphasis continues to be on the performances of individual subjects.

These three types of single-subject design are sufficiently different from one another to require separate treatment. The next sections describe the logic of baseline designs and indicate how to analyze and interpret the results obtained from such designs. We then focus briefly on dynamic designs. Finally, the last part of the chapter describes the discrete trials approach and examines the issues surrounding the use of statistical techniques with single-subject designs.

## BASELINE DESIGNS

The group-based experimental designs we discussed in previous chapters depend on averaging to even out across the various treatment conditions the effects of any uncontrolled, extraneous variables on the dependent variable. You perform the experiment and then use inferential statistics to evaluate the significance of any differences in mean performance that do emerge between treatments. The statistical analysis is used to decide whether those differences are *reliable.* If the results are reliable, then you would expect to reproduce essentially the same results if you were to repeat, or *replicate,* the study.

In contrast to group-based designs, a **baseline design** focuses on the behavior of a single subject both within and across the experimental treatments and does not rely on averaging to deal with uncontrolled variability. Within a treatment condition, the behavior of interest is sampled repeatedly over time and plotted to create a **behavioral baseline**. This baseline typically changes over time as the effect of the exposure to the treatment condition develops and also in response to the effects of uncontrolled variables. For example, the baseline may rise for a time and then show no further change except for small, unsystematic fluctuations. The subject typically remains under a given experimental treatment until the baseline meets a **stability criterion**, which imposes an objective rule for deciding that the baseline has stabilized. When the behavior has stabilized in this way, the subject is then exposed to the next treatment condition during which the baseline is again plotted until it becomes stable.

After the subject has been exposed to each experimental treatment, these conditions are then repeated. In the simplest case, the design would involve exposing the subject to two conditions: a **baseline phase**, to assess behavior in the absence of the treatment, and an **intervention phase**, to assess behavior during application of the treatment. The subject would be exposed to each of these phases twice, yielding what is called an **ABAB design**, where A and B represent the two phases. This immediate **intrasubject replication** of each phase allows you to establish the reliability of your observations within each phase. To the extent that your observations are reliable, the level of baseline observed under one exposure to a phase will be recovered during reexposure to that same phase. In other words, intrasubject replication helps you establish the *internal validity* of your findings.

**TABLE 12-1    Characteristics of the Single-Subject Baseline Design**

1. Individual subjects are observed under each of several phases. Each phase exposes subjects to a specific treatment condition.

2. Extensive observations are made during a given phase to establish a behavioral baseline against which any between-phase changes due to treatment effects can be seen.

3. Each subject is observed under all phases, with each treatment phase repeated at least once. This repetition, or *intrasubject replication*, establishes the reliability (internal validity) of the findings.

4. Subjects usually remain in each phase until a *stability criterion* is met.

5. Multiple subjects may be included in the experiment. This *intersubject replication* helps establish the generality of the findings across subjects (external validity).

When you move from baseline to intervention and then back to baseline, this return to a previous phase is termed a **reversal strategy** and is designed to assess whether any changes in baseline level produced by the intervention are reversible. If so, then you should be able to recover the original baseline.

Despite the name "single-subject design," most studies of this kind include more than one subject to provide what is termed **intersubject replication**. The purpose of intersubject replication is to establish the *external validity* of your findings. To the extent that different subjects show similar changes in baseline levels across the experimental conditions, you demonstrate that your effects are not unique to a particular subject.

Table 12-1 summarizes the characteristics of the single-subject baseline design.

## An Example Baseline Experiment: Do Rats Prefer Signaled or Unsignaled Shocks?

To illustrate the baseline approach to single-subject design, we describe a typical example, part of a larger experiment that investigated whether rats prefer a schedule of signaled shocks over an equivalent schedule of unsignaled shocks (Badia & Culbertson, 1972). The subjects were tested individually in a small operant conditioning chamber equipped with a response lever, a house light, and a floor of metal rods that could be electrified to deliver a brief shock to the rat's feet. (The shocks are similar to static electric pokes and do not harm the rat.)

In the baseline phase, each subject received a series of training sessions to familiarize the rat with the characteristics of each shock schedule and to establish a behavioral baseline. At times the chamber house light was off, and at other times it was on. When the light was off, shocks occurred unpredictably according to a random schedule at an average rate of one shock every two minutes (unsignaled schedule). When the light was on, shocks continued to occur on the same schedule, but each shock was immediately preceded by a 5-second warning tone (signaled schedule). Each session provided equal experience with the two schedules.

During the baseline phase, responses on the lever had no effect on conditions, but the number of responses during each session was recorded. At the end of each session, the percentage of responses out of the total possible was calculated and plotted to provide the behavioral baseline. The investigators continued to train each rat until three successive points on the baseline remained within a 10% range (stability criterion). The subject was then placed in the intervention phase of the experiment.

During the intervention phase, the rat was placed on the unsignaled schedule (identified by darkness). Pressing the lever now "bought" the rat 1 minute of time on the signaled schedule. The house light turned on to indicate that the signaled schedule was now in effect, and any shocks that happened to be programmed during the minute were preceded by the warning tone. When this 1-minute "changeover period" ended, the house light was extinguished, and the unsignaled schedule was automatically reinstated. At this time, the rat could buy another minute in the signaled schedule by again pressing the lever. The number of "changeover responses" on the lever was recorded, and as in the baseline phase, the percentage of responses out of the total possible was calculated and plotted. Intervention-phase sessions continued until the stability criterion was again met. The baseline phase was then repeated, followed by a second exposure to the intervention phase, to provide an intrasubject replication of each phase.

Note that the two shock schedules were identical except for the signal and that the rat could neither avoid nor escape the shocks. Would the rats nevertheless press the lever to get into the signaled schedule during the intervention phases? The answer to this question can be found in Figure 12-1, which shows the level of responding during the final three sessions in each phase for each rat.

During the initial baseline phase (during which responses had no programmed consequences), the level of responding of each rat remained low, typically around 10% of the maximum possible rate (see the first panel of Figure 12-1). However, note the dramatic changes that occurred when subjects were placed in the intervention phase: Response rates zoomed up to over 85% (second panel). The subsequent return to baseline conditions produced an equally dramatic effect as response rates fell back to the low levels obtained during the first baseline phase (third panel). Finally, response rates jumped back to high levels when subjects were returned to the intervention phase (fourth panel).

The fact that response rates were high in the intervention phases would mean little without the comparison provided by responding in the baseline phases when responses did not produce the signaled schedule. This comparison shows that response rates were high *only* when responses did produce the signaled schedule.

Badia and Culbertson (1972) concluded from this experiment that rats strongly prefer the signaled shock schedule over an equivalent unsignaled schedule although it was unclear why. Evidently, the signaled schedule contains a powerful source of reinforcement that was capable of generating high rates of responding during the intervention phase. The findings, which could not be explained adequately by known principles of conditioning, led to an extensive series of follow-up studies that sought to clarify the sources of reinforcement and their impact on preference responding (reviewed in Badia, Harsh, & Abbott, 1979).

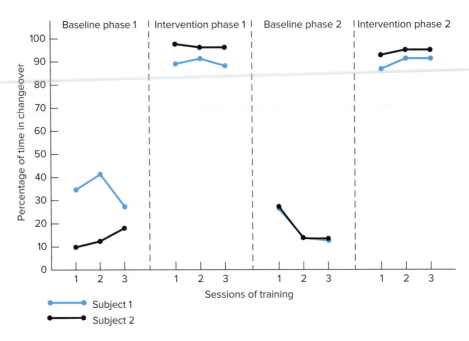

**FIGURE 12-1**    Results of a single-subject experiment on rat preference for scheduled shock over unscheduled shock.

SOURCE: Badia and Culbertson, 1972, table 3.

## QUESTIONS TO PONDER

1. How were single-subject designs used in the early days of behavioral research?
2. What are the major characteristics of the single-subject baseline design?
3. What is a behavioral baseline?
4. Why is it important to establish a behavioral baseline in a single-subject design?
5. What is a stability criterion, and why is it important?
6. What is an ABAB design, and how does it relate to intrasubject replication?
7. What are intrasubject and intersubject replication, and what do they tell you?

### Issues Surrounding the Use of Baseline Designs

When using baseline designs, you may have to grapple with a number of issues. These include what stability criterion (if any) to adopt, how to deal with uncontrolled variability (unstable or drifting baselines), and how to cope with irreversible baselines.

*Choosing a Stability Criterion*    Systematic changes such as those due to learning or habituation show up in the behavioral baseline as trends toward increasing or decreasing values. Such trends usually occur immediately after a change to a new phase when behavior is in transition from one stable level to another. Optimally, your stability criterion should guarantee that your subjects will remain in a given phase only until the baseline shows no further systematic changes.

Choosing a good stability criterion is something of an art. If your stability criterion is too stringent, your baseline may never achieve it, and you will not be able to proceed to the next phase. Yet if your stability criterion is too lax, you may proceed to the next phase before your subject's performance has actually stabilized. As a result, your "stable" baseline values will not accurately reflect the effect of your independent variable. Developing a good stability criterion may require some pilot work in which you observe your baseline until it shows no long-term trends. You then attempt to identify a stability criterion that would have allowed you to stop sooner without including transitional data. In the example experiment, experience with the percentage measure used indicated that the baseline was likely to remain stable if the data remained within 10% across three successive sessions.

Because only the stable performances truly represent the long-term effect of an independent variable on the dependent variable, you usually report only the data that meet the stability criterion. This was done in the Badia and Culbertson (1972) example: Figure 12-1 omits the transitional data from the plot.

During the experiment, the only way to determine whether your baseline has met the stability criterion is to update your plot after each session and then examine it. If you fail to keep your plot current, you may be shocked to discover that you have run your subject through another session under the previous phase when you should have changed to a new phase. Because this is both a waste of time and a violation of experimental procedure, you can appreciate how important it is to keep the baseline up to date.

**Transitional Behavior and the Stability Criterion**    By imposing a stability criterion, the single-subject baseline approach removes transitional data (when behavior is changing between stable levels) from the analysis. Of course, if the focus of the experiment is on transitional behavior, then using a stability criterion will not reduce the variability in the data of interest. However, it is still useful because it indicates that the transition is over and you can stop collecting data within that phase.

**Stability Criterion Versus Fixed Time or Trials**    The group approach encourages you to design experiments in which all subjects receive the same amount of exposure to each treatment. If some subjects reach stable levels of performance in the allotted time and others do not, then the data from each treatment will reflect varying mixtures of average transition rates and average levels of steady-state performance. Such differences between treatments may turn out to be statistically significant yet misleading. Employing a stability criterion in such cases helps ensure that the data will reflect terminal levels of performance for all subjects under a given treatment condition.

There are times, however, when it is important for experimental reasons to keep the amount of exposure to a given treatment constant across subjects prior to introducing the next treatment. In that case, you would probably choose to end the phase according to some criterion other than a stable baseline (e.g., after a certain amount of time in the phase). However, because you continue to monitor the baseline of each subject, you can determine how stable each individual's behavior was in the final stages of exposure to the phase.

Melissa Anglesea, Hannah Hoch, and Bridget Taylor (2008) provide an example of the use of an ABAB design in an applied setting. In such settings, the decision to end a phase often depends on factors such as time constraints rather than the meeting of an explicit stability criterion. Anglesea et al. were concerned with the eating behavior of three teenage boys with autism. Although the boys were capable of feeding themselves, they wolfed down their meals. To get the boys to eat at a normal rate, Anglesea et al. attached a vibrating pager to each boy's belt and trained each boy (using physical guidance of the boy's hand, verbal reinforcement, and a fading procedure) to place his hand on the pager, wait until the pager vibrated, and then take a bite of a target food. During the baseline phase, the pager was deactivated. During the intervention phase, the pager vibrated every so many seconds, an interval that matched the eating rate of a normal adult. Figure 12-2 shows the total seconds of eating time and the total number of bites taken during the observation periods across the several sessions of each phase. The intervention clearly increased eating time without affecting the amount eaten per bite, as the total number of bites required to consume the food remained essentially constant across phases. Note the success of both the intrasubject and intersubject replications.

*Judging Differences in Stable Performance Across Phases*    Large and consistent differences in performance levels across phases stand out when there is comparatively little variation within each phase, as in the Anglesea et al. (2008) data just presented. Judging whether reliable differences exist is more difficult when baselines are more variable and the difference between their levels is relatively small. Matyas and Greenwood (1990) had students taking a postgraduate course in single-case design and analysis evaluate computer-generated graphs depicting simulated data from an AB design (a baseline phase followed by an intervention phase). The graphs differed in effect size, level of variability, and autocorrelation. False alarm rates (declaring that the intervention was effective when it was not) were "surprisingly high" (16% to 84%) and sensitive to both the level of variability and degree of positive autocorrelation. However, miss rates (declaring that the intervention was not effective when it was) were "relatively low" (0% to 16%). These results suggest that the traditional "eyeball" evaluation may be less conservative with respect to the identification of treatment effects than commonly realized. Similar concerns about the visual evaluation of data from single-subject designs were raised by Kazdin (1978).

Such concerns have led some researchers to propose alternative methods of evaluation. For example, Fisher, Kelley, and Lomas (2003) have developed a "conservative dual criterion" (CDC) method to evaluate differences in trend across phases. Steward, Carr, Brandt, and McHenry (2007) found that this method was superior to the use of lectures to train six university students to visually inspect AB-design graphs. (See Fisher et al., 2003, for a description of the CDC method.)

Ideally, the differences in performance across the phases of a single-subject baseline design are such as to make reliable changes easy to judge. Such changes may be less clear, however, in some applied settings where control over extraneous variables may be unavoidably weak and where it may not be convenient to use a stability criterion. Isis Bulté and Patrick Onghena (2011) developed a software package called "R"

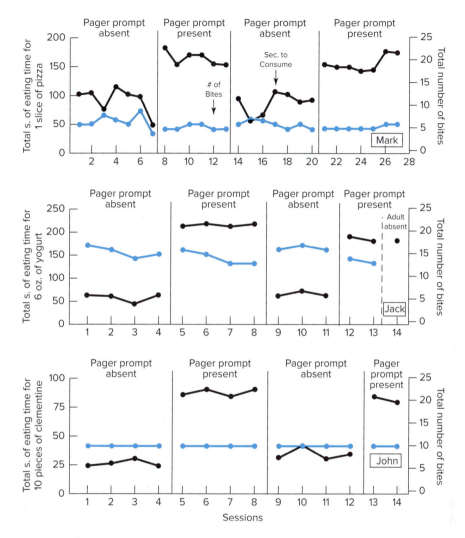

**FIGURE 12-2** Results of the eating-behavior study.

SOURCE: Anglesea, M. M., Hoch, H., & Taylor, B. A. (2008). "Reducing rapid eating in teenagers with autism: Use of a pager prompt". *Journal of Applied Behavior Analysis*, *41*, 107–111. doi: 10.1901/jaba.2008.41–107.

to aid visual analysis in such cases. Using R, a researcher can graph the data from a single-subject baseline design, superimpose horizontal lines to indicate the central tendency of points within a phase, visualize baseline trends, generate "range lines" to indicate the variability of the points, and even extract raw data from published graphs. Another approach, assessed by Ruman Manolov, Antonio Solanas, and David Leiva (2010), supplements visual inspection of the graphs with measures of *effect size*. Effect size in this context basically reflects the size of the change in performance between baseline and intervention phases relative to the amount of overlap in the data points.

Two of the three effect size measures they evaluated performed well on simulated data from an AB design, discriminating data in which an effect was present from those in which an effect was not present (see Manolov et al., 2010, for details).

Other researchers have proposed using statistical methods, such as randomization tests, to discriminate differences in baseline levels, but the suitability of such tests is still controversial. We discuss this issue near the end of this chapter.

## Dealing with Uncontrolled Variability

Within the single-subject approach, extraneous variables produce uncontrolled variability of the baseline within each phase. In the group approach, this variability is handled by averaging data across subjects, but in single-subject designs it is handled instead by tight experimental control. Uncontrolled variability can be reduced only if you can identify its sources. Consequently, the single-subject researcher makes an effort to identify the possible sources of variability. The first step in this process is to graph the data from each subject and look for uncontrolled variability in the baseline, which will be evident when the data points on your graph show moderate to high levels of instability across observation periods.

It is, of course, unreasonable to expect a given subject to show exactly the same pattern of behavior across observational periods or to expect different subjects to display identical patterns of behavior in a given phase. You must decide how much variation is acceptable. If the observed variation is within acceptable limits, then you (much like the group researcher) consider the observed effects to be reliable. Unlike the group researcher, however, you may still be concerned with uncontrolled variation, despite the emergence of a clear relationship between the independent and dependent variables. In your next experiment, you would then take steps to bring this variation under control.

The difference between the single-subject and group approach is a philosophical one. The group approach assumes that if experimental controls fail to reduce uncontrolled variation, then statistical methods should be used to control it. The single-subject approach assumes that if experimental controls fail to reduce uncontrolled variation, then one should endeavor to identify the extraneous variables responsible for it and bring them under experimental control.

When extraneous variables contribute strongly to variation in the dependent variable, identifying them should help you to better understand the behavior in question. The single-subject approach strongly encourages you to identify these important sources of behavioral influence. The group approach does not do this because the effects of the sources are hidden from view during the averaging process.

Of course, data collected across replications of a given phase usually will be similar, not identical. How similar do they have to be, and in what ways, before you can say that the results have been replicated? The answer depends on the degree of control you have over the dependent variable within a treatment condition (its stability) and on the questions that the experiment was designed to answer.

If you have a relatively high degree of control over your dependent variable within a phase, variation in the baseline across successive observations will be minimal. Any effect of the independent variable will be clearly visible as a shift in performance upward or downward relative to this baseline. If each replication of a given condition produces levels of performance that overlap the levels observed in previous administrations of the same conditions, then the reliability of the data is unquestionable.

If your degree of control over the dependent variable is relatively low, the baseline will be variable and the effect of the independent variable will be more difficult to detect. Variation in baseline levels may occur both within and between replications of the same conditions. Variations between replications can occur both as a result of chance (the data points are varying and happen to be higher or lower during replication) and as a result of carryover. Nevertheless, changes in behavior induced by a particular treatment may be consistent in direction and approximate size.

Figure 12-3 shows an example of such a case. The graph indicates the percentage of study behavior during class for Robbie, a disruptive third-grader (Hall, Lund, & Jackson, 1968). During the baseline phase, Robbie's study behavior varied a fair amount but never exceeded 45%. When the teacher began to give Robbie special attention for studying (intervention phase), Robbie's study behavior increased dramatically. Withdrawal of the special attention (reversal phase) was accompanied by a reduction in studying, but the original baseline was not recovered. The return to the intervention phase brought a gradual return to previous reinforcement levels.

In this example, the baseline obtained during the original baseline phase was not recovered during replication. Nevertheless, the change in response rates from the baseline phase to the reinforcement phase is similar on both occasions, and there is little doubt that this change is reliable even if the amount of change is not.

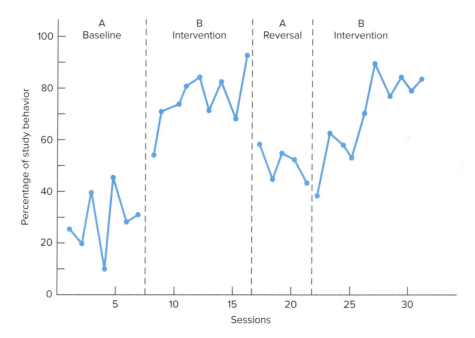

**FIGURE 12-3**  Percentage of study behavior during baseline and reinforcement showing intrasubject replication.
Source: Hall, R. V., Lund, D., and Jackson, D. (1968). Effects of teacher attention on study behavior. *Journal of Applied Behavior Analysis, 1*, 1–12.

Whether you would consider the intrasubject replication shown in Figure 12-3 successful would depend on your experimental question. If your question asked whether reinforcement increases the rate of studying, then the answer is yes, and the replication was successful. Studying increased relative to the baseline phase on both occasions. If your question asked by what amount studying increases, however, then the answer differs from first to second administration, and the replication was not successful.

## Determining the Generality of Findings

As previously noted, single-subject baseline designs use intersubject replication (typically with three to six subjects) to establish whether the findings generalize across subjects. Intersubject replication does not always succeed.

A classic example of a failure of intersubject replication was provided by George Reynolds (1961). In this experiment, two pigeons were trained to peck at a translucent response key. Pecking on the key when it displayed a triangle against a red background led to occasional food reward. Pecking on the key when it displayed a circle against a green background led to nonreward. Both pigeons quickly learned to peck during triangle/red and not to peck during circle/green. They were then tested to see how much they would peck at the key when it displayed each stimulus shape or color separately. One pigeon pecked when the key displayed the triangle but not when it displayed the red color, even though both stimuli had been associated with reward during training. The other pigeon pecked when the key was red but not when the triangle was present.

To explain this failure to obtain intersubject replication, several theorists have suggested that each bird must have attended to different aspects of the original stimuli on which they had been trained. Apparently, one pigeon must have focused on the shapes and the other on the colors. The phenomenon has been termed *overshadowing* and has been used to support theories of selective attention.

Note that although the intersubject replication failed in the Reynolds (1961) experiment, the failure itself revealed a general principle: Learning to discriminate a complex stimulus on the basis of one aspect of it blocks learning about other, equally predictive aspects. The fact that the two birds' key-pecking behaviors came under the influence of different stimuli within the compound stimulus suggests that uncontrolled determining factors were at work. These factors could be the subject of further research. Such factors tend to be hidden by the averaging process when a group approach is used.

Intersubject replication establishes the generality of results across subjects, but establishing the generality of findings across experimental settings requires a different approach. Results are usually double-checked in new experiments. These experiments build on the original findings while extending the range of assessed variables, the types of variables manipulated, and/or the kinds of subjects tested. For example, the patterns of responding generated under various schedules of reinforcement have been replicated by using such varied reinforcers as food, water, chocolate milk, and cigarettes with such diverse subjects as goldfish, rats, pigeons, cats, dogs, monkeys, dolphins, and humans. Such extensions that incorporate aspects of the original experiment while changing others are termed **systematic replications** to distinguish them **direct replications** which replicate the original study exactly. (Sidman, 1960).

## QUESTIONS TO PONDER

1. What factors affect your decision concerning choosing a stability criterion?
2. How is uncontrolled variability handled in the single-subject approach?
3. How do the single-subject and group approaches differ in how they deal with uncontrolled variability?
4. How is the generality of research findings established in single-subject research?

## Dealing with Problem Baselines

In addition to excessive uncontrolled variability, problems you may have to deal with in baseline designs include drifting baselines, unrecoverable baselines, unequal baselines between subjects, and inappropriate baseline levels.

*Drifting Baselines*    In some cases, it may prove impossible to stabilize a baseline against slow, systematic changes (drift). For example, during an experiment in which the dependent measure is basal skin conductance (a psychophysiological measure of arousal), conductance may gradually drift upward or downward as time passes during the experiment. If attempts fail to control this drift, you may be able to deal with the drift by effectively subtracting it out.

Figure 12-4 shows the results from a hypothetical ABAB experiment in which the baseline drifted systematically. Note that the baseline drifted gradually upward within each phase. Because the drift was consistent, it is possible to estimate the position (dashed lines) that the baseline would have reached at any point during the experiment had the treatment not been introduced. The effect of the treatment is clearly discernible after allowing for the drift.

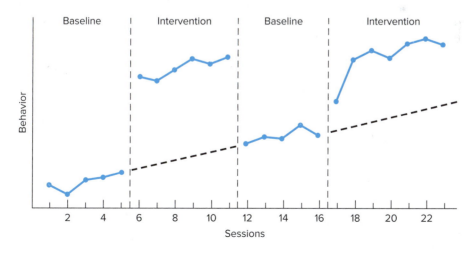

**FIGURE 12-4**  Hypothetical single-subject data showing a drifting baseline.

*Unrecoverable Baselines*    Another potentially serious problem arises if baseline levels of performance cannot be recovered during reversal. Such changes are considered carryover effects, the familiar problem discussed in Chapter 10 that plagues within-subjects designs. Some carryover effects render the baseline completely unrecoverable (in which case it becomes impossible to conduct a successful intrasubject replication). Special designs are required to deal with such completely irreversible changes. A discussion of these special designs appears later in the chapter. Other carryover effects are less of a problem because they render the baseline at least partially recoverable.

Such partially recoverable baselines frequently occur when learning develops during a treatment condition. In a simple operant conditioning experiment, for example, rats may rarely press a lever during the initial baseline phase (before reinforcement is introduced). During the reinforcement phase, subjects learn that pressing the lever produces food, and the reinforcing effect of this contingency generates high response rates. Return to baseline conditions at this point often fails to produce a full return to baseline levels of responding.

Despite the lack of reinforcement for lever pressing, the rats repeatedly approach the lever and press it in a series of widely spaced "bursts" of responding that are characteristic of extinction conditions. As a result, the rate of responding (although considerably lower than that obtained during reinforcement) remains somewhat elevated relative to the initial baseline rate. The rats are no longer naive concerning the potential result of lever pressing.

Partial reversals such as this present few problems for analysis as long as a clear, replicable change remains in the levels of performance across treatments. You may even be able to remove some such carryover effects by taking appropriate steps. For example, if partial reversal results from fatigue or adaptation, you can minimize the effects of these variables by providing rest periods between your experimental treatments.

*Unequal Baselines Between Subjects*    The baselines of different subjects in an experiment may level off at very different values even though the conditions imposed on the subjects are nominally identical. For example, after the same number of hours of deprivation, one rat may press a lever vigorously to earn a food reward whereas another may respond in a lackluster fashion. These initial differences in response rates may then produce different rates of learning in the treatment condition and result in apparently different functional relationships, a failure of intersubject replication.

In this case, identical levels of deprivation generate different levels of motivation because physiological differences exist between the subjects. To reduce the differences in motivation, you may increase the level of deprivation of the rat with the lower response rate. A little experimentation may provide a level that produces response rates similar to those of the first rat. With the baseline rates equated, the two subjects may now perform similarly across treatments.

Because the dependent variable is repeatedly measured during the baseline conditions, such steps may be taken to fine-tune the baseline to meet desired characteristics of stability and comparability. If comparable baselines are established across subjects, achieving intersubject replication may become more likely.

*Inappropriate Baseline Levels*    Even if all subjects show similar baseline levels during the baseline phase, the particular levels obtained may not be useful for evaluating the effect of subsequent manipulations. A low baseline is desirable if you expect the treatment to increase the level of responding, but it is clearly undesirable if you expect the treatment to *decrease* the level of responding. Studies of the effects of punishment on behavior fall into the latter category. Detecting any suppressive effect of punishment would be difficult if the dependent variable were already near zero (the floor of this measure) before the punishment contingency was introduced. Similarly, you will not be able to detect a facilitating effect of a treatment on behavior if the baseline starts at a value near its ceiling.

The solution to these problems is usually obtained by adjusting the experimental conditions to produce the desired baseline levels. In the punishment experiment, for example, you might increase the baseline response rates by reinforcing responses according to a variable interval schedule. You could then adjust the schedule to produce any desired level of responding. You would maintain the same schedule in the punishment condition. Thus, you could attribute any difference between these two conditions in the rate of responding to the effect of punishment contingency.

## QUESTIONS TO PONDER

1. What is a drifting baseline, and how can you deal with one?
2. What is an unrecoverable baseline, and what can you do if you have one?
3. What can you do if you have unequal baselines between subjects?
4. What can you do if you have an inappropriate baseline?

## Types of Single-Subject Baseline Design

As yet, no widely accepted nomenclature exists to describe the wide variety of single-subject designs, although a few descriptive terms have emerged. This section differentiates among designs that manipulate a single independent variable (single-factor designs), those that manipulate two or more independent variables (multifactor designs), those that measure several dependent variables (multiple-baseline designs), and those that systematically vary the criterion used to initiate a new phase (changing criterion designs).

*Single-Factor Designs*    We have focused attention thus far on the ABAB design, which offers a complete intrasubject replication of the baseline (A) and intervention (B) phases of an experiment. Although less common, AB and ABA designs are also used. The AB design presents only a single administration of each condition and thus lacks intrasubject replication. Confounding by time-related factors is a serious problem with this design. The ABA design includes a reversal phase in which baseline conditions are reestablished after exposure to the treatment. This baseline reassessment allows you to determine whether the observed changes in behavior after treatment introduction were caused by the treatment. However, it lacks the final return to the B phase and thus fails to establish the recoverability of the baseline in the intervention phase. AB designs may be necessary if the intervention phase produces irreversible changes or (in an applied setting) if it is desirable to continue a treatment once it has been initiated. ABA designs may be appropriate if it is desirable to return the subject to preexperimental conditions prior to the termination of the study.

These basic procedures can be extended to include multiple levels of the independent variable. As in group designs, if these levels represent quantitative differences, the design is said to be *parametric.*

Using multiple levels of the independent variable presents certain problems for single-subject designs. Because only one or a few subjects are tested, completely counterbalancing the order of treatments across subjects is not usually possible. Instead, each subject may be exposed to the treatments repeatedly in different orders to assess the degree of carryover.

As an example of this counterbalancing strategy, consider a parametric single-factor experiment in which the three levels of the independent variable are A, B, and C. A single subject might be exposed to these treatments in the following order: A, B, A, C, B, C. This order provides transitions between close values of the independent variable (A–B, B–C, C–B), as well as a transition between distant values (A–C). Additional subjects might be tested with different orders. (Note that this particular design imposes a single replication of each treatment and thus represents a logical extension of the ABAB design.)

Sometimes what starts out as an ABAB design may end up being extended and modified in the light of the initial findings. Kelly Therrien, David Wilder, Manuel Rodriguez, and Byron Wine (2005) ended up with an ABABC design in this way when conducting research in an applied setting. The study was carried out at one location of a sandwich restaurant chain to assess the effect of an intervention on the percentage of customers who were greeted by an employee within 3 seconds of entering the store. Therrien et al. (2005) defined a greeting as "any verbal acknowledgment given by an employee" (p. 412), (e.g., "Hello" and "What can I get you?"). Three or four employees were behind the service counter at all times.

The intervention consisted of having the manager behind the counter and a chime that rang each time the door opened. Data were collected by observers, posing as customers, who sat at a nearby table and surreptitiously recorded the percentage of customers who were greeted by an employee (other than the manager) within 3 seconds of entering the shop. Data were first collected during a baseline (A) phase in which the intervention was absent. After seven daily baseline sessions, the "manager + chime" intervention (B) phase was imposed. This continued for five sessions and was followed by a return to the baseline (A) phase. After a further six sessions in the baseline phase, the intervention (B) phase was imposed again. Because the level of performance during the intervention was not as high as desired, a final (C) phase was added that continued the intervention but added feedback to it. During this phase, immediately following each session, the manager graphed each employee's greeting performance and individually showed each employee the graph. The employee was praised if the new point was higher than the previous one (e.g., "You guys look great!") but said nothing otherwise.

Figure 12-5 shows the results averaged across employees. (Results were said to be similar for most individuals.) The data clearly show that the intervention was effective in raising the level of customer greeting and that this effect was reversible. The

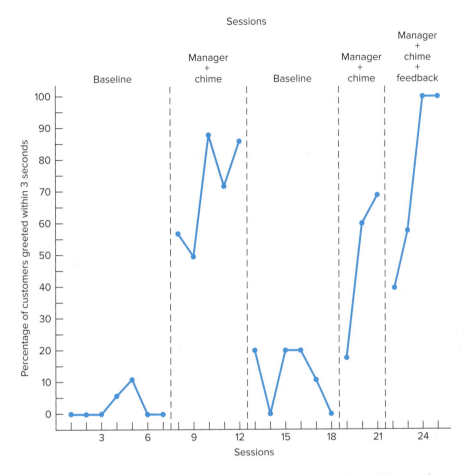

**FIGURE 12-5**   Results of the customer-greeting study for the baseline and intervention phases. The original ABAB design was extended by the addition of a final manager+ chime + feedback phase.

SOURCE: Therrian, K., Wilder, D. A., Rodriques, M, and Wine, B. (2005). Preintervention analysis and improvement of customer greeting in a restaurant. *Journal of Applied Behavior Analysis, 38,* 411–415.

addition of feedback seems to have brought about additional improvement, although the reliability of this effect was not assessed in the study through replication.

This applied study did not employ a stability criterion to determine when to move to the next phase. (As noted previously, often in real-world settings, factors such as time constraints limit the ability to impose such a criterion.) Even so, the effects of the interventions are clearly evident in the graphs.

If you must test a number of levels of your independent variable and are concerned about possible drift in your baseline, you may want to include a return to the baseline phase after each exposure to a treatment phase. One of us (Abbott) and Pietro Badia (1979) used this technique with rat subjects. As in the Badia and Culbertson

(1972) study, this experiment assessed the preference for signaled over unsignaled foot shocks. Signaled shocks were preceded by a warning tone whereas unsignaled shocks were not. Subjects could choose to receive signaled shocks by pressing a lever. Each response produced 1 minute on the signaled shock schedule, identified by illumination of a house light. At other times, unsignaled shocks were delivered.

The independent variable was the length of the signal, which was systematically varied across treatments from 0.5 second to 2.0 seconds (in half-second steps). Baseline response levels were collected during training phases, which also familiarized subjects with the signaled and unsignaled schedules prior to each test phase. Each training phase provided a given signal length and was followed by a test phase at the same length.

Figure 12-6 shows the results of the Abbott and Badia (1979) experiment. The dependent variable (percentage of time in changeover) reflects the number of minutes in the signaled condition "bought" by responses as a percentage of total session time.

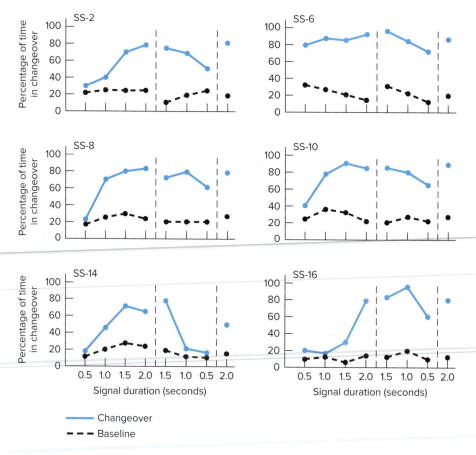

**FIGURE 12-6**    Results of an experiment in which baselines (the dashed lines) were repeatedly assessed. Each graph represents the performance of a single subject.
SOURCE: Abbott, B, and Badia, P. (2005). Choice for signaled over unsignaled shock as a function of signal length. *Journal of the Experimental Analysis of Behavior, 32,* 413.

During training, the responses actually had no effect, but the number of minutes that would have been bought by these responses served to provide the baseline. The average percentage of time in changeover is shown across the final three stable sessions in each condition during the baseline (the black line) and testing (the red line) phases as a function of signal length. Each graph represents the performance of a different subject.

The levels of changeover responding during testing were generally low during initial testing at a signal length of 0.5 second. These levels increased as the signals were lengthened across treatments until they reached nearly maximum values. When signals were then shortened, responding tended to decline. These changes were not caused simply by baseline drift. This is shown by the fact that the baselines collected during training phases remained relatively low throughout the experiment.

Also note the failure to recover the original levels of responding on return to the 0.5-second signal length in four of the subjects (all but SS-6 and SS-14). This indicates that carryover effects were present. Even so, the effect of signal length on changeover responding is clear. Shorter signals supported weaker responding than did longer signals.

*Multifactor Designs*    Single-subject designs can include more than one independent variable. As in factorial group designs, you can assess the main effects of independent variables and their interactions. Murray Sidman (1953) provided an example of this design during an investigation of responding on the free operant avoidance schedule that bears his name. The Sidman avoidance schedule delivers a brief shock at regular intervals (e.g., every 5 seconds) during the shock–shock (S–S) interval. A response, usually a lever press, terminates the S–S interval and starts another interval, the response–shock (R–S) interval. If the subject fails to respond during the R–S interval, a shock occurs and a new S–S interval begins. If the subject responds during the R–S interval, no shock is delivered, and the timer is reset to the beginning of the R–S interval. Thus, if the subject always responds during the R–S interval, all scheduled shocks can be avoided.

Sidman (1953) investigated the effect of varying the length of both the S–S and R–S intervals. Thus, this experiment had two factors: length of the S–S interval and length of the R–S interval. Rats were exposed to several levels of each independent variable in every combination.

Figure 12-7 shows the results from this two-factor single-subject experiment. The figure shows the rates of lever pressing generated under each combination of S–S and R–S intervals. The graph shows portions of each condition in which the stability criterion was met. As you can see, the number of responses per minute was affected by the lengths of both intervals.

Because the data from multifactor single-subject experiments are not submitted to a statistical analysis, omitting some cells of the factorial matrix presents no special analytical problems. If the functional relationships between independent and dependent variables follow regular patterns (as is usually the case), then it is possible to "sweep out" the functions. You can do this by providing data points at well-placed intervals rather than at every possible combination of levels. Each subject must be exposed to every combination of levels for which a point is required. Using less than the full factorial number of combinations can result in considerable savings in the time required to complete the experiment.

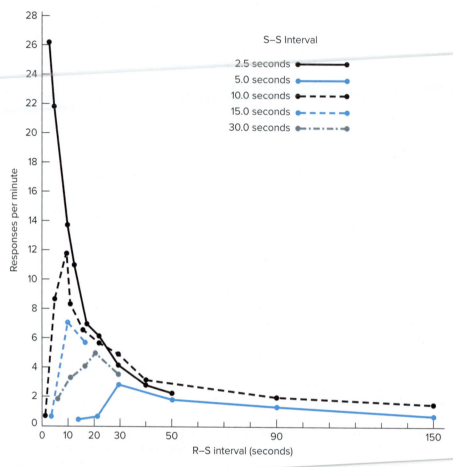

**FIGURE 12-7** Performance of a single subject in a two-factor design in which R–S and S–S intervals both were manipulated.

SOURCE: Sidman, Murray. Two temporal perimeters of the maintenance of avoidance behavior by the white rat. *Journal of Comparative and Physiological Psychology, 46,* 253–261.

*Multiple-Baseline Designs*    Some treatments cause irreversible changes in behavior, and a special approach is required to deal with this problem. **Multiple-baseline designs** provide one solution. These designs simultaneously sample several behaviors within the experimental context to provide multiple behavioral baselines.

As an example, imagine you have developed a new technique for eliminating undesirable habits. You expect the changes to be relatively permanent, so a reversal design is clearly inappropriate. You decide to use a multiple-baseline design.

To test your technique, you identify a few individuals who have at least two undesirable habits they wish to kick: smoking and excessive coffee drinking. You begin your study by simply observing and recording the frequencies of these two behaviors across a number of days to establish a baseline for each behavior. You then introduce

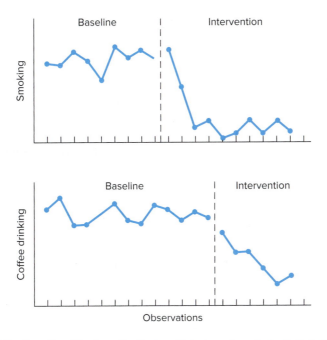

**FIGURE 12-8**   Results of the hypothetical multiple-baseline study. Both behaviors are collected simultaneously from a single subject.

your treatment but apply it to only *one* of the behaviors. For one subject, you choose to attack smoking and for the other, coffee drinking.

The treatment appears to be successful. The treated behavior soon declines to levels well below the baseline. At the same time, however, the untreated behavior remains at its previous baseline levels. When the treated behavior stabilizes, you begin to apply the treatment to the remaining behavior. This too, now declines to low levels.

Figure 12-8 shows the data collected from one participant in the hypothetical multiple-baseline study. Note that each behavior changes only after the treatment is introduced for that behavior.

The multiple-baseline design uses the untreated behavior as a partial control for time-correlated changes that may confound the effect of the independent variable. It is possible that the change in the treated behavior would have happened when it did even if the treatment had not been introduced. However, if this change was not caused by the treatment, the untreated behavior likely would have changed as well. In addition, the untreated behavior most likely would not subsequently change as soon as the treatment was applied to it.

For the multiple-baseline design to be effective, the behaviors chosen for observation should be relatively independent of one another. If the behaviors are correlated, then applying the treatment to one of the behaviors will affect both. Your ability to discriminate treatment-induced changes from changes induced by time-correlated confounding factors will be seriously hampered.

Debbie Westerlund, Elizabeth Granucci, Peter Gamache, and Hewitt Clark (2006) used the multiple-baseline design to assess the effectiveness of peer mentoring of four female cosmetology students afflicted with specific learning disabilities and/or severe emotional disturbances. For each student, the researchers identified two behaviors in need of intervention. Two students received peer mentoring for hair-roller setting (the proper steps followed, rollers correctly sized for the hairstyle, and hair properly distributed among the rollers, etc.) and for combing out (the proper steps followed, hair combed out properly for the hairstyle, etc.). The other two students received peer mentoring for comfort inquiry (asking the client such questions as "Is the water temperature comfortable?") and for suggestion statements about such things as hairstyling products and recommended haircuts.

The peer mentors assisted the students in ways designed to minimize embarrassing them. Such assistance included demonstrations, corrective feedback offered as suggestions, and verbal prompts delivered quietly or away from patrons. The mentors explained or modeled the behavior, allowed the student to demonstrate the behavior, and provided descriptive praise for portions of the behavior that were correctly demonstrated.

The multiple-baseline design was implemented in three phases. In the first, baseline phase, target behaviors were monitored, and their levels recorded over several sessions. In the second phase, the intervention commenced for one of the two target behaviors. Several sessions later, intervention commenced for the second target behavior.

Figure 12-9 shows the results for one of the students. (Similar results were obtained for the other three.) The graph shows the percentage of steps completed for roller setting and for combing out during the baseline and intervention sessions. As the figure indicates, the percentage of steps completed was low for both behaviors during the baseline phase. The intervention for roller setting commenced on session 5 and produced an immediate and substantial improvement in performance that continued over the remainder of the sessions. Meanwhile, the second behavior, combing out, continued to be performed poorly. On session 7, the intervention for combing out began, and this behavior too showed an immediate and substantial benefit. In each case, the improvement in a behavior began only after peer mentoring had commenced for that behavior, so it is unlikely that the timing of these changes is coincidental.

*Changing Criterion Design*    In therapeutic settings, it is sometimes desirable to set a criterion level of performance with respect to some target behavior. In a smoking-cessation program, for example, the ultimate goal is to smoke zero cigarettes per day. However, having a client attempt to quit "cold turkey" often leads to failure. In such cases, a gradual reduction in the number of cigarettes smoked per day may prove more effective. The **changing criterion design** was developed for such cases (Hartman & Hall, 1976). You begin with a baseline phase to assess the current level of the target behavior. Then, for the first intervention phase, you set an initial target criterion for the behavior, one that requires only a relatively small change. The intervention commences and continues until the criterion level of the behavior is achieved. You then adjust the criterion another small step toward the ultimate goal. You continue this process until the final goal is achieved.

A nice example of the changing criterion design was provided by Christopher Skinner, Amy Skinner, and Kevin Armstrong (2000), who used the changing criterion

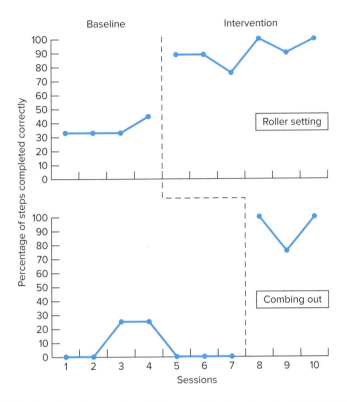

**FIGURE 12-9** Results of the peer-mentoring multiple-baseline study for one participant. Source: Westerlund, D., Granucci, E. A., Gamache, P., and Clark, H. B. (2006). Effects of peer mentors on work-related performance of adolescents with behavioral and/or learning disabilities. *Journal of Positive Behavior Interventions, 8,* 244–251.

design to increase the number of pages being read each day by a young adult man ("Kevin") diagnosed with schizophrenia. Although Kevin wanted to read, he found it difficult to sustain his concentration on the task and typically gave up before he had completed a single page. He therefore agreed to participate in a study that was designed to increase the number of pages read without interruption. During the study, Kevin read from books of his choosing.

The procedure began with a baseline phase that assessed his current level of uninterrupted reading, which, as previously noted, was less than one page. Next, Kevin was exposed to an intervention phase. The initial criterion was set to two pages, and Kevin was given one opportunity each day to earn a soft-drink reward for achieving this criterion. This phase continued until Kevin met or exceeded the criterion on three successive occasions. The criterion was then raised by one page and the procedure repeated using the new criterion until the new criterion was met. This process was repeated until Kevin decided to end his participation 8 weeks later. By this time, he was consistently reading six to eight pages at a time. Moreover, staff later observed that Kevin continued to read on his own.

Establishing the criteria to use in a changing criterion design requires a bit of judgment. The changes in successive criteria must be small enough that each new criterion has a good chance of being achieved, but large enough to discern reliable changes in the target behavior. If the behavior at criterion is highly stable, then even small changes will be visible. Changes will be harder to see if the behavior continues to vary a fair amount from data point to data point. In that case, the changes in criteria may need to be larger.

Sometimes, a subject will fail to achieve a new criterion. When this happens, it may become necessary to return to the previous value and then either make a second attempt at the failed value or try one that is closer to the current value.

## QUESTIONS TO PONDER

1. What are the characteristics of the single-factor baseline design?
2. What are the characteristics of the multifactor baseline design?
3. What is a multiple-baseline design, and when would you use one?
4. Describe the changing criterion design. When is it used?

## DYNAMIC DESIGNS

Although baseline designs afford the opportunity to examine moment-to-moment changes in behavior within each baseline or treatment phase, their primary use is to establish how behavior differs from one level of an independent variable to another in the steady state. Adaptation to new conditions may require time and experience; if so, behavior observed immediately after a switch from one treatment to another may not typify the stable pattern that may emerge after more extensive exposure. For this reason, subjects are kept under each treatment condition until behavior shows no sign of further systematic change.

This emphasis on steady-state behavior fosters the use of designs in which independent variables are manipulated in discrete levels even when the variable itself is continuous. For example, the key-pecking behavior of pigeons may be examined at several widely separated levels of food deprivation (e.g., 80%, 90%, and 100% of free-feeding body weight). Subjects are maintained at each level of deprivation until their behavior stabilizes and then are moved to the next level. In such designs, behavior immediately following the change in level (described as *transitional* to distinguish it from steady-state behavior) can be observed to determine what has been called *behavioral dynamics*—regular patterns of behavioral change over time. A nice example of this approach is provided by William Palya, Don Walter, Robert Kessel, and Robert Lucke (1996), who investigated behavioral dynamics following an unsignaled step transition from variable-interval reinforcement to extinction in pigeons. To emphasize the regularities in these dynamics, the curves relating response rate to time following the transition were averaged across repeated transitions (but not across subjects). Figure 12-10 depicts the reinforcement rates and response rates as functions of time (in seconds) for four birds. The step transition to extinction occurs at 200 seconds in each graph. Each bird showed a rapid decrease in response rate, which began within seconds of the transition.

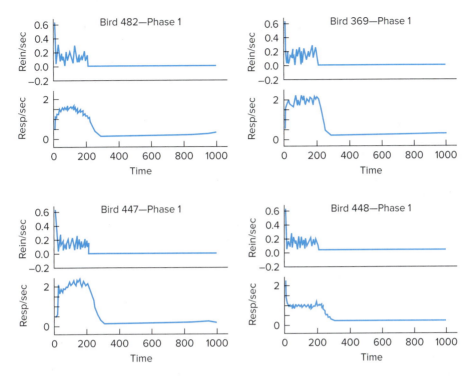

**FIGURE 12-10** Step-transition data from four pigeons.

SOURCE: Palya, W. L., Walter, D., Kessel, R., and Lucke, R. (1996). Investigating behavioral dynamics with a fixed-time extinction schedule and linear analysis. *Journal of the Experimental Analysis of Behavior, 66,* 391–409.

Step changes in the level of the independent variable may reveal interesting regularities in transitional behavior, but it may be at least as informative to record behavior during *continuous variation* of the independent variable as long as (1) the rate of variation is not so fast that the behavioral changes cannot "keep up" and (2) the changes are more or less reversible. Such a design lacks the discrete values of the independent variable that serve to distinguish the baseline and intervention phases of the baseline design, so, strictly speaking, it may not be appropriate to refer to studies using continuous independent variable variation as baseline designs. For this reason, we have chosen to identify designs that employ a continuously varying independent variable as **dynamic designs**.

A typical dynamic design was used in a "compensatory tracking" experiment described by William T. Powers (1978). An individual participant was given the task of keeping a cursor (a short, vertical line) aligned with a target (another short, vertical line), simultaneously presented on a computer screen. Although the target remained fixed in position on the screen, the cursor could be moved left and right by manipulating a joystick. However, an invisible force or "disturbance" seemed to be acting on the cursor, causing it to drift erratically left and right on its own. To keep the cursor on the target, the participant had to compensate for the cursor's drift by moving the joystick.

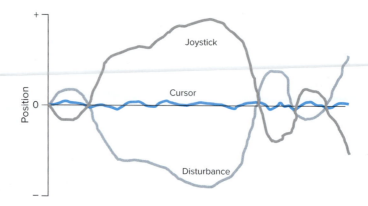

**FIGURE 12-11**    Continuous data from a dynamic design. The participant moved a joystick to keep a cursor horizontally aligned with a target mark at position zero over a period of 60 seconds (see text). Horizontal scale indicates time; vertical scale indicates vertical distances from target mark.

SOURCE: Powers, W. T. (1978). Quantitative analysis of purposive systems: Some spadework at the foundations of scientific psychology. *Psychological Review, 85*, 417–435.

The independent variable in this experiment was the disturbance, which varied smoothly and continuously in size and direction over a programmed range of values. The continuously monitored dependent variable was the position of the joystick. Together with the target position, these values were used to compute the moment-by-moment position of the cursor and the error (difference between target and cursor positions).

Figure 12-11 shows the data from one 60-second experimental run. One line shows the variation in the disturbance (independent variable) over the course of the run. The second line shows the position of the joystick, scaled to screen coordinates. Notice how this line is almost a mirror image of the first. As the cursor moved in one direction, the participant had to move the joystick in the opposite direction to cancel out the cursor's movement and keep it over the target. The third line (which varies over a much smaller range than the other two) shows the position of the cursor relative to the target. The fact that cursor excursions were generally small shows that the participant was highly successful in keeping the cursor near the target. The data from such experimental runs were used to evaluate a mathematical model (derived from control theory) that used the moment-by-moment disturbance values to predict the participant's joystick movements. The joystick positions predicted by the model matched the observed positions almost perfectly.

Although we have distinguished between baseline and dynamic designs, it is important to understand the close relation between the two types. The Palya et al. (1996) design described earlier can be thought of as a baseline design involving discrete values of the independent variable. However, it also could be viewed as a dynamic design in which the independent variable changes as a step function, swinging instantly between extreme values. More important than the label you choose to describe the design is the kind of information the study was designed to collect. In the Palya et al. study, the focus was on the dynamics of behavioral change.

The method of continuously varying the independent variable while observing continuous, dynamic changes in the dependent variable has been used infrequently in the behavioral sciences but should become more common as interest in behavioral dynamics increases. In May 1992, the *Journal of the Experimental Analysis of Behavior* devoted an entire issue to the topic of behavioral dynamics. There you can find a number of examples of this continuous approach to single-subject research.

## DISCRETE TRIALS DESIGNS

Although baseline and dynamic designs can be powerful tools for discovering causal relationships in the single subject, they will not work in every experimental situation. Imagine, for example, that you are interested in studying the ability of an air traffic controller to detect a radar signal representing a single airplane in trouble (the "signal") against a radar screen full of radar signals from other airplanes (the "noise"). In one condition of your experiment, you present the target radar "blip" embedded within other radar blips ("signal + noise," in signal-detection theory terms). In the second condition, the target blip is absent (only the other radar blips are present—"noise only"). After each trial, your participant indicates whether the target blip was present on the radar screen.

Using the baseline approach, you should first expose all your participants to a series of signal + noise trials. After every 50 trials, you calculate the number of yes responses and plot these numbers to provide the behavioral baseline. You then continue the signal + noise treatment until the baseline stabilizes and then switch over to the noise-only treatment. Can you see any problem with this design?

If you said yes, you're right! During the signal + noise treatment, your participant would soon begin to suspect that the target radar blip (the signal) was present on every trial. Before long you would discover that your baseline had jumped to 100% yes responses and would stay there, inducing a ceiling effect. The baseline would not provide a true reflection of your participant's ability to detect the target blip because on many of the trials the participant would respond yes simply out of habit and not because the signal had actually been detected.

In such cases, the baseline approach must be abandoned in favor of a design that will discourage the participant from establishing a response set, as was the case in the previous example. Fortunately, such a design exists: the **discrete trials design**. Like baseline designs, discrete trials designs focus on the behavior of the individual participant (e.g., your air traffic controller) rather than on group behavior.

### Characteristics of the Discrete Trials Design

Both the baseline and discrete trials designs seek to rigidly control extraneous sources of variance, to make the effect of the independent variable readily visible. Unlike the baseline design, however, the discrete trials design does not produce a continuous within-treatment baseline that can be adjusted and fine-tuned. Instead, behavior measured over a series of discrete trials must be averaged to provide relatively stable indices of behavior under the various treatment conditions. The major characteristics of the discrete trials design are shown in Table 12-2.

---

**TABLE 12-2    Characteristics of the Discrete Trials Design**

1. Individual subjects receive each treatment condition of the experiment dozens (perhaps hundreds) of times. Each exposure to a treatment, or trial, produces one data point for each dependent variable measured.

2. Extraneous variables that might introduce unwanted variability in the dependent variable are tightly controlled.

3. If feasible, the order of presenting the treatments is randomized or counter-balanced to control order effects.

4. The behavior of individual subjects undergoing the same treatment may be compared to provide intersubject replication.

---

The single-subject designs commonly used in experimental psychology prior to the 1920s were generally discrete trials. They continue in use today, especially in psychophysics (which studies the relationship between physical stimuli and the sensations they generate), as well as in some areas of human judgment and decision making.

An example of such a design is provided by a classic experiment on signal detection reported by Wilson Tanner, John Swets, and David Green (1956). The problem in signal detection is to determine how good a given observer is at detecting a signal that may be almost buried in noise. This is traditionally indexed by the observer's "hit rate," which is the proportion of trials on which the observer reported detecting the signal when the signal was actually present. However, the hit rate is affected by more than the observer's ability to separate the signal from the noise. It also is determined by the observer's *response bias,* or willingness to decide that a signal was present when he or she is uncertain about that. Observers with a "liberal" response bias will tend to guess yes whereas those with a "conservative" response bias will tend to guess no. Guessing yes increases the hit rate, so, everything else being equal, those with a liberal response bias will *seem* to be better at detecting the signal than those with a conservative response bias. Thus, in traditional experiments, the ability to detect the signal is confounded by response bias.

The Tanner et al. (1956) experiment was designed to eliminate this confound by separately measuring the observer's response bias and ability to detect the signal. Part of the strategy involved measuring not only the hit rate but also the "false-alarm" rate. This is the proportion of trials on which the observer reported detecting the signal when it was *not* actually present. Guessing yes when uncertain not only increases the hit rate (on trials when the signal was present) but also increases the false-alarm rate (on trials when the signal was not present).

In the experiment, two participants were exposed to a series of trials in which an auditory signal was either present or absent against a background of noise. On each trial, the participants were required to respond yes if they thought they heard the signal and no if they did not.

The participants' response biases were manipulated by systematically varying the probability of the signal being present on a trial. When the probability was low, participants would most often be right when guessing if they guessed no and therefore adopted a conservative response bias. When the probability was high, participants

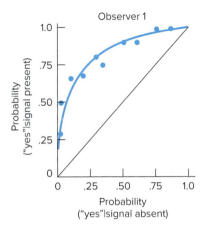
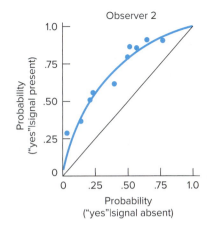

**FIGURE 12-12** Results for two observers in a signal-detection study.
SOURCE: Tanner, Swets, and Green, 1956.

would most often be right when guessing if they guessed yes and therefore adopted a liberal response bias. In the experiment, the probability of signal presentation was systematically varied across days from 0.1 (1 out of 10 trials) to 0.9 (9 out of 10 trials). Participants received 300 trials per day and spent 2 days at each probability level.

Figure 12-12 shows the results for each participant. The figure depicts the hit rate (probability of saying yes when the signal was present) plotted against the false-alarm rate (probability of saying yes when the signal was absent). The diagonal line represents the points at which hits equal false alarms, a situation that indicates no ability to detect the signal. Points falling above the diagonal indicate cases in which the hit rate exceeded the false-alarm rate and thus demonstrate some ability to detect the signal above the noise. All points falling along the same curve indicate the same sensitivity to the signal, and curves lying farther above the diagonal indicate greater sensitivity than those lying closer to the diagonal. The position of a point along a given curve indicates the response bias, ranging from conservative (closer to the lower left) to liberal (closer to the upper right).

## Analysis of Data from Discrete Trials Designs

Analysis of data from discrete trials single-subject experiments usually begins by averaging the responses across the repeated presentations of a particular treatment. A large number of presentations helps ensure that the resulting mean provides a stable and representative estimate of the population mean (i.e., of the mean that would be obtained if an infinite number of trials could be given to the same subject under the treatment conditions). The means obtained from the different treatment conditions may then be compared to determine whether they appear to differ. This comparison may or may not include assessment through inferential statistics to determine whether the observed differences are reliable.

The analysis applied to the data of discrete trials single-subject experiments is usually determined by a theory or model of the behavior being examined. For example, in the area of human judgment and decision making, a lens model analysis has often been applied to data collected from single subjects. Another example is the theory of signal detectability that provided the analytical model for the signal-detection experiment previously described. Often these analyses yield a small number of descriptive statistics, such as the $d'$ (a measure of sensitivity) and $\beta$ (a measure of response bias) in signal detection. If a relatively large number of subjects have been tested, these descriptive measures (although derived from a single-subject analysis) may be used as data for a between-subjects analysis.

Used in this way, inferential statistics are not applied to analyze the data of an individual subject but groups of subjects. Some investigators have argued for the application of inferential statistics to single-subject data (see Kazdin, 1976).

## INFERENTIAL STATISTICS AND SINGLE-SUBJECT DESIGNS

Those who advocate applying inferential statistics to data from single-subject designs would not want to use them as a substitute for control over variables and replication. However, they argue that in some cases, the desired level of control is difficult to achieve (e.g., in some clinical situations). For these cases they suggest that inferential statistics may provide a solution.

If you choose to take this route, be aware that the usual statistical procedures developed for group designs cannot be applied to data from single-subject designs without modification, and even then problems may exist (Kazdin, 1976).

The most straightforward approach is to use the multiple observations taken within a treatment to provide an estimate of uncontrolled error variance (in group designs, this estimate is provided by within-treatment observations of multiple subjects). This estimate is then compared with the variance of scores between treatments to give an estimate of the probability that the treatment deviations were the product of chance (Chassan, 1967).

Unfortunately, this approach is upset by the serial dependency across data points. That is, scores from adjacent observations within a treatment are more likely to be similar to each other than to scores from more widely separated observations. This is similar to the problem of correlated scores that appears in within-subjects designs (see Chapter 10). For reasons not discussed here, it is a more serious problem for single-subject designs. Several ways to deal with serial dependency have been proposed, but none is entirely satisfactory. In fact, Manolov, Solanas, Bulté, & Onghena (2010) state that "[h]ow to analyze single-subject data is a question yet to be answered" (p. 191). These authors found in a study of simulated data from ABAB designs that randomization test results were distorted by the presence of autocorrelation (a measure of serial dependency) and strongly affected by the relative lengths of the four phases. For a discussion of the general problem and a review and assessment of options available at the time, see Kazdin (1976, 1978). See Manolov et al. (2010) for a more contemporary discussion of these issues.

## ADVANTAGES AND DISADVANTAGES OF THE SINGLE-SUBJECT APPROACH

A design that affords advantages in one arena often carries disadvantages in another. In this section, we explore some of the major advantages and disadvantages of the single-subject approach.

The main advantage of the single-subject approach is its focus on controlling error variance. By focusing on behavior of individual subjects (as opposed to looking at group means), you may better identify potential sources of error and control them. On a related note, focusing on individual subjects may lead to a truer estimation of the impact of the independent variable. Individual patterns of behavior often reveal nuances obscured by averaging used in the group approach. (This issue is discussed again in more detail in Chapter 13.)

Single-subject designs in general (and baseline designs in particular) require that a single subject's behavior be followed over a relatively large number of observations. A perhaps extreme example was provided by an experiment conducted by one of the authors of this text (Abbott) in which the same rat subjects were tested in various conditions of the experiment for more than a year. This experiment included two independent variables. Each assessment phase was preceded by a training phase in which baselines were established. About nine days, on the average, were required to reach the stability criterion for the behavior, and each phase had to be replicated.

Of course, not many single-subject designs require this much time to test a subject, but most do require much more time than the equivalent group design would. This intensive investigation of the behavior of a single subject is both a strength and a weakness of the single-subject approach. It is a strength in that the long observational period often reveals nuances of behavior that might be missed in a short-term design. The ability to adjust and fine-tune the baseline over time provides an extended opportunity to identify previously unsuspected important variables. The intensive investigation is a weakness in that the strategy commits the investigator to a relatively long-term project that may be disrupted by uncontrolled factors such as illness or breakdowns of equipment.

On the bright side, even the breakdown of equipment can sometimes lead to new discoveries. Sidman (1960) documents how a sticking relay in his operant conditioning equipment resulted in the accidental delivery of unavoidable shocks to a rat that had been successfully responding to an avoidance schedule. The baseline of responding had been stable, but now began to climb to high rates. The finding was unexpected and generated a whole new direction of research.

Another advantage of single-subject designs is the fact that causal relationships can be established by using even just one subject. This is particularly important in clinical settings in which the objective of the research may be to identify an effective treatment for the behavioral disorder of a specific client. When more than one subject is used, the single-subject design permits the investigator to compare individual responses to the independent variable. Each subject may be found to exhibit reliable yet idiosyncratic responses to the same variable. Comparing subject-related variables may then suggest which differences between the subjects might be responsible for the differential responses. A design with only one subject may provide a good demonstration that a variable has an effect on behavior. However, to elevate the demonstration to the status of a general finding, the results should be replicated with additional subjects.

A disadvantage of single-subject designs is that the design is inappropriate for many research applications. For example, potential carryover effects may confound the effects of the independent variable. If carryover effects are severe enough to cause irreversible changes, then the single-subject approach may have to be abandoned in favor of the between-subjects approach. In addition, some research questions simply do not lend themselves to a single-subject design. Much of the research in social and developmental psychology could not be run as single-subject designs.

Moreover, the results from single-subject designs sometimes are of limited generality. By tightly controlling the experimental situation to reduce error variance, you may be creating a highly artificial environment within which the behavior of interest is observed. For example, if you study the effects of positive reinforcement on the behavior of autistic children in a tightly controlled laboratory, you cannot be sure that your results will apply to autistic children in a hospital setting. In short, tight experimental control of extraneous variables increases internal validity. However, remember that when you increase internal validity, you often reduce external validity.

A final disadvantage of the single-subject approach is that, despite all attempts to control extraneous variables, some variables cannot be easily controlled. Subject variables such as personality and intelligence cannot be controlled by tight experimental design. In research in which a homogeneous strain of rats serves as the subject population, this problem may not be important. However, when you apply single-subject research design to humans (such as in a clinical setting), extraneous variables may come into play, and there is no easy way to eliminate their effects. The only option may be to measure those variables and statistically control their effects.

Consider single-subject research as an alternative to group-based research when appropriate. You should not try to fit every research question into a single-subject design. However, keep this option open when your research question could be best answered with a single-subject approach. Finally, even if you use a group design, you can apply some of the logic of the single-subject approach. Do not ignore individual subject behavior and look only at average performance. In many cases, looking at the scores of individual subjects within your experiment can help you to interpret your data.

## QUESTIONS TO PONDER

1. What are the characteristics of a dynamic design?
2. What are the major characteristics of the discrete trials design?
3. How are inferential statistics used in single-subject designs?
4. What are the advantages and disadvantages of the single-subject approach?

## SUMMARY

Single-subject (or small-$n$) designs allow you to establish causal relationships among independent and dependent variables while focusing on the behavior of one or a few subjects. These designs work by collecting large numbers of observations of a subject's behavior within each treatment condition, rigidly controlling extraneous variables that might contribute to unwanted variability in the dependent measure, focusing primarily on relatively powerful independent variables whose effects (given the small amount of uncontrolled variation in the dependent measure) are easily detected by inspecting graphs, and repeating each treatment condition to establish reliability through intrasubject replication.

Single-subject designs dominated psychological research prior to the 1920s but were overshadowed by group-based designs following the development of inferential statistics. Experiments based on single-subject designs were difficult to publish in the past, but today the single-subject approach has regained wide acceptance. This acceptance has arisen especially in applied areas such as clinical psychology in which the primary interest is in assessing the effectiveness of therapeutic procedures on individual clients.

Single-subject designs fall into three broad categories: baseline designs, dynamic designs, and discrete trials designs. Baseline designs repeatedly record the subject's score on the dependent measure within each treatment exposure to plot a baseline for the behavior. Steps are taken to identify and control extraneous variables so that the variability and drift of the baseline are reduced to the minimum level. Usually the baseline must meet a stability criterion before the next treatment condition can be introduced. Each treatment is repeated at least once (intrasubject replication) to determine the reliability of the findings. If more than one subject is tested (intersubject replication), comparison across subjects is performed to establish the generality of results. Generality and reliability are also assessed through systematic replication. This replication examines the same independent and dependent variables under conditions somewhat different from those of the original experiment (for example, different species of subject or different reinforcer).

Baseline designs include single-factor designs (which include one independent variable), multifactor designs (two or more independent variables), and multiple-baseline designs (more than one dependent variable). Single-factor designs commonly follow an AB, ABA, or ABAB format. The AB type evaluates behavior during a baseline (A) condition and then in a treatment (B) condition. The lack of intrasubject replication makes this design subject to confounding by time-related factors and therefore undesirable. The ABA design controls time-related factors by adding a second baseline evaluation after the treatment evaluation. The ABAB design provides a complete intrasubject replication of the experiment. The ABAB design is preferable to the ABA design, especially if it would be unethical to end the experiment after returning the subject's behavior to an undesirable state in the second baseline evaluation. The ABAB design format can be extended for multilevel variables. When such variables are quantitative, the design is said to be parametric.

Multifactor baseline designs require that different combinations of the independent variables be tested across the study. A factorial design may be used (in which every combination is evaluated) or specific combinations of interest may be tested. In either case, each treatment is evaluated at least twice to provide intrasubject replication. These designs can become extremely time consuming to conduct if the number of variable combinations to be tested is large.

Multiple-baseline designs provide a partial solution to the problem of irreversible treatment effects. Different behaviors are observed, and a baseline established for each. The treatment is then introduced separately for each behavior in staggered fashion across time. The treatment is judged effective if the level of each behavior changes only after the treatment is applied to it. The multiple-baseline approach requires that each behavior be relatively independent of the others.

Changing criteria designs impose a criterion of performance that must be reached before the next phase can begin. Subsequent phases change the criterion by small amounts to gradually move performance toward an ultimate target level. This approach is used when behavior must be shaped gradually toward its final level.

Dynamic designs are similar to baseline designs but employ a continuously vary-ing independent variable. The behavior of interest is monitored continuously to deter-mine the dynamic response of the behavioral system to the ongoing changes in the independent variable. Such designs focus more on transitions of behavior as opposed to the steady state.

Discrete trials designs expose subjects to a series of trials, with each trial providing one exposure to a given treatment and yielding one score for each dependent measure. Each treatment is repeated a large number of times to provide stability to the treatment means. These designs are used in areas such as psychophysics, human judgment, and decision making, in which the interest focuses on the perceptual or decision-making abilities of individuals. Such designs often follow from a theoretical analysis of the behavior and yield descriptive statistics that are then evaluated in light of the theory. If a relatively large number of subjects are thus tested, the summary statistics from each subject may provide the data for a group-based inferential statistical analysis.

Some interest has been expressed in developing inferential statistics that can be applied to single-subject data. These statistics would be employed when the data can-not be stabilized or the independent variables are too weak to produce results that can be visually analyzed. A problem with such analyses is the serial dependency (or cor-relation) between successive observations of a single subject. Serial dependency seri-ously biases the traditional statistical tests (such as the $t$ test or analysis of variance). Despite attempts to deal with serial dependency, the various proposed solutions are controversial and not yet widely accepted.

Single-subject designs have both advantages and disadvantages. Advantages include the ability to obtain functional relationships that apply to a single subject, the avoidance of artifacts that may emerge in group studies because of averaging data across subjects with differing behaviors, the potential identification of new important variables while attempting to stabilize baselines, and the ability to conduct experi-ments with an extremely limited number of available subjects. Disadvantages include the length of time required to test each subject through all the conditions of the experi-ment (increasing the possibility of subject loss because of attrition or equipment fail-ure), the inability to detect the effects of weak variables when behavior is not well controlled, the difficulty in assessing the effects of variables that cause irreversible changes, and possibly limited external validity.

## KEY TERMS

| | |
|---|---|
| baseline design | intersubject replication |
| behavioral baseline | systematic replication |
| stability criterion | direct replication |
| baseline phase | multiple-baseline design |
| intervention phase | changing criterion design |
| ABAB design | dynamic design |
| intrasubject replication | discrete trials design |
| reversal strategy | |

## CHAPTER 13

# Describing Data

Once you have conducted your research, the next step is to organize, summarize, and describe your data. This chapter reviews strategies that you can use to effectively organize, summarize, and describe data. The sections on descriptive statistics are intended to provide a brief review of these statistics. Computation is addressed in this chapter only where necessary to explain a particular statistic. If you need more information on these statistics, see one of the many introductory statistics texts available (such as Gravetter & Wallnau, 2017, or Pagano, 2013).

## DESCRIPTIVE STATISTICS AND EXPLORATORY DATA ANALYSIS

**Descriptive statistics** allow you to summarize the properties of an entire distribution of scores with just a few numbers. Although descriptive statistics are commonly used to address the specific questions that you had in mind when you designed your study, they also can be employed to help you discover important but perhaps hidden patterns in your data that may shed additional light on the problems you are interested in resolving. The search for such patterns in your data is termed **exploratory data analysis (EDA)**. Over the past 50 years or so, a whole new set of descriptive tools has been developed to aid you in this search, many of which are graphical in nature.

When research has been designed to answer a specific question or set of questions, there is a strong temptation to rush directly to the inferential statistical techniques that will assess the "statistical significance" of the findings and to request only those descriptive statistics related directly to the analysis, such as group means, standard deviations, and standard errors. Resist this temptation. As we explain in Chapter 14, many of the most commonly used inferential statistics make certain crucial assumptions about the populations from which the scores in your data set were drawn. If these assumptions are violated, the results of the statistical analysis may be misleading.

Some exploratory techniques help you spot serious defects in your data that may warrant taking corrective action before you proceed to the inferential analysis. Others help you determine which summary statistics would be appropriate for a given set of data. Still others may reveal unsuspected influences. In this chapter, we introduce you to a number of descriptive tools (both numerical and graphical) for describing data and revealing secrets that hide within.

## ORGANIZING YOUR DATA

Before you can interpret your data, you must first organize and summarize them. How you organize your data depends on your research design (whether you have conducted a survey, observational study, or experiment), how many variables were observed and recorded, and how observations were grouped or subdivided. A few representative examples follow.

For *survey data,* a data summary sheet like that shown in Figure 13-1 would be appropriate. The data are organized into a series of columns, one for numbering the respondents, one for each question asked, and one for each demographic item. To save space, the identifiers over the columns should be kept short. Here, we have simply labeled each question Q1, Q2, and so on. If space permits, you may invent more descriptive labels. Each row gives the data for one respondent. In the example, certain demographic variables have been dummy-coded. **Dummy codes** identify category values as numbers (e.g., sex of respondent: 1 = female, 2 = male). By using dummy codes, you simplify data entry (e.g., you enter a "1" instead of "female").

Data sheets like the one shown in Figure 13-1 can go on for pages. A good strategy is to lay out your first data sheet and, before entering any data, copy it. In this way you avoid having to enter the column and row labels by hand on each new page. In addition,

| Resp. | Q1 | Q2 | Q3 | Q4 | Q5 | Sex | Age | Marit. | Time |
|---|---|---|---|---|---|---|---|---|---|
| 1 | 3 | 4 | 4 | 4 | 2 | 2 | 25 | 2 | 1 |
| 2 | 4 | 3 | 5 | 5 | 2 | 1 | 20 | 2 | 3 |
| 3 | 3 | 3 | 4 | 4 | 3 | 1 | * | 1 | 1 |
| 4 | 1 | 4 | 4 | 4 | 2 | 2 | 22 | 2 | 1 |
| 5 | 3 | 4 | 4 | 4 | 2 | 2 | 29 | 1 | 3 |
| 6 | 3 | 3 | 4 | 4 | 3 | 1 | 19 | 2 | 1 |
| 7 | 2 | 4 | 3 | 4 | 1 | 2 | 19 | 2 | 1 |
| 8 | 2 | 4 | 4 | 5 | 4 | 2 | 25 | 2 | 3 |
| 9 | 2 | 3 | 3 | 3 | 3 | 1 | 21 | 2 | 1 |
| 10 | 2 | 3 | 2 | 3 | 3 | 2 | 20 | 2 | 1 |
| 11 | 4 | 3 | 4 | 4 | 3 | 2 | 18 | 2 | 3 |
| 33 | 2 | 4 | 3 | 4 | 2 | 1 | 24 | 1 | 1 |
| 34 | 2 | 3 | 2 | 4 | 3 | 1 | 24 | 2 | 1 |
| 35 | 1 | 2 | 4 | 4 | 4 | 2 | 31 | 3 | 2 |
| 36 | 2 | 4 | 5 | 5 | 3 | 1 | 26 | 2 | 3 |

**FIGURE 13-1**    Example data summary sheet for survey data (* = missing data).

you should make out a single "key" or "code sheet" that describes the scale(s) used for the questions, gives a fuller description of the question or variable in each column, and indicates what each dummy code represents. Figure 13-2 shows the code sheet that accompanies the data sheet shown in Figure 13-1. The code sheet shows the Likert-scale codes used in conjunction with each attitude item, the five attitude statements, the three demographic items, and the dummy codes used to represent the category values of sex, marital status, and time of class attendance. It is worth noting that if you use a commercial survey program (e.g., Qualtrics), you can set up your codes beforehand in the program and the data will be automatically entered into your data sheet as they come in.

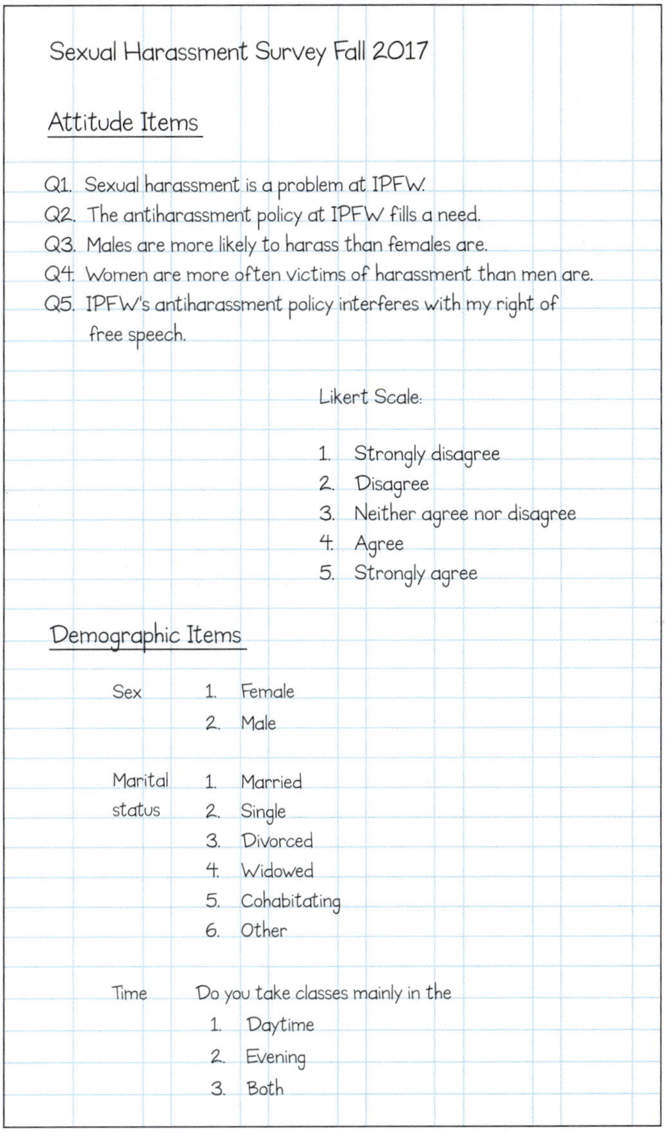

Sexual Harassment Survey Fall 2017

Attitude Items

Q1. Sexual harassment is a problem at IPFW.
Q2. The antiharassment policy at IPFW fills a need.
Q3. Males are more likely to harass than females are.
Q4. Women are more often victims of harassment than men are.
Q5. IPFW's antiharassment policy interferes with my right of
    free speech.

Likert Scale:

1.  Strongly disagree
2.  Disagree
3.  Neither agree nor disagree
4.  Agree
5.  Strongly agree

Demographic Items

Sex           1.  Female
              2.  Male

Marital       1.  Married
status        2.  Single
              3.  Divorced
              4.  Widowed
              5.  Cohabitating
              6.  Other

Time          Do you take classes mainly in the
              1.  Daytime
              2.  Evening
              3.  Both

**FIGURE 13-2**  Code sheet for the data summary sheet of Figure 13-1.

| Subject number | Words/3 sec | Words/18 sec | CCCs/3 sec | CCCs/18 sec |
|---|---|---|---|---|
| 1 | 19 | 19 | 16 | 16 |
| 2 | 18 | 17 | 16 | 06 |
| 3 | 19 | 14 | 20 | 14 |
| 4 | 19 | 16 | 15 | 14 |
| 5 | 19 | 15 | 19 | 13 |
| 6 | 19 | 17 | 13 | 07 |
| 7 | 20 | 20 | 18 | 13 |
| 8 | 19 | 19 | 14 | 06 |
| 9 | 20 | 19 | 17 | 14 |
| 10 | 18 | 13 | 05 | 02 |
| 11 | 19 | 16 | 14 | 11 |
| 12 | 18 | 17 | 08 | 02 |
| 13 | 18 | 13 | 11 | 00 |
| 14 | 16 | 06 | 11 | 03 |
| 31 | 19 | 19 | 14 | 08 |
| 32 | 20 | 17 | 19 | 17 |
| 33 | 19 | 14 | 07 | 00 |
| 34 | 20 | 14 | 16 | 10 |

**FIGURE 13-3** Data summary sheet for a 2 × 2 within-subjects factorial experiment presented in an unstacked format.

| Subject number | Item type (1 = word, 2 = ccc) | Retention interval (1 = 3s, 2 = 18s) | Number correct |
|---|---|---|---|
| 1 | 1 | 1 | 19 |
| 1 | 1 | 2 | 19 |
| 1 | 2 | 1 | 16 |
| 1 | 2 | 2 | 16 |
| 2 | 1 | 1 | 18 |
| 2 | 1 | 2 | 17 |
| 2 | 2 | 1 | 16 |
| 2 | 2 | 2 | 06 |
| 3 | 1 | 1 | 19 |
| 3 | 1 | 2 | 14 |
| 3 | 2 | 1 | 20 |
| 3 | 2 | 2 | 14 |
| 34 | 1 | 1 | 20 |
| 34 | 1 | 2 | 14 |
| 34 | 2 | 1 | 16 |
| 34 | 2 | 2 | 10 |

**FIGURE 13-4** Data summary sheet for the same data as shown in Figure 13-3, presented in stacked format.

Experimental or quasi-experimental designs break down the dependent variable according to treatments or categories. You can organize data from these designs in two distinct ways. One way (called an *unstacked format*) is to create a separate column for the scores from each treatment. Figure 13-3 shows a simple summary sheet organized in this way for a 2 × 2 within-subjects factorial experiment. The subject numbers appear in the leftmost column. Because each subject was exposed to all the treatments, only one column of subject numbers was needed. Reserve space at the bottom of the data summary sheet for column summary statistics such as the mean and standard deviation. You can enter these after you have analyzed the data.

The second way to organize your data is to use a *stacked format*. In this format, you create one column for the participant IDs, a column for the treatment levels (dummy-coded), and a column for each dependent variable. Figure 13-4 redisplays a portion of the data of Figure 13-3 in this way. The stacked format works better than the unstacked format when your data include multiple independent or dependent variables. These are easily accommodated by including additional columns to indicate the treatment levels or observed values of the additional variables. Also, many computer statistical analysis packages expect the data to be entered in this format. A disadvantage of the stacked format is that, unlike the unstacked format, it does not provide a simple way to display treatment summary statistics.

More complex designs involving several independent and/or quasi-independent variables can be accommodated within either format. Figure 13-5 displays data in unstacked format from individual subjects for a 2 × 4 between-subjects design in a study by Bordens and Horowitz (1986) on the effects of joining multiple criminal offenses in a single trial (a procedure known as "joinder of offenses"). Each column provides the data from one treatment. In this two-factor between-subjects design, each treatment represented one level of "Charges judged" (the first independent variable) combined with one of the four levels of "Charges filed" (the second independent variable). The bottom two rows display summary measures (the mean and standard deviation) for each treatment.

A useful data summary sheet must be clearly labeled. Note that the columns of data in Figure 13-5 are clearly labeled with the levels of the independent variable in effect for each group. The top headings indicate the two levels of charges judged. The second level of headings indicates the level of charges filed as appropriate to each group.

| | Charges judged | | | | | | | |
| | One charge | | | | Two charges | | | |
| Charges filed | 1 | 2 | 3 | 4 | 1 | 2 | 3 | 4 |
|---|---|---|---|---|---|---|---|---|
| | 3 | 5 | 6 | 2 | 6 | 3 | 4 | 5 |
| | 3 | 4 | 3 | 4 | 4 | 5 | 6 | 5 |
| | 3 | 4 | 4 | 5 | 4 | 5 | 4 | 5 |
| | 4 | 4 | 4 | 5 | 5 | 5 | 5 | 6 |
| | 4 | 5 | 5 | 5 | 4 | 4 | 5 | 5 |
| | 3 | 3 | 5 | 5 | 5 | 5 | 4 | 4 |
| | 2 | 3 | 4 | 5 | 5 | 4 | 4 | 5 |
| | 5 | 4 | 5 | 4 | 3 | 5 | 5 | 5 |
| | 6 | 4 | 3 | 6 | 3 | 5 | 5 | 6 |
| | 5 | 5 | 4 | 6 | 5 | 3 | 6 | 6 |
| Mean | 3.8 | 4.1 | 4.3 | 4.7 | 4.4 | 4.4 | 4.8 | 5.2 |
| Standard deviation | 1.23 | 0.74 | 0.95 | 1.16 | 0.97 | 0.84 | 0.79 | 0.63 |

**FIGURE 13-5**  Data summary sheet for a 2 × 4 between-subjects design.
Source: Bordens and Horowitz, 1986.

The organization just described works well for a $2 \times 4$ factorial experiment and can be expanded to handle more levels of each factor or more factors. Other designs may require a different organization.

## Organizing Your Data for Computer Entry

If you are going to submit your data to computer analysis, you should find out how the statistical analysis software that you intend to use expects the data to be organized. Many packages require the data to be entered in stacked format, some require the unstacked format, and some will accept either.

If you have not already done so on your original data sheets, you may have to code your variables before entering the data into the computer. Most software for data analysis looks for a numeric or alphabetic code to determine the levels or values of your independent and dependent variables. You must decide how to code these variables.

Coding independent variables involves assigning values to corresponding levels. For a quantitative independent variable (e.g., number of milligrams of a drug), simply record on your coding sheet the number of milligrams administered to subjects in each treatment group (e.g., 10, 20, or 30). For qualitative independent variables, you must assign an arbitrary number to each level. For example, if your independent variable were the loudness of a tone in an auditory discrimination experiment (low, moderate, and high), you might code the levels as 1 = low, 2 = moderate, 3 = high. As noted, this assignment of numbers to the levels of a qualitative independent variable is called *dummy coding*.

For quantitative data (e.g., if your participants rated the intensity of a sound on a scale ranging from 0 to 10), simply transfer each participant's score to your coding sheet. If, however, your dependent measure were qualitative (e.g., yes/no), you must dummy-code your dependent variable. For example, you could code all yes responses as 1 and all no responses as 2.

When coding your dependent variables, transfer the data (numeric or dummy-coded) to your coding sheet exactly as they are. Don't be concerned with creating new variables (e.g., by adding together existing ones) or with making special categories. Most statistical analysis software have commands that let you manipulate data in a variety of ways (adding numbers, doing data transformations such as a log transformation, etc.). So don't waste time creating new variables when preparing your data for input.

## Entering Your Data

Personal computer versions of statistical software have easy-to-use spreadsheet interfaces that allow you to enter data quickly and make corrections easily. If you don't like the data-entry provision in a particular program, the program may allow you to enter your data into a stand-alone spreadsheet program such as Microsoft's Excel and then read the spreadsheet file into the statistical program's data editor.

You can make data entry easier by organizing your data-coding sheet the way your data editor expects the data to be entered. For example, if your data will be entered one column at a time, organize the data into columns on the sheet. Then simply read down the columns while entering your data.

Errors climb when fatigue sets in, so if you are entering a large amount of data, take frequent breaks. Be sure to save any data that you have entered before you leave the keyboard. At this time, you also should make a backup copy of your data on a removable disk or some other device such as a USB drive.

When you save your data, you create a *data file* from which the data will be read when the computer conducts your analysis. Try to think of a descriptive file name that will uniquely identify the data. When you have several data files, using descriptive file names makes it easier to find the correct file. It is also a good idea to add a date to your file name so that you will know which is the most recent version (e.g., MemoryApril10.dat).

After you have entered your data, check for errors. Because the computer cannot detect incorrectly entered data, it is up to you to catch any mistakes if you are to avoid invalid results. If you have had someone else enter the data for you, don't assume that the other person has already done the checking.

As was the case for survey data, you can save a great deal of time and effort by using a commercial program to control your experiments and collect your data (e.g., Empirisoft's MediaLab). If you use MediaLab, your data are automatically stored to a file that can be entered directly into Microsoft Excel or a statistical analysis software package such as SPSS. Doing this will not only save you the time needed to code and enter data by hand, but will also virtually eliminate data entry errors. Having said this, you should always check your electronic data files for errors. If, for example, you made an error in the program you created to collect data, there will be errors in your data file.

*Examining Your Data*    Typically, the data from individual groups or conditions are used to compute summary statistics, such as the group average, that represent group or condition as a whole. When you calculate an average, you have one score that characterizes an entire distribution. You then can refer to the performance of subjects in a group by citing the average performance. If your data will be submitted to a statistical analysis based on treatment means, you will be treating your data in this way.

Although convenient, group averages do have two important limitations. First, the average score may not represent the performance of individual subjects in a group. An average score of 5 can result if all 10 subjects in a group scored 5 or if half scored 0 and half scored 10. In the former case, the average accurately reflects the individual performance of each subject. In the latter case, it does not. We examine this idea in more detail during the discussion of the mean.

The second limitation of using grouped data is that a curve resulting from plotting averaged data may not reflect the true nature of the psychological phenomenon being studied. In a learning experiment, for example, in which rats must meet a learning criterion (e.g., three consecutive error-free trials), a graph showing how the group average changes across trials might suggest that learning is a gradual process. Inspection of graphs of each individual subject's behavior might tell a different story. It might be that each rat evidences no learning for some variable number of trials, then suddenly masters the task, and after that never makes another error. Such a pattern of data would suggest that learning is an all-or-none proposition rather than the process of gradual improvement implied by the group average.

Unfortunately, researchers too often fall into the pattern of collecting data and then calculating an average without considering the individual scores constituting the average. A good strategy to adopt is to look at both the grouped and individual data. When you have repeated measures of the same behavior, examining individual data shows how each subject performed in your study. This may provide insights into the psychological process being studied that are not afforded by grouping data.

When you collect only a single score for each subject, you should still examine the distribution of individual scores. This usually entails plotting the individual scores on a graph and carefully inspecting the graph.

## QUESTIONS TO PONDER

1. Why is it important to scrutinize your data using exploratory data analysis (EDA)?
2. How do you organize your data in preparation for data analysis?
3. What are the problems inherent in entering your data for computer data analysis?
4. Why is it important to examine individual scores even when your analysis will be based on group averages?

## GRAPHING YOUR DATA

Whether you have chosen a grouped or an individual strategy for dealing with your data, you will often find it beneficial to plot your data on a graph. Graphing helps you make sense of your data by representing them visually. The next sections describe the various types of graphs and indicate their uses. For details on drawing graphs, see Chapter 16.

### Elements of a Graph

A basic graph represents your data in a two-dimensional space. The two dimensions (horizontal and vertical) are defined by two lines intersecting at right angles, called the *axes* of the graph. The horizontal axis is called the *abscissa* or *x-axis* of the graph, and the vertical axis is called the *ordinate* or *y-axis*. (The terms *x-axis* and *y-axis* are used in this discussion.)

When graphing data from an experiment, you normally represent levels of your independent variable along the *x*-axis and values of the dependent variable along the *y*-axis. A pair of values (one for the *x*-axis and one for the *y*-axis) defines a single *point* within the graph. You can present data within the two-dimensional space of a graph as a bar graph, line graph, scatter plot, or (abandoning the Cartesian *x*-axis, *y*-axis geometry) pie graph.

### Bar Graphs

A **bar graph** presents your data as bars extending away from the axis representing your independent variable (usually the *x*-axis although this convention is not always followed). The length of each bar reflects the value of the dependent variable.

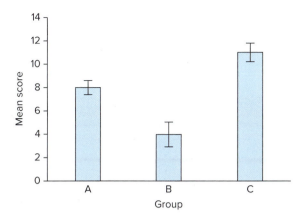

**FIGURE 13-6** Bar graph from a hypothetical one-factor design, showing means and standard errors of the mean.

Figure 13-6 shows group means from a one-factor, three-group experiment plotted as a bar graph. The three bars in Figure 13-6 represent the three levels of the independent variable for which data were collected. The length of each bar along the *y*-axis represents the mean score obtained on the dependent variable. Note that each bar straddles the *x*-axis value that it represents. The width of each bar has no meaning and is chosen to provide a pleasing appearance.

The bars usually represent estimates of population values based on sample data, such as the sample mean. In such cases the graph may also present an indication of the precision of the estimate in the form of *error bars,* whiskers that extend from the tops of the bars. The error bars show the variability of scores around the estimate. Figure 13-6 displays error bars depicting the standard error of the mean.

You also can use a bar graph to represent data from a multifactor design. Figure 13-7 shows a bar graph of the data from a two-factor time-estimation experiment (Waldum & McDaniel, 2016). The two factors were participant age (young adult or older adult) and number of songs played in the background (none, 2, or 4) while participants answered a series of trivia questions. After completing the task, participants estimated how much time they had taken.

A bar graph is the best method of graphing when your independent variable is categorical (such as the type of drug administered). In this case, the distance along the *x*-axis has no real meaning. A line graph (which visually emphasizes that distance) would be misleading. The bar graph makes the arbitrary ordering of categories apparent, whereas a line graph would inappropriately suggest the presence of trends in these data.

In addition to displaying such statistical values as treatment means, bar graphs may be used to display certain kinds of data distributions, discussed later in the chapter.

## Line Graphs

A **line graph** represents data as a series of points connected by a line. It is most appropriate when your independent variable, represented on the *x*-axis, is continuous and *quantitative* (e.g., the number of seconds elapsing between learning and recall). This

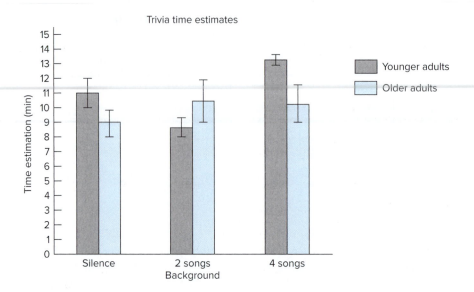

**FIGURE 13-7**    Bar graph of means from a two-factor design; error bar depicts standard errors.
SOURCE: Waldum, Emily A and Mark A. McDaniel, "Why Are You Late? Investigating the Role of Time Management in Time-Based Prospective Memory" *Journal of Experimental Psychology*, Vol. 145, No.8., Figure 2. Copyright 2016  by American Psychological Association.

is in contrast to a bar graph, which is most appropriate when your independent variable is categorical or *qualitative* (e.g., categories representing grades on an exam). Line graphs are also appropriate when you want to illustrate functional relationships among variables. A *functional relationship* is one in which the value of the dependent variable varies as a function of the value of the independent variable. Usually, the depicted functional relationship is causal.

Figure 13-8 illustrates a line graph that depicts the group means from a single-factor experiment with a continuous independent variable. The error bars extending vertically in both directions depict the precision with which the points estimate the population parameter. These same data were shown in Figure 13-6 in the form of a bar

**FIGURE 13-8**    Line graph showing means and standard errors from a one-factor design.

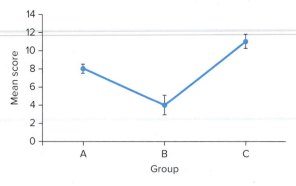

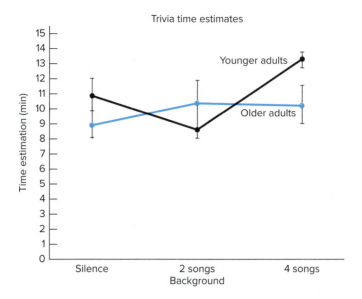

**FIGURE 13-9**    Line graph of means from a two-factor design; error bar depicts standard errors.

SOURCE: Waldum, Emily A and Mark A. McDaniel, "Why Are You Late? Investigating the Role of Time Management in Time-Based Prospective Memory" *Journal of Experimental Psychology*, Vol. 145, No.8., Figure 2.  Copyright 2016 by American Psychological Association.

graph. Notice the difference in how the two types of graphs visually represent the means.

A line graph also can be used to depict the means from multifactor experiments. Figure 13-9 shows such a line graph for the two-factor experiment on time estimation (Waldum & McDaniel, 2016) described earlier. The levels of one factor are represented along the *x*-axis, just as in a single-factor experiment. The levels of the other factor are represented by using different symbols or line styles. In the figure, all points collected under the same value of the second factor are connected by a line of the same color.

*Shapes of Line Graphs*    Relationships depicted on a line graph can take a variety of shapes. Figure 13-10 shows a graph on which the curve is *positively accelerated*. A positively accelerated curve is relatively flat at first and becomes progressively steeper

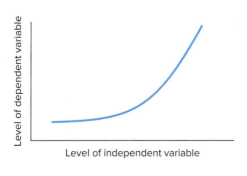

**FIGURE 13-10**    Line graph of positively accelerated functional relationship.

**FIGURE 13-11**   Line graph of negatively accelerated functional relationship.

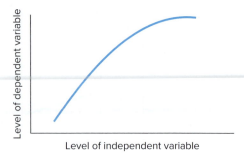

Level of independent variable

**FIGURE 13-12**   Line graph of nonmonotonic functional relationship.

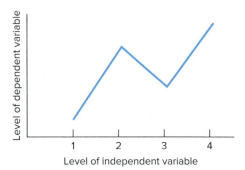

Level of independent variable

as it moves along the *x*-axis. Positive acceleration can occur both in the upward and downward directions along the *y*-axis.

A curve also may be *negatively accelerated,* as shown in Figure 13-11. Here the curve is steep at first but becomes progressively flatter as it moves along the *x*-axis. Eventually, the curve "levels off" at some maximum or minimum value. The function is said to be *asymptotic* at this value. The *asymptote* of a curve is its theoretical limit, or the point beyond which no further change in the value of the dependent variable is expected. In Figure 13-11 the relationship is asymptotic.

Whether positively or negatively accelerated, any curve also may be characterized as *increasing* or *decreasing,* which refers to whether the values along the *y*-axis increase or decrease, respectively, as the value along the *x*-axis increases. For example, a negatively accelerated, increasing function would approach a ceiling value at the asymptote whereas a negatively accelerated, decreasing function would approach a floor value.

A graph also may vary in complexity. The curves depicted in Figures 13-10 and 13-11 are *monotonic.* That is, the curve represents a uniformly increasing or decreasing function. A *nonmonotonic* function contains reversals in direction, as illustrated in Figure 13-12. Notice how the curve changes direction twice by starting off low, rising, falling off, and then rising again.

## Scatter Plots

In research using a correlational strategy, the data from the two dependent measures are often plotted as a **scatter plot**. On a scatter plot, each pair of scores is represented as a point on the graph. Consider the data shown in Table 13-1. To make a scatter plot of these data, you plot the values of variable A along the *x*-axis and the values of variable B along the *y*-axis (or vice versa, it really does not matter). Then each pair of values is represented by a point within the graph. Figure 13-13 shows a scatter plot of the data in Table 13-1.

Scatter plots often include a "best-fitting" straight line (not shown in the figure) to indicate the general trend of the data points shown in the plot. In those cases the graph may also include the equation for this line and the coefficient of correlation. (We discuss these in the section on correlation and regression.)

## Pie Graphs

If your data are in the form of proportions or percentages, then you might find a **pie graph** is a good way to represent the value of each category in the analysis. A pie graph represents the data as slices of a circular pie. Figure 13-14 shows two representative pie graphs. The pie graph to the left indicates the proportion of various behaviors observed in rat subjects during a half-hour coding period. The pie graph to the

| TABLE 13-1 Bivariate Data for a Scatterplot | | |
|---|---|---|
| SUBJECT NUMBER | VARIABLE A | VARIABLE B |
| 1 | 5 | 5 |
| 2 | 4 | 2 |
| 3 | 9 | 8 |
| 4 | 2 | 1 |
| 5 | 6 | 7 |
| 6 | 3 | 4 |

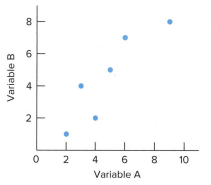

**FIGURE 13-13** Scatter plot of the bivariate data presented in Table 13-1.

**FIGURE 13-14**   Pie graph and exploded pie graph.

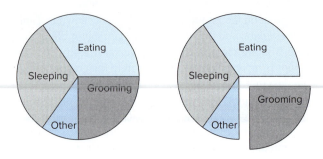

right, called an *exploded pie graph,* displays the same proportions while emphasizing the proportion of time devoted to grooming.

## The Importance of Graphing Data

You can use either tables or graphs to summarize your data. If you organize data in tables, you present the numbers themselves (averages and/or raw score distributions). If you display the data in a graphical format, you lose some of this numerical precision. The value of a point usually can only be approximated by its position along the *y*-axis of the graph. However, graphing data is important for two major reasons, discussed in the next sections.

*Showing Relationships Clearly*   The saying "One picture is worth a thousand words" applies to graphing data from your research. Although summarizing data in a table is fine, proper graphing adds a degree of clarity no table can provide. The graph brings out subtleties in the relationships that may not be apparent from inspecting a table.

*Choosing Appropriate Statistics*   In addition to making it easier to see relationships in your data, graphs allow you to evaluate your data for the application of an appropriate statistic. Before you apply any statistic to your data, graph your sample distributions and examine their shapes. Your choice of statistic will be affected by the manner in which scores are distributed, as described in the next section.

Graphing your data on a scatter plot is helpful when you intend to calculate a measure of correlation. Inspecting a scatter plot of your data can help you determine which measure of correlation is appropriate for your data. What you would look for and how your findings would affect your decision are taken up during the discussion of correlation measures later in the chapter.

## THE FREQUENCY DISTRIBUTION

One of the first steps to perform when analyzing your data is to create a frequency distribution for each dependent variable in an experiment or for each variable in a correlational study. A **frequency distribution** consists of a set of mutually

**TABLE 13-2  Frequency Distribution Table of Hypothetical IQ Data**

| CLASS | $f$ |
|-------|-----|
| 125–134 | 5 |
| 115–124 | 12 |
| 105–114 | 22 |
| 95–104 | 25 |
| 85–94 | 26 |
| 75–84 | 7 |
| 65–74 | 3 |
| $\Sigma f$ | 100 |

exclusive categories (*classes*) into which you sort the actual values observed in your data, together with a count of the number of data values falling into each category (*frequencies*). The classes may consist of response categories (e.g., for political party affiliation, they might consist of Democrat, Republican, Independent, and Other) or ranges of score values along a quantitative scale (e.g., for IQ, they might consist of 65–74, 75–84, 85–94, 95–104, 105–114, 115–124, and 125–134).

## Displaying Distributions

Frequency distributions take the form of tables or graphs. Table 13-2 presents a hypothetical frequency distribution of IQ scores using the classes just given. Because IQ scores are quantitative data, the classes are presented in order of value from highest to lowest. To the right of each class is its frequency ($f$), the number of data values falling into that class. Because there were no IQ scores below 65 or above 134, classes beyond these limits are not tabled.

Although a table provides a compact summary of the distribution, it is not particularly easy to extract useful information from it about center, spread, and shape. Graphical or semi-graphical displays are much better for this purpose. Here we describe two: the histogram and the stemplot.

*The Histogram*    Figure 13-15 displays our IQ frequency distribution as a histogram. **Histograms** resemble bar graphs, with each bar representing a class. Unlike the bars in a bar graph, those in a histogram are drawn touching to indicate that there are no gaps between adjacent classes. Also, on a histogram, the *y*-axis represents a frequency: a count of the number of observations falling into a given category (e.g., the number of exam scores falling into the categories of A, B, C, D, or F). On a bar graph, the *y*-axis typically represents a mean score (e.g., the time estimates shown in Figure 13-7).

The scale on which the variable was measured appears along the *x*-axis with the bars positioned appropriately to cover their respective ranges along the scale. The

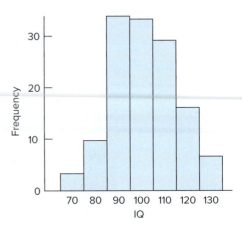

**FIGURE 13-15** Hypothetical IQ data displayed as a histogram.

*y*-axis denotes the frequency; thus, a given bar's length indicates the frequency of scores falling within its range.

A histogram's appearance changes depending on how wide you make the classes. Make the classes too narrow, and you produce a flat-looking histogram with many empty or nearly empty classes. Make the classes too wide, and you produce a tall histogram lacking in detail. The goal is to create a histogram that indicates the shape of the distribution—one that is neither too wide and flat nor too narrow and tall.

*The Stemplot*    As a quick alternative to the histogram, you might consider using a **stemplot** (also known as a stem-and-leaf plot), which was invented by statistician John Tukey (1977) to simplify the job of displaying distributions. To create a stemplot of your data, you simply break each number into two parts: stem and leaf. The stem part consists of the leftmost number or numbers and the leaf, the rightmost number. Thus, an IQ score of 67 would be broken into its leftmost number, or stem (6), and rightmost number, or leaf (7). After finding the lowest and highest stems, make a column that includes all the stem numbers in ascending order from lowest to highest. Then draw a vertical line immediately to the right of the stem column. Finally, for each score in your data, find its stem number in the stem column, then write its leaf number to the right of the vertical line on the same row as the stem. So, the IQ score of 67 would look like the first entry at the top of Figure 13-16. You do this for each number in your distribution. The final result would look something like Figure 13-16, which plots some hypothetical IQ data as a stemplot.

Stemplots are easy to construct and display and have the advantage over histograms and tables of preserving all the actual values present in the data. However, you

**FIGURE 13-16** Hypothetical IQ data displayed as a stemplot.

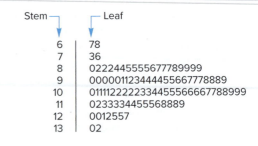

do not have much freedom to choose the class widths because stemplots inherently create class widths of 10 (the span of a stem). Stemplots are not especially useful for larger data sets because the number of leaves becomes too large.

## Examining Your Distribution

When examining a histogram or stemplot of your data, look for the following important features. First, locate the center of the distribution along the scale of measurement. In the IQ distribution plotted earlier, were the scores centered around 100 IQ points (an average value for the population as a whole) or somewhere else? The location of the center of a distribution tells you where the scores tended to cluster along the scale of measurement.

Second, note the spread of the scores. Do they tend to bunch up around the center or spread far from it? The spread of the scores indicates how variable they are.

Third, note the overall shape of the distribution. Is it hill-shaped, with a single peak at the center, or does it have more than one peak? If hill-shaped, is it more or less *symmetrical,* or is it skewed? A **skewed distribution** has a long "tail" trailing off in one direction and a short tail extending in the other. A distribution is *positively skewed* if the long tail goes off to the right, upscale [see Figure 13-17(a)] or *negatively skewed* if the long tail goes off to the left, downscale [see Figure 13-17(b)]. Many variables encountered in psychology tend to produce a distribution that follows more or less a mathematical form known as the **normal distribution**, which is symmetric and hill-shaped—the well-known bell curve. Because many common inferential statistics assume that the data follow a normal distribution, check the distribution of your data to see whether this assumption seems reasonable.

Finally, look for *gaps,* or **outliers**. Outliers are extreme scores that lie far from the others, well outside the overall pattern of the data (Moore & McCabe, 2015). Outliers may be perfectly valid (although unusual) scores, but sometimes they represent

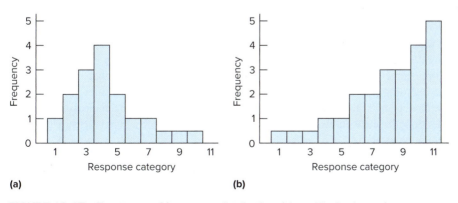

(a)     (b)

**FIGURE 13-17**  Two types of frequency distribution: (a) positively skewed and (b) negatively skewed.

mistakes made in data collection or transcription. These bogus values can destroy the validity of your analysis. When you find an outlier, examine it carefully to determine whether it represents an error. Correct erroneous values or, if this is not possible, delete them from your analysis.

If you can find no valid reason for removing an outlier, you will have to live with it. However, you can minimize its effects on your analysis by using **resistant measures**, so called because they tend to resist distortion by outliers. We describe some of these measures next in our discussions of measures of center and spread.

## QUESTIONS TO PONDER

1. How do various types of graphs differ, and when should each be used?

2. How do negatively accelerated, positively accelerated, and asymptotic functional relationships differ?

3. Why is it important to graph your data and inspect the graphs carefully?

4. How do you graph a frequency distribution as a histogram and as a stemplot?

5. What should you look for when examining the graph of a frequency distribution?

## DESCRIPTIVE STATISTICS: MEASURES OF CENTER AND SPREAD

In many research situations, it is convenient to summarize your data by applying descriptive statistics. This section reviews two categories of descriptive statistics: measures of center and measures of spread. The next section describes another category of descriptive statistics, measures of association.

### Measures of Center

A **measure of center** (also known as a *measure of central tendency*) gives you a single score that represents the general magnitude of scores in a distribution. This score characterizes your distribution by indicating a score value that falls at or near the middle of the distribution. The most common measures of center are the mode, the median, and the mean (also called the *arithmetic average*). Each measure of center has strengths and weaknesses. Also, situations exist in which a given measure of center cannot be used.

*The Mode*    The **mode** is simply the most frequent score in a distribution. To obtain the mode, count the number of scores falling into each response category. The response category with the highest frequency is the mode. The mode of the distribution 1, 2, 4, 6, 4, 3, 4 is 4, because 4 is the most frequent score.

No mode exists for a distribution in which all the scores are different. Some distributions, called *bimodal distributions,* have two modes. Figure 13-18 shows a bimodal distribution of hypothetical scores (percentage correct) on an Introductory psychology exam.

Although the mode is simple to calculate, it is limited because it does not take into account the values of scores outside of the most frequent score. The only information yielded by the mode is the most frequent score. Consequently, two distributions may have similar modes and yet look very different. Consider the following two distributions of scores: 2, 2, 6, 3, 7, 2, 2, 5, 3, 1 and 2, 2, 21, 43, 78, 22, 33, 72, 12, 8. In both these distributions, the mode is 2. Looking only at the mode, you might conclude that the two distributions are similar. Obviously, this conclusion is incorrect. It is clear that the second distribution is very different from the first. The mode may not represent a distribution very well and would not be the best measure to use when comparing distributions.

*The Median*   A second measure of center is the median. The **median** is the middle score in a distribution. To calculate the median, follow these steps:

1. Order the scores in your distribution from lowest to highest (or highest to lowest, it does not matter).

2. Count down through the distribution and find the score in the middle of the distribution. This score is the median of the distribution.

What is the median of the following distribution: 7, 5, 2, 9, 4, 8, 1? The correct answer is 5. The ordered distribution is 1, 2, 4, 5, 7, 8, 9, and 5 is the middle score.

You may be wondering what to do if you have an even number of scores in your distribution. In this case, there is no middle score. To calculate a median with an even number of scores, you order the distribution as before and then identify the *two* middle scores. The median is the average of these two scores. For example, with the ordered distribution of 1, 3, 6, 7, 8, 9, the median is 6.5 (6 + 7 = 13; 13/2 = 6.5).

The median takes more information into account than the mode. However, it is still a rather insensitive measure of center because it does not take into account the

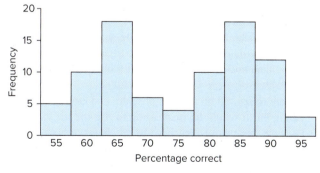

**FIGURE 13-18**   A bimodal frequency distribution of test scores.

magnitudes of the scores above and below the median. As with the mode, two distributions can have the same median and yet be very different in character. For this reason, the median is used primarily when the mean is not a good choice.

*The Mean*    The **mean** (denoted as *M*) is the most sensitive measure of center because it takes into account all scores in a distribution when it is calculated. It is also the most widely used measure of center. The computational formula for the mean is

$$M = \frac{\Sigma X}{n}$$

where $\Sigma X$ is the sum of the scores and *n* is the number of scores in the distribution. To obtain the mean, simply add together all the scores in the distribution and then divide by the total number of scores (*n*).

The major advantage of the mean is that, unlike the mode and the median, its value is directly affected by the magnitude of each score in the distribution. However, this sensitivity to individual score values also makes the mean susceptible to the influence of outliers. One or two such outliers may cause the mean to be artificially high or low. The following two distributions illustrate this point. Assume that distribution A contains the scores 4, 6, 3, 8, 9, 2, 3, and distribution B contains the scores 4, 6, 3, 8, 9, 2, 43. Although the two distributions differ by only a single score (3 versus 43), they differ greatly in their means (5 versus 10.7, respectively).

The mean of 5 appears to be more representative of the first distribution than the mean of 10.7 is of the second. The median is a better measure of center for the second distribution. The medians of the two distributions are 4 and 6, respectively—not nearly as different from one another as the means. Before you choose a measure of center, carefully evaluate your data for skewness and the presence of deviant, outlying scores. Do not blindly apply the mean just because it is the most sensitive measure of center.

*Choosing a Measure of Center*    Which of the three measures of center you choose depends on two factors: the scale of measurement and the shape of the distribution of the scores. Before you use any measure of center, evaluate these two factors.

Chapter 5 described four measurement scales: nominal (qualitative categories), ordinal (rank orderings), interval (quantities measured from an arbitrary zero point), and ratio (quantities measured from a true zero point). The measurement scale that you chose when you designed your experiment will now influence your decision about which measure of center to use.

If your data were measured on a nominal scale, you are limited to using the mode. It makes no sense to calculate a median or mean sex, even if the sex of subjects has been coded as 0s (males) and 1s (females). What would it mean to say that the mean sex in a sample is 1.4?

If your data were measured on an ordinal scale, you could properly use either the mode or the median, but it would be misleading to use the mean as your measure of center. This is because the mean is sensitive to the distance between scores. With an ordinal scale, the actual distance between points is unknown. You cannot assume that scores equally distant in terms of rank order are equally far apart, but you do assume this (in effect) if you use the mean.

The mean can be used if your data are scaled on an interval or ratio scale. On these two scales, the numerical distances between values are meaningful quantities.

Even if your dependent measure were scaled on an interval or ratio scale, the mean may be inappropriate. One of the first things you should do when summarizing your data is to generate a frequency distribution of the scores. Next, plot the frequency distribution as a histogram or stemplot and examine its shape. If your scores are normally distributed (or at least nearly normally distributed), then the mean, median, and mode will fall at the same point in the middle of the distribution, as shown in Figure 13-19. When your scores are normally distributed, use the mean as your measure of center because it is based on the most information.

As your distribution deviates from normality, the mean becomes a less representative measure of center. The two graphs in Figure 13-20 show the relationship between the three measures of center with a positively skewed distribution and a negatively skewed distribution. Notice the relationship between the mean and median for these skewed distributions. In a negatively skewed distribution, the mean underestimates the center. Conversely, in a positively skewed distribution, the mean overestimates the center. Because the median is much less affected by skew, it provides a more representative picture of the distribution's center than does the mean and should be preferred whenever your distribution is strongly skewed.

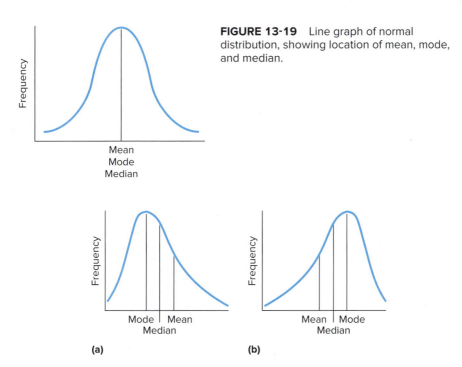

**FIGURE 13-19**  Line graph of normal distribution, showing location of mean, mode, and median.

**FIGURE 13-20**  Line graph of (a) positively and (b) negatively skewed distributions, showing relationship between mean, mode, and median.

**FIGURE 13-21**    Stemplot of hypothetical scores (percent correct) from an introductory psychology test. Equivalent grades are shown at left.

| | | |
|---|---|---|
| F | 5 | 4 |
| | 5 | 6666789 |
| D | 6 | 112222222333444 |
| | 6 | 55555666667789999 |
| C | 7 | 2 |
| | 7 | 5556889 |
| B | 8 | 011122233444 |
| | 8 | 55667777777777888999 |
| A | 9 | 0012234 |

Deviations from normality also create problems when deciding on an inferential statistic. Chapter 14 discusses inferential statistics and ways to deal with data that are not normally distributed. Neither the mean nor the median will accurately represent the center if your distribution is bimodal. With a bimodal distribution, both measures of center underrepresent one large cluster of scores and overrepresent the other.

Figure 13-21 presents a stemplot of hypothetical scores from an introductory psychology exam that generated a bimodal distribution. The mean for these scores is 75.4 and the median is 77, both in the grade C range. However, few students actually received a C. The mean and median underrepresent the large cluster of scores in the grade B category and overestimate the large cluster of scores in the grade D category. Thus, neither the mean nor the median would be an appropriate measure of center for these scores.

To summarize the discussion to this point, the three measures of center are the mean, the median, and the mode. The mean is the most sensitive measure of center because it takes into account the magnitude of each score in the distribution. The mean is also the preferred measure of center. The median is less sensitive to the distribution of scores than the mean but is preferred when your distribution is skewed or contains serious outliers. Which measure of center you can legitimately use depends on the scale on which the dependent variable was measured and on the manner in which the scores are distributed.

## Measures of Spread

Another important descriptive statistic you should apply to your data is a **measure of spread** (also known as a *measure of variability*). If you look again at some of the sample distributions described thus far (or at the data presented in Table 13-1), you will notice that the scores in the distributions differ from each other. When you conduct an experiment, it is extremely unlikely that your subjects will all produce the same score on your dependent measure. A measure of spread provides information that helps you to interpret your data. Two sets of scores may have highly similar means yet very different distributions, as the following example illustrates.

Imagine that you are a scout for a professional baseball team and are considering one of two players for your team. Each player has a .263 batting average over 4 years of college. The distributions of the two players' averages are as follows:

Player 1: .260, .397, .200, .195

Player 2: .263, .267, .259, .263

Which of these two players would you prefer to have on your team? Most likely, you would pick player 2 because he is more "consistent" than player 1. This simple example illustrates an important point about descriptive statistics. When you are evaluating your data, you should take into account both the center *and* the spread of the scores. This section reviews four measures of spread: the range, the interquartile range, the variance, and the standard deviation.

*The Range*   The **range** is the simplest and least informative measure of spread. To calculate the range, you simply subtract the lowest score from the highest score. In the baseball example, the range for player 1 is .202, and the range for player 2 is .008.

Two problems with the range are that it does not take into account the magnitude of the scores between the extremes and that it is very sensitive to outliers in the distribution. Compare the following two distributions of scores: 1, 2, 3, 4, 5, 6 and 1, 2, 3, 4, 5, 31. The range for the first distribution is 5, and the range for the second is 30. The two ranges are highly discrepant despite the fact that the two distributions are nearly identical. For these reasons, the range is rarely used as a measure of spread.

*The Interquartile Range*   The **interquartile range** is another measure of spread that is easy to calculate. To obtain the interquartile range, follow these steps:

1. Order the scores in your distribution.

2. Divide the distribution into four equal parts (quarters).

3. Find the score separating the bottom 25% of the distribution (quartile 1, or $Q_1$) and the score separating the top 25% ($Q_3$) from the rest of the distribution. The interquartile range is equal to $Q_3$ minus $Q_1$.

The interquartile range is less sensitive than the range to the effects of extreme scores. It also takes into account more information because more than just the highest and lowest scores are used for its calculation. The interquartile range may be preferred over the range in situations in which you want a relatively simple, rough measure of spread that is resistant to the effects of skew and outliers.

*The Variance*   The **variance** ($s^2$) is the average squared deviation from the mean. The defining formula is

$$s^2 = \frac{\Sigma(X - M)^2}{n - 1}$$

where $X$ is each individual score making up the distribution, $M$ is the mean of the distribution, and $n$ is the number of scores. Table 13-3 shows how to use this formula by means of an example worked out for one distribution of scores.

*The Standard Deviation*   Although the variance is frequently used as a measure of spread in certain statistical calculations, it does have the disadvantage of being expressed in units different from those of the summarized data. However, the variance can be easily converted into a measure of spread expressed in the *same* unit of measurement as the original scores: the **standard deviation** ($s$). To convert from the variance to the standard deviation, simply take the square root of the variance. The standard deviation of the data in Table 13-3 is 2.61 ($\sqrt{6.8}$). The standard deviation is the most popular measure of spread.

| TABLE 13-3 | Calculation of a Variance | | | |
|---|---|---|---|---|
| | $X$ | $X^2$ | $(X - M)$ | $(X - M)^2$ |
| | 3 | 9 | −2 | 4 |
| | 5 | 25 | 0 | 0 |
| | 2 | 4 | −3 | 9 |
| | 7 | 49 | 2 | 4 |
| | 9 | 81 | 4 | 16 |
| | 4 | 16 | −1 | 1 |
| $\Sigma$ | 30 | 184 | | 34 |

$M = 30/6 = 5.0$

$s^2 = 34/5 = 6.8$

*Choosing a Measure of Spread*    The choice of a measure of center is affected by the distribution of the scores, and the same is true for the choice of a measure of spread. Like the mean, the range and standard deviation are sensitive to outliers. In cases in which your distribution has one or more outliers, the interquartile range may provide a better measure of spread.

In addition to noting the presence of outliers, you should note the shape of the distribution (normal or skewed) when selecting a measure of spread. Remember that the mean is not a representative measure of center when your distribution of scores is skewed and that the mean is used to calculate the standard deviation. Consequently, with a skewed distribution, the standard deviation does not provide a representative measure of spread. If your distribution is seriously skewed, use the interquartile range instead. Like the median, the interquartile range is resistant to the effects of skew and outliers.

## Boxplots and the Five-Number Summary

The **five-number summary** provides a useful way to boil down a distribution into just a few easily grasped numbers, several of which are resistant to the effects of skew and outliers and all of which are based on the ranks of the scores. Included in the five-number summary are the following: the minimum, the first quartile, the median (second quartile), the third quartile, and the maximum. The minimum and maximum are simply the smallest and largest scores in the distribution; these are not resistant measures for the simple fact that the most extreme outliers will fall at the ends of the distribution and therefore are likely to *be* the maximum or minimum scores. The three center values (the first quartile, median, and third quartile) are resistant measures. From the five-number summary, you can easily calculate the range (maximum − minimum) and interquartile range ($Q_3 - Q_1$); the latter is of course a resistant measure of spread. By examining the five-number summary, you can quickly determine the center, spread, and range of the distribution in question.

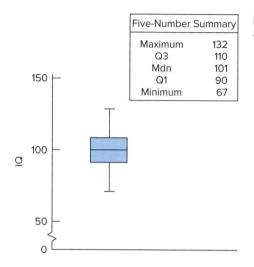

| Five-Number Summary | |
| --- | --- |
| Maximum | 132 |
| Q3 | 110 |
| Mdn | 101 |
| Q1 | 90 |
| Minimum | 67 |

**FIGURE 13-22**  Five-number summary and boxplot of the IQ data.

An even better approach is to display the five-number summary as a **boxplot**. Figure 13-22 shows the five-number summary for our IQ distribution and displays these numbers as a boxplot. The first and third quartiles form the ends of the box, which encloses a line marking the median. The two "whiskers" reach out from the box to mark the minimum and maximum scores.

If you have data from several treatments or samples, you can easily compare the distributions from each using *side-by-side* boxplots, as shown in Figure 13-23. Each box should depict the distribution of the same variable.

You often can discern the general shape of the distribution from the boxplot by noting the position of the median within the box and the relative lengths of the two whiskers. In a symmetric distribution, the median will fall close to the middle of the box, and the two whiskers will be similar in length. In a positively skewed distribution, the median will be pushed toward the left end or bottom of the box (nearer $Q_1$), and the right or top whisker will usually be longer than the left or bottom one. In a negatively skewed distribution, the reverse pattern will be found.

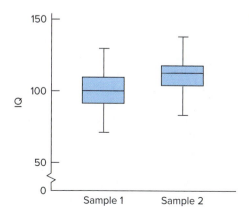

**FIGURE 13-23**  Side-by-side boxplots showing IQ data from two samples.

## QUESTIONS TO PONDER

1. What is a measure of center?
2. How do the mode, median, and mean differ, and under what conditions would you use each?
3. What is a measure of spread?
4. What measures of spread are available, and when would you use each?
5. How are the variance and standard deviation related, and why is the standard deviation preferred?
6. What is the five-number summary, and how can you represent it graphically?
7. What is a *resistant measure*?

## MEASURES OF ASSOCIATION, REGRESSION, AND RELATED TOPICS

In some cases, you may want to evaluate the direction and degree of relationship (correlation) between the scores in two distributions. For this purpose, you must use a **measure of association**. This section discusses several measures of association, along with the related topics of linear regression, the correlation matrix, and the coefficient of determination.

### The Pearson Product-Moment Correlation Coefficient

The most widely used measure of association is the **Pearson product-moment correlation coefficient, or Pearson *r***. You would use it when you scale your dependent measures on an interval or a ratio scale. The Pearson correlation coefficient provides an index of the direction and magnitude of the relationship between two sets of scores.

The value of Pearson *r* can range from +1 through 0 to −1. The sign of the coefficient tells you the direction of the relationship. A positive correlation indicates a *direct relationship* (as the values of the scores in one distribution increase, so do the values in the second). A negative correlation indicates an *inverse relationship* (as the value of one score increases, the value of the second decreases). Figure 13-24 illustrates scatter plots of data showing positive, negative, and no correlation.

The magnitude of the correlation coefficient tells you the degree of *linear relationship* (straight line) between your two variables. A correlation of 0 indicates that no relationship exists. As the strength of the relationship increases, the value of the correlation coefficient increases toward either +1 or −1. Both +1 and −1 indicate a perfect linear relationship. The sign is unrelated to the magnitude of the relationship and simply indicates the direction of the relationship. Figure 13-25 shows three correlations of differing strengths. Panel (a) shows a correlation of +1; panel (b), a correlation of about +.8; and panel (c), a correlation of 0.

*Factors That Affect the Pearson r*    Before you use the Pearson *r*, examine your data much as you do when deciding on a measure of center. Several factors affect the magnitude and sign of the Pearson *r*.

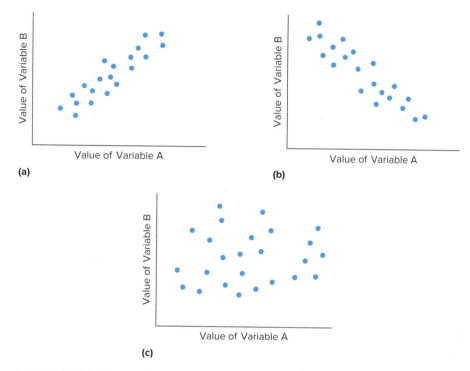

**FIGURE 13-24**   Scatter plots showing (a) positive, (b) negative, and (c) no correlation.

The presence of outliers is one factor that affects the Pearson $r$. An outlier can drastically change your correlation coefficient, affecting its magnitude, its sign, or both. This is especially true if you use a small number of pairs of scores to compute the Pearson $r$.

Restricting the range over which the variables vary also can affect Pearson $r$. For example, if you were to examine the relationship between IQ and grade point average (GPA) in a group of college students, you would probably find a weaker correlation than if you examined the same two variables using high school students. Because IQ varies less among college students than among high school students, any variation in GPA that relates to IQ also will tend to vary less. As a result, the impact of extraneous variables such as motivation will be relatively larger, leading to a reduced correlation.

The Pearson $r$ is sensitive not only to the range of the scores but also to the shapes of the score distributions. The formula used to calculate the coefficient uses the standard deviation for each set of scores. Recall that you use the mean to calculate the standard deviation. If the scores are not normally distributed, the mean does not represent the distribution well. Consequently, the standard deviations will not accurately reflect the variability of the distributions, and the correlation coefficient will not provide an accurate index of the relationship between your two sets of scores. Hence, you should inspect the frequency distributions of each set of scores to ensure that they are normal (or nearly normal) before using the Pearson $r$.

Finally, Pearson $r$ reflects the degree to which the relationship between two variables is linear. Because of this assumption, take steps to determine whether the

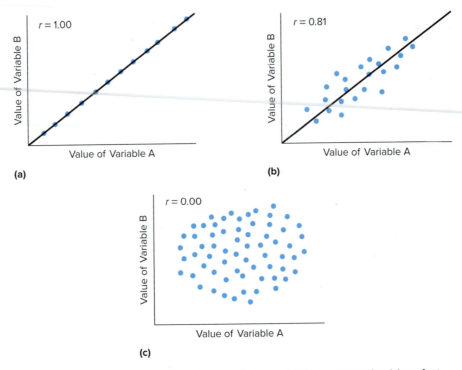

**FIGURE 13-25**    Scatter plots showing correlations of differing strengths: (a) perfect positive correlation, (b) strong positive correlation, and (c) zero correlation.

relationship appears to be linear. You can do this by constructing a scatter plot and then determining whether the points appear to scatter symmetrically around a straight line. Figure 13-26 shows a scatter plot in which the measures have a *curvilinear relationship* (rather than a linear relationship).

When the relationship between variables is nonlinear, the Pearson $r$ underestimates the degree of relationship between the variables. For example, the Pearson correlation between the variables illustrated in Figure 13-26 is zero. However, the two variables are obviously systematically related. There are special correlation techniques for nonlinear data, which are not discussed here.

Pearson $r$ is used when both of your variables are measured along a continuous scale. You may need to correlate variables when one (or both) of them is not measured

**FIGURE 13-26**    Scatter plot showing a curvilinear relationship.

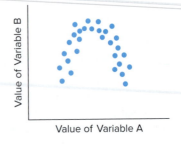

along a continuous scale. Special correlation coefficients are designed for these purposes, three of which are discussed in the next sections.

## The Point-Biserial Correlation

You may have one variable measured on an interval scale and the other measured on a nominal scale. For example, perhaps you want to investigate the relationship between self-rated political conservatism (measured on a 10-point scale) and whether or not a person voted for a particular referendum (yes or no). Because one variable is continuous and the other dichotomous (having only two possible values), you would apply the **point-biserial correlation**.

Although there is a special formula for the point-biserial correlation, in practice you can use the formula for the Pearson $r$ to compute it. The dichotomous variable is dummy-coded as 0 for one response and 1 for the other.

*Factors That Affect the Point-Biserial Correlation*    You should know a couple of things about the point-biserial correlation. First, its magnitude partly depends on the proportion of participants falling into each of the dichotomous categories. If the number of participants in each category is equal, then the maximum value the point-biserial can attain is $\pm 1.0$ (just as with the Pearson $r$). However, if the number of participants in each category is *not* equal, then the maximum attainable value for the point-biserial correlation is less than $\pm 1.0$. Consequently, the degree of relationship between the two variables may be underestimated. You should examine the proportion of participants using each category of the dichotomous variable and, if the proportions differ greatly, temper your conclusions accordingly.

The magnitude of the point-biserial correlation also is affected by the limited variation of the dichotomous variable (i.e., only two values possible). If the underlying variable is continuous but has been dichotomized for the analysis (e.g., anxiety level specified as either low or high), the point-biserial correlation will tend to underestimate the true strength of the relationship.

## The Spearman Rank-Order Correlation

The **Spearman rank-order correlation**, or **rho** ($\rho$), is used either when your data are scaled on an ordinal scale (or greater) or when you want to determine whether the relationship between variables is monotonic (Gravetter & Wallnau, 2017). The rank-order correlation is relatively easy to calculate and can be interpreted in much the same way as a Pearson $r$.

## The Phi Coefficient

The **phi coefficient** ($\varphi$) is used when *both* of the variables being correlated are measured on a dichotomous scale. You can calculate the phi coefficient with its own formula. However, like the point-biserial correlation, phi is usually calculated by dummy-coding the responses as 1s and 0s and then plugging the resulting scores into the formula for Pearson $r$. The same arguments concerning restriction of range that apply to the point-biserial correlation also apply to phi—only doubly so.

## QUESTIONS TO PONDER

1. What do measures of association tell you?
2. What are the measures of association available to you, and when would you use each?
3. What affects the magnitude and direction of a correlation coefficient?

## Linear Regression and Prediction

A topic closely related to correlation is **linear regression**. With simple correlational techniques, you can establish the direction and degree of relationship between two variables. With linear regression, you can estimate values of a variable based on knowledge of the values of others. The following section introduces you to simple bivariate (two-variable) regression (also included are some calculations to help you understand regression). Chapter 15 extends bivariate regression to the case in which you want to consider multiple variables together in a single analysis.

*Bivariate Regression*    The idea behind **bivariate linear regression** is to find the straight line that best fits the data plotted on a scatter plot. Consider an example using the data presented in Table 13-4, which presents the scores for each of 10 subjects on two measures ($X$ and $Y$). Figure 13-27 shows a scatter plot of these data. You want to find the straight line that best describes the linear relationship between $X$ and $Y$.

**TABLE 13-4    Data for Linear Regression Example**

| $X$ | $Y$ | $(X - M)$ | $(Y - \bar{Y})$ | $(X - M)(Y - \bar{Y})$ | $(X - M)^2$ |
|---|---|---|---|---|---|
| 7 | 8 | 1.40 | 1.30 | 1.82 | 1.96 |
| 3 | 4 | −2.60 | −2.70 | 7.02 | 6.76 |
| 2 | 4 | −3.60 | −2.70 | 9.72 | 12.96 |
| 10 | 9 | 4.40 | 2.30 | 10.12 | 19.36 |
| 8 | 9 | 2.40 | 2.30 | 5.52 | 5.76 |
| 7 | 7 | 1.40 | 0.30 | 0.42 | 1.96 |
| 9 | 8 | 3.40 | 1.30 | 4.42 | 11.56 |
| 6 | 8 | 0.40 | 1.30 | 0.52 | 0.16 |
| 3 | 4 | −2.60 | −2.70 | 7.02 | 6.76 |
| 1 | 6 | −4.60 | −0.70 | 3.22 | 21.16 |
| $M_X = 5.6$ | $M_Y = 6.7$ | | | $SP = 49.8$ | $SS_X = 88.4$ |

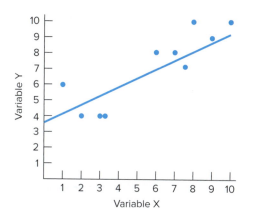

**FIGURE 13-27** Scatter plot of data from Table 13-4.

The best-fitting straight line is the one that minimizes the sum of the squared deviations of each data point from the line, as measured along the y-axis. This line is called the **least-squares regression line**. At any given value of $X$ found in the data, the position of the line indicates the value of $Y$ predicted from the linear relationship between $X$ and $Y$. You can compare these predicted values with the values actually obtained. The best-fitting straight line minimizes the squared differences between the predicted and obtained values.

The following formula describes the regression line mathematically:

$$\hat{Y} = a + bX$$

where $\hat{Y}$ ("y-hat") is the predicted $Y$ score, $b$ is the slope of the regression line (also called the *regression weight*), $X$ is the value of the $X$ variable, and $a$ is the y-intercept (Pagano, 2013). The constants $a$ and $b$ define a particular regression line. You can use the following formula to determine the value of $b$ for a given set of data points (Gravetter & Wallnau, 2017):

$$b = \frac{SP}{SS_X}$$

where $SP = \Sigma (X - M_X)(Y - M_Y)$, $SS_X = \Sigma (X - M_X)^2$, and $M_X$ and $M_Y$ are the means for the $X$ and $Y$ scores, respectively.

Using the numbers from Table 13-4, we have

$$b = \frac{49.8}{88.4} = 0.56$$

The formula for the y-intercept ($a$) is

$$a = M_Y - bM_X$$

For this example,

$$a = 6.7 - 0.56(5.6) = 3.56$$

Substituting these values for $b$ and $a$ in the regression equation gives

$$\hat{Y} = 3.56 + 0.56X$$

This equation allows you to predict the value of $Y$ for any given value of $X$. For example, if $X = 6$, then

$$\hat{Y} = 3.56 + 0.56(6) = 6.92$$

Thus, if $X$ is 6, then based on the regression line, $Y$ is predicted to have a value of 6.92.

***Residuals and Errors in Prediction***    For each actual value of $Y$ in your data, the regression equation allows you to compute a predicted value, $(\hat{Y})$. The difference between $Y$ and $\hat{Y}$ is a *residual*. Residuals will be low when the regression equation generates values of $\hat{Y}$ that are close to the actual values of $Y$.

Perfectly correlated variables result in no error in prediction (the predicted and actual values of $Y$ will always agree). However, when your correlation is less than perfect, there will be error in predicting $Y$ from $X$. You can estimate the amount of error in prediction by calculating the **standard error of estimate**, which is a measure of the distance between your data points and your computed regression line (Gravetter & Wallnau, 2017). The following formula is used to compute the standard error of estimate (Gravetter & Wallnau, 2017; *df* stands for "degrees of freedom"):

$$s_{est} = \sqrt{\frac{SS_{error}}{df}} = \sqrt{\frac{\Sigma(Y - \hat{Y})}{n - 2}}$$

In the current example, $s_{est} = 1.008$.

A close but inverse relationship exists between the magnitude of $s_{est}$ and the magnitude of the correlation between $X$ and $Y$. If $X$ and $Y$ are highly correlated, the data points will be clustered tightly around the regression line, and $s_{est}$ will be small. As the strength of the relationship between $X$ and $Y$ decreases, $s_{est}$ increases.

## The Coefficient of Determination

The square of the correlation coefficient (whether Pearson $r$, point-biserial, Spearman rho, or phi) is called the **coefficient of determination**. The coefficient of determination provides a measure of the amount of variance that two variables being tested share. It indicates how much of the variability in one of the scores can be "explained" by the variability in the other score. For example, if variation in score $X$ actually *caused* variations to occur in score $Y$, the coefficient of determination would indicate what proportion of the total variation in score $Y$ was caused by variation in score $X$.

As an example, assume that you investigated the relationship between intelligence and school performance and found a correlation of .60. Then the coefficient of determination is .60², or .36. This means that 36% of the variation in school performance is accounted for by the variation in intelligence.

Of course, you usually don't know if the relationship is truly a causal one or in which direction the causal arrow points. Consequently, you should interpret this statistic with caution. Perhaps the most enlightening use of this statistic is to subtract it from 1.0. The resulting number, called the **coefficient of nondetermination**, gives the proportion of variance in one variable *not accounted for* by variance in the other variable. This is in effect *unexplained* variance caused by unmeasured factors. If the coefficient of nondetermination is large, then your measured variables are having little impact on each other relative to these unmeasured factors. If this happens, then perhaps you should try to identify these unmeasured variables and either hold them constant or measure them.

## QUESTIONS TO PONDER

1. What is linear regression, and how is it used to analyze data?
2. How are regression weights and standard error used to interpret the results from a regression analysis?
3. What is the coefficient of determination, and what does it tell you?
4. What it the coefficient of nondetermination, and what does it tell you?

### The Correlation Matrix

If you have computed all the possible correlations among a number of variables, you can make the relationships among the variables easier to comprehend by displaying the correlation coefficients in a table called a **correlation matrix**. Table 13-5 shows a hypothetical correlation matrix for five variables (1 to 5). The variables being correlated in the matrix are shown in the headings along the top and left side of the matrix. Each number within the matrix is the correlation between the two variables whose row and column intersect at the position of the number. For example, the correlation between variables 5 and 3 can be found by reading across the row labeled "variable 5" to the column labeled "variable 3." The correlation found at that intersection is .06.

Note that the numbers along the diagonal are omitted from the table. This is because the diagonal positions represent the correlations of each variable with itself, which are necessarily 1.0. You also omit the correlations above the diagonal because they simply duplicate the correlations already given below the diagonal. For example, the correlation of variable 5 with variable 3 (below the diagonal) is the same as the correlation of variable 3 with variable 5 (which would appear above the diagonal).

**TABLE 13-5   A Correlation Matrix**

|  | VARIABLES | | | |
| VARIABLES | *1* | *2* | *3* | *4* |
| --- | --- | --- | --- | --- |
| 2 | .54 | | | |
| 3 | .43 | .87 | | |
| 4 | .52 | .31 | .88 | |
| 5 | .77 | .44 | .06 | .39 |

## Multivariate Correlational Techniques

The measures of correlation and linear regression discussed in this chapter are all bivariate. Even if you calculate several bivariate correlations and arrange them in a matrix, your conclusions are limited to the relationships between pairs of variables. Bivariate correlation techniques are certainly useful and powerful tools. In many cases, however, you may want to look at three or more variables simultaneously. For example, you might want to know what the relationship between two variables is with the effect of a third held constant. Or you might want to know how a set of predictor variables relates to a criterion variable. In these cases and related others, the statistical technique of choice is *multivariate analysis.* Multivariate analysis is a family of statistical techniques that allow you to evaluate complex relationships among three or more variables. Multivariate correlational analyses include multiple regression, discriminant analysis, part and partial correlation, and canonical correlation. Chapter 15 provides an overview of these and other multivariate techniques.

## QUESTIONS TO PONDER

1. What is a correlation matrix, and why should you construct and inspect one?
2. How does a multivariate correlational analysis differ from a bivariate correlational analysis?

## SUMMARY

When you have finished conducting your research, you begin the task of organizing, summarizing, and describing your data. The first step is to organize your data so that you can more easily conduct the relevant analyses. A good way to gain some understanding of your data is to graph the observed relationships. You can do this with a bar graph, line graph, scatter plot, or pie graph, whichever is most appropriate for your data.

A frequency distribution shows how the scores in your data vary along the scale of measurement. Although a frequency distribution can be presented in tabular format, you can grasp its essential features more easily by graphing it as a histogram or by creating a stemplot. When examining these, you should look for several important features: the center, around which the scores tend to vary; the spread, or degree to which the scores tend to vary from the center; the overall shape of the distribution (e.g., symmetric or skewed); and the presence of gaps or outliers—deviant points lying far from the rest. Examine any outliers carefully and correct or eliminate any that resulted from error. Descriptive statistics are methods for summarizing your data. Descriptive statistics include measures of central tendency, measures of variability, and measures of correlation.

The mode, median, and mean are the three measures of center. The mode is the most frequent score in your distribution. The median is the middle score in an ordered distribution. The mean is the arithmetic average of the scores, obtained by summing the scores and dividing the sum by the total number of scores.

Which of the three measures of center you should use depends both on the scale that the data were measured on and on the shape of the distribution of scores. The mean should be used only with data scaled on either a ratio or an interval scale and normally distributed. In cases in which the data are skewed or bimodal, the mean does not provide a representative measure of center and the median or mode should be considered. Ordinally scaled data are best described with the median, and nominally scaled data are best described with the mode.

Measures of spread include the range, interquartile range, variance, and standard deviation. The range is simply the difference between the highest and lowest scores in your distribution. Although simple to calculate, the range is rarely used. Serious limitations of the range are that it is strongly affected by extreme scores and takes into account only the highest and lowest scores (thus ignoring the remaining scores in the distribution). The interquartile range takes into account more of the scores in the distribution and is less sensitive than the range to extreme scores. The variance uses all the scores in its calculation but has the disadvantage that its unit of measurement differs from that of the scores from which it derives. This problem can be overcome by taking the square root of the variance. The resulting statistic, the standard deviation, is the most commonly used measure of spread.

Your decision about which of the measures of spread to use is affected by the same two factors that affect your decision about central tendency (scale of measurement and distribution of scores). The standard deviation is a good measure of spread when your scores are normally distributed. As scores deviate from normality, the standard deviation becomes a less representative measure of spread. When your data are skewed, use the interquartile range.

The five-number summary provides a concise view of your distribution by providing the minimum, first quartile, median, third quartile, and maximum. Displaying these five numbers as a boxplot helps visualize the center, spread, and shape of the distribution. You can quickly compare distributions of the same variable from different treatments or samples by creating side-by-side boxplots.

Measures of association provide an index of the direction and degree of relationship between two variables. The most popular measure of association is the Pearson product-moment correlation coefficient ($r$). This coefficient can range from $-1$ through 0 to $+1$. A stronger relationship is indicated as the coefficient approaches $\pm1$. A negative correlation indicates that an increase in the value of one variable is associated with a decrease in the value of the second (inverse relationship). A positive correlation indicates that the two measures increase or decrease together (direct relationship).

The Pearson $r$ is applied to data scaled on either an interval or a ratio scale. Other measures of correlation are available for data measured along other scales. The point-biserial correlation is used if one variable is measured on an interval or ratio scale and the other on a dichotomous scale. Spearman's rho is used if both variables are measured on at least an ordinal scale. The phi coefficient is used if both variables are dichotomous.

Linear regression is a statistical procedure closely related to correlation. With linear regression, you can estimate the value of a criterion variable given the value of a predictor. In linear regression, you calculate a least-squares regression line, which is the straight line that best fits the data on a scatter plot. This line minimizes the sum of the squared distances between each data point and the line, as measured along the *y*-axis (least-squares criterion), and minimizes the difference between predicted and obtained values of *y*. A measure of the difference between the predicted and actual values is provided by the standard error of estimate. The magnitude of the standard error is related to the magnitude of the correlation between your variables. The higher the correlation, the lower the standard error.

By squaring the correlation coefficient, you obtain the coefficient of determination, an index of the amount of variation in one variable that can be accounted for by variation in the other. Subtracting the coefficient of determination from 1.0 gives you the coefficient of nondetermination, the proportion of variance *not* shared by the two variables. The larger this number, the larger the effect of unmeasured sources of variance relative to that of the measured variables.

Multivariate statistical techniques are used to evaluate more complex relationships than simple bivariate statistics. With multivariate correlational statistics, you can analyze the degree of relationship between a set of predictor variables and a criterion variable or look at the correlation between two variables with the effect of a third variable held constant.

## KEY TERMS

descriptive statistics

exploratory data analysis (EDA)

dummy code

bar graph

line graph

scatter plot

pie graph

frequency distribution

histogram

stemplot

skewed distribution

normal distribution

outlier

resistant measure

measure of center

mode

median

mean

measure of spread

range

interquartile range

variance

standard deviation

five-number summary

boxplot

measure of association

Pearson product-moment correlation coefficient, or Pearson *r*

point-biserial correlation

Spearman rank-order correlation (rho)

phi coefficient ($\varphi$)

linear regression

bivariate linear regression

least-squares regression line

regression weight

standard error of estimate

coefficient of determination

coefficient of nondetermination

correlation matrix

# Using Inferential Statistics

C hapter 13 reviewed descriptive statistics that help you character-ize and describe your data. However, they do not help you assess the reliability of your findings. A reliable finding is repeatable whereas an unreliable one may not be. Statistics that assess the reli-ability of your findings are called **inferential statistics** because they let you infer the characteristics of a population from the characteris-tics of the samples comprising your data.

This chapter reviews the most widely used inferential statistics. The discussion focuses on issues of application and interpretation; for the most part we do not present computational formulas or worked examples.

## INFERENTIAL STATISTICS: BASIC CONCEPTS

Before introducing some of the more popular inferential statistics, we explore the basic concepts underlying these statistics. You should understand these concepts before tackling the discussion of inferential statistics that follows. If you need a more comprehensive refresher on these concepts, consult a good introductory statistics text.

### Sampling Distribution

Our discussion of distributions in Chapter 13 focused on distributions of individual scores, which are sometimes referred to as raw-score distributions. However, imagine repeatedly taking samples of a cer-tain size (e.g., $n = 10$ scores) from a given population, computing the mean of each sample, and then creating a distribution of these sample means. If you could take *every possible* sample of $n$ scores from the population, you would have what is known as the *sampling distribu-tion of the mean.* Statistical theory reveals that this distribution will tend to closely approximate the normal distribution, even when the population of scores from which the samples were drawn is far from normal in shape. Thus, you can use the normal distribution as a theoretical model that will allow you to make inferences about the likely value of the population mean, given the mean of a single sample from that population.

The sample mean is not the only statistic for which you can obtain a sampling distribution. In fact, each sample statistic has its own theoretical sampling distribution. To name just a few, the $z$ statistic, Student's $t$, the $F$ ratio, and chi-square each have an associated sampling distribution. Inferential statistics rely on these sampling distributions to draw conclusions about the reliability of data.

## Sampling Error

When you draw a sample from a population of scores, the mean of the sample, $M$, will probably differ from the population mean, $\mu$ (pronounced "mu"). An estimate of the amount of variability in sample means expected across a series of such samples is provided by the **standard error of the mean** (or *standard error* for short). It may be calculated from the standard deviation of the sample as follows:

$$s_M = \frac{s}{\sqrt{n}}$$

where $s$ is the standard deviation of the sample and $n$ is the number of scores in the sample. The standard error estimates the standard deviation of the sampling distribution of the mean for the population from which the sample was drawn.

## Degrees of Freedom

In any distribution of scores with a known mean, a limited number of data points yield independent information. For example, if you have a sample of 10 scores and a known mean (e.g., 6.5), only 9 scores are free to vary. That is, once you have selected 9 scores from the population, the value of the 10th must have a particular value that will yield the mean. Thus, the **degrees of freedom (*df*)** for a single sample are $n - 1$.

You can extend this logic to the analysis of an experiment. If you have three equally sized groups in your experiment with means on the dependent variable of 2, 5, and 10 points, the grand mean (the sum of all the scores divided by the total number of scores) is then 5.7 points. If you know the grand mean and the means for two of your groups, the final mean must have a particular value that is determined by these other means. Hence, the degrees of freedom for a three-group experiment are $k - 1$ (where $k$ is the number of groups). The degrees of freedom are used in the computation of the inferential statistics in the evaluation of statistical significance.

## Parametric Versus Nonparametric Statistics

Inferential statistics can be classified as either *parametric* or *nonparametric*. A *parameter* in this context is a characteristic of a population, whereas a *statistic* is a characteristic of your sample. A *parametric statistic* estimates the value of a population parameter from the characteristics of a sample. When you use a parametric statistic, you are making certain assumptions about the population from which your sample was drawn. A key assumption of a parametric test is that your sample was drawn from a normally distributed population of scores. Another is that your data fall along at least an interval scale of measurement.

In contrast to a parametric statistic, a *nonparametric statistic* makes no assumptions about the distribution of scores underlying your sample. Nonparametric statistics are used if your data do not meet the assumptions of a parametric test. They are especially well suited for analyzing data that fall on a nominal or ordinal scale of measurement.

## QUESTIONS TO PONDER

1. Why are sampling distributions important in inferential statistics?
2. What is sampling error, and why is it important to know about?
3. What are degrees of freedom, and how do they relate to inferential statistics?
4. How do parametric and nonparametric statistics differ?

## THE LOGIC BEHIND INFERENTIAL STATISTICS

Whenever you conduct an experiment, you expose subjects to different levels of your independent variable. Although a given experiment may contain several groups, assume for the present discussion that the experiment in question includes only two: an experimental group and a control group. The data from each group can be viewed as a sample of scores obtained from a target population in which everyone was exposed to that group's treatment. Each treatment mean provides an estimate of the mean of the population from which the samples were drawn.

Consider first the case in which the experimental treatment had no effect on the scores. In that case, the experimental and control group scores could be viewed as two independent samples taken from the *same* population. Figure 14-1 illustrates this situation. At the top is the distribution of scores from the population and below it the distributions of the two samples drawn from this population. Because the two samples were drawn from the same population and thus estimate the same population mean, you would expect the two sample means to differ only because of sampling error.

Now let's consider the case in which the experimental treatment does affect the scores, perhaps by shifting them up-scale. Figure 14-2 illustrates this situation. At top now are *two* population distributions representing populations of individuals exposed to the experimental and control treatments, respectively. The population distribution underlying the experimental group is shifted upward and away from that of the control group by the effect of the experimental treatment. This new, shifted distribution resembles the old one in standard deviation, but its mean is higher.

The bottom part of the figure shows two possible sample distributions—one for the control group and one for the experimental treatment group. These two sample means provide estimates of two *different* population means. Because of sampling error, the two sample means might or might not differ even though a difference exists between the population means. (In this illustration, they do differ.)

Your problem (as a researcher) is that you do not know whether the treatment really had an effect on the scores. You must decide this based on your observed sample

**FIGURE 14-1**  Frequency distributions showing the relationship between samples and population, assuming that the experimental treatment had no effect on the dependent variable ($M_1$, mean of sample 1; $M_2$, mean of sample 2).

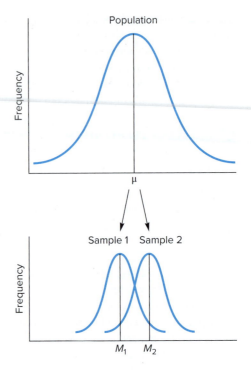

**FIGURE 14-2**  Frequency distributions showing the relationship between samples and population, assuming that the treatment had an effect on the dependent variable.

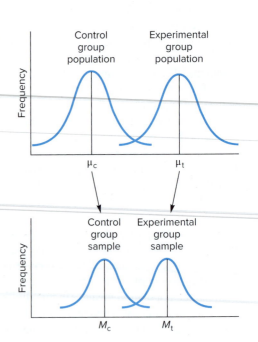

means (which may differ by a certain amount) and the sample standard deviations. From this information, you must decide whether the two sample means were drawn from the same population (the experimental treatment had no effect on the sample scores) or from two different populations having different means owing to the effect of the treatment. Inferential statistics help you make this decision.

These two possibilities (different or the same populations) can be viewed as statistical hypotheses to be tested. The hypothesis that the means were drawn from the same population (i.e., $\mu_c = \mu_t$) is referred to as the *null hypothesis* ($H_0$). The hypothesis that the means were drawn from different populations ($\mu_c \neq \mu_t$) is called the *alternative hypothesis* ($H_1$).

Inferential statistics use the characteristics of the two samples to evaluate the validity of the null hypothesis. Put another way, they assess the probability that the means of the two samples would differ *by the observed amount or more* if they had been drawn from the same population of scores. If this probability is sufficiently small (i.e., if it is very unlikely that two samples this different would be drawn by chance from the same population), then the difference between the sample means is said to be *statistically significant,* and the null hypothesis is rejected.

When you reject the null hypothesis, you are concluding that the two samples did not come from populations having the same mean. It implies that your treatment had an effect on your dependent measure, shifting the distribution of experimental treatment scores away from that of the untreated population.

## Statistical Errors

When making a comparison between two sample means, there are two possible states of affairs (the null hypothesis is true or it is false) and two possible decisions you can make (to reject the null hypothesis or not to reject it). In combination, these conditions lead to four possible outcomes, represented by the four boxes shown in Table 14-1.

The lower left-hand box represents the situation in which the null hypothesis is true (the independent variable had no effect), and you correctly decide not to reject the null hypothesis. This is a disappointing outcome, but at least you made the right decision.

**TABLE 14-1   Statistical Errors**

|  | TRUE STATE OF AFFAIRS | |
| --- | --- | --- |
| **DECISION** | *$H_0$ True* | *$H_0$ False* |
| Reject $H_0$ | Type I error | Correct decision |
| Do not reject $H_0$ | Correct decision | Type II error |

The upper left-hand box represents a more disturbing outcome. Here the null hypothesis is again true, but you have incorrectly decided to reject the null hypothesis. In other words, you decided that your independent variable did have an effect when in fact it did not. In statistics this mistake is called a **Type I error**. In signal-detection experiments, the same kind of mistake is called a "false alarm" (saying that a signal was present when actually it was not).

The lower right-hand box in Table 14-1 represents a second kind of error. In this case, the null hypothesis is false (the independent variable did have an effect), but you have incorrectly decided not to reject the null hypothesis. This is called a **Type II error** and represents the case in which you concluded your independent variable had no effect when it really did have one. In signal-detection experiments, such an outcome is called a "miss" (not detecting a signal that was present).

Ideally, you would like to minimize the probability of making either a Type I or a Type II error. Unfortunately, some of the things that you can do to minimize a Type I error actually increase the probability of a Type II error, and vice versa.

## Determining Statistical Significance

In inferential statistics, the **p-value** is the estimated probability of obtaining an apparent treatment effect (difference between samples) *at least as large as* the one you actually found, *given that the null hypothesis is true*. By setting a criterion probability for rejecting the null hypothesis, you can set the rate at which you will commit Type I errors. This criterion, called the **alpha level ($\alpha$)**, is the probability of making a Type I error. The smaller you make alpha, the less likely you are to make a Type I error. In theory, you can reduce the probability of making a Type I error to any desired level. For instance, you could average less than one Type I error in 1 million experiments (for which the null hypothesis was true) by choosing an alpha level of .000001. There are good reasons, discussed later, why you do not ordinarily adopt such a conservative alpha level.

By convention, the minimum acceptable alpha traditionally has been set at .05, or 5 chances in 100 that sampling error alone could have produced an effect at least as large as the one observed. The particular level of alpha you adopt is called the *level of significance*. If the difference between means yields a *p* value that is less than or equal to alpha, you declare that difference to be *statistically significant*.

If you are using statistical software to conduct your analysis, the software will compute the value of the test statistic and the associated *p*-value for you. If you are doing the calculations by hand, however, computing *p* can be challenging. To avoid this problem, statisticians created tables of *critical values* for popular tests. To determine whether the value of your test statistic is significant, you compare it to the critical value obtained from the table. If your observed value *equals or exceeds* the critical value, you declare your effect statistically significant.

## One-Tailed Versus Two-Tailed Tests

The critical values of a statistic depend on such factors as the number of observations per treatment, the number of treatments, and the desired alpha level. They also depend on whether the test is one-tailed or two-tailed.

Figure 14-3 shows two examples of the sampling distribution for the $z$ statistic. This distribution is normal and therefore symmetric about the mean. The left distribution shows the **critical region** (shaded area) for a *one-tailed test,* assuming alpha has been set to .05. This region contains 5% of the total area under the curve, representing the 5% of extreme cases in this region whose $z$ scores occur by chance with a probability of .05 or less. The $z$ values falling into this critical region are judged to be statistically significant.

The right distribution in Figure 14-3 shows the *two* critical regions for the *two-tailed test,* using the same .05 alpha value. To keep the probability at .05, the total percentage of cases found in the two tails of the distribution must equal 5%. Thus, each critical region must contain 2.5% of the cases. Consequently, the $z$ scores required to reach statistical significance must be more extreme than was the case for the one-tailed test.

You would conduct a one-tailed test if you were interested only in whether the obtained value of the statistic falls in one tail of the sampling distribution for that statistic. This is usually the case when your research hypotheses are directional. For example, you may want to know whether a new therapy is measurably *better* than the standard one. However, if the new therapy is not better, then you really do not care whether it is simply as good as the standard method or is actually worse. You would not use it in either case.

In contrast, you would conduct a two-tailed test if you wanted to know whether the new therapy was either better *or* worse than the standard method. In that case, you need to check whether your obtained statistic falls into either tail of the distribution.

The major implication of all this is that for a given alpha level you must obtain a greater difference between the means of your two treatment groups to reach statistical significance if you use a two-tailed test than if you use a one-tailed test. The one-tailed test is therefore more likely to detect a real difference if one is present (i.e., it is more powerful). However, using the one-tailed test means giving up any information about the reliability of a difference in the other, untested direction.

The use of one-tailed versus two-tailed tests has been a controversial topic among statisticians. Strictly speaking, you must choose which version you will use *before* you see the data. You must base your decision on such factors as practical considerations (as in the therapy example), your hypothesis, or previous knowledge. If you wait until after you have seen the data and then base your decision on the direction of the obtained outcome, your actual probability of falsely rejecting the null hypothesis will be greater

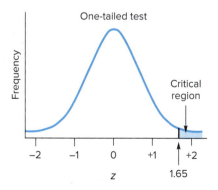
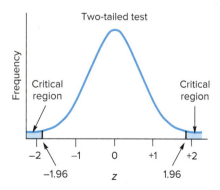

**FIGURE 14-3**   Graphs showing critical regions for one-tailed and two-tailed tests of statistical significance.

than the stated alpha value. You have used information contained in the data to make your decision, but that information may itself be the result of chance processes and unreliable.

If you conduct a two-tailed test and then fail to obtain a statistically significant result, the temptation is to find some excuse why you "should have done" a one-tailed test. You can avoid this temptation if you adopt the following rule of thumb: Always use a two-tailed test unless there are compelling *a priori* reasons not to.

## QUESTIONS TO PONDER

1. What is the general logic behind inferential statistics?
2. What are Type I and Type II errors, and how are they related?
3. What does statistical significance mean?
4. When should you use a one-tailed or a two-tailed test?

### Statistical Power

Inferential statistics are designed to help you determine the validity of the null hypothesis. Consequently, you want your statistics to detect real population differences when they exist. The **power** of a statistical test is its ability to detect these real differences. Put in statistical terms, the *power* of a statistical test is the probability that it will reject the hull hypothesis *when the null hypothesis is false* and is one minus the probability of a Type II error. A powerful statistic is one that is more likely to detect the effects of your independent variables when they are present.

The issue of the power of your statistical test is an important one. If your statistical test is low in power, you may fail to detect an effect that is really there, leading you to abandon a potentially fruitful line of research. Consequently, you want to be reasonably sure that your failure to reject the null hypothesis is not caused by a lack of power in your statistical test.

A number of factors, reviewed next, affect how much power your statistical test will have.

*Alpha Level*   As you reduce your alpha level (e.g., from .05 to .01), you reduce the probability of making a Type I error. Adopting a more conservative alpha level makes it more difficult to reject the null hypothesis. Unfortunately, it also reduces power. Given a constant error variance, a larger difference between means is required to obtain statistical significance with a more conservative alpha level (e.g., .01 instead of .05). This loss of power is the reason we do not use highly conservative alpha levels, such as .00001.

*Sample Size*   The power of your statistical test increases with the size of your sample because larger samples provide more stable estimates of population parameters. In particular, the standard errors of the means get smaller, so the likely positions of the population means fall within narrower bounds. Consequently, it is easier to detect small differences in population means and thus to reject the null hypothesis when it is false.

*One-Tailed Versus Two-Tailed Tests*    A two-tailed test is less powerful than a one-tailed test. This can be easily demonstrated by looking at the critical values of $z$ for one versus two tails. The critical value at $\alpha = .05$ for a one-tailed test is 1.65. For a two-tailed test, the critical value is 1.96. It is thus easier to reject the null hypothesis with the one-tailed test than with the two-tailed test.

*Effect Size*    The degree to which the manipulation of your independent variable changes the value of the dependent variable is termed the **effect size**. To facilitate comparison across variables and experiments, effect size is usually reported as a proportion of the variation in scores *within* the treatments under comparison; for example, the effect size for the difference between two treatment means might be reported as $(M_2 - M_1)/s$, where $s$ is the pooled sample standard deviation (Cohen, 1988). Measured in this way, effect size estimates the amount of overlap between the two population distributions from which the samples were drawn. Large effect sizes indicate relatively little overlap: The mean of population 2 lies far into one tail of the distribution of population 1, so a real difference in population means is likely to be detected in the inferential test (good power). Small effect sizes indicate a large overlap in the population distributions and thus, everything else being equal, relatively little power.

In the past, effect sizes were reported rarely, but a growing recognition of their importance in the interpretation of data has led to a dramatic change in publication practices. In fact, according to the *Publication Manual of the American Psychological Association* (6th ed.), "For the reader to appreciate the magnitude or importance of a study's findings, it is almost always necessary to include some measure of effect size in the Results section" (APA, 2010, p. 34).

*Determining Power*    Because the business of inferential statistics is to allow you to decide whether or not to reject the null hypothesis, the issue of power is important. You want to be reasonably sure that your decision is correct. Failure to reject the null hypothesis can be caused by many factors. Your independent variable actually may have no effect, or your experiment may have been carried out so poorly that the effect was buried in error variance. Or maybe your inferential statistic simply was not powerful enough to detect the difference.

Although alpha (the probability of making a Type I error can be set directly, it is not so easy to determine what the power of your analysis will be. However, you can work backward from a desired amount of power to estimate the sample sizes required to obtain it. To calculate these estimates, you must be willing to state the level of power required, the size of the difference you expect to find, and the expected error variance. [See Gravetter & Wallnau (2017) or Keppel (1982) for a discussion on how to estimate the required sample size.]

You can estimate the expected difference between means and the expected error variance from pilot research, from theory, or from previous research in your area. Unfortunately, the proper amount of power is not easy to establish. There is no agreed-on acceptable or desirable level of power (Keppel, 1982). Too much power can be as bad as too little. If you tested enough subjects, you could conceivably obtain statistical significance even in the most minute and trivial of differences. Similarly, when you use a correlation, you can achieve statistical significance even with small correlations if you include enough subjects. Consequently, your sample should be large enough to be sensitive to differences between treatments but not so large as to produce significant but trivial results.

The possibility of your results being statistically significant and yet trivial may seem strange to you. If so, the next section may clarify this concept.

## QUESTIONS TO PONDER

1. What is statistical power and what factors affect it?

2. What is an effect size, and why is it important to include some measure of effect size along with the results of your statistical test?

3. How is the power of a statistical test determined?

## Statistical Versus Practical Significance

To say that results are significant (statistically speaking) merely indicates that the observed sample differences are unlikely to have occurred as mere products of chance. Consequently, you can have increased confidence that they resulted from the effects of your treatment. Confusion arises when you give the word *significant* its more common meaning. Something "significant" in this more common sense is important or worthy of note.

The fact that the treatment means of your experiment differ significantly may or may not be important. If the difference is predicted by a particular theory and not by others, then the finding may be important because it supports that theory over the others. The finding also may be important if it shows that one variable strongly affects another. Such findings may have practical implications by demonstrating, for example, the superiority of a new therapeutic technique. In such cases, a statistically significant (i.e., reliable) finding also may have *practical significance.*

Advertisers sometimes purposely blur the distinction between statistical and practical significance. A number of years ago, Bayer aspirin announced the results of a "hospital study on pain other than headache." Evidently, groups of hospital patients were treated with Bayer aspirin and with several other brands. The advertisement glossed over the details of the study, but apparently the patients were asked to rate the severity of their pain at some point after taking Bayer or brand X (the identities of both brands were probably concealed). According to the ad, "the results were significant—Bayer was better." However, the ad did not say in what way the results were significant. Evidently, the results were statistically significant and thus unlikely given that only chance was operating to produce the difference. Without any information about the pain ratings, however, you do not know if this finding has any practical significance. It may be that the Bayer and brand X group ratings differed by less than 1 point on a 10-point scale. Although this average difference may have been reliable, it also may be the case that no individual could tell the difference between two pains so close together on the scale. In that case, the statistically significant difference would have no practical significance and would provide no reason for choosing Bayer over other brands of aspirin.

If a difference is *not* statistically significant, then it can have no *practical* significance, no matter how big the difference is. It is not reliable; therefore, even a large difference likely reflects nothing more than the effect of extraneous variables on your measure.

Given that your results are statistically significant, your measure of effect size can help you to gauge the practical significance of your finding. Effect size tells you how large the effect is, relative to the amount of overlap in the data from your two conditions. A stronger effect stands out more clearly against the background of extraneous variation and may, therefore, have greater practical utility.

If your measure of effect size is the difference between the condition means, divided by the pooled standard deviation (Cohen, 1988), then you can think of it as a standard $z$-score. Robert Coe (2002) suggests that one way to visualize what effect size means is to determine, for a given effect size, the percentage of individuals from, say, a control group who would score lower (or higher, depending on the direction of the effect) than the average person from an experimental group. Imagine that you tested a new treatment for depression. If you obtained an effect size of .50, then 69% of your control group would have scored higher on your measure of depression than the average person who received the treatment. For an effect size of .80, this number rises to 79%. From these numbers, it would seem that a fair number of individuals are benefiting from your new treatment—enough, perhaps, to make it worth using.

## Recent Changes in Reporting Practices

Standard practices for evaluating and reporting the results of inferential statistical calculations have recently been undergoing changes in response to a number of criticisms leveled against them. One is the evaluation of $p$ by comparing its value to a chosen alpha level (e.g., .05) in order to declare whether a given effect is statistically significant. This imposes an artificial standard on significance that is hard to justify (e.g., why is .05 to be preferred over some other alpha?). This, together with the availability of statistical analysis software that can compute exact $p$ values, has led to the recommendation to publish these exact values so that researchers can apply their own criteria when deciding whether to judge some difference as statistically significant.

Another criticism against the evaluation of $p$ for statistical significance is that the result only indicates whether the evidence justifies rejecting the null hypothesis. It does not indicate a range showing how large the effect is likely to be in the population. The APA offers the following solution. For point estimates (e.g., sample means), always report an associated measure of variability (e.g., the standard error). For parameter estimates (such as the difference between means in the population), report confidence intervals. *Confidence intervals* replace the point estimate associated with significance testing with a range of values within which the true difference (e.g., between treatment means) is likely to lie. A 95% confidence interval, for example, indicates the range of values within the true difference will lie in 95% of cases. In addition, one can still determine statistical significance: If the range of values does not overlap a zero difference, then the difference is significant (at, e.g., the .05 level if using a 95% CI).

Neither exact $p$ values nor confidence intervals provide direct information as to the likely size of an effect in the population; this fact has led to the current practice of including measures of effect size along with the traditional $p$ values, as noted earlier in our discussion of statistical power.

## Balancing Type I Versus Type II Errors

In the behavioral sciences, an alpha level of .05 (or 1 chance in 20) is usually considered the maximum acceptable rate for Type I errors. This level provides reasonable protection against Type I errors while also maintaining a reasonable level of power for most analyses. Of course, if you want to guard more strongly against Type I errors, you can adopt a more stringent alpha level, such as the .01 level (1 chance in 100).

Whatever alpha level you determine is reasonable for your purposes, remember that this number does nothing more than provide a criterion for deciding whether the differences you have obtained are reliable. A difference is either reliable or it is not. If your results are significant at the .0001 level, they are not any more reliable than if they were significant at the .05 level. It does not mean your results are "more significant" or "more reliable" than significant results obtained at the .05 level. If the results are statistically significant at your chosen alpha level, it simply means you are willing to believe that the differences are real. However, lower alpha levels (moving from .05 to .01) allow you greater confidence in your decision about your results.

The importance of Type I errors may vary depending on the type of research and the purposes to which the information may be put. For example, applied research may be better evaluated at a less conservative alpha level (for example, $p < .10$). If you were testing the effectiveness of a new form of judicial instruction on the reduction of bias against Black defendants, a Type II error might be more serious than a Type I error. If you retain the null hypothesis when it is false, more Black defendants may be convicted as a result.

Ultimately, it is up to you to decide on an appropriate balance between Type I and Type II errors. Unfortunately, most journals will not publish a finding unless it is significant at least at the $p < .05$ level. Chapter 3 examined this issue in the discussion of publication practices.

## QUESTIONS TO PONDER

1. What are statistical and practical significance and how are they different?
2. How have reporting practices affected how you report statistical significance?
3. Why is it important to consider how to balance Type I and Type II errors?

## PARAMETRIC STATISTICS

As previously noted, there are two types of inferential statistics: parametric and nonparametric. The type you apply to your data depends on the scale of measurement used and how your data are distributed. Parametric statistics are designed for use when your data fall on at least an interval scale.

## Assumptions Underlying a Parametric Statistic

Three assumptions underlie parametric inferential tests (Gravetter & Wallnau, 2017): (1) The scores have been sampled randomly from the population, (2) the sampling distribution of the mean is normal, and (3) the within-groups variances are homogeneous. Assumption 3 means the variances of the different groups are highly similar. In statistical inference, the treatment is assumed to affect the mean but not the variance.

Serious violation of one or more of these assumptions may bias the statistical test. Such bias will lead you to commit a Type I error either more or less often than the stated alpha probability and thus undermine the value of the statistic as a guide to decision making. We examine the effects of violations of these assumptions later during a discussion of the statistical technique known as the *analysis of variance*.

## Inferential Statistics with Two Samples

Imagine you have conducted a two-group experiment on whether "death-qualifying" a jury (i.e., removing any jurors who could not vote for the death penalty) affects how simulated jurors perceive a criminal defendant. Participants in your experimental group were death qualified, whereas those in your control group were not. Participants then rated on a scale from 0 to 10 the likelihood that the defendant was guilty as charged of the crime. You run your experiment and then compute a mean for each group. You find that the two means differ (the experimental group mean is 7.2, and the control group mean is 4.9).

Your means may represent a single population and differ only because of sampling error. Or your means may reliably represent two different populations. Your task is to decide which of these two conditions is true. Is the observed difference between means reliable, or does it merely reflect sampling error? This question can be answered by applying the appropriate statistical test, which in this case is a *t* test.

## The *t* Test

Use the *t* **test** when your experiment includes only two levels of the independent variable (as in the jury example). Special versions of the *t* test exist for designs involving independent samples (e.g., randomized groups) and for those involving correlated samples (e.g., matched-pairs designs and within-subjects designs).

*The t Test for Independent Samples*   You use the *t* **test for independent samples** when you have data from two groups of participants who were assigned at random to the two groups. The test comes in two versions, depending on the error term selected. The *unpooled* version computes an error term based on the standard error of the mean provided separately by each sample. The *pooled* version computes an error term based on the two samples combined, under the assumption that both samples come from populations having the same variance. The pooled version may be more sensitive to any effect of the independent variable, but it should be avoided if there are large differences in sample sizes and standard errors. Under these conditions, the probability estimates given by the pooled version may be misleading.

*The t Test for Correlated Samples*   When the two means being compared come from samples that are not independent, the formula for the *t* test must be adjusted to take into account any correlation between scores; the adjusted version is called the *t* **test for correlated samples**. In such cases, the scores from the two samples come in pairs arising from two observations of the same variable on the same participant or from single observations taken on each of a matched pair of participants. Within-subjects and matched-pairs experimental designs and some correlational designs meet this requirement.

The *t* test for correlated samples produces a larger *t* value than the *t* test for independent samples when applied to the same data *if* the scores from the two samples are at least moderately correlated, and this tends to make the correlated samples test more powerful. However, this advantage tends to be offset by the correlated sample *t* test's smaller degrees of freedom [equal to $n - 1$, where $n$ is the number of *pairs* of scores, as opposed to the $(n_1 - 1) + (n_2 - 1)$ degrees of freedom of the *t* test for independent samples, where $n_1$ and $n_2$ are the number of scores in the two samples]. When the correlation between samples is 0, the *t* values given by the correlated samples and independent samples *t* tests (pooled version) are identical; with its reduced degrees of freedom, the correlated samples *t* test will then be less powerful than the independent samples *t* test.

## An Example from the Literature: Contrasting Two Groups

Spinal cord injuries (SCI) represent a major source of physical disabilities (Hess, Marwitz, & Kreutzer, 2003). SCIs are often the result of automobile accidents or falls that involve rapid deceleration of the body and may result in mild traumatic brain injury (MTBI). Hess et al. note that when a patient with an SCI is rushed into the emergency room, the possibility that MTBI exists is often overlooked because of the seriousness of SCIs. Often, patients with SCI show cognitive impairments normally associated with MTBI, such as memory loss, attention deficits, and problems with processing information (Hess et al., 2003). The problem is that it is sometimes difficult to determine whether cognitive impairments are the result of MTBI or the emotional trauma associated with SCI.

David Hess, Jennifer Marwitz, and Jeffrey Kreutzer (2003) conducted a study to differentiate between patients with MTBI (without SCI) and patients with SCI. Participants were patients with SCI or MTBI who had been treated at a medical center. Participants' neuropsychological functioning was measured using a battery of tests assessing attention (two tests), motor speed, verbal learning, verbal memory (two tests), visuospatial skills, and word fluency. Mean scores were computed on each measure for patients with SCI and MTBI. Hess et al. used a series of *t* tests to determine if the SCI and MTBI patients differed significantly on any of the neuropsychological tests. They found significant differences between the two groups on 5 of the 10 tests. The results (shown in Table 14-2) indicated that, as a rule, patients with SCI performed better than patients with MTBI. Hess et al. also found that a high percentage of SCI patients had significant impairment on several of the cognitive measures (even though they scored better than the MTBI patients). Hess et al. suggest that SCI patients might benefit from a comprehensive rehabilitation program that targets cognitive functioning as well as emotional well-being.

If you are conducting your *t* tests on a computer, the statistical package will compute the exact *p* value for the test, given the obtained *t* and degrees of freedom. For example, in Table 14-2, the *t* given for the written attention test (2.40 with 18 degrees of freedom) yields an exact *p* of .027427 for a two-tailed test. Simply compare your obtained *p* values to your chosen alpha level. If *p* is less than or equal to alpha, the difference between your groups is statistically significant at the stated alpha level. In our example, the exact *p* obtained in the first *t*-test is less than .05 and therefore is significant at the .05 level.

**TABLE 14-2  Means and *t* Values from the Five Significant Differences Found by Hess et al. (2003)**

| TEST | SCI | MTBI | *t(df)* |
|------|-----|------|---------|
| Written attention test | 41.6 | 30.4 | 2.40 (18) |
| Motor speed | 91.4 | 126.1 | –2.20 (31) |
| Verbal learning | 47.1 | 37.9 | 2.40 (34) |
| Verbal memory (immediate recall) | 25.9 | 18.7 | 3.16 (49) |
| Verbal memory (delayed recall) | 21.4 | 10.7 | 4.73 (44) |

If published today, the Hess et al. (2003) paper would include an estimate of effect size for each statistical test, such as that provided by Cohen's *d*. For the written attention test, $d = .76$—a moderately strong effect.

Hess et al. (2003) presented differences between means and evaluated the statistical significance of these differences using a stated alpha level and the *t* test for independent samples. However, many journals now strongly suggest reporting confidence intervals rather than *p*, holding that confidence intervals are more informative than *p* values. For the Hess et al. (2003) study, we computed the 95% CI around the difference between the experimental and control group sample means for the written attention test, based on the information presented in Table 14-2. The result was $11.2 \pm 9.4$ points. Thus, there is a 95% chance that the true difference between the means (in the population as a whole) is between 1.8 and 20.6 points. The confidence interval reminds us that the true effect in the population may differ fairly widely from the observed difference in sample means. Because a difference of zero lies outside the 95% CI, we can conclude that the effect is statistically significant at the .05 level.

### The *z* Test for the Difference Between Two Proportions

In some research, you may have to determine whether two proportions are significantly different. In a jury simulation in which participants return verdicts of guilty or not guilty, for example, your dependent variable might be expressed as the proportion of participants who voted guilty. A relatively easy way to analyze data of this type is to use a *z* **test for the difference between two proportions**. The logic behind this test is essentially the same as for the *t* tests. The difference between the two proportions is evaluated against an estimate of error variance.

### QUESTIONS TO PONDER

1. What are the assumptions underlying parametric statistics?

2. Which parametric statistics would you use to analyze data from an experiment with two independent groups?

3. Which parametric statistic is appropriate for a matched two-group design?

## Beyond Two Groups: Analysis of Variance (ANOVA)

When your experiment includes more than two groups, the statistical test of choice is **analysis of variance (ANOVA)**. As the name implies, ANOVA is based on the concept of analyzing the variance that appears in the data. For this analysis, the variation in scores is divided, or *partitioned,* according to the factors assumed to be responsible for producing that variation. These factors are referred to as *sources of variance.* The next sections describe how variation is partitioned into sources and how the resulting source variations are used to calculate a statistic called the *F* ratio. The *F* ratio is ultimately checked to determine whether the variation among means is statistically significant.

*Partitioning Variation*    The value of any particular score obtained in a between-subjects experiment is determined by three factors: (1) characteristics of the subject at the time the score was measured, (2) measurement or recording errors (together called *experimental error*), and (3) the value of the independent variable (assuming the independent variable is effective). Because subjects differ from one another (factor 1) and because measurement error fluctuates (factor 2), scores will vary even when all subjects are exposed to the same treatment conditions. Scores will vary even more if subjects are exposed to different treatment conditions and the independent variable is effective.

Figure 14-4 shows how the total variation in the scores from a given experiment can be partitioned into two sources of variability (between-groups variability and within-groups variability). Notice that the example begins with a total amount of variability among scores. Again, this total amount of variability may be attributable to one or more of three factors: your independent variable, individual differences, and experimental error (Gravetter & Wallnau, 2017).

The first component resulting from the partition is the *between-groups variability.* The between-groups variability may be caused by the variation in your independent variable, by individual differences among the different subjects in your groups, by experimental error, or by a combination of these (Gravetter & Wallnau, 2017). The second component, the *within-groups variability,* may be attributed to error. This error can arise from either or both of two sources: individual differences between subjects treated alike within groups and experimental error (Gravetter & Wallnau, 2017). Take note that variability caused by your treatment effects is unique to the between-groups variability.

**FIGURE 14-4**    Partitioning total variation into between-groups and within-groups sources.

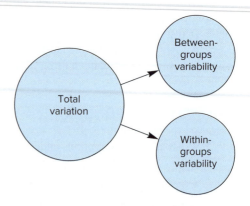

*The F Ratio*   The statistic used in ANOVA to determine statistical significance is the **F ratio**. The *F* ratio is simply the ratio of between-groups variability to within-groups variability. Both types of variability that constitute the ratio are expressed as variances. (Chapter 13 described the variance as a measure of spread.) However, statisticians perversely insist on calling the variance the *mean square*, perhaps because the term is more descriptive. The *F*-ratio and its associated degrees of freedom determine the obtained *p*, based on where the *F*-ratio falls in the sampling distribution of *F*. If *p* is less than or equal to your chosen alpha, then your *F* is statistically significant at that level.

## The One-Factor Between-Subjects ANOVA

Use the one-factor between-subjects ANOVA when your experiment includes only one factor (with two or more levels) and has different subjects in each experimental condition. As an example, imagine you have conducted an experiment on how well participants can detect a signal against a background of noise, measured in decibels (db). Participants were exposed to different levels of background noise (no noise, 20 db, or 40 db) and asked to indicate whether or not they heard a tone. The number of times that the participant correctly stated that a tone was present represents your dependent variable. You found that participants in the no-noise group detected more of the tones (36.4) than participants in either the 20-db (23.8) or 40-db (16.0) group. Table 14-3 shows the distributions for the three groups.

Submitting your data to a one-factor between-subjects ANOVA, you obtain an *F* ratio of 48.91. The obtained *p* for this *F*-ratio depends on this value and the degrees of freedom associated with both the numerator and denominator of the *F*-ratio. For the numerator this is $k - 1$, where $k$ is the number of groups. For the denominator, it is $k(n - 1)$, where $n$ is the number of subjects in each group. In this case, the degrees of freedom for the numerator and denominator are 2 and 12, respectively.

Given *F* and the degrees of freedom for both the numerator and denominator, your statistical package will compute the exact *p*-value. For $F(2, 12) = 48.91, p = .00000170$, which is significant at the .000002 level.

**TABLE 14-3   Data from Hypothetical Signal-Detection Study**

|  | NO NOISE | 20 DECIBELS | 40 DECIBELS |
|---|---|---|---|
|  | 33 | 22 | 17 |
|  | 39 | 24 | 14 |
|  | 41 | 25 | 19 |
|  | 32 | 21 | 11 |
|  | 37 | 27 | 19 |
| $\Sigma X$ | 182 | 119 | 80 |
| $\Sigma X^2$ | 6,684 | 2,855 | 1,328 |
| $M$ | 36.4 | 23.8 | 16.0 |

*Interpreting Your F Ratio*    A significant *F* ratio tells you that at least some of the differences among your means are probably not caused by chance but rather by variation in your independent variable. The only problem, at this point, is that the *F* ratio fails to tell you where among the possible comparisons the reliable differences actually occur. To isolate which means differ significantly, you must conduct specific comparisons between pairs of means. These comparisons can be either planned or unplanned.

*Planned Comparisons*    **Planned comparisons** (also known as *a priori comparisons*) are used when you have specific preexperimental hypotheses. For example, you may have hypothesized that the no-noise group would differ from the 40-db group but not from the 20-db group. In this case, you would compare the no-noise and 40-db groups and then the no-noise and 20-db groups. These comparisons are made using information from your overall ANOVA (see Keppel, 1982). Separate *F* ratios (each having 1 degree of freedom) or *t* tests are computed for each pair of means. The resulting *F* ratios or values are then are evaluated to determine the obtained *p*-values for each comparison and, based on these, their statistical significance.

You can conduct as many of these planned comparisons as necessary. However, a limited number of such comparisons yield unique information. For example, if you found that the no-noise and 20-db groups did not differ significantly and that the 40- and 20-db groups did, you have no reason to compare the no-noise and 40-db groups. You can logically infer that the no-noise and 40-db groups differ significantly. Those comparisons that yield new information are known as *orthogonal comparisons.* Any set of means has $(k - 1)$ orthogonal comparisons, where *k* is the number of treatments.

You can use planned comparisons in lieu of an overall ANOVA if you have highly specific preexperimental hypotheses. In this case, you would not have the information required to use the ANOVA-based formula for planned comparisons. A simple alternative is to conduct multiple *t* tests. You should not perform too many of these comparisons even if the relationships were predicted before you conducted your experiment. Performing multiple tests on the same data increases the probability of making a Type I error across comparisons through a process called *probability pyramiding* (discussed in the next section).

*Unplanned Comparisons*    If you do not have a specific preexperimental hypothesis concerning your results, you must conduct **unplanned comparisons** (also known as *post hoc comparisons*). Unplanned comparisons are often "fishing expeditions" in which you are simply looking for any differences that might emerge. In experiments with many levels of an independent variable, you may be required to perform a fairly large number of unplanned comparisons to fully analyze the data.

Two types of error must be considered when making many comparisons: **per-comparison error** and **familywise error**. Per-comparison error is the alpha for each comparison between means. If you set an alpha level of .05, the per-comparison error rate is .05. The familywise error rate (Keppel, 1982) takes into account the increasing probability of making at least one Type I error as the number of comparisons increases (i.e., probability pyramiding). You compute familywise error with the following formula:

$$\alpha_{FW} = 1 - (1 - \alpha)^c$$

where *c* is the number of comparisons made and alpha is your per-comparison error rate. For example, if you are making four comparisons ($c = 4$) and $\alpha = .05$, then $\alpha_{FW} = 1 - (1 - .05)^4 = 1 - .95^4 = 1 - .815 = .185$. Thus the chance of getting at least one significant difference by chance in four comparisons is more than three times the stated alpha level, assuming that only chance is at work to produce these differences.

Special tests can be applied to control familywise error, but it is beyond the scope of this chapter to discuss each of them individually. Table 14-4 lists the tests most often used to control familywise error and gives a brief description of each. For more information about these tests, see Keppel (1982, Chapter 8).

*Sample Size*   You can still use an ANOVA if your groups contain unequal numbers of subjects, but you must use adjusted computational formulas. The adjustments can take one of two forms, depending on the reasons for unequal within-cell sample sizes.

Unequal sample sizes may simply be a by-product of the way you conducted your experiment. If you conducted your experiment by randomly distributing your materials to a large group, for example, you would not be able to keep the sample sizes equal. In such cases, unequal sample sizes do not result from the properties of your treatment conditions.

Unequal sample sizes also may result from the effects of your treatments. If one of your treatments is painful or stressful, participants may drop out of your experiment because of the aversive nature of that treatment. Death of animals in a group receiving highly stressful conditions is another example of subject loss related to the experimental manipulations that result in unequal sample sizes.

*Unweighted Means Analysis*   If you end up with unequal sample sizes for reasons *not* related to the effects of your treatments, one solution is to equalize the groups by randomly discarding the excess data from the larger groups. Even then, discarding data may not be a good idea, especially if the sample sizes are small to begin with. The loss of data inevitably reduces the power of your statistical tests.

Rather than dropping data, you could use an *unweighted means analysis* that involves a minor correction to the ANOVA. This analysis gives each group in your design equal weight in the analysis, despite unequal group sizes.

*Weighted Means Analysis*   If the inequality in sample sizes was planned or reflects actual differences in the population, you should use a *weighted means analysis* (Keppel, 1973). In a weighted means analysis, each group mean is weighted according to the number of subjects in the group. As a result, means with higher weightings (those from larger groups) contribute more to the analysis than do means with lower weights. See Keppel (1973, 1982) or Gravetter and Wallnau (2017) for more information about unequal sample size in ANOVA.

## The One-Factor Within-Subjects ANOVA

If you used a multilevel within-subjects design in your experiment, the statistical test to use is the *one-factor within-subjects ANOVA*. As in a between-subjects analysis, the between-treatments sum of squares can be affected by the level of the independent variable and by experimental error (Gravetter & Wallnau, 2017). However, unlike the between-subjects case, individual differences no longer contribute to the between-treatments sum of squares because the same subjects are in each experimental treatment. The within-subjects source of variance(s) also can be partitioned into two factors: variability within a particular treatment (i.e., different subjects reacting differently to the same treatment) and experimental error.

**TABLE 14-4    Post Hoc Tests**

| TEST | USE | COMMENTS[a] |
|------|-----|-------------|
| Scheffé test | To keep familywise error rate constant regardless of the number of comparisons to be made | Very conservative test; Scheffé correction factor corrects for all possible comparisons, even if not all are made |
| Dunnett test | To contrast several experimental groups with a single control group | Not as conservative as the Scheffé test because only the number of comparisons made is considered in the familywise error rate correction |
| Tukey-a HSD test | To hold the familywise error rate constant over an entire set of two-group comparisons | Not as conservative as the Scheffé test for comparisons between pairs of means; less powerful than the Scheffé for more complex comparisons |
| Tukey-b WSD test | Alternative Tukey test | Not as conservative as Tukey's HSD test, but more conservative than the Newman–Keuls test |
| Newman–Keuls test | To compare all possible pairs of means and control per-comparison error rate | Less conservative than the Tukey test; critical value varies according to the number of comparisons made |
| Ryan's Test (REGWQ) | Modified Newman–Keuls test in which critical values decrease as the range between the highest and lowest means decreases | Controls familywise error better than the Newman–Keuls test but is less powerful than the Newman–Keuls test |
| Duncan test | To compare all possible pairs of means | Computed in the same way as the Newman–Keuls test; with more than two means to be compared, it is less conservative than the Newman–Keuls |
| Fisher test | To compare all possible combinations of means | Powerful test that does not overcompensate to control familywise error rate; no special correction factor used; significant overall $F$ ratio justifies comparisons |

[a]A conservative test is one with which it is more difficult to achieve statistical significance than with a less conservative test. "Power" refers to the ability of a test to reject the null hypothesis when the null hypothesis is false.
SOURCE: Keppel, 1982, pp. 153–159; Pagano, 2013; Winer, 1971; and information found at www2.chass.ncsu.edu/garson/pa765/anova.htm.

The contribution of individual differences is estimated by treating subjects as a factor in the analysis ($S$). You then subtract $S$ from the usual within-groups variance. This subtraction reduces the amount of error in the denominator of the $F$ ratio, thus making the $F$ ratio more sensitive to the effects of the independent variable (i.e., more powerful)—a major advantage.

*The Latin Square ANOVA*   Latin square designs are used to counterbalance the order in which subjects receive treatments in within-subjects experiments (see Chapter 10). If present, carryover effects tend to inflate the error term used to calculate your $F$ ratio. Consequently, they must be removed before you calculate $F$. This is done by treating practice effects as a factor in the analysis. For more information on the Latin square ANOVA, see Keppel (1982, pp. 385–391).

*Interpreting Your F Ratio*   A significant overall $F$ ratio tells you that significant differences exist among your means, but, as usual, it does not tell you where these significant differences occur. To determine which means differ, you must further analyze your data. The tests used to compare your means are similar to those used in the between-subjects analysis. Once again, they can be either planned or unplanned.

## QUESTIONS TO PONDER

1. When would you need to use a one-factor ANOVA rather than a $t$ test to analyze your data?

2. Why should you normally use ANOVA to analyze data from more than two treatments, rather than conducting multiple $t$ tests?

3. When would you do a planned versus an unplanned comparison, and why?

4. What is the difference between weighted and unweighted means analysis, and when would you use each?

5. What is a post hoc test, and what does it control?

6. How does a Latin Square ANOVA deal with possible carryover effects?

## The Two-Factor Between-Subjects ANOVA

Chapter 10 discussed the two-factor between-subjects design. In this design, you include two independent variables and randomly assign different subjects to each condition. In addition, you combine independent variables across groups so that you can extract the independent effect of each factor (the main effects) and the combined effect of the two factors (interaction) on the dependent variable. (If you are unclear about the meanings of these terms, review Chapter 10.) The analysis appropriate to data from this design is the *two-factor between-subjects ANOVA*. This ANOVA is necessarily more complicated than a one-factor ANOVA because it must determine the statistical significance of each main effect and of the interaction as well.

*Main Effects and Interactions*   If you find significant main effects and a significant interaction in your experiment, you must be careful about interpreting the main effects.

When you interpret a main effect, you are suggesting that your independent variable has an effect on the dependent variable, regardless of the level of your other independent variable. The presence of an interaction provides evidence to the contrary. The interaction shows that neither of your independent variables has a simple, independent effect. Consequently, you should avoid interpreting main effects when an interaction is present.

You should also be aware that certain kinds of interactions can cancel out the main effects. The independent variables may have been effective, and yet the statistical analysis will fail to reveal statistically significant main effects for these factors. To see how this can happen, imagine you have conducted a two-factor experiment with two levels of each factor. Figure 14-5 graphs the cell means for this hypothetical experiment.

The diagonal lines depict the functional relationship between factor A and the dependent variable at the each level of factor B. The fact that the lines are not parallel indicates the presence of an interaction. Notice that factor A strongly affects the level of the dependent variable at *both* levels of factor B but that these effects run in opposite directions.

The dashed line in Figure 14-5 represents the main effect of factor A, computed by averaging the upper and lower points to collapse across the levels of factor B. This dashed line is horizontal, indicating that there is no change in the dependent variable across the two levels of factor A (collapsed over factor B). Although factor A has strong effects on the dependent variable at each level of factor B, its average (main) effect is zero.

Logically, if the interaction of two variables is significant, then the two variables themselves have reliable effects. Consequently, if you have a significant interaction, do not interpret the main effects. The effects of the factors involved in the interaction are reliable whether or not the main effects are statistically significant.

Finally, most of the time you are more interested in the significant interaction than in main effects, even before your experiment is conducted. Hypothesized relationships among variables are often stated in terms of interactions. Interactions tend to be inherently more interesting than main effects. They show how changes in one variable alter the effects on behavior of other variables.

*Sample Size*    Just as with a one-factor ANOVA, you can compute a multifactor ANOVA with unequal sample sizes. The unweighted means analysis can be conducted

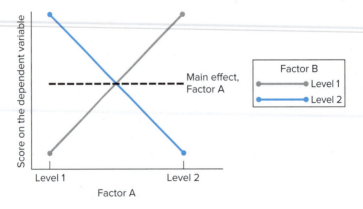

**FIGURE 14-5**    Graph showing a two-way interaction that masks main effects.

on a design with two or more factors (the logic is the same). For details on modifications to the basic two-factor ANOVA formulas for weighted means and unweighted means analyses, see Keppel (1973, 1982).

*ANOVA for a Two-Factor Between-Subjects Design: An Example*    An experiment conducted by Doris Chang and Stanley Sue (2003) provides an excellent example of the application of ANOVA to the analysis of data from a two-factor experiment. Chang and Sue investigated how the race of a student affected a teacher's assessments of the student's behavior and whether those assessments were specific to certain types of issues. Teachers (163 women and 34 men) completed a survey on which they evaluated the behavior of three hypothetical children. Each survey included a photograph of a child who was either Asian American, African American, or Caucasian. The survey also included a short description of the child's behavior, which was depicted as falling into one of three "problem" types: (1) "overcontrolled" (anxious to please and afraid of making mistakes), (2) "undercontrolled" (disobedient, disruptive, and easily frustrated), or (3) "normal" (generally follows rules, fidgets only occasionally, etc.). These two variables comprise the two independent variables in a 3 (race of child) × 3 (problem type) factorial design. The survey also included several measures on which teachers evaluated the child's behavior (e.g., seriousness, how typical the behavior was, attributions for the causes of the behavior, and academic performance).

We limit our discussion of the results to one of the dependent variables: typicality of the behavior. The data were analyzed with a two-factor ANOVA. The results indicated a significant main effect of problem type, $F (2, 368) = 46.19, p < .0001$. Normal behavior ($M = 6.10$) was seen as more typical than either undercontrolled ($M = 4.08$) or overcontrolled ($M = 4.34$) behavior. The ANOVA also revealed a statistically significant race by problem–type interaction, $F (4, 368) = 7.37, p = .00001018$.

*Interpreting the Results*    This example shows how to interpret the results from a two-factor ANOVA. First, consider the two main effects. There was a significant effect of problem type on typicality ratings. Normal behavior was rated as more typical than overcontrolled or undercontrolled behavior. If this were the only significant effect, you could then conclude that race of the child had no effect on typicality ratings because the main effect of race was not statistically significant. However, this conclusion is not warranted because of the presence of a significant interaction between race of learner and problem type.

The presence of a significant interaction suggests that the relationship between the two independent variables and your dependent variable is complex. Figure 14-6 shows the data contributing to the significant interaction in the Chang and Sue (2003) experiment. Analyzing a significant interaction like this one involves making comparisons among the means involved.

Because Chang and Sue (2003) predicted the interaction, they used planned comparisons (*t* tests) to contrast the relevant means. The results showed that the typicality of the Asian American child's behavior was evaluated very differently from that of the Caucasian or African American child. Teachers saw the normal behavior of the Asian American child as less typical than the normal behavior of either the Caucasian or African American child. Teachers saw the overcontrolled behavior of the Asian American

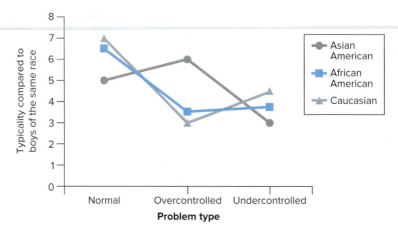

**FIGURE 14-6**    Graph showing an interaction between race and problem type.
SOURCE: Chang, D. F., & Sue, S. (2003). The effects of race and problem type on teachers' assessments of student behavior. *Journal of Consulting and Clinical Psychology, 71*, 235–242. Copyright 2003 by American Psychological Association.

child as more typical than the same behavior attributed to the African American or Caucasian child. The undercontrolled behavior was seen as less typical for the Asian American child than for the African American and Caucasian children, respectively. So the race of the child did affect how participants rated the typicality of a behavior, but the nature of that effect depended on the type of behavior attributed to the child.

## The Two-Factor Within-Subjects ANOVA

All subjects in a two-factor within-subjects design are exposed to every combination of levels of your two independent variables. Use a *two-factor within-subjects ANOVA* to analyze these designs. This analysis applies the same logic developed for the one-factor within-subjects ANOVA. As in the one-factor case, subjects are treated as a factor along with your manipulated independent variables.

The major difference between the one- and two-factor within-subjects ANOVA is that you must consider the interaction between each of your independent variables and the subjects factor (A × S and B × S), in addition to the interaction between your independent variables (A × B). You can find a complete example of the two-factor within-subjects ANOVA in Keppel (1973).

## Mixed Designs

In some situations, your research may call for a design mixing between-subjects and within-subjects components. This design was discussed briefly in Chapter 11. If you use such a design (known as a *mixed* or *split-plot design*), you can analyze your data with an ANOVA. The computations involve calculating sums of squares for the between factor and for the within factor.

The most complex part of the analysis is the selection of an error term to calculate the *F* ratios. The within-groups mean square is used to calculate the between-subjects

*F* whereas the interaction of the within factor with the within-groups variance is used to evaluate both the within-subjects factor and the interaction between the within-subjects and between-subjects factors. Keppel (1973, 1982) provides an excellent discussion of this analysis and a complete worked example.

## Higher-Order and Special-Case ANOVAs

Variations of ANOVA exist for just about any design used in research. For example, you can include three or four factors in a single experiment and analyze the data with a *higher-order ANOVA*. In a three-factor ANOVA, for example, you can test three main effects (A, B, and C), three two-way interactions (AB, AC, and BC), and a three-way interaction (ABC). As discussed in Chapter 10, it may be difficult to interpret the higher-order interactions that occur when your design includes more than four factors.

A special ANOVA is used when you have included a continuous correlational variable in your experiment (such as age). This type of ANOVA, called the **analysis of covariance** (**ANCOVA**), allows you to examine the relationship between experimentally manipulated variables while statistically controlling another variable that may be correlated with them. Keppel (1973, 1982) provides clear discussions of these analyses and other issues relating to ANCOVA.

## ANOVA: Summing Up

To summarize, ANOVA is a powerful parametric statistic used to analyze one-factor experiments (either within-subjects or between-subjects) with more than two treatments and to analyze multifactor experiments. It is intended for use when your dependent variable is scaled on at least an interval scale. The assumptions that apply to the use of parametric statistics in general (such as homogeneity of variance and normally distributed sampling distributions) apply to ANOVA.

ANOVA involves forming a ratio between the variance (mean square) caused by your independent variable plus experimental error and the variance (mean square) caused by experimental error alone. The resulting score is called an *F* ratio. A significant *F* ratio tells you that at least one of your means differs significantly from the other means. To determine where the significant differences occur you must apply special follow-up (post hoc) tests.

## QUESTIONS TO PONDER

1. If you have two independent variables in your experiment, what type of ANOVA should be used to analyze your data?

2. What are main effects and interactions, and how are they analyzed?

3. What is a higher-order ANOVA? What difficulties arise as the number of orders increases?

4. What is ANCOVA, and what does it do that ANOVA does not do?

## NONPARAMETRIC STATISTICS

Thus far, this discussion has centered on parametric statistical tests. In some situations, however, you may not be able to use a parametric test. When your data do not meet the assumptions of a parametric test or when your dependent variable was scaled on a nominal or ordinal scale, consider a nonparametric test. This section discusses three nonparametric tests: chi-square, the Mann–Whitney $U$ test, and the Wilcoxon signed ranks test. You might consider using many other nonparametric tests. For a complete description of these, see Siegel and Castellan (1988). Table 14-5 summarizes some information on these and other nonparametric tests.

### Chi-Square

When your dependent variable is a dichotomous decision (such as yes/no or guilty/not guilty) or a frequency count (such as how many people voted for candidate A and how many for candidate B), the statistic of choice is **chi-square** ($\chi^2$). Versions of chi-square exist for studies with one and two variables. This discussion is limited to the two-variable case. For further information on the one-variable analysis, see either Siegel and Castellan (1988) or Roscoe (1975).

*Chi-Square for Contingency Tables*    *Chi-square for contingency tables* (also called the *chi-square test for independence*) is designed for frequency data in which the relationship, or contingency, between two variables is to be determined. In a voter preference study, for example, you might have measured sex of respondent in addition to candidate preference. You may want to know whether the two variables are related or independent. The chi-square test for contingency tables compares your *observed cell frequencies* (those you obtained in your study) with the *expected cell frequencies* (those you would expect to find if chance alone were operating).

A study reported by Herbert Harari, Oren Harari, and Robert White (1985) provides an excellent example of the application of the chi-square test to the analysis of frequency data. Harari et al. investigated whether male participants would help the victim of a simulated rape. Previous research on helping behavior suggested that individuals are less likely to help someone in distress if they are with others than if they are alone. Harari et al. conducted a field investigation of this effect. Participants (either walking alone or in noninteracting groups) were exposed to a mock rape (a male confederate of the experimenters grabbed a female confederate and dragged her into some bushes). Observers recorded whether participants helped the female rape victim. Table 14-6 shows the frequencies of participants helping under the two conditions. The results of a chi-square test performed on these data indicated that participants in groups were significantly more likely to help than those who were alone.

*Limitations of Chi-Square*    If any of your expected cell frequencies is less than five, the value of chi-square may be artificially inflated (Gravetter & Wallnau, 2017). You have three options to deal with this problem. First, you could increase your sample size. Second, you could combine cells (if it is logical to do so); for example, you could categorize subjects into three categories rather than five. Third, you could consider a different test. The Fisher exact probability test (see Roscoe, 1975, or Siegel & Castellan,

**TABLE 14-5   Nonparametric Tests**

| TEST | MINIMUM SCALE OF MEASUREMENT | COMMENTS |
|---|---|---|
| *One-Sample Tests* | | |
| Binomial | Nominal | |
| Chi-square | Nominal | |
| Kolmogorov–Smirnov | Ordinal | Can be used as a more powerful alternative to chi-square |
| *Two Independent Samples* | | |
| Chi-square | Nominal | |
| Fisher exact probability | Nominal | Alternative to chi-square when expected frequencies are small |
| Kolmogorov–Smirnov | Ordinal | More powerful than the Mann–Whitney $U$ test |
| Wald–Wolfowitz runs | Ordinal | |
| Moses test of extreme reactions | Ordinal | Less powerful than Mann–Whitney $U$ test |
| Randomization test | Interval | Tests the difference between means without assuming normality of data or homogeneity of variance |
| Mann–Whitney $U$ | Ordinal or above | Good alternative to $t$ test when assumptions violated |
| *Two Related Samples* | | |
| McNemar | Nominal | Good test when you have a before–after hypothesis |
| Sign | Ordinal | Good when quantitative measures are not possible, but you can rank data |
| Wilcoxon matched pairs | Ordinal | Good alternative to $t$ test when normality assumption is violated |
| Walsh test | Interval | Good nonparametric alternative to the $t$ test; data must be distributed symmetrically |
| Randomization test for matched pairs | Interval | |

**TABLE 14-5   Nonparametric Tests** *continued*

| *More Than Two Related Samples* | | |
|---|---|---|
| Cochran Q test | Nominal | Most useful when data fall into natural dichotomous categories |
| Friedman two-way ANOVA | Ordinal | |
| *More Than Two Independent Samples* | | |
| Chi-square | Nominal | |
| Kruskal–Wallis one-way ANOVA | Ordinal | Good alternative to a one-factor ANOVA when assumptions are violated |

SOURCE: Roscoe, 1975; and Siegel and Castellan, 1988.

**TABLE 14-6   Number of Participants Helping Mock Rape Victim, in Two Conditions**

| | HELPED | DID NOT HELP | |
|---|---|---|---|
| **PARTICIPANTS IN GROUPS** | 34 | 6 | 40 |
| **PARTICIPANTS ALONE** | 26 | 14 | 40 |
| | 60 | 20 | |

SOURCE: Harari, Harari, and White, 1985.

1988) is an alternative to chi-square when you have small expected frequencies and a $2 \times 2$ contingency table (Roscoe, 1975).

A significant chi-square indicates that your two variables are related. It does not tell you where the significant differences lie when more than two categories of each variable exist. To determine the locus of the significant effects, you can conduct separate chi-square tests on specific cells of the contingency table.

## The Mann–Whitney *U* Test

Another powerful nonparametric test is the **Mann–Whitney *U* test**. Use the Mann–Whitney *U* test to evaluate the significance of a difference between two independent groups when your dependent variable is scaled on at least an ordinal scale. It is a good alternative to the *t* test when your data do not meet the assumptions of the *t* test (when the scores are not normally distributed or when the variances are heterogeneous).

## The Wilcoxon Signed Ranks Test

If you conduct a single-factor experiment using a within-subjects or matched-pairs design, the **Wilcoxon signed ranks test** is a good alternative to the correlated samples *t* test when your data do not meet the *t* test's assumptions. For more information on the Wilcoxon signed ranks test, see Siegel and Castellan (1988).

## Parametric Versus Nonparametric Statistics

Nonparametric statistics are useful when your data do not meet the assumptions of parametric statistics. If you have a choice, choose a parametric statistic over a nonparametric one because parametric statistics are generally more powerful. That is, the parametric statistic usually provides a more sensitive test of the null hypothesis than does an equivalent nonparametric statistic.

Unfortunately, appropriate nonparametric tests are not always available for complex designs. Consequently, when designing your study, you should try to scale your dependent measures so an ANOVA or other suitable parametric statistic can be used.

## QUESTIONS TO PONDER

1. What is a nonparametric statistic? Under what conditions would you use one?
2. When would you use the chi-square test for contingency tables?
3. When would you use a Mann-Whitney *U* test or a Wilcoxon signed ranks test?

## Data Transformations

Sometimes you may find it necessary to transform your data to a new scale. For example, a simple transformation can be accomplished by subtracting a constant from your data. (You might do this if the original numbers are very large.) When you compute some statistics, large numbers make the computations difficult. Subtracting a constant from each score can make the numbers manageable without affecting the relationships within the data. Conversely, you might add a constant to each score in order to eliminate negative numbers.

When you add or subtract a constant, the shape of the original frequency distribution does not change. The mean of the distribution changes, but its standard deviation does not. When you multiply or divide by a constant, both the mean and standard deviation change. Such transformations, called *linear transformations,* simply change the magnitude of the numbers representing your data, but they do not change the scale of measurement.

Certain statistics can be used only if your data meet certain assumptions. If your data do not meet these assumptions, you might choose a nonparametric statistic. Unfortunately an appropriate nonparametric substitute may not be available. Another solution is to consider using a data transformation that will tend to correct the problem (e.g., by changing a skewed distribution of scores into a normal one or by removing heterogeneity of variance). Different problems with the data require different transformations to correct them. Table 14-7 lists some of the more popular data transformations and the conditions under which each might be used.

**TABLE 14-7    Data Transformations and Uses**

| TRANSFORMATION | FORMULA | USE |
|---|---|---|
| *Square root* | $X' = \sqrt{X}$ <br> *or* <br> $X' = \sqrt{X + 1}^{\text{a}}$ | When cell means and variances are related, this transformation makes variances more homogeneous; also, if data show a moderate positive skew |
| *Arcsin* | $X' = 2 \text{ arcsin } \sqrt{X}$ <br> *or* <br> $X' = 2 \text{ arcsin } \sqrt{X \pm (1/2n)}^{\text{b}}$ | When basic observations are proportions and have a binomial distribution |
| *Log* | $X' = \log X$ <br> *or* <br> $X' = \log (X + 1)^{\text{c}}$ | Normalizes data with severe positive skew |

[a]Formula used if basic observations are frequencies or if values of $X$ are small.
[b]Formula used if values of $X$ are close to 0 or 1.
[c]Formula used if value of $X$ is equal to or near 0.
SOURCE: Tabachnick and Fidell, 2013, and Winer, 1971.

Data transformations to make data conform to the assumptions of a statistic are being used less and less frequently (Keppel, 1973). ANOVA, perhaps the most commonly used inferential statistic, appears to be very robust against even moderately serious violations of the assumptions underlying the test. For example, Winer (1971) has demonstrated that even if the within-cell variances vary by a 3:1 ratio, the $F$ test is not seriously biased. Transformations of the data may not be necessary in these cases. Also, when you transform your data, your conclusions must be based on the transformed scale and not the original. In most cases, this is not a problem. However, Keppel (1973) provides an example in which a square root transformation changed significantly the relationship between two means. Prior to transformation, the mean for group 1 was lower than the mean for group 2. The opposite was true after transformation.

Use data transformations only when absolutely necessary because they can be tricky. Sometimes transformations of data correct one aspect of the data (such as restoring normality) but induce new violations of assumptions (such as heterogeneity of variance). If you must use a data transformation, before going forward with your analysis, check to be sure that the transformation had the intended effect.

## ALTERNATIVES TO TRADITIONAL INFERENTIAL STATISTICS

We close the chapter by examining alternatives to traditional significance testing, beginning with a Bayesian approach.

## A Bayesian Approach to Inferential Statistics

Although null hypothesis significance testing (NHST) remains highly popular for the assessment of the reliability of research findings, its use has come under increasing criticism in recent years. Perhaps the most serious criticism is that NHST does not tell researchers what they want to know:

> In scientific inference, what we want to know is the probability that the null hypothesis $(H_0)$ is true given that we have obtained a set of data $(D)$; that is, $p(H_0|D)$. What null hypothesis significance testing tells us is the probability of obtaining these data or more extreme data if the null hypothesis is true, $p(D|H_0)$. (Kirk, 1996, p. 747)

In practice, researchers treat the $p$ values yielded by significance testing as if they do, in fact, tell us something about the probability that the null hypothesis is true. The logic is as follows: If obtaining an effect as large or larger than the one observed in the data is highly unlikely to occur simply by chance (e.g., $p < .05$), then I will assume that chance was not responsible for the observed effect on this occasion. After all, the odds are against it! In effect, researchers assume that because $p(D|H_0)$ is small, then $p(H_0|D)$ must be small as well. But is this assumption justified? Raymond Nickerson (2000) has argued that in most cases, a small $p$ *does* provide evidence against the null hypothesis, although this evidence is not as strong as usually assumed.

Nickerson reached this conclusion by conducting a Bayesian analysis under some reasonable assumptions. The Bayesian analysis allows one to compute what researchers actually want—the probability of the null hypothesis, given the data—based on what $p$ provides—the probability of the data, given the hypothesis—and some additional information, using the following formula:

$$p(H_0|D) = \frac{p(D|H_0)p(H_0)}{p(D|H_0)p(H_0) + p(D|H_A)p(H_A)}$$

The left-hand term in this equation is called the *posterior probability* of the null hypothesis. The terms $p(H_0)$ and $p(H_A)$ are the *prior probabilities* of the null and alternative hypotheses, respectively. The equation offers a principled way to adjust what is called the *credibility* of the null hypothesis based on the data (i.e., the change from its prior to its posterior probability.

To apply this equation, we need to specify the prior probabilities. These values may be based on prior research but typically are quite subjectively based on a researcher's intuitions. The conditional probability at top on the right-hand side is, of course, simply the $p$ value obtained in a traditional significance test.

Nickerson evaluated this equation under several reasonable assumptions and concluded that the credibility of the null hypothesis, given the data, is likely to be small when $p$ is small. However, it was not as small as one might be led to conclude based on $p$ alone, suggesting that an alpha level of .05 may lead a true null hypothesis to be rejected more often than the alpha level would indicate. Nevertheless, Nickerson's analysis does support the supposition that low $p$ values typically would be associated with low probabilities of the null hypothesis.

Although Nickerson's analysis may provide some justification for the use of null hypothesis significance testing, other arguments against such testing are not so easily dispatched. One is that this practice pits the researcher's hypothesis against only one alternative: the null hypothesis of no difference. This encourages testing theories that make only weak predictions (e.g., merely that a treatment will have an effect), which will be supported by rejection of the null hypothesis no matter how large or small the effect. Researchers who evaluate theories that make strong predictions (e.g., concerning the size and direction of an effect) want to know whether the observed effect matches predictions, not just that it differs significantly from no effect (Kruschke, 2013). A further problem is that traditional significance testing has no mechanism for accepting the null hypothesis: Failure to reject the null hypothesis merely indicates that the evidence was insufficient for rejection (Kruschke, 2013). This is similar to a jury's decision not to convict a defendant—failure to convict does not prove innocence but indicates only that the evidence was insufficient for conviction.

To address the problems inherent in NHST, many researchers advocate using a Bayesian analysis instead. Kruschke (2013) notes several advantages to this approach. First, a Bayesian analysis can provide an answer to the question researchers want NHST to answer: What is the probability of the null hypothesis, given the data? Second, Bayesian estimation can be used with strong theories to identify the parameters that give the most accurate predictions. Third, the Bayesian approach allows one to evaluate the credibility of a null value. (In many cases it is just as important to know that a treatment has no effect as that it has some effect. Consider the time, effort, money, and even lives that could be saved by ruling out ineffective treatments!)

We have already noted the push to substitute confidence intervals for $p$ values in published research and to include a measure of statistical power in the results. The former represents an effort to avoid the dichotomous reject/fail to reject decision making normally associated with NHST, whereas the latter provides information about the strength of an effect that is lacking when only a $p$ value is provided. However, supporters of the Bayesian approach note that it can provide similar information while also taking account of the prior credibility of the null and alternative hypotheses. Space does not permit us to provide a detailed account of these Bayesian methods here, but we wanted you to have at least some acquaintance with the Bayesian approach as an alternative to NHST. For a brief introduction to Bayesian analysis, see Chapter 2 of Kruschke (2015), which currently is available free for download from the Web at https://sites.google.com/site/doingbayesiandataanalysis/.

## Alternatives to Inferential Statistics

Inferential statistics cannot always be applied to assess the reliability of your results. You may have too few subjects (such as in single-subject or small-$n$ research designs). Or you may have data that badly violate the assumptions of parametric tests with no appropriate nonparametric statistic to use instead. In these cases, you may test the reliability of your data by replication.

*Replication* means that you repeat your experiment. If your data are reliable, you should find a highly similar pattern of results after each replication. Replication does not mean that you have to conduct exactly the same experiment each time. Often a subsequent experiment in a series will include conditions that replicate those of the original experiment. The subsequent experiment may include conditions designed to test the effects of changing some parameters within the original context. The new experiment will provide a check on the original findings while providing new information.

Keep in mind that replication is not limited to small-*n* designs or situations in which violations of assumptions occur. You can include an element of replication in any study. Moreover, you need not limit yourself to replicating your own findings. If previous research shows a certain effect, you may wish to replicate that finding in your own research before extending your observations to new situations. Indeed, such replications are the heart of the scientific method. When successful, they demonstrate the reliability of findings both within the original context and across experimenters, subjects, and laboratories. When unsuccessful, they point to potentially important variables that may limit the generality of findings to particular situations and parameters. Either result can be important for the advancement of scientific knowledge.

Inferential statistics were developed to assess the reliability of findings within the confines of a single set of observations. By providing an index of probable reliability, they reduce the need for direct replication and thus save time and money by reducing the requirement for subjects. Nevertheless, they should not be viewed as a substitute for replication. Probably no finding in psychology has been accepted on the basis of a single experiment that was statistically significant at some alpha level. The value of inferential statistics is found not so much in the elimination of replication as in their warning that the effects apparent in research data may result from nothing more than random factors. Human beings are extremely good at recognizing patterns even when such patterns are simply the result of "noise." Inferential statistics can control the human tendency to interpret every apparent trend or difference in the data as if it were meaningful.

Inferential statistics sometimes may lack sufficient power and therefore may fail to detect effects that are clearly shown by replication. A case in point is provided by a series of experiments conducted by one of the authors of this text (Abbott) to test the effect of predictable versus unpredictable shock schedules on pain sensitivity. In each experiment, three groups of eight rats were exposed to a schedule of predictable shock, unpredictable shock, or no shock. The subjects were then tested in the same apparatus for pain sensitivity by means of the "tail-flick" test. In the tail-flick test, a hot beam of light was focused on the rat's tail. The length of time elapsing until the rat flicked its tail out of the beam (a protective reflex) indicated the degree of pain sensitivity.

The results of the first experiment indicated that the two groups exposed to shock were less sensitive to the heat than the group exposed to no shock, replicating a well-established finding. In addition, the group exposed to unpredictable shock seemed less sensitive than the group exposed to predictable shock. However, this effect was not statistically significant ($p > .05$).

Parameters of the experiment were twice altered in ways that were expected to increase the size of the predictability effect (if it existed), and the experiment was replicated. However, each replication produced virtually the identical result. On each occasion, the unpredictable shock group demonstrated less sensitivity to pain than the predictable shock group, and each time this difference was not statistically significant.

The problem could be dealt with by taking measures to increase the power of the statistical test (such as increasing sample sizes or going to a matched groups design). However, to do so would appear to be a waste of resources. In this case, the reliability of the finding was already established through replication even though the statistical analysis itself indicated that the results were probably not reliable.

Inferential statistics are simply a guide to decision making and are not the goal of the research project. As such, you should not design and conduct your research in a particular way simply because a particular inferential statistic is available to analyze such a design. Much like designing your experiment before developing hypotheses, choosing a statistical test before designing a study can place unwanted restrictions on your research. For example, you may not be able to manipulate your independent variable the way you would like and may miss some important relationships. Instead, design your study to answer your research questions in the clearest way possible and then select the method of analysis (whether inferential statistic or replication) that works best for that design.

## QUESTIONS TO PONDER

1. When are data transformations used, and what should you consider when using one?
2. How does a Bayesian analysis help you evaluate the credibility of the null hypothesis beyond using a $p$-value?
3. What are the alternatives to inferential statistics for evaluating the reliability of data?

## SUMMARY

This chapter has reviewed some of the basics of inferential statistics. Inferential statistics go beyond simple description of results. They allow you to determine whether the differences observed in your sample are reliable. Inferential statistics allow you to make a decision about the viability of the null hypothesis (which states that there is no difference among treatments) while controlling the probability of rejecting the null hypothesis when it is in fact true (Type I error).

It is important to understand some of the basic concepts behind inferential statistics before they are used. First is a sampling distribution of the mean, which is obtained when all samples of a given size are drawn from a population and sample means are calculated. Sampling error is the amount of variance in the sample means across a series of such samples and is represented by the standard error of the mean. Each statistic has its own sampling distribution, which is used to determine statistical significance. Second is degrees of freedom, which is the number of values in a distribution free to vary in a given sample and is usually $n - 1$. Degrees of freedom come into play when computing inferential statistics and their associated $p$-values.

The two types of inferential statistics are parametric and nonparametric. Parametric tests (such as the $t$ test and ANOVA) make assumptions about the populations underlying your samples. For example, these tests assume that the sampling distribution of the mean is normal and that there is homogeneity of within-cell variances. Parametric statistics are designed for use when your data are scaled on at least an interval scale. If your data seriously violate the assumptions of a parametric test or your data are scaled on a nominal or ordinal scale, a nonparametric statistic can be used (such as chi-square or the Mann–Whitney $U$ test). These tests are usually easier to compute than parametric tests. However, they are less powerful and more limited in application. Nonparametric statistics may not be available for higher-order factorial designs.

In an experiment the data from each group can be viewed as a sample of scores obtained from a target population in which everyone was exposed to that group's treatment. Each treatment mean provides an estimate of the mean of the population from which the sample was drawn. If an experimental treatment has no effect, then the experimental and control group scores could be viewed as two independent samples taken from the same population. If the treatment was effective, then the two sample means are representative of two different populations. The hypothesis that the means were drawn from the same population (i.e., $\mu_c = \mu_t$) is referred to as the null hypothesis ($H_0$). The hypothesis that the means were drawn from different populations ($\mu_c \neq \mu_t$) is called the alternative hypothesis ($H_1$). Inferential statistics help you decide the validity of the null hypothesis. If you decide that your independent variable had an effect when in fact it did not, you have made a Type I error. On the other hand, if you decide that your independent variable had no effect when in fact it did, you have made a Type II error.

Statistical significance indicates that the difference between your means was unlikely if only chance were at work. It suggests that your independent variable had an effect. Two factors contribute to a statistically significant effect: the size of the difference between means and the variability among the scores. You can have a large difference between means, but if the variability is high, you may not obtain statistical significance. Conversely, you may have a very small difference and yet obtain a significant effect if the variability is low. Measures of effect size can help to assess how strong your treatment differences are relative to the within-treatment variability of your scores. Most journals now insist that some measure of effect size be included along with the $p$ values from your statistical analysis.

An alpha level of .05 is the largest generally acceptable level for concluding that a difference between treatments is statistically significant. This value has been chosen because it represents a reasonable compromise between Type I and Type II errors. When using statistical software to conduct your analysis, the software will compute the value of the test statistic and the associated $p$-value for you. If you are doing the calculations by hand, however, computing $p$ can be challenging. To avoid this problem, statisticians created tables of critical values for popular tests.

A statistical test can be one-tailed or two-tailed, depending on how the critical regions are distributed in the sampling distribution of the statistic. In a one-tailed test, the critical region is limited to one end of the sampling distribution. You would conduct a one-tailed test if you were interested only in whether the obtained value of the statistic falls in one tail of the sampling distribution for that statistic. This is usually the case when your research hypotheses are directional (e.g., a new therapy is better than an old one, rather than merely different). In a two-tailed test, critical regions are split between the two ends of the sampling distribution. Use a two-tailed test when you do not have a directional hypothesis. Generally, a one-tailed test is more sensitive to differences between means than a two-tailed test. However, in most cases you should use a two-tailed test.

Consider the power of your statistical test when evaluating your results. If you do not obtain statistical significance, perhaps no differences exist. Or it could mean that your test was not sensitive enough to detect small differences that do exist. The power of a test is affected by the alpha level selected (with power being reduced as a more conservative alpha level is adopted) and sample size (the larger the sample, the more powerful the statistic), whether you use a one- or two-tailed test (one-tailed tests are more powerful), and the size of the effect produced by your independent variable (larger effects produce more power). There are methods for determining optimal sample sizes for obtaining a given level of power. However, to use them you must be able to specify an expected magnitude of the treatment effect, an estimate of error variance, and the desired power. The first two can be estimated from pilot data or previous research. Unfortunately, there is no agreed-on acceptable level of power.

There is a difference between statistical and practical significance. Statistical significance merely indicates that the observed differences between sample means are unlikely to have occurred by chance. Consequently, you can have increased confidence that they resulted from the effects of your treatment. Practical significance refers to whether an observed difference is important in the real world. An effect can be statistically significant, but be of little practical importance.

The practice of reporting the results of a statistical analysis simply in terms of $p$ values has come under criticism in recent years. One problem is that $p$ does not provide any indication of the range of values within which the true difference may fall in the population, given the observed sample difference. A significant difference only leads us to conclude that it is unlikely to be zero. Therefore, many journals now either require or strongly advise researchers to report confidence intervals within which the population value is likely to lie, rather than $p$.

There are parametric statistics available for two-group experiments. Use the $t$ test for independent samples when different subjects are randomly assigned to the two groups; use the $t$ test for correlated samples when the same subjects are used in both groups. Use the $z$ test for proportions to determine if the difference between two proportions is statistically significant. For multi-group experiments, use the analysis of variance (ANOVA). The analysis of variance involves calculating an $F$-ratio, which is the ratio of between-subjects variation to within-subjects variation. You compare the obtained value of $F$ against a critical value to determine significance. There are versions of the ANOVA for designs that include more than one factor. These test the significance of the main effect of each factor plus any interactions. Do not interpret main effects when a significant interaction is present. After finding a significant overall effect, you explore it further using either planned or unplanned comparisons.

Use nonparametric statistics when your data do not meet the assumptions of a parametric test or when your dependent variable was scaled on a nominal or ordinal scale. Chi-square is used when your dependent variable is a dichotomous decision or a frequency count. Chi-square for contingency tables is designed for frequency data in which the relationship, or contingency, between two variables is to be determined. This test is not valid if the expected frequency in one or more cells falls below five. Use the Mann–Whitney $U$ test when your dependent variable is scaled on at least an ordinal scale or as an alternative to the $t$ test when your data do not meet the assumptions of the $t$ test. The Wilcoxon signed ranks test is used when conducting a single-factor experiment using a correlated-samples or matched-pairs design. There are additional nonparametric tests (e.g., the Fisher exact probabilities test, Cochran Q test) for other designs.

Nonparametric statistics are useful when your data do not meet the assumptions of parametric statistics. If you have a choice, choose a parametric statistic over a nonparametric one because parametric statistics are generally more powerful. Nonparametric statistics are not always available for complex designs. Consequently, you may want to design your study to use dependent variables that allow parametric statistics to be used.

Data transformations are available for those situations in which your data are in some way abnormal. You may transform data if the numbers are large and unmanageable or if your data do not meet the assumptions of a statistical test. The transformation of data to meet assumptions of a test, however, is being done less frequently because inferential statistics tend to be robust against the effects of even moderately severe violations of assumptions. Transformations should be used sparingly because they change the nature of the variables of your study.

Some researchers have advocated that null hypothesis significance testing (NHST) be abandoned in favor of a Bayesian approach to data analysis, which, among other advantages, offers a way to assess what researchers want to know: the probability of the null hypothesis, given the data, as opposed to what the NHST-based $p$ value delivers, which is the probability of the data, given that the null hypothesis is true. For the present, however, NHST remains the dominant choice among researchers.

Inferential statistics are not the only means available for assessing the reliability of your findings. Where samples are necessarily small or an appropriate inferential statistic is not available for your research design, don't forget that you can still assess reliability by actual replication of your study.

## KEY TERMS

inferential statistics

standard error of the mean

degrees of freedom (*df*)

Type I error

Type II error

*p* value

alpha level ($\alpha$)

critical region

power

effect size

*t* test

*t* test for independent samples

*t* test for correlated samples

*z* test for the difference between two proportions

analysis of variance (ANOVA)

*F* ratio

planned comparisons

unplanned comparisons

per-comparison error

familywise error

analysis of covariance (ANCOVA)

chi-square ($X^2$)

Mann–Whitney *U* test

Wilcoxon signed ranks test

data transformation

# 15

# Using Multivariate Design and Analysis

During discussions of experimental and nonexperimental design, previous chapters assumed a **univariate strategy**: Only one dependent variable was included, or multiple dependent variables were analyzed in separate statistical analyses. Although many research questions can be addressed with a univariate strategy, others are best addressed by considering dependent variables together in a single analysis. A **multivariate strategy** includes two or more dependent measures in a single analysis.

This chapter introduces the major multivariate analysis techniques. Keep in mind that providing an in-depth introduction to these techniques in the confines of one chapter is impossible. Such a task is better suited to an entire book. Also, the complex and laborious calculations needed to compute multivariate statistics are better left to computers. Consequently, this chapter does not discuss the mathematics behind these statistical tests except for those cases in which some mathematical analysis is required to understand the issues. Instead, this chapter focuses on practical issues: applications of the various statistics, the assumptions that must be met, and interpretation of results. If you want to use any of the statistics discussed in this chapter, read *Using Multivariate Statistics* (Tabachnick & Fidell, 2013) or one of the many monographs published by Sage Publications (such as Asher, 1976, or Levine, 1977).

## CORRELATIONAL AND EXPERIMENTAL MULTIVARIATE DESIGNS

When you design an experimental or correlational study, you may decide to include multiple measures. In this case, you are using a **multivariate design**. In such a design, you might include multiple dependent variables in an experiment. For example, in an experiment on the factors that affect jury decision making, you might include measures of defendant guilt, defendant credibility, and how well jurors understand evidence. In a nonexperimental study, you could measure a number of variables, some designated as predictor variables and others as criterion variables. For example, you could analyze actual trials and record the defendant's race, gender, the severity of the crime committed, and jury verdicts. You could then use race, gender, and crime severity as predictor variables and the verdict as the criterion variable. When you use a multivariate design, whether experimental or correlational, and want to analyze measures in a single analysis, you would use one of the multivariate statistics available. The following sections describe some of these multivariate statistical tests.

## Correlational Multivariate Design

If you include multiple measures in a correlational study, you could calculate separate bivariate correlations (e.g., Pearson correlations) for all possible pairs of those measures. Or you could use a *multivariate correlational analysis* in which you include all your measures in a single analysis.

Several multivariate analyses are designed to assess complex correlational relationships among multiple dependent variables. For example, the goal of **multiple regression** is to explain the variation in one variable (the dependent or *criterion variable*) based on variation in a set of others (the *predictor variables*). What constitutes a "predictor variable" and a "criterion variable" is not related to anything inherent in the variable itself. Rather, you decide which variables to use as predictors based on your research question. Relevant previous research, theory, or practical experience should guide your decision about which variables should be measured and what role each variable should play in your analysis.

Two other multivariate techniques used to evaluate relationships in a correlational study are discriminant analysis and canonical correlation. **Discriminant analysis** is a variation of multiple regression in which your criterion variable is measured nominally (e.g., yes/no). **Canonical correlation** allows you to evaluate the relationship between two *sets* of variables, one of which may be identified as a predictor variable set and the other as the criterion variable set.

In some research situations (e.g., questionnaire and test construction), you may reduce a large set of variables to smaller sets that consist of variables relating to one another. Factor analysis is used for this purpose. In **factor analysis**, several dependent variables are analyzed to find out if any of them share common underlying dimensions called *factors*. You examine the dependent variables that make up the factors to identify the dimension that those factors represent.

*Advantages of the Correlational Multivariate Strategy*        Single multivariate analysis has two major advantages over multiple bivariate analyses. First, if you conduct a large number of independent bivariate correlation analyses, you increase your risk of finding relationships that occur merely by chance. Multivariate statistics allow you to look at complex relationships while controlling such statistical errors. Second, independent univariate analyses allow you to evaluate relationships only between *pairs* of variables. You may discover that variable *X* correlates highly with variable *Y*. However, what you do not know is whether this high correlation will persist when you consider a third variable, $Z$. It may be that $X$ is correlated with $Y$ only because $Z$ is highly correlated with $X$. Multivariate statistics provide the information needed to evaluate the importance of a predictor variable for explaining variability in the criterion variable, given the effects of other predictor variables.

*Causal Inference*    Multivariate techniques allow you to draw some *tentative* causal inferences from your correlational data. At the least, when properly applied, they allow you to have greater confidence in possible causal connections among variables. However, remember that you are still using correlational data, so any causal inferences you draw must be discussed with caution.

   *Path analysis* and *structural equation modeling* are two techniques that allow you to explore causal models relating your variables. Path analysis, which applies multiple regression analysis to the investigation of possible causal relationships among variables, begins with a theory or model specifying a causal chain of events involving several variables and a behavior. For example, a model may suggest that a consumer's buying behavior will not occur until the consumer first finds out about a product, then generates positive ideas about the product, and finally forms an intention to buy the product. You could obtain measures on the degree to which the consumer was familiar with the product, had positive ideas about it, and intended to buy it. You could then enter the measures into a series of multiple regression analyses. Based on the results, you could test the validity of your theory or model and begin to form some tentative conclusions about possible causal relationships among your variables. Structural equation modeling is related to path analysis and allows you to more completely explore potential causal models linking your variables.

## Experimental Multivariate Design

The logic of univariate experimental design applies to multivariate design. That is, you manipulate one or more independent variable(s) and look for changes in the values of your dependent variables. The major difference between a univariate experimental strategy and a multivariate experimental strategy is how dependent variables are handled. When you use a univariate strategy, multiple dependent measures are analyzed separately with multiple statistical tests. In contrast, when you use a multivariate strategy, multiple dependent variables are combined statistically (based on the correlations among them) and analyzed with a single statistical test.

   Implied in your choice of a multivariate design over a univariate design is that your dependent measures are correlated. Typically, you include multiple dependent measures because you have some reason to believe that those measures are important to the phenomenon under study and that those measures relate in some way to one another. Multivariate statistical techniques take into account the correlations among your dependent measures and, in most cases, use them to your advantage.

*Multivariate Statistical Tests for Experimental Designs*    The two multivariate statistics most widely used to analyze multiple dependent variables in an experimental design are **multivariate analysis of variance (MANOVA)** and *multivariate analysis* *of covariance (MANCOVA)*. Another multivariate statistic that is commonly used when your dependent variable is categorical (e.g., guilty or not guilty) is *multiway frequency analysis*. As with univariate statistics, these tests help you evaluate the reliability of the relationship between your independent variable (or variables) and your dependent variables.

*Advantages of the Experimental Multivariate Strategy*    A multivariate experimental strategy has several advantages over a univariate strategy. First, collecting several dependent measures and treating them as a correlated set may reveal relationships that might be missed if a traditional univariate approach were taken. Because multivariate statistical tests consider the correlations among dependent variables, they tend to be more powerful than separate univariate tests of those same dependent variables. Second, because all your dependent variables are handled in a single analysis, complex relationships among variables can be studied with less chance of making a Type I error than when using multiple univariate tests (Bray & Maxwell, 1982).

A third advantage of the multivariate strategy is realized when you have used a within-subjects design. A fairly restrictive set of assumptions underlies the univariate within-subjects ANOVA that are often difficult to satisfy. Using MANOVA allows you to analyze your data with less concern over these restrictive assumptions.

## ASSUMPTIONS AND REQUIREMENTS OF MULTIVARIATE STATISTICS

Before using multivariate statistics, you must check to see that your data meet the assumptions and requirements underlying the statistic to be used. These assumptions include linearity, normality, and homoscedasticity. In addition, you must evaluate your data for the presence of outliers and measurement error and for sufficient sample size.

### Linearity

An assumption underlying bivariate correlational statistics is that the relationship between continuously measured variables is linear (see Chapter 13 for a more complete discussion). Violation of this assumption leads to an underestimation of the degree of relationship between variables. Multivariate statistics, which are all based on correlations (even MANOVA), also assume that the relationships among continuously measured variables are linear. You check for linearity by visually inspecting scatter plots of pairs of variables. If your data are linear, then all the points should follow a straight line. Nonlinear data, in contrast, will show a horseshoe-shaped function (Tabachnick & Fidell, 2013).

Whereas mild deviations from linearity probably will not lead to a serious underestimation of a relationship by multivariate statistics, moderate to serious deviations may. If your data are nonlinear, you may be able to correct the problem by transforming your data. You may have to transform both offending variables in order to restore linearity. After any transformation, you should again inspect the scatter plots to see if the transformation had its intended effect.

## Outliers

The presence of extreme scores, or *outliers,* in a distribution can also distort the results from a multivariate analysis. Recall that multivariate statistics are all based on calculating bivariate correlations. Bivariate correlational statistics work by fitting the best straight line to the data. This regression line minimizes the distance of the data points from the line according to some statistical criterion (usually a least-squares criterion). If your data set has outliers, the regression line may not represent the trend shown by the majority of scores. Outliers change the slope of the regression line calculated from your data. They also affect both the magnitude and the sign of the calculated correlation. (See Chapter 13 for a more complete discussion.)

*Identifying Outliers*    Two types of outliers that must be considered in multivariate statistics are univariate outliers and multivariate outliers. A *univariate outlier* is a deviant score on one measure from a given source (e.g., from a single subject), whereas a *multivariate outlier* is a deviant score on a combination of variables from a single source.

Univariate outliers may be detected by converting raw scores to $z$ scores. If the $z$ score is very deviant (such as 3), then that raw score is considered to be a univariate outlier, especially with a large sample (Tabachnick & Fidell, 2013). Another way to look for outliers is to evaluate the amount of skewness in your data. If your data are skewed, then outliers probably exist. However, note that measures of skewness (see Chapter 13) detect skewness if outliers exist only in one tail of your distribution.

Detecting multivariate outliers is more difficult than detecting univariate outliers. Multivariate outliers can be detected either statistically or graphically (Tabachnick & Fidell, 2013). Using the statistical method, you obtain a statistic called the *Mahalanobis Distance* from a statistical program such as SPSS. The Mahalanobis Distance represents the distance between a particular case and the centroid (the point created by the means of all the variables in the analysis) of remaining cases. The statistical program also calculates a discriminant analysis that tells you which case separates from the other cases in the analysis (Tabachnick & Fidell, 2013). A multivariate outlier with an unusual combination of scores will be weighted heavily in the discriminant function equation, yielding a significant Mahalanobis Distance of the outlier from other cases. There are other statistical techniques you can use to detect multivariate outliers (see, e.g., Tabachnick & Fidell, 2013). You also can detect multivariate outliers by inspecting plots of residuals provided by multiple regression programs. Any point on the plot that is distant from other points is a multivariate outlier. Screening for multivariate outliers should be done again after the data are cleaned up because some outliers may "hide" behind others (Tabachnick & Fidell, 2013).

*Dealing with Outliers*    There are several ways to deal with outliers. If outliers are causing a positive skew in your data, you can use a data transformation to normalize the distribution (Tabachnick & Fidell, 2013). Data with a moderate positive skew should be transformed with a square root transformation. For a more serious positive skew, you should use a logarithmic transformation. Again, transformations such as these reduce the impact of outliers if they are found only in one tail of your distribution. If outliers exist in both tails, transformations may not help (Tabachnick & Fidell, 2013).

If your data are negatively skewed, you use a *reflecting strategy.* Reflecting involves transforming a negatively skewed distribution to a positively skewed distribution. The first step in reflecting is to subtract each score from the highest score in the distribution and add 1 to this difference score. You then apply either a square root or logarithmic transformation to the now positively skewed data. Which transformation you use depends on the degree of positive skewness.

Another way to deal with outliers is to delete from the analysis either all data from the variable containing the outlier or from the subject with the outlying scores. The disadvantage to this procedure is that you lose data. If you start with a relatively small sample, the loss of data may preclude using multivariate statistics.

Finally, you should check for transcription and other data-entry errors. Sometimes outliers are caused by entering the wrong numbers or by telling the computer to look for data in the wrong positions. Any erroneous data should be corrected.

Of all the requirements of multivariate statistics, detecting outliers is probably the most important. The presence of just a single multivariate outlier can change the results of your analysis and affect your conclusions. Consequently, you should check and correct for both univariate and multivariate outliers.

## Normality and Homoscedasticity

As is the case with bivariate statistics, multivariate statistics assume that the population distribution underlying your sample distribution is normal. This is the assumption of *normality.* Transform skewed data with one of the indicated transformations, in order to normalize the distributions, before using any multivariate statistic.

*Homoscedasticity* is related to normality and is the assumption that "the variability in scores on one variable is roughly the same at all values of the other variable" (Tabachnick & Fidell, 2013). Figure 15-1 shows two scatter plots of two hypothetical variables. Panel (a) shows the pattern of data indicating homoscedasticity. Notice that the shape of the scatter plot created by the data points is elliptical. If both variables are normally distributed, homoscedasticity results.

Contrast the scatter plot shown in panel (b) of Figure 15-1 with the one shown in panel (a). Notice how the shape of the scatter plot has changed from elliptical to

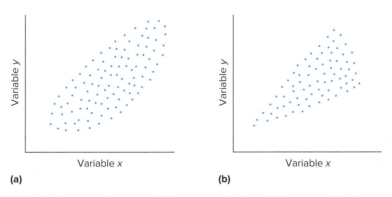

**(a)**                                                    **(b)**

**FIGURE 15-1** Homoscedasticity and heteroscedasticity: (a) homoscedasticity between two variables and (b) heteroscedasticity between two variables.

conical. The conical pattern of data points indicates that *heteroscedasticity* is present. Heteroscedasticity usually occurs because the distribution of one or more variable(s) included in the analysis is skewed. To eliminate heteroscedasticity, apply one of the data transformations previously discussed.

## Multicollinearity

*Multicollinearity* results when variables in your analysis are highly correlated (Tabachnick & Fidell, 2013). The impact of multicollinearity is complex and beyond the scope of this chapter. If two variables are highly correlated, one of them should be eliminated from the analysis. The high correlation means the two variables are measuring essentially the same thing, so little is lost by eliminating one of them.

## Error of Measurement

The heart of the research process is identifying important variables to study, measuring those variables, establishing relationships among the variables, and drawing conclusions about behavior based on those relationships. Drawing valid conclusions about the behavior under study requires that your variables be accurately measured. Inaccurate measurement may lead to an inordinate number of Type II errors. For example, you may conclude that a theoretical model is invalid when the reason for rejecting the model was in fact an inaccurate measurement of variables.

In a perfectly ordered world with perfect measuring devices, you could obtain the *true value* of your dependent variable. Unfortunately, we do not live in a perfectly ordered world, nor do we have perfect measuring devices. Consequently, the best you can do is to *estimate* the true value of a variable by obtaining an *observed value*. The difference between the true value of a variable and your observed value is the *error of measurement* (or simply, *measurement error*). Figure 15-2 shows the relationship between a variable's true value, observed value, and measurement error. Notice that the observed value is a function of both the true value of the variable and the measurement error (Asher, 1976).

Error of measurement is a problem for both multivariate and univariate research. It is particularly troublesome when you adopt a multivariate strategy because it leads to an underestimation of the correlations among variables that are used to compute the various multivariate statistics (Asher, 1976; Hunter, 1987). This leads to Type II errors.

Measurement error can arise from many sources, including incomplete, inaccurate, or biased sources of information. For example, if you were interested in studying the relationship between three predictor variables (gender, socioeconomic status, and

**FIGURE 15-2**   The observed value of any variable (top) is a function of the true value of that variable and the measurement error (bottom).

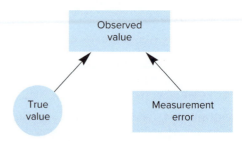

education level) and crime rate, you need a good source for each of these four variables. Consider the crime rate. You could obtain records of crimes reported to the police, but this source may not be complete because many crimes go unreported. The best way to avoid this source of measurement error is to use multiple sources of information.

Another source of measurement error is inaccurate or invalid measurement devices. Defects in mechanical recording devices, poorly designed rating scales, and the like all contribute to measurement error. To avoid this source of error, be sure that your equipment is in working order and that you have adequately pretested your measures.

## Sample Size

Fairly large sample sizes are needed for multivariate analyses. The large sample size is necessary because the correlations used to calculate these statistics are not very stable when based on small samples. A multivariate analysis that uses a small sample may result in an unacceptable Type II error rate. This occurs because unstable correlations tend to provide less reliable estimates of the degree of relationship among your variables.

Tabachnick and Fidell (2013) offer the following formula for computing the sample size required for a multiple regression analysis:

$$N \geq 50 + 8m$$

where $m$ = the number of predictor variables. So, if you have five predictor variables, you would need a minimum of 90 participants in your sample. Larger samples may be needed if your data are skewed, there is substantial measurement error, or you anticipate weak relationships among variables (Tabachnick & Fidell, 2013). Tabachnick and Fidell also caution that you can have *too large* a sample. With overly large samples, very weak relationships that may have neither theoretical nor practical value can achieve statistical significance.

To summarize, several factors should be considered before using multivariate statistics. Make sure that your data meet the assumptions of the test you are going to use (i.e., normality, linearity, and homoscedasticity), that you have removed any outliers or minimized their effects through transformation, that you have considered error of measurement, and that you have gathered a sufficiently large sample. If you violate the assumptions of the test or fail to take into account the other important factors, the results that you obtain may not be valid.

## QUESTIONS TO PONDER

1. What statistics are used to evaluate correlational and experimental multivariate relationships?

2. What are the key assumptions and requirements of multivariate statistics?

3. How do various violations of the assumptions underlying multivariate statistics affect your data analysis?

## CORRELATIONAL MULTIVARIATE STATISTICAL TESTS

Now that you are familiar with the general logic behind multivariate statistics and understand the assumptions and requirements of these tests, we can explore some of the more popular multivariate data analysis techniques. This discussion begins with factor analysis, then examines the techniques used to analyze multivariate data from experimental designs (e.g., MANOVA and multiway frequency analysis), and, finally, examines techniques for causal modeling.

### Factor Analysis

Imagine you are interested in measuring the degree to which males conform to male social norms. Before you conduct your study, you need to find a way to define just what those norms are. While reviewing the literature, you discover that there are several male social norms that are relevant to male social behavior. You decide to design a questionnaire including 100 items to measure male social norms and administer it to a sample of male participants.

After all your participants have completed the questionnaire, you now face the task of determining the underlying nature of male social norms. Do the questions on your questionnaire measure a single dimension (such as aggressiveness) or several dimensions (such as aggressiveness, competitiveness, and dominance)? Your search for the dimensions underlying male social norms lends itself perfectly to factor analysis.

Factor analysis operates by extracting as many significant factors from your data as possible, based on the bivariate correlations between your measures. A *factor* is a dimension that consists of any number of variables. In your study of male social norms, for example, you may find that your 100 questions actually measure three underlying dimensions (e.g., aggressiveness, competitiveness, and dominance). Factor analysis involves extracting one factor (such as aggressiveness) and then evaluating your data for the existence of additional factors.

The successive factors extracted in factor analysis are not of equal strength. Each successive factor accounts for less and less variance. Typically, the first two or three factors will be the strongest (i.e., account for the most variance). The strength of a factor is indicated by its *eigenvalue* (for a more complete discussion of eigenvalues, see Tatsuoka, 1971, or Tabachnick & Fidell, 2013). Factors with eigenvalues of less than 1.0 usually are not interpreted.

*Factor Loadings*    To determine the dependent variables constituting a common factor, *factor loadings* are computed. Each factor loading is the correlation between a measure and the underlying factor. A positive factor loading means that a variable positively correlates with the underlying dimension extracted whereas a negative loading means that a negative correlation exists. By convention, loadings are interpreted only if they are equal to or exceed .30.

*Rotation of Factors*    After you have obtained your factor loadings, you must interpret them. The factor loadings computed initially are often difficult to interpret because they are somewhat ambiguous. *Factor rotation* is used to make the factors distinct by maximizing high correlations and minimizing low correlations (Tabachnick & Fidell, 2013). Rotated factors will include more distinct clusters of factor loadings than unrotated factors and are thus easier to interpret. Two types of rotation are orthogonal rotation and oblique rotation.

In *orthogonal rotation,* the axes representing the factors remain perpendicular when rotated around fixed points representing your data. Orthogonal rotation assumes that your measures are uncorrelated and consequently that the factors extracted are uncorrelated. Generally, orthogonal rotation is preferred over oblique rotation because the results are easier to interpret. The most popular orthogonal rotation method is *varimax,* which maximizes the variance of loadings on each factor and simplifies factors (Tabachnick & Fidell, 2013).

In *oblique rotation,* the angle between the axes, as well as the orientation of the axes in space, may change. Oblique rotation assumes that your measures and factors are correlated. If you have good reason to believe that your measures are correlated, oblique rotation might be a better choice than orthogonal rotation.

*Principal Components and Principal Factors Analysis*　　Two types of factor analysis are *principal components analysis* and *principal factors analysis.* Panel (a) of Table 15-1 shows a standard three-variable correlation matrix. Remember, such correlations are used to calculate factor loadings. Panel (b) shows the same correlation matrix completed by filling in the correlations missing from the matrix in panel (a). Notice that the values on the diagonal of the matrix are all 1s. In principal components analysis, the diagonal of the completed correlation matrix is filled with 1s. In contrast, principal factors analysis completes the correlation matrix with *communalities* along the diagonal. Essentially, communality is a measure of a variable's reliability and is fairly easy to obtain after factor analysis. However, you need these

**TABLE 15-1**　**Two Correlation Matrices for Three Variables**

**(A) HYPOTHETICAL CORRELATION MATRIX**

|  | *Variable 1* | *Variable 2* | *Variable 3* |
|---|---|---|---|
| Variable 1 |  |  |  |
| Variable 2 | .71 |  |  |
| Variable 3 | .61 | .74 |  |

**(B) COMPLETED CORRELATION MATRIX**

|  | *Variable 1* | *Variable 2* | *Variable 3* |
|---|---|---|---|
| Variable 1 | 1.00 | .71 | .61 |
| Variable 2 | .71 | 1.00 | .74 |
| Variable 3 | .61 | .74 | 1.00 |

values before analysis. Various techniques have been proposed for estimating communalities (see Bennett & Bowers, 1976), none of which is much better than any other.

Your choice between principal components and principal factors analysis rests on the goals of the analysis. Principal components analysis is most appropriate under two circumstances: if you do not have a theoretical or empirical basis for relationships among variables or if you want to reduce a large number of variables down to a smaller set and obtain an empirical summary of the data. Principal factors analysis is most appropriate when you have theoretically or empirically based predictions (Tabachnick & Fidell, 2013). In the absence of any clear information on which technique is best, you should probably use principal components analysis.

*Exploratory Versus Confirmatory Factor Analysis*    A distinction also is made between exploratory factor analysis and confirmatory factor analysis. *Exploratory factor analysis* is used when you have a large set of variables that you want to describe in simpler terms and you have no a priori ideas about which variables will cluster together. Exploratory factor analysis is often used in the early stages of research to identify the variables that cluster together. From such an analysis, research hypotheses can be generated and tested. *Confirmatory factor analysis* is used in later stages of research where you can specify how variables might relate given some underlying psychological process (Tabachnick & Fidell, 2013).

## QUESTIONS TO PONDER

1. When is factor analysis used, and what do factor loadings tell you?
2. Why are factors rotated in factor analysis?
3. What is the difference between principal components and principal factors analysis?
4. When do you use exploratory or confirmatory factor analysis?

## Partial and Part Correlations

Sometimes two variables are both influenced by a third variable. If this third variable was not held constant when the data were collected, it can affect the apparent relationship between the two variables of interest. However, if you have recorded the values of the third variable along with the other two, you can statistically evaluate the impact of the third variable. Partial correlation and part correlation (also called the *semipartial correlation*) are two statistics that determine the correlation between two variables while statistically controlling for the effect of a third.

*Partial Correlation*    **Partial correlation** allows you to examine the relationship between two variables with the effect of a third variable *removed* from both of these variables. For example, suppose you are interested in the factors relating to performance on the Scholastic Assessment Test (SAT). You obtain the SAT scores from 500

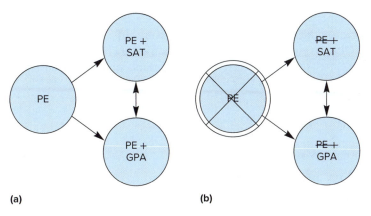

**FIGURE 15-3** Partial correlation. Panel (a) shows the relationship between SAT and GPA with the effect of PE in both. Panel (b) shows the relationship between SAT and GPA with the effect of PE removed from both.

high school seniors, as well as their grade point averages (GPA). You also collect data on the parents' educational level (PE) in the belief that it may affect SAT scores. Specifically, you are interested in the relationship between GPA and SAT scores. For example, perhaps you believe that students with high GPAs will score higher on the SAT than students with low GPAs. However, you are concerned that PE may confound the relationship between GPA and SAT. If causal relationships exist between PE and GPA and between PE and SAT, then any variation in PE will cause changes in both SAT and GPA. What you really want to do is look at the relationship between GPA and SAT with any effect of PE removed. This is a problem that can be solved with partial correlation.

Figure 15-3 shows how partial correlation works. In panel (a), you can see that PE is affecting both SAT and GPA. Any correlation between GPA and SAT will include the influence of PE (shown by the fact that PE is added to both GPA and SAT). Panel (b) shows what happens when you remove the effects of PE from both SAT and GPA. In effect, PE is subtracted from both GPA and SAT. The resulting SAT and GPA scores are known as *residual scores*. Partial correlation is the correlation between the SAT and GPA residual scores.

Partial correlation is not limited to three-variable cases. You can examine the relationship between two variables with the effects of several others removed. You can learn more about these more complex partial correlations in Thorndike (1978).

*Part Correlation*   In some cases, you may want to examine the relationship between two variables when the influence of a third is removed from only *one* of these variables. **Part correlation** (also known as *semipartial correlation*) is used in this situation.

Conceptually, part correlation is similar to partial correlation. As with partial correlation, the relationship between one variable (such as SAT) and the variable to be removed (such as PE) is determined, and residual scores are calculated. This yields an

SAT score for each participant with the effect of PE held constant (Thorndike, 1978). These residual scores are then correlated with the *raw* scores (the original scores) of the other variable (GPA) to yield the part correlation coefficient (Thorndike, 1978).

In practice, part correlation is computed by using a formula similar to that used for partial correlation.

## QUESTIONS TO PONDER

1. What do partial and part correlations tell you?
2. When would you use partial correlation?
3. When would you use part correlation?

## Multiple Regression

Assume that you are interested in studying the variables correlated with college students' attitudes toward seeking counseling for personal problems. You are interested in investigating those variables that relate to a student having either a positive or negative attitude toward seeking professional counseling. Multiple regression analysis is the best statistic to address such an issue. You will have a single measure of attitude toward counseling (the criterion or dependent variable) and several measures that might relate to that attitude (predictor variables).

*The Multiple Regression Equation*    Chapter 13 discussed bivariate linear regression and provided the linear equation for that analysis. The logic developed for the bivariate case easily can be extended to the multivariate case. The linear equation for multiple regression is

$$\hat{Y} = b_1X_1 + b_2X_2 + b_3X_3 + b_4X_4 + b_5X_5 + constant$$

where $\hat{Y}$ is the predicted criterion score; $b_1$, $b_2$, $b_3$, $b_4$, and $b_5$ are the regression weights associated with the predictors; $X_1$, $X_2$, $X_3$, $X_4$, and $X_5$ are the values of the predictors; and *constant* is the *y*-intercept of the regression line.

*Types of Regression Analysis*    The several types of regression analysis include simple, hierarchical, and stepwise analyses. The major difference between these types is how your predictor variables are entered into the regression equation, which may affect the regression solution.

In *simple regression analysis* (the type used in the example to follow), all predictor variables are entered together. Each predictor variable is assessed as if it had been entered after each of the other predictors had been entered (Tabachnick & Fidell, 2013). In *hierarchical regression,* you specify the order in which your variables are entered into the regression equation. You use hierarchical regression if you have a well-developed theory or model suggesting a certain causal order. In *stepwise regression,* the order in which variables are entered is based on a statistical decision, not on a theory.

When you enter variables into a stepwise regression analysis, the order in which predictors are entered is determined by the qualities of the sample data. The first variable entered is the one accounting for the most variance in the dependent measure. The next variable entered is the one that adds most to the ability of the regression equation to account for the variance in the dependent variable (i.e., increases $R$-square the most). Variables are entered one at a time until none of the remaining variables add significantly to $R$-square.

Your choice of regression strategies should be based on your research questions or underlying theory. If you have a theoretical model suggesting a particular order of entry, use hierarchical regression. In the absence of any well-specified theory, you should usually choose simple regression. Stepwise regression is used infrequently because it tends to capitalize on chance. Sampling and measurement error tend to make unstable correlations among variables in stepwise regression. Thus, the statistical decisions used to determine order of entry may vary considerably from sample to sample. The resulting regression equation may be unique to a particular sample.

***Multiple R and R-Square***     **Multiple $R$** is the correlation between the predicted values of $Y$ ($\hat{Y}$) and the observed values of $Y$. **$R$-square** is simply the square of multiple $R$ and provides an index of the amount of variability in the dependent variable accounted for by the predictor variables (Roscoe, 1975). There is a problem with $R$-square. Because of sampling error, $R$-square tends to overestimate the variance accounted for, especially with small samples (Tabachnick & Fidell, 2013). *Adjusted R-square* compensates for this overestimation. You should use the adjusted $R$-square as a measure of variance accounted for rather than the unadjusted $R$-square. You also should pay attention to the standard error. The standard error gives you an indication of how much variability there is around the calculated regression line. The lower the value, the better it is.

***Regression Weights***     *Regression weights* are used to interpret the results from a multiple regression analysis. There are two types of regression weights: raw and standardized. A raw regression weight ($b$) is calculated based on the raw scores (the original scores on your dependent variables) entered into the regression analysis. A standardized regression weight is calculated after your raw scores have been transformed to standard scores. The standardized regression weights are known as **beta weights** (abbreviated with the Greek symbol $\beta$). When you use a computer program (such as SPSS) to conduct a regression analysis, you can determine if a beta weight is statistically significant by looking at the $p$-value the $t$ test provided. A statistically significant beta weight tells you that a predictor variable is significantly related to your criterion variable.

For most applications in psychological research, you should use the standardized regression weights (beta weights) because they can be directly compared—even if the variables to which they apply were measured on very different scales. For example, even though variables such as intelligence, GPA, and socioeconomic status are all measured on different, nonequivalent scales (IQ points, grade point average, and dollars, respectively), the beta weights can be directly compared because all of the scores from these measures were converted to standard scores. This is not the case for the raw regression weights. Only when your variables are measured on the same standard scale should you use the raw score regression weights.

*Interpretation of Regression Weights*   If your regression analysis is significant, you may want to know how much of the variability in your dependent variable can be accounted for by a given predictor variable. You might be tempted to use a beta weight for this purpose. However, you should avoid this temptation because a beta weight does not tell you the unique contribution of a given predictor to variability in the dependent variable.

A beta weight for a given predictor variable may be high because it directly produces most of the variance in the dependent variable. However, that same predictor variable may simply be correlated with another statistically significant predictor variable, making it appear that it causes the variance in the dependent variable when it is the other one that is the actual cause (Tabachnick & Fidell, 2013). Similarly, a beta weight for a given predictor variable may be low, and yet that predictor may have a strong causal influence on the dependent variable. This situation can occur when another predictor variable in the analysis correlates with the predictor variable with the low beta weight. The analysis mistakenly may assign weight to the correlated variable instead of the one actually causing the variability in the dependent variable. A variable that masks the true effect of another variable is termed a *suppressor variable.*

An alternative to using beta weights to determine the unique contribution of each predictor is to use *squared semipartial correlations* instead (Tabachnick & Fidell, 2013). The results of a computer regression analysis will provide a semipartial (part) correlation for each predictor variable (if it doesn't automatically do so, you can request them). Simply square the semipartial correlation for each variable. The squared semipartial correlations indicate the amount of variability in the dependent variable accounted for by each variable. Keep in mind that the squared semipartial correlations may or may not sum to $R$-square. (See Tabachnick & Fidell, 2013 for a detailed discussion of this issue.)

*An Example of Multiple Regression*   Because multiple regression is commonly used and underlies many other multivariate statistics, we here present an extended example. Recall the previously mentioned study of the factors correlating with a student's attitude toward seeking counseling for personal problems. David Vogel and Stephen Wester (2003) actually conducted such a study. They had 209 college students (143 male and 66 female) complete a measure of their attitude toward seeking counseling. The students also completed measures concerning their willingness to disclose personal information about themselves, how risky they felt such disclosures were, and whether they had sought counseling in the past. These latter measures, along with participant gender, yielded five predictor variables for a multiple regression analysis: willingness to self-disclose personal information, risk of disclosing emotional information, utility of disclosing emotional information, gender, and previous counseling.

The results showed a significant regression analysis, $F(5, 190) = 25, p < .001$. The $R^2$ was .40, and the adjusted $R^2$ was .39, indicating that 39% of the variance was accounted for by the regression analysis. Table 15-2 shows how each predictor variable related to the dependent variable and whether each predictor variable contributed significantly to the regression analysis. The first column shows the raw score regression weights. Remember, we don't use them to interpret a regression analysis. The third column shows the standard error of the regression weights. The beta weights (standardized regression weights) are shown in the fourth column. These are the ones that we use to interpret the regression analysis.

**TABLE 15-2   Results from Vogel and Wester's (2003) Multiple Regression Analysis**

| CRITERION VARIABLE | b | $SE_b$ | β | t | p |
|---|---|---|---|---|---|
| Self-disclosure of distressing information | 4.1 | .84 | .29 | 4.8 | <.001 |
| Anticipated risk of emotional self-disclosure | −1.9 | .63 | −.18 | −3.1 | <.01 |
| Anticipated utility of emotional self-disclosure | 2.9 | .69 | .24 | 4.1 | <.001 |
| Participant gender | 7.5 | 1.7 | .27 | 4.5 | <.001 |
| Previous counseling | −5.4 | 1.6 | −.20 | −3.4 | <.01 |

SOURCE: Vogel, D., & S., Wester, (2003). To seek help, or not to seek help: The risks of self-disclosure. *Journal of Counseling Psychology, 50*, 351–361. Copyright 2003 by American Psychological Association.

As you can see, the strongest predictor of attitude toward seeking counseling is a person's willingness to disclose distressing information. The positive regression weight tells us that individuals who are more willing to self-disclose are more likely to have a positive attitude toward seeking counseling. Another strong predictor is the anticipated utility of self-disclosing emotional information (β = .24), indicating that individuals who see emotional self-disclosure as useful have a more positive attitude toward seeking help. Notice that the anticipated risk of emotional self-disclosure is negatively related to help-seeking attitude (β = −.18), indicating that those who see emotional self-disclosure as risky have a more negative attitude toward seeking help.

## QUESTIONS TO PONDER

1. For what research applications would you use the various types of multiple regression analysis?

2. How are multiple $R$, $R^2$, and adjusted $R^2$ used to interpret the results from a multiple regression analysis?

3. What is the difference between the raw and standardized regression weights, and why are the standardized weights used when interpreting the results from a regression analysis?

4. What is the squared semipartial correlation, and when is it used?

### Discriminant Analysis

Discriminant analysis is a special case of multiple regression. It is used when your dependent variable is categorical (e.g., male–female or Democrat–Republican–Independent) and you have several predictor variables. Discriminant analysis allows you to predict membership in a group (one of the discrete categories of your dependent variable) based on a set of predictor variables. You can use discriminant analysis to identify a simple rule for classifying participants into groups or to determine which of your predictor variables contributes most heavily to the separation of groups. The analysis works by forming *discriminant functions*. For each dependent variable group, a discriminant function score is calculated according to the following formula (Tabachnick & Fidell, 2013):

$$D_i = d_{i1}z_1 + d_{i2}z_2 + \cdots + d_{in}z_n$$

where $D_i$ is the discriminant function score calculated for each participant, $d_i$ is the regression weight, and $z$ is the standardized raw score on a particular predictor. In discriminant analysis, a new variable $(D_i)$ is calculated for each participant. This variable is the best linear combination of predictor variables, just as in multiple regression. When the discriminant function scores have been calculated for each group, a centroid can then be determined. The *centroid* is simply the average of the discriminant function scores within a group.

More than one discriminant function can link your predictors with your dependent variable. However, the number of functions is limited to the number of predictors or to the number of levels of the dependent variable minus 1, whichever is smaller. For example, if you had seven predictors and three levels of the dependent variable, the number of possible functions is 2 (3 − 1). Each discriminant function represents a different linkage between the predictors and the dependent variable. The first one calculated maximizes the separation between levels of the dependent variable. Subsequent functions represent progressively weaker linkages between the predictors and the dependent variable.

Because the computations needed to perform a discriminant analysis are complex, you will probably use a computer program to conduct a discriminant analysis. SPSS conducts a discriminant analysis within its Analyze subprogram. The output of the SPSS analysis gives you several important pieces of information. First, the output will indicate the number of discriminant functions extracted, along with tests of statistical significance. Second, you can request several other statistics needed to interpret your results. These include the standardized discriminant function coefficients (analogous to beta weights) and pooled within-groups correlations between the discriminant functions and predictor variables (structure correlations).

You can use a discriminant analysis in two ways. First, you can evaluate the amount of variability accounted for by each function. You would do this by conducting a dimension reduction analysis that provides a canonical correlation coefficient and significance tests for each function. The squared canonical correlation coefficient gives a measure of the variability accounted for by a specific function. By looking at the dimension reduction analysis, you can determine the significance of each function and the variability accounted for by each function.

The second way you can use the discriminant analysis is to evaluate the degree of contribution of each predictor (within a function) to the separation of groups. One strategy is to look at the standardized discriminant function coefficients. However, these weights (like beta weights) do not reveal how much each individual predictor contributes to variation in the dependent variable. Another strategy is to look at the structure correlations, which can be interpreted much like factor loadings. By convention, you typically consider those structure correlations that exceed .30. The structure correlations can help you determine what each discriminant function represents. However, they are not good indicators of the predictor's degree of unique contribution to discriminating among dependent variable groups (Tabachnick & Fidell, 2013).

Rather than looking at beta weights or structure correlations, you could conduct a set of specific contrasts in which each dependent variable group is contrasted with all others. You then look for which predictor variables separate a particular group from the rest (see Tabachnick & Fidell, 2013).

## Canonical Correlation

Multiple regression determines the relationship between a set of predictors and a *single* dependent variable. To determine the relationship between a set of predictors and a *set* of dependent variables, you use canonical correlation. Canonical correlation works by creating two new variables for each subject, called *canonical variates.* A canonical variate is computed both for the dependent and predictor sets. The canonical variate is simply the score predicted from a regression equation based on the variables within a set. The correlation between the two canonical variates is the *canonical correlation.*

Canonical correlation does not appear much in published psychological literature because, at this point in its development, it is a purely descriptive strategy. It can be used to describe the relationship between two sets of variables, but it cannot be used to infer causal relationships. Consequently, this technique is not discussed further. If you want to know more about the technique, see Tabachnick and Fidell (2013) and Levine (1977).

## QUESTIONS TO PONDER

1. What is discriminant analysis, and when is it used?
2. What do discriminant functions tell you?
3. What are the two main applications of discriminant analysis?
4. What is canonical correlation, and when is it used?

## EXPERIMENTAL MULTIVARIATE STATISTICAL TESTS

In this section, we review two multivariate statistical analysis techniques used to analyze data from multivariate experimental designs: multivariate analysis of variance and multiway frequency analysis.

## Multivariate Analysis of Variance

Assume you are required to conduct an experiment for a senior thesis. Your major area of interest is in the development of a concept of death among school-aged children. You have reviewed the literature and have found most of the current research to be correlational. You decide there is room for some experimental work in the area, but you also decide to draw on the existing correlational research to help you develop your measures. You find that the previous research suggests that several important measures should be applied to assessing children's concepts of death. So you decide to include three measures in your experiment.

The existing literature suggests that development of a child's concept of death can be accelerated by exposure to experience with the concept of death. So you decide to conduct a single-factor experiment with three groups. The first group is simply exposed to a film about a character who dies. The second group role-plays a dying animal. The third group, a control group, receives no special treatment.

After running your experiment, you are faced with the problem of how to analyze your three dependent measures. Of course, you could simply conduct three separate one-factor ANOVAs. You are uncomfortable with this strategy because the existing literature indicates that your three chosen measures are correlated. You might miss some important relationships among your variables if you simply use a series of univariate tests. In this situation, a viable alternative is to use a MANOVA to analyze your data. Like canonical correlation and discriminant analysis, MANOVA operates by forming a new linear combination of dependent variables for each effect in your design. For example, for a two-factor between-subjects design, a different linear combination of scores is formed for each of the two main effects and for the interaction.

*An Example of MANOVA*    Suppose you conducted the one-factor experiment looking at the effect of a training program on children's concepts of death. Your measure of the concept of death consisted of a questionnaire containing several important questions concerning death (e.g., "What happens when you die?" "What can you do to bring something dead back to life?" and "Do dead people feel pain?"). Children simply answered the questions. Independent raters then indicated how mature the concept of death was in each response. Because your measures were related to the same concept, you decide to use a MANOVA rather than separate ANOVAs to analyze the data.

Table 15-3 shows some hypothetical data that might be generated from such a study. Table 15-4 shows part of the output from an SPSS MANOVA analysis of

**TABLE 15-3** Data from Hypothetical Experiment on Developing a Concept of Death

| | FILM | | | ROLE PLAYING | | | CONTROL | | |
|---|---|---|---|---|---|---|---|---|---|
| *Subject* | $X_1$ | $X_2$ | $X_3$ | $X_1$ | $X_2$ | $X_3$ | $X_1$ | $X_2$ | $X_3$ |
| 1 | 6 | 3 | 5 | 8 | 7 | 9 | 1 | 2 | 1 |
| 2 | 5 | 5 | 3 | 7 | 9 | 5 | 2 | 2 | 4 |
| 3 | 6 | 4 | 2 | 9 | 9 | 7 | 1 | 1 | 2 |
| 4 | 4 | 2 | 2 | 6 | 8 | 8 | 3 | 3 | 3 |
| 5 | 3 | 2 | 6 | 7 | 8 | 9 | 4 | 1 | 2 |

NOTE: $X_1$, $X_2$, and $X_3$ refer to the three dependent measures listed in the text.

**TABLE 15-4**   **Partial SPSS Output for Hypothetical Experiment on Developing a Concept of Death**

### MULTIVARIATE TESTS OF SIGNIFICANCE ($S = 2, M = 0, N = 4$)

| Test Name | Value | Approx. F | Hypoth. df | Error df | Sig. of F |
|-----------|-------|-----------|------------|----------|-----------|
| Pillai's | 1.21442 | 5.66832 | 6.00 | 22.00 | .001 |
| Hotelling's | 17.82643 | 26.73964 | 6.00 | 18.00 | .000 |
| Wilks's | .03962 | 13.41251 | 6.00 | 20.00 | .000 |
| Roy's | .94583 | | | | |

Note: $F$ statistic for Wilks's Lambda is exact.

### EIGENVALUES AND CANONICAL CORRELATIONS

| Root No. | Eigenvalue | Pct. | Cum. Pct. | Canon Cor. |
|----------|-----------|------|-----------|-----------|
| 1 | 17.459 | 97.940 | 97.940 | .973 |
| 2 | .367 | 2.060 | 100.000 | .518 |

### DIMENSION REDUCTION ANALYSIS

| Roots | Wilks's L | F Hypoth. | df | Error df | Sig. of F |
|-------|-----------|-----------|-----|----------|-----------|
| 1 TO 2 | .03962 | 13.41251 | 6.00 | 20.00 | .000 |
| 2 TO 2 | .73140 | 2.01981 | 2.00 | 11.00 | .179 |

### ROY–BARGMAN STEPDOWN F TESTS

| Variable | Hypoth. MS | Error MS | Stepdown | F Hypoth. df | Error df | Sig. of F |
|----------|-----------|----------|----------|--------------|----------|-----------|
| DIE | 33.80000 | 1.56667 | 21.57447 | 2 | 12 | .000 |
| LIFE | 13.73684 | 1.06132 | 12.94322 | 2 | 11 | .001 |
| FEEL | 7.89738 | 2.47695 | 3.18835 | 2 | 10 | .085 |

### CORRELATIONS BETWEEN DEPENDENT AND CANONICAL VARIABLES

| | Canonical Variable | |
|---|---|---|
| VARIABLE | 1 | 2 |
| DIE | −.436 | .870 |
| LIFE | −.735 | −.198 |
| FEEL | −.376 | −.025 |

these data. The top part of Table 15-4 shows the multivariate tests of significance. Although the results from a number of such tests are shown, you decide to use the Wilks's test (the reasons why you choose one test over another are not important here because, in most cases, there will be little difference among them). The Wilks's test indicates that the effect of the treatment was significant, $F(6, 20) = 13.14$, $p < .001$. This tells you that your independent variable reliably affected the value of the linear dependent variable created in the MANOVA. When you conduct a single-factor MANOVA, you get essentially the same analysis as a canonical correlation analysis. As in canonical correlation, SPSS MANOVA extracts as many discriminant functions as possible (two in this case). The second section of Table 15-4 shows the statistics relevant to the discriminant functions extracted. Here, the canonical correlations are presented ("Canon Cor.") along with the percentage of variance accounted for ("Pct.") and the associated eigenvalues. Eigenvalues are not discussed here. See Tabachnick and Fidell (2013) for a discussion of these values.

The third section of Table 15-4 presents the results of a dimension reduction analysis. This analysis reveals that only the first function was significant ($p < .001$).

The significant $F$ ratio in the multivariate test indicates a reliable effect of the training program on concepts of death. As a next step, you assess each dependent variable's contribution to this significant effect. There are several ways to do this. You could simply look at the univariate $F$ tests produced by SPSS. This strategy has limitations, especially if your dependent variables are correlated with one another (Tabachnick & Fidell, 2013). An alternative strategy is to examine the *Roy–Bargman stepdown analysis* shown in the fourth section of Table 15-4.

In the Roy–Bargman stepdown analysis, the first dependent variable is entered and tested for significance. Then the second variable is entered, and the first variable is treated as a covariate. This test tells you whether each dependent variable explains variability over and above the variability already explained by those previously entered. The Roy–Bargman stepdown analysis is similar in concept to hierarchical regression. The main drawback to this analysis is that it can be used only when you can specify the order in which variables are entered. In the absence of a theoretically or empirically based order of entry, the Roy–Bargman test should not be used.

Finally, you also could look at the structure correlations shown at the bottom of Table 15-4 (labeled "Correlations Between Dependent and Canonical Variables"). The structure correlations are similar to factor loadings and can be interpreted as such.

In addition to these analyses, you might want to conduct some post hoc analyses to determine the specific effect of the independent variable on the dependent variables. These tests are similar to those used in univariate ANOVA but are more complex.

### Using MANOVA for Within-Subjects Designs

Chapters 10 and 14 discussed within-subjects designs and analyses. Each subject in a within-subjects design is exposed to all levels of your independent variable. Chapter 14 indicated that a repeated-measures

ANOVA can be used to analyze data from this design. Data from within-subjects (and mixed) designs also can be analyzed with MANOVA.

The within-subjects ANOVA assumes homogeneity of both within-cell variances and within-cell covariances. The first assumption states that variance should be homogeneous across treatments. This assumption applies to both the between-subjects and within-subjects analyses. However, the assumption of homogeneity of covariance (also called the assumption of sphericity) applies only to the within-subjects ANOVA. The following example illustrates the idea of homogeneity of covariances.

Figure 15-4 shows a simple one-factor within-subjects design. Notice that the behavior of each subject is evaluated under each level of the independent variable. This being the case, you can form pairs of conditions and subtract the scores associated with each subject within those two conditions (Keppel, 1982). You can then obtain variances based on the resulting difference scores. This variance is called *covariance*. In the design illustrated in Figure 15-4, you can form three pairs of conditions ($C_1$ with $C_2$, $C_2$ with $C_3$, and $C_1$ with $C_3$) and three concomitant covariances. If the covariances are not homogeneous, then the sphericity assumption has been violated.

In a between-subjects ANOVA, mild to moderate violations of the homogeneity of variance assumption do not strongly affect the validity of the statistical test. In a within-subjects ANOVA, however, violations of sphericity lead to a serious positive bias: rejecting the null hypothesis more often than you should at a given alpha level. Thus, you are making more Type I errors than are acceptable.

Another problem with the univariate within-subjects analysis is that when you add a second independent variable, the analysis becomes somewhat controversial. The controversy surrounds selecting an error term appropriate to test the main effects and

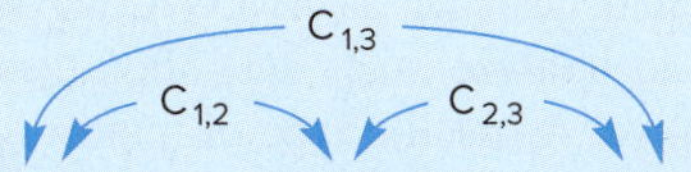

**FIGURE 15-4**
Three-treatment within-subjects design showing covariances.

| Subject | Level 1 | Level 2 | Level 3 |
|---------|---------|---------|---------|
| 1 | $X_{1,1}$ | $X_{2,1}$ | $X_{3,1}$ |
| 2 | $X_{1,2}$ | $X_{2,2}$ | $X_{3,2}$ |
| 3 | $X_{1,3}$ | $X_{2,3}$ | $X_{3,3}$ |
| 4 | $X_{1,4}$ | $X_{2,4}$ | $X_{3,4}$ |
| 5 | $X_{1,5}$ | $X_{2,5}$ | $X_{3,5}$ |

$C_{1,3}$, $C_{1,2}$, $C_{2,3}$

Note: $X_{i,j}$ represents a subject's score, where $i$ = the level of the independent variable and $j$ = the subject number. $C_{i,j}$ indicates the covariances that could be calculated, where $i$ and $j$ are the levels of the independent variable.

interactions. You can select a "pooled" error term and use this same term for all the within-subjects factors, or you can use separate error terms for each. Unfortunately, the two choices may lead to different outcomes of the statistical analysis, and there is little agreement on which choice is best.

Because MANOVA circumvents the problems with the homogeneity assumptions and error-term selection, it has been suggested as an alternative to standard within-subjects ANOVA (O'Brien & Kaiser, 1985; Tabachnick & Fidell, 2013). In the MANOVA, the repeated measures taken on each subject are treated as correlated dependent variables and analyzed accordingly. Rather than assuming sphericity, MANOVA takes into account the covariances actually present in the data. For information on using MANOVA to analyze within-subjects designs, see O'Brien and Kaiser (1985).

## QUESTIONS TO PONDER

1. When would you use a multivariate analysis of variance (MANOVA) to analyze your data?

2. How are the results of a MANOVA interpreted?

3. Why would you use a MANOVA to analyze data from a within-subjects design?

## Multiway Frequency Analysis

Most of the powerful inferential statistics discussed in this chapter and in Chapter 14 require that your variables be measured along at least an interval scale. However, there are research situations in which you may want to measure or manipulate categorical variables (e.g., sex of subject). Statistics such as ANOVA, MANOVA, and multiple regression are not appropriate to analyze such data. For these cases, **multiway frequency analysis** is an alternative. A specific type of multiway frequency analysis used for categorical or qualitative variables is loglinear analysis.

**Loglinear analysis** is analogous to chi-square (see Chapter 14) in that you use observed and expected frequencies to evaluate the statistical significance of your data. An important difference between chi-square and loglinear analysis is that loglinear analysis can be easily applied to experimental research designs that include more than two independent variables whereas chi-square is normally limited to the two-variable case.

*Applications of Loglinear Analysis*    Loglinear analysis has a wide range of applications. You can use loglinear analysis if you conducted a correlational study with several categorical variables; loglinear analysis is well suited to this task. You also can use loglinear analysis if you conducted an experiment including a categorical dependent variable (e.g., guilty/not guilty) even if your independent variables were quantitative.

Loglinear analysis is also a useful tool for testing and building theoretical models. In this application, you specify how variables should be entered into the analysis for the models that you wish to test. Loglinear analysis is then used to test the relative adequacy of each model.

Finally, because loglinear analysis is a nonparametric statistic, you can use it if your data violate the assumptions of parametric statistics (such as ANOVA). In this instance, you can use loglinear analysis even if your dependent variable was measured along an interval or ordinal scale (Tabachnick & Fidell, 2013). However, one important requirement must still be met.

Like chi-square, loglinear analysis uses observed and expected cell frequencies to compute your test statistic. To obtain valid results, your expected cell frequencies must be relatively large. Tabachnick and Fidell (2013) recommend having five times as many subjects as cells to ensure adequate expected frequencies. So, for example, if you have a $2 \times 2 \times 2$ design, you should have $2 \times 2 \times 2 \times 5 = 40$ subjects to ensure sufficiently large expected cell frequencies.

You should inspect all expected frequencies to ensure that they are all larger than one and that no more than 20% of them fall below five (Tabachnick & Fidell, 2013). If you find small expected frequencies, Tabachnick and Fidell suggest several remedies. First, you could accept and live with the reduced power of the analysis caused by low expected frequencies. Second, categories can be collapsed or combined to increase frequencies within each category. Third, you could delete variables to reduce the number of categories in your analysis. This latter strategy should be done with caution, and you should not delete variables that are correlated with other variables in the analysis (Tabachnick & Fidell, 2013).

*How Loglinear Analysis Works* When you use ANOVA or multiple regression to analyze your data, your analysis uses group means as a basis for analysis. When you have categorical data, however, you must deal with proportions instead of means. For example, if you used a three-factor design with a categorical dependent variable (yes/no), you would summarize your data according to the proportion of subjects falling into each category.

In a standard analysis of proportional data from a two-factor experiment in which you are interested in a single relationship between two variables, chi-square is used to evaluate that relationship. However, when evaluating more than one relationship (i.e., two main effects and an interaction), chi-square is not the best test statistic because the component chi-squares do not sum to the total chi-square. In this case, a likelihood ratio ($G^2$) is used in place of chi-square. Although similar to chi-square (in that cell expected and observed frequencies are compared), $G^2$ involves taking the natural log (ln) of the ratio of observed cell frequency to the expected cell frequency, according to the following formula (Tabachnick & Fidell, 2013):

$$G^2 = 2(f_o)\ln(f_o/f_e)$$

where $f_o$ is the observed cell frequency and $f_e$ is the expected cell frequency. A $G^2$ is computed for each main effect and interaction in your design and is interpreted in the same way as chi-square. For detailed discussions of loglinear analysis, see Agresti and Finlay (1986) and Tabachnick and Fidell (2013).

## QUESTIONS TO PONDER

1. What is multiway frequency analysis, and when is it used?

2. What is loglinear analysis, and when is it used?

3. What is $G^2$, and how is it used in loglinear analysis?

## MULTIVARIATE STATISTICAL TECHNIQUES AND CAUSAL MODELING

In this section, we discuss two applications of multivariate statistics to causal modeling: path analysis and structural equation modeling.

### Path Analysis

Unlike the other analytic techniques already discussed, **path analysis** is not a statistical procedure in and of itself. Rather, it is an application of multiple regression techniques to the testing of causal models. Path analysis allows you to test a model specifying the causal links among variables by applying simple multiple regression techniques.

Always remember that path analysis is designed to test causal models, not to sift through data for interesting relationships among variables. Developing a clearly articulated causal model is crucial in path analysis. The model should not rest on flimsy ideas and unsupported conjecture. Instead, the causal relationships proposed in the model should rest on a strong theoretical or empirical base.

Translating theoretical propositions into a clearly defined path model can be tricky. You always are tempted to determine how to measure your variables first and then derive the model. This method may not be the best. It may limit the possible causal relationships within your model and consequently may not allow you to adequately test your theory. Instead, first develop a list of the causal links among variables as suggested by your theory (Hunter & Gerbing, 1982). Then show these links among variables in a *path diagram*. After developing the path model and diagram, you can then decide how to measure your variables.

*Causal Relationships*    The heart of path analysis is developing a causal model and identifying causal relationships. Causal relationships among variables can take many forms. The simplest of these is shown in panel (a) of Figure 15-5, where variable A (independent variable) causes changes in variable B (dependent variable). Another possible causal relationship is shown in panel (b). Here, two variables impinge on variable B. This model suggests that variation in the dependent variable has multiple causes. These causal variables can be uncorrelated as shown in panel (b). Panel (c) shows a situation in which two variables believed to cause changes in the dependent variable are correlated. In Figure 15-5 (and in path analysis, in general), straight arrows denote causal relationships and are called *paths*. Curved, double-headed arrows denote correlational relationships.

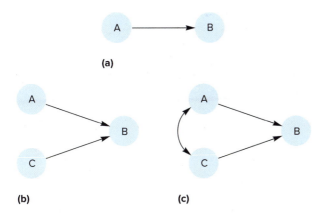

**FIGURE 15-5** Three possible causal relationships. (a) Variable A causes changes in B; (b) uncorrelated variables A and C contribute to changes in the value of B; (c) correlated variables A and C cause changes in the value of B.

The simple causal relationships just described can be combined to form more complex causal models. One such model is the *causal chain* in which a sequence of events leads ultimately to variation in the dependent variable. To illustrate a simple causal chain, consider a modification of a previous example in which you were trying to determine what variables correlated with SAT scores.

Suppose you believe that parental education (PE) and student motivation (SM) relate to variation in SAT scores. You have reason to believe that a causal relationship exists. So you develop a causal model like the one illustrated in panel (a) of Figure 15-6. Your model suggests that PE causes changes in SM, which then causes changes in SAT scores. Notice that you are proposing that PE does not directly cause changes in SAT but rather operates through SM.

When developing simple causal chains (and more complex causal models), keep in mind that the validity of your causal model depends on how well you have done your homework and conceptualized your model. Perhaps SM does not directly cause changes in SAT scores as conjectured but rather operates through yet another variable, such as working hard (WH) in class. Panel (b) of Figure 15-6 shows a causal chain including WH. If you excluded WH from your model, the causal relationships and the model you develop may not be valid.

You can progress from simple causal chains to more complex models quite easily. Figure 15-7 shows three examples of more complex causal models. In panel (a), the

**FIGURE 15-6** (a) Three-variable causal chain and (b) four-variable causal chain.

**FIGURE 15-7**   Three complex causal models.

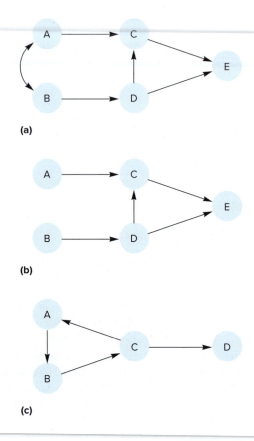

(a)

(b)

(c)

causal model suggests variables A and B are correlated (indicated with the curved arrow). Variable A is believed to exert a causal influence on variable C, and B on D. Variable D is hypothesized to cause changes in C, and both D and C are believed to cause changes in E.

*Types of Variables and Causal Models*   Variables A and B in panel (a) of Figure 15-7 are called *exogenous variables.* Exogenous variables begin the causal sequence. Notice that no causal paths lead to variable A or B. All the other variables in the model shown in panel (a) are *endogenous variables.* These variables are internal to the model, and changes in them are believed to be caused by other variables. Variables C, D, and E are all endogenous variables. Panel (b) of Figure 15-7 shows essentially the same model as panel (a), except that the two exogenous variables are not correlated.

The models in panels (a) and (b) are both known as *recursive models.* Notice that there are no loops of variables. That is, causal relationships run in only one direction (e.g., D causes C, but C does not cause D). In contrast, panel (c) of Figure 15-7 shows a *nonrecursive model,* which has a causal loop. In this case, variable A is believed to be a cause of C (operating through B), but C also can cause A. In general, recursive models are much easier to deal with conceptually and statistically (Asher, 1976).

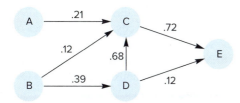

**FIGURE 15-8** Path diagram showing path coefficients.

*Estimating the Degree of Causality*    After you have developed your causal models and measured your variables, you obtain estimates, called *path coefficients,* of the causal relationships among your variables. Figure 15-8 shows a causal model with the path coefficients indicated for each causal path.

Path coefficients are determined by using a series of multiple regression analyses. Each endogenous variable is treated as a dependent variable in the regression analysis. All the variables in the model assumed to cause changes in the dependent variable are treated as predictors. For example, the path coefficients for A–C and D–C in Figure 15-8 are obtained by using C as the dependent variable and A, B, and D as predictors. The path coefficients are the standardized regression weights (beta weights) from these analyses.

*Interpreting Path Analysis*    Path analysis is used to test the validity of a presumed causal model. To that end, you look at the path coefficients and determine whether the pattern expected by the model has emerged. In addition to looking at the path coefficients (which give you estimates of the direct effects of variables on other variables), you also decompose the paths into indirect effects. Decomposition can be done according to Wright's rules (see Asher, 1976).

## QUESTIONS TO PONDER

1. What is path analysis, and how is it used in the research process?

2. Why is it important to develop a causal model when using path analysis?

3. What are the different types of variables used in a path analysis?

4. How are path coefficients used to interpret a path analysis?

## Structural Equation Modeling

**Structural equation modeling (SEM)** is a variant of path analysis. With path analysis, variables that are directly observed and measured are included in the analysis. Sometimes, however, you deal with variables that are not directly observable but rather are manifested in a number of behaviors (Streiner, 2006). Variables that are not directly observable are known as *hypothetical constructs.* In the language of SEM, a hypothetical construct is called a **latent variable**, which is not measured directly. For example, depression is a hypothetical construct because it is not measured directly. Instead, we can measure several behaviors that relate to depression (e.g., suicidal thoughts, loss of energy, and sleep disturbances). You could have participants indicate how many times a week they have suicidal thoughts, rate their energy levels on a 10-point scale, and indicate how many hours of sleep they get a night. Each of these three variables is called a **measured variable** in SEM because they are measured directly. From the values of the measured variables, you can determine the value of the latent variable. One advantage of SEM over path analysis is that in SEM, you can evaluate the relationships among measured variables *and* hypothetical constructs within the models you test (Streiner, 2006). With path analysis, you evaluate only measured variables.

SEM is normally used as a confirmatory procedure and not an exploratory one (Garson, 2006). That is, you start with a theoretical or empirical model that predicts certain patterns of relationships among variables. G. David Garson suggests that there are three confirmatory applications of SEM:

1. *Strictly confirmatory approach:* You test a model to see if data that you collected are consistent with the predictions of the model.

2. *Alternative models approach:* You test two or more alternative models to see which one (if any) best fits the data collected.

3. *Model development approach:* You use SEM to develop a model by combining exploratory and confirmatory approaches. You then test the model, and if you find that it does not fit the data very well, you make modifications to the model and retest it. You keep doing this until you find the model that best fits the data.

An important fact to keep in mind about SEM is that it requires you, as the researcher, to develop a model to test based on existing theory and research. You do not simply go on a "fishing expedition" by throwing variables into an SEM analysis and hope to find meaningful relationships and causal connections. However, as noted earlier, SEM can serve an exploratory function. Even this, however, requires that you specify a coherent model to be tested.

Developing a model for SEM analysis starts with a verbal statement of how variables relate (e.g., according to a theory) (Hershberger, Marcoulides, & Parramore, 2003). Next, you draw out the model using boxes, ovals, and arrows. Boxes represent measured variables; their names are written inside the boxes. Ovals denote latent variables. Arrows specify the relationships among variables: straight arrows for causal relationships and curved arrows for correlational relationships.

As you saw in our discussion of path analysis, path coefficients are derived by using multiple regression analysis. In SEM specialized statistical techniques are used to derive coefficients. The most popular program used for this purpose is LISREL, published by Scientific Software International (SSI). The LISREL package includes programs for various types of modeling. For details, visit the SSI website at www.ssicentral.com.

## MULTIVARIATE ANALYSIS: A CAUTIONARY NOTE

The bare-bones overview of the major multivariate techniques in this chapter could not provide a detailed discussion of the controversies surrounding the use of these tests. Although some researchers characterize multivariate statistics such as MANOVA as "a powerful and rich methodology to characterize group difference" (Bray & Maxwell, 1982, p. 363), others advocate extreme caution in applying multivariate statistics (Hunter, 1987). In our experience, caution is called for when using multivariate statistics.

The computer can analyze multivariate data quickly and efficiently. In fact, the computer has made multivariate statistical techniques readily available to most researchers. With such easy access inevitably comes misapplication. The computer can grind out pages and pages of output in an amazingly short period of time. It cannot interpret the results for you, however. Much of the controversy over the use of multivariate statistics lies in the area of interpretation.

In multiple regression, for example, is it really better to use the standardized regression weights or the unstandardized weights to interpret the data? Or should you heed the advice of Tabachnick and Fidell (2013) to calculate semipartial correlations? In discriminant analysis, should you use the standardized coefficients or the structure correlations? In factor analysis, should you use orthogonal or oblique rotation? Unfortunately, there are no universally agreed-on answers to these and other major questions concerning multivariate analyses.

This chapter has discussed some of the advantages of multivariate statistics over univariate statistics. Unfortunately, multivariate statistics are not simple substitutions for univariate statistics. In a univariate ANOVA, for example, the effect of an independent variable on a dependent variable is evaluated by determining if the observed means change as a function of changes in the independent variable. Fine-grained analyses are then conducted to determine which means differ significantly. MANOVA, however, produces results that are more difficult to interpret. Instead of performing simple fine-grained analyses to localize significant effects, you set up contrasts with discriminant analyses. In short, interpreting results from a MANOVA is more complex than interpreting results from univariate ANOVAs.

The most prudent thing that you can do at this point is to spend some time learning about the intricacies of these tests so that you can identify and avoid these hidden traps. Thoroughly familiarize yourself with the assumptions of multivariate statistics and with how these statistics operate before attempting to use them.

Also, pay close attention to how you design your study. In many cases, failure to uncover relationships with a multivariate test is caused by faulty logic more during the design phase than during the analysis phase (Asher, 1976). Multivariate statistics cannot make sense out of poorly conceived and measured variables. There is no substitute for a carefully designed multivariate study that has a sound theoretical or empirical base and a well-defined measurement model.

## QUESTIONS TO PONDER

1. What is structural equation modeling, and how does it differ from path analysis?

2. What are the three confirmatory applications of structural equation modeling?

3. What is a latent variable, and how is it used in structural equation modeling?

4. Why should you exercise caution when using multivariate data analysis?

## SUMMARY

Whenever you include several related measures in the same study, you are using a multivariate design. Analysis of your data is then done with one of the many multivariate statistical tests. There are multivariate tests for experiments with multiple dependent measures (MANOVA and MANCOVA) and tests for correlational designs (multiple regression, canonical correlation, discriminant analysis, and factor analysis). These tests allow you to identify complex relationships while controlling statistical errors.

Like univariate and bivariate statistics, multivariate statistics make assumptions that must be met. Your variables must be linearly related and normally distributed. Violations of these assumptions may lead to invalid conclusions. In addition, you must identify and deal with both univariate and multivariate outliers because outliers can drastically affect the correlations used to compute multivariate statistics. Outliers can be handled either by deleting cases or variables or by using an appropriate data transformation. Also, make an effort to develop a sound measurement model to avoid the problem of error of measurement. Error of measurement can lead to an unacceptable number of Type II errors.

Factor analysis is used either to reduce a large set of variables to a smaller set or to confirm that certain variables measure the same underlying factor. Two types of factor analysis are principal components and principal factors. The difference between the two is found in the values placed on the diagonal of the correlation matrix used to extract factors. In principal components analysis, 1s are placed on the diagonal. In principal factors analysis, communalities are placed on the diagonal. These communalities are difficult to derive before factor analysis. Principal components analysis is therefore more popular.

Factor analysis extracts as many significant factors as possible. For each factor, a variable will have a certain loading. These loadings are the correlations between the original variable and the factor extracted. You should rotate the factors before interpreting the loadings. The most popular rotation method is varimax.

Partial and part correlation analyses are used when you want to evaluate the relationship between two variables while controlling for a third. Partial correlation evaluates the relationship between two variables with the effect of a third variable removed from both of the variables being correlated. A part correlation (also known as a semipartial correlation) evaluates the relationship between two variables with the effect of a third removed from only one of them.

Multiple regression is used when you have identified a single, continuously measured dependent variable and several predictor variables. The analysis operates by determining regression weights based on the correlations among your variables. Two types of regression weights are raw and standardized weights. In general, you should use the standardized weights to help interpret your results. Unfortunately, the standardized weights do not tell you how much each variable contributes to explaining variability in your dependent variable. To do this, you should calculate the squared semipartial correlations. These correlations can then be used to determine the degree to which each variable independently contributes to variation in the dependent variable.

Discriminant analysis is an extension of multiple regression. It is used when your dependent variable is categorical. Essentially, you are trying to predict group membership based on knowledge of your predictor variables. Interpretation is made by examining the amount of variability accounted for by each of the extracted discriminant functions and by setting up contrasts between your dependent variable groups. The former tells you how important each function is, and the latter how important each variable is to the solution.

In situations in which you have two sets of variables, the analysis of choice is canonical correlation. One set of variables may be identified as the dependent variable set and the other, the predictor variable set. Canonical correlation computes for each set a new variable called a canonical variate. The correlation between the canonical variates is the canonical correlation. Interpretation of a canonical analysis can be made by looking at the structure correlations. These can be interpreted much like factor loadings in factor analysis.

MANOVA is used when you have an experiment with several related dependent measures. The analysis is essentially an extension of discriminant analysis to experimental data. Interpretation is based on the significance of the discriminant functions extracted for each effect, the Roy–Bargman stepdown test, and the structure correlations.

MANOVA also can be used to analyze data from a within-subjects design. Because of the restrictive assumptions of the univariate within-subjects ANOVA and the controversy surrounding error term selection for that analysis, MANOVA should be considered as an alternative. In MANOVA, the repeated measures taken from each subject are treated as correlated dependent variables. Using MANOVA in this capacity circumvents many of the problems associated with the traditional within-subjects ANOVA.

Multiway frequency analysis is a nonparametric multivariate statistic with a variety of applications. It can be used to analyze categorical data from an experiment or categorical variables from a correlational study. It also can be used on interval or ratio data in instances in which your data do not meet the assumptions of the analysis of variance. One form of multiway frequency analysis commonly used is loglinear analysis.

Path analysis is used to test a clearly specified causal model. Using a theory, you develop a causal model, measure your variables, and then use a series of simple multiple regression analyses to derive path coefficients. The path coefficients are used as estimates of the magnitude of causal relationships among variables. Interpretation is facilitated by looking at both direct and indirect effects of variables. Causal models can be of several types. Simple causal chains propose that there is a linear path from one variable to another. More complex models can involve complex path linkages. Models can be either recursive (which contain no causal loops) or nonrecursive (which contain causal loops). Conceptually, recursive models are easier to analyze and interpret. Structural equation modeling is a technique related to path analysis. It differs from path analysis in that it allows you to look at hypothetical variables called latent variables in your model. Finally, multivariate analyses are complex and tricky to use. Don't try to use them until you have a sound understanding of how they work, what assumptions they make, and how results can be interpreted.

## KEY TERMS

univariate strategy

multivariate strategy

multivariate design

multiple regression

discriminant analysis

canonical correlation

factor analysis

multivariate analysis of variance
(MANOVA)

partial correlation

part correlation

multiple $R$

$R$-square

beta weight

multiway frequency analysis

loglinear analysis

path analysis

structural equation modeling (SEM)

latent variable

measured variable

# Reporting Your Research Results

Y our journey through the world of research has taken you through the steps involved in choosing a research question, developing hypotheses, choosing a general strategy and specific design to test your hypotheses, and describing and analyzing your data. The final step in this process is to tell the world what you did and what you found.

Reporting your research results is perhaps the most important step because it is only by this reporting that science progresses. Other scientists working in the field need to know what you have done: the questions you have asked, the methods you have used to address them, and the answers you have found. This step is not only essential for progress but also required to assess the reliability of your findings and the soundness of your conclusions. Only when your research has been reported can others attempt to replicate and extend your findings.

Effectively communicating the results of your research requires you to know what must be said and how to communicate it clearly and in the proper format. This chapter discusses how to organize and present your research findings. Even if you are not planning to pursue a career in psychological research, you will find that much of the information contained in this chapter is valuable. Many occupations—especially those at a managerial or technical level— require you to organize facts, to draw conclusions, and to present the facts and conclusions clearly and logically in a written report. Although the format and contents of your reports are likely to differ from those of the scientific report described here, the general principles of organization and composition will be the same.

## APA WRITING STYLE

Regardless of the scientific discipline, scientific journals require a specific *writing style* for manuscripts submitted for publication. This writing style specifies the rules that must be followed when preparing your manuscript. For example, it will specify how to set up margins, which fonts are acceptable, what sections must be included, and how to format tables and graphs.

In psychology, most journals follow the style established by the American Psychological Association (APA) in the *Publication Manual of the American Psychological Association* (6th ed., 2010). We refer to this manual simply as the APA publication manual. When you follow the manual, your manuscript conforms to APA style.

Sometimes you may come across a journal that does not completely follow APA style. Nevertheless, these journals usually follow APA style closely with only a few minor exceptions. (These exceptions are usually indicated on or near an inside cover of each journal issue or on the journal's website, under a heading such as "Notes to Authors.") Therefore, most of what you learn about APA style will apply even to non-APA psychology journals. The following discussion provides a condensed description of how to write a research report in APA style. We cannot present a comprehensive review of APA style in the space available here. (For additional details, consult the APA publication manual. You can also consult Purdue University's Owl Online Writing Lab at https://owl.english.purdue.edu/owl/resource/560/01/ for a good condensed presentation of APA style.) In this chapter, we also discuss how to avoid some common errors of composition and grammar and how to prepare a conference presentation.

## WRITING AN APA-STYLE RESEARCH REPORT

There are seven main sections in an APA-style research report manuscript: the title page, abstract, introduction, method, results, discussion, and references. There are many guidelines to follow when you are preparing an APA-style manuscript. For example, specific instructions govern margins, line spacing, the content of each section, and how to present information in tables and figures. In this section, we discuss some of the basic guidelines for preparing an APA-style manuscript.

### Getting Ready to Write

For this discussion, we assume that you will be creating your manuscript by using word processing software (such as Microsoft Word or Google Docs). Before you begin to type, make sure the settings of your word processor conform to the requirements of an APA-style manuscript. Pay attention in particular to the settings for paper size, font (typeface and size), margins, line spacing, hyphenation, and justification.

To create an APA-style manuscript, select the 8½- × 11-inch paper size (usually the default). As for typeface, APA prefers Times New Roman. A *serif* typeface such as this is preferred for the body of the manuscript (i.e., typeface that has lines extending from the beginnings and ends of letters) because it is easier to read. You may use a *sans serif* (without the lines) such as Arial for figures because this typeface gives a very clean, clear look. Set the font size to 12 points. Be sure to turn off any setting that compresses the typeface or reduces the spacing between characters. Also, be sure to change the default setting that inserts an extra blank line between paragraphs.

Use double spacing throughout your manuscript. This goes for the spaces between lines of text, between lines in the title, and after headings, footnotes, quotations, references, figure captions, and all elements of a table (although you may use single spacing in tables or figures). You may use more space before or after an equation, but you should *not* use single or one-and-a-half spacing in your manuscript, except in some cases in figures and tables (APA, 2010). Spacing after punctuation marks varies according to where a punctuation mark occurs. Use a single space after commas, colons, and semicolons. Use a single space after periods appearing in references and after initials. Use double space after periods that end sentences in the body of your manuscript.

Be sure to turn off right justification so that the last words of the lines on a page form a ragged right edge. Also, check to be sure that you disable automatic hyphenation. APA style requires that a word too long to fit on a given line appear in its entirety on the next line. This will happen only if automatic hyphenation is off.

All margins for an APA-style manuscript must be at least 1 inch (top, bottom, left, and right). With most word processors, 1 inch margins are usually the default. A typed line has a maximum length of 6½ inches.

Most likely you will be required to submit your manuscript to a journal electronically. If this is the case, you should check the journal's electronic submission guidelines to see if there are any additional requirements. For example, a journal might require a word count or a special watermark in the manuscript. If you are going to submit a hard copy, print the completed manuscript on 8½- × 11-inch heavy white bond paper. Use a high-quality printer (e.g., inkjet or laser printer) and check to be sure that the manuscript is free of defects such as light printing.

*Formatting a Page*    Each page of an APA manuscript includes a **running head** and a page number. The running head is a shortened version of your title having no more than 50 characters (including punctuation and spaces). Use your word processor's page header function to create the text and set up automatic page numbering so that the running head and page number appear on every page of your manuscript automatically. Position the running head flush left and the page number flush right on the same line.

Indent the first line of all paragraphs and footnotes (with the exception of the abstract, the first paragraph of block quotes, titles and headings, table titles and notes, and figure captions). Set the tabs on your word processor to give an indent of from five to seven spaces (or one-half inch).

*Heading Structure*    Headings within a manuscript identify different sections and subsections. In an APA-style manuscript, you can have anywhere from one to five levels of headings. The structure for these five levels is as follows (APA, 2010, p. 62):

    **Centered, boldface, upper and lowercase** (Level 1)

**Flush left, boldface, upper and lowercase** (Level 2)

    **Indented, boldface lowercase paragraph heading ending with a period.** (Level 3)

Running head: CONTEXTUAL INFORMATION AND PERCEPTION OF ART          1

Contextual Information, Artistic Style, and the Perception of Art

Kenneth S. Bordens

Indiana University-Purdue University Fort Wayne

Author Note

Kenneth S. Bordens, Department of Psychology, Indiana University-Purdue University Fort Wayne.

Everyone is still at the same place. However, if an author had taken a new position it would be disclosed in this second paragraph.

We thank Bruce B. Abbott for his advice on the design of the present experiment and data analysis.

Correspondence concerning this article should be addressed to Kenneth Bordens, Department of Psychology, Indiana University-Purdue University Fort Wayne, hisemail@ipfw.edu.

**FIGURE 16-1**    Sample title page.

*Indented, boldface italicized, lowercase paragraph heading ending with a period.* (Level 4)

> *Indented, italicized, lowercase paragraph heading ending with a period.* (Level 5)

In most cases, you will use only a three-level heading structure. However, you may use the other levels depending on the needs of your paper. A three-level heading structure looks like this:

**Method** (Level 1)

**Participants** (Level 2)

**Participants not meeting requirements.** (Level 3)

For manuscripts requiring more than three levels of headings, consult the APA publication manual (2010, pp. 62–63).

## QUESTIONS TO PONDER

1. How do you set up a paper using APA writing style?
2. What is the heading structure used in an APA-style manuscript?

# PARTS AND ORDER OF MANUSCRIPT SECTIONS

Each section of an APA-style manuscript includes important information that informs your reader what your paper is about, how you conducted your study, what you found, how your results relate to previous research and theory, and a list of references. In the sections that follow, we present information about each major section of an APA-style paper. The order in which we present these sections is the order in which they should appear in your paper.

## The Title Page

The **title page** includes (in order) your running head and page number, the title of your paper, author name, the author's institutional affiliation, and any author notes. On the title page *only,* prefix the running head with "Running head:" and follow this with your running head typed in all capital letters. Place the title, author, and institutional affiliation information on the top half of the title page centered between the left and right margins. Figure 16-1 shows how to format a title page for a single author. Consult the APA publication manual (2010) to see how to format a title page for other types of authorship.

*Title*    When researchers looking for relevant articles on a particular topic scan the table of contents of a journal or an abstract in PsycINFO, the title of an article first captures attention. If the title fails to communicate clearly what the paper is about, readers may skip the paper.

An unread paper is useless. To avoid this fate for your paper, make your title concise yet informative. Avoid using words that add little to the meaningfulness of your title (e.g., "An Experimental Investigation of . . ." and "A Correlational Field Study of . . ."). Keep your title short enough to avoid confusion about your research, but not so short that it fails to convey the topic of your paper. The recommended length for a title is no more than 12 words.

Taking our cue from the story of "Goldilocks and the Three Bears," we present the following examples showing a title that is too long, a title that is too short, and one that is just right:

*Too long:* An Experimental Study of the Effect of Delay of

Reinforcement on Discrimination Learning in White Rats

*Too short:* The Effect of Reinforcement on Learning

*Just right:* Effect of Delay of Reinforcement on Discrimination

Learning in Rats

In the first example, the words "An Experimental Study of " and "White" add extraneous words to your title. The second title is too general. A potential reader has only a vague idea about the focus of your study. The third example concisely conveys the essence of your study.

Center your title between the left and right margins. If multiple lines are required, double-space them just as you do other text. Capitalize the first letter of the first word and of all subsequent words (except for articles, prepositions of three letters or less, and conjunctions).

***Author Name(s) and Affiliation(s)***    If you are the sole author of the paper, your name goes one double-spaced line beneath the title. Include your given name, middle initial(s), and last name (in that order), centered between the margins. To avoid confusion you should use the same format for your name for all papers you prepare. Do not include any titles (such as Mr., Ms., Dr.) or degrees (B.A., M.A., Ph.D., M.D., etc.).

Your affiliation identifies where you were when you conducted your research. This is usually the organization that provided the local facilities and/or support for your research (usually a university or college). Its name appears one double-spaced line below yours on the title page, centered between the margins.

If there are two or more authors, how you organize the information depends on whether everyone has the same affiliation. Consult the APA publication manual for details. With multiple authors, the APA publication manual directs that multiple authors must be listed in order of their degree of contribution to the paper. If all authors contributed equally, they should work out some method for listing (e.g., alphabetically). If you do this, you should note it in the manuscript in an "author note."

***Author Note***    Published APA-style journal articles include an **author note**, which is a small footnote at the bottom of the title page to identify each author's departmental affiliation, provide acknowledgments, state disclaimers or conflicts of interest, and indicate how readers can contact the author. Author notes are not numbered, nor should you refer to them in the body of your paper.

Center the words "Author Note" below the author affiliation (see Figure 12-1) and arrange the author note itself in four paragraphs (APA, 2010). The first paragraph identifies the author's affiliation when the study was conducted. The second paragraph lists any changes in author affiliation since the study was conducted. The third paragraph includes acknowledgments such as grants that supported the research or the names of those who made special contributions to the research (such as informal review, assistance with the research design, or statistical analysis). It also indicates any special circumstances concerning the paper (such as that the study was a replication of an earlier one or that the study was done as a requirement for a degree). The fourth paragraph presents the "point of contact." Here you provide a complete mailing address (including, if desired, an e-mail address at the end of the paragraph) where readers can contact you. An author note is also used to indicate any conflicts of interest or biases an author may have.

## The Abstract

The **abstract** is a concise summary of your paper. Each journal has its own requirements concerning the length of your abstract. In most cases, the length of your abstract will be between 150 and 250 words (APA, 2010, p. 27). The content of your abstract will depend on the nature of your paper. In the abstract for an empirical study, include the following (APA, 2010, p. 26):

1. Information on the problem under study (preferably in one sentence).

2. The nature of the subject sample (e.g., age and sex).

3. A description of the methods used, including equipment, procedures for gathering data, names of tests, and so on.

4. A statement of the findings, including information on levels of statistical significance, effect sizes, and confidence intervals.

5. A statement of the conclusions drawn and any implications or applications of your results.

Although short, the abstract is important. Abstracts of papers appear at the beginning of the journal article and in databases such as PsycINFO. A potential reader will use your abstract to decide whether to read your paper as part of a literature search. If your abstract is poorly written, readers may fail to understand the significance of your work and may pass it by. Thus, you should put effort into writing a clear, concise abstract.

Your abstract is the first substantive section of your paper. However, you typically write it *after* you have written the rest of your paper, when you will have a clearer idea about what must be included in the abstract.

The APA manual defines four qualities that make for a good abstract. First, your abstract must be *accurate*. This means that the information in your abstract reflects what is in the body of your paper. Do not include any information in the abstract that does not appear in your paper. Second, your abstract should be *nonevaluative*. You should report on your study and avoid adding any comments on what is in your paper. Third, your abstract should be *coherent and readable*. Write your abstract using clear and concise language. Generally, write in the active rather than passive voice and write in the present tense (except when describing specific manipulations or results). Fourth, make your abstract as *concise* as possible. Include only the most important information and write in concise sentences. Remember, you have a limited number of words, so make them count.

*Formatting the Abstract*   Type your abstract on a separate page, immediately after your title page and number it as page 2. Type the word "Abstract" (not in boldface) centered on the line following your running head and page number. On the next line, begin your abstract. Do *not* indent the first line of the abstract. Include a list of keywords, centered immediately below your abstract (see Figure 16-2).

## QUESTIONS TO PONDER

1. What information is included on the title page, and in what order would you find that information (from the top of the page to the bottom of the page)?

2. What is an abstract, and why is it so important?

3. What information goes into an abstract, and how long should an abstract be?

## The Introduction

The text of the paper begins with the **introduction**. The primary function of the introduction is to describe the problem studied and your basic research strategy. Before writing your introduction, the APA manual suggests asking yourself the following questions (APA, 2010, p. 27):

1. Why is the issue studied important?

CONTEXTUAL INFORMATION AND PERCEPTION OF ART                    2

### Abstract

An experiment was conducted to determine if providing contextual information about various artistic styles would increase liking and lead to more positive perceptions of examples of art. Participants were 172 male and female artistically naive undergraduate students. Participants evaluated four artworks from one of four styles (Dada, Outsider, Impressionism, and Renaissance) on several rating scales. Results showed that when no contextual information was presented perceived match between an artwork and an internal concept of art was higher than if contextual information was presented and that Dada art received the lowest match scores followed by Outsider, Impressionist, and Renaissance art. Dada art was liked significantly less than Outsider, Impressionist, or Renaissance art. Factor analysis of bipolar semantic differential scales revealed four dimensions underlying perception of art and that different styles could be separated based on these dimensions.

*Keywords:* artistic styles, perception of art, context, judgment of art

**FIGURE 16-2**   Sample abstract.

2. How does your study relate to previous research in the area and how does it differ from other studies on the same issue?

3. What are the hypotheses and objectives of your study and how do they relate to relevant theory (if they do)?

4. How do your hypotheses relate to your research design?

5. What are the theoretical and practical implications of your study?

Your introduction should include three essential elements (APA, 2010): an exploration of the importance of the problem examined, a description of relevant previous research and theory, and a clear statement of your hypotheses and how they relate to your research design. To help the reader understand why you conducted your study, your introduction should include the following information:

1. An introduction to the topic under study.

2. A brief review of the research findings and theories related to the topic.

3. A statement of the problem to be addressed by the research (identifying an area in which knowledge is incomplete).

4. A statement of the purpose of the research (always to solve the problem identified but perhaps only a specific aspect of it).

5. A brief description of the research strategy, intended to establish the relationship between the question being addressed and the method used to address it.

6. A description of any predictions about the outcome and of the hypotheses used to generate those predictions.

Your goal in the introduction is to present this information in an easily understandable way. To accomplish this, you should structure your introduction to move from a general to a specific level. This general structure is shown in Figure 16-3. In the opening paragraph of your introduction, present a general discussion of the issue you chose to study. Next, present a review of research relating directly to your study. This will help you develop the underlying logic and rationale for your study in more specific terms. Next, identify the specific problem addressed by your research and state the purpose of your study. Finally, show how your study addresses the question, and state your specific hypotheses.

If your introduction includes information of a controversial nature, you should present this information in a fair and balanced manner. You should avoid expressing strong opinions on one side or another of the controversial issue. If you must express a personal opinion in the introduction, you should offer it without hostility and without making personal attacks on those with whom you disagree. When using citations to support your view or your research, you must present the research fairly and not out of context (APA, 2010).

Students often have difficulty determining what should go into the literature review of previous findings. Should it include a comprehensive review of *all* relevant research or be limited to a few papers that relate specifically to your research? The answer: Try for something between these extremes.

You can assume that your reader has some knowledge of the basic psychological concepts that underlie your study. Your job is to bring your reader up to date on the literature that most directly relates to your study. For example, if you investigated the effect of amount of reinforcement on behavior modification of developmentally delayed children, you need not review all research on operant conditioning and reinforcement. You can assume that your reader has some knowledge of the basic concepts of operant conditioning. Instead, focus on the important issues relating directly to using operant conditioning to modify the behavior of developmentally delayed persons.

Assume you have decided to focus your introduction on the important issues. You then begin your literature search and, to your shock and horror, you find 200 articles that relate in some way to your research topic. Just how many of these must be included in your literature review? Of course, you cannot hope to review them all.

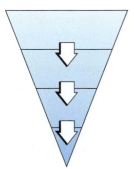

Present general introduction to your topic.

Review literature.

Link your literature review to your topic.

State your hypotheses.

**FIGURE 16-3**   General-to-specific organization of an APA-style introduction.

In fact, such a comprehensive literature review is inappropriate for a research paper. Your review should focus on those issues that are most important for establishing the rationale of your study. Therefore, you should identify all the papers most directly relevant to the issues raised by your introduction. Within this narrower area, you can cite all or at least many of the relevant papers.

*Formatting the Introduction*    To follow APA style, begin the introduction on a new page with your running head and page number (page 3) in the page header. Next, center the title of the paper at the top of the page and start the introduction immediately below the title. The title is the same one you used on the title page. Do *not* type the heading "Introduction." In addition, neither your name nor your affiliation appears on the first page of the introduction. Figure 16-4 shows a sample introduction. Notice how the author followed the general-to-specific structure suggested in Figure 16-4 by beginning with a statement of the problem to study, followed by a review of relevant literature. It ends with a statement of the hypothesis to be tested (not shown).

## The Method Section

You have established the rationale for your study and stated your hypotheses in the introduction. Now you must tell your reader exactly how you conducted your study. You do this in the **method section**, which describes in detail the characteristics of your subjects, materials, and apparatus used, research design, and procedures followed. The level of detail should be sufficient to allow another researcher to replicate your study. If your paper uses a methodology described before, you may give a brief summary of the methods used and refer the reader to the previously published account.

The method section is divided into subsections to improve organization and readability. APA style permits considerable flexibility in how you divide and label the various subsections. The most common format contains the following subsections: *participants* (or *subjects* if you used animals), *apparatus* (or *materials* if this descriptor is more appropriate), and *procedure*. If you consider it necessary, you also may include a *design* subsection to clarify your design for your readers. A design subsection is particularly useful when your study used an unconventional or complex design. You also can combine subsections if this improves the clarity of the report. A description of each subsection follows.

*Participants or Subjects*    If humans participated as subjects in your study, describe them in a **participants subsection**. In this section, you specify the nature and size of the sample used in your study. Specify the number of participants and provide information on relevant demographic variables (such as sex, age, race, ethnicity), the procedures used for selecting participants and assigning them to treatments, any special agreements made with participants (such as payment for their participation), and information on personal characteristics of the participants that are relevant to your research (such as IQ and personality). Also, report any special characteristics of your participants, such as mental impairment, psychopathology, or special abilities.

If your subjects were animals, describe them in a **subjects subsection**. Describe the genus, species, strain, and any other important relevant information (such as the

CONTEXTUAL INFORMATION AND PERCEPTION OF ART                    3

Contextual Information, Artistic Style and the Perception of Art

Understanding and enjoyment of art is partially dependent on the degree to which viewers understand and can make sense of a work of art (Russell, 2003). This is especially true of nonrepresentational, modern styles of art which place greater information processing demands on the viewer (Leder, Belke, Oeberst, & Augustin, 2004). Evidence shows that not only does nonrepresentational art place greater processing demands on observers, but also that viewers typically like nonrepresentational art less than more conventional forms of representational art (Clemmer & Bordens, 1987; Cupchik & Gebotys, 1988; Leder Carbon, & Ripsas, 2006; Schimmel & Förster, 2008).

Art is much like any other categorical concept and exhibits characteristics common to other natural categories. Wittgenstein (1953) argued that natural categories exhibit "family resemblance," meaning that members of a category have characteristics that occur together with no single feature defining membership in a category. Modern cognitive theory follows this idea by postulating that natural categories have "centrality" (Best, 1999) and that some categories serve as better exemplars than others. This fits with Rosch's (1975) idea that categories are represented by a "prototype" which represents the center point of a category and is an internalized image of the best fitting member of a category. Hence, the prototypical bird looks something like a robin. Adajian (2005) has written that prototype theory in cognitive psychology extends to art. He suggests that the concept of "artwork" is organized around prototypes and that some artworks are more central to the concept of artwork than others. This conceptualization suggests that some works of art more closely match an internal prototype for art than others and will be more closely associated with the concept of "artwork."

**FIGURE 16-4**  Sample introduction.

supplier). Also, give the number of animals used in the study and their sex, age, weight, and physical condition. Provide details of the care and housing of the animals (e.g., whether they were housed individually or in groups, whether they were given free access to food and water, and the scheduling of light and darkness in the colony room). In this section, you also specify the number of subjects assigned to each condition in your experiment and any other information (such as special handling) that your reader needs to know in order to replicate your study. Finally, in either subsection, indicate that you treated your participants or subjects in accordance with APA ethical codes.

*Apparatus or Materials*[1]    You describe the equipment or any materials used to measure behavior in this section. If you used primarily equipment (e.g., video cameras, operant chambers, computers), describe that equipment in an **apparatus subsection**. If you used primarily written materials (e.g., a questionnaire, summaries of criminal cases, or rating scales), describe them in a **materials subsection**. In either case, the level of detail necessary in your description depends on the nature of the equipment or materials.

If you used a commercial piece of laboratory equipment (e.g., an operant chamber or a computer), you do not have to detail its characteristics. Instead, simply provide the name of the manufacturer and the model number of the equipment. Similarly, if you used a standardized test (such as the Stanford–Binet or the Bem Sex Roles Inventory), simply name the test (and the version, if relevant), and describe how it was obtained.

If you designed special equipment or developed a new measure, you must describe the equipment or measure in detail. If you designed a special operant chamber, for example, give its dimensions, materials of construction, and the types, characteristics, and locations of attached equipment (such as feeders, houselights, response levers, and sound sources). In short, provide any information that your reader would need to reproduce your chamber in its essential details. Similarly, describe any measures you developed (e.g., questionnaires).

Although you should provide enough information to enable another researcher to replicate your study, it is not feasible to reproduce extensive materials (such as a 250-item questionnaire or lengthy instructions) in your method section. If you used such materials, inform your readers where and how they can obtain them. Some journals allow you to reproduce such materials in an appendix.

*Procedure*    In the **procedure subsection**, tell your reader precisely the procedure you followed throughout the course of the study. Describe the conditions to which subjects were exposed or under which they were observed, what behaviors were recorded, how the behaviors were measured or scored, when the measures were taken, and any debriefing procedures. Provide enough information about the procedure so that another researcher could reproduce its essential details.

If you used animal subjects, describe the following: how you handled the animals, the length of the experimental sessions, any special deprivation schedules, and to what manipulations the subjects were exposed. If humans were used, include details about the instructions they received (if you cannot reproduce them, describe them in detail), informed-consent procedures, procedures for assigning subjects to conditions, debriefing, and how the experimental manipulations were introduced.

*Formatting the Method Section*    The method section begins immediately after the end of the introduction (do not necessarily start it on a new page). Center the word "Method" (not "Methods," a common error we see often) as a level 1 heading. On the next double-spaced line, type the word "Participants" beginning at the left margin as a level 2 heading. Again, move down a double-spaced line, indent, and start the first

---

[1]Although the APA manual (2010) no longer makes a formal distinction between apparatus and materials sections, it is still a useful distinction, and we recommend using it.

CONTEXTUAL INFORMATION AND PERCEPTION OF ART                                    24

## Method

### Participants

Participants were 172 male ($N$ = 54) and female ($N$ = 118) undergraduate students enrolled in Elementary Psychology classes at a Midwestern regional university campus in the United States. Participants received credit in their Elementary Psychology classes for their voluntary participation. Participants ranged in age between 17 and 51 ($M$ = 21.88, $SD$ = 6.44). Additionally, participants reported relatively little formal training in art ($M$ = 2.42, $SD$ = 1.45, on a 7-point scale), infrequent visits to art museums ($M$ = 1.94, $SD$ = 1.22, on a 7-point scale), and low levels of knowledge about art ($M$ = 2.22, $SD$ = 1.31, on a 7-point scale). However, participants reported a moderate level of interest in the arts ($M$ = 3.55, $SD$ = 1.62, on a 7-point scale). Participants had not taken many college level art courses. Specifically, 84.1% reported that they had taken no art or art appreciation courses at the college level, 11.6% completed 1 to 2 courses, 3.5% had taken 3 to 4 courses and 1.7% completed 5, 6 or more than 6 courses.

### Design

The experiment used a 2 (type of contextual information provided) × 4 (style of art judged) × 2 (order of artwork presentation) between-subjects design. Participants received either information providing a historical context for the artworks they judged (contextual information) or with a general introduction to art excluding the contextual information (no contextual information). Participants judged four examples from one of four artistic styles (Dada art, Impressionist art, Outsider art, or Renaissance art). The order in which the artworks were judged was counterbalanced across artistic style conditions.

### Materials

**Artworks.** For each art style color pictures of two paintings and two sculptures were selected.  The artworks in each style were chosen after the author reviewed a large number of works. The works used were chosen because they were representative of the works in a style, but were not extreme examples. The exception to this rule was Duchamp's *Fountain* which is a controversial work. Two styles (Impressionist and Renaissance) were chosen because they exemplified more "conventional" representational styles of art and two styles (Dada and Outsider) were chosen because they exemplified "less conventional" nonrepresentational styles.

**FIGURE 16-5**   First page of a method section. The method section begins immediately after the end of the introduction, not necessarily on a new page.

paragraph of the participants (or subjects) subsection. Follow the same format you used with the participants subsection for the apparatus (or materials) and procedure subsections. Figure 16-5 shows an example method section with participants, design, materials, and procedure subsections. Note how each subsection contributes to your understanding of the described experiment.

## QUESTIONS TO PONDER

1. What information is included in the introduction to an APA-style paper? How is the introduction organized?
2. What information would you expect to find in the method section?
3. Describe the various subsections of the method section.

## The Results Section

The purpose of your **results section** is to report your findings. You should present all relevant data summaries and analyses. As a rule, do not present raw (unanalyzed) or individual data unless the focus of the study was on the behavior of individual subjects (e.g., case history or single-subject design). If your analysis is complex, you may want to provide an overview of your strategy for data analysis in the opening paragraph. Outline for the reader which statistical tests you applied and in what order.

Your results section should be primarily a verbal description where you describe what you found. Make this verbal description the driving force behind your results section. The results of descriptive and inferential statistics also will appear in your results section. However, these statistics should support your verbal descriptions. Too often, students make the mistake of throwing in everything but the kitchen sink by giving just about every statistic shown on a computer output. What results is a compilation of numbers with little coherence. Remember, you should verbally describe what you found and refer to the relevant statistics to support what you say.

In most cases, you will use generally available statistics such as $t$ tests, analyses of variance, or correlation coefficients. However, in some cases, you may have used statistics that are not as widely used or readily available. In this case, you should give a specific description of these analyses and indicate how your reader can obtain information about them. Next, report the results of any tests used to establish that your data met the requirements of the applied statistical tests (e.g., homogeneity of variance and normality). Report any data transformations that you applied to your data.

After you have presented this preliminary information, you can report your results. Include values of any descriptive (e.g., means and standard deviations) and inferential statistics (e.g., $t$ tests, analyses of variance) that you calculated, along with the relevant $p$ values. The APA manual strongly suggests reporting confidence intervals (95% or 99%) and effect size statistics for all significant effects. Do not interpret or discuss your findings in the results section (APA, 2010); you do this in the next section of your paper.

*Formatting the Results Section*    Start your results section immediately after the method section on the same page as the end of the method section, if there is room. The results section should be a continuation of your paper. Center the heading "Results" (level 1 heading), double-space, and indent to start the first paragraph of your new section. Figure 16-6 shows the first page of an example results section.

CONTEXTUAL INFORMATION AND PERCEPTION OF ART                    33

**Results**

Data were analyzed using SPSS-PC Version 15. Alpha level was set at $p < .05$ for all analyses of variance (ANOVA). *Post hoc* analyses were done using an LSD test.

**Match Between Artwork and Participant Concept of Art**

**Averaged match ratings.** An average "match" score was calculated for each subject by averaging each participant's rating of the degree to which each artwork within an artistic style matched their internal concept of what constitutes a work of art. For example, a participant's average match score for Dada art was obtained by summing the match scale rating scores for *Nude on a Staircase*, *Configuration*, *Dada Head*, and *Fountain* and dividing by four. The resulting averaged match scores were analyzed with a three factor (style × contextual information × order) ANOVA. The results showed a significant main effect for contextual information, $F(1, 156) = 5.78$, $p = .017$, $\eta^2 = .04$. When no contextual information was presented the average match score was higher ($M = 5.31$, $SD = 1.18$, 95% CI [5.08, 5.54]) than if contextual information was presented ($M = 4.90$, $SD = 1.25$, 95% CI [4.68, 5.14]). There was also a significant main effect for art style, $F(3, 156) = 12.68$, $p < .001$, $\eta^2 = .20$. Dada art received the lowest averaged match score ($M = 4.34$, $SD = 1.05$, 95% CI [4.02, 4.67]) followed by Outsider art ($M = 4.97$, $SD = 1.25$, 95% CI [4.64, 5.30]), Impressionist art ($M = 5.48$, $SD = 1.02$, 95% CI [5.15, 5.81]), and Renaissance art ($M = 5.65$, $SD = 1.15$, 95% CI [5.32, 5.98]). *Post hoc* pair wise comparisons using an LSD test showed that Dada art was rated as matching significantly less than the other three styles of art. Similarly, Outsider art was rated as matching internal concepts of art significantly lower than Impressionist and Renaissance art. Dada and Outsider art did not differ significantly, nor did Impressionist and Renaissance art. Generally, Dada and Outsider art were rated as matching internal concepts of art significantly lower than Impressionist and Renaissance art.

**FIGURE 16-6** First page of a results section. The results section begins immediately after the end of the method section, not necessarily on a new page.

The results section is where you discuss any tables or figures that present data from your study. Although these will appear in the body of the *published* text, they do *not* appear in the body of the manuscript. Instead, you refer to the figure or table at the appropriate place. However, when referring to a figure or table, do not refer to its position. For example, *do not* say, "Figure 1, shown above, illustrates . . ." because the figure may not appear where you expected it to be placed in the published article. Simply refer to the figure by number in your manuscript: "Figure 1 shows the relationship between . . ."

Presenting the results of a statistical test is a bit tricky but not difficult once you become familiar with the process. You usually report the results of a statistical test in sentence format. The sentence states the effect being evaluated, whether or not the difference between treatment levels was statistically significant, the critical statistic used, the degrees of freedom, the value obtained for the statistic, the level of significance achieved, the measure of effect size used, and the effect size. Table 16-1 presents examples of how to report other statistics. In cases in which your analysis is very complex, you could present the results of your statistical tests in a table.

When reporting the results from an inferential statistical analysis, it is a good idea to begin by stating the alpha used to evaluate statistical significance. For example, you might say:

All statistical tests employed an alpha level of .05.

Alternatively, you can indicate the alpha level when you report the results of your statistical analysis;

At the .05 alpha level, the main effect of stimulus complexity was statistically significant, $F(2, 35) = 12.45$, $p = .034$, $\eta^2 = .06$.

When reporting the actual values of your statistical tests, include the value obtained for the test (e.g., the $F$-value), degrees of freedom, $p$-value, and an effect size statistic (e.g., eta squared, abbreviated $\eta^2$). When reporting $p$-values, report the exact value obtained from your computer printout to two or three decimal places. You should report $p$-values that are lower than .001 as $p < .001$ (and not for example, $p < .00001$). The following example shows how you should report the results of an inferential statistical test if you have previously stated your chosen alpha level:

The main effect of stimulus complexity was statistically significant, $F(2, 35) = 12.45$, $p = .032$, $\eta^2 = .06$.

In your results section you must report descriptive statistics associated with any significant effects you found. You should report the means, standard deviations, and confidence intervals associated with each statistically significant effect. You have two

**TABLE 16-1    Commonly Used Statistical Citations**

| STATISTIC | FORMAT |
|---|---|
| Analysis of variance | $F(1, 85) = 5.96$, $p = .026$, $\eta^2 = .06$. |
| Chi-square | $\chi^2(3, N = 100) = 11.34$, $p < .001$ |
| $t$ test | $t(56) = 4.78$, $p = .013$ |
| $z$ test | $z = 2.04$, $p = .033$ |
| Pearson correlation | coefficient $r = .87$ or $r = -.87$ |
| Mean | $M = 6.56$ |
| Standard deviation | $SD = 1.96$ |
| Confidence interval | 95% CI [5.67, 7.98] |

Note: Numbers in parentheses are the degrees of freedom. For the analysis of variance, the first number in the parentheses is the degrees of freedom for the numerator and the second number the degrees of freedom for the denominator (error).

options for reporting these statistics. You can organize descriptive statistics in a table. Use this option if you have many means relating to a complex interaction. The other option is to report the descriptive statistics in the body of your report. In this case, use the following format:

> Participants in the simple stimulus group identified more stimuli correctly ($M = 12.56$, $SD = 2.43$, 95% CI [11.2, 14.51]) than participants in the complex stimulus group ($M = 9.24$, $SD = 2.66$, 95% CI [7.32, 11.22]).

Putting the previous two example sentences together, your results section might contain the following:

> The main effect of stimulus complexity was statistically significant, $F(2, 35) = 12.45$, $p = .032$, $\eta^2 = .06$. Participants in the simple stimulus group identified more stimuli correctly ($M = 12.56$, $SD = 2.43$, 95% CI [11.2, 14.51]) than participants in the complex stimulus group ($M = 9.24$, $SD = 2.66$, 95% CI [7.32, 11.22]).

As you can see from these examples, APA style follows a consistent format for reporting statistical results. For statistical symbols, use the normal typeface for Greek letters and for acronyms (e.g., ANOVA) but italicize all other symbols that use standard alphabetical characters (e.g., $F$, $df$, $p$). Table 16-2 shows the abbreviations used for common statistics.

## The Discussion Section

In the **discussion section**, you interpret your results, draw conclusions, and relate your findings to previous research or theory. The structure of your discussion section, as

---

**TABLE 16-2   Abbreviations for Statistical Symbols**

| ABBREVIATION | MEANING |
| --- | --- |
| CI | Confidence interval |
| $df$ | Degrees of freedom |
| $F$ | $F$ ratio |
| $M$ | Arithmetic average (mean) |
| $N$ | Number of subjects in entire sample |
| $n$ | Number of subjects in limited portion of a sample |
| $p$ | $p$ value |
| $SD$ | Standard deviation |
| $t$ | $t$ statistic |
| $z$ | Results from $z$ test or a $z$ score |
| $\mu$ | Population mean (mu) |
| $\alpha$ | Alpha level |
| $\beta$ | Beta |
| $d$ | Cohen's $d$ (effect size statistic) |
| $\eta^2$ | Eta squared (effect size statistic) |
| $\omega^2$ | Omega squared (effect size statistic) |

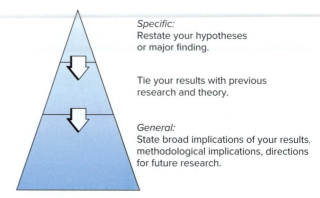

**FIGURE 16-7** Specific-to-general organization of an APA-style discussion section.

*Specific:*
Restate your hypotheses or major finding.

Tie your results with previous research and theory.

*General:*
State broad implications of your results, methodological implications, directions for future research.

shown in Figure 16-7, reverses that of the introduction; rather than moving from general to specific, it moves from specific research findings to general implications.

Begin your discussion section with a brief restatement of your hypotheses. Next, briefly indicate whether your data were consistent with your pre-experimental hypotheses. Use the remainder of the discussion section to integrate your findings with previous research and theory. Discuss how consistent your findings are with previous work in the area.

If your study yielded results that are discrepant from previous work, you should speculate on why the discrepancies emerged. Also, point out any problems encountered during the course of your research that might temper any conclusions drawn from your study. You should report on any methodological problems that became evident when you actually ran your study. Finally, indicate what implications your findings have for future research in the area. Point out any specific areas that need to be investigated further.

In the discussion section, you have license to speculate on the importance of your findings. Avoid the temptation to overstep the bounds of that license. You must base your interpretations on your data, data from previous research, and/or established theory. Avoid the temptation to make unsubstantiated interpretations even if they make intuitive sense to you.

Figure 16-8 shows an example of the first page of a discussion section. The author of this paper followed the specific-to-general organization shown in Figure 16-7. He began with a brief statement of what was found and then integrated these findings with those of other research in the area.

*Formatting the Discussion Section*    Start your discussion section immediately after the results section, on the same page if there is room. Center the heading "Discussion" (level 1 heading), double-space, and indent to start the first paragraph of your new section.

## QUESTIONS TO PONDER

1. What would you expect to find in the results section of a manuscript?
2. How is the results section formatted, and how are statistics reported?
3. How is the discussion organized, and what would you expect to find in the discussion section?

CONTEXTUAL INFORMATION AND PERCEPTION OF ART                39

**Discussion**

The results of this study provided only partial support for the pre-experimental hypotheses. Hypothesis 1 stated that providing contextual information would increase ratings of how well examples of those styles match participants' internal concepts of art. Hypothesis 1 was not supported. In fact, the opposite occurred. Providing contextual information led to participants perceiving examples of the various styles of art as matching less well with their internal standards than when no contextual information was presented. There are a number of possible explanations for this finding.

First, initial classification of art is an automatic process (Leder et al., 2004). Providing contextual information may bring this early stage of processing of art under more conscious control, making the issue of just what defines art more consciously available to participants. This greater conscious processing may have led participants to be more critical of the artworks and a corresponding tendency to distance the artworks from their internal prototypes of what constitutes art. Second, there is evidence that enhancing abstract thought is related to individuals willingness to include unconventional styles of art in their internal concept of art than enhancing concrete thought (Schimmel & Förster, 2008). Providing concrete, contextual information on the different styles of art may have encouraged participants to think more concretely about art and thus may have caused them to perceive the examples of art judged as more distant from their internal concept of art than if no contextual information was presented. In fact, in the no contextual information condition, various definitions of art were presented which were less concrete and may have enhanced abstract thought about art resulting in greater acceptance of less conventional art styles. Third, like many category-based judgments, individuals have prototypes representing best-fitting examples of a category. People tend to show a greater preference for exemplars that closely match their internal prototypes. Art is a natural category that may have fuzzy and fluid boundaries defining what constitutes art. Providing contextual information may have caused the prototypes to become more rigid and better defined, making it more likely that particular exemplars would be viewed as less representative of a category than in the no context condition.

**FIGURE 16-8**   First page of a discussion section. The discussion section begins immediately after the end of the results section, not necessarily on a new page.

## The Reference Section

The **reference section** provides a bibliographical list of the references cited in the report. You must list in the reference section all articles, books, or other sources (e.g., conference presentations) you cited in the body of your paper. Conversely, you *must* cite in your paper any references listed in the reference section. If you read hundreds of papers but only cited three of them, your reference section should contain only the three papers actually cited. Start your reference section on a new page. Type the word "References" (not in boldface) centered on the top line and begin your first reference on the next line. Figure 16-9 shows how you format a reference section in APA style.

Use a hanging indent when typing each APA-style reference, as shown in Figure 16-9. Your word processor should allow you to do this easily. For a journal reference, italicize the title of the journal, volume number, and associated punctuation marks. Do not italicize the page numbers, however. Remember to leave a single space after all punctuation marks in a reference. Also include the *DOI system number* (digital object identifier) if provided. You can find the DOI number with the bibliographic information

CONTEXTUAL INFORMATION AND PERCEPTION OF ART                    41

References

Adajian, T. (2005). On the prototype theory of concepts and the definition of
     art. *Journal of Aesthetics and Art Criticism, 63*, 231–236.
     doi:10.1111/j.0021-8529.2005.00203.x

Best, J. B. (1999). *Cognitive psychology*. Belmont, CA: Brooks/Cole
     Wadsworth.

Bartlett, F. C. (1932). *Remembering: A study in experimental and social
     psychology*. Cambridge, England: Cambridge University Press.

Clemmer, E. J., & Bordens, K. S. (1987, July). Semantic-differential profiles of
     esthetic experience: Abstract and impressionist paintings. Paper
     presented at the Second International Congress of  Applied
     Psycholinguistics, University of Kassel, Kassel, Federal Republic of
     Germany.

Cupchik, G. C., & Gebotys, R. (1988). The experience of time, pleasure, and
     interest during aesthetic episodes. *Empirical Studies of the Arts,
     6*, 1–12.

Halberstadt, J. (2006). The generality and ultimate attractiveness of
     prototypes. *Personality and Social Psychology Review, 10*, 166–183.

Halberstadt, J., & Rhodes, G. (2003). Its not just average faces that are
     attractive: Computer-manipulated averageness makes birds, fish,
     and automobiles attractive. *Psychonomic Bulletin and Review, 10*,
     149–156.

Hekkert, P. (2006). Design aesthetics: Principles of pleasure in design.
     *Psychology Science, 48*, 157–172.

**FIGURE 16-9**    First page of a reference section. Start the reference section on a new page.

provided in a journal article (usually at the top or bottom of the first page of an article) or in its listing in an electronic database. The DOI is not italicized and no period is used after it. A specific reference would look like this:

Schmiege, S. J., Broaddus, M. R., Levin, M., & Bryan, A. D. (2009). Randomized trial of group interventions to reduce HIV/STD risk and change theoretical mediators among detained adolescents. *Journal of Consulting and Clinical Psychology, 77,* 38–50. doi:10.1037/a0014513

If the journal is one that starts each issue on page 1 (most journals in psychology do not, but if in doubt you should check), include the issue number in parentheses after the volume number with the issue number not italicized (e.g., . . . *36*(1)). Do not include the issue number for articles appearing in journals that number pages continuously across issues (i.e., issue 1 ends on page 243 and issue 2 begins on page 244).

Table 16-3 provides examples of reference formats for the more commonly cited reference types. If you encounter a reference of a type not covered in the table, consult the APA (2010) publication manual.

For some reason students seem to have a great deal of trouble formatting references properly. We have seen a myriad of errors in reference list entries. With a little attention to detail, you can avoid many of the errors we commonly see. The following example embodies several of these errors. Compare the reference that follows to the one preceding and see if you can identify the errors.

Hardy, Charlie, L., and Van Vugt, Mark. (2006). Nice Guys Finish First: The Competitive Altruism Hypothesis. *Personality and Social Psychology Bulletin, 32*(10), 1402–1413.

See how many of the following errors that you found:

1. You do not provide authors' full first names (Charlie and Mark). Use the initials only.

2. The "&" sign is used before the last author's name, not the word *and.*

3. Only the first word of the article title is capitalized. Subsequent words use lowercase font (except for the word after the colon or proper nouns).

4. You do not provide the issue number after the volume number of the journal (the 10 shown in parentheses in the example) unless the journal is one of the rare ones that starts each issue on page 1.

You list entries in your reference section alphabetically according to the last name of the first author. If there are two articles by the same author from different years, list them in order from oldest to newest, for example, Smith (2005) before Smith (2007). If you have two (or more) references by the same author published in the same year, list them alphabetically according to the title (excluding prepositions such as "a" or "the"). Place lowercase letters immediately after each date, which will correspond to letters assigned to in-text citations for these entries. For example:

Smith, A. B. (2006a). Control mechanisms in . . .

Smith, A. B. (2006b). A replication of . . .

**TABLE 16-3    Format for Common Reference Sources**

### JOURNAL ARTICLE

*Print or Electronic Source: DOI Available*

Schmiege, S. J., Broaddus, M. R., Levin, M., & Bryan, A. D. (2009). Randomized trial of group interventions to reduce HIV/STD risk and change theoretical mediators among detained adolescents. *Journal of Consulting and Clinical Psychology, 77,* 38–50. doi:10.1037/a0014513

*Print Source: DOI Not Available*

Sciangula, A., & Morry, M. M. (2009). Self-esteem and perceived regard: How I see myself affects my relationship satisfaction. *Journal of Social Psychology, 149,* 143–158.

*Electronic Source: DOI Not Available*

Stepanova, E. V., & Strube, M. J. (2009). Making of a face: Role of facial physiognomy, skin tone, and color presentation mode in evaluations of racial typicality. *Journal of Social Psychology, 149,* 66–81. Retrieved from http://www.heldref.org/pubs/soc/about.html

### REPORT FROM A PRIVATE ORGANIZATION FROM ITS WEBSITE

Alan Guttmacher Institute (2003, September/October). *Services for men at publicly funded family planning agencies, 1998–1999*. Retrieved from http://www.agi-usa.org/pubs/journals/3520203.html

### BOOK

*Print Version*

Lifton, R. J. (1986). *The Nazi doctors: Medical killing and the psychology of genocide*. New York: Basic Books.
Tabachnick, B. G., & Fidell, L. S. (2013). *Using multivariate statistics* (6th ed.). Boston: Allyn and Bacon.

*Electronic Version of a Print Book*

Baldwin, J. M. (1905). *Mental development of the child and the race* (3rd ed.) [Mead Project Version]. Retrieved from http://www.brocku.ca/MeadProject/Baldwin/Baldwin_1906/Baldwin_1906_toc.html

*Article in an Edited Book*

Austin, W. G. (1986). Justice in intergroup conflict. In S. Worchel & W. G. Austin (Eds.), *Psychology of intergroup relations* (pp. 153–176). Chicago: Nelson-Hall.

### PAPER OR POSTER SESSION AT A CONFERENCE

Seeley, W. P. (2008, August). Effects of interpretation of emotional and energetic cost in picture perception. Paper presented at the Twentieth Biennial Congress of the International Association of Empirical Aesthetics, Chicago, IL.

One-author entries come before multiple-author entries in which the first author is the same as the single author. So, for example,

Adams, J. K. (2004) . . .

Adams, J. K., & Smith, B. D. (2001) . . .

Entries with more than two authors are alphabetized by the last name of the first author, then by the second author, and then by the third author and so on. For example,

Adams, J. K., Charles, S. L., & Smith, B. D. (2003) . . .

Adams, J. K., Smith, B. D., & Charles, S. L. (2003) . . .

There are other rules for ordering reference entries. For more information see the APA manual (2010, pp. 181–183).

It is increasingly common to find resources published in an electronic medium such as the Internet. For a reference from a journal you obtained online for which a DOI is provided (e.g., through *PsycARTICLES* or EBSCO), use the same format as for the same article in a printed journal (see the first example in Table 16-3). If, on the other hand, you use an online version of an article and no DOI is available, provide the home website address of the journal (APA, 2010, p.199) as shown in the following example:

Stepanova, E. V., & Strube, M. J. (2009). Making of a face: Role of facial physiognomy, skin tone, and color presentation mode in evaluations of racial typicality. *Journal of Social Psychology, 149,* 66–81. Retrieved from http://www.heldref.org/pubs/soc/about.html

Provide the home web page for the journal and *not* the web address of the database you used to find the article. You do this because the website information included in a database may change frequently, and presumably, the journal's will be more constant (APA, 2010). Do not hyperlink the website or put a period at the end of the web address. Finally, do not provide the date on which you retrieved the document.

One final point about formatting your references: Databases such as PsycINFO provide full APA citations (click on Cite on the page with the abstract). It is tempting just to copy and paste this citation into your references section. However, use caution because the citations provided may contain formatting errors. Some of the errors are flagrant and some are subtle. Here is an example of one from PsycINFO that has a number of flagrant errors. See if you can find them.

KARMARKAR, U. R., & TORMALA, Z. L. (2010). Believe Me, I Have No Idea What I'm Talking About: The Effects of Source Certainty on Consumer Involvement and Persuasion. *Journal Of Consumer Research, 36*(6), 1033–1049.

Here is a list of the errors in this citation:

1. The names of the authors should not be in all capital letters.

2. Only the first letter of the first word and the word after the colon are capitalized. All others must be lowercase.

3. The "of" in the title of the journal should not be capitalized.

4. The issue number should not be provided.

The bottom line is that you should not copy and paste a citation found in PsycINFO (or any other database) without looking for and correcting errors.

## Footnotes

APA writing style specifies two types of footnote. A *content footnote* clarifies a point made in the text of the paper, or to provide additional details that would detract from the flow of your discussion at that point. A *copyright permission footnote* acknowledges the source of copyrighted quoted material, figures, or tables.

In the body of your paper, you number content and copyright footnotes consecutively using Arabic numerals. At the point in the text at which the reader should consult the footnote, simply place a superscript number (beginning with 1 for the first footnote), as in the following example:

The trial, used previously (Horowitz & Bordens, 1988), consisted of a 4-hour audiotape.[1]

There are two options for footnote placement in your manuscript. You may place each footnote on the bottom of the page on which the noted material appears. You can do this easily by using the footnote function of your word processor. Alternatively you may place the footnotes on a separate page after your references, entitled "Footnotes."

## QUESTIONS TO PONDER

1. Where do you begin the reference section in an APA-style manuscript?

2. What information do you include in an APA-style reference, and how is a reference entry formatted?

3. Why should you not copy and paste a reference from a database directly into your reference section?

4. How are footnotes used in an APA-style manuscript, and where are they placed?

## Tables

Tables present complex information that you cannot easily summarize in the body of your paper. For example, they can illustrate the design of your study or present summary data (e.g., tables of means and standard errors, correlation matrices). Tables are somewhat time consuming to make and expensive to reproduce, so use them only when necessary.

Tables prepared according to APA specifications include a title, a number, headings, a body, and if necessary, notes. Create a separate page for each table, which should appear as shown in Figure 16-10. Place the title and number of the table at the

CONTEXTUAL INFORMATION AND PERCEPTION OF ART                47

Table 1

*Means for Significant Style × Order Interaction*

| Style | Order | |
| | Order 1 | Order 2 |
| Dada | 3.88 (1.02) | 4.81 (0.88) |
| Outsider | 5.21 (1.23) | 4.74 (1.25) |
| Impressionist | 5.49 (1.18) | 5.49 (1.13) |
| Renaissance | 5.72 (1.33) | 5.59 (1.12) |

*Note:* Standard deviations shown in parentheses.

**FIGURE 16-10**   Sample APA-style table.

top of the page, as illustrated. The headings of your table should clearly tell your reader what information is presented in your table. In the body of the table, include the information that you want your reader to see. Finally, as shown in Figure 16-10, use notes to explain the meaning of symbols in the table or to provide information not included in the table itself. Place pages with tables after your reference section.

## Figures

Use figures in your paper to provide graphic illustrations of complex material or relationships that cannot be adequately described in text. Although figures appear most often in the results section of your paper, they also can appear in any other section. For example, you could use a figure in your method section to illustrate the materials used in your study or in the introduction to show an important theoretical relationship. Because figures are difficult to prepare and are expensive to reproduce in journals, use them sparingly.

Graphs, drawings, and photographs are three commonly used types of figures. Use graphs to illustrate complex relationships among variables. Use drawings and photographs to illustrate equipment, materials, or stimuli you used in your study. You might use photographs to convey aspects of results that you cannot adequately describe in the text of your paper. For example, articles about physiological psychology may present photographs of histological sections to show the location of a lesion or stimulating electrode in the brain.

A simple rule to follow when preparing graphs is to make them simple and accurate. A visually confusing graph adds little to your paper. An improperly drawn graph can confuse your reader or make small, albeit statistically significant, effects look unnaturally large. Carefully plan and draw your graphs.

Figure 16-11 illustrates how the scaling of an axis on a graph can influence the reader's impression of the size of an effect. Participants scanned a one-page document

**FIGURE 16-11**
(a) Graph that
exaggerates size of a
relationship;
(b) graph that
accurately depicts a
relationship.

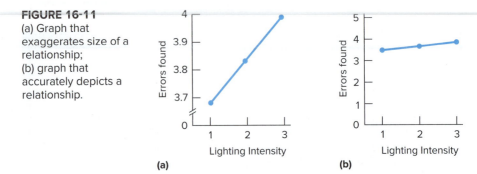

(a)                                                    (b)

for typographical errors under dim, medium, and bright lighting. The document contained five errors. Panel (a) displays the average number of errors found (vertical axis) as a function of lighting intensity (horizontal axis). A cursory look at this graph conveys the impression that lighting intensity had a large influence on the number of errors detected. However, the examination of the scale along the vertical axis reveals that the entire range of values varies only between 3.6 and 4 errors. The graph shown in panel (b) gives a more accurate impression of the influence of lighting intensity on the number of errors detected. Here the scale of errors presented along the horizontal axis covers the entire range of possible values (0 to 5). The small differences among means are represented fairly, and your reader is not misled.

In some cases, you may find it necessary to break an axis to fit all your data on a graph. For example, if values of the dependent variable can range from 0 to 50 but participants used only numbers between 0 and 3 and between 32 and 40, you may want to show the data on a graph similar to the one shown in Figure 16-12. Notice that the *y*-axis is broken by slash marks. This shows your reader that a range of values along the *y*-axis has been skipped over. You should also break any lines within the graph that cross the broken part of an axis, as shown in the figure.

Some graphs require a *legend* to identify the meanings of the symbols or line styles used in the graph. The legend appears within the figure itself. Look at Figure 16-13, which shows how an APA-style figure page looks. The legend at the top of the graph tells the reader which line represents which level of art style.

**FIGURE 16-12**    Graph showing
a broken axis.

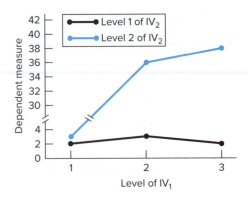

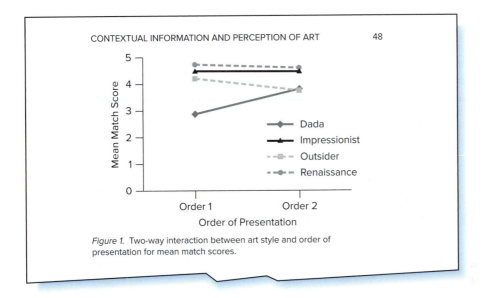

CONTEXTUAL INFORMATION AND PERCEPTION OF ART
48
5
4
3
2
1
0
Mean Match Score
Dada
Impressionist
Outsider
Renaissance
Order 1
Order 2
Order of Presentation
*Figure 1.* Two-way interaction between art style and order of presentation for mean match scores.

**FIGURE 16-13** Sample APA-style figure.

You must also include a caption for your figure. The caption provides the title for your figure along with any other necessary explanatory information (e.g., the source of a figure, information about what specific numbers mean). Type the caption immediately below your figure using the format shown in Figure 16-13.

If you have more than one figure, each goes on its own page. Each page must include the running head and page number. Position the figure pages after any table pages.

## QUESTIONS TO PONDER

1. When are tables used in an APA-style manuscript?
2. How are the tables used in an APA-style manuscript formatted?
3. When do you use figures in an APA-style manuscript?
4. How do you format a figure page, and what is included on it?

## ELEMENTS OF APA STYLE

In addition to knowing about the different sections of an APA-style manuscript and what goes in them, you must also know some things about conventions used in APA style. These include citing references in your paper, citing quoted material, using numbers in your paper, and avoiding biased language. We discuss these conventions next.

## Citing References in Your Report

In some writing styles, you indicate citations in the body of your paper with numbers. In APA style, however, citations are made by providing the name(s) of the author(s), the publication date of the source, and (when needed) specific pages within the source.

The format of a citation within the text of your manuscript depends on how you choose to write a sentence that includes the citation. If the citation is included as an integral part of the sentence, you give the last name(s) of the author(s) and, in parentheses, the year in which the work was published. Here is an example with two authors:

> According to Smith and Jones (2009), memory for meaningful information is much better than memory for meaningless information.

If the citation is "tacked on" to the sentence, enclose the citation in parentheses, as follows:

> Memory for meaningful information tends to be much better than memory for meaningless information (Smith & Jones, 2009).

The two examples just provided are *multiple-author citations*. Notice that when you cite the names of two authors in the sentence itself (the first example), you use the word *and* to connect the authors' names. When the names are used in parentheses (as in the second example), you use an ampersand (&) to connect them.

When you have more than two authors, the citation takes the following form:

> According to Smith, Jones, and Harris (2009), memory for meaningful information is better than memory for meaningless information.

or

> Memory for meaningful information is better than memory for meaningless information (Smith, Jones, & Harris, 2009).

When a citation is from a source with only two authors, *always* provide the names of both authors each time you cite the source. However, if you must cite an article with three or more authors several times in your paper, writing each name repeatedly becomes tedious. In this case, provide all of the authors' names the first time you cite the source (e.g., Smith, Jones, & Harris). Thereafter, provide only the first author's name followed by "et al." (Latin for "and others"). Here is an example:

> Memory for meaningful information is much better than memory for meaningless information (Smith, Jones, Harris, Baker, & Thomas, 2009) . . . Smith et al. also point out that . . .

If you cite a source with more than five authors, use the "et al." device for the first and all subsequent citations. In the reference section, provide last names and initials for up to seven authors. For eight or more, list the first six authors, then three dots (ellipsis points), then the last author.

What happens if you have two citations from the same authors in different orders from the same year (e.g., Smith, Jones, Harris, & Baker, 2008, and Smith, Harris, Jones, & Baker, 2008)? Using the et al. device would be confusing because your reader would not know to which source you are referring. In this case, you provide as many author names as needed to distinguish between the two sources (e.g., Smith, Jones, et al., 2008, and Smith, Harris, et al., 2008).

Finally, several special in-text citations are sometimes used. These are summarized in Table 16-4.

## Citing Quoted Material

Whenever you directly quote a source, you must indicate the source. You must include the author's name, year of publication, and page or pages where you found the quoted material. For electronic sources without page numbers, provide the paragraph number (e.g., para. 2). If the electronic source has headings, provide the section title (e.g., Results section, para. 3). For shorter quotes (40 words or less) include the quoted material in your paragraph and enclose the quoted material in quotation marks. As with reference citations, the form to follow depends on the sentence structure. For example,

> Although research does suggest that television has the potential to aid in the socialization of children, there is still reason to be cautious. In fact, according to Liebert, Sprafkin, and Davidson (1982, p. 209), "Although most studies suggest that prosocial television can have desired effects, our ability to magnify these effects and minimize undesirable ones is in its infancy."

or

> Even though research does suggest that television has the potential to aid in the socialization of children, "our ability to magnify these effects and minimize undesirable ones is in its infancy" (Liebert, Sprafkin, & Davidson, 1982, p. 209).

or

> Even though research does suggest that television has the potential to aid in the socialization of children, Liebert, Sprafkin, and Davidson (2006) say that "our ability to magnify these effects and minimize undesirable ones is in its infancy" (p. 209).

For longer quotes (40 or more words), set the quoted material off in a block paragraph format without quotation marks. Indent the entire block quote about a half inch from the left margin. Provide appropriate citation information at the end of the paragraph if you did not provide it in the sentence that introduced the quoted material. For example:

For example, John Watson once famously said

> Give me a dozen healthy infants, well formed, and my own specified world to bring them up in and I'll take any one at random and train him to become any type of specialist I might select—doctor, artist, lawyer, merchant-chief and, yes, even beggar-man and thief, regardless of his talents, penchants, tendencies, abilities, vocations, and race of his ancestors (Watson, 1930, p. 104).

**TABLE 16-4    APA-Style, In-Text Citations**

| APPLICATION | CITATION FORMAT |
|---|---|
| | *Single Author* |
| AUTHOR NAMED IN SENTENCE | |
| One article: | Jones (2010) |
| Two articles (same year): | Jones (2010a, 2010b) |
| Two articles (different years): | Jones (2009, 2010) |
| Personal communication: | Smith (personal communication, July 15, 2010)[a] |
| AUTHOR NAMED IN PARENTHESES | |
| One article: | (Jones, 2010) |
| Two articles (same year): | (Jones, 2010a, 2010b) |
| Two articles (different years): | (Jones, 2009, 2010) |
| Personal communication: | (Smith, personal communication, July 15, 2010)[a] |
| | *Multiple Authors[b]* |
| AUTHORS NAMED IN SENTENCE | |
| Two authors: | Smith and Jones (2010) |
| More than two authors: | Smith, Jones, and Key (2010) |
| AUTHORS NAMED IN PARENTHESES | |
| Two authors: | (Smith & Jones, 2010) |
| More than two authors: | (Smith, Jones, & Key, 2010) |
| Multiple citation for same idea: | (Harris, 2008; Jones, 2010; Smith & Jones, 2006) |
| | *Special Citations* |
| LEGAL CITATIONS | |
| Litigants named in sentence: | *Ballew v. Georgia* (1976) |
| Litigants named in parentheses: | (*Ballew v. Georgia*, 1976) |

[a]Personal communication items are *not* placed in the reference list.
[b]Format for multiple articles follows that for single authors.
SOURCE: American Psychological Association, Copyright 2010.

These examples cited a direct quotation. Even when you simply paraphrase some-one's ideas or words, you still cite the source (although you do not provide page numbers for paraphrased ideas). We discuss source attribution again in the section on plagiarism.

## QUESTIONS TO PONDER

1. What are the general rules for in-text citations?
2. How do you cite quoted material in your paper?

## Using Numbers in the Text

As a rule, you spell out numbers lower than 10 (e.g., five), and express numbers 10 and above numerically (e.g., 23). A few exceptions to this rule are as follows (APA, 2010):

1. Use numerals when a number immediately precedes a unit of measurement (e.g., a 5-mg dose).
2. Use numerals when representing statistical or mathematical functions, percentages, ratios, percentiles, and quartiles (e.g., multiplied by 4; the 2nd percentile).
3. Use numerals when representing time, dates, ages, sample or population sizes, specific numbers of subjects in an experiment, scores and points on a scale, sums of money, and numerals as numerals (e.g., the longitudinal study took 4 years; numbers on the scale ranged from 0 to 10). An exception to this rule is to write out numbers that refer to approximated time periods (e.g., approximately sixteen years).
4. Use numerals when discussing a specific place in an ordered series, parts of books, and each number in a list of four or more numbers (e.g., Grade 2; Table 1).
5. Use numerals for all numbers that appear in the abstract of a paper or in graphical displays.

Express numbers in words in the following cases (APA, 2010):

1. Any number that begins a sentence, title, or heading is written out (e.g., Twenty subjects were assigned; Three subjects were dropped from the analysis, leaving 58 subjects). However, consider rewriting sentences or headings that begin with numbers so that they do not begin with a number.
2. Write out numbers representing common fractions (e.g., two-thirds of the class).
3. Write out numbers for universally accepted usages (e.g., Five Books of Moses, the Twelve Apostles).

For other cases see the APA publication manual (2010, pp. 111–115).

## Avoiding Biased Language

**Biased language** occurs when you inadvertently use language that presupposes that one group is preferred over another or that might be offensive to a group of people. For example, by using the male pronoun *he* to express ideas generically, we fall into the trap of biased writing. The APA publication manual gives three guidelines to follow to avoid biased language.

Guideline 1 refers to providing descriptions at the appropriate level of specificity. For example, when you describe ethnic groups, avoid using general terms such as *Asian* or *Hispanic*. Instead, be specific. If your participants were Chinese or Puerto Rican, use those more specific terms. When you refer to sexual orientation, rather than using the term "gay" to refer to men and women, use "gay men" or "lesbian women" instead (APA, 2010). There may also be some confusion over when to use the term "gender" or "sex." The term "gender" is used when referring to men and women in a social or cultural context. The term "sex" is a biological term and is used when referring to biological differences between men and women (APA, 2010). There are two general rules to follow with respect to describing groups. First, when in doubt always use a more specific term; second, use group descriptors only when they are relevant (APA, 2010).

Guideline 2 deals with the issue of "labeling." You should be sensitive to the labels you attach to people. Avoid labeling groups of people. For example, the label "the elderly" categorizes people as if they were objects (APA, 2010). The term "elderly people" is preferred (APA, 2010). Also in this category is writing that elevates one's own group above others. For example, the phrase "men and wives" implies that males are the standard by which women are to be judged (APA, 2010). In this case, "husbands and wives" would be better. Finally, be aware of the fact that the order in which you list groups may imply superiority of one group over another. For example, always mentioning White participants before Black participants may imply a superiority of Whites over Blacks. To avoid this, mix the order in which you present group identifiers. Finally, be aware that the appropriateness of labels may change over time. For example, the term "homosexual" is no longer accepted in scientific writing because of the negative connotations attached to the term in the past. Instead, the term "same-sex orientation" is preferred currently. Try to find out which terms of reference are acceptable.

Guideline 3 suggests you refer to individuals who participate in your research in a way that acknowledges their participation. For example, rather than saying, "Participants were run in groups of four," say, "Participants completed the experiment in groups of four." The latter sentence conveys that the participants were active in the experiment, which they were.

The APA publication manual (2010, pp. 70–77) provides an extended discussion of the three guidelines just outlined as well as discussions of specific areas of concern (e.g., racial and ethnic identity, gender, sexual preference, and disabilities). Keep in mind, however, that avoiding biased language should not come at the expense of precision and accuracy. An attempt to avoid offending anybody may obscure important information. The APA urges that you use good judgment rather than a set of rigid rules concerning what is acceptable writing.

## QUESTIONS TO PONDER

1. What are the general rules for using numbers in the text of a manuscript? What are the main exceptions to the general rules for using numbers?

2. What is biased language, and why should you avoid using it?

3. What are the three APA guidelines for avoiding biased language?

## EXPRESSION, ORGANIZATION, AND STYLE

The previous sections explained the general conventions to follow when writing an APA-style paper. Unfortunately, merely knowing about subsections and citation formats does not guarantee that you will write a quality paper. You also must know how to present your ideas in a clear and organized way.

As a rule, you should write using the active voice in a sentence. That is, sentences should follow a subject–verb–object organization. Note the differences in the two sentences below:

*Passive voice:* A questionnaire was given to each participant to complete.

*Active voice:* I gave a questionnaire to each participant to complete.

Using the personal pronouns *I* or *we* is acceptable in APA style and is even preferable because it encourages writing in the active voice. In years past, authors were encouraged to write in the third person. Current APA style allows you to write in the first person.

Perhaps the most common flaws in student papers are poorly expressed ideas, unorganized presentation of ideas, and sloppy presentation style. You can have a good handle on your research topic, procedures, and results but still be unable to communicate them well to your readers. Unclear writing and a disorganized presentation obscure important points. In your writing, you should express your ideas clearly and concisely to your readers.

### Precision and Clarity of Expression

Improper grammar can seriously interfere with the precision and clarity of your manuscript. Unfortunately, students often do not pay close enough attention to the grammatical structure of their sentences. A result of this can be ambiguous sentences. Consider the following example:

The experimenter recorded how fast each rat ran the maze with a stopwatch.

In this example, the writer's intention was to say that the experimenter used a stopwatch to time the rat's running speed. Instead, you get the image of a rat running the maze while holding a stopwatch! The problem here is that the modifier "with a stopwatch" is misplaced in such a way that it refers to the rat, not to the experimenter. The following rewritten sentence is unambiguous and consequently much clearer:

Using a stopwatch, the experimenter timed each rat's running speed.

Here, the modifier is properly attached to the experimenter.

Another common grammatical error is disagreement between subject and verb. In the following incorrect sentence, the verb goes with the word "records" and not "one":

Only one of the subject's *records were* included in the analysis.

This sentence should be corrected as follows:

Only *one* of the subject's records *was* included in the analysis.

Of course, this chapter cannot explore all the common grammatical errors. But you should make an effort to reduce grammatical errors in your writing. Some good guides that may help you are Crews (1980); Hall (1979); Leggett, Mead, and Charvat (1978); Strunk and White (1979); and Chapter 3 of the APA publication manual (2010). You can also use an online source such as the Purdue University Owl website (http://owl.english.purdue.edu/owl/). A grammar checker, included with most word processors, may also help (but is not always correct).

Proper word choice is the second aspect of clear writing. Make sure you select words that convey your ideas as you intend. For example, in general writing, the words *feel* and *believe* are used interchangeably. In scientific writing, however, they may mean very different things (APA, 2010). Choose the word that most accurately conveys your meaning. If you mean *believe,* then say *believe.*

Unnecessary qualifiers also reduce clarity of expression. Phrases such as "approximately equal" and "particularly strong" are imprecise, and different readers may interpret them differently. Be specific when referring to quantity estimates. Moreover, be careful about using pronouns in place of nouns, especially in long sentences. Following the meaning of a sentence with multiple mentions of "they," "it," and so on is difficult.

Avoid using complex words when simple words would suffice. For example, don't say *masticate* when you mean *chew,* or *cogitate* when you mean *think* (Hall, 1979, p. 84). In addition, never utilize the word *utilize*—use *use* instead. Constant use of fancy words becomes tedious to read. Base your choice on how well a word conveys your meaning, not on how intelligent you think it makes you sound. If a complex word best conveys your meaning (e.g., *clandestine* implies much more than *secret*), use it. In other cases, use the preferred simple word.

Using jargon can also reduce clarity. *Jargon* refers to the use of technical vocabulary even when that vocabulary is not relevant. Not all readers will know what you mean by these terms, so it is best to avoid them if possible. For example, using the term *voir dire* throughout an article may confuse readers who are not familiar with legal terminology. It would be better to use the term *jury selection.*

There are other flaws that can affect precision and clarity. See the APA manual (pp. 68–70) for a discussion of these flaws.

## Economy of Expression

You should express your ideas in a concise, economical manner (APA, 2010). Three major flaws in writing threaten economy of expression: wordiness, redundancy, and unit length (APA, 2010).

*Wordiness* refers to using more words than necessary to express an idea clearly. Consider the following examples:

*Wordy:* There were several participants who required additional assistance.

*Better:* Several participants required additional assistance.

The currently popular phrase "the exact same" is not only grammatically suspect ("exactly the same" would be better); it uses three words when one will do: "identical."

*Redundancy* occurs when words duplicate a meaning already conveyed by other words. In the following example, the word *past* is redundant: "The participant's past history was examined." *Unit length* concerns the length of sentences within a paragraph. Using too many short sentences creates a choppy style. Using excessively involved, long sentences can be confusing. Vary the length of the sentences within a paragraph to establish and maintain the interest of your reader. Attention to unit length also extends to the length of paragraphs (APA, 2010), a topic we discuss in the next section.

## Organization

Whereas clarity of expression relates most closely to the structure of sentences, organization relates to how you organize those sentences into paragraphs and how you weave paragraphs into an entire paper. You can write the most beautiful, grammatically correct sentences yet fail to convey your ideas clearly. A paragraph is more than a collection of grammatically correct sentences. You must weave those sentences into a coherent, unified entity that clearly conveys information to your readers.

Paragraphs can include four types of sentences (Crews, 1980). These are theme sentences, support sentences, limiting sentences, and transitional sentences. The *theme sentence,* which is usually the first sentence in a paragraph, conveys to your reader the topic of the paragraph. *Support sentences* follow the theme sentence and support and elaborate the theme. *Limiting sentences* indicate possible limits to the assertion made in the theme sentence. Finally, *transitional sentences* smoothly shift from one idea to another within a paragraph. These four types of sentences should be combined to achieve unity.

Crews (1980) suggests four general rules to help you attain unity within paragraphs:

1. Make only one major point within a paragraph.

2. Make your theme sentence the most general sentence within a paragraph. All subsequent sentences should focus on the theme stated in the theme sentence.

3. Stick to the theme stated at the outset of the paragraph. Unity is disrupted when you stray from the point.

4. Use complete sequences of limiting or supporting sentences. That is, if you have something positive to say about a topic, list all the positive elements before turning to the negative.

The following paragraph exemplifies these points:

> Piaget's view of the development of object permanence was based on rather informal tests with infants. In a typical test, Piaget hid an object, and the infant was required to engage in a visual or manual search for it. From the results of such tests, Piaget concluded that infants do not demonstrate object permanence until they are 6 months old and do not achieve a full understanding that objects continue to exist when out of sight until the end of the sensorimotor stage. However, later research suggests that infants may acquire the concept of object permanence long before Piaget suggested they do.

The first sentence in the paragraph is the theme sentence because it tells the reader that the paragraph is about Piaget's views on object permanence. The subsequent sentences discuss issues relevant to the theme sentence. The next two support the theme sentence, whereas the last one limits it.

In addition to unity, a paragraph should have coherence. Coherence is disrupted when sentences that relate only tangentially to a topic are included in a paragraph (Hall, 1979, p. 193). Two problematic sentences are italicized in the following paragraph. The first disrupts unity, and the second disrupts coherence.

> Methodological problems were apparent in the Jones and Smith (2010) experiment. *Smith was only a graduate student at the time of the study.* The methodological problems stemmed from use of outdated equipment. *Some of the equipment was so old that it could hardly be kept working.* This equipment did not have the sensitivity to record accurately the subtle changes in the subjects' behavior.

The first italicized sentence is irrelevant to the topic introduced at the beginning of the paragraph. The second italicized sentence, although tangentially related, is not necessary. It serves only to break up the important points in the previous and subsequent sentences (points that you should link directly). The two italicized sentences together add little to the discussion and disrupt the unity of the paragraph.

Without these two unnecessary statements, the paragraph still conveys the important idea that the Jones and Smith study was flawed because of archaic equipment:

> Methodological problems were apparent in the Jones and Smith (2010) experiment. The methodological problems stemmed from use of outdated equipment. This equipment did not have the sensitivity to record accurately the subtle changes in the subjects' behavior.

Paragraphs can become confusing when too long. Overly long paragraphs are a common error we have encountered in student writing. If a paragraph runs longer than one double-spaced manuscript page, look for places to break the paragraph into shorter ones (APA, 2010). Breaking long paragraphs into shorter ones provides pauses for your readers and is preferable to a single, overly long paragraph. As a general rule, deal with only one major topic in a paragraph. Weave together paragraphs to create a unified and consistent narrative that will hold your readers' interest. Avoid confusing your readers with too much information packed into too little space.

On a similar note, you also should avoid using a sequence of overly short paragraphs. Overusing one- or two-sentence paragraphs breaks up the flow of your writing and makes it abrupt and difficult to read (APA, 2010). If you find you have many short paragraphs, see if you can reorganize your ideas to create fewer but longer paragraphs.

You should organize each section of your paper into units. For example, you might organize your introduction into three subsections (even if they are not labeled as such). In the first subsection, you introduce your topic (using perhaps two paragraphs). In the second subsection, you might review relevant literature (five paragraphs). Finally, in the third subsection, you might summarize the research you reviewed and state your hypotheses (three paragraphs). You should organize the information in your method, results, and discussion sections in a similar fashion.

The best way to avoid disorganization is to make an outline of your paper before you begin writing and then stick to the outline. Indicate the main sections (introduction, method, etc.), and identify the subtopics to be handled within the major sections.

## Style

Your final paper is a reflection of you as well as of your work. A paper can be well organized and clearly written yet still make a negative impression on your reader because of sloppy presentation. Frequent misspellings, misused words, and typographical errors detract significantly from your paper. Work to eliminate them.

You can best avoid misspellings by using a dictionary (we recommend *Webster's 11th edition, Webster's Third New International edition,* or the Merriam-Webster Online Dictionary [https://www.merriam-webster.com]). If you have difficulty with spelling (as many of us do), have your paper read by a good speller. The spelling checker that comes with your word processing program also can help identify some spelling errors. However, it will not catch errors involving "sound-alike" words (such as using "witch" when you meant "which") or the wrong grammatical form (e.g., typing "our" when you meant "your"). Some, but not all, of these errors might be flagged by a grammar checker. In addition, the spelling checker may not recognize certain technical terms even when these are spelled correctly. For those you will need to keep your dictionary handy.

Misused words also detract from your paper. For example, "affect" and "effect" are commonly confused. As a verb, "affect" means "to act on," and "effect" means "to bring about" (see Table 16-5 for a list of commonly misused words). Avoiding these errors involves acquiring a good vocabulary. If you have trouble in this area, have your paper read by someone who has a good vocabulary. The grammar checker in your word processor also can help by flagging possible grammatical errors and suggesting alternative constructions. Although these are not always completely accurate, they do help you to spot potential trouble spots.

**TABLE 16-5    Commonly Misused Words**

| WORDS | TRUE MEANINGS AND COMMENTS |
|---|---|
| affect/effect | *affect:* to influence<br>*effect:* the result of; to implement |
| accept/except | *accept:* to take willingly<br>*except:* excluding; to exclude |
| among/between | *among:* used when you refer to more than two<br>*between:* used when you refer to only two |
| amount/number | *amount:* refers to quantity<br>*number:* refers to countable elements |
| analysis/analyses | *analysis:* singular form<br>*analyses:* plural form |
| cite/site | *cite:* make reference to<br>*site:* location |
| datum/data | *datum:* singular form<br>*data:* plural form |
| every one/everyone | *every one:* each one<br>*everyone:* everybody |
| few/little | *few:* refers to number<br>*little:* refers to amount |
| its/it's | *its:* possessive pronoun<br>*it's:* contraction of "it is" |
| many/much | *many:* refers to countable elements<br>*much:* refers to quantity |
| principle/principal | *principle:* strongly held belief<br>*principal:* foremost |
| than/then | *than:* conjunction used when making a comparison<br>*then:* refers to the past in time |
| that/which | *that:* used to specify a crucial aspect of something: "the study that was conducted by Smith (1984)"<br>*which:* used to offer a qualification that is not crucial to something: "the study, which was published in 1984" (*which* is always preceded by a comma; *that* takes no comma) |
| there/their/they're | *there:* refers to a place<br>*their:* possessive pronoun<br>*they're:* contraction of "they are" |
| whose/who's | *whose:* the possessive of "who"<br>*who's:* contraction of "who is" |
| your/you're | *your:* possessive pronoun<br>*you're:* contraction of "you are" |

SOURCE: Crews, 1980; Hall, 1979; Leggett, Mead, and Charvat, 1978; and Strunk and White, 1979.

Frequent stylistic errors detract from your work. Careful proofreading is essential. Correct any errors you find before you submit your work. Make these corrections on your word processor, not pencil them in on the printed manuscript.

## QUESTIONS TO PONDER

1. Why are precision and clarity of expression, organization, and style so important to consider when preparing a manuscript?
2. What factors contribute to or detract from precision and clarity of expression?
3. What factors contribute to or detract from good organization?
4. What can you do to ensure that your paper has proper style?

### Making It Work

A goal you should strive to achieve is to produce a well-written report of your results that is clear, organized, and visually pleasing. Most writers, even professionals, cannot produce a "finished product" after only a single writing. The best way to approach writing a paper (especially in the early stages of your writing career) is to prepare a rough draft and then make careful revisions. If your university or college has a writing center (or other similar resource), you can have someone there read the draft of your paper. This person can point out flaws and give you ideas about correcting those flaws.

During the revision process, look for three major things. First, read through your paper, paragraph by paragraph, and check for unity, coherence, and proper word usage. Second, read your paper for organization between paragraphs and sections. Finally, carefully comb your paper for typographical errors, misused words, and other stylistic errors. Only after you have completed several cycles of writing and revising should you submit your paper to your instructor or to a journal.

### Avoiding Plagiarism and Lazy Writing

Reference citations must be included in your paper to give credit to others who have published or presented ideas you have drawn upon. If you use someone else's words or ideas without proper citation, you are guilty of **plagiarism**, which is at best unethical and at worst illegal. Penalties for plagiarism can range from a failing grade on an assignment to civil litigation (if the plagiarized work is published).

A broad rule of thumb to avoid plagiarism is to provide a citation whenever another person's work influenced your thinking. Of course, this means citing more than direct quotations and paraphrases of someone else's writing. If an idea you present in your paper is not originally yours, then you must cite the source.

A writing deficiency closely related to plagiarism is lazy writing (Rosnow & Rosnow, 1986). In **lazy writing**, an individual simply lifts paragraph after paragraph out of one or more sources and presents them as a paper (Unfortunately, this practice has become rampant since the advent of electronic copy-and-paste!). The difference between plagiarism and lazy writing is that in lazy writing, the individual properly cites the source of the material.

Although lazy writing is technically not plagiarism, few instructors will accept a paper that relies heavily on quoted material. Keep the following rules of thumb in mind when writing a paper:

1. Always properly cite the source of words and ideas that are not your own.

2. Always paraphrase information from another source and provide a proper citation.

3. Enclose directly quoted material in quotation marks or set longer passages off in a block paragraph style and provide the proper citation, which includes the page number(s) where the material can be found in the original source.

4. Use quoted material sparingly and *only* to support something you have written *in your own words*.

5. Make sure any written assignment you turn in is written in your own words. Never turn in a paper that consists of large amounts of material taken from other sources with little of your own writing. This is true even if you made some minor, cosmetic changes to the original material and properly cited the original source.

For further information on lazy writing, go to the website supporting this text. There you will find extended examples of plagiarism and lazy writing as well as advice on how to avoid these two writing flaws. You also will find links to a number of websites that deal with plagiarism.

## QUESTIONS TO PONDER

1. What are plagiarism and lazy writing?
2. How can you avoid plagiarism and lazy writing?

## TELLING THE WORLD ABOUT YOUR RESULTS

Having put the finishing touches on your paper, your next step is to make its results known to the scientific community. You could present your results at a local, regional, or national scientific convention (e.g., the Annual Meeting of the Midwestern Psychological Association), an option we discuss later. You also can have your results published in a scientific journal.

### Publishing Your Results

Before submitting your paper to a scientific journal for possible publication, you have to make a couple of preliminary decisions. First is where to send your paper. Some journals publish research on a broad variety of topics, whereas others focus more narrowly on specific fields of research such as perception, animal learning, or personality.

To identify an appropriate journal for your paper, one approach is to check the references you cited to see where they were published. You might also try reading the descriptions that journals provide on their websites detailing the kinds of papers and topics they accept.

A second decision is whether to send your paper to a refereed or nonrefereed journal. As stated in Chapter 3, papers sent to a refereed journal are reviewed before publication, but those sent to a nonrefereed journal are not reviewed. A refereed journal is preferred because your work will likely receive more serious attention by the scientific community. Your paper may be published more rapidly in a nonrefereed journal, but you may have to pay a fee to cover publication costs.

*Submitting Your Paper for Publication*    Most scientific journals require you to submit your manuscript electronically in a particular file format. For APA journals, formats allowed include the rtf format (available as option within most word processors) and Microsoft Word's doc or docx format. In addition to your manuscript, the APA requires you to include the following: a cover letter; a "Certification of Compliance with APA Ethical Principles" form; and, if there are any potential conflicts of interest involved in the research, a "Disclosure of Interests" form. For these and other general details pertaining to *APA journal submission, read the APA Manuscript Submission Guidelines for All Authors*, which is available online at http://www.apa.org/pubs/authors/instructions.aspx.

The APA also recommends that you review its *Checklist for Manuscript Submission* before submitting your manuscript. A version of this checklist appears in the APA publication manual (2010) and online at http://www.apa.org/pubs/authors/manuscript-check.aspx.

*The Publication Process*    After submission to a refereed journal, your manuscript goes through a standard procedure for review and publication. First, your paper is sent out for review. After the initial review, you receive a decision about acceptance or rejection. The editor of the journal may accept or reject your paper outright. In many cases, however, papers are given a conditional acceptance. The editor then asks you to revise and resubmit your paper. After resubmission, the paper may be sent out for another review if the revisions are extensive.

Once accepted, your paper goes to a *copy editor,* who looks for stylistic errors. In most cases, the copyedited manuscript is returned to you for review. At this point, you may still make limited changes to the manuscript. You then return the copyedited manuscript to the editor.

Next, the publisher typesets your manuscript. Once this is done, you receive *proofs,* which are copies of your paper as it will appear in the journal. You read these proofs to be sure that they agree with your manuscript and that there are no errors. Errors may be of two types: printer errors and author errors. A *printer error* occurs when the text in the proofs does not match the submitted manuscript. *Author errors* are errors you did not catch in copy editing. For example, you may discover that you reported a statistic incorrectly. You can correct both types of errors. However, the publisher might charge you for corrections of author errors. After reviewing the proofs and correcting any errors, you return them to the publisher for publication in the journal.

The cycle of submission-review-revision and resubmission-acceptance-publication is a relatively long one. After your initial submission to a refereed journal, two months or more may pass before you receive your first feedback. After revision, another two months or more may pass (depending on whether the editor sent your paper out for a second review). The entire process (from submission to publication) can take a year or more. Chapter 3 discussed this and other publication-related issues in greater detail.

## Paper Presentations

In addition to publication, you can communicate your research results through a paper presentation. Paper presentations can range from class presentations to more formal seminars to presentations at professional meetings. Two methods of presenting the results of your research are used at professional meetings. You can deliver an oral presentation before an audience, or you can present your findings in a poster session.

*Oral Presentations*    For an *oral presentation,* you are usually given a limited time to present your information. At paper sessions at professional meetings, for example, you are given 15 minutes. In that brief time, you must communicate to your audience the rationale behind your study, your methods, results, and conclusions. Because of the time limit, it is helpful if you distribute a written summary of your paper (including figures and tables) to your audience. Some conferences may require that you do this. Even if they do not, you should prepare handouts.

When preparing for an oral presentation, follow a few general rules. First, organize your talk. Do not go in and try to "wing it." Instead, develop an outline of your talk and stick to it. Second, do not read your paper. Store what you want to say in your head. Use your notes only as a guide. Third, use appropriate visual aids whenever possible. Computerized slide shows and printed handouts provide quick, easy ways to present complex methods and results. Rather than waste precious time describing methods and complex results, refer to your visual aids and restrict your discussion to the most important aspects of your research. Fourth, take some time to practice your presentation, perhaps in front of some colleagues. This will allow you to tell whether the length of your presentation is appropriate, whether you are communicating clearly, and whether you left out any elements. Feedback from your colleagues during a practice session can be valuable in identifying the strong points and weak points of your presentation.

A common mistake during oral presentations is giving an overly detailed account of the methods and procedures. It is not easy to communicate these complexities verbally. Listeners can retain only so much information and may become lost if you give too much. Try to boil down a complex method to its essential elements. To understand your study, listeners may need to know that you tested rats in an operant chamber. They may become lost in the details if you try to explain that the rats were Long–Evans females weighing between 250 and 350 grams and housed individually in 7- × 7- × 14-inch wire cages, and that the chamber was 25 × 25 × 30 centimeters (cm), constructed from aluminum sheet and fitted with a floor consisting of 0.8-cm-diameter stainless-steel bars spaced 1.2 cm apart. If your procedure is complicated, diagram it and present it on a slide or handout rather than attempting to explain it all verbally.

A final rule to follow is to avoid being pedantic and pompous. Some presenters are so consumed with self-importance that they choose to bore the audience with unnecessary details of their lives and research. Pomposity is manifested when the presenter is 13 minutes into his or her presentation and has yet to say anything about the methods and results of the study. Your audience will appreciate your presentation more and get more out of it if you focus your presentation on central issues of the research being reported.

*Poster Sessions*    In a *poster session,* you prepare a poster to present the rationale behind your study and your hypotheses, method, results, and conclusions. Unlike the oral presentation, you have as long as an hour to present your research. Many posters on related topics are presented within each session.

The main advantage of a poster session is that you can speak extensively with other people who are doing research in your area. During oral presentations, interaction with the audience may be limited to a few questions immediately following your presentation or a few minutes after the paper session. In a poster session, an interested person can take time to read your poster and perhaps formulate more meaningful questions and input.

Poster sessions usually require more time and effort on your part than oral presentations. Posters may be time consuming to make and difficult to transport although technology and the advent of vinyl posters have cut down on these logistical problems. Despite the difficulties, in some ways the poster format is superior to the oral presentation. It allows you greater freedom of presentation, more time for discussion, and less superficial interactions with other researchers in your area.

Conferences differ in the guidelines you must follow to format your poster (e.g., what elements must be included, placement of sections, typeface style and size). If you are planning to present a poster, you should obtain a copy of the guidelines used at the conference at which you will be presenting. You should have your poster prepared professionally. Your university may provide services for poster preparation. If not, you can use a commercial company (e.g., an online company or Kinkos). In many cases you can have your poster professionally prepared at relatively low cost. You should not show up at your poster session with several 8.5 × 11-inch pages printed out on your home printer. Not only is this a tacky way of presenting your research, it may also be difficult for your audience to read. In addition, as was the case for the oral presentation, you should prepare a written version of your poster to distribute to interested individuals.

## The Ethics of Reporting or Publishing Your Results

Reporting or publishing your results in a public forum carries with it important responsibilities. You must consider a number of ethical issues, including avoiding plagiarism, giving proper publication credit (e.g., granting authorship status and deciding on an order of authorship), not publishing previously published results, and sharing data with qualified scientists who might want to reanalyze the data. See the APA manual (2010) for an extensive discussion of this issue.

## QUESTIONS TO PONDER

1. What is typically the sequence of events involved in submitting a paper for publication?
2. What are an oral presentation and a poster session, and how do they differ?
3. What are the ethical obligations involved in reporting or publishing your results?

## SUMMARY

After you have designed and conducted a study and have analyzed your data, you then prepare a report of your results. Two ways of reporting your results are the written report and the presentation. The written report establishes a permanent record of your results that is less susceptible to misunderstanding and misinterpretation than is a presentation. The presentation format gives a forum to disseminate results quickly.

Psychological research is reported using APA style (or a close variant of it), which specifies how a paper must be prepared. An APA-style paper consists of a title page, an abstract, an introduction, a method section, a results section, a discussion section, and a reference list, plus additional pages for author notes, footnotes, tables, and figures.

The title page of your paper includes the title of your paper, your name, institutional affiliation, and author notes. The abstract is a brief but concise summary of your research and is the last part of your paper that you write. The introduction of your paper introduces your topic, reviews relevant research, and states your hypotheses. It begins with a general discussion of issues and then moves to a specific discussion of your research. Its major purpose is to provide a logical justification for the study being reported.

The method section describes exactly how you conducted your study. Separate subsections provide information about participants or subjects, apparatus or materials, and procedures. The goal of the method section is to provide enough information that another researcher could replicate your study in all its essential details.

Your results are presented in the results section, which provides a detailed report of the findings (illustrated if necessary with tables and figures) and the results of any statistical analyses of the data.

The results are discussed in the discussion section. The section usually begins with a brief summary of the results to be discussed and a restatement of any hypotheses bearing on these results. The discussion indicates whether these hypotheses were supported by the results. The findings are then related to previous knowledge in the field and conclusions are drawn.

Figures and tables are used to communicate complex information about methods or results that cannot be adequately described verbally. Graphs of relationships must be carefully drawn to avoid misleading the reader. Graphs should not be drawn to make small, albeit statistically significant, effects look large. Clear legends and captions must be included on the figure itself. Tables, like figures, can help summarize complex information. Each table consists of a number, a title, a body, and (if needed) notes describing the table. Because figures and tables are time consuming to prepare and expensive to reproduce in journals, they should only be used to illustrate complex materials or relationships.

Certain conventions are followed when you prepare an APA-style paper. References in the body of your paper are not footnoted. Instead, the author(s) of a reference is included in the text, along with the date of publication of the reference. Each reference cited in the body of your paper should be listed in expanded format in your reference section.

In a well-prepared paper, ideas must be clearly expressed, organized, and presented in a visually pleasing way. Clarity of expression requires grammatically correct sentences, properly chosen words, and economical expression. Ideas can be obscured by grammatically incorrect sentences (i.e., ambiguous sentences), poorly chosen words, and wordy sentences. Poor organization, like unclear expression, can obscure important points in your paper. Organization can be enhanced by developing and sticking to an outline.

Finally, a paper can be well written and organized yet still make a bad impression on the reader. Frequent misspellings, typographical errors, and improper word usage make your paper appear poor to your reader. Have someone proofread your paper to identify spelling and grammatical errors. Make corrections professionally by retyping rather than penciling in or crossing out information.

Plagiarism is using the words or ideas of another person without giving credit to the source. Plagiarism is unethical and, in a published work, may result in legal action against you. Lazy writing is writing that consists primarily of quoted (although properly cited) material. Although lazy writing is not as serious a problem as plagiarism, it is still inappropriate. To avoid both, make sure that your paper consists mainly of your own writing and ideas. Use quoted material and reference citations to support your ideas, not to present them.

After you have prepared your APA-style paper, you may want to submit it to a journal for publication. If you submit your paper to a refereed journal, it will be reviewed by outside reviewers. The editor of the journal can decide (based on the reviews) either to unconditionally accept or reject a paper or to ask you to revise and resubmit your paper. If you revise and resubmit your paper, it may be sent out for a second review. Typically, the entire cycle of initial review, second review, acceptance, and publication takes almost a year.

You also can communicate your research findings through a presentation. In an oral presentation, you stand before an audience and present your results. In a poster session, you prepare a poster and answer questions about your work. The poster session affords more time and deeper communication with others in your field than does an oral presentation.

Finally, concern over ethics does not end with the completion of your research project. Ethical practice dictates that you give proper credit to the ideas and findings of others presented in your research report, properly order the authors' names to reflect the relative importance of their contributions to the research, avoid submitting for publication findings that have already been published elsewhere, and make your data available to fellow researchers who request them.

## KEY TERMS

running head

title page

author note

abstract

introduction

method section

participants subsection

subjects subsection

apparatus subsection

materials subsection

procedure subsection

results section

discussion section

reference section

biased language

plagiarism

lazy writing

# GLOSSARY

**ABAB design**  In a single-subject baseline design, the baseline (A) and intervention (B) phases are each repeated to provide an immediate intrasubject replication.

**abstract**  A concise summary of an APA-style manuscript that includes a brief description of the rationale for the study, methods, results, and conclusions.

**accuracy**  Agreement of a measurement with a known standard.

**alpha level (α)**  The probability of obtaining a difference at least as large as the one actually obtained, given that the difference occurred purely as a result of chance factors. By convention, the maximum acceptable alpha level is .05 (5 chances in 100 or 1 chance in 20).

**analogical theory**  A theory that explains a relationship through analogy to a well-understood model.

**analysis of covariance (ANCOVA)**  Variant of the analysis of variance used to analyze data from experiments that include a correlational variable (covariate).

**analysis of variance (ANOVA)**  An inferential statistic used to evaluate data from experiments with more than two levels of an independent variable or data from multifactor experiments. Versions are available for between-subjects and within-subjects designs.

**apparatus subsection**  Subsection of the method section of an APA-style manuscript in which any equipment, materials, and measures are described in detail. Sometimes called the *materials* subsection.

**applied research**  Research carried out primarily to investigate a real-world problem.

**archival research**  A nonexperimental research strategy in which you make use of existing records as your basic source for data.

**author note**  An element of the title page providing author, departmental affiliation, acknowledgments, disclaimers or conflicts of interest, and author contact information.

**bar graph**  A graph on which data from groups of subjects are represented by bars of differing heights tied to the value of the dependent variable for the group.

**baseline design**  A single-subject experimental design in which subjects are observed under each of several treatment conditions. Observations made during baseline periods (no treatment) are compared with observations made during intervention periods (treatment introduced).

**baseline phase**  Phase of a single-subject, baseline design in which you establish the level of performance on the dependent measure before introducing the treatment.

**basic research**  Research carried out primarily to test a theory or empirical issues.

**behavioral baseline**  Level of behavior under the baseline and intervention phases of a single-subject, baseline design. It is used to determine the amount of uncontrolled variability in the data.

**behavioral categories**  The general and specific classes of behavior to be observed in an observational study.

**behavioral measure**  A measure of a subject's activity in a situation, for example, the number of times a rat presses a lever (frequency of responding).

**belief-based explanation**   An explanation for behavior that is accepted without evidence because it comes from a trusted source or fits within a larger framework of belief.

**Belmont Report**   A report issued in 1979 presenting three basic principles of ethical treatment of human participants that underlie all medical and behavioral research (respect for persons, beneficence, and justice).

**beneficence**   An ethical principle in the Belmont Report stating that researchers will do no harm to participants and will strive to maximize benefits to the participant while minimizing harm.

**beta weight (β)**   Standardized regression weight used to interpret the results of a linear regression analysis. A beta weight can be interpreted as a partial correlation coefficient.

**between-subjects design**   An experimental design in which different groups of subjects are exposed to the various levels of the independent variable.

**biased language**   Language used in writing where you inadvertently presuppose that one group is preferred over others.

**biased sample**   A sample that is not representative of the population it is supposed to represent.

**bivariate linear regression**   A statistical technique for fitting a straight line to a set of data points representing the paired values of two variables.

**boxplot**   A graphical display of the values of the five-number summary of a distribution.

**canonical correlation**   Multivariate statistical techniques used to correlate two sets of variables.

**carryover effect**   A problem associated with within-subjects designs in which exposure to one level of the independent variable alters the behavior observed under subsequent levels.

**case history**   A nonexperimental research technique in which an individual case is studied intensively to uncover its history (e.g., a patient in therapy).

**causal relationship**   A relationship in which changes in the value of one variable cause changes in the value of another.

**changing criterion design**   A single-subject baseline design that employs as a stability criterion a specified level of performance, which is altered in gradual steps across phases in order to shape performance toward a target level.

**chi-square ($\chi^2$)**   Nonparametric inferential statistic used to evaluate the relationship between variables measured on a nominal scale.

**circular explanation (or tautology)**   An explanation of behavior that refers to factors whose only proof of existence is the behavior they are being called on to explain.

**cluster sampling**   A sampling technique in which naturally occurring groups (such as students in an elementary school class) are randomly selected for inclusion in a sample.

**coefficient of determination**   Statistic indicating the proportion of variance in one variable accounted for by variation in a second variable.

**coefficient of nondetermination**   Statistic indicating the proportion of variance in one variable not accounted for by variation in a second variable.

**Cohen's Kappa (κ)**   A popular statistic used to assess interrater reliability. It compares the observed proportion of agreement to the proportion of agreement that would be expected if agreement occurred purely by chance.

**cohort-sequential design**   A developmental design including cross-sectional and longitudinal components.

**commonsense explanations**   Loose explanations for behavior that are based on what we believe to be true about the world.

**concurrent validity**   The validity of a test established by showing that its results can be used to infer an individual's value on some other, accepted test administered at the same time.

**confirmation bias**   The human tendency to seek out information that confirms what is already believed.

**confirmational strategy**   A strategy for testing a theory that involves finding evidence that confirms the predictions made by the theory.

**confounding**   Two variables that vary together in such a way that the effects of one cannot be separated from the effects of the other.

**construct validity**   Validity that applies when a test is designed to measure a "construct" or variable "constructed" to describe or explain behavior on the basis of theory (e.g., intelligence). A test has construct validity if the measured values of the construct predict behavior as expected from the theory (e.g., those with higher intelligence scores achieve higher grades in school).

**content analysis**   A nonexperimental research technique that is used to analyze a written or spoken record for the occurrence of specific categories of events.

**content validity**   Validity of a test established by judging how adequately the test samples behavior representative of the universe of behaviors the test was designed to sample.

**control group**   A group of subjects in an experiment that does not receive the experimental treatment. The data from the control group are used as a baseline against which data from the experimental group are compared.

**correlation matrix**   A matrix giving the set of all possible bivariate correlations among three or more variables.

**correlational relationship**   A relationship in which the value of one variable changes systematically with the value of a second variable.

**correlational research**   Research in which no independent variables are manipulated. Instead, two or more dependent variables are measured to identify possible correlational relationships.

**counterbalancing**   A technique used to combat carryover effects in within-subjects designs. Counterbalancing involves assigning the various treatments of an experiment in a different order for different subjects.

**covariate**   A correlational variable (usually a characteristic of the subject) included in an experiment to help reduce the error variance in statistical tests.

**criterion-related validity**   The ability of a measure to produce results similar to those provided by other, established measures of the same variable.

**critical region**   Portion of the sampling distribution of a statistic within which observed values of the statistic are considered to be statistically significant. Usually the 5% of cases found in the upper and/or lower tail(s) of the distribution.

**cross-sectional design**   A developmental design in which participants from two or more age groups are measured at about the same time. Comparisons are made across age groups to investigate age-related changes in behavior.

**data transformation**   Mathematical operation applied to raw data, such as taking the square root or arcsine of the original scores in a distribution. Often applied to data that violate the assumptions of parametric statistical tests to help them meet those assumptions.

**debriefing**   A session, conducted after an experimental session, in which participants are informed of any deception used and the reasons for the deception.

**deception**   A research technique in which participants are misinformed about the true nature and purpose of a study. Deception is ethical if the researcher can demonstrate that important results cannot be obtained in any other way.

**Declaration of Helsinki**   A declaration on ethical treatment of research participants issued by the World Medical Association in 1964. It stated that the health, welfare, and dignity of research participants be protected by researchers and that research be based on accepted research practices and existing research.

**deductive reasoning**   Reasoning that goes from the general to the specific. Forms the foundation of the rational method of inquiry.

**degrees of freedom (*df*)**   The number of scores that are free to vary in a distribution of a given size having a known mean.

**demand characteristics**   Cues inadvertently provided by the researcher or research context concerning the purposes of a study or the behavior expected from participants.

**demonstration**   A nonexperimental technique in which some phenomenon is demonstrated. No control group is used.

**dependent variable**   The variable measured in a study. Its value is determined by the behavior of the subject and may depend on the value of the independent variable.

**descriptive statistics**   Statistics that allow you to summarize the properties of an entire distribution of scores with just a few numbers.

**descriptive theory**   A theory that simply describes the relationship among variables without attempting to explain the relationship.

**direct replication** Exactly replicating an experiment. No new variables are included in the replication.

**directionality problem** A reason not to infer causality from correlational research, stating that the direction of causality is sometimes difficult to determine.

**disconfirmational strategy** A method of testing a theory that involves conducting research to provide evidence that disconfirms the predictions made by the theory.

**discrete trials design** A single-subject experimental design in which subjects receive each treatment condition dozens or hundreds of times. Each trial (exposure to a treatment) produces one data point, and data points are averaged across trials to provide stable estimates of behavior.

**discriminant analysis** Multivariate statistical technique used when you have multiple predictor variables and a categorical criterion variable.

**discussion section** The section of an APA style manuscript that includes the author's interpretation of the findings of a study and conclusions drawn from the data.

**domain** The range of situations to which a theory applies. Also called the *scope* of a theory.

**double-blind technique** Neither the participants in a study nor the person carrying out the study knows at the time of testing which treatment the participant is receiving.

**dummy code** In a data file, numbers used to stand for category values; for example, $0 = $ male, $1 = $ female.

**dynamic design** An experimental design in which the independent variable is varied continuously over time while monitoring the response of the dependent variable.

**effect size** The amount by which a given experimental manipulation changes the value of the dependent variable in the population, expressed in standard deviation units.

**empirical question** A question that can be answered through objective observation.

**equivalent time samples design** A variation of the time series design in which a treatment is administered repeatedly, with each administration followed by an observation period.

**error variance** Variability in the value of the dependent variable that is related to extraneous variables and not to the variability in the independent variable.

**Ethical Principles of Psychologists and Code of Conduct 2002** A comprehensive document from the American Psychological Association stating the ethical responsibilities of psychologists and researchers.

**ethnography** A nonquantitative technique used to study and describe the functioning of cultures through a study of social interactions and expressions between people and groups.

**expectancy effect** When a researcher's preconceived ideas about how subjects should behave are subtly communicated to subjects and, in turn, affect the subjects' behavior.

**experimental group** A group of subjects in an experiment that receives a nonzero level of the independent variable.

**experimental research** Research in which independent variables are manipulated and behavior is measured while extraneous variables are controlled.

**experimenter bias** When the behavior of the researcher influences the results of a study. Experimenter bias stems from two sources: expectancy effects and uneven treatment of subjects across treatments.

**exploratory data analysis (EDA)** Examining data for potentially important patterns and relationships, especially through the use of simple graphical techniques and numerical summaries.

**external validity** The extent to which the results of a study extend beyond the limited sample used in the study.

**extraneous variable** Any variable that is not systematically manipulated in an experiment but that still may affect the behavior being observed.

***F* ratio** The test statistic computed when using an analysis of variance. It is the ratio of the between-groups variance to within-groups variance.

**face-to-face interview** Method of administering a questionnaire that involves face-to-face interaction with the participant. Two types are the structured and unstructured interview.

**face validity** How well a test appears to measure (judging by its contents) what it was designed to measure. Example: A measure of mathematical ability would have face validity if it contained math problems.

**factor analysis** Multivariate statistical technique that uses correlations between variables to determine the underlying dimensions (factors) represented by the variables.

**factorial design** An experimental design in which every level of one independent variable is combined with every level of every other independent variable.

**familywise error** The likelihood of making at least one Type I error across a number of comparisons.

**file drawer phenomenon** A problem associated with publication practices and meta-analysis that occurs because results that fail to achieve statistical significance often fail to be published (i.e., get relegated to the researcher's file drawer).

**five-number summary** A set of five numbers used to summarize the characteristics of a distribution: the minimum, first quartile, median, third quartile, and maximum.

**frequency distribution** A graph or table displaying a set of values or range of values of a variable, together with the frequency of each.

**functional explanation** An explanation for a phenomenon given in terms of its function, that is, what it accomplishes.

**fundamental theory** A theory that proposes a new structure or underlying process to explain how variables and constants relate.

**generalization** Applying a finding beyond the limited situation in which it was observed.

**higher-order factorial design** Experimental design that includes more than two independent variables (factors).

**histogram** A graph depicting a frequency distribution in which the frequencies of class intervals are represented by adjacent bars along the scale of measurement.

**hypothesis** A tentative explanation for an observation, phenomenon, or scientific problem that can be tested by further investigation. Scientific hypotheses must be posed in a form that allows them to be tested.

**Implicit Association Test (IAT)** A popular measure of implicit attitudes that uses responses that are not under direct conscious control.

**independent variable** The variable that is manipulated in an experiment. Its value is determined by the experimenter, not by the subject.

**inferential statistics** Statistical procedures used to infer a characteristic of a population based on certain properties of a sample drawn from that population.

**information extraction** A specialized form of content analysis in which language processing software is used to analyze large databases of information.

**informed consent** Agreeing to serve as a research participant after being informed about the nature of the research and the participant's rights and responsibilities. The participant typically reads and signs a form specifying the purpose of a study, the methods to be used, requirements for participation, costs and benefits of research participation, that participation is voluntary, and that the participant is free to withdraw from the study at any time without penalty.

**institutional animal care and use committee (IACUC)** A committee that screens proposals for research using animal subjects and monitors institutional animal-care facilities to ensure compliance with all local, state, and federal laws governing animal care and use.

**institutional review board (IRB)** A committee that screens proposals for research using human participants for adherence to ethical standards.

**interaction** When the effect of one independent variable on the dependent variable in a factorial design changes over the levels of another independent variable.

**internal validity** The extent to which a study evaluates the intended hypotheses.

**Internet survey** Survey conducted on the Internet, typically by having participants fill out a web-based questionnaire. Such surveys are subject to potential respondent bias as only those having access to the Internet can respond.

**interquartile range** A measure of spread in which an ordered distribution of scores is divided into four groups. The score separating the lower 25% is subtracted from the score separating the upper 25%. The resulting difference is divided by 2.

**interrater reliability** The degree to which multiple observers agree in their classification or quantification of behavior.

**interrupted time series design** A variation of the time series design in which changes in behavior are charted as a function of time before and after some naturally occurring event.

**intersubject replication**   The behaviors of multiple subjects used in a single-subject design are compared to establish the reliability of results.

**interval scale**   A measurement scale in which the spacing between values along the scale is known. The zero point of an interval scale is arbitrary.

**intervention phase**   Phase of a single-subject, baseline design in which the treatment is introduced and the dependent measure evaluated.

**interview**   *See* **face-to-face interview.**

**intraclass correlation coefficient ($r_I$)**   A measure of agreement between observers that can be used when your observations are scaled on an interval or ratio scale of measurement.

**intrasubject replication**   In a single-subject experiment, each treatment is repeated at least once for each subject and behavior is measured. This helps establish the reliability of the results obtained from a single-subject experiment.

**introduction**   The first substantive section of an APA-style manuscript, which includes the rationale for the study, a literature review, and usually a statement of the hypothesis to be tested.

**justice**   An ethical principle in the Belmont Report stating that the researcher and participant should share in the costs and benefits of the research.

**latent variable**   A variable in structural equation modeling that is not directly observable and must be estimated from other measures.

**law**   A relationship that has been substantially verified through empirical test.

**lazy writing**   Flaw in writing, closely related to plagiarism, that involves using too much quoted (albeit properly cited) material in a manuscript.

**least-squares regression line**   Straight line, fit to data, that minimizes the sum of the squared distances between each data point and the line.

**line graph**   A graph on which data relating the variables are plotted as points connected by lines.

**linear regression**   Statistical technique used to determine the straight line that best fits a set of data.

**literature review**   A review of relevant research and theory conducted during the early stages of the research process to identify important variables and accepted methods and to establish a rationale for research hypotheses.

**loglinear analysis**   A nonparametric, multivariate statistical technique used primarily to evaluate data from multifactor research with a nominal dependent variable. It can also be used on interval or ratio data that violate the assumptions of the analysis of variance.

**longitudinal design**   A developmental design in which a single group of subjects is followed over a specified period of time and measured at regular intervals.

**mail survey**   Method of administering a survey that involves mailing questionnaires to participants. Nonresponse bias may be a problem.

**main effect**   The independent effect of one independent variable in a factorial design on the dependent variable. There are as many main effects as there are independent variables.

**manipulation check**   Measures included in an experiment to test the effectiveness of the independent variables.

**Mann–Whitney $U$ test**   Nonparametric inferential statistic used to evaluate data from a two-group experiment in which the dependent variable was measured along at least an ordinal scale. It can also be used on interval or ratio data if the data do not meet the assumptions of the $t$ test for independent samples.

**matched-groups design**   Between-subjects experimental design in which matched sets of subjects are distributed, at random, one per group across groups of the experiment.

**matched-pairs design**   A two-group matched groups design.

**materials subsection**   A subsection of the method section of an APA-style manuscript in which primarily written materials used in a study (e.g., questionnaires) are described.

**mean**   The arithmetic average of the scores in a distribution. The most frequently reported measure of center.

**measure of association**  A measure used to evaluate the direction and degree of relationship (correlation) between the scores in two distributions.

**measure of center**  A single score, computed from a data set, that represents the general magnitude of the scores in the distribution.

**measure of spread**  A single score, computed from a data set, that represents the amount of variability of the scores in the distribution (i.e., how spread out they are).

**measured variable**  A variable in structural equation modeling that is measured directly.

**mechanistic explanation**  An explanation for a phenomenon given in terms of a mechanism that is assumed to produce it through an explicit chain of cause and effect.

**median**  The middle score in an ordered distribution.

**meta-analysis**  A statistics-based method of reviewing literature in a field that involves comparing or combining the results of related studies.

**method of authority**  Relying on authoritative sources (e.g., books, journals, scholars) for information.

**method section**  The section of an APA-style manuscript in which the methods used in a study are described in detail.

**mixed design**  An experimental design that includes between-subjects as well as within-subjects factors. Also called a *split-plot design.*

**mixed-mode survey**  A survey method that employs more than one type of survey (e.g., both mail and Internet).

**mode**  The most frequent score in a distribution. The least informative measure of center.

**model**  Specific application of a general theoretical view. The term *model* is sometimes used as a synonym for *theory.*

**multiple-baseline design**  Simultaneously sampling several behaviors in a single-subject, baseline design to provide multiple baselines of behavior. Used if your independent variable produces irreversible changes in the dependent variable.

**multiple control group design**  Single-factor, experimental design that includes two or more control groups.

**multiple *R***  The correlation between the best linear combination of predictor variables entered into a multiple regression analysis and the dependent variable.

**multiple regression**  Multivariate linear regression analysis used when you have a single criterion variable and multiple predictor variables.

**multistage sampling**  A variant of cluster sampling in which naturally occurring groups of subjects are identified and randomly sampled. Individual subjects are then randomly sampled from the groups chosen.

**multivariate analysis of variance (MANOVA)**  Multivariate analog to the analysis of variance used to analyze data from an experimental design with multiple dependent variables.

**multivariate design**  A research design in which multiple dependent or predictor variables are included.

**multivariate strategy**  A data analysis strategy in which multiple dependent measures are analyzed with a single, multivariate statistical test.

**multiway frequency analysis**  A class of alternatives to ANOVA, MANOVA, or regression analysis for use when you want to measure or manipulate categorical variables.

**naturalistic observation**  Observational research technique in which subjects are observed in their natural environments. The observers remain unobtrusive so that they do not interfere with the natural behaviors of the subjects being observed.

**nested design**  An experimental design with a within-subjects factor in which different levels of one independent variable are included under each level of a between-subjects factor.

**nominal scale**  A measurement scale that involves categorizing cases into two or more distinct categories. This scale yields the least information.

**nonequivalent control group design**  A time series experiment that includes a control group that is not exposed to the experimental treatment.

**nonparametric design**  Experimental research design in which levels of the independent variable are represented by different categories rather than different amounts.

**nonparticipant observation**   An observational research technique in which the observer attends group functions and records observations without participating in the group's activities.

**nonrandom sample**   A specialized sample of subjects used in a study who are not randomly chosen from a population.

**nonrefereed journal**   A journal in which articles do not undergo prepublication editorial review.

**nonresponse bias**   A problem associated with survey research, caused by some participants not returning a questionnaire, resulting in a biased sample.

**normal distribution**   A specific type of frequency distribution in which most scores fall around the middle category. Scores become less frequent as you move from the middle category. Also referred to as a *bell-shaped curve.*

**Nuremberg Code**   An early code of ethical treatment of research participants developed after World War II, resulting from the Nuremberg trials of Nazi war criminal doctors.

**Office of Research Integrity (ORI)**   An office within the U.S. Department of Health and Human Services that oversees the integrity of the research process. The ORI documents and investigates cases involving research fraud.

**open-ended item**   Questionnaire item that allows the subject to fill in a response rather than selecting a response from provided alternatives.

**operational definition**   A definition of a variable in terms of the operations used to measure it.

**ordinal scale**   A measurement scale in which cases are ordered along some dimension (e.g., large, medium, or small). The distances between scale values are unknown.

**outliers**   Values of a variable in a set of data that lie far from the other values.

*p* **value**   In a statistical test, the probability, estimated from the data, that an observed difference in sample values arose through sampling error. *p* must be less than or equal to the chosen alpha level for the difference to be statistically significant.

**paper session**   A meeting at a scientific convention at which the most up-to-date research results are presented. A paper session may involve disseminating data by reading a paper or presenting a poster.

**parallel-forms reliability**   Establishing the reliability of a questionnaire by administering parallel (alternate) forms of the questionnaire repeatedly.

**parametric design**   An experimental design in which the amount of the independent variable is systematically varied across several levels.

**parsimonious explanation**   An explanation or theory that explains a relationship using relatively few assumptions.

**part correlation**   Multivariate correlational statistic used to examine the relationship between two variables with the effect of a third variable removed from one of them.

**partial correlation**   Multivariate correlational statistic used to examine the relationship between two variables with the effect of a third variable removed from both of them.

**partially open-ended item**   Questionnaire item that provides participants with response-categories but includes an "other" response category with a space for participants to define the category.

**participant observation**   An observational research technique in which a researcher insinuates him- or herself into a group to be studied and participates in the group's activities.

**participants subsection**   A subsection of the method section of an APA-style manuscript used when humans are employed in a study and describing the nature of the sample.

**path analysis**   An application of multiple regression used to develop and test causal models using correlational data.

**Pearson product-moment correlation (Pearson *r*)**   The most popular measure of association. Indicates the magnitude and direction of a correlational relationship between variables.

**peer review**   Process of editorial review used by refereed journals. Manuscripts are usually sent out to at least two reviewers who screen the research for quality and importance.

**per-comparison error**   The alpha level for each of any multiple comparisons made among means.

**personal communication**   Information obtained privately from another researcher (e.g., by letter or phone).

**phi ($\varphi$) coefficient**   Measure of correlation used when both variables are measured on a dichotomous scale.

**physiological measure**  A measure of a bodily function of subjects in a study (e.g., heart rate).

**pie graph**  Type of graph in which a circle is divided into segments. Each segment represents the proportion or percentage of responses falling in a given category of the dependent variable.

**pilot study**  A small, scaled-down version of a study used to test the validity of experimental procedures and measures.

**plagiarism**  A serious flaw in writing that involves using another person's words or ideas without properly citing the source. *See also* **lazy writing.**

**planned comparisons**  Hypothesis-directed statistical tests made after finding statistical significance with an overall statistical test (such as ANOVA).

**point-biserial correlation**  A variation of the Pearson correlation used when one variable is measured on a dichotomous scale.

**population**  All possible individuals making up a group of interest in a study. For example, all U.S. women constitute a population. A small proportion of the population is selected for inclusion in a study (*see* **sample**).

**poster session**  A way of disseminating research results at a conference, in which a presenter prepares a poster providing information about the research being reported.

**power**  The ability of an experimental design or inferential statistic to detect an effect of a variable when an effect is present.

**predictive validity**  The ability of a measure to predict some future behavior.

**pretest–posttest design**  A research design that involves measuring a dependent variable (pretest), then introducing the treatment, and then measuring the dependent variable a second time (posttest).

**primary source**  A reference source that contains the original, full report of a study. It includes all the details needed to replicate and interpret the study.

**probability sampling**  A sampling technique in which each member of a population has a known probability of being in the sample.

**procedure subsection**  The subsection of the method section of an APA-style manuscript that provides a detailed description of the procedures used in a study.

**proportionate sampling**  A variation of stratified sampling in which the proportion of subjects sampled from each stratum is matched to the proportion of subjects in each stratum in the population.

**protoscience**  Science at the edges of current scientific understanding; fringe science.

**pseudoexplanation**  An explanation proposed for a phenomenon that simply relabels the phenomenon without really explaining it.

**pseudoscience**  A set of ideas based on theories put forth as scientific when they are not scientific.

**PsycARTICLES**  A computerized source of articles, downloadable in PDF format, that were published in the journals of the American Psychological Association.

**PsycINFO**  A computerized database system that indexes journals and book chapters relevant to psychology and related fields.

**Q-sort methodology**  A qualitative measurement technique that involves establishing evaluative categories and sorting items into those categories.

**qualitative data**  Data in which the values of a variable differ in kind (quality) rather than in amount.

**qualitative theory**  A theory in which terms are expressed verbally rather than mathematically.

**quantitative data**  Data collected that are represented by numbers that can be analyzed with widely available descriptive and inferential statistics.

**quantitative theory**  A theory in which terms are expressed mathematically rather than verbally.

**quasi-experimental design**  A design resembling an experimental design but using quasi-independent rather than true independent variables.

**quasi-independent variable**  A variable resembling an independent variable in an experiment, but whose levels are not assigned to subjects at random (e.g., the subject's age).

**$R$-square**  The square of the multiple $R$ in a multiple regression analysis. Provides a measure of the amount of variability in the dependent measure accounted for by the best linear combination of predictor variables.

**random assignment**  The process of assigning subjects to experimental treatments randomly.

**random sample**   A sample drawn from the population such that every member of the population has an equal opportunity to be included in the sample.

**randomized two-group design**   A between-subjects design in which subjects are assigned to groups randomly.

**range**   The least informative measure of spread; the difference between the lowest and highest scores in a distribution.

**range effects**   A problem in which a variable being observed reaches an upper limit (ceiling effect) or lower limit (floor effect).

**ratio scale**   Highest scale of measurement; it has all of the characteristics of an interval scale plus an absolute zero point.

**rational method**   Developing explanations through a process of deductive reasoning.

**refereed journal**   A journal whose articles have undergone prepublication editorial review by a panel of experts in the relevant field.

**reference section**   The section of an APA-style manuscript providing an alphabetical list of the bibliographic information for all works cited in a manuscript.

**regression weight**   Value computed in a linear regression analysis that provides the slope of the least squares regression line. *See also* **beta weight.**

**reliability**   Whether a measure or question-naire produces the same or similar responses with multiple administrations of the same or a similar instrument.

**representative sample**   A sample of subjects in which the characteristics of the population are adequately represented.

**resistant measure**   Statistics that are not strongly affected by the presence of outliers or skewness in the data.

**respect for persons**   An ethical principle in the Belmont Report stating that research partici-pants are free to make their own decisions and that individuals with diminished autonomy must be protected.

**restricted item**   Questionnaire item that pro-vides participants with response alternatives from which the participant selects an answer.

**results section**   The section of an APA-style man-uscript that contains a description of the findings of a study. The section normally reports the values of descriptive and inferential statistics obtained.

**reversal strategy**   Running a second baseline phase after the intervention phase in a single-subject, baseline design.

**role attitude cue**   An unintended cue in an experiment that suggests to the participants how they are expected to behave.

**role playing**   Alternative to deception that involves having participants act as though they had been exposed to a certain treatment.

**running head**   A shortened version of the title to a manuscript (no more than 50 characters) that appears on each page of a manuscript.

**sample**   A relatively small number of individu-als drawn from a population for inclusion in a study. *See also* **population.**

**sampling error**   The deviation between the characteristics of a sample and a population.

**scatter plot**   A plot used to display correla-tional data from two measures. Each point represents the two scores provided by each subject, one for each measure, plotted against one another.

**science**   A set of methods used to collect infor-mation about phenomena in a particular area of interest and build a reliable base of knowl-edge about them.

**scientific explanation**   A tentative explanation for a phenomenon, based on objective obser-vation and logic, and subject to empirical test.

**scientific method**   The method of inquiry pre-ferred by scientists. It involves observing phe-nomena, developing hypotheses, empirically testing the hypotheses, and refining and revis-ing hypotheses.

**scientist**   A person who adopts the methods of science in his or her quest for knowledge.

**secondary source**   A reference source that summarizes information from a primary source and includes research reviews and the-oretical articles.

**self-report measure**   A measure that requires participants to report on their past, present, or future behavior.

**semipartial correlation**   *See* **part correlation.**

**simple main effect**   In a factorial analysis of variance (ANOVA), the effect of one factor at a given level (or combination of levels) of another factor (or factors).

**simple random sampling**   A sampling tech-nique in which every member of a population has an equal chance of being selected for a sample and in which the sampling is done on a purely random basis.

**simulation**    A laboratory research technique in which you attempt to re-create as closely as possible a real-world phenomenon.

**single-blind technique**    The person testing subjects in a study is kept unaware of the hypotheses being tested.

**single-subject design**    An experimental design that focuses on the behavior of an individual subject rather than groups of subjects.

**skewed distribution**    A frequency distribution in which most scores fall into categories above or below the middle category.

**sociogram**    A graphical representation of the pattern of interpersonal relationship choices.

**sociometry**    A nonexperimental research technique involving identifying and measuring interpersonal relationships within a group.

**Solomon four-group design**    An expansion of the pretest–posttest design that includes control groups to evaluate the effects of administering a pretest on your experimental treatment.

**Spearman rank-order correlation (rho)**    A measure of correlation used when variables are measured on at least an ordinal scale.

**split-half reliability**    A method of assessing reliability of a questionnaire using a single administration of the instrument. The questionnaire is split into two parts, and responses from the two parts are correlated.

**stability criterion**    Criterion used to establish when a baseline in a single-subject, baseline design no longer shows any systematic trends. Once the criterion is reached, the subject is placed in the next phase of the experiment.

**standard deviation**    The most frequently reported measure of spread. The square root of the variance.

**standard error of estimate**    A measure of the accuracy of prediction in a linear regression analysis. It is a measure of the distance between the observed data points and the least squares regression line.

**standard error of the mean**    An estimate of the amount of variability in expected sample means across a series of samples. It provides an estimate of the deviation between a sample mean and the underlying population mean.

**stemplot**    A graphical display of a distribution of scores consisting of a column of values (the stems) representing the leftmost digit or digits of the scores and, aligned with each stem, a row of values representing the rightmost digit of each score having that particular stem value.

**stratified sampling**    A sampling technique designed to ensure a representative sample that involves dividing the population into segments (strata) and randomly sampling from each stratum.

**strong inference**    A strategy for testing a theory in which a sequence of research studies is systematically carried out to rule out alternative explanations for a phenomenon.

**structural equation modeling (SEM)**    A variant of path analysis in which variables that are indirectly observed and measured are included in the analysis, allowing you to evaluate relationships involving hypothetical constructs.

**subjects subsection**    A subsection of the method section of an APA-style manuscript in which the nature of the subject sample employed is described. This section is called *subjects* if animals were employed in a study.

**systematic replication**    Conducting a replication of an experiment while adding new variables for investigation.

**systematic sampling**    A sampling technique in which every $k$th element is sampled after a randomly determined start.

*t* **test**    An inferential statistic used to evaluate the reliability of a difference between two means. Versions exist for between-subjects and within-subjects designs and for evaluating a difference between a sample mean and a population mean.

*t* **test for correlated samples**    A parametric inferential statistic used to compare the means of two samples in a matched-pairs or a within-subjects design in order to assess the probability that the two samples came from populations having the same mean.

*t* **test for independent samples**    A parametric inferential statistic used to compare the means of two independent, random samples in order to assess the probability that the two samples came from populations having the same mean.

**tautology**    *See* **circular explanation.**

**telephone survey**   Method of conducting a survey that involves calling participants on the telephone and asking them questions from a prepared questionnaire.

**test–retest reliability**   A method of assessing the reliability of a questionnaire by administering repeatedly the same or parallel form of a test.

**theory**   A plausible or scientifically acceptable, well-substantiated explanation of some aspect of the natural world; an organized system of accepted knowledge that applies in a variety of circumstances to explain a specific set of phenomena and predict the characteristics of as-yet-unobserved phenomena.

**third-variable problem**   A problem that interferes with drawing causal inferences from correlational results. A third, unmeasured variable affects both measured variables, causing the latter to appear correlated even though neither variable influences the other.

**time series design**   A research design in which behavior of subjects in naturally occurring groups is measured periodically both before and after introduction of a treatment.

**title page**   The first page of an APA-style manuscript, including the running head, title, author name(s) and institutional affiliation(s), and author notes.

**treatment**   A level of an independent variable applied during an experiment. In multifactor designs, a specific combination of the levels of each factor.

**Type I error**   Deciding to reject the null hypothesis when, in fact, the null hypothesis is true. Also referred to as an *alpha error*.

**Type II error**   Deciding not to reject the null hypothesis when, in fact, the null hypothesis is false. Also referred to as a *beta error*.

**univariate strategy**   A data analysis strategy in which multiple dependent measures are analyzed independently with separate statistical tests.

**unplanned comparison**   Comparison between means that is not directed by your hypothesis and is made after finding statistical significance with an overall statistical test (such as ANOVA).

**validity**   The extent to which a measuring instrument measures what it was designed to measure.

**variable**   Any quantity or quality that can take on a range of values.

**variance**   A measure of spread. The averaged square deviation from the mean.

**volunteer bias**   Bias in a sample that results from using volunteer participants exclusively.

**Wilcoxon signed ranks test**   A nonparametric statistical test that can be used when the assumptions of the $t$ test for correlated samples are seriously violated.

**within-subjects design**   An experimental design in which each subject is exposed to all levels of an independent variable.

**$z$ test for the difference between two proportions**   A parametric inferential statistic used to determine the probability that two independent, random samples came from populations having the same proportion of "successes" (e.g., persons favoring a particular candidate).

# REFERENCES

Abbott, B., & Badia, P. (1979). Choice for signaled over unsignaled shock as a function of signal length. *Journal of the Experimental Analysis of Behavior, 32,* 409–417.

Adair, J. G. (1973). *The human subject: The social psychology of the psychological experiment.* Boston, MA: Little, Brown.

Agresti, A., & Finlay, B. (1986). *Statistical methods for the social sciences.* San Francisco, CA: Dullen.

Aguinis, H., & Henle, C. A. (2001). Empirical assessment of the bogus pipeline. *Journal of Applied Social Psychology, 31,* 352–375.

Allport, G. W. (1954). Historical background of modern social psychology. In G. Lindzey (Ed.), *Handbook of social psychology* (Vol. 1, pp. 3–56). Cambridge, MA: Addison-Wesley.

Allport, G. W., & Postman, L. (1945). The basic psychology of rumor. *Transactions of the New York Academy of Sciences, 11,* 61–81.

American Psychological Association. (1973). *Ethical principles in the conduct of research with human participants.* Washington, DC: Author.

American Psychological Association. (2002). Ethical principles of psychologists and code of conduct. *American Psychologist, 57,* 1060–1073. doi:10.1037/0003-066X.57.12.1060

American Psychological Association. (2010). *Publication manual of the American Psychological Association* (6th ed.). Washington, DC: Author.

American Psychological Association. (2012). Guidelines for ethical conduct in the care and use of nonhuman animals in research. Retrieved from http://www.apa.org/science/leadership/care/care-animal-guidelines.pdf.

American Psychological Association. (2016). Bullying. Retrieved from http://www.apa.org/topics/bullying/

Anastasi, A. (1976). Psychological testing (4th ed.). New York, NY: Macmillan.

Anderson, C. A., Lindsay, J. J., & Bushman, B. J. (1999). Research in the psychological laboratory: Truth or triviality? *Current Directions in Psychological Science, 8,* 3–9.

Anderson, N. (1968). A simple model for information integration. In R. P. Abelson, E. Aronson, W. J. McGuire, T. M. Newcomb, M. J. Rosenberg, & P. Tannenbaum (Eds.), *Theories of cognitive consistency: A sourcebook* (pp. 731–743). Chicago, IL: Rand McNally.

Andersson, M. (1982). Female choice selects for extreme tail length in a widowbird. *Nature, 299,* 818–820.

Anglesea, M. M., Hoch, H., & Taylor, B. A. (2008). Reducing rapid eating in teenagers with autism: Use of a pager prompt. *Journal of Applied Behavior Analysis, 41,* 107–111. doi:10.1901/jaba.2008.41–107

Applebaum, M. I., & McCall, R. B. (1983). Design and analysis in developmental psychology. In P. H. Mussen & W. Kessen (Eds.), *Handbook of child psychology: Vol. 1. History, theory, and methods* (pp. 415–476). New York, NY: Wiley.

Aronson, E., & Carlsmith, J. M. (1968). Experimentation in social psychology. In G. Lindzey & E. Aronson (Eds.), *Handbook of social psychology* (Vol. 1, pp. 1–79). Reading, MA: Addison-Wesley.

Asher, H. B. (1976). Causal modeling. *Sage University paper series on quantitative applications in the social sciences* (Series No. 07003). Beverly Hills, CA: Sage.

**Association of Internet Researchers. (2012).** Ethical decision-making and internet research: Recommendations from the AoIR Ethics Committee. Retrieved from http://aoir.org/reports/ethics2.pdf

**Ax, A. F. (1953).** The physiological differentiation between fear and anger in humans. *Psychosomatic Medicine, 15,* 432–442.

**Badia, P., & Abbott, B. B. (1984).** Preference for signaled over unsignaled shock schedules: Ruling out asymmetry and response fixation as factors. *Journal of the Experimental Analysis of Behavior, 41,* 45–52.

**Badia, P., & Culbertson, S. (1972).** The relative aversiveness of signalled vs. unsignalled escapable and inescapable shock. *Journal of the Experimental Analysis of Behavior, 17,* 463–471.

**Badia, P., & Runyon, R. P. (1982).** *Fundamentals of behavioral research.* Reading, MA: Addison-Wesley.

**Badia, P., Harsh, J., & Abbott, B. (1979).** Choosing between predictable and unpredictable shock conditions: Data and theory. *Psychological Bulletin, 86,* 1107–1131.

**Bakeman, R., & Gottman, J. M. (1997).** *Observing interaction: An introduction to sequential analysis* (2nd ed.). Cambridge, England: Cambridge University Press.

**Baker, M. (2011).** Inside the minds of mice and men. *Nature, 475,* 123–128.

**Bartneck, C., Duenser, A., Moltchanova, E., & Zawieska, K. (2015).** Comparing the similarity of responses received from studies in Amazon's Mechanical Turk to studies conducted online and with direct recruitment. *PLOS ONE, 10,* 1–23. doi:10.1371/journal.pone.0121595

**Baumans, V. (2004).** Use of animals in experimental research: An ethical dilemma? *Gene Therapy, 11,* S64–S66.

**Baumeister, R. F. (2015).** Recognizing and coping with our own prejudices: Fighting liberal bias without conservative input. *Behavioral and Brain Sciences, 38,* 15–16. doi:10.1017/S0140525X14001423, e132

**Baumrind, D. (1964).** Some thoughts on the ethics of research: After reading Milgram's "Behavioral study of obedience." *American Psychologist, 26,* 887–896.

**Baumrind, D. (1985).** Research using intentional deception: Ethical issues revisited. *American Psychologist, 40,* 165–174.

**Bell, R. (1992).** *Impure science: Fraud, compromise and political influence in scientific research.* New York, NY: Wiley.

**Belmont Report. (1979).** Ethical principles and guidelines for the protection of human subjects of research. Retrieved from http://www.hhs.gov/ohrp/human-subjects/guidance/belmont.htm#xbasic

**Bennett, S., & Bowers, D. (1976).** *An introduction to multivariate techniques for social and behavioral sciences.* New York, NY: Wiley.

**Berg, B. L. (2009).** *Qualitative research methods for the social sciences* (7th ed.). Boston, MA: Allyn and Bacon.

**Bernstein, D. M., Laney, C., Morris, E. K., & Loftus, E. F. (2005).** False memories about food can lead to food avoidance. *Social Cognition, 23,* 11–34.

**Bethell, C., Fiorillo, J., Lansky, D., Hendryx, M., & Knickman, J. (2004).** Online consumer surveys as a methodology for assessing the quality of the United States health care system. *Journal of Medical Internet Research, 6*(1). Retrieved from http://www.jmir.org/2004/

**Blatchley, B., & O'Brien, K. R. (2007).** Deceiving the participant: Are we creating the reputational spillover effect? *North American Journal of Psychology, 9,* 519–534.

**Block, G. (2003).** The moral reasoning of believers in animal rights. *Society and Animals, 11,* 167–180.

**Bode, N. W., & Codling, E. A. (2013).** Human exit route choice in virtual crowd evacuations. *Animal Behaviour, 86,* 347–358. doi:10.1016/j.anbehav.2013.05.025

**Bolt, M., & Myers, D. G. (1983).** *Teacher's resource and test manual to accompany social psychology.* New York, NY: McGraw-Hill.

**Bordens, K. S. (1984).** The effects of likelihood of conviction, threatened punishment, and assumed role on mock plea bargain decisions. *Basic and Applied Social Psychology, 5,* 59–74.

**Bordens, K. S., & Horowitz, I. A. (1986).** Prejudicial joinder of multiple offenses: The relative effects of cognitive processing and criminal schemata. *Basic and Applied Social Psychology, 7,* 243–258.

**Bornmann, L., & Daniel, H-D. (2009).** Reviewer and editor bias in journal peer review: An investigation of manuscript refereeing at Angewandte Chemie International Edition. *Research Evaluation, 18,* 262–272.

Borsuk, R. M., Aarsen, L. W., Budden, A. E., Koricheva, J., Leimu, R., Tregenza, T., & Lortie, C. J. (2009). To name or not to name: The effect of changing author gender on peer review. *BioScience, 59,* 985–989. doi: 10.1525/bio.2009.59.11.10

Bosnjak, M., Neubarth, W., Couper, M. P., Bandilla, W., & Kaczmirek, L. (2008). Prenotification in Web-based access panel surveys: The influence of mobile text messaging versus e-mail on response rates and sample composition. *Social Science Computer Review, 26,* 213–222.

Boynton, M. H., Portnoy, D. B., & Johnson, B. T. (2013). Exploring the ethics and psychological impact of deception in psychological research. *IRB: Ethics & Human Research, 35,* 7–13.

Boynton, P. (2003). "I'm just a girl who can't say no"?: Women, consent, and sex research. *Journal of Sex and Marital Therapy, 29,* 23–32.

Braithwaite, R. B. (1953). *Scientific explanation.* New York, NY: Harper & Row.

Bray, J. H., & Maxwell, S. E. (1982). Analyzing and interpreting significant MANOVAs. *Review of Educational Research, 52,* 340–367.

Brick, J. M., Williams, D., & Montaquila, J. M. (2011). Address-based sampling for subpopulation surveys. *Public Opinion Quarterly, 75,* 409–428. doi:10.1093/poq/nfr023

Broad, W., & Wade, N. (1983). *Betrayers of the truth.* New York, NY: Simon & Schuster.

Broca, P. P. (1861). Loss of speech, chronic softening and partial destruction of the anterior left lobe of the brain. Retrieved from http://psychclassics.yorku.ca/Broca/perte-e.htm

Brody, J. L., Gluck, J. P., & Aragon, A. S. (2000). Participants' understanding of the process of psychological research: Debriefing. *Ethics and Behavior, 10,* 13–25.

Brown, S. R. (1996). Q methodology and qualitative research. *Qualitative Health Research, 6,* 561–567. Retrieved from http://www.rz.unibw-muenchen.de/~p41bsmk/qmethod/srbqhc.htm

Bulté, I., & Onghena, P. (2011). When the truth hits you between the eyes: A software tool for the visual analysis of single-case experimental data. *Methodology, 8,* 104–114. doi:10.1027/1614-2241/a000042

Butler, B. E., & Petrulis, J. (1999). Some further observations concerning Cyril Burt. *British Journal of Psychology, 90,* 155–160.

Byington, K. W., & Schwebel, D. C. (2013). Effects of mobile internet use on college student pedestrian injury risk. *Accident Analysis and Prevention, 51,* 78–83. doi:10.1016/j.aap.2012.11.001

Calif, M E., Mooney, R., & Cohn, D. (2004). Bottom-up relational learning of pattern matching rules for information extraction. *Journal of Machine Learning Research, 4,* 177–210. doi:10.1162/153244304322972685

Callahan, C. A., Hojat, M., & Gonnella, J. S. (2007). Volunteer bias in medical education research: An empirical study of over three decades of longitudinal data. *Medical Education, 41,* 746–753.

Callaway, E. (2011). Report finds massive fraud at Dutch universities. *Nature, 479*(7371), 15. doi:10.1038/479015a

Cameron, L., & Rutland, A. (2006). Extended contact through story reading in school: Reducing children's prejudice toward the disabled. *Journal of Social Issues, 62,* 469–488.

Campbell, D. T. (1969). Prospective: Artifact and control. In R. Rosenthal & R. L. Rosnow (Eds.), *Artifact in behavioral research* (pp. 351–382). New York, NY: Academic Press.

Campbell, D. T., & Stanley, J. C. (1963). *Experimental and quasi-experimental designs for research.* Chicago, NY: Rand McNally.

Carnahan, T., & McFarland, S. (2007). Revisiting the Stanford prison experiment: Could participant self-selection have led to the cruelty? *Personality and Social Psychology Bulletin, 33,* 603–614.

Carroll, R. T. (2006). Pseudoscience. Retrieved from http://skepdic.com/pseudosc.html

Cate, O., Brewster, D., Cruess, R., Calman, K., Rogers, W., Supe, A., & Gruppen, L. (2013). Research fraud and its combat: What can a journal do? *Medical Education, 47,* 638–640. doi:10.1111/medu.12197

Ceci, S. J., Bruck, M., & Loftus, E. F. (1998). On the ethics of memory implantation research. *Applied Cognitive Psychology, 12,* 230–240.

Chandler, J., Mueller, P., & Paolacci, G. (2014). Nonnaïveté among Amazon Mechanical Turk workers: Consequences and solutions for behavioral researchers. *Behavior Research Methods, 46,* 112–130. doi:10.3758/s13428-013-0365-7

Chang, D. F., & Sue, S. (2003). The effects of race and problem type on teachers' assessments of student behavior. *Journal of Consulting and Clinical Psychology, 71,* 235–242.

Chassan, J. B. (1967). *Research design in clinical psychology and psychiatry.* New York, NY: Appleton-Century-Crofts.

Chomsky, N. (1965). *Aspects of a theory of syntax.* Cambridge, MA: MIT Press.

Church, A. H. (1993). Estimating the effects of incentives on mail survey return rates: A meta-analysis. *Public Opinion Quarterly, 57,* 62–79.

Cialdini, R. B. (1994). A full-cycle approach to social psychology. In G. G. Brannigan & M. R. Merrens (Eds.), *The social psychologists: Research adventures* (pp. 52–72). New York, NY: McGraw-Hill.

Coe, R. (2002, September). *It's the effect size, stupid: What effect size is and why it's important.* Paper presented at the meeting of the British Educational Research Association, Exeter, England.

Cohen, J. (1988). *Statistical power analysis for the behavioral sciences* (2nd ed.). Hillsdale, NJ: Erlbaum.

Cohen, J. M., Bankert, E., & Cooper, J. A. (2005). History and ethics. Retrieved from http://www.citiprogram.org/members/courseandexam/moduletext.asp? strKey ID=0332B55E-959E-49B2-A091-4B344164DA45-1045638

Cohen, R. J., Swerdlik, M. E., & Sturman, E. D. (2013). *Psychological testing and assessment: An introduction to tests and measures* (9th ed.). Boston, MA: McGraw-Hill.

Coker, R. (2007). Distinguishing science from pseudoscience. Retrieved from http://web2.ph.utexas.edu/~coker2/index.files/distinguish.htm

Conrad, E., & Maul, T. (1981). *Introduction to experimental psychology.* New York, NY: Wiley.

Cooper, H. M., & Rosenthal, R. (1980). Statistical versus traditional methods for summarizing research findings. *Psychological Bulletin, 87,* 442–449.

Cooper, M. L. (2009). Problems, pitfalls, and promise in the peer-review process: Commentary on Trafimow & Rice (2009). *Perspectives on Psychological Science, 4,* 84–90. doi:10.1111/j.1745-6924.2009.01109.x

Cooperman, E. (1980). Voluntary subjects' participation in research: Cognitive style as a possible biasing factor. *Perceptual and Motor Skills, 50,* 542.

Cornell University Library. (2015). Distinguishing scholarly journals from other periodicals. Retrieved from http://olinuris.library.cornell.edu/content/distinguishing-scholarly-journals-other-periodicals

Correll, J., Park, B., Judd, C. M., & Wittenbrink, B. (2002). The police officer's dilemma: Using ethnicity to disambiguate potentially threatening individuals. *Journal of Personality & Social Psychology, 83,* 1314–1329. doi:10.1037//0022-3514.83.6.1314

Crane, D. (1967). The gatekeepers of science: Some factors affecting the selection of articles for scientific journals. *American Sociologist, 32,* 195–201.

Crano, W. D., & Brewer, M. B. (1986). *Principles and methods of social research.* Boston, MA: Allyn and Bacon.

Cressy, D. (2011). Animal research: Battle scars. *Nature, 470*(7335), 452–453. doi:10.1038/470452a

Crews, F. (1980). *The Random House handbook* (3rd ed.). New York, NY: Random House.

Crump, M. C., McDonnell, J. V., & Gureckis, T. M. (2013). Evaluating Amazon's Mechanical Turk as a tool for experimental behavioral research. *PLOS ONE, 8,* 1–18. doi:10.1371/journal.pone.0057410

Dal Grande, E., Chittleborough, C. R., Campostrini, S., Dollard, M., & Taylor, A. W. (2016). Pre-survey text messages (SMS) improve participation rate in an Australian mobile telephone survey: An experimental study. *PLOS ONE, 11,* 1–10. doi:10.1371/journal.pone.0150231

Dattalo, P. (2008). *Determining sample size: Balancing power, precision, and practicality.* Oxford, England: Oxford University Press.

Davidson, B., Worall, L., & Hickson, L. (2003). Identifying communication activities of older people with aphasia: Evidence from naturalistic observation. *Aphasiology, 17,* 243–264.

Davidson, P. R., & Parker, K. C. H. (2001). Eye movement desensitization and reprocessing (EMDR): A meta-analysis. *Journal of Consulting and Clinical Psychology, 69,* 216–316.

Davis, A. J. (1984). Sex-differentiated bias in nonsexist picture books. *Sex Roles: A Journal of Research, 11,* 1–16.

Davis, M. H., Mitchell, K.V., Hall, J. A., Lothert, J., Snapp, T., & Meyer, M. (1999). Empathy, expectations, and situational preferences: Personality influences on the decision to participate in volunteer helping behaviors. *Journal of Personality, 67,* 469–503.

De Beuckelear A., & Lievens, F. (2009). Measurement equivalence of paper-and-pencil and Internet organisational surveys: A large scale examination in 16 countries. *Applied Psychology: An International Review, 58,* 336–361. doi:10.1111/j.1464-0597.2008.00350.x

DeSantis, A. D. (2003). A couple of White guys sitting around talking: The collective rationalization of cigar smokers. *Journal of Contemporary Ethnology, 32,* 432–466.

Dillman, D. A. (2000). *Mail and Internet surveys: The tailored design method* (2nd ed.). New York, NY: Wiley.

Dillman, D. A., Christian, L. M., & Smyth, J. D. (2014). *Internet, phone, mail, and mixed-mode surveys: The tailored design method* (4th ed.). New York, NY: John Wiley and Sons.

Dillman, D., & Messer, B. L. (2010). Mixed-mode surveys. In P. V. Mardsen & J. D. Wright (Eds.). *Handbook of survey research* (2nd ed.) (pp. 551–574). Bingley, United Kingdom: Emerald Group Publishing Ltd.

DiNitto, D. M., Busch-Armendariz, N. B., Bender, K., Woo, H., Tackett-Gibson, M., & Dyer, J. (2009). Testing telephone and web surveys for studying men's sexual assault penetration behaviors. *Journal of Interpersonal Violence, 23,* 1483–1493. doi: 10.1177/0886260508314341

Drews, F. A., Pasupathi, M., & Strayer, D. L. (2008). Passenger and cell conversations in simulated driving. *Journal of Experimental Psychology: Applied, 14,* 392–400. doi: 10.1037/a0013119

Duarte, J. L., Crawford, J. T., Stern, C., Haidt, J., Jussim, L., & Tetlock, P. E. (2014). Political diversity will improve social psychological science. *Behavioral and Brain Sciences, 38.* doi:10.1017/S0140525X14000430

Dutch News. (2012). Five questions about: The Diederik Stapel affair. Retrieved from http://www.dutchnews.nl/features/2011/11/five_questions_about_the_diede.php

Ebbinghaus, H. E. (1964). *Memory: A contribution to experimental psychology.* New York, NY: Dover. (Original work published 1885.)

Edwards, A. L. (1953). *Techniques of attitude scale construction.* New York, NY: Appleton-Century-Crofts.

Edwards, A. L. (1985). *Experimental design in psychological research* (5th ed.). New York, NY: Harper & Row.

Eggerston, L. (2010). *Lancet* retracts 12-year-old article linking autism to MMR vaccines. *CMAJ: Canadian Medical Association, 182,* E199–200.

Ellis, C. (1993). "There are survivors": Telling a story of sudden death. *Sociological Quarterly, 34,* 711–730.

Enochson, K., & Culbertson, J. (2015). Collecting psycholinguistic response time data using Amazon Mechanical Turk. *PLOS ONE, 10,* 1–17. doi:10.1371/journal.pone.0116946

Enserink, M. (2012). Fraud-detection tool could shake up psychology. *Science, 337*(6090), 21–22.

Epley, N., & Huff, C. (1998). Suspicion, affective response, and educational benefit as a result of deception in psychology research. *Personality and Social Psychology Bulletin, 24,* 759–768.

Ethical Research Involving Children (ERIC) Project. (2013). Ethical research involving children. Retrieved from http://childethics.com/wp-content/uploads/2013/10/ERIC-compendium-approved-digital-web.pdf

Fancher, R. E. (1979). *Pioneers of psychology.* New York, NY: Norton.

Fancher, R. E. (1985). *The intelligence men: Makers of the IQ controversy.* New York, NY: Norton.

Ferguson, A. (2012). Revenge of the sociologists: The perils of politically incorrect academic research. *The Weekly Standard, 17*(43), 24–28.

Ferreira-Valente, M. A., Pais-Ribeiro, J. L., & Jensen, M. P. (2011). Validity of four pain intensity rating scales. *Pain, 152,* 2399–2404. doi:10.1016/j.pain.2011.07.005

Festinger, L. (1957). *A theory of cognitive dissonance.* Stanford, CA: Stanford University Press.

Fischer, H., Anderson, J. L. R., Furmark, T., Wik, G., & Fredrikson, M. (2002). Right-sided human prefrontal brain activation during acquisition of conditioned fear. *Emotion, 2,* 233–241.

Fisher, W. W., Kelley, M. E., & Lomas, J. E. (2003). Visual aids and structured criteria for improving visual inspection and interpretation of single-case designs. *Journal of Applied Behavior Analysis, 36,* 387–406.

**Fiske, D. W., & Fogg, L. (1990).** But the reviewers are making different criticisms of my paper! *American Psychologist, 45,* 591–598.

**Fiske, S. T. (2009).** Institutional review boards: From bane to benefit. *Perspectives on Psychological Science, 4,* 30–31. doi:10.1111/j.1745-6924.2009.01085.x

**Fleming, C., & Bowden, M. (2009).** Web-based surveys as an alternative to traditional mail methods. *Journal of Environmental Management, 90,* 284–292. doi:10.1016/j.jenvman.2007.09.011

**Forscher, B. K. (1963).** Chaos in the brickyard. *Science, 42*(3590), 339. doi:10.1126/science.142.3590.339.

**Foundation for Biomedical Research. (2005).** Poll shows a majority of Americans favor animal research. Retrieved from http://www.fbresearch.org/Journalists/Releases/Polls/HartPoll_4_15_05.htm

**Freedman, J. L. (1969).** Role playing: Psychology by consensus. *Journal of Personality and Social Psychology, 13,* 107–114.

**French-Lazovik, G., & Gibson, C. L. (1984).** Effects of verbally labeled anchor points on the distributional parameters of rating measures. *Applied Psychological Measurement, 8,* 49–57. doi:10.1177/014662168400800106

**Fry, D. P. (1992).** "Respect for the rights of others is peace": Learning aggression versus non-aggression among the Zapotec. *American Anthropologist, 94,* 621–639.

**Gabriel, K. I., Rutledge, B. H., & Barkley, C. L. (2012).** Attitudes on animal research predict acceptance of genetic modification technologies by university undergraduates. *Society & Animals, 20,* 381–400. doi:10.1163/15685 306-12341261

**Gaither, G. A., Sellbom, M., & Meier, B. P. (2003).** The effect of stimulus content on volunteering for sexual interest research among college students. *Journal of Sex Research, 40,* 240–248.

**Gamson, W. A., Fireman, B., & Rytina, S. (1982).** *Encounters with unjust authority.* Homewood, IL: Dorsey Press.

**Garcia, J., & Koelling, R. A. (1966).** Relation of cue to consequences in avoidance learning. *Psychonomic Science, 4,* 123–124.

**Garson, D. G. (2006).** Structural equation modeling. Retrieved from http://www2.chass.ncsu.edu/garson/pa765/structur.htm

**GazetteOnline. (2005).** Skorton testifies in D.C. about lab vandalism. Retrieved from http://www.gazetteonline.com/2005/05/18/Home/News/skortontestimony.prt

**Geggie, D. (2001).** A survey of newly appointed consultants' attitudes towards fraud in research. *Journal of Medical Ethics, 27,* 344–346.

**Gibbon, J. (1977).** Scalar expectancy theory and Weber's law in animal timing. *Psychological Review, 84,* 279–325.

**Gibbs, A., & Lawson, A. E. (1992).** The nature of scientific thinking as reflected by the work of biologists and by biology textbooks. *The American Biology Teacher, 54,* 137–152.

**Glass, G. V. (1978).** In defense of generalization. *The Behavioral and Brain Sciences, 1*(3), 394–395.

**Godlee, F., Smith, J., & Marcovitch, H. (2011, January 8).** Wakefield's article linking MMR vaccine and autism was fraudulent. *BMJ: British Medical Journal, 342,* 64–66. doi:10.1136/bmj.c7452

**Gold, P. E. (1987).** Sweet memories. *American Scientist, 75,* 151–155.

**Goldiamond, I. (1965).** Stuttering and fluency as manipulable operant response classes. In L. Krasner & L. P. Ullman (Eds.), *Research in behavior modification* (pp. 106–156). New York, NY: Holt, Rinehart & Winston.

**Goldstein, I. (2003).** Sexual dysfunction after hysterectomy. Retrieved from http://www.bumc.bu.edu/sexualmedicine/informationsessions/sexual-dysfunction-after-hysterectomy/

**Goldstein, J. H., Rosnow, R. L., Goodstadt, B. E., & Suls, J. E. (1972).** The good subject in verbal operant conditioning research. *Journal of Experimental Research in Personality, 28,* 29–33.

**Gonzales, J. E., & Cunningham, C. A. (2015).** The promise of pre-registration in psychological research. *Psychological Science Agenda, 29*(8). Retrieved from http://www.apa.org/science/about/psa/2015/08/pre-registration.aspx

**Gottman, J. M., & Roy, A. K. (2008).** *Sequential analysis: A guide for behavioral researchers.* New York, NY: Cambridge University Press.

**Gowin, J. L., Swann, A. C., Moeller, F. G., & Lane, S. D. (2010).** Zolmitriptan and human aggression: Interaction with alcohol. *Psychopharmacology, 210,* 521–531. doi:10.1007/s00213-010-1851-6

Gravetter, F. J., & Wallnau, L. B. (2017). *Statistics for the behavioral sciences* (10th ed.). Belmont, CA: Cengage Learning.

Greenberg, B. S. (1980). *Life on television: Current analyses of U.S. TV drama.* Norwood, NJ: Ablex.

Greene, E., & Loftus, E. F. (1984). What's in the news? The influence of well-publicized news events on psychological research and courtroom trials. *Basic and Applied Social Psychology, 5,* 211–221.

Greenwald, A. G., McGhee, D. E., & Schwartz, J. L. K. (1998). Measuring individual differences in implicit cognition: The implicit association test. *Journal of Personality and Social Psychology, 74,* 1464–1480.

Grice, G. R. (1966). Dependence of empirical laws upon the source of experimental variation. *Psychological Bulletin, 66,* 488–498.

Griggs, R. A. (2014). The continuing saga of Little Albert in introductory psychology textbooks. *Teaching of Psychology, 41,* 309–317. doi:10.1177/0098628314549702

Grod, O. N., Budden, A. E., Tregenza, T., Koricheva, J., Leimu, R., Aarsen, L. W., & Lortie, C. J. (2008). Systematic variation in reviewer practice according to country and gender in the field of ecology and evolution. *PLOS ONE, 3,* e3202. doi:10.1371/journal.pone.0003202

Guéguen, N. (2015). High heels increase women's attractiveness. *Archives of Sexual Behavior, 44,* 2227–2235. doi:10.1007/s10508-014-0422-z

Gundersen, D. A., Peters, K. R., Conner, A., Dayton, J., & Delnevo, C. D. (2014). Stability of sample quality for a national random-digit dialing cellular phone survey of young adults. *American Journal of Epidemiology, 180,* 1047–1049. doi:aje/kwu271

Hall, D. (1979). *Writing well.* Boston, MA: Little, Brown.

Hall, R. V., Lund, D., & Jackson, D. (1968). Effects of teacher attention on study behavior. *Journal of Applied Behavior Analysis, 1,* 1–12.

Halpern, S. D., Kohn, R., Dornbrand-Lo, A., Metkus, T., Asch, D. A., & Volpp, K. G. (2011). Lottery-based versus fixed incentives to increase clinicians' response to surveys. *Health Services Research, 46,* 1663–1674. doi:10.1111/j.1475-6773.2011.01264.x

Hamby, S., Sugarman, D. B., & Boney-McCoy, S. (2006). Does questionnaire format impact reported partner violence rates? An experimental study. *Violence and Victims, 21,* 507–518.

Hamilton, D. K., & Stichler, J. F. (2015). Institutional Review Boards and peer-reviewed publication. *Health Environments Research & Design Journal, 8,* 81–84. doi:10.1177/1937586714567647

Haney, C., Banks, C., & Zimbardo, P. (1973). Interpersonal dynamics in a simulated prison. *International Journal of Criminology and Penology, 1,* 69–87.

Harari, H., Harari, O., & White, R. V. (1985). The reaction to rape by American male by-standers. *Journal of Social Psychology, 125,* 653–658.

Hartman, D. P., & Hall, R. V. (1976). The changing criterion design. *Journal of Applied Behavior Analysis, 9,* 527–532.

Hehman, E., Graber, E. C., Hoffman, L. H., & Gaertner, S. (2012). Warmth and competence: A content analysis of photographs depicting American presidents. *Psychology of Popular Media Culture, 1,* 46–52. doi:10.1037/a0026513

Helmstetter, F. J., & Fanselow, M. S. (1987). Strain differences in reversal of conditional analgesia by opioid antagonists. *Behavioral Neuroscience, 101,* 735–737.

Hempel, C. G. (1966). *Philosophy of natural science.* Englewood Cliffs, NJ: Prentice Hall.

Herrmann, D., & Yoder, C. (1998). The potential effects of the implanted memory paradigm on child subjects. *Applied Cognitive Psychology, 12,* 198–206.

Herrnstein, R. J. (1970). On the law of effect. *Journal of the Experimental Analysis of Behavior, 13,* 243–266.

Herrnstein, R. J., & Prelec, D. (1992). Melioration. In G. Loewenstein & J. Elster (Eds.), *Choice over time* (pp. 235–263). New York, NY: Russell Sage.

Hershberger, S. L., Marcoulides, G. A., & Parramore, M. M. (2003). Structural equation modeling: An introduction. In B. H. Pagesek, A. Tomer, & A. von Eye (Eds.), *Structural equation modeling* (pp. 3–41). New York, NY: Cambridge University Press. Retrieved from http://www.loc.gov/catdir/samples/cam033/2002035067.pdf

Hertwig, R., & Ortmann, A. (2008). Deception in experiments: Revisiting the arguments in its defense. *Ethics and Behavior, 18,* 59–92. doi:10.1080/10508420701712990

Hess, D. W., Marwitz, J., & Kreutzer, J. (2003). Neuropsychological impairments after spinal cord injury: A comparative study with mild traumatic brain injury. *Rehabilitation Psychology, 48*, 151–156.

Hicks, A. L., Martin Ginnis, K. A., Pelletier, C. A., Ditor, D. S., Foulon, B., & Wolfe, D. L. (2011). The effects of exercise training on physical capacity, strength, body composition and functional performance among adults with spinal cord injury: A systematic review. *Spinal Cord, 49*, 1103–1127. doi:10.1038/sc.2011.62

Higbee, K. L., Millard, R. J., & Folkman, J. R. (1982). Social psychology research during the 1970s: Predominance of experimentation on college students. *Personality and Social Psychology Bulletin, 8*, 182–183.

Hite, S. (1976). *The Hite report: A nationwide study on female sexuality.* New York, NY: Macmillan.

Hite, S. (1983). *The Hite report on male sexuality.* New York, NY: Ballantine Books.

Hojat, M., Gonnella, J. S., & Caelleigh, A. S. (2003). Impartial judgment by the "gatekeepers" of science: Fallibility and accountability in the peer review process. *Advances in Health Sciences Education, 8*, 75–96.

Hollingdale, J., & Greitemeyer, T. (2014). The effect of online violent video games on levels of aggression. *PLOS ONE, 9*, 1–5. doi:10.1371/journal.pone.0111790

Holmes, D. S. (1976a). Debriefing after psychological experiments, I: Effectiveness of postdeception dehoaxing. *American Psychologist, 31*, 858–867.

Holmes, D. S. (1976b). Debriefing after psychological experiments, II: Effectiveness of postdeception desensitizing. *American Psychologist, 31*, 868–875.

Holsti, O. R. (1969). *Content analysis for the social sciences and humanities.* Reading, MA: Addison-Wesley.

Hooke, R. (1983). *How to tell the liars from the statisticians.* New York, NY: Dekker.

Horowitz, I. A. (1969). The effects of volunteering, fear arousal, and number of communications on attitude change. *Journal of Personality and Social Psychology, 11*, 34–37.

Horowitz, I. A. (1985). The effects of jury nullification instructions on verdicts and jury functioning in criminal trials. *Law and Human Behavior, 9*, 25–36.

Horowitz, I. A., & Bordens, K. S. (1988). The effects of outlier presence, plaintiff population size, and aggregation of plaintiffs on simulated jury decisions. *Law and Human Behavior, 13*, 209–229.

Horowitz, I. A., & Rothschild, B. H. (1970). Conformity as a function of deception and role playing. *Journal of Personality and Social Psychology, 14*, 224–226.

Horowitz, I. A., Bordens, K. S., & Feldman, M. S. (1980). A comparison of verdicts obtained in severed and joined criminal trials. *Journal of Applied Social Psychology, 10*, 444–456.

Howard, S., & Hughes, B. M. (2008). Expectancies, not aroma, explain impact of lavender aromatherapy on psychophysiological indices of relaxation in young healthy women. *British Journal of Health Psychology, 13*, 603–617. doi:10.1348/135910707X238734

Huang, H-M. (2005). Do print and Web surveys provide the same results? *Computers in Human Behavior, 22*, 334–350.

Huck, S. W., & Sandler, H. M. (1979). *Rival hypotheses: Alternative explanations of data based conclusions.* New York, NY: Harper & Row.

Hudson, J. M., & Bruckman, A. (2004). "Go away": Participant objections to being studied and the ethics of chatroom research. *The Information Society, 20*, 127–139.

Huefner, J. C., & Ringle, J. L. (2012). Examination of negative peer contagion in a residential care setting. *Journal of Child Family Studies, 21*, 807–815. doi:10.1007/s10826-011-9540-6

Hunter, J. E. (1987). Multiple dependent variables in program evaluation. In M. M. Mark & R. L. Shotland (Eds.), *Multiple methods.* San Francisco, CA: Jossey-Bass.

Hunter, J. E., & Gerbing, D. W. (1982). Unidimensional measurement, second-order factor analysis and causal models. *Research in Organizational Behavior, 4*, 267–320.

Hunter, J. E., & Schmidt, F. L. (2004). *Methods of meta-analysis: Correcting error and bias in research findings* (2nd ed.). Thousand Oaks, CA: Sage Publications.

Inbar, Y., & Lammers, J. (2012). Political diversity in Social and Personality Psychology. *Perspectives on Psychological Science, 7*, 496–503. doi:10.1177/1745691612448792

**Innacchione, V. G. (2011).** Research synthesis: The changing role of address-based sampling in survey research. *Public Opinion Quarterly, 75,* 556–575. doi:10.1093/poq/nfr017

**Institute for Scientific Information. (1988).** SSCI journal citation reports: A bibliometric analysis of social science journals in the ISI data base. *Social Sciences Citation Index, 6.*

**Ipsos MORI (2012).** Views on the use of animals in scientific research. Retrieved from http://www.ipsos-mori.com/DownloadPublication/1512_sri-BIS_animal_research_2012_final_report_September_published_final.pdf

**IRB Advisor (2011, January 1).** Facebook research poses unique ethical concerns. Retrieved from http://go.galegroup.com/ps/i.do?id=GALE%7CA246123298&v=2.1&u=iulib_fw&it=r&p=HRCA&sw=w

**James, J. M., & Bolstein, R. (1992).** Large monetary incentives and their effect on mail survey response rates. *Public Opinion Quarterly, 56,* 442–453.

**James, L., Vila, B., & Daratha, K. (2013).** Results from experimental trials testing participant responses to White, Hispanic, and Black suspects in high-fidelity deadly force judgment and decision-making simulations. *Journal of Experimental Criminology, 9,* 189–212.

**Janis, I., & Mann, L. (1965).** Effectiveness of emotional role playing in modifying smoking habits and attitudes. *Journal of Experimental Research in Personality, 1,* 84–90.

**Jones, R. A. (1994).** The ethics of research in cyberspace. *Internet Research, 4,* 30–35.

**Joynson, R. B. (1989).** *The Burt affair.* London, England: Routledge.

**Kalichman, M., & Friedman, P. (1992).** A pilot study of biomedical trainees' perceptions concerning research ethics. *Academic Medicine, 67,* 769–775.

**Kanuk, L., & Berenson, C. (1975).** Mail surveys and response rates: A literature review. *Journal of Marketing Research, 12,* 440–453.

**Katz, J. (1972).** *Experimentation with human beings.* New York, NY: Russell Sage Foundation.

**Kazdin, A. E. (1976).** Statistical analyses for single-case experimental designs. In M. Hersen & D. H. Barlow (Eds.), *Single-case experimental designs: Strategies for studying behavior change* (pp. 265–316). New York, NY: Pergamon Press.

**Kazdin, A. E. (1978).** Methodological and interpretive problems of single-case experimental designs. *Journal of Consulting and Clinical Psychology, 46,* 629–642.

**Keeter, S., Kennedy, C., Dimock, M., Best, J., & Craighill, P. (2006).** Gauging the impact of growing nonresponse on estimates from a National RDD telephone survey. *Public Opinion Quarterly, 70,* 759–779. doi:10.1093/poq/nfl035

**Keller, H. B., & Lee, S. (2003).** Ethical issues surrounding human participants research using the Internet. *Ethics & Behavior, 13,* 211–219.

**Kelly, G. (1963).** *A theory of personality: The psychology of personal constructs.* New York, NY: Norton.

**Kelman, H. C. (1967).** The use of human subjects: The problem of deception in social psychological experiments. *Psychological Bulletin, 67,* 1–11.

**Keppel, G. (1973).** *Design and analysis: A researcher's handbook.* Englewood Cliffs, NJ: Prentice Hall.

**Keppel, G. (1982).** *Design and analysis: A researcher's handbook* (2nd ed.). Englewood Cliffs, NJ: Prentice Hall.

**Keusch, F. (2012).** How to increase response rates in list-based web survey samples. *Social Science Computer Review, 30,* 380–388. doi:10.1177/0984439311409709

**Key, W. B. (1973).** *Subliminal seduction.* New York, NY: Signet.

**Kimmel, A. J., Smith, C. N., & Klein, J. G. (2011).** Ethical decision making and research deception in the behavioral sciences: An application of social contract theory. *Ethics & Behavior, 21,* 222–251. doi:10.1080/10508422.2011.570166

**Kirk, R. E. (1996).** Practical significance: A concept whose time has come. *Educational and Psychological Measurement, 56,* 746–759.

**Kish, L. (1965).** *Survey sampling.* New York, NY: Wiley.

**Knäuper, B., Stich, C., Yugo, M., & Tate, C. (2008).** Stretched rating scales cause guided responding. *Health Communication, 23,* 253–258. doi:10.1080/10410230802056230

**Kowalski, R. M., Giumetti, G. W., Schroeder, A. N., & Lattanner, M. R. (2014).** Bullying in the digital age: A critical review and meta-analysis of cyberbullying research among youth. *Psychological Bulletin, 140,* 1073–1137. doi:10.1037/a0035618

Krantz, J. H., & Dalal, R. (2000). Validity of Web-based research. In M. H. Birnbaum (Ed.), *Psychological experiments on the Internet* (pp. 35–57). San Diego, CA: Academic Press.

Krippendorff, K. (2004). *Content analysis: An introduction to its methodology.* Thousand Oaks, CA: Sage.

Kruschke, J. K. (2013). Bayesian estimation supersedes the t test. *Journal of the Experimental Psychology: General, 142,* 573–603. doi:10.1037/a0029146

Kruschke, J. K. (2015). *Doing Bayesian data analysis* (2d ed.). Waltham, MA: Academic Press/Elsevier.

Kruse, C. R. (1999). Gender, views of nature, and support for animal rights. *Society and Animals, 7,* 179–198.

Kuhn, T. S. (1970). *The structure of scientific revolutions* (2nd ed.). Chicago, IL: University of Chicago Press.

Laguilles, J. S., Williams, E. A., & Saunders, D. B. (2011). Can lottery incentives boost Web survey response rates? Findings from four experiments. *Research in Higher Education, 52,* 537–553. doi:10.1007/s11162-010-9203-2

Lam, L. T., Cheng, Z., & Liu, X. (2013). Violent online games exposure and cyberbullying/victimization among adolescents. *Cyberpsychology, Behavior & Social Networking, 16,* 159–165. doi:10.1089/cyber.2012.0087

Lam, T. C. M., & Kolic, M. (2008). Effects of semantic incompatibility on rating response. *Applied Psychological Measurement, 32,* 248–260. doi:10.1177/0146621607301094

Landy, E., & Aronson, E. (1969). The influence of the character of the criminal and his victim on the decisions of simulated jurors. *Journal of Experimental Social Psychology, 5,* 141–152.

Latané, B. (1981). The psychology of social impact. *American Psychologist, 36,* 343–356.

Lavrakas, P. J. (2010). Telephone surveys. In P. M. Marsden & J. D. Wright (Eds.). *Handbook of survey research* (2nd ed.) (pp. 471–498). Bingley, United Kingdom: Emerald Group Publishing Ltd.

Lavrakas, P. J., Shuttles, C. D., Steeh, C., & Fienberg, H. (2007). The state of surveying

cell phone numbers in the United States: 2007 and beyond. *Public Opinion Quarterly, 71,* 840–854. doi:10.1093/poq/nfm054

Leaton, R. N., & Borszcz, G. S. (1985). Potentiated startle: Its relation to freezing and shock intensity in rats. *Journal of Experimental Psychology: Animal Behavior Processes, 11,* 421–428.

Lee, C. M., & Hunsley, J. (2015). Evidence-based practice: Separating science from pseudoscience. *Canadian Journal of Psychiatry, 60,* 534–540.

Leggett, G., Mead, C. D., & Charvat, W. (1978). *Prentice Hall handbook for writers* (7th ed.). Englewood Cliffs, NJ: Prentice Hall.

Levine, M. S. (1977). Canonical analysis and factor comparison. *Sage University paper series on quantitative applications in the social sciences* (Series No. 07-006). Beverly Hills, CA: Sage.

Lewis, J. E. (2008). Dream reports of animal rights activists. *Dreaming, 18,* 181–200. doi:10.1037/a0013393

Lilienfeld, S. O. (2005). The 10 commandments of helping students distinguish science from pseudoscience in psychology. *APS Observer, 18(9).* Retrieved from http://www.psychologicalscience.org/observer/the-10-commandments-of-helping-students-distinguish-science-from-pseudoscience-in-psychology#.WJUDy_krLIU

Lilienfeld, S. O. (2015). Introduction to special section on pseudoscience in psychiatry. *Canadian Journal of Psychiatry, 60,* 531–533.

Lilienfeld, S. O., Lynn, S. J., & Lohr, J. M. (2003). Science and pseudoscience in clinical psychology: Initial thoughts, reflections, and considerations. In S. O. Lilienfeld, S. J. Lynn, & J. M. Lohr (Eds.). *Science and pseudoscience in clinical psychology* (pp. 1–14). New York, NY: Guilford Press.

Lindsey, D. (1978). *The scientific publication system in social science.* San Francisco, CA: Jossey-Bass.

Link, M. W., & Mokdad, A. (2005). Effects of survey mode on self-reports of alcohol consumption: A comparison of mail, web, and telephone approaches. *Journal of Studies on Alcohol, 66,* 239–245.

Lomborg, S. (2013). Personal internet archives and ethics. *Research Ethics, 9,* 20–31. doi:10.1177/1747016112459450

Longino, H. E. (1990). *Science as social knowledge.* Princeton, NJ: Princeton University Press.

Lönnqvist, J-E., Paunonen, S., Verkaslo, M., Leikas, S., Tuulio-Henrikkson, A., & Lönnqvist, J. (2006). Personality characteristics of research volunteers. *European Journal of Personality, 21,* 1017–1030. doi:10.1002/per.655

Lord, F. M. (1953). On the statistical treatment of football numbers. *American Psychologist, 8,* 750–751.

Lorenz, K. (1950). The comparative method in studying innate behavior patterns. *Symposium of the Society for Experimental Biology, 4,* 221–268.

Lu, X., Battistuzzo, C. R., Zoghi, M., & Galea, M. P. (2015). Effects of training on upper limb function after cervical spinal cord injury: A systematic review. *Clinical Rehabilitation, 29,* 3–13. doi:10.1177/0269215514536411

Macaulay, D. (1979). *Motel of the mysteries.* Boston, MA: Houghton Mifflin.

Mahoney, M. J. (1977). Publication prejudices: An experimental study of confirmatory bias in the peer review system. *Cognitive Therapy and Research, 1,* 161–175.

Mandel, F. S., Weiner, M., Kaplan, S., Pelcovitz, D., & Labruna, V. (2000). An examination of bias in volunteer subject selection: Findings from an in-depth child abuse study. *Journal of Traumatic Stress, 13,* 77–88.

Manne, S., & Fatima, S. S. (2011). A novel approach for text categorization of unorganized data based with information extraction. *International Journal on Computer Science & Engineering, 3,* 2846–2854.

Manolov, R., Solanas, A., & Leiva, D. (2010). Comparing "visual" effect size indices for single-case designs. *Methodology, 6,* 49–58. doi:10.1027/1614-2241/a000006

Manolov, R., Solanas, A., Bulté, I., & Onghena P. (2010). Data-driven-specific robustness and power of randomization tests for ABAB designs. *The Journal of Experimental Education, 78,* 191–214. doi:10.1080/00220970903292827

Mans, G., & Stream, C. (2006). Relationship between news media coverage of medical research and academic medical centers and people volunteering for clinical trials. *Public Relations Review, 32,* 196–198.

Marcus, B., & Schütz, A. (2005). Who are the people reluctant to participate in research? Correlates of four different types of nonresponse as inferred from self- and observer ratings. *Journal of Personality, 73,* 959–964.

Markham, A., & Buchanan, E. (2012). Ethical decision-making and Internet research: Recommendations from the AoIR Working Committee *(Version 2.0). Retrieved from http://aoir.org/reports/ethics2.pdf*

Markowitz, D. M., & Hancock, J. T. (2014). Linguistic races of a scientific fraud: The case of Diederik Stapel. *PLOS ONE, 9,* 1–5. doi:10. 1371/journal.pone.0105937

Marsh, H. W., Bornmann, L., Mutz, R., Daniel, H-D., & O'Mara, A. (2009). Gender effects in the peer reviews of grant proposals: A comprehensive meta-analysis comparing traditional and multi-level approaches. *Review of Educational Research, 79,* 1290–1326. doi:10.3102/0034654309334143

Martin, A. L., & Katz, J. (2010). Inclusion of authorized deception in the informed consent process does not affect the magnitude of the placebo effect for experimentally induced pain. *Pain, 149,* 208–215. doi:10.1016/j.pain.2009.12.004

Matfield, M. (2002). Animal experimentation: The continuing debate. *Nature Reviews, 1,* 149–152.

Matyas, T. A., & Greenwood, K. M. (1990). Visual analysis of single-case time series: Effects of variability, serial dependence, and magnitude of intervention effects. *Journal of Applied Behavior Analysis, 23,* 341–351.

Mayo, C., & LaFrance, M. (1977). *Evaluating research in social psychology.* Monterey, CA: Brooks/Cole.

McFarland, C., Cheam, A., & Buehler, R. (2007). The perseverance effect in the debriefing paradigm: Replication and extension. *Journal of Experimental Social Psychology, 43,* 223–240.

McFarland, S. (1981). Effects of question order on survey responses. *Public Opinion Quarterly, 48,* 208–215.

McGraw, K. O., & Wong, S. P. (1996). Forming inferences about some intraclass correlation coefficients. *Psychological Methods, 1,* 30–46.

McNemar, Q. (1946). Opinion-attitude methodology. *Psychological Bulletin, 43,* 289–374.

Messer, B. L., & Dillman, D. A. (2011). Surveying the general public over the Internet using address-based sampling and mail contact procedures. *Public Opinion Quarterly, 75,* 429–457. doi:10.1093/poq/nfr021

Meystre, S. M., Savava, G. K., Kipper-Schuler, K. C., & Hurdle, J. F. (2008). Extracting information from textual documents in the electronic health record: A review of recent research. *Yearbook of Medical Informatics, 3,* 128–144.

Michael, R. T., Gagnon, J. H., Laumann, E. O., & Kolata, G. (1994). *Sex in America: A definitive survey.* Boston, MA: Little, Brown.

Milgram, S. (1963). Behavioral study of obedience. *Journal of Abnormal and Social Psychology, 67,* 371–378.

Milgram, S. (1974). *Obedience to authority.* New York, NY: Harper & Row.

Mitchell, G. (2012). Revisiting truth or triviality: The external validity of research in the psychological laboratory. *Psychological Science, 7,* 109–117. doi:10.1177/1745691143 2343

Mitchell, S. K. (1979). Interobserver agreement, reliability, and generalizability of data collected in observational studies. *Psychological Bulletin, 86,* 376–390.

Montee, B. B., Miltenberger, R. G., & Wittrock, D. (1995). An experimental analysis of facilitated communication. *Journal of Applied Behavior Analysis, 28,* 189–200.

Mook, D. G. (1983). In defense of external validity. *American Psychologist, 38,* 379–387.

Moore, D. S., & McCabe, G. P. (2015). *Introduction to the practice of statistics* (8th ed.). New York, NY: Freeman.

Morrison, R. S. (1990). Disreputable science: Definition and detection. *Journal of Advanced Nursing, 15,* 911–913. doi:10.1111/1365-26 48.ep8529161

Moser, C. A., & Kalton, G. (1972). *Survey methods in social investigation.* New York, NY: Basic Books.

Mosteller, F., & Tukey, J. W. (1977). *Data analysis and regression.* New York, NY: Addison-Wesley.

Mutz, R., Bornmann, L., & Daniel, H-D. (2012). Does gender matter in grant peer review? An empirical investigation using the example of the Austrian Science Fund. *Zeitschrift fur Psychologie, 220,* 121–129. doi:10.1027/2151-2604/a000103

Myers, D. (2008). *Social psychology* (9th ed.). New York, NY: McGraw-Hill.

Myers, D. G. (1999). *Social psychology* (6th ed.). New York, NY: McGraw-Hill.

National Research Council. (2011). *Guide for the care and use of laboratory animals* (8th ed.). Retrieved from http://grants.nih.gov/grants/olaw/Guide-for-the-Care-and-Use-of-Laboratory-Animals.pdf

Neisser, U. (1976). *Cognition and reality: Principles and implications for cognitive psychology.* San Francisco, CA: Freeman.

Nerb, J., & Spada, H. (2001). Evaluation of environmental problems: A coherence model of cognition and emotion. *Cognition and Emotion, 15,* 521–551.

Nickerson, R. S. (2000). Null hypothesis significance testing: A review of an old and continuing controversy. *Psychological Methods, 5,* 241–301. doi:10.1037//1082-989X.5.2.241

Nirenberg, T. D., Wincze, J. P., Bansal, S., Liepman, M. R., Engle-Friedman, M., & Begin, A. (1991). Volunteer bias in a study of male alcoholics' sexual behavior. *Archives of Sexual Behavior, 20,* 371–379.

O'Brien, R. G., & Kaiser, M. K. (1985). MANOVA method for analyzing repeated measures designs: An extensive primer. *Psychological Bulletin, 97,* 316–333.

Ockham's Razor (n.d.). Retrieved from http://www.2think.org/occams_razor.shtml

Oczak, M., & Niedźwieńska, A. (2007). Debriefing in deceptive research: A proposed new procedure. *Journal of Empirical Research on Research Ethics, 2,* 49–59. doi:10.1525/jer.2007.2.3.49

Oei, A., & Hartley, L. R. (2005). The effects of caffeine and expectancy on attention and memory. *Human Pharmacology, 20,* 193–202.

Office of Research Integrity. (n.d.). Whistleblower Bill of Rights. Retrieved from http://ori.hhs.gov/Whistleblower-Rights

Office of Research Integrity. (1995). Handling misconduct-whistleblowers. Retrieved from http://ori.hhs.gov/guidelines-whistleblowers

Office of Research Integrity. (2006). Case summaries. *ORI Newsletter, 14(2),* 11–11. Retrieved from http://ori.dhhs.gov/documents/newsletters/vol14_no2.pdf

Office of Research Integrity. (2013). Complainant. Retrieved from http://ori.hhs.gov/complainant

**Office of Research Integrity. (2016).** Frequently asked questions: What is research misconduct?. Retrieved from http://ori.hhs.gov/content/frequently-asked-questions#5

**Orbell, S., & Hagger, M. (2006).** Temporal framing and the decision to take part in type 2 diabetes screening: Effects of individual differences in consideration of future consequences on persuasion. *Health Psychology, 25,* 537–548.

**Oreskes, N. (2004).** The scientific consensus on climate change. *Science, 306*(5702), 1686. doi:10.1126/science.1103618.

**Ormandy, E. H., & Schuppli, C. A. (2014).** Public attitudes toward animal research: A review. *Animals, 4,* 391–408. doi:10.3390/ani4030391

**Ormandy, E. H., Schuppli, C. A., & Weary, D. M. (2013).** Public attitudes toward the use of animals in research: Effects of invasiveness, genetic modification and regulation. *Anthrozoös, 26,* 165–184. doi:10.2752/175303713X13636846944240

**Orne, M. T. (1962).** On the social psychology of the psychological experiment with particular reference to demand characteristics and their implications. *American Psychologist, 17,* 776–783.

**Ornstein, P. A., & Gordon, B. N. (1998).** Risk versus rewards of applied research with children: Comments on "The potential effects of the implanted memory paradigm on child participants" by Douglas Herrmann and Carol Yoder. *Applied Cognitive Psychology, 12,* 241–244.

**Padilla-Walker, L. M., Zamboanga, B. L., Thompson, R. A., & Schmersal, L. A. (2005).** Extra credit as incentive for voluntary research participation. *Teaching of Psychology, 32,* 150–153. doi:10.1207/s15328023top3203_2

**Paolacci, G., & Chandler, J. (2014).** Inside the Turk: Understanding Mechanical Turk as a participant pool. *Current Directions in Psychological Science, 23,* 184–188. doi:10.1177/0963721414531598

**Pagano, R. R. (2013).** *Understanding statistics in the behavioral sciences* (10th ed.). Belmont, CA: Wadsworth.

**Palya, W. L., Walter, D., Kessel, R., & Lucke, R. (1996).** Investigating behavioral dynamics with a fixed-time extinction schedule and linear analysis. *Journal of the Experimental Analysis of Behavior, 66,* 391–409.

**Pazouki, E., & Rahmati, M. (2009).** A novel multimedia data mining framework for information extraction of a soccer video stream. *Intelligent Data Analysis, 13,* 833–857. doi: 10.3233/IDA-2009-0395

**Peplau, L. A., & Conrad, E. (1989).** Beyond nonsexist research: The perils of feminist methods in psychology. *Psychology of Women Quarterly, 13,* 379–400.

**Peters, D. P., & Ceci, S. J. (1982).** Peer-review practices of psychological journals: The fate of published articles, submitted again. *Behavioral and Brain Sciences, 5,* 187–255.

**Peterson, L. R., & Peterson, M. J. (1959).** Short-term retention of individual verbal items. *Journal of Experimental Psychology, 58,* 193–198.

**Petrie, M. (1994).** Improved growth and survival of offspring of peacocks with more elaborate trains. *Nature, 371*(6498), 598–599. doi:10.1038/371598a0.

**Pew Research Center. (2009).** The Internet's role in campaign 2008. Retrieved from http://pewinternet.org/Reports/2009/6—The-Internets-Role-in-Campaign-2008.aspx

**Pew Research Center. (2012, September).** The state of the 2012 election—mobile politics. Retrieved from http://pewinternet.org/Reports/2012/Election-2012-Mobile.aspx

**Pew Research Center (2013).** Cell phone activities 2013. Retrieved from http://www.pewinternet.org/files/old-media//Files/Reports/2013/PIP_Cell%20Phone%20Activities%20May%202013.pdf

**Pew Research Center (2014).** Cell phones, social media and campaign 2014. Retrieved from http://www.pewinternet.org/2014/11/03/cell-phones-social-media-and-campaign-2014/

**Pfungst, Oskar. (1911).** *Clever Hans (the horse of Mr. von Osten): A contribution to experimental animal and human psychology* (Trans. C. L. Rahn). New York, NY: Henry Holt. (Originally published in German, 1907).

**Phillips K. J., Mudford O. C., Zeleny J. R., & Elliffe D. (2014),** Using calibration and interobserver agreement algorithms to assess the accuracy and precision of data from electronic and pen-and-paper continuous recording methods. *Behavioral Interventions, 29,* 315–330. doi:10.1002/bin.1395

**Piaget, J. (1952).** *The origins of intelligence in children.* New York, NY: Norton.

**Pittenger, D. J. (2003).** Internet research: An opportunity to revisit classic ethical problems in behavioral research. *Ethics and Behavior, 13,* 45–60.

Pittinger, D. J. (2002). Deception in research: Distinctions and solutions from the perspective of utilitarianism. *Ethics and Behavior, 12,* 117–142.

Platt, J. R. (1964). Strong inference. *Science, 146*(3642), 347–353.

Plous, S. (1996). Attitudes toward the use of animals in psychological research and education: Results from a national survey of psychologists. *American Psychologist, 51,* 1167–1180.

Plous, S. (1998). Signs of change within the animal rights movement: Results from a follow-up survey of activists. *Journal of Comparative Psychology, 112,* 48–54.

Powers, W. T. (1978). Quantitative analysis of purposive systems: Some spadework at the foundations of scientific psychology. *Psychological Review, 85,* 417–435.

Probst, T. (2003). Exploring employee outcomes of organizational restructuring. *Group and Organization Management, 28,* 416–439.

Quas, J. A., Malloy, L. C., Melinder, A., Goodman, G. S., D'Mello, M., & Schaaf, J. (2007). Developmental differences in the effects of repeated interviews and interviewer bias on young children's event memory and false reports. *Developmental Psychology, 43,* 823–837. doi:10.1037/0012-1649.43.4.823

Rayner, E., Baxter, S. M., & Ilicic, J. (2015). Smoker's recall of fear appeal imagery: Examining the effect of fear intensity and fear type. *Australasian Marketing Journal, 23,* 61–66. doi:10.1016/j.ausmj.2014.11.003

Reed, D. D., Critchfield, T. S., & Martins, B. K. (2006). The generalized matching law in elite sport competition: Football play calling as operant choice. *Journal of Applied Behavior Analysis, 39,* 281–297. doi:10.1901/jaba.2006.146-05

Regenberg, A., Mathews, D. H., Blass, D. M., Bok, H., Coyle, J. T., & Duggan, P. (2009). The role of animal models in evaluating reasonable safety and efficacy for human trials of cell-based interventions for neurologic conditions. *Journal of Cerebral Blood Flow & Metabolism, 29,* 1–9.

Renfrey, G., & Spates, C. R. (1994). Eye movement desensitization: A partial dismantling study. *Journal of Behavioral Therapy and Experimental Psychiatry, 25,* 231–239.

Rescorla, R. A. (1999). Summation and overexpectation with qualitatively different outcomes. *Animal Learning & Behavior, 27,* 50–62.

Rescorla, R. A., & Wagner, A. R. (1972). A theory of Pavlovian conditioning: Variations in the effectiveness of reinforcement and nonreinforcement. In A. H. Black & W. F. Prokosy (Eds.), *Classical conditioning II: Current research and theory* (pp. 64–99). New York, NY: Appleton-Century-Crofts.

Research Triangle Institute (1995). *Consequences of whistleblowing for the whistleblower in misconduct in science cases: Final report.* Retrieved from http://ori.hhs.gov/images/ddblock/consequences_0.pdf

Resnick, J. H., & Schwartz, T. (1973). Ethical standards as an independent variable in psychological research. *American Psychologist, 28,* 134–139.

Resnik, D. B., Gutierrez-Ford, C., & Peddada, S. (2008). Perceptions of ethical problems with scientific journal peer review: An exploratory study. *Science & Engineering Ethics, 14,* 305–310. doi:10.1007/s11948-008-9059-4

Resnik, D., & Elmore, S. (2016). Ensuring the quality, fairness, and integrity of journal peer review: A possible role of editors. *Science & Engineering Ethics, 22,* 169–188. doi:10.1007/s11948-015-9625-5

Reynolds, G. S. (1961). Attention in the pigeon. *Journal of the Experimental Analysis of Behavior, 4,* 203–208.

Reynolds, M. D., Tarter, R. E., & Kirisci, L. (2004). Characteristics of men with substance use disorder consequent to illicit drug use: Comparison of a random sample and volunteers. *Drug and Alcohol Dependence, 75,* 241–251. doi:10.1016/j.drugalcdep.20 04.03.009

Rhodes, J. C., Kjerulff, K. H., Langenberg, P. W., & Guzinski, G. M. (1999). Hysterectomy and sexual functioning. *Journal of the American Medical Association, 282,* 1934–1941.

Riva, G., Teruzzi, T., & Anolli, L. (2003). The use of the Internet in psychological research: Comparison of online and offline questionnaires. *CyberPsychology and Behavior, 6,* 73–80.

Roberts, J. V. (1985). The attitude–memory relationship after 40 years: A meta-analysis of the literature. *Basic and Applied Social Psychology, 6,* 221–242.

Roberts, L. M., Wilson, S., Roalfe, A., & Bridge, P. (2004). A randomised controlled trial to determine the effect on response of including a lottery incentive in health surveys. *BMC Health Services Research, 4,* 30–38. doi:10.1186/1472-6963-4-30

Rogers, T. B. (1995). *The psychological testing enterprise: An introduction.* Pacific Grove, CA: Brooks/Cole.

Roscoe, J. T. (1975). *Fundamental statistics for the behavioral sciences* (2nd ed.). New York, NY: Holt, Rinehart & Winston.

Rosenberg, M. S. (2005). The file-drawer problem revisited: A general weighted method for calculating fail-safe numbers in meta-analysis. *Evolution, 59,* 464–468. doi:10.1111/j.0014-3820.2005.tb01004.x

Rosenthal, R. (1976). *Experimenter effects in behavioral research* (enlarged ed.). New York, NY: Irvington.

Rosenthal, R. (1979). The "file drawer problem" and tolerance for null results. *Psychological Bulletin, 86,* 638–641.

Rosenthal, R. (1984). Meta-analytic procedures for social research. *Applied Social Research Methods* (Vol. 6). Beverly Hills, CA: Sage.

Rosenthal, R., & Rosnow, R. L. (1975). *The volunteer subject.* New York, NY: Wiley.

Rosnow, R. L., & Rosnow, M. (1986). *Writing psychology papers.* Monterey, CA: Brooks/Cole.

Ross, L., Lepper, M. R., & Hubbard, M. (1975). Perseverance in self-perception and social perception: Biased attributional processes in debriefing paradigms. *Journal of Personality and Social Psychology, 32,* 880–892.

Saad, L. (2010). Four moral issues sharply divide Americans. Retrieved from http://www.gallup.com/poll/137357/Four-Moral-Issues-Sharply-Divide-Americans.aspx

Saini, J., Kuczynski, E., Gretz, H. F., III, & Sills, E. S. (2002). Supracervical hysterectomy versus total abdominal hysterectomy: Perceived effects on sexual function. *BMC Women's Health, 1.* Retrieved from http://www.pubmedcentral.nih.gov/articlerender.fcgi?artid=65528

Saks, M. J. (1986). The law does not live by eyewitness testimony alone. *Law and human behavior, 10,* 279–280.

Saunders, D. R. (1980). Definition of Stroop interference in volunteers and non-volunteers. *Perceptual and Motor Skills, 51,* 343–354.

Schaie, K. W. (1965). A general model for the study of developmental problems. *Psychological Bulletin, 64,* 92–107.

Schouten, J. W., & McAlexander, J. H. (1995). Subcultures of consumption: An ethnography of the new bikers. *Journal of Consumer Research, 22,* 43–61.

Schreer, G. E., Smith, S., & Thomas, K. (2009). "Shopping while Black": Examining racial discrimination in a retail setting. *Journal of Applied Social Psychology, 39,* 1432–1444. doi:10.1111/j.1559-1816.2009.00489.x

Schuler, H. (1982). *Ethical problems in psychological research.* New York, NY: Academic Press.

Schwarz, N., Knäuper, B., Hippler, H-J., Noel-Neumann, E., & Clark, L. (1991). Rating scales: Numeric values may change the meaning of scale labels. *Public Opinion Quarterly, 55,* 570–582. doi:10.1086/269282

Scott, S. (2013). Pre-registration would put science in chains. *Times Higher Education.* Retrieved from http://www.timeshighereducation.com/comment/opinion/pre-registration-would-put-science-in-chains/2005954.article

Seligman, M. E. P. (1970). On the generality of the laws of learning. *Psychological Review, 77,* 406–418.

Seligman, M. E. P., & Hager, J. L. (1972). *Biological boundaries of learning.* New York, NY: Appleton-Century-Crofts.

Shaffer, D. (1985). *Developmental psychology: Theory, research, and applications.* Monterey, CA: Brooks/Cole.

Shanks, N. (2003). Animal rights in the light of animal cognition. *Social Alternatives, 22,* 12–18.

Shapiro, F. (1989). Eye movement desensitization: A new treatment for post-traumatic stress disorder. *Journal of Behavioral Therapy and Experimental Psychiatry, 20,* 211–217.

Shattell, M. M., Chinn, P., Thomas, S. P., & Cowling III., W. R. (2010). Authors' and editors' perspectives on peer review quality in three scholarly nursing journals. *Journal of Nursing Scholarship, 42,* 58–65. doi:10.111 1/j.1547-5069.2009.01331.x

Sheridan, C. E. (1979). *Methods of experimental psychology.* New York, NY: Holt, Rinehart & Winston.

Sherman, L. W., & Strang, H. (2004). Experimental ethnography: The marriage of qualitative and quantitative research. *The Annals of the American Academy of Political and Social Science, 595,* 204–222. doi: 10.1177/0002716 204267481

Shin, Y. H., (1999). The effects of a walking exercise program on physical function and emotional state of elderly Korean women. *Public Health Nursing, 16,* 146–154.

Shohat, M., & Musch, J. (2003). Online auctions as a research tool: A field experiment on ethnic discrimination. *Swiss Journal of Psychology, 62,* 139–145.

Shrout, P. E., & Fleiss, J. L. (1979). Intraclass correlations: Uses in assessing rater reliability. *Psychological Bulletin, 86,* 420–428.

Sidman, M. (1953). Two temporal parameters of the maintenance of avoidance behavior by the white rat. *Journal of Comparative and Physiological Psychology, 46,* 253–261.

Sidman, M. (1960). *Tactics of scientific research: Evaluating experimental data in psychology.* New York, NY: Basic Books.

Sieber, J. E., Iannuzzo, R., & Rodriguez, B. (1995). Deception methods in psychology: Have they changed in 23 years? *Ethics and Behavior, 5,* 67–85.

Siegel, S., & Castellan, N. J. (1988). *Nonparametric statistics for the behavioral sciences* (2nd ed.). New York, NY: McGraw-Hill.

Siegfried, T. (2015). P value ban: Small step for a journal, giant leap for science. Retrieved from http://www.sciencenews.org/blog/context/p-value-ban-small-step-journal-giant-leap-science

Sigelman, L. (1981). Question order effects on presidential popularity. *Public Opinion Quarterly, 45,* 199–207.

Signal, T. D., & Taylor, N. (2006). Attitudes to animals in the animal protection community compared to a normative community sample. *Society and Animals, 14,* 265–275. doi: 10.1163/156853006778149181

Silberman, G., & Kahn, K. L. (2011). Burdens on research imposed by institutional review boards: The state of the evidence and its implications for regulatory reform. *Milbank Quarterly, 89,* 599–627. doi: 10.1111/j.1468-0009.2011.00644.x

Silverman, I., Shulman, A. D., & Weisenthal, D. L. (1970). Effects of deceiving and debriefing psychological subjects on performance in later experiments. *Journal of Personality and Social Psychology, 14,* 203–212.

Simonsohn, U. (2013). Just post it: The lesson from two cases of fabricated data detected by statistics alone. *Psychological Science, 24,* 1875–1888. doi:10.1177/0956797613480366

Simpson, S. S., Bouffard, L. A., Garner, J., & Hickman, L. (2006). The impact of legal reform on the probability of arrest in domestic violence cases. *Justice Quarterly, 23,* 297–316.

Singer, P. (1975). *Animal liberation: A new ethics for our treatment of animals.* New York, NY: Avon Books.

Singer, P. (2002). *Animal liberation.* New York, NY: HarperCollins Publishers.

Sinkowitz-Cochran, R. L. (2013). Survey design: To ask or not to ask? That is the question . . . *Clinical Infectious Diseases, 56,* 1159 –1164.

Skinner, B. F. (1949). Are theories of learning necessary? *Psychological Review, 57,* 193–216.

Skinner, C. H., Skinner, A. L., & Armstrong, K. J. (2000). Analysis of a client-staff-developed shaping program designed to enhance reading persistence in an adult diagnosed with schizophrenia. *Psychiatric Rehabilitation, 24,* 52–57.

Slovic, P., & Fischoff, B. (1977). On the psychology of experimental surprise. *Journal of Experimental Psychology: Human Perception and Performance, 3,* 544–551.

Smit, H. J., & Rogers, P. J. (2000). Effects of low doses of caffeine on cognitive performance, mood and thirst in low and higher caffeine consumers. *Psychopharmacology, 152,* 167–173.

Smith, S. S., & Richardson, D. (1983). Amelioration of deception and harm in psychological research: The important role of debriefing. *Journal of Personality and Social Psychology, 44,* 1075–1082.

Smith, T. E., Sells, S. P., & Clevenger, T. (1994). Ethnographic content analysis of couple and therapist perceptions in a reflecting team setting. *Journal of Marital and Family Therapy, 20,* 267–286.

Snowdon, C. T. (1983). Ethnology, comparative psychology, and animal behavior. *Annual Review of Psychology, 34,* 63–94.

Sohl, J. E. (2004). What is science, what is not? Retrieved from http://planet.weber.edu/Critical_Thinking.htm

Sommers, R., & Miller, F. G. (2013). Forgoing debriefing in deceptive research: Is it ever ethical?. *Ethics & Behavior, 23,* 98–116. doi: 10.1080/10508422.2012.732505

Sontag, M. (2012). Research ethics and institutional review boards. *Politics & the Life Sciences, 31,* 67–79. doi:10.2990/31_1-2_67

Stanovich, K. E. (1986). *How to think straight about psychology.* Glenview, IL: Scott, Foresman.

Stavrinos, D., Byington, K. W., & Schwebel, D. C. (2011). Distracted walking: Cell phones increase injury risk for college pedestrians. *Journal of Safety Research, 42,* 101–107. doi:10.1016/j.jsr.2011.01.004

Steen, R. G. (2011). Retractions in the scientific literature: Is the incidence of research fraud increasing? *Journal of Medical Ethics, 37,* 249–253. doi:10.1136/jme.2010.040923

Steinberg, J. A. (2002). Misconduct of others: Prevention techniques for researchers. *APS Observer, 15, 1.* Retrieved from http://www.psychologicalscience.org/observer/0102/misconduct.html

Stephenson, L. B., & Crête, J. (2010). Studying political behavior: A comparison of Internet and telephone surveys. *International Journal of Public Opinion Research, 23,* 24–54. doi:10.1093/ijpor/edq025

Stevens, S. S. (1946). On the theory of scales of measurement. *Science, 103*(2684), 677–680.

Stevenson, M. R. (1995). Is this the definitive sex survey? *Journal of Sex Research, 32,* 77–91.

Steward, K. K., Carr, J. E., Brandt, C. W., & McHenry, M. M. (2007). An evaluation of the conservative dual-criterion method for teaching university students to visually inspect AB-design graphs. *Journal of Applied Behavior Analysis, 40,* 713–718.

Stolle, D. P., Robbennolt, J. K., Patry, M., & Penrod, S. D. (2002). Fractional factorial designs for legal psychology. *Behavioral Sciences and the Law, 20,* 5–17.

Streiner, D. L. (2006). Building a better model: An introduction to structural equation modeling. *Canadian Journal of Psychiatry, 51,* 317–324.

Strunk, W., & White, E. B. (1979). *The elements of style* (3rd ed.). New York, NY: Macmillan.

Stryjewski, T. P., Kalish, B. T., Silverman, B., & Lehmann, L. S. (2015). The impact of institutional review boards (IRBs) on clinical innovation. *Journal of Empirical Research on Human Research Ethics, 10,* 481–487. doi:10.1177/1556264615614936

Suls, J., & Martin, R. (2009). The air we breathe: A critical look at practices and alternatives in the peer-review process. *Perspectives on Psychological Science, 4,* 40–50.

Swami, V., Furnham, A., & Christopher, A. N. (2008). Free the animals? Investigating attitudes toward animal testing in Britain and the United States. *Scandinavian Journal of Psychology, 49,* 249–276. doi:10.1111/j.1467-9450.2008.00636.x

Tabachnick, B. G., & Fidell, L. S. (2013). *Using multivariate statistics* (6th ed.). Boston, MA: Allyn and Bacon.

Tanner, W. P., Jr., Swets, J. A., & Green, D. M. (1956). *Some general properties of the hearing mechanism* (Tech. Rep. No. 30). Ann Arbor, MI: University of Michigan, Electronic Defense Group.

Tatsuoka, M. M. (1971). *Multivariate analysis: Techniques for educational and psychological research.* New York, NY: Wiley.

Taylor, W. C., Obitz, F. W., & Reich, J. W. (1985). Experimental bias resulting from using volunteers in alcoholism research. *Journal of Studies on Alcohol and Drugs, 43,* 240–251.

Therrien, K., Wilder, D. A., Rodriguez, M., & Wine, B. (2005). Preintervention analysis and improvement of customer greeting in a restaurant. *Journal of Applied Behavior Analysis, 38,* 411–415.

Thorndike, R. M. (1978). *Correlational procedures for research.* New York, NY: Gardner Press.

Tinbergen, N. (1951). *The study of instinct.* London, England: Oxford University Press.

Treadway, M., & McCloskey, M. (1987). Cite unseen: Distortions of Allport and Postman's rumor study in the eyewitness testimony literature. *Law and Human Behavior, 11,* 19–26.

Trujillo, N. (1993). Interpreting November 22: A critical ethnography of an assassination site. *Quarterly Journal of Speech, 79,* 447–466.

Tsang, J-A. (2006). Gratitude and prosocial behaviour: An experimental test of gratitude. *Cognition and Emotion, 20,* 138–148.

Tucker, W. H. (1997). Re-reconsidering Burt: Beyond a reasonable doubt. *Journal of the History of the Behavioral Sciences, 33,* 145–162.

Tukey, J. W. (1977). *Exploratory data analysis.* Reading, MA: Addison-Wesley.

U.S. Department of Agriculture, National Agricultural Library. (2013). Animal welfare act and animal welfare regulations. Retrieved from http://www.aphis.usda.gov/animal_welfare/downloads/Animal%20Care%20Blue%20Book%20-%202013%20-%20FINAL.pdf

U.S. Department of Commerce. (2013). Computer and Internet use in the United States: Population characteristics. Retrieved from http://www.census.gov/prod/2013pubs/p20-569.pdf

U.S. Department of Health and Human Services. (2009). Basic HHS policy for protection of human research subjects. Retrieved from https://www.hhs.gov/ohrp/regulations-and-policy/regulations/45-cfr-46/

U.S. Department of Health and Human Services. (2009). Protection of human subjects: Title 45 code of federal regulations, part 46. Retrieved from http://www.hhs.gov/ohrp/regulations-and-policy/regulations/45-cfr-46/index.html

U.S. National Academy of Sciences. (2013). Definitions of evolutionary terms. Retrieved from http://nationalacademies.org/evolution/Definitions.html

Uebersax, J. (2016). The myth of chance-corrected agreement. Retrieved from http://john-uebersax.com/stat/kappa2.htm on 7/14/2016

Ullman, D., & Jackson, T. (1982). Researchers' ethical concerns: Debriefing from 1960–1980. *American Psychologist, 37,* 972–973.

Underwood, M. K., Scott, B. L., Galperin, M. B., Bjornstad, G. J., & Sexton, A. M. (2004). An observational study of social exclusion under varied conditions: Gender and developmental differences. *Child Development, 75,* 1538–1555.

Unger, R. K. (1983). Through the looking glass: No wonderland yet. *Psychology of Women Quarterly, 8,* 9–32.

Unger, R., & Crawford, M. (1992). *Women and gender: A feminist psychology.* New York, NY: McGraw-Hill.

Vandell, D. L., & Hembree, S. E. (1994). Peer social status and friendship: Independent contributors to children's social and academic adjustment. *Merrill-Palmer Quarterly, 40,* 461–477.

Velleman, P. F., & Wilkinson, L. (1993). Nominal, ordinal, interval, and ratio typologies are misleading. *American Statistician, 47,* 65–72.

Vicente, P., & Reis, E. (2010). Using questionnaire design to fight nonresponse bias in web surveys. *Social Science Computer Review, 28,* 251–267. doi:10.1177/09844 39309340751

Vinacke, W. E. (1954). Deceiving experimental subjects. *American Psychologist, 9,* 155.

Vogel, D., & Wester, S. (2003). To seek help, or not to seek help: The risks of self-disclosure. *Journal of Counseling Psychology, 50,* 351–361.

Vollmer, T. A., & Bourret, J. (2000). An application of the matching law to evaluate the allocation of two- and three-point shots by college basketball players. *Journal of Applied Behavior Analysis, 33,* 137–150.

Wadman, M. (2011). Chimpanzee research on trial. *Nature, 474,* 268–271. doi:10.1038/474268a

Wadsworth, B. J. (1971). *Piaget's theory of cognitive development.* New York, NY: McKay.

Wakefield, A. J., Murch, S. H., Anthony, A., Linnell, J., Casson, D. M., & Malik, M., et al. (1998). Ileal-lymphoid-nodular hyperplasia, non-specific colitis, and pervasive developmental disorder in children. *The Lancet, 351,* 637–641. doi:10.1016/S0140-6736(97)11096-0 [Retracted]

Waldum, E. R., & McDaniel, M. A. (2016). Why are you late? Investigating the role of time management in time-based prospective memory. *Journal of Experimental Psychology: General, 145,* 1049–1061. doi:10.1037/xge0000183

Wallien, M. S. C., Veenstra, R., Kreukels, B. P. C., & Cohen-Kettenis, P. T. (2010). Peer group status of gender dysphoric children: A sociometric study. *Archives of Sexual Behavior, 39,* 553–560. doi:10.1007/s10508-009-9517-3

Walster, E., Berscheid, E., Abrahams, D., & Aronson, V. (1967). Effectiveness of debriefing following deception experiments. *Journal of Personality and Social Psychology, 6,* 371–380.

Walster, E., Walster, G. W., & Berscheid, E. (1978). *Equity theory and research.* Boston, MA: Allyn and Bacon.

Warner, J. L., Berman, J. J., Weyant, J. M., & Ciarlo, J. A. (1983). Assessing mental health program effectiveness: A comparison of three client follow-up methods. *Evaluation Review, 7,* 635–658.

Watson, J. B., & Rayner, R. (1920). Conditioned emotional reactions. Retrieved from http://psychclassics.yorku.ca/Watson/emotion.htm

Weijters, B., Cabooter, E., & Schillewaert, N. (2010). The effect of rating scale format on response styles: The number of response categories and response category labels. *International Journal of Research in Marketing, 27,* 236–247. doi:10.1016/j.ijresmar.2010.02.004

Weinfurt, K. P., & Bush, P. J. (1995). Peer assessment of early adolescents solicited to participate in drug trafficking: A longitudinal analysis. *Journal of Applied Social Psychology, 25,* 2141–2157.

Westerlund, D., Granucci, E. A., Gamache, P., & Clark, H. B. (2006). Effects of peer mentors on work-related performance of adolescents with behavioral and/or learning disabilities. *Journal of Positive Behavior Interventions, 8,* 244–251.

Williams, C. D. (1959). The elimination of tantrum behavior by extinction procedures. *Journal of Abnormal and Social Psychology, 59,* 269.

Winer, B. J. (1971). *Statistical principles in experimental design* (2nd ed.). New York, NY: McGraw-Hill.

Winkel, G. H., & Sasanoff, R. (1970). An approach to objective analysis of behavior in architectural space. In H. M. Proshansky, W. H. Ittelson, & L. G. Rivlin (Eds.), *Environmental psychology: Man and his environment* (pp. 619–630). New York, NY: Holt, Rinehart & Winston.

Winters, K. E. (2008). Investigative summary regarding allegations that NASA suppressed climate change science and denied media access to Dr. James E. Hansen, a NASA scientist. Retrieved from http://oig.nasa.gov/investigations/OI_STI_Summary.pdf

Wolchik, S. A., Spencer. S. L., & Lisi, I. S. (1983). Volunteer bias in research employing vaginal measures of sexual arousal. *Archives of Sexual Behavior, 12,* 399–408.

Wolfensohn, S., & Maguire, M. (2010). What has the animal rights movement done for animal welfare? *Biologist, 57,* 2–27.

Wong, D., and Baker, C. (1988). Pain in children: Comparison of assessment scales. *Pediatric Nursing, 14,* 9–17.

Wood, C. (1979). The I-knew-it-all-along effect. *Journal of Experimental Psychology: Human Perception and Performance, 43,* 345–353.

World Medical Association Declaration of Helsinki. (1964). Retrieved from http://www.wma.net/e/policy/b3.htm

Wright, D. E., Titus, S. L., & Cornelison, J. B. (2008). Mentoring and research: An analysis of research mentoring in closed ORI cases [Electronic version]. *Science, Engineering and Ethics, 14,* 323–336. doi: 10.1007/s11948-008-9074-5

Wueest, B., Clematide, S., Bünzli, A., Laupper, D., & Frey, T. (2011). Electoral campaigns and relation mining: Extracting semantic network data from newspaper articles. *Journal of Information Technology & Politics, 8,* 444–463. doi:10.1080/19331681 .2011.567387

Wuensch, K. L., & Poteat, G. M. (1998). Evaluating the morality of animal research: Effects of ethical ideology, gender, and purpose. *Journal of Social Behavior and Personality, 13,* 139–150.

Wundt, W. (1897). *Outlines of psychology.* Retrieved from http://psychclassics.yorku.ca/Wundt/Outlines/

Yaremko, R. M., Harari, H., Harrison, R. C., & Lynn, E. (1982). *Reference handbook of research and statistical methods.* New York, NY: Harper & Row.

Zeidner, M. (2006). Gender group differences in coping with chronic terrorism: The Israeli scene. *Sex Roles, 54,* 297–310.

# NAME INDEX

# SUBJECT INDEX